CANADIAN CRIMINAL
Justice Policy

Contemporary Perspectives

Edited by KARIM ISMAILI • JANE B. SPROTT • KIM VARMA

OXFORD
UNIVERSITY PRESS

OXFORD

UNIVERSITY PRESS

Oxford University Press is a department of the University of Oxford.
It furthers the University's objective of excellence in research, scholarship,
and education by publishing worldwide. Oxford is a registered trade mark of
Oxford University Press in the UK and in certain other countries.

Published in Canada by
Oxford University Press
8 Sampson Mews, Suite 204,
Don Mills, Ontario M3C 0H5 Canada

www.oupcanada.com

Copyright © Oxford University Press Canada 2012

The moral rights of the author have been asserted

Database right Oxford University Press (maker)

Library and Archives Canada Cataloguing in Publication

Ismaili, Karim, 1967–
Canadian criminal justice policy : contemporary
perspectives / Karim Ismaili, Jane B. Sprott, and Kim Varma.

Includes index.
ISBN 978–0–19–543941–0

1. Criminal justice, Administration of—Canada.
2. Crime—Government policy—Canada.   I. Sprott, Jane B.
II. Varma, Kimberly N., 1968–   III. Title.

HV9960.C2I86 2012   364.971   C2012-901760-4

Cover image: Tyler Boley/Getty Images

Oxford University Press is committed to our environment.
This book is printed on Forest Stewardship Council® certified paper
and comes from responsible sources.

MIX
Paper from
responsible sources
FSC   FSC® C004071
www.fsc.org

Printed and bound in Canada

3 4 — 16 15 14

CONTENTS

Preface and Acknowledgements **v**
Contributors **vii**

**INTRODUCTION   Thinking about Criminal Justice Policy
in Canada   viii**
Karim Ismaili, Jane B. Sprott, and Kim Varma

Suggested Readings and Websites **xxvii**

PART 1 THE CRIMINAL JUSTICE SYSTEM

Overview   1
Karim Ismaili, Jane B. Sprott, and Kim Varma

1   **Canadian Police and Policing Policy, Post-9/11   5**
Christopher Murphy

2   **Back to the Future? Policy Development in Pre-trial Detention
in Canada   30**
Anthony N. Doob and Cheryl Marie Webster

3   **A Trip from Thoughtful to Thoughtless: Murder Sentencing
in Canada   58**
Allan Manson

4   **Maintaining Our Balance: Trends in Imprisonment Policies
in Canada   79**
Cheryl Marie Webster and Anthony N. Doob

5   **Youth Justice Policy Reform: The Youth Criminal Justice Act   110**
Richard Barnhorst

6   **Aboriginal Justice Policy in Canada   135**
Scott Clark and Tammy Landau

7   **Domestic Violence and Problem-Solving Courts   160**
E. Jane Ursel

Suggested Readings and Websites **182**

PART 2 RELATED POLICY AREAS

Overview   185
Karim Ismaili, Jane Sprott, and Kim Varma

8   Drug Law and Policy Canada: Torn between Criminal Justice
     and Public Health   188
     Benedikt Fischer, Meagan Bibby, Elena Argento, Thomas Kerr,
     and Evan Wood

9   Terrorism and National Security Policy-Making in Canada   222
     Kent Roach

10   The Criminalization of Poverty: Welfare Reform and the Policing
      of Welfare in Canada   248
      Wendy Chan

11   Immigration Penality and the Crime-Security Nexus:
      The Case of Tran Trong Nghi Nguyen   273
      Anna Pratt

12   Policy and Politics: The Evolution of Organized Crime Policies
      in Canada   298
      Margaret E. Beare

13   Internet Law and Policy from a Canadian Perspective   326
      Sara M. Smyth

      Suggested Readings and Websites   358

      Index   361

PREFACE and ACKNOWLEDGEMENTS

PREFACE

Our goal in putting together this edited collection of essays was to fill what we saw as a gap within the Canadian criminological literature—namely, insufficient attention to the development of various types of criminal justice, and criminal justice–related, policies. Canada has a unique history and distinctive constitutional arrangements, which means that policy development here differs from that of other countries and is thus an area of unique interest.

In this volume, we have gathered together the writings of some of the foremost Canadian experts in their respective fields. The accounts they provide about various policy developments are, we believe, informative and help to carve out an understanding of the place of policy within criminal justice and related fields. Several of the authors trace the history behind our policies, providing insight into the ways in which policies succeed, fail, or work in collaboration with other areas of public policy (i.e., social policy, national security policy, telecommunications policy, etc.). The analyses presented here help us to understand not only how we got to where we are, but also where we may be heading. We have been, of course, limited by space, and thus not every policy area could be represented within this collection. Nevertheless, we feel we have managed to capture many interesting standard criminal justice polices (e.g., policing, courts, corrections, youth justice, Aboriginal justice) as well as some closely related policies (e.g., immigration, terrorism, welfare, drugs, etc.). We hope the readers of this edited collection are left with an understanding of this incredibly dynamic and largely under-examined field of criminal justice policy in Canada.

ACKNOWLEDGEMENTS

Karim Ismaili would like to thank the students in his CRM 404 class (Criminal Justice Policy) at Ryerson University for helping him think through the framework of the book; he also thanks Richard Vengroff (Kennesaw State University) for sharing his wisdom and experience. Jane Sprott would like to acknowledge the support she received from a Social Sciences and Humanities Research Council of Canada (SSHRC) grant. Kim Varma and Jane Sprott would like to thank the faculty and staff in the Department of Criminal Justice and Criminology, Ryerson University. The editors would like to thank Carla Cassidy (Ryerson University) for her continued support and encouragement. We also wish to thank Judith Turnbull for her careful and insightful copy-editing. We thank as well Nancy Reilly and Tamara Capar (Oxford University Press) for their exceptional support and guidance. We doubt this project would have been completed were it not for their patience, understanding, and, when necessary, 'gentle' reminders. Finally, we would all like to acknowledge the broad support that our two institutions—Ryerson University and Kennesaw State University—have provided us throughout the writing of this text.

CONTRIBUTORS

Elena Argento
Centre for Applied Research in Mental
Health & Addiction
Simon Fraser University

Richard Barnhorst
Senior Legal Counsel, Youth Justice
Policy Section
Department of Justice Canada

Margaret E. Beare
Department of Sociology
York University

Meagan Bibby
Centre for Applied Research in Mental
Health & Addiction
Simon Fraser University

Wendy Chan
Department of Sociology and
Anthropology
Simon Fraser University

Scott Clark
Department of Criminal Justice and
Criminology
Ryerson University

Anthony N. Doob
Centre for Criminology and Sociolegal
Studies
University of Toronto

Benedikt Fischer
Faculty of Health Sciences
Simon Fraser University

Thomas Kerr
Department of Medicine
University of British Columbia

Tammy Landau
Department of Criminal Justice and
Criminology
Ryerson University

Allan Manson
Faculty of Law
Queen's University

Christopher Murphy
Department of Sociology and Social
Anthropology
Dalhousie University and University of
King's College

Anna Pratt
Department of Social Science
York University

Kent Roach
Faculty of Law
University of Toronto

Sara M. Smyth
School of Criminology
Simon Fraser University

E. Jane Ursel
Department of Sociology
University of Manitoba

Cheryl Marie Webster
Department of Criminology
University of Ottawa

Evan Wood
Department of Medicine
University of British Columbia

INTRODUCTION

Thinking about Criminal Justice Policy in Canada

Karim Ismaili, Jane B. Sprott, and Kim Varma

Crime is a social phenomenon that touches the lives of countless Canadians on a daily basis. It disrupts relationships, causes harm to person and property, and evokes strong feelings and emotional responses. Crime is also a complex social phenomenon; it is neither easily explained nor easily addressed. Its subject matter is vast, as are its motivations and consequences for individuals, communities, and societies. In an increasingly interconnected world, crime spans the local and the global and can take place in actual and virtual spaces. And since it is socially constructed, crime is an ever-changing phenomenon: what is suitable to view as a crime, who is suitable to cast as a criminal, and how society ultimately responds to both crime and criminals emerge from a context that must be analyzed rather than taken for granted (Christie, 2004, p. 10). In addition to being complex, crime and criminal justice permeate the popular culture, occupy a dominant place in the public imagination, and are increasingly significant topics of political and public discussion in Canada. These features—along with the fact that providing for the safety and security of its citizens is a core, if not *the* core, responsibility of government—set the policies designed to address crime apart from other public policy areas, rendering the nexus of crime and public policy fascinating to explore.

Exploring contemporary Canadian criminal justice policy is precisely what this book aims to do. The 13 chapters that follow this introduction present the policy-oriented research of some of the foremost thinkers on criminal justice in Canada. The contributions tackle pressing contemporary policy issues facing the justice system (Part I) and explore the intersection of crime policy with subject areas that fall outside the relatively narrow and traditional confines of the criminal justice system (Part II). Put another way, the book explores topics that have enjoyed a long and established history of criminal justice analysis (e.g., policing, courts, corrections, Aboriginal justice, and youth justice) with others that are newly emergent or recast in a manner that poses unique challenges for policy-makers, for the criminal justice system, and for society (e.g., terrorism, immigration, organized crime, welfare, drugs, and technology). The contributors were each asked to scrutinize their topic through a policy lens and were guided to consider the following sorts of questions along the way:

- How did the issue come to the attention of policy-makers? Were special interest groups advancing agendas? Was there some spectacular event? Did bureaucrats or government officials perceive the issue as a problem? How were policy issues defined and framed? What characterizations were dominant? Was there a struggle over ideas?

- What was the reform process? Who was involved? How were reforms presented to the public? Or did the issue not even make it into the public debate? Did the reforms succeed or fail to make it through the legislative process?

- What effect did the policy have? Did it change anything? Why or why not? What does the future hold?

- Is there a symbolic dimension to the policy?

- What was the impact on those who were affected by this policy?

- How did this policy affect other policies or legislation already in place? For example, did addressing one area cause a spillover into other areas?

- Were there implementation challenges?

- Has the policy been evaluated? What were the findings?

- How does the policy balance security, equity, liberty, and efficiency? What does the analysis reveal about crime policy in Canada? What does it reveal about the Canadian political system? What does it reveal about Canada's connection to the world?

We contend that if we explore topics through a policy lens and consider questions such as those presented above, our understanding of crime and criminal justice in Canada can be enhanced. Through the various contributions in this book, readers will come to appreciate some of the distinctive features of Canadian criminal justice policy, along with other features that are shared with nations such as Australia, Great Britain, and the United States. Highlighting these differences and similarities is only one of the myriad reasons this book was developed. An equally compelling rationale relates to the observation that while the study of crime policy in Canada has matured significantly in recent years, evidence of that maturity is not as visible as it could be. Part of the reason for this is simply because the work of scholars and practitioners is dispersed across a wide range of academic, governmental, and popular publication venues. Added to that is the reality that localism and regionalism remain enduring features of Canada. As will become clear, local and regional contexts matter: the lessons learned from policies pursued in Ontario, Vancouver, or Winnipeg, for example, often resonate beyond provincial borders, providing ample opportunity for others to learn from their experience. This book can thus be viewed as an attempt to bring coherence and visibility to the study of Canadian criminal justice policy via the work of experts located across the country. Our goal is to provide a foundation from which policy-makers, practitioners, scholars, students, and members of the public can discuss and debate important ideas, trends, and controversies, and do so in an informed manner.

Before outlining some of the unique aspects of Canadian criminal justice policy, we will first discuss of some key concepts and distinctive features of criminal justice policy. We will provide a brief overview of the factors that have contributed to the recent interest in this policy area. When these are viewed together, it will become clear that the time has come for Canadian criminal justice policy to establish itself as a focus of research and analysis and as an applied field of study.

THE STUDY OF CRIMINAL JUSTICE POLICY
Some Important Concepts

Although its meaning is often variable and contingent, individuals, groups, agencies, businesses, political parties, institutions, and governments use the term 'policy' in everyday talk and everyday action. Policy has been alternatively described as 'a course of action or inaction rather than specific actions or decisions'; a 'web of decisions and actions that allocate values'; 'a set of interrelated decisions concerning the selection of goals and the means of achieving them within a specified situation'; 'a stance which, once articulated, contributes to the context within which a succession of future decisions will be made'; and, in the words of a senior British civil servant, 'rather like an elephant—you recognize it when you see it but cannot easily define it.' The concept of policy is thus difficult to treat as a very specific and concrete phenomenon; it requires shape and needs to be situated (Ham & Hill, 1984, p. 11). Policy is both a process and a product: it refers to the process of decision-making and also to the product of that process. Policy 'may be explicit or implicit, purposeful or accidental, decided at one time or evolve gradually. Policies may constitute the sources of regularities in practice, but they also represent initiatives which never get implemented' (Solomon, 1981, p. 6).

The term 'policy' has many uses: for example, it can serve as a label for a field of activity (e.g., criminal justice policy, educational policy, welfare policy, etc.); as a general purpose or desired state of affairs; as a specific proposal (put forward by an elected leader, government agency, or interest group); as a decision of government (often arising from a crucial moment of choice); as a formal authorization (e.g., a specific act or statute); as a program of activity (e.g., a legislative package that includes a mandate, organizational structure, and resources); as an output (i.e., what governments actually deliver as opposed to what is promised or envisioned); as a product of a particular activity; as a theory (if we do X, then Y will follow); and as a process that unfolds over a period of time (Hogwood & Gunn, 1984, pp. 12–19). Such descriptions provide insight into the sheer range of activities that constitute policy, and serve to highlight why it is important to consider the specific context in which the term is used.

Public policy is a decision or action of government that addresses a public problem or issue. It is widely accepted that for a policy to be considered public policy, 'it must to some degree have been generated or at least processed within the framework of governmental procedures, influences and organizations' (Hogwood & Gunn, 1984, p. 24). Unlike the vast majority of private sector policies, public policies are funded through public resources and backed up by the legal system. This latter feature is particularly important to criminal justice policy, since it is the threat of sanctions—including the loss of liberty—that is a defining characteristic in this policy area.

All public policy—including criminal justice policy—is the outcome of a process that is important to uncover and explore. That process has been conceptualized in a number of ways, with the most popular images emphasizing a series of stages and/or a series of steps. The former might include the identification of a problem, agenda setting, the formulation of policy proposals, policy adoption, policy implementation, and evaluation. Deborah Stone (1988, p. 5) summarizes the steps commonly associated with the policy process in the following manner: 'identify objectives; identify alternative courses of action for achieving objectives; predict and evaluate the possible consequences of each alternative; select the alternative that maximizes the attainment of objectives.'

While useful, both conceptualizations have been criticized for not capturing the reality of the policy process. For example, policy-making rarely proceeds in a linear and wholly rational manner. This observation has prompted the development of alternative models that highlight the 'somewhat anarchic' nature of policy-making (Jones & Newburn, 2005, p. 61). One such model—the structured interaction perspective—'does not assume a single decision-maker, addressing a clear policy problem: it focuses on the range of participants in the game, the diversity of their understandings of the situation and the problem, the ways in which they interact with one another, and the outcomes of this interaction. It does not assume that this pattern of activity is a collective effort to achieve known and shared goals' (Colebatch, 1998, p. 102). Far from policy-making being a rational enterprise, these models point to the volatility that is characteristic of the everyday policy-making process. Value differences, the role of interest groups, shifts in public mood, and decisions based on political ambitions and institutional constraints are only a few of the many challenges encountered in contemporary policy environments. Such forces, critics contend, make rational policy action unlikely, especially in fields like criminal justice. The reality is more dynamic, volatile, and even chaotic. This debate among policy researchers should not, however, diminish the importance of examining the policy process. As the political scientist Peter Solomon has noted (1981, p. 5), such an examination can facilitate our understanding of how the political process negotiates change, helps us identify the constraints the process places upon the translation of ideas and analysis into action, describes the degree to which various actors influence the movement of criminal justice proposals through the policy process, and provides insight into how politics determines what is and can be implemented. While dominated by governments and their duly constituted public agencies, the policy-making process is not restricted to state actors. A diverse array of stakeholders, including those from civil society and the private sector, take an active role in attempting to shape the substance and direction of policy (see, for example, Hyshka, 2009).

Finally, it is important to note that crime policies have multiple purposes: they identify and define those behaviours deemed unacceptable to society and thus punishable by law; they nurture and support the informal social controls that reduce the incidence of crime in society; they provide a framework through which the formal apparatus of social control—the criminal justice system—operates; they both authorize and constrain the behaviour of criminal justice officials; and they trigger a course of action that can lead to the deprivation of individual liberty, the ultimate punishment provided for in Canadian criminal law. While the criminal justice system functions to provide safety and security where other informal social controls have weakened or otherwise broken down, its authority must be exercised within the rule of law and, ideally, be implemented free of favour or bias.

It will become apparent when reading the various contributions to this book that the authors ascribe different meanings to policy, identify a range of purposes to the policies they examine, employ different methods to study policy, and bring a variety of theoretical perspectives to bear when examining and evaluating policies and the processes that created them. Although some may view this lack of agreement as an impediment to sound and systematic criminal justice policy analysis, we contend that it is an important starting point from which to build a comprehensive understanding of the challenges and dilemmas confronting those thinking about and working within this policy area.

Distinctive Features of Criminal Justice Policy

Observers of criminal justice have noted some distinctive features of the field that are important to consider when embarking on policy research and analysis. While these features are characteristic of criminal justice in most liberal democracies, the degree to which they influence public policy varies from jurisdiction to jurisdiction. For example, an ongoing debate within the criminal justice literature involves the degree to which the state agencies and departments involved in the administration of justice act as a coherent and unified 'system'. Critics argue that the major components of the system—policing, courts, and corrections—carry out their respective mandates independently, generating systemic or institutional fragmentation. Diverse organizational objectives and differences in the use of discretionary powers exacerbate the fragmentation, leading some to describe the criminal justice system as 'a network of interrelated, yet independent, individuals and agencies, rather than as a system *per se*' (Griffiths & Verdun-Jones, 1994, p. 9). In such an environment, the development of coherent criminal justice policy that reflects the needs and expectations of each component of the 'system' becomes a significant challenge. And in situations where a degree of consensus on policy is secured, differences can often arise at the implementation phase.

A further explanation for institutional fragmentation is advanced by Nagel and his associates, who contend that fragmentation is the result of differences in training, status, and ideology among police, courts, and corrections personnel. These differences reflect 'the kinds of authority relationships that exist in the sub-system organizations. Positive sanction and normative power are more prevalent among legally trained professionals in the system. Negative sanctions and coercive power tend to be stressed in law enforcement and, at least in relation to custodial work, in correctional organizations. All of these factors lead to diverse organizational climates that surround the different components of the system' (1983, p. 9). It is worth noting that institutional fragmentation can also exist within subsystem organizations. For example, it is not uncommon to find police leaders and rank-and-file officers, or Crown counsel and defence lawyers, holding contrasting views on important policy issues.

Because criminal law and criminal justice policy are expected to embody fundamental principles of society, a further distinctive characteristic of the field is the symbolic quality of the content involved (Gusfield, 1963; Hagan, 1983; Newburn & Jones, 2007). Crime and criminal justice are also symbols that have the potential to arouse, widen, and deepen public interest by appealing to ideological or moral concerns (Edelman, 1988; Scheingold, 1984, 1991). They condense a number of stresses that people experience in their day-to-day lives, and are powerful because they relate to the moral, ethical, and cultural concerns of the social order (Nagel et al., 1983, p. 11). Their potential to evoke strong and often emotional responses suggests that crime and criminal justice symbols are especially vulnerable to transformation for strategic purposes: 'The symbolic implications of the criminal law and of law and order politics are particularly interesting because the emotional issues involved easily lend themselves to demagogic excesses. This is especially true in light of the fact that the workings of the criminal justice system are quite complex and not well understood by the public, which tends to oversimplify the issues that are involved' (Nagel et al., 1983, pp. 11–12). The symbolic dimension of crime and criminal justice can also be used strategically. Newburn and Jones recently made this point in their examination of the international popularity of *zero tolerance* in contemporary criminal justice. Zero tolerance, they argue, is now widely used by politicians, policy-makers, and criminal justice officials 'when there is a need to indicate strong measures and clear resolve' (2007, p. 222). In this sense, the term has been deployed to 'convey a mood and to impress an audience rather than in any concrete way to describe a set of policies or to frame particular objectives' (2007, p. 236). The variability of both the meaning of criminal justice and the symbols underlying that meaning compels an analysis of the evolving material basis of the symbol, as well as the shifting socio-political environment in which it is lodged (Edelman, 1988; Hagan, 1983; Majchrzak, 1984).

Recent Interest in Criminal Justice Policy

The study of policy has recently emerged as an important focus within criminal justice and criminology, a development that is part of a larger movement calling for a more vital and engaged *public criminology* (see Uggen & Inderbitzen, 2010). Paul Rock has described the movement as one that seeks 'greater academic engagement with "issues of public concern" in civic, policy, and political debates about crime, criminal justice, and criminal law' (Rock, 2010, p. 751). Its impact has been significant and can be seen in the founding of new criminal justice policy journals devoted to bridging 'the gap between policy relevant findings and criminal justice policy' (Clear & Frost, 2007, p. 633), in the criminology and criminal justice conferences that now regularly feature panels on various aspects of policy, in the colleges and universities that have recruited faculty members and designed policy-focused courses and programs, and in the general intellectual and financial investments that have generated a proliferation of research on a broad range of substantive crime policy issues.

Although complex and still unfolding, the origins of the movement can be traced back to a three-decade–long transformation in governance that has witnessed the rise of neo-liberalism in a number of Western industrialized democracies (including Canada, but most notably in the United States and the UK), along with a shift in politics that has, among other things, generated a highly charged symbolic and politicized discourse regarding crime and criminal justice. While there is significant national variation in the actual impact of this transformation (see Webster and Doob's chapter in this volume for a comparative perspective on this issue), there is little doubt that it has ushered in a period of decline in the role that criminological expertise plays in the policy-making process (see Haggerty, 2004). Part of this has to do with the 'fact that in a society saturated with "crime talk", [criminologists] have utmost difficulty in communicating with politicians, policy-makers, professionals and the public. Criminological reasoning is now mediated and contested by a range of vociferous interest groups, activists and a multitude of institutional actors and public opinions. And criminologists are alienated from late modern political culture because crime, policing and punishment are defining electoral issues' (Chancer & McLaughlin, 2007, p. 157).

The political significance of crime has been apparent for decades. Walter Miller, writing in a seminal 1973 article, argued that '[i]deology is the permanent hidden agenda of criminal justice' (p.142). He defined ideology as a set of 'general and abstract beliefs or assumptions about the correct or proper state of things, particularly with respect to the moral order and political arrangements, which serve to shape one's positions on specific issues' (ibid.). The ideological basis for criminal justice commands strong, emotional, partisan allegiance and has consequences for the processes of planning, program, and policy in criminal justice (ibid.). According to Miller, the ideological right perceives excessive leniency toward lawbreakers, the favouring of offender rights over those of victims, the erosion of respect for authority, the costs of crime being unfairly born by law-abiding citizens, and a culture of permissiveness eroding society. Those who subscribe to this world view contend, among other things, that individuals are responsible for their behaviour and that the moral and legal order must be enforced firmly and fairly by duly constituted authorities. The ideological left, on the other hand, is concerned with over-criminalization, labelling and social stigmatization, over-institutionalization, and over-centralization and discriminatory bias in state institutions, including the criminal justice system. The result is a world view that sees the social order as the primary cause of crime. Those on the left note that the criminal law and its enforcement must be cognizant of social inequalities, including the unequal distribution of power (Miller, 1973).

As a basic framework for understanding the American political context during the tumultuous period of the late 1960s and 1970s, Miller's work nicely captures the fundamental ideological differences that separated Republicans (the right) from Democrats (the left). While these ideological differences remain, they are less stark today. Crime and disorder became a political issue, one that Republicans convinced voters they could respond to more effectively than Democrats. Crime was successfully framed as the rational choice of offenders, crime policy became a matter of 'law and order', and a 'get tough' approach to offenders dominated the operation of the criminal justice system. Politically popular, the approach was eventually co-opted in the 1990s by President Bill Clinton, a Democrat. The result of this strategic shift by Democrats is visible in a criminal justice system and approach to crime policy that today reflects the values of the ideological right over the ideological left.

Whereas in the United States ideology has had a dramatic impact on criminal justice policy and on society, its significance in Canada has been far more muted. As will be discussed later in this chapter and throughout the book, federalism, the judiciary, the role of the public service, and other insulating political and cultural factors have shielded policy-makers from the highly politicized environment found in the United States. That is not to say that ideological differences do not exist in Canada; they do, but they have been generally less consequential from a policy standpoint because of the moderating impact of these same insulating factors. One sees evidence of the original left/right dichotomy described by Miller in the pronouncements and political documents disseminated by the major political parties, with the Conservative Party occupying the right and the Liberal, New Democratic, Bloc Québécois, and Green Parties each located to the left of the Conservatives on the ideological spectrum. As in the United States, Canada too has seen a drift rightward in the discourse on crime and criminal justice. This is most apparent in campaigns and elections, which, since the mid- to late 1980s, have routinely featured debate and discussion on crime and criminal justice, and the response to these issues, as policy differences between political parties that matter (see Hatt et al., 1992). While this makes for lively interchanges between political candidates and may indeed be consequential to the public in terms of election outcomes, the story of Canadian criminal justice is one of general resistance to the volatility that is so often associated with ideological and partisan preferences.

Whether this will remain the case is difficult to say, and there are indications that the resistance (or insulating factors) is weakening. This can be a source of frustration for criminologists, who find that it is increasingly the case that empirical research about crime has an uneasy relationship with the values and needs that often dominate the world of politics and policy (Hawkesworth, 1988, ch. 3). Indeed, the belief that scholarly knowledge alone determines policy outcomes is naive (Laub, 2004, p. 18). If there is one lesson to be learned from the decline of criminological influence in the contemporary period, it is that pure reason competes with politics in shaping state responses to the crime 'problem' (Zajac, 2002, p. 252). As Henry Ruth and Kevin Reitz have said:

> There is no doubt that data and empirical evidence supply only some of the inputs that influence the making of policy, and that they can be overridden by contrary moral sentiments, the tides of cultural change, the vagaries of politics, emotionalism, sensationalism, residual ignorance, and the inertial forces of laziness, habit, and vested interests. All of the messiness of real-world decision-making, even when fully acknowledged and experienced, does not diminish the importance of striving for an improved knowledge base. (2003, pp. 39–40)

The desire for crime policy to be rational and based on the best possible evidence remains a basic—albeit elusive—goal for many criminologists and policymakers. While the increasingly complex policy environment suggests that this goal may not be attainable, it has not deterred an influential group of criminologists to argue that 'rational and evidence-based crime policy' is the only way to counter the various forces described above (see Welsh & Farrington, 2005; Mears, 2007). Those who identify with this perspective point to a variety of problems that can be found in many criminal justice policies. Mears (2007) has noted several such problems: the lack of an empirically justified need for the policy in the first place; problematic design issues, such as gaps between the theory guiding the policy and the policy ultimately pursued; implementation problems of various sorts; the lack of evaluation, or an undue emphasis on the results of evaluations conducted; and, finally, the lack of effective cost-benefit analyses that might serve to guide investment decisions. Whether an evidence-based crime policy can fulfill its ambition of using the 'highest quality scientific evidence in the development of public policy' remains to be seen (Welsh & Farrington, 2005, p. 350). Nevertheless, we see this ambition as a further indication of how the study of criminal justice policy can contribute to improving an underdeveloped knowledge base and help begin to reverse the decline in influence experienced by criminologists in recent years (Beckett, 1997; Garland, 2001; Gest, 2001; Ruth & Reitz, 2003; Currie, 2007; Clear, 2010).

CRIMINAL JUSTICE POLICY IN CANADA
Origins and Sources
In Canada, the legal authority to develop public policy flows primarily from the Constitution Act, 1867. The Act defines a federal system of government and outlines the division of labour between the federal Parliament (the Parliament of Canada) and provincial legislatures. Parliament is empowered to make laws for the whole of Canada with respect to matters assigned to it by the Constitution. Likewise, a provincial legislature is empowered to make and implement laws in areas assigned to it and which fall within its territorial borders. The distribution over criminal matters is found primarily in sections 91(27) and 92(14) of the Constitution Act, 1867. The federal Parliament, in section 91(27), is conferred with the power to make laws in relation to 'the criminal law, except the constitution of courts of criminal jurisdiction, but including the procedure in criminal matters.' The provincial role in criminal justice is found in section 92(14). It confers on provincial legislatures the power to make laws in relation to 'the administration of justice in the province, including the constitution, maintenance, and organization of provincial courts, both of civil and criminal jurisdiction, and including procedure in civil matters in those courts'. The provincial responsibility for the administration of justice authorizes the provinces to establish a provincial police service with the power to enforce federal criminal laws, and to oversee municipal police services insofar as they relate to municipal institutions and the administration of justice. Jurisdiction over correctional institutions is divided between the two levels of government: section 91(28) authorizes the federal Parliament governance over 'penitentiaries', which hold offenders sentenced to imprisonment for two years or more; provinces, under section 92(16), have jurisdiction over 'prisons', which hold offenders sentenced to imprisonment for less than two years. In short, the federal government is responsible for framing the criminal law and supervising penitentiaries, while the provincial governments administer the law through their responsibilities for policing and the operation of the lower courts (Rock, 1986, p. 4).

The jurisdictional responsibilities assigned in Canada stand in contrast to other federal jurisdictions, such as the United States and Australia, where the criminal law is a state responsibility. As the noted constitutional scholar Peter Hogg has noted:

> The argument accepted by the United States and Australia that criminal law should reflect local conditions and sentiments was rejected by the fathers of confederation in favor of a national body of law. However . . . for the most part, the Criminal Code is enforced by the provinces; and the decisions to investigate, charge and prosecute offenses are therefore matters of provincial policy which will no doubt be framed in response to local

conditions and sentiments. In this way, the criminal law is not as centralized as other fields of federal legislative competence, where federal administration normally follows federal enactment. (1985, p. 398)

While the constitutional and legal authority for federal and provincial involvement in criminal justice policy is entrenched in the Constitution, it would be inaccurate to suggest that the two levels of government hold a monopoly in this area. In practice, much of the actual development, administration, and implementation of justice policy remain in the hands of local officials and professionals, in institutions that are effectively beyond the reach of both levels of government (Solomon, 1981, p. 7). This can be traced back to the tradition, prominent in the United Kingdom and Canada, of keeping the administration of justice free from political interference. The result is judicial and law enforcement policy that is set locally, often with unique features that can only be understood in reference to what Solomon calls the 'local legal culture'. Indeed, it is the local legal culture, rather than centrally determined policy, that is often cited as the dominant 'source of judicial and policy practice' (Solomon, 1981, p. 7).

Since 1982, the Charter of Rights and Freedoms has functioned as part of Canada's supreme law, guaranteeing 'a set of civil liberties that are regarded as so important that they should receive immunity, or at least special protection, from state action' (Hogg, 1985, p. 651). These include freedoms such as the freedom of expression, the right to vote, mobility rights, various minority rights, and rights guaranteeing fairness during legal proceedings. Protection of these fundamental rights and freedoms is accomplished through the courts. If a law is challenged and found to violate Charter rights, it is voided, thus guaranteeing that civil liberties are protected from the actions of legislators, state agencies, and state officials. The entrenchment of the Charter of Rights and Freedoms dramatically expanded the courts' scope of judicial review, as well as their policy-making function (the chapter by Roach in this volume discusses the interplay between the courts and Parliament in the shaping of recent national security policy).

The expanded policy-making role of the courts has had a significant impact on the administration of justice and, by extension, on the content of criminal justice policy in Canada. Generally, cases are pursued to determine whether state action and/or legislation violates one or more of the legal rights guaranteed in sections 7–14 of the Charter (e.g., the right to counsel, the right to be secure from unreasonable search and seizure, the right to a speedy trial, the right to be presumed innocent, and the right to not be subjected to cruel and unusual punishment). If it is determined that violations have occurred, either through the actions of state officials or through the laws themselves, the courts can impose a remedy for those so aggrieved (via s. 24(1) of the Charter). This provision has dramatically increased the use of litigation as a form of interest-group activity, deeply embedding in Canada the expression of political demands in the language of rights. Whereas traditional interest-group activity emphasized interactions with bureaucrats, legislators, political parties, and, to a lesser extent, the courts, section 24(1) offers a path of judicial review considerably more powerful and more accessible than was previously available to citizens. This not only provides a concrete example of how the Charter has been transformative for individuals and groups, but also highlights the significant impact it has had on all policy, including criminal justice policy.

The Policy Community

Public policy is shaped and influenced by a wide range of actors with a direct or indirect interest in the policy field. These actors can include government agencies, pressure groups, media people, and individuals, including academics, consultants, and other 'experts' (Pross, 1986). Each actor occupies a role in the *policy community*, which Pross defines as a 'part of a political system that—by virtue of its functional responsibilities, its vested interests, and its specialized knowledge—acquires a dominant voice in determining government decisions in a specific field of public activity, and is generally permitted by society at large and the public authorities in particular to determine public policy in that field' (p. 98). The policy community subdivides into two segments: the sub-government and the attentive public. The sub-government is composed of government agencies and institutionalized associations that actually make policy within the sector (Coleman & Skogstad, 1990, p. 25). It normally consists of a very small group of people who work at the core of the policy community. The attentive public, on the other hand, is less tightly knit and more loosely defined. Its composition varies, but it usually contains important, though less central, government agencies, private institutions, pressure groups, specific interests, and individuals. As Pross states, 'the attentive public lacks the power of the sub-government but still plays a vital role in policy development' (1986, p. 99). Researchers have demonstrated that the structure and function of policy communities vary from policy field to policy field (Pross, 1986, p. 106; see Coleman & Skogstad, 1990). Similarly, the relationships between actors in policy communities also vary. A *policy network* is a concept used to capture the relationships that emerge between both individuals and organizations that are in frequent contact with one another around issues of importance to the policy community (Atkinson & Coleman, 1992; Coleman & Skogstad, 1990).

When one considers the decentralization and fragmentation inherent in the field of criminal justice, it seems reasonable to question whether a distinct policy community exists in Canada. We believe that such a community does exist, although it must constantly work to manage the tensions that arise from these characteristics; like the criminal justice system itself, it is a community that features relationships of *independent interdependence*. At the federal level, for example, responsibility for criminal justice is divided between two agencies—Public Safety Canada and the Department of Justice Canada—each with separate leading roles in operational and legislative matters. While both possess independent mandates, their day-to-day substantive concerns emphasize interdependence. A similar pattern emerges in the context of intergovernmental relations. The division of powers over criminal matters in Canada has fostered the development of provincial policy communities that are primarily concerned with the administration of justice within provincial boundaries. However, the independent interdependence that characterizes the relationship between federal agencies is duplicated at the intergovernmental level, serving to bridge the gap between otherwise independent policy communities. So just as the federal criminal justice policy community is connected to provincial policy communities by virtue of the provincial power over the administration of justice, provincial policy communities are linked to the wider criminal justice policy community by virtue of the federal criminal law power.

Richard Simeon (1972) has pointed out that federalism is about the artful skill of diplomacy. Diplomacy involves tact and patience, but most importantly it involves communication. Thus, 'there is much talk in official Canada, much conscious deliberation and reflection, and a clear articulation of policies' (Rock, 1986, p. 46). That talk is sometimes informal and sometimes structured. It is practised in a number of federal-provincial arenas: in committees, task forces, working groups, meetings of deputy ministers, and meetings of ministers (p. 45). While Canada's *intra-* and *intergovernmental* relations have been, and continue to be, generally productive in criminal justice, disagreements can arise, as was the case with respect to Quebec's position on the Youth Criminal Justice Act (see the chapter by Barnhorst in this volume for a more detailed discussion of these issues). There is little doubt that federalism represents a source of complexity for the criminal justice policy community, as it does for many other areas of public policy in Canada. However, it is important to note that traits and experiences shared across jurisdictional and geographic boundaries can also serve to unify federalism's diverse elements. As we will see, all criminal justice policy communities are encountering policy environments with increasingly diverse and rapidly maturing interest groups. All contain sub-governments dominated by a hierarchy of professional interests. And all are experiencing the pressures of an expanding attentive public (Ismaili, 2006, 2011).

The Sub-Government and the Attentive Public

As has been discussed, federalism implies that intergovernmental relations will constitute a significant feature of any policy community in Canada. Many federal and provincial officials are deeply involved in criminal justice policy; some are de facto members of the sub-government. Those who play a central role include the prime minister, the premiers, the minister of justice and attorney general of Canada, the minister of public safety, and various provincial and territorial counterparts. Elected officials who serve on criminal justice legislative committees can also be viewed as being important members of the sub-government, as, occasionally, are mayors and members of city councils involved in pressing or high-profile local criminal justice matters that resonate regionally or nationally. Finally, judicial actors exert both a strong and a steady influence on the work of the sub-government through their decisions on the application, review, and interpretation of law. While not active participants in the work of the sub-government in a conventional sense, they are nonetheless of central importance to the criminal justice policy community.

Directly responsible for translating the political priorities of elected officials into public policy, the public servants who head criminal justice government departments and agencies are central participants in the policy community sub-government. Also active in the initiation and screening of proposals for change in criminal justice policy are bureaucrats at all levels of government who have no operational responsibilities, but who concern themselves with monitoring policies and advising elected officials (Solomon, 1991, p. 161). While government departments and individual bureaucrats (or policy-makers) are not part of the formal criminal justice 'system', it is important to consider them in terms of their efforts to reduce institutional fragmentation. The relationships that are struck between government policy-making agencies and the various components of the justice system are essential to its smooth functioning. Bureaucrats thus engage in a precarious balancing act in the attempt to accommodate the diverse needs and demands of the various 'system' components, along with those of politicians, interest groups, and other interested members of the public.

A wide range of interest groups also populate the criminal justice policy community. Each group is committed to influencing the outcome of public policy, although the degree to which it is ultimately successful is subject to considerable variation. Stolz (2002) has identified eight distinct types of interest group that attempt to influence criminal justice policy: professional, business, social welfare, civic, ad hoc, victims, ex-offender, and offender-oriented interest groups mobilize resources and press their respective positions at various decision points in the policy process. The interest groups that have traditionally had the most influence on criminal justice policy are those that represent professionals and other officials involved in the operation of the criminal justice system—police associations, bar associations, judicial organizations, and correctional associations (Fairchild, 1981). As active members of the policy community sub-government, these interest groups represent professions with an institutionalized stake in the operation of the criminal law and the criminal justice system (Fairchild, 1981). Their influence is enhanced by the high degree of public deference accorded them, especially on policy matters concerning the day-to-day operation of the criminal justice system.

Policy Networks

When analyzing criminal justice policy, it is important to consider the relationships that develop among the various actors in the policy community. Governments, for example, can ill afford to develop policy that will be met with criticism from professionals. Close ties with professional groups are cultivated to preclude such occurrences. Views are solicited and perspectives shared. The opinions of professionals are considered vital, and their support essential (Pross, 1986, p. 98). Similarly, professional organizations seek to ensure that their positions on issues are represented at various stages of the policy process. Their involvement goes a long way toward ensuring that that objective is met. It is this close and privileged access to the policy development process that often distinguishes the influence of professionally oriented groups from other interests in the criminal justice policy community.

In cases where a crime or criminal justice issue is in the public spotlight, elected officials are particularly responsive to public concerns and pay correspondingly less attention to the views of policy professionals, including criminologists. It is therefore inaccurate to state that non-professional interest groups are completely shut out from the sub-government in the criminal justice policy community. The views of a number of reform-oriented interest groups are considered vital and essential to the policy process, particularly those with an established presence in the policy community. Indeed, if there is one trend that has characterized the policy community over the past three decades, it is the increasing number of maturing interests that have developed around issues of criminal justice. Institutionalized victims' groups, groups working toward the elimination of violence against women, and others focused on the needs of minorities are proliferating. All are seeking to influence the shape and direction of public policy.

The attentive public in the criminal justice policy community is also expanding. As Fairchild has noted, 'Matters of criminal law go to the heart of questions about governmental legitimacy, state authority, and other popular conceptions of right and wrong, and are thus of closer concern to many individuals than are most other legislative issues' (1981, p. 189). This explains, in large part, the increase in the number of ad hoc and single-issue reform interests that have recently been created around various criminal justice issues. The attentive public obtains much of its information about crime and the criminal justice system from the media. Because the coverage of crime is so prominent in 'all means of mass communications, including daily and weekly newspapers, television, radio, news magazines, and so on' (Marion, 2002, p. 39), both the quantity and nature of media imagery can have a significant influence on how crime is perceived and, ultimately, on which criminal justice policies are pursued. Viewed in this light, the manner in which crime and criminal justice issues are framed by the mainstream media becomes a significant contextual feature of the policy community. As Marion has stated:

> The media is important because it educates the public about crime. Unfortunately, the media's coverage of crime events does not reflect reality. The media tend to cover crimes that occur less frequently such as mass shootings and extremely violent offenses. Although they make for good media ratings, these types of crimes are rare. In addition to misrepresenting the types of crimes committed, television shows tend to depict stereotypes of criminals, prisoners, and victims that are usually not accurate. (2002, p. 40)

Perceptions are, by their very nature, malleable. When perceptions relate to crime, they are rarely grounded on sound, accurate information. What remains is an apparent gulf between two related but independent domains: attitudes about crime and knowledge about crime (Roberts, 1994, p. 1). It is difficult to narrow this gulf in a policy sector where political reaction to the public's anxiety over crime is commonplace. This is especially troubling because it is these very reactions that often serve to reinforce and perpetuate the inaccurate perceptions held by a large segment of the population.

POLICY CHALLENGES, CONTEMPORARY AND LONG-STANDING

A number of the chapters in this book point to the influence that the 11 September 2001 terrorist attack on the United States (and the subsequent attacks on Spain and England) has had on Canada's justice system. The impact has been dramatic, affecting the administration of justice, the nature of criminal justice policy, and the relationship between the state and society. As will become clear as one reads the various chapters in this book, the response to the threat of terrorism has also redefined the manner in which migration, national security, organized crime, and telecommunications are viewed in relation to crime and crime control. It may well be that what we are now experiencing in Canada is a transformation in governance similar to that which commentators argue has been underway in the United States for a number of years. Described by Jonathon Simon as 'governing through crime' (2007, p. 11), that transformation caused people to act against crime and other troubling behaviours across a variety of institutional settings and resulted in the migration of technologies, discourses, and metaphors of crime and criminal justice into all kinds of institutions where they easily gravitated into new opportunities for governance. Indeed, '[j]ust as we now see the war on terrorism as requiring a fundamental recasting of American governance, the war on crime has already wrought such a transformation—one which may now be re-legitimized as a 'tough' response to terrorism' (p. 11). While Canada's political culture is in many ways distinct from that of the United States, our proximity to that nation, our intertwined histories, and the ease with which policies travel in the contemporary world should lead us to think seriously about the diffusion of crime control strategies (Jones & Newburn, 2002, 2007). But Canadians should not stop there. We are *influenced by* and in turn *influence* the policy debates of many nations. This too is deserving of in-depth study.

Policies are made in a variety of settings, ranging from the local to the global, and involve a variety of actors, some more powerful than others. It is essential that these processes, settings, and actors be viewed as central to the study of criminal justice policy. And while it is critical that Canadians examine how policies are made and who participates in the policy-making process, policy outcomes must also be assessed in terms of their impact on society (Sheehy, 2004). A number of chapters in this volume point to policies and practices in Canada that are deeply troubling and that serve to control, criminalize, and punish those who are already marginalized in society. Other chapters argue that the criminal justice system is ill-equipped to address complex social problems and social conditions. It is our hope that this book will provide readers with an opportunity to learn about some of the many challenges and dilemmas confronting the field of criminal justice in Canada, and will stimulate a broader discussion about the goals and objectives of policy and the capacity for criminal justice reform.

CRITICAL THINKING QUESTIONS

1. What evidence can be presented to support the contention that Canadian criminal justice policy has become politicized in recent years?

2. What makes crime a particularly potent symbol? What are the implications of this for criminal justice policy?

3. Does the Canadian version of federalism help or hinder the development of criminal justice policy?

4. Select a criminal justice issue and use the policy community framework to highlight the actors and networks that will likely influence the policy-making process.

5. How does ideology manifest itself in Canadian criminal justice policy?

REFERENCES

Atkinson, M., & Coleman, W. D. (1992). Policy networks, policy communities and problems of governance. *Governance: An International Journal of Policy and Administration, 5*, 155–80.

Beckett, K. (1997). *Making crime pay: Law and order in contemporary American politics.* New York: Oxford University Press.

Canada. *Constitutional Documents.* Ottawa: Department of Justice. Retrieved 7 June 2011 from http://laws.justice.gc.ca/eng/Const/

Chancer, L., & McLaughlin, E. (2007). Public criminologies: Diverse perspectives on academia and policy. *Theoretical Criminology, 11*(2), 155–73.

Christie, N. (1993). *Crime control as industry: Towards gulags, Western style?* London: Routledge.

———. (2004). *A suitable amount of crime.* London: Routledge.

Clear, T. (2010). Policy and evidence: The challenge to the American Society of Criminology. *Criminology, 48*(1), 1–25.

———, & Frost, N. (2007). Informing public policy. *Criminology and Public Policy, 6*(4), 633–40.

Colebatch, H. (1998). *Policy.* Buckingham, UK: Open University Press.

Coleman, W. D., & Skogstad, G. (Eds.). (1990). *Policy communities and public policy in Canada.* Mississauga: Copp Clark Pitman.

Currie, E. (2007). Against marginality: Arguments for a public criminology. *Theoretical Criminology, 11*(2), 175–90.

Edelman, M. (1988). *Constructing the political spectacle.* Chicago: University of Chicago Press.

Fairchild, E. S. (1981). Interest groups in the criminal justice process. *Journal of Criminal Justice, 9*, 181–94.

Garland, D. (2001). *The culture of control: Crime and social order in contemporary society.* Chicago: University of Chicago Press.

Gest, T. (2001). *Crime and politics: Big government's erratic campaign for law and order.* New York: Oxford University Press.

Griffiths, C. T., & Verdun-Jones, S. N. (1994). *Canadian criminal justice.* Toronto: Harcourt, Brace and Company.

Gusfield, J. (1963). *Symbolic Crusade.* Urbana: University of Illinois Press.

Hagan, J. (1983). The symbolic politics of criminal sanctions. In S. Nagel et al. (Eds.), *The political science of criminal justice* (pp. 27–39). Illinois: Thomas Books.

Haggerty, K. (2004). Displaced expertise: Three constraints on the policy relevance of criminological thought. *Theoretical Criminology, 8*(2), 211–31.

Ham, C., & Hill, M. (1984). *The policy process in the modern capitalist state.* Sussex: Harvestor Press.

Hatt, K., Caputo, T., & Perry, B. (1992). Criminal justice policy under Mulroney, 1984–1990: Neo-conservatism, eh? *Canadian Public Policy, 18*(3), 245–60.

Hawkesworth, M. E. (1988). *Theoretical issues in policy analysis.* Albany: SUNY Press.

Hogg, P. (1985). *Constitutional Law of Canada.* Toronto: Carswell.

Hogwood, B. W., & Gunn, L. A. (1984). *Policy analysis for the real world.* New York: Oxford University Press.

Hyshka, E. (2009). The saga continues: Canadian attempts to reform cannabis law in the twenty-first century. *Canadian Journal of Criminology and Criminal Justice, 51*(1), 73–91.

Ismaili, K. (2006). Contextualizing the criminal justice policy-making process. *Criminal Justice Policy Review, 17*(3), 255–69.

———. (2011). Thinking about criminal justice policy: Process, players, and politics. In K. Ismaili (Ed.), *U.S. criminal justice policy: A contemporary reader* (pp. 1–18). Sudbury, MA: Jones and Bartlett Publishers.

Jones, T., & Newburn, T. (2002). Policy convergence and crime control in the USA and UK: Streams of influence and levels of impact. *Criminal Justice, 2*(2), 173–203.

———. (2005). Comparative criminal justice policy-making in the United States and the United Kingdom: The case of private prisons. *British Journal of Criminology, 45*(1), 58–80.

———. (2007). *Policy transfer and criminal justice.* Maidenhead, UK: Open University Press.

Laub, J. H. (2004). The life course of criminology in the United States. *Criminology, 42*(1), 1–26.

Majchrzak, A. (1984). *Methods for Policy Research.* London: Sage Publications.

Marion, N. E. (2002). *Criminal justice in America: The politics behind the system.* Durham, NC: Carolina Academic Press.

Mears, D. P. (2007). Towards rational and evidence-based crime policy. *Journal of Criminal Justice, 35*, 667–82.

Miller, W. B. (1973). Ideology and criminal justice policy: Some current issues. *Journal of Criminal Law and Criminology, 64*(2), 141–62.

Nagel, S., et al. (1983). Introduction: General relations between political science and criminal justice. In S. Nagel et al. (Eds.), *The political science of criminal justice* (pp. ix–xii). Illinois: Thomas Books.

———. (1983). Introduction. In S. Nagel et al. (Eds.), *The political science of criminal justice* (pp. 5–13). Illinois: Thomas Books.

Newburn, T., & Jones, T. (2007). Symbolizing crime control: Reflections on zero tolerance. *Theoretical Criminology, 11*(2), 221–43.

Pross, A. P. (1986). *Group politics and public policy.* Toronto: Oxford University Press.

Roberts, J. (1994). *Public knowledge of crime and justice: An inventory of Canadian findings.* Ottawa: Department of Justice.

Rock, P. (1986). *A view from the shadows: The Ministry of the Solicitor General of Canada and the making of the justice for victims of crime initiative.* Oxford: Clarendon Press.

———. (2010). Comment on 'public criminologies'. *Criminology and Public Policy, 9*(4), 751–67.

Ruth, H., & Reitz, K. R. (2003). *The challenge of crime: Rethinking our response.* Cambridge, MA: Harvard University Press.

Scheingold, S. A. (1984). *The politics of law and order: Street crime and public policy.* New York: Longman.

———. (1991). *The politics of street crime: Criminal process and cultural obsession.* Philadelphia: Temple University Press.

Sheehy, E. (2004). Advancing social inclusion: The implications for criminal law and policy. *Canadian Journal of Criminology and Criminal Justice, 46*(1), 73–95.

Simeon, R. (1972). *Federal-provincial diplomacy.* Toronto: University of Toronto Press.

Simon, J. (2007). *Governing through crime: How the war on crime transformed American democracy and created a culture of fear.* New York: Oxford University Press.

Solomon, P. (1981). The policy process in Canadian criminal justice: A perspective and research agenda. *Canadian Journal of Criminology, 23,* 5–25.

———. (1991). Politics and crime: A survey. In J. Gladstone et al. (Eds.), *Criminology: A Readers Guide* (pp. 157–76). Toronto: University of Toronto, Centre of Criminology.

Stolz, B. A. (2002). The roles of interest groups in US criminal justice policy-making: Who, when, and how. *Criminal Justice, 2*(1), 51–69.

Stone, D. (1988). *Policy paradox and political reason.* Boston: Scott, Foresman/Little.

Uggen, C., & Inderbitzin, M. (2010). Public criminologies. *Criminology and Public Policy, 9*(4), 725–49.

Welsh, B. C., & Farrington, D. P. (2005). Evidence-based crime prevention: Conclusions and directions for a safer society. *Canadian Journal of Criminology and Criminal Justice, 47*(2), 337–54.

Zajac, G. (2002). Knowledge creation, utilization and public policy: How do we know what we know in criminology? *Criminology and Public Policy, 1*(2), 251–4.

INTRODUCTION

SUGGESTED READINGS

Clear, T., & Frost, N. (2008). Rules of engagement: Criminology and criminal justice policy. *Criminal Justice Matters, 72*, 37–8.

Currie, E. (2007). Against marginality: Arguments for a public criminology. *Theoretical Criminology, 11*(2), 175–90.

Doob, A., & Webster, C.M. (2006). Countering punitiveness: Understanding stability in Canada's imprisonment rate. *Law and Society Review, 40*, 325–67.

Lafree, G. (2007). Expanding criminology's domain. *Criminology, 45*(1), 501–32.

Rock, P. (1995). The opening stages of criminal justice policy-making. *British Journal of Criminology, 35*, 1–16.

SUGGESTED WEBSITES

Children and Youth, Crime Prevention through Social Development. http://www.ccsd.ca/cpsd/ccsd/index.htm

Department of Justice Canada. http://www.justice.gc.ca/eng/cons/rt-tr/index.html

Department of Justice Canada, Policy Centre for Victim Issues. http://www.justice.gc.ca/eng/pi/pcvi-cpcv/index.html

International Centre for Criminal Law Reform and Criminal Justice Policy. http://www.icclr.law.ubc.ca/Index.htm

Public Safety Canada. http://www.publicsafety.gc.ca/pol/index-eng.aspx

PART 1
The Criminal Justice System

OVERVIEW

Part I of our text explores policy developments among the more traditional aspects of the criminal justice system—policing, pre-trial detention, sentencing, and the use of imprisonment in Canada. Specific attention has also been devoted to policy developments within the areas of youth justice, Aboriginal justice, and domestic violence courts. Those topics, we felt, deserved their own focus because they have their own histories, policy developments, and debates that set them apart from the other aspects of the criminal justice system. There are, however, similar themes that emerge in all of the chapters. All of the authors explore the evolution of policy over time—some focusing on improvements, however slight (e.g., Ursel; Barn-horst; Clark and Landau), others describing a rather sad story of principled debate evolving into simplistic, punitive-sounding slogans and catchy phrases (e.g., Doob and Webster; Manson; Webster and Doob). All of the chapters emphasize that these criminal justice issues may appear deceptively simple (e.g., one law that the federal government is responsible for), but there are complexities owing to the division of powers between federal and provincial governments. In some cases, while the federal government is responsible for the law (e.g., pre-trial detention, sentencing, youth justice, etc.), the provinces are responsible for the administration of the law and thus there is considerable provincial variation and competing interests. In other cases, the provinces have more responsibility for crafting policy than the federal government (e.g., policing and domestic violence courts), which leads to enormous variation across Canada that can prove difficult for those trying to understand changes in policy.

Murphy, in chapter 1, describes how pre-9/11 'public' police in most Western societies were in institutional decline. Neo-liberal initiatives to diminish government expenditures and limit responsibilities for services like public policing resulted in the expansion of 'alternative' forms of private, community, and self-policing. However, the terrorist attacks in New York, London, and Spain dramatically changed the role and direction of policing policy in most Western countries. Murphy discusses the key macro-level policy drivers of Canadian policing since 9/11 (e.g., globalization and crime; policing global-local terrorism; the politicization of post-9/11 policing) and details their impact on current police policy and practice in Canada (e.g., reinvestment in public policing; diversification of the public policing role; intelligence-led policing). He argues that Canadian policing is in a critical transition period as it faces a myriad of local and national pressures to respond to demands to become more rational and national in its structure and operations. However, Canada does not have a strong 'federal' notion of national policing, and thus it may be that Canadian policing will remain predominately local in orientation, concerned more about managing immediate community-level (or provincial) policing problems, than about participating in the creation of an integrated national and strategic policing policy response.

Doob and Webster, in their chapter on pre-trial detention (chapter 2), examine changes in legislation from the 1960s onward. Historically, there was considerable concern about the detention of legally innocent people and having release based on cash bail. These concerns led to the 1971 Bail Reform Act, which, among other things, created a system of non-cash bail and a presumption against detention. However, as Doob and Webster argue, the law in the Criminal Code and the law as it actually operates in bail court often do not look very much alike. Thus, the presumption against detention has been a principle that, one could argue, is not seen in practice. Currently, the number of people in provincial institutions who have not been sentenced exceeds the number who are serving sentences. Doob and Webster examine the reasons for this and discuss the recent amendments to the Criminal Code that affect bail. They conclude that while recent amendments were supported by all political parties, political gain appears to have been more important than the need to deal with the complexities around pre-trial detention.

Manson (chapter 3) traces the evolution of sentencing policy for murder cases from capital punishment to life imprisonment. What started as a principled debate appears, over time, to have deteriorated into a series of emotional debates with little substance or evidence. Many of the titles of the bills that have recently been introduced are misleading and do not accurately reflect the proposed changes.

Moreover, the debates that occur within Parliament appear overly simplistic and emotional, rather than based on the evidence and facts relating to how the system actually operates. Manson persuasively argues that the changes introduced, and passed, were clearly intended to make the government appear 'tough on crime' and to address the perceived 'needs of victims' rather than any real problems with the administration of law. In addition, there are serious problems inherent in basing criminal justice responses solely on what victims want. Manson notes that, sadly, this legislative strategy succeeded with little or no opposition and that the committees that had provided valuable insight in the past are now 'rubber stamps'.

In chapter 4, Webster and Doob explore some reasons for Canada's surprising stability in the use of imprisonment. While Canada has issued official policy statements about what should happen to prisoners when in prison, it does not have an explicit set of policies on who should be sent to prison. Nevertheless, over the last 100 years—in fact, until very recently—Canada has had relative stability in the use of imprisonment. Webster and Doob examine possible explanations for this stability, focusing on historical, structural, and cultural factors. In all three domains, there appears to be consensus that restraint in the use of imprisonment is necessary. The restrained approach of Canada's political parties is somewhat surprising and clearly stands in stark contrast to the longer-term politicization of crime in nations like the United States or England and Wales. Most recently, there have been slight increases in the use of imprisonment in Canada, and Webster and Doob consider whether or not these increases may be signalling a break with our long-standing tradition of stability.

Barnhorst, in chapter 5, examines the long policy process that resulted in the passing of the Youth Criminal Justice Act (YCJA) in 2003. The YCJA was developed to address some key concerns around the implementation of the previous youth justice legislation (the Young Offenders Act). While some provinces—and members of the public—were concerned about apparent 'leniency', the Department of Justice was concerned about the evidence that suggested that court and custody were being overused for minor offences. The substantial changes contained in the YCJA were the result of a difficult seven-year reform process in which compromises were made in an attempt to address concerns raised by the provinces, academics, policing organizations, and victims groups. In the end, the YCJA became law and saw great success in achieving its main objectives. Barnhorst provides insight into some of the factors that contributed not only to the passing of the Act, but also to the success in its implementation.

In chapter 6, Clark and Landau recognize the history of criminal justice failures with respect to dealing with Aboriginal peoples. Whether one looks provincially or federally, Aboriginal peoples are overrepresented in court and in custody facilities. Clark and Landau explore this overrepresentation and the reasons for it. They explore the relevance of systemic discrimination as an explanatory framework and the kinds of policy initiatives that have been developed to address the problem of overrepresentation. While some progress has been made in terms of the policies developed, many challenges remain. In particular, some of the problems faced by Aboriginal peoples, such as those that contribute to their overrepresentation in correctional facilities (e.g., poverty, unemployment, marginalization), lie beyond the purview of the criminal justice system.

Finally, Ursel, in chapter 7, investigates the proliferation of domestic violence courts across Canada and situates the growth within the larger context of 'problem–solving' courts that have been developing throughout the United States and Canada. Domestic violence was initially thought of as a personal, private issue, but as the feminist movement gained support and momentum throughout the 1970s and 1980s, domestic violence was transformed into a serious social problem. Traditional responses (e.g., charging and prosecuting) seemed inadequate and did not sufficiently address the needs of victims or the complexity of the issue. In short, there was fertile ground for domestic violence courts to take root. Ursel's chapter investigates the growth of these courts across Canada, focusing on one such Winnipeg court in considerable detail. While the problem of domestic violence remains, there is no question that people's understanding of this complex issue has improved over time.

1

Canadian Police and Policing Policy, Post-9/11

Christopher Murphy

Prior to the game-changing terrorist attack in New York on 9/11/2001, the academic narrative on public policing argued that the public police in most Western societies were in institutional decline, subject to neo-liberal initiatives to diminish government expenditures and limit responsibilities for public services like policing (Bayley & Shearing, 1998; Murphy, 1998). Despite continuing demand, public policing in the decade before the attacks had become increasingly, rationalized, responsibilized, privatized, diversified, and pluralized (Jones & Newburn, 2002). Government spending restraints and concerns about rapidly growing policing costs and expanding policing commitments dramatically limited police growth (Murphy, 2002) while encouraging the expansion of 'alternative' forms of private, community, and self-policing. However, the horrific, but successful, terrorist attacks in New York, London, and Spain dramatically changed the role and direction of public policing and policing policy in most Western countries, amplifying some existing trends and stimulating various new developments (Ransly & Mazerolle, 2009). This chapter (a) examines the key macro-level policy drivers of Canadian policing since 9/11; (b) discusses their impact on current police policy and practice in Canada; and (c) explores emerging policing policy issues. However, before we engage in an analysis of Canadian policing policy, it is useful to first reflect on what we mean by policing and police policy, and try to untangle the complex relationships between them.

POLICE AND POLICING POLICY IN CANADA

Building on important conceptual distinctions made by Shearing and Stenning (1987) and later by Brodeur (2007), 'policing' in this article refers to a broad set of regulatory and coercive activities that are designed to maintain public order, safety, and security, and can be engaged in by a variety of public and private agencies. The 'police' are a government agency, authorized by law and public and political consent to provide a variety of policing services, the most central being the enforcement of law and order. While this article focuses primarily on the 'public police', it is important to recognize that there are a number of other possible policing agencies whose roles and relationships are changing in late or postmodern Canada.

'Policy' for the purposes of this essay refers to a planned course of action intended to influence and determine specific institutional outcomes or practices. Policies are in most cases formally articulated or written as an institutional or organizational response to a set of external or internal circumstances or pressures. Policies can be *proactive* in the sense that they are intended to initiate a preferred or desired police response or practice (e.g., minority recruitment), or they can be *reactive* in the sense that they are *ex post facto* attempts to reflect and incorporate a change in existing practice. Policy-making in policing is complicated by the unclear governance relationship between the broader public and political policy environment and the traditional operational autonomy of public policing. A semi-autonomous relationship between political governance and internal police policy development suggests that police policy-making is often the result of a negotiated external and internal political process. There are occasions where political or public pressure results in the development of new or adjusted policing policies and practices (e.g., community policing, police response to domestic violence), and there are also instances where public policy pressures are ignored (e.g., police taser policy).

A variety of relations between policing policy and police practices can be observed. It is quite possible that changes at the operational level aren't always reflected in formal police policy, or the reverse, that formal policy changes are not reflected in policing practice. Without the benefits of ongoing operational research and evaluation, it is difficult to say whether police policies are actually working as intended or not. Thus the question of policy and practice remains an empirical question, one that varies in accordance with each policy-related issue.

Policy analysis examines the broad external policy environment of public policing as it produces changes in internal strategic or operational policies and practice. However, the development of strategic policy in Canada is an uncertain product of a loosely federated governance and policy environment, one fragmented by various federal, provincial, and municipal political jurisdictions and interests. So, while the federal government is responsible for changes to the Criminal Code and uses the RCMP in a national policing policy capacity, the basic governance responsibility for all non-federal policing rests with provincial and municipal governments. Thus, Canadian policing policy is seldom the result of a federally led national policy planning process, but is more often a product and mix of shared national and local policing politics and policy concerns.

Despite governance decentralization, the basic operational policies that govern the structure, organization, and delivery of police services in Canada are essentially

> **BOX 1.1**   Evidence-Free Policing—Only in Canada
> You Say—Pity!
>
> Compared to countries such as the United States, Great Britain, and Aus-
> tralia, Canada has a limited academic and applied police research environ-
> ment. Neither Canadian police nor the different levels of government
> responsible for police services are willing to invest in research or policy
> evaluation. While there are some outstanding Canadian police academics
> and researchers dispersed throughout the country and some larger police
> services have reasonably well-developed internal operations research pro-
> grams, there is no national centre or agency dedicated to social science
> research on policing. Canada doesn't have the equivalent of the US Police
> Executive Research Forum, the Police Foundation, the National Institute of
> Justice, or, in the UK, the Home Office Police Research Unit, the Scottish
> Institute for Policing Research, or the various police research programs and
> institutes in Australian universities. Though the absence of a centre for Can-
> adian police research has been increasingly acknowledged as a problem, the
> practices of developing policy without a research foundation, of imple-
> menting policy without evaluation, and of adopting police policy and research
> from other countries unfortunately characterizes the current Canadian
> police policy environment. So when major policy or operational problems
> arise and public investigation and commissions follow, there is often no
> existing body of Canadian research knowledge or capacity to address the
> issues involved. This curiously Canadian disregard for critical policy reflec-
> tion and empirical evidence is especially problematic in the era of so-called
> intelligence-based policing and evidence-based policy-making.

standardized through a common set of legal powers and procedural rules (e.g., the
Criminal Code) and the homogenizing influences of specific federal legislation,
regulations, and statutes. In addition, Canadian policing has evolved an institutional culture where policing policies and procedures are often exchanged and
best practices shared. As a result, most police services have similar operational policies, regulations, standards, and operating procedures for most aspects of routine
police work. While all police services may not perform these functions in identical
ways, there is at least at the operational policy level a significant degree of uni-
formity in Canadian policing policy.

Finally, when we compare the general strategic nature and direction of policing policy and practice in Canada (e.g., community policing), it is remarkably
similar to general international policing policy trends and developments. In the
global era of the Internet, local police policy response often adopts or adapts to
policing policy and practice from other regional, national, or international policy
centres. Global policy transfer (Newburn, 2002) in public policing is now a

pervasive and organized enterprise. The challenge for developing policing policy in Canada is to resist the tendency to overlook distinctive national or local policing contexts before adopting generic policy responses. For example, Canadian 'use of force' policies, technologies, and training have been largely imported from the United States without much modification for our distinctive Canadian cultural and sociological context, sometimes with unfortunate consequences. So, while Canada is an active part of the global policing policy environment, we must also recognize that Canada has its own distinctive history, culture, and politics that should affect the way police policy issues are perceived and addressed. Box 1.2 proposes some distinctive Canadian contextual qualities that could be said to distinguish Canadian policing.

BOX 1.2   What's Canadian about Canadian Policing?
Generalizations and Hypotheses

1. Canada historically has had a conservative political culture, one that values 'peace, order, and good government'. Canadians' belief in 'government and governance' is reflected in their supportive attitudes to public police and policing in general.
2. Public police in Canada enjoy an unusually high level of public and political support. Gallup polls rank the police as one of the most trusted occupations, with higher status than in the United States or the UK.
3. Canadian police may be the best-paid public police in the world and also the most expensive. Canadians spend more per capita on public policing than do comparable countries such as the United States, England, and Australia.
4. However, Canada has fewer police per capita than do those same comparison countries. We have developed a model of public policing that pays high salaries to fewer police officers, while these other countries have elected to have more police but pay them less.
5. Canadian police history suggests that Canadian police operate with a high degree of political independence and that Canadian policing does not have the same history of political corruption as police in the United States and Australia.
6. Canada allocates police and policing governance responsibilities to all three levels of government: municipal, provincial, and federal. This makes our police system less centralized than Great Britain's but more centralized than that in the United States.
7. Canada has no 'national' police force. The RCMP is often regarded as such because it has a broad policing mandate. It has distinct federal policing functions, it provides national police support services to Canadian police, it has contractual policing agreements for provincial policing in seven provinces, it serves as municipal police in more than 200 municipalities

and a number of Aboriginal communities, and it has responsibilities for some international policing functions.

8. However, the RCMP does not operate as the provincial police in two of the most populous provinces in Canada (Ontario and Quebec), and it doesn't police any major urban municipalities in Canada (except Burnaby, BC). So approximately 70 per cent of the Canadian population are not directly policed by the RCMP but by municipal or provincial police services.

POST-9/11 POLICY DRIVERS OF CANADIAN POLICING

Canadian policing over the last 10 years has been shaped by many of the same global forces that are influencing policing and security policy and practices everywhere in the Western world. The following describes how some of these global pressures are being translated at the national and local levels in Canadian policing.

Globalization and Crime

Globalization describes an array of interrelated social, economic, and political forces and change processes (Eriksen, 2007). A global market economy, rapid and pervasive communication systems, and increased mobility are creating new possibilities for both traditional and new criminal and political threats to domestically policed local order and security. As a result, globalization and the processes and technologies associated with it are changing not only what the police do but also how they do it. Globalization complicates and expands the threat of traditional crime by introducing new non-local or externally linked actors and products into locally policed environments. As a result, responding to global or nationally linked crime and terrorism networks and linkages has become a new national and local policing priority.

Nationally and federally, this has meant that global or internationally organized crime has become a bigger priority for both the federal government and the RCMP and has led to increased demand for already limited federal policing resources and capacities (see chapter 12 by Margaret Beare in this volume). The RCMP has in the last 10 years made global organized crime one of its five key operational priorities, and it is devoting more of its resources to expanding its own international policing capacity through enhanced intelligence and international policing partnerships.

The globalization of crime has also affected municipal and local policing in Canada. Because an increasing amount of 'local' crime is not local in origin and often has global roots and connections, municipal police in Canada must now increasingly respond to crimes and criminals with international and local linkages, such as transnational smuggling networks, budding homegrown terrorist cells, cross-border drug and human smuggling rings, online global cybercrime groups, complex multinational fraud and money-laundering schemes, and organized crime and local grow-ops. These crimes have only recently become municipal police concerns and in varying degrees are a shared responsibility with the federal RCMP. While both federal RCMP and municipal police have responsibilities granted to them by the federal Criminal Code, the federal RCMP have a leadership role in crime areas of mutual interest, such as organized crime, drug crimes, border and port security, financial crimes, national security, and cybercrime. Operationally, the federal policing role is determined by case complexity, jurisdictional requirements, the need for specialized and dedicated investigative resources, and the organizational capacity and resources to support complex, lengthy, and expensive investigations.

BOX 1.3	The Federal RCMP Policing Mandate

The federal policing mandate of the RCMP is described in various ways. Formally, the RCMP enforces 250 federal statutes and shares a responsibility with all other Canadian police services to enforce the federal Criminal Code. Operationally, this federal Criminal Code mandate translates into a variety of federal policing priorities, such as border integrity (e.g., customs and excise, immigration and passport enforcement); drugs and organized crime (e.g., various Criminal Code offences related to drug enforcement and organized crime); financial and commercial crime (e.g., investigations into proceeds of crime, integrated market enforcement, and related Criminal Code offences); and policing activities related to national security and international policing. The increasingly transnational and global nature of crime and the rise of international and domestic terrorism have given new importance to the federal policing role of the RCMP.

Because of the shared local and federal nature of these crimes, federal and municipal policing interests often overlap and require some kind of operating relationship and collaborative or joint response. Though federal-municipal police relationships are extensive, they vary by location, enforcement issues, political context, and interpersonal and institutional history, resulting in fragmented, sometimes competitive, and often inconsistent police responses. The lack of a *national policing policy* in Canada, one that would set national and local policing standards and develop a funding formula and protocols to ensure police collaboration, undermines the effectiveness of the required national policing response to national and international crime.

Policing Global-Local Terrorism

RCMP Priority 2: National security and the threat of terrorism remain top priorities for Canadians. The RCMP will detect, disrupt/prevent and investigate terrorist criminal activity in Canada and abroad; ensure border integrity; and, working with a number of Canadian police agencies and federal departments, prepare a counter-radicalization strategy for the entire Canadian law enforcement and security community. (RCMP website: retrieved 15 April 2011 from http://www.rcmp-grc.gc.ca/prior/index-eng.htm)

Globalization has been linked in a variety of ways with the recent emergence of global and domestic terrorism in the West (Nassar, 2005). The globally linked domestic terrorist event of 9/11 changed forever the Canadian public perception that terrorism was a limited and primarily foreign phenomenon. While external and domestic terrorism clearly existed in Canada before 9/11, as the Air India terrorist attack so clearly revealed, the threat of terrorism was viewed by governments and police as a relatively minor and low policing priority. The recently released report (Commission of Inquiry into the Investigation of the Bombing of Air India Flight 182, 2010) on the mishandled Air India investigation reveals that Canadian police and security at that time were clearly caught off-guard and were unprepared about how to prevent or indeed investigate such an event. However, the 9/11 attack and the subsequent aggressive US government response galvanized the Canadian federal government and the RCMP into developing Canada's first national security policy and led to the creation of an impressive new national policing and security assemblage.

For Canadian police, adding security policing responsibilities to conventional crime control is a significant new development (Brodeur, 2007; Murphy, 2007). New security powers, along with the need to include local municipal police in a vague but evolving role in national security, are a departure from the conventional crime-control police model. Policing crime is definable and limited by law and results in public and legally framed police responses, such as a referral, warning, charge, or arrest. However, security, a vague policing objective, is open to interpretation, manipulation, and discretion (Zedner, 2003). Security policing as a policing style is more anticipatory, proactive, and preventative, as police must reorient their operations from responding to real events or actions to trying to predict their occurrence and prevent them from happening, effectively moving from 'probable cause' to 'possible cause'.

While in theory the RCMP alone are responsible for the law enforcement aspects of national security, the operational reality of security policing has proved to be more complex and confusing, as law enforcement and security intelligence functions are related and often overlap. Role confusion and conflict are evident in reports on the Air India investigation (Commission of Inquiry into the Investigation of the Bombing of Air India Flight 182, 2010) and in various submissions to the Arar Commission. The Arar Commission's first report (Commission of Inquiry into the Actions of Canadian Officials in Relation to Maher Arar, 2006a) cites questionable RCMP security policing decisions and activities, and explains why the report's first recommendation is that 'the RCMP should ensure that its activities in matters relating to national security are properly within its mandate as a law enforcement agency' (2006a, p. 312).

A national security policy has also made the relationship of the federal RCMP to other provincial and municipal police services in Canada more important, as it makes the RCMP the lead police agency in the development of a nationally integrated policing and security response. Since 9/11, municipal police forces are at least in theory to be regarded as policing and security partners in an RCMP-led 'national security policing response'. However, while much has been made at the policy level of the need for police agency collaboration and an integration of national and local security policing efforts, there has been little articulation of just what those distinctive and collaborative policing roles and responsibilities should be. Despite extra federal funding for RCMP security policing, there has been little or no funding allocated to municipal policing to cover the costs of their national security policing responsibilities. Nevertheless, there have been some clearly successful collaborative joint security policing efforts at the local operational level between the federal RCMP and Toronto, Montreal, and Vancouver police, suggesting that collaborative police practice is not necessarily a product of formal policy, but is driven by necessity and shared policing interests.

Politicization: The Politics of Post-9/11 Policing

The post-9/11 politics of public security and public safety are in part related to the development of the new threats of global organized crime and domestic terrorism and the emergence of a more supportive political environment for public policing in Canada. Growing public concern, amplified by a combination of both sensationalized media and opportunistic political discourse, has created a supportive post-9/11 context for the growth of policing and security in Canada. Though linked to a dramatized increase in certain 'signal' crimes, such as urban gang and gun violence and the pervasive but vague threats of both domestic and imported terrorism, policing has become part of the new conservative politics of law and order. While overall crime rates may be decreasing and the threat of terrorism remains low relative to that in other countries, the federal conservative government has made 'law and order' and 'national security' hot-button public policy issues. Concentrating primarily on creating more punitive laws, expanding minimum sentences, and building new prisons, the war against crime and criminals has also meant more federal and provincial funding support for more police on the streets. In addition, the federal government has been especially responsive to police concerns about limited resources, legal restraints, and the need for new powers (e.g., Internet privacy). The 'tough on crime and criminals' atmosphere tends to validate traditional law enforcement ideologies and practices while undermining more liberal community policing and non-police responses such as community-based crime prevention. Only a politicized and securitized environment, with unrestricted confidence in the police and an ideological commitment to law and order at any cost, could support and defend the recent extraordinary $1-billion policing and security event—the policing of the G-20 meetings in Toronto.

Finally, the politicization of public policing has occurred even more directly than at the G-20 meeting, but in reverse. While police themselves are quick to reject any 'political' involvement or any interference in the management of policing, increasingly Canadian police unions and police leaders are becoming involved in local and federal party politics by either publicly supporting candidates who are perceived to be supportive of police interests or running themselves for public office. The most recent example is the election and appointment to the federal cabinet of Julian Frantino, former chief of Toronto police and commissioner of the Ontario Provincial Police (OPP). An increasing influence of police in the political process and on the policies that affect policing and criminal justice in general is a trend that bears ongoing scrutiny, especially as we move into an era where the power and resources of the police may well become more important in an increasingly uncertain and unstable world.

BOX 1.4	Policing the Toronto G-20

This event was a post-9/11 example of both the politicization and the securitization of Canadian public policing and public safety. Deployed ostensibly to prevent external terrorist attacks on 20 world leaders meeting in Toronto, the Canadian government spent $1 billion, primarily on public policing, to demonstrate to the world Canada's capacity to guarantee public order, safety, and security. Using a variety of existing and questionable legal powers, new force technology, and imported crowd-control techniques, more than 10,000 police officers from various police agencies worked collaboratively with the RCMP and the Toronto police to provide the political leaders meeting in Toronto with a high degree of personal safety. Public safety and public order were translated in practice into a public security event, and providing security to political elites was a policing priority. This required the aggressive policing of a largely peaceful 'public'. The resulting shocking policing images of thousands of heavily armed and armoured riot police, firing rubber bullets and tear gas at largely peaceful demonstrators, surrounding groups and forcefully 'kettling' them for hours, and then aggressively using mass arrest and special-purpose detention centres as ways of managing protesters, were for most Canadians inconsistent with their views of Canada and Canadian policing. Whatever one's view of the potential security threat posed by 'black block' provocations, the message communicated by police was that they would do anything necessary to secure their view of public order, an approach that did not seem to distinguish between legitimate political demonstration and violent rioters. The traditional model of public police as public protectors, limited by law and publicly accountable to the community, was transformed by a security-based state policing model that seemed free to assert its authority through the aggressive use of force and intimidation aimed at protecting the security priorities of government. The seemingly experimental and inconsistent nature of police responses to the protestors suggested police were practising strategies for possible future political protests and anti-terrorism scenarios. Subsequent critical media and public debate has led to a number of public and government enquiries about the enormous cost of security at the G-20 meeting and the questionable police tactics. This debate, however, has been politically framed by the federal government as anti-government and anti-police rather than as a reasonable demand by the public for police accountability in a democratic society.

CURRENT POLICE POLICY AND PRACTICE TRENDS IN CANADA

As a consequence of the activation of these major macro-level social, political, and cultural forces, the role, mandate, and style of policing in Canada are evolving in new ways.

Reinvesting in Public Policing

The most obvious result of these broad social and political changes in terms of both perceived and real increases in global and domestic threats is the dramatic reinvestment by governments in the police as a central government or governance agency. The neo-liberal narrative of the decline of the government role in the provision of public safety in Canada virtually stopped with the terrorist events of 9/11, and a new government narrative evolved in which governments and their police and security services became vital to threatened local and national public safety and security. The 10-year period of fiscal rationalization of public policing that preceded 2001 changed abruptly after 9/11, as government investment in all forms of policing and security grew dramatically. A special 'security budget' allocated an extra $7.8 billion over five years to fit an expanded concept of national security. In addition to new funding for the RCMP, large funding increases were allocated to other national security agencies, including the Canadian Security Intelligence Service (CSIS), the Communication Security Establishment (CSE), and Military Intelligence. Other old or newly created institutions were also given funding for the creation of new security functions or operations such as the coast guard, the new border services agency, overseas immigration offices, public health, and emergency planning. Indeed, so much money was spent on so many different agencies for so many different security initiatives that the federal auditor general conducted a special review of security spending (Auditor General of Canada, 2004).

As Table 1.1 indicates, governments have increased their contributions to public policing significantly since 2000, particularly in comparison to the 10 years prior to the 9/11 attack. Government expenditures on policing rose from $6.8 billion in 2000 to $12.3 billion in 2009, an increase of 81 per cent over nine years; this is partially related to a 20 per cent increase in the number of police officers, a major expansion over the previous nine years. This post-9/11 period has seen the largest percentage increase in government expenditure on public policing in history.

Fear of urban crime and concern about national security combine to explain the political economy of this recent period of remarkable police growth. However, this same period has also seen a dramatic increase in the cost of policing for governments, making the maintenance of growth during a period of economic restraint problematic; this would become a public policy issue in the near future.

TABLE 1.1   Recent growth in Canadian policing

	Police Officers	%	Policing Costs	%	Per Capita Cost per Officer	%
1991	56,766	100.0	$5,426,887,000	100.0	$189	100.0
2000	55,954	98.6	$6,798,531,000	125.3	$222	117.5
2009	67,299	118.6	$12,316,896,000	227.0	$365	193.1

Source: Statistics Canada (2010).

Diversification of the Public Policing Role

Consistent with government's reinvestment in police services has been a gradual and almost imperceptible broadening and diversification of the public police mandate. The conventional, but never accurate, notion that public police are primarily involved in law enforcement and crime control has been replaced by a much broader and more diversified general 'policing and security' mandate. The rationalization of police response or focus on crime control into a more general risk and security policing model (Ericson & Haggerty, 1997) is in part a product of the various kinds of new activities that almost by default now constitute modern urban police work. The new post-9/11 mandate of public safety (Brody, 2009) and public security broadens the notion of public policing to include almost any threat or risk to public order and public safety, broadly conceived. This would include a variety of forms of anti-terrorism policing, such as responses to natural and man-made emergencies, crisis in public-order policing, and the policing of public and political protest—all involving partnering with a variety of other public and private agencies. These diverse policing activities require public police to become far more engaged with other, often quite different, public and private sector partners, and to establish new and unusual inter-agency relationships. 'Interoperability' is a new policy direction for policing, one that promotes the increasing participation of police with other public and private agencies. This means that police will be expected to share and exchange information, technologies, analyses, and techniques, and ultimately to develop collaborative shared multi-agency response strategies, which will mean a blurring of long-established traditional institutional and operational distinctions.

This new broader police mandate of crime control, public safety, and security invariably has an impact on more traditional police crime-control functions. Limited resources mean that traditional police functions must compete with new policing and security functions. As a result, most urban police agencies are increasingly operating as 'serious' crime-response agencies, dealing with serious crimes and limiting wherever possible their involvement with less serious crimes and public order problems. Thus, while public policing after 9/11 has expanded the mandate and scope of public policing activities, it has broadened its reach by limiting its response to more conventional police services such as street patrol, minor crime, and private property protection. The resulting decrease in public and private safety helps explain the ongoing expansion of private policing and security.

Private Policing Growth

Canadian criminologists, Shearing and Stenning (1982, 1983), in a series of classic articles on the nature and growth of private security, and Rigakos (2002), in more recent work on internal organizational dynamics, suggest that today's growth and diversification of private security are simply a recognition or return to a model of policing that existed prior to the growth of the modern welfare state. The continued growth and expansion of private policing had been going on for sometime before 9/11. A review of the most recent available statistics (Statistics Canada, 2008) suggests that private security growth rates have actually outpaced the growth rates in public policing post-9/11. In 2001, there were 84,000 private security personnel (62,860 public police officers), while in 2006, this number had grown to 101,525 private security personnel (68,860 public police officers), a 21 per cent increase in the five-year period, more than double the rate of increase in public police officers during the same period. The continued and expanded growth of private security suggests that a public and private demand for all forms of policing and security have grown since 9/11. While the role of the public police has expanded and diversified since 9/11, policing in general as a collective enterprise, as well as security as a marketable commodity, have also clearly increased. The continuing growth in demand for more private policing and security has implications for public policing.

The role of private policing and security in Canada remains a public policy issue that has yet to be addressed in any comprehensive and coherent national policy framework. Some countries (e.g., England) are establishing formal public-private policing partnerships and regulatory relationships as a way to defend and extend the reach and influence of public policing (Johnston, 2003). The relationship between public and private police in Canada has been characterized more by competition, suspicion, and a reluctant recognition of the legitimacy of the private police function. Police unions concerned about protecting their monopoly on the provision of police services have tried to limit the legitimacy as well as the growth and expansion of private security, especially where it encroaches on traditional public police and public safety functions. Though understandable from a union perspective, the ongoing view that private policing represents competition rather than partnership and a potential expansion of general policing capacity. This view inhibits the development of more progressive integrated models of policing in Canada—models in which a limited but a privately partnered public police force could provide both more policing and broader policing governance. In the meantime, the expansion of private space and private security continues unabated, and the issues of private justice and public accountability remain largely unaddressed.

Policing Risk

Risk and security are linked concepts. Security-oriented policing activities are mobilized by real or perceived security risks. Prior to 9/11, some policing scholars, notably Richard Ericson and Kevin Haggerty, were already arguing that conventional policing in the late modern era had become less focused on crime control and more focused on the surveillance and management of risk. In their 1997 book *Policing the Risk Society*, the authors contend that Canadian policing had begun to shift its emphasis from preventing and responding to crime to the policing of broadly defined 'risk populations' through various surveillance, information, and risk-based strategies, calculations, and analyses. While this may have been a novel hypothesis in 1997, risk rhetoric and risk logic now increasingly dominate policing discourse and practice. Police routinely claim that they do risk assessment, risk management, and risk analysis. The risk of terrorism, more than the risk of crime, provides police with a new rationale for the aggressive collection, integration, and analysis of security information. But risk analysis is itself risky. Security-based risk analysis requires the collection of broad information from a variety of sources and involves highly interpreted and predictive forms of analysis. The variety and range of information collected, the scope of the analysis, the predictive nature of the exercise, and the uncertainty of the outcome produce a high probability of error. When conventional crime-control policing shifts to risk-oriented security policing, it goes from responding to and acting on publicly and legally defined violations and violators to the more nebulous and discretionary goals of monitoring, managing, and anticipating possible security threats or risks. 'Better safe than sorry', the logic of security-based risk, produces justifiable errors and mistakes: the arrests of possible terrorists are made on the basis of limited information; potential terrorists are targeted for surveillance based on unconfirmed sources; a terrorist suspect is handed over to foreign police for interrogation; and suspects with possible links to terrorists can be denied entry or citizenship. Ericson (2006) suggests that these are some of the demonstrated costs of trying to manage the risk of terrorism.

Intelligence-Led Policing

The recent popularity of *intelligence-led policing* (ILP) in government and policing circles is not surprising. In theory, ILP emphasizes aggressive surveillance, information gathering, and analysis as a basis for selective police action (Gill, 2000). Canada's national security policy identifies improved security intelligence as the central pillar of its national security strategy, dedicating an entire chapter to its promotion (Public Safety and Emergency Preparedness Canada, 2004). In particular, the report argues for enhanced security capabilities and the creation of a 'Threat Assessment Centre' for more effective integration and analysis of the information provided by multiple policing and security agencies. While ILP was already an established neo-liberal managerial policing reform (McGuire, 2000), since 9/11, it has rapidly replaced community policing as the new policing rationale and strategy for many Canadian police services.

Instead of the community being a partner in policing, it becomes a problem, a source of intelligence, and a possible target for police action. The RCMP has identified ILP as one of its major organizational priorities, and a number of major municipal police services refer to it as their new operational philosophy (Deukmedjian, 2006). Shifting the discourse of 'community' to the more security-resonant tropes of 'intelligence, information, and risk' suggests that it is now security, not crime, that increasingly rationalizes modern policing. The irresistible combination of neo-liberal rationality, managerial promise, and professional, scientific validation is reassuring in a risk-averse environment. ILP also resonates with traditional police values, as it is police based and proactive, and offers a less restricted and operationally aggressive response, one that is also less publicly visible and accountable.

Security-Based Community Policing

For the last 20 years 'community policing' has been the official 'progressive' model of Western public policing. However, after 9/11, public policing priorities shifted and the discourse of terrorism provided a rationale for police services to question and in some cases abandon community policing, seeing it as a no longer relevant or effective policing model for the more threatening and insecure post-9/11 era. The security crisis of 9/11 also transformed some urban communities into security problems. Communities went from being potential partners to potential suspects, from having a crime problem to being a security problem, and from being communities *at* risk to being communities *of* risk. The 'community as security problem' has become a legitimate space for new domestic security-oriented anti-terrorism policing operations, such as pre-emptive disruption strategies, broad community surveillance, paid community informants, and other forms of social penetration (Haggerty & Ericson, 2000). Suspect communities are pressured to demonstrate their citizenship by 'watching, calling, and sharing' information on suspicious neighbours, friends, and relatives. While using local community policing for national security purposes may be desirable from a security perspective, the heavy-handed use of local police and their local community relationships to meet national security goals may subvert and undermine long-established local police-community relationships while potentially alienating and radicalizing some community members. So, while anti-terrorism provides a strong rationale for securitizing local community policing, it runs the risk of undermining the often fragile police relationships with suspect communities and of discrediting community policing as a viable model for local policing in diverse communities.

However, Canadian police, since 9/11, have generally shown a degree of cultural sensitivity to the challenges of policing suspect ethnic or minority communities. For example, the Cross-Cultural Roundtable on Security was created as an initiative of the national security policy in order to engage minority Canadians and the government of Canada in a long-term dialogue on matters related to national security. The roundtable brings together citizens who are designated leaders in their respective communities and focuses on emerging developments in national security matters and their impact on the communities. While, predictably, the roundtable has its fair share of critics, its creation at least demonstrates an awareness that anti-terrorism and security puts the government and especially its policing agencies in a more complicated and problematic relationship with certain communities.

Taser Policing

Leaving aside the curious absence of any public policy consultation or discussion on the use of 'conducted energy weapons', or tasers, we should note that these weapons have been adopted more broadly and quickly in Canada than in almost any other country in the world. Internal policy shifts that initially classified the taser as a restricted 'alternative to deadly force' weapon and later reclassified it as a lower-risk 'intermediate weapon' with much broader deployment options led to a number of questionable public taser incidents, some resulting in death. Despite a series of serious public and political concerns raised by various critical public inquiries (Braidwood Commission on Conducted Energy Weapon Use, 2009, 2010; Commission for Public Complaints against the RCMP, 2010), Canadian police have vigorously defended their continued discretionary usage policies and the taser's questionable safety record. Police defence of the taser as a 'necessary use of force' option for patrol officers in routine police situations may indicate that police view their current working environment as being increasingly risky and threatening to their personal safety. This perception is fuelled by training scenarios that privilege police safety over public safety and encourage a risk-averse policing style—where actions such as resisting police authority or posing even a minor threat to police officer safety are deemed legitimate grounds for the deployment of a range of potentially lethal weapons and tactics. One wonders whether the use of tasers and other alternative new force technologies and strategies, many of them on trial at the recent policing of the G-20 summit, is not an indication of a new harder-edged post-911 policing style.

EMERGING POLICING POLICY ISSUES

As a result of these post-9/11 pressures and practices, the following issues constitute current and future points of policy tension, debate, and development: police
and policing integration; police capacity and sustainability; and police governance
and accountability. These issues are reviewed in the following sections.

Police and Policing Integration

The terrorist events of 9/11 demonstrated the ability of global-local terrorist networks and relationships to produce threats to public safety and security almost
anywhere in the world. The failure of local police and security agents to anticipate
these terrorist attacks was, in part, a failure of communication among the various
policing and security agencies involved, both nationally and internationally, thus
demonstrating the limitations of traditionally insular and often competitive police
and security agencies. With the rise of global terrorism and the increasingly global
nature of organized crime, more integrated, collaborative, and co-operative policing has become desirable and perhaps inevitable. Various models of police and
policing integration have been offered for consideration in Canada, but they
remain works in progress.

The integration of policing and security was one of the central components of
Canada's national security policy. In a major policy statement (Public Safety and
Emergency Preparedness Canada, 2004), the federal government advocates a variety of measures to 'fully integrate' diverse government departments, systems,
agencies, and the private sector into one integrated national security system. Policing integration is identified in the RCMP's 2005 Strategic Plan, which cites 'the
development of an integrated policing model operating at all levels and in all locations, supporting broad information-sharing, joint national security enforcement
teams, integrated border teams, and joint intelligence and analysis teams.'

Since 9/11, the federal government has given the RCMP a greater role in the
development of a national security response by emphasizing its role in developing
integrated national security policing. 'Police integration' is designed to make individual
policing and security agencies and services more connected, collaborative, and co-
ordinated in order to produce a more nationally focused and coherent police
response to domestic and foreign terrorism. Integrated policing emphasizes the
importance of collaborative and interoperable policing relationships and partnerships. This integrated national policing model is an RCMP-centred or -managed
model that assumes the RCMP to be the logical and appropriate co-ordinator of
all international, national, regional, and local policing and security efforts, while
local municipal police play a support or limited partnership role. This integration
philosophy is evident in a number of recent policing and security (or 'horizontal'
policing) initiatives generated by federal RCMP policing functions. Integrated
Border Enforcement Teams (IBETS), designed to enhance border security between
Canada and the United States, combine senior officials from five core agencies, the

RCMP, the Canada Border Services Agency, US Homeland Security, US Customs and Immigration, and the US Coast Guard. Integrated Market Enforcement Teams (IMET) are inter-agency teams of capital market specialists focusing on enforcement related to the Criminal Code. Integrated National Security Enforcement Teams (INSETS) are located in Vancouver, Toronto, Montreal, and Ottawa, and operate in a co-ordinated way to detect, prevent, disrupt, and investigate terrorist targets in Canada. They work with multiple municipal, provincial, and federal government agencies and other police forces and security agencies. These specific operational initiatives have had varying degrees of success, while the more general notion of a nationally integrated RCMP-led policing response has proven to be far more difficult to develop formally. Operational issues such as governance costs and concerns, the relative priority given to different federal, provincial, and municipal security concerns, and traditional organizational resistance to shared operations typically undermine the success of national police integration efforts.

Integrated policing reinforces and facilitates the blurring of security and policing, as both police and security agencies are part of the same policing network, sharing information, engaging in joint operations, and pursuing overlapping policing and security objectives. Integration is not simply a technical, organizational, or communications arrangement, but a rationale for combining or co-ordinating different kinds of policing and security entities, each with its own interests, values, and practices. It tries to blend them into one compatible or interoperable network, somehow combining quite different goals, institutional competencies, legal limits, and professional standards. Established historical, political, and legal differences in policy, law, rights, and due process protections must often be subordinated to the needs of the network and the demands of reciprocity and partnership. This can create problems, as clearly illustrated in the Maher Arar case, where the RCMP, in meeting its international information-sharing obligations, passed on unreliable or incomplete information about Arar, a Canadian citizen, to US border security police. Different US information standards, risk tolerance, and security practices resulted in Arar being identified erroneously as a terrorist suspect by US security, and he was sent to Syria, where he was brutally tortured. The Arar case illustrates the potential danger of integrating national policing and intelligence agencies across nation-states with different legal values, procedural standards, and security mandates, and highlights the importance of developing effective forms of internal, public, and political governance and accountability for this new type of distributed and de-centred policing operations.

Given the importance attached to developing integrated, multi-sited policing and security environments or networks (Shearing, 2005; Dupont, 2004) and the potential for mistakes or errors, serious questions have been raised about the adequacy of conventional institutional governance and public accountability mechanisms designed to monitor and prevent such problems. While the more fragmented, pluralistic, domestic policing environment of pre-9/11 was perhaps less efficient and effective, it was arguably more governable and democratic.

Nevertheless, the future of Canadian policing would appear to be one in which significant efforts will go into enhancing police and security integration and general interoperability among municipal, provincial, and federal police, as well as into developing external linkages between the federal RCMP police and the various transnational police and security networks.

Police Capacity and Sustainability

While the cost of Canadian policing has always been substantial, post-9/11 saw a significant increase in government expenditures on all forms of policing and security. Increased police expenditures at the federal, provincial, and municipal levels, together with the expansion of security-related policing functions, happened during a period of general government growth and increasing public expenditures. However, the recent near collapse of the global economy followed by debt-based government stimulus spending has created a new and more restrictive fiscal environment for policing. Government debt loads at the federal, provincial, and, especially, municipal levels will limit the current growth trends in public policing and lead to another period of the pre-9/11 type of restraint, reduction, and rationalization. As police budgets continue to expand their proportion of government spending, especially for municipal governments, they raise serious questions about the value and sustainability of the current model of public policing. The previous neo-liberal rationalization of public policing may once again make economic and political sense in an era in which governments will be forced to limit and choose between public services like policing, education, health care, and so on. This has already happened in Great Britain, where the British police have been asked to sustain 20 per cent cuts in their operating budget, which will result in the loss of more than 5,000 police officers. In the United States, a number of major and small cities have sustained similar cutbacks as their municipal and state governments face potential bankruptcy.

While Canada's economic situation is marginally better, the cost projections as indicated in Figure 1.1 for Canadian policing are higher than in either Great Britain or the United States. Thus, the debate over fiscal restraint and necessary reductions in government spending has just begun at both the federal and municipal level. Already the RCMP and a number of police services in urban centres such as Winnipeg and Toronto are being asked to make cuts to their budgets. Maintaining the current level of police service will be challenging given the current trend of 5 per cent annual increases in police salaries and costs. Budget freezes and personnel cutbacks will inevitably mean a reduction and rationalization of existing police services, although this time it will be more challenging given the previous rationalization of police services during the 1990s. Maintaining core police services will remain a priority, but will inevitably require withdrawal of police resources from less serious but nevertheless valued public policing services such visible patrol, traffic, community policing, and crime prevention. The under-the-radar transfer of policing responsibilities back to individuals, the community,

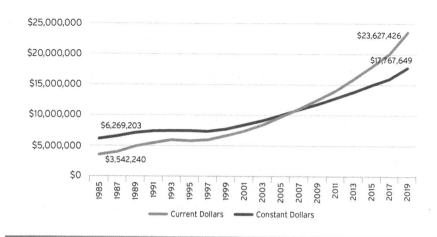

FIGURE 1.1   Police expenditures and projections 1985–2020, current and constant $000's

and private and commercial enterprises will continue to spur growth in personal and private security responses and declining public satisfaction with the police.

The expensive and inefficient traditional police-only service model may prove to be difficult to maintain given its expensive reliance on highly paid, trained, and legally empowered police constables to provide virtually all policing and security services. There will be pressures to change the standard model of service delivery and experiment with more diverse and cheaper alternative service delivery models. Other countries, such as England and selected jurisdictions in the United States, are already experimenting with various versions of police-civilian service delivery, such as community constables and civilian investigators. Canadian policing, with its strong union presence and limited government leadership, has resisted innovations that challenge any diminution of the conventional 'police only' model. Given the choice between cutting costs through diminution of traditional police services and experimenting with more cost-efficient police alternatives, Canadian police—like many of their public service colleagues—opted for the former rather than weaken their commitment to traditional modes of service delivery.

At the federal level, the fiscal investment in the RCMP is already becoming more limited despite the federal government's commitment to federally led policing and security. The current unwieldy, complex, and expensive policing and security mandate of the RCMP may not be fiscally sustainable, and given its recent series of institutional problems, it may also not be entirely manageable. RCMP costs promise to escalate dramatically in the near future if the current proposal for RCMP unionization proceeds successfully. The prospects of a unionized RCMP will no doubt improve the personal safety and financial security of individual police officers but will be achieved through higher policing expenditures and a reduction in the nature and extent of traditional RCMP police services. As these costs increase and service levels drop, the sustainability of the current multi-dimensional RCMP model of policing may well become a public and political issue of substance, while the 'federal only' RCMP model becomes both fiscally and politically more appealing.

Police Governance and Accountability

While public attitudes toward the police in most Western countries remain generally supportive, there has been a shift in recent public discourse regarding police governance of their own behaviour, especially deviant behaviour. Though reflective of more general suspicion of all authoritative institutions, the misuse or the abuse of police powers and police corruption has lately been central to public discourse and discussion. Changing public attitudes toward police were revealed in a recent Ipsos Read poll (2011) that found that trust in the police in Canada had fallen from a high of 73 per cent in 2003 to 57 per cent in 2011—a significant 16 per cent drop. Shifts like this are usually stimulated by high-profile police incidents or cases, and lead to questions regarding the desirability and effectiveness of police regulating and governing their own actions and behaviour. The privileged status and powers of all professions, together with their claims to self-regulation and operational autonomy, are under attack as part of a general postmodern scepticism about all authoritative institutions. Traditional claims for operational autonomy are being challenged by more public and political demands for demonstrable external accountability (Stenning, 2005).

BOX 1.5   Cellphones and Police Surveillance

Reinforcing the trend toward accountability is the increasing surveillance of police activities through public technologies such as video cameras and video-phones. Some police actions that were once private or backstage are now on public display for anyone with a television or an Internet connection. For example, current public outrage and policy change over the use of conducted energy weapons (tasers) by the RCMP were clearly animated by a random bystander's video-phone recording of one such event, and the policing of the G-20 summit was captured extensively on camera by the participants. The growing pervasiveness of the technology of public police surveillance means that the police themselves are increasingly being monitored by the public, which makes it even harder for them to protect themselves from public criticism, review, or opinion (Ericson & Haggerty, 1997). Increasing new social-media scrutiny and public techno-surveillance dramatically amplify incidents and elements of police deviance or error, feeding public arguments for more accountability civilian review and regulation.

The increasingly broad and diverse nature of modern policing and the broad mandate of public safety and security, coupled with ongoing efforts to expand police collaboration and integration with other agencies of government, the private sector, and community agencies, have created a sense of urgency among policing scholars and commissions of inquiry about the need for new, more effective, and empowered structures for police governance (Sheptycki, 1995, 2002). Canadian policing has, in the last few years, seen an unprecedented number of public inquiries and government investigations into various kinds of police and policing problems and wrongdoing. Public inquiries and commissions have been struck to investigate a variety of problematic police activities and functions, such as political interference in policing (Ipperwash Inquiry, 2007), the RCMP role in the Mahar Arar wrongful terrorism conviction and torture case (Commission of Inquiry into the Actions of Canadian Officials in Relation to Maher Arar, 2006a, 2006b), RCMP and CSIS competence in the Air India terrorism investigation (Commission of Inquiry into the Investigation of the Bombing of Air India Flight 182, 2010), a number of high-profile taser-related inquiries (Braidwood Commission on Conducted Energy Weapon Use, 2009, 2010; Commission for Public Complaints against the RCMP, 2010), two investigations into senior RCMP management and leadership (Public Safety and Emergency Preparedness Canada, 2007; Commission for Public Complaints against the RCMP, 2009), and most recently a report on the policing of the Toronto G-20 meetings (Ombudsman of Ontario, 2010). These high-profile and critical public investigations have revealed a number of general problems with the traditional reliance on the internal police investigation of police wrongdoing and with the limited capacity and reach of external police governance agencies. Virtually all of the recent public inquiries regarding Air India, Maher Arar, and tasers concluded that more independent and effective civilian investigation and governance mechanisms needed to be established to ensure more acceptable and effective police governance of policing.

Governance and accountability structures that do not have to rely on traditional internal mechanisms of police self-governance as a basis for external review suggest a trend toward civilian review and alternative models to those of police investigating themselves. Civilian investigation and external review have become more apparent in a number of recent developments such, as the ongoing activities of the Special Investigations Unit in Ontario, the creation of the Alberta Law Enforcement Review Board, and the proposed creation of a civilian-led Serious Incident Response Team in Nova Scotia. Recent indications that the RCMP will allow its members to be subject to various provincial models of police governance and accountability are also a significant step toward acknowledging increasing demands for more local accountability and external investigation of police misconduct or wrongdoing. Related provincial government initiatives that try to encompass both public and private policing support arguments for new models of 'policing' as opposed to police governance (Stenning, 2009).

Thus, the recent growth, diversity, and reach of post-9/11 policing are challenging the capacity and mechanisms of conventional police governance and public accountability, suggesting that we are now in a period of governance catch-up. The need to create more powerful governance agencies that can independently monitor and investigate the use of new police powers, capacities, and inter-agency relationships in ways that are consistent with both public interest and policing and security concerns will be the major policing policy challenge of the next era.

CONCLUSION: THE UNCERTAIN FUTURE OF CANADIAN POLICING

The globalization of policing and security, the expansion of the public police role beyond crime to public safety, the diversification of agents and agencies involved in policing and security, and increasing pressures to link, collaborate, and integrate policing in a more coherent national policing and security mandate suggest both a validation and a challenge to the academic narrative of policing development after 9/11. Canadian policing is in a critical transition period, as it faces a myriad of local and national pressures to respond to demands to become more rational and national in structure and operations. However, this kind of collective response requires overcoming long-established institutional, jurisdictional, and cultural differences, and moving away from a generally decentralized, largely unintegrated, and often parochial and competitive assemblage of federal, provincial, and municipal police agencies.

BOX 1.6   Toward a National Policing Policy for Canada?

Dissatisfaction with the ambiguous state of federal 'national' and 'local' provincial or municipal policing in Canada has recently been publicly articulated by the Federation of Canadian Municipalities (FCM) and the Canadian Association of Chiefs of Police (CACP). A report commissioned by the CACP strongly endorsed the need to create 'a policing public policy framework to address the goals of interagency co-operation and jurisdictional challenges that have been identified as a major challenge . . . and should be endorsed by all levels of government and developed around the concept of collaboration and systematic accountability.' This was followed by a report by the Institute for Strategic International Studies (2006) that similarly endorsed the need for a new national policing arrangement or new deal that is described in the report as 'a nationally co-ordinated locally effective policy and funding framework'. Currently, the CACP is on record as supporting the development of a new national policing framework through a process of consultation and negotiation with all levels of government. The federal government and the RCMP have to date not officially responded.

Despite serious global and local challenges facing Canadian policing, the traditionally decentralized policy and governance framework suggests that Canada will continue to adopt a reactive approach to police and policing policy and governance problems and issues. Lacking a strong, central, and activist 'federal' notion of national policing, Canadian policing may well remain local and parochial in orientation, concerned more about managing immediate local policing problems than about participating in the creation of an integrated national and strategic policing policy response.

CRITICAL THINKING QUESTIONS

1. What are the relevant 'Canadian' values and traditions that shape and influence Canadian policing policy and practice?

2. Should policing policy in Canada be driven from the centre by the federal government or as is now the case in a more decentralized and loosely co-ordinated federal-, provincial-, and municipal-based policing model? Which model do you think offers the best approach for dealing with postmodern Canadian policing issues and problems?

3. The increasingly expensive model of policing we have developed in Canada may not be fiscally or politically sustainable in the near future. What are the implications for Canadian policing and public safety?

4. The future of policing in Canada and elsewhere is complicated by a new set of globally connected threats or risks such as new forms of organized crime and terrorism. Do you think domestic Canadian police are prepared to deal with these new threats?

5. As domestic policing in Canada becomes more powerful, diverse, and complex, what are the implications for effective police accountability and transparency?

REFERENCES

Auditor General of Canada. (2004). *2004 Report of the Auditor General of Canada to the House of Commons.* Chapter 3, National security in Canada—The 2001 anti-terrorism initiative. Ottawa: Government of Canada.

Bayley, D., & Shearing, C. (1998). The future of policing. In G.P. Alpert & A.R. Piquero (Eds.), *Community policing: Contemporary readings.* Prospect Heights, IL: Waveland Press.

Braidwood Commission on Conducted Energy Weapon Use. (2009). *Restoring public confidence: Restricting the use of conducted energy weapons in British Columbia.* Victoria: Government of British Columbia.

Braidwood Commission on the Death of Robert Dziekanski. (2010). *Why?: The Robert Dziekanski tragedy.* Victoria: Government of British Columbia.

Brodeur, J.-P. (2007). High and low policing in post-9/11 times. *Policing, A Journal of Policy and Practice, 1*(1), 25–37.

Brody J. (2009). From social security to public safety. *University of Toronto Quarterly, 78*(2), 687–708.

Commission for Public Complaints against the RCMP. (2009). *Police investigating police: Final public report: A chair-initiated complaint and public interest investigation into public concerns about the impartiality of RCMP members conducting criminal investigations into other RCMP members in cases involving serious injury or death.* Ottawa : Government of Canada.

———. (2010). *RCMP use of the conducted energy weapon (CEW): January 1, 2009 to December 31, 2009: Special report of June 24, 2010.* Ottawa : Government of Canada.

Commission of Inquiry into the Actions of Canadian Officials in Relation to Maher Arar. (2006a). *Report of the events relating to Maher Arar: Analysis and recommendations.* Ottawa: Government of Canada.

———. (2006b). *A new review mechanism for the RCMP's national security activities.* Ottawa: Government of Canada.

Commission of Inquiry into the Investigation of the Bombing of Air India Flight 182. (2010). *Air India Flight 182: A Canadian tragedy.* Ottawa: Government of Canada.

Deukmedjian, J. (2006). *From community to intelligence: Recent trends and transformations in Canadian policing.* Presented at the annual meeting of the American Society of Criminology, Toronto, 5 October.

Dupont, B. (2006). Security in the age of networks. *Policing and Society, 14*(1), 76–91.

Ericson, R.V. (2006). Ten uncertainties of risk management. *Canadian Journal of Criminology and Criminal Justice, 48*(3), 345–57.

Ericson, R.V., & Haggerty, K.D. (1997). *Policing the risk society.* Toronto: University of Toronto Press.

Eriksen, T.H. (2007). *Globalization: The key concepts.* Oxford: Berg.

Gill, P. (2000). *Rounding up the usual suspects?: Developments in contemporary law enforcement intelligence.* Aldershot: Ashgate Publishing.

Haggerty, K.D., & Ericson, R.V. (2000). The surveillant assemblage. *British Journal of Sociology, 51*(4), 605–22.

Institute for Strategic International Studies. (2006). *A New reality for police leadership in Canada.* Ottawa: Canadian Association of Chiefs of Police.

Ipperwash Inquiry. (2007). *Report of the Ipperwash Inquiry.* Toronto: Government of Ontario.

Ipsos Reid. (2011). *A matter of trust.* Toronto: Ipsos North America.

Johnston, L. (2003). From 'pluralisation' to 'the police extended family': Discourses on the governance of community policing in Britain. *International Journal of the Sociology of Law, 31*(3), 185–204.

Jones, T., & Newburn, T. (2002). The transformation of policing? Understanding current trends in policing systems. *British Journal of Criminology, 42*(1), 129–46.

McGuire, M. (2000). Policing by risks and targets: Some consequences of intelligence-led crime control. *Policing and Society, 9*(1), 315–36.

Murphy, C. (1998). Policing postmodern Canada. *Canadian Journal of Law and Society, 3*(2), 1–26.

———. (2002). *The rationalization of Canadian public policing: A study of the impact and implications of resource limits and market strategies in public policing.* Canadian Association of Chiefs of Police: The Police Futures Group, Electronic Series, No. 1.

————. (2007). 'Securitizing' Canadian policing: A new policing paradigm for the post-9/11 security state. *Canadian Journal of Sociology, 32*(4), 449–62.

Nassar, J.R. (2005). *Globalization and terrorism: The migration of dreams and nightmares.* Oxford: Rowman and Littlefield Publishers.

Newburn, T. (2002). Atlantic crossings: Policy transfer and crime control in the USA and Britain. *Punishment & Society, 4*(2), 165–94.

Ombudsman of Ontario. (2010). *Caught in the act: Investigation into the Ministry of Community Safety and Correctional Services' conduct in relation to Ontario Regulation 233/10 under the Public Works Protection Act.* Toronto: Government of Ontario.

Public Safety and Emergency Preparedness Canada. (2004). *Securing an open society: Canada's national security policy.* Ottawa: Government of Canada.

————. (2007). *Rebuilding the trust: Task Force on Governance and Cultural Change in the RCMP.* Ottawa: Government of Canada.

Ransly, J., & Mazerolle, L. (2009). Policing in an era of uncertainty. *Police Practice and Research, 10*(4), 365–81.

Rigakos, G.S. (2002). *The new parapolice: Risk markets and commodified social control.* Toronto: University of Toronto Press.

Shearing, C.D. (2005). Nodal security. *Police Quarterly, 18*(1), 57–63.

————, & Stenning, P.C. (1982). *Private security and justice: The challenge of the 80s.* Montreal: Institute for Research on Public Policy.

————, & ————. (1983). Private security: Implications for social control. *Social Problems, 30*(5), 498–505.

————, & ————. (1987). Re-framing the police: An introduction. In C.D. Shearing & P.C. Stenning (Eds.), *Private policing.* Beverley Hills, CA: Sage Publications.

Sheptycki, J. (1995). Transnational policing and the makings of a postmodern state. *British Journal of Criminology, 35*(4), 613–35.

————. (2002). Accountability across the policing field: Towards a general cartography of accountability for post-modern policing. *Policing and Society, 12*(4), 323–38.

Statistics Canada. (2008). *Private security and public policy.* Ottawa: Canadian Centre for Justice Statistics, Catalogue No. 85-002-X.

————. (2010). *Police resources in Canada.* Ottawa: Canadian Centre for Justice Statistics, Catalogue No. 85-225-X.

Stenning, P. (2005). *The idea of the political independence of the police: International interpretations and experiences.* Research paper, commissioned by the Ipperwash Inquiry.

————. (2009). Governance and accountability in a plural policing environment—The story so far. *Policing, A Journal of Policy and Practice, 3*(1), 22–33.

Zedner, L. (2003). Too much security. *International Journal of Sociology of Law, 31*(3), 155–84.

2

Back to the Future?
Policy Development in
Pre-trial Detention in Canada

Anthony N. Doob and Cheryl Marie Webster

INTRODUCTION

Canada's legal system—like many others—has assumed that there is no controversy about a simple principle: people are presumed to be innocent until proven
guilty by a fair and impartial court (s. 11(d) of the Charter). The fact that a police
officer (or anyone else, for that matter) may think that a person is guilty does not
make that person guilty. Rather, the presumption of innocence is fervently maintained throughout the criminal justice process until proven otherwise.

As an extension of this central legal principle, it is natural to assume that punishment cannot be imposed by the state unless the accused person has been found
guilty of an offence. To many people's surprise, this belief turns out to be untrue—
at least in terms of effect. In fact, Canadian courts regularly imprison individuals
who have merely been accused (rather than found guilty) of an illicit act through
the imposition of pre-trial detention. In this case, pre-trial custody constitutes the
detention of persons charged with a criminal offence who are awaiting either a
bail determination (i.e., the judicial decision of whether they will be released or
detained until trial) or—having been formally detained as the result of a bail hearing—the completion of their case.

Indeed, section 11(e) of the Charter of Rights and Freedoms and, in pre-
Charter days, both the Canadian Bill of Rights and normal criminal practice
clearly contemplate that some people will be held in pre-trial custody. Moreover,
this is not a recent practice. As Manson (2004/5, p. 292) reminds us, while
'imprisonment as a form of sentence is a relatively new addition to the criminal
justice system . . . imprisonment pending trial dates back to ancient communities
and the days of dungeons, dragons, chains, and torture.' Nor is this practice
innocuous. Although pre-trial detention constitutes a legitimate criminal

procedure whose legal purpose is preventative (i.e., averting an accused person's failure to appear for trial or inhibiting further offending), its punitive bite is unambiguous. As Ontario Court of Appeal Justice Rosenberg noted in *R. v. McDonald*, '[t]o pretend that pre-sentence imprisonment does not occasion a severe deprivation and that it is not punitive would result in a triumph of form over substance.'

In fact, criminological research has repeatedly called attention to numerous deleterious collateral effects of pre-trial detention on the accused. Notably, pre-trial custody imposes serious criminal justice consequences. Most obviously, it may negatively impact the ability of the accused to defend him- or herself (e.g., rendering it more difficult to hire and communicate with a lawyer, find evidence or witnesses to support one's case, procure employment or engage in other activities that would demonstrate intent to 'mend one's ways') (Hill et al., 2004; Trotter, 2010; Hagan & Morden, 1981). In addition, pre-trial detention can affect an accused person's decision to plead guilty (Friedland, 1965; Kellough & Wortley, 2002)—an effect that also appears to differ across races. Further, detained suspects are more likely to receive custodial sanctions than those who are released, even across cases in which the most serious offences are relatively similar in nature (Friedland, 1965; Koza & Doob, 1975b). In addition, those who are held in custody awaiting trial are likely to be *seen* as being guilty (Doob & Cavoukian, 1977; Koza & Doob, 1975a).

Furthermore, pre-trial detention can have non-criminal justice ramifications with equally devastating effects on an accused's life (Trotter, 2010). Beyond possible job loss and its collateral effects on family members relying on this income, the stigmatization of the accused (and family) has also been noted in the literature (National Council for Welfare, 2000; Manns, 2005). Moreover, anecdotal evidence (Ritchie, 2005; Kellough & Wortley, 2002) suggests that pre-trial detention—even for short periods—is onerous for the accused, who is often housed in overcrowded detention centres with no recreational, educational, or rehabilitative programs. These harmful consequences are only exacerbated when one recalls that a non-trivial proportion of those held in pre-trial detention are ultimately never found guilty (Webster, 2007).

Within this context, it is perhaps unsurprising that pre-trial detention became a focus of concern in Canada (as well as elsewhere) in the 1960s. While this criminal procedure is arguably a necessary evil, the presumption of innocence—coupled with other fundamental principles of justice (e.g., restraint, fairness, equality)—would seem to demand its careful scrutiny in order to ensure the least intrusive, the least abrasive, and, more generally, the least punitive policies and practices. Evaluated in light of these 'rights-protecting' parameters (Trotter, 2010), the bail system was found to be sadly lacking—a recognition that subsequently inspired radical reform. The final product was the 1972 Bail Reform Act, which constituted nothing less than a complete overhaul and codification of the law of bail in Canada (Trotter, 2010).

This new legislation arguably constituted a turning point in Canadian bail law. Certainly in comparison with the past, the reform movement significantly enhanced civil liberties within the bail system. In fact, it has been asserted that Canada—under the Bail Reform Act—enjoys a 'liberal and enlightened' bail system (cited in Trotter, 2010, pp. 1–14). While not minimizing these fundamental gains, we would nonetheless argue that many of these protections have been gradually eroded over the past several decades. At least in some parts of Canada, it would seem that Canadians are well on their way to returning to a situation that existed 50 years ago—albeit under a legal regime that is quite different from that which existed in the 1960s.

Part I of this chapter describes the 'bail landscape' in the 1960s that sparked the reform movement and the various remedies contained in the Bail Reform Act. Part II explores several of the changes in pre-trial detention subsequent to this new legislation that have arguably undermined many of the rights-protecting ideals of the early 1970s. Part III discusses several potential explanations driving this recent turn in Canada's bail system.

PART I: THE EARLY DAYS OF DETENTION BEFORE TRIAL

Concern with the bail system in Canada was brought to the forefront in the 1960s by a landmark study by Martin Friedland of the operation of the Toronto bail courts. One of the central problems identified by this scholar was rooted in the overuse of pre-trial detention. Friedland (1965) observes that 'detention *after* trial (i.e., sentencing) . . . touches the lives of significantly fewer persons than detention *before* trial' (3, emphasis in the original). This reality whereby a greater number of accused were being held in custody before—rather than after—being found guilty was considered by this scholar to be a flagrant disregard for the principles of justice.

And, in fact, in the 6,000 cases that Friedland examined (which arrived at court for the first time in late 1961 or early 1962), only about 8 per cent of those accused of offences were summoned to court. The alternative to being summoned to court—occurring in the remaining 92 per cent of the cases—is complex. It involves being arrested, booked by the police at a police station, placed in a police cell, and then held until (or unless) released by a judicial officer—usually at court but occasionally by a justice of the peace at the police station. Remarkably, the low rate of being summoned to court did not differ between those charged with indictable offences (generally more serious offences) and those charged with non-indictable offences. However, a larger proportion of women (12%) were summoned to court than men (7.5%). For those who were 16 and 17 years old (then considered adults in Ontario), 95 per cent were arrested and brought to court by the police.

Friedland (1965, p. 22) also notes that traditionally, 'criminal law has interposed the independent scrutiny of a justice of the peace between the police and the accused as a safeguard against unwarranted arrests.' However, in practice (at the time of his study), the police controlled the initial detention (before trial), since most arrests (95%) were carried out without a warrant. Not surprisingly, he recommended increased use of the summons (rather than the use of the power of arrest and detention), arguing that the attendance of many of the accused could be just as easily secured by less intrusive means.

For those arrested and brought to court, release, at that time, usually meant posting bail—cash, or occasionally, property. Friedland (1965, p. 127) points out that '[a] sound system would presumably have amounts of bail high enough reasonably to ensure the appearance of the accused and yet low enough to afford him a reasonable chance of raising it.' The problem with cash bail—as it worked in Toronto in the early 1960s—was that the amount of cash bail became standardized. Essentially, it was a tariff that was offence based rather than offender or 'risk' based. Friedland observes that for the 169 prostitution cases in his sample for which bail was set, bail was *exactly* $500 in all but one case. Indeed, he notes that there were standardized amounts for certain offences, 'the existence of [which] negates the concept of judicial discretion exercised mainly on the likelihood of the individual appearing for his trial' (p. 128). Partly as a result of this standardization, bail was not met (i.e., the accused was held in detention awaiting trial) in 62 per cent of the cases in which bail was set.

Equally problematic, since most accused did not have sufficient cash to meet bail, professional 'bondsmen' would, in effect, lend the bail money to the accused (or they would pay the bond directly to the court). In the 1960s, bail bondsmen in Toronto were performing this 'service' for a fee of 15 per cent of the amount of bail. Given that the bail bondsmen were the people at risk of losing the money paid to the court to ensure the release of the accused, it was, in effect, these individuals who performed the 'risk assessment' on the accused, ultimately determining who would be released. The process of having a third party pay for the accused person's release was, as Friedland notes, almost certainly illegal. For this reason as well as others, he notes that 'the arguments against any form of professional bondsman are overwhelming' (1965, p. 155).

Most importantly, Friedland (1965) suggests that Canada move to a non-cash system whereby the accused would deposit no funds, but in the case that he or she did not appear for trial, there would be a fixed amount of money, as legal debt, owed to the Crown (p. 178). This debt might be attributed to the accused person him- or herself or a third party—a surety—might be asked to shoulder the risk. Sureties are typically people who are related to or are friends of the accused who undertake to 'guarantee' that the accused appear when required (as well as obey other conditions of release). If the accused does not comply with the conditions of release, the surety can be asked to pay the guaranteed amount. In either way, security would no longer be required in advance as a condition prior to release.

As an academic text, Friedland's book received an enormous amount of publicity (Friedland, 2007, p. 100). The *Globe and Mail* published three long excerpts—on three successive weeks—just prior to its publication. In addition, the *Globe* published a full-length editorial on the issue and the CBC devoted two half-hour programs to Friedland's findings and recommendations. Further, the news magazine *Maclean's* reviewed the book and posters for it appeared prominently in Toronto bookstores. As Friedland himself commented, nobody but his proud parents would have expected such a reaction.

Perhaps even more importantly, the Canadian Committee on Corrections ('Ouimet Committee') relied heavily on Friedland's book when it drafted its chapter on bail in 1969. Rooted in the same rights-protecting philosophy that dictated significant restraint in the use of pre-trial detention, the committee's recommendations were blunt, proposing that people should be summoned to court unless there was good reason to do otherwise. Specifically, it suggested that 'the Criminal Code be amended to provide that the justice shall issue a summons rather than a warrant unless it is made to appear that the public interest requires the issue of a warrant rather than a summons' (p. 93).

Equally notable was the committee's view that charging someone with a criminal offence should not create a licence for the state to hold a person in custody simply because someone thought that he or she might commit a crime. Rather, detention should be permitted only within a strict set of criteria. Specifically, the committee argued that

> [p]re-trial detention, in the view of the Committee, can only be justified where it is *necessary* in the public interest: (i) To ensure the appearance of the accused at his trial. (ii) To protect the public pending the trial of the accused. Pre-trial detention is justified where it is *necessary* to prevent criminal misconduct by the accused pending his trial. The offences sought to be prevented may be offences similar to those in respect of which the accused has been arrested, or may be offences related to his trial such as: (a) The destruction of evidence or the tampering with witnesses. (b) Otherwise attempting to pervert the course of justice. (Canadian Committee on Corrections, 1969, p. 97, italics in original)

Based largely on the committee's recommendations as well as on Friedland's 1965 work, sweeping legislative changes to the procedure for granting bail in Canada were proposed in 1970. As Friedland (2007) observes, John Turner (minister of justice under Prime Minister Pierre Trudeau) indicated early in his term that he wanted new legislation on bail. Given that Trudeau (later the prime minister responsible for the Charter of Rights and Freedoms) had been minister of justice prior to the 1968 election and the Liberals, for the first time in that decade, had achieved a majority government, it is unsurprising that amendments to the provisions of the Criminal Code relating to bail were proposed. Further, the substance of these changes was clear. As Friedland (2007) notes, he and Irwin Cotler (then executive assistant to the minister of justice and subsequently, from 2003 to 2006, minister of justice of Canada) were involved in their drafting.

Despite significant opposition from the police, the Bail Reform Act became law in 1971, ushering in a new era in the law of bail in Canada. Its guiding philosophy was one of enhanced civil liberties, with a focus on restraint in the use of pre-trial detention (Trotter, 2010). As originally written, this legislation presumed that accused people should not be brought to court for a bail hearing. Police were conferred vast new powers of release to avoid unnecessary arrest and detention (Trotter, 2010). In particular, peace officers were told to issue an appearance notice to someone whom they had arrested unless certain specified circumstances existed. The law also required a review of any detention by the arresting officer's 'officer in charge', who could subsequently release the accused or, for reasons similar to those of the arresting officer, decide that it was necessary to hold the accused for a bail hearing before a judicial officer.

In addition, the Bail Reform Act stipulated specific criteria for the determination of an accused person's suitability for release. Specifically, the new legislation originally allowed the judicial officer to detain an accused for only one of two reasons. Friedland (2007) notes that the primary ground—ensuring that the accused shows up for trial—was uncontroversial. The secondary ground—the possibility that the accused would commit further offences—was much more controversial. The original wording of the grounds for detention was as follows:

> For the purposes of this section, the detention of the accused in custody is justified only on either of the following grounds, namely:
>
> (a) on the primary ground that his detention is necessary to ensure his attendance in court in order to be dealt with according to law; and
>
> (b) on the secondary ground (the applicability of which shall be determined only in the event that and after it is determined that his detention is not justified on the primary ground referred to in paragraph [a]) that his detention is necessary in the public interest or for the protection or safety of the public, having regard to all the circumstances including any substantial likelihood that the accused will, if he is released from custody, commit a criminal offence involving serious harm or an interference with the administration of justice.' (Section 457[7][b], as it was then numbered)

Equally consistent with the philosophy of the Bail Reform Act, which encouraged the release of accused persons, this legislation made it clear that the Crown must prove that the accused should be detained in custody. That is, it was not the accused person's responsibility to prove that he or she should be released; rather, the onus was placed on the prosecutor to justify the accused person's detention. This provision clearly reflected the 'presumption of innocence' and 'right to reasonable bail' then contained in the 1960 Bill of Rights.

As a corollary of this principle, the new legislation also created new forms of release for the courts, as well as restricted the use of cash deposits. Most importantly, a justice or judge was henceforth directed to release the accused on an undertaking without conditions 'unless the prosecutor . . . shows cause why the detention of the accused is justified or why an order under any other provision of this section should be made' (s. 457[1], as it was then numbered). An undertaking—as the preferred form of release—constituted the least onerous manner in which an accused person might be released, as he or she did not acknowledge any indebtedness to the Crown nor deposit any money or valuable security (Trotter, 2010). Even the more burdensome forms of release (e.g., release on an undertaking with conditions; release on a recognizance with or without sureties and with or without deposit of money or valuable security) were organized according to a 'ladder principle' favouring less onerous conditions unless cause was shown for more onerous grounds.

PART II: THE LATTER DAYS OF DETENTION BEFORE TRIAL

As Trotter (2010) notes, the general structure and much of the substantive content of the bail provisions created by the Bail Reform Act have remained intact over the last 40 years. However, it is equally true that many of these provisions have also been regularly amended. Taken together, the modifications that the Bail Reform Act has undergone have arguably diluted the rights-protecting philosophy underlying the bail reform movement. Indeed, almost without exception, the principal amendments have made it more difficult to obtain bail and have resulted in more stringent release orders (Trotter, 2010). With increasing restrictions on access to liberty at the front end of the criminal justice system, some might say that we are returning to a past in which fewer protections of civil liberties existed in the bail system.

Perhaps the most obvious manifestation of this erosion of the rights-protecting philosophy of the 1970s is reflected in the current remand (i.e., unsentenced prisoners) problem in Canada. While the Canadian total provincial imprisonment rate (top line in Figure 2.1) has been relatively stable over the past half-century,[1] this overall stability masks a fundamental change in the nature of the offenders being housed in provincial prisons. Specifically, while the provincial sentenced population has decreased steadily over the past 30 years, this decline has been almost perfectly compensated for by the continual rise in the provincial remand population over the same period.[2] Despite the focus on restraint in the use of pre-trial detention underlying the Bail Reform Act, an increasing number of accused persons have been held in pre-trial detention every year. In fact, according to the most recent year of available data (2008), a greater number of people are detained (for at least one day) in pre-trial custody in Canada than are currently admitted to provincial institutions to serve their sentences—a situation clearly reminiscent of the 1960s.

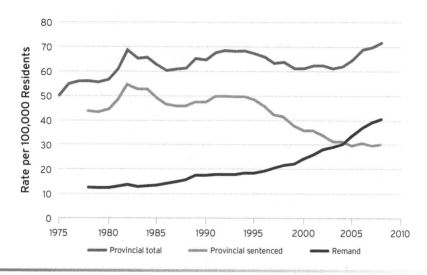

FIGURE 2.1   The components of Canada's overall provincial/ territorial imprisonment rate (average daily counts per 100,000 residents)

However, even this (disconcerting) fact obscures the variation that exists across the country. Figure 2.2 presents the proportion of those admitted to provincial/ territorial correctional institutions in Canada's 13 jurisdictions who are in remand. This figure shows that for the majority of Canadian jurisdictions, there was—in 2008—a greater number of people admitted to provincial/territorial correctional facilities as unsentenced than sentenced prisoners.[3] For instance, one can observe that just under 75 per cent of all admissions to custody in Quebec were to remand. That is, approximately three times as many people in Quebec entered prison not having been sentenced to prison as were sent to prison to serve their sentences in 2008. Only in Prince Edward Island, Newfoundland and Labrador, Nunavut, New Brunswick, and the Northwest Territories (five of the smallest Canadian jurisdictions) as well as Manitoba were more people admitted to prison after rather than before being sentenced.

If one examines count rather than admission data, the story changes very little. Count data represent the number of individuals—in our particular case, those on remand—who are in a provincial prison on any given day. Admissions data describe the number of individuals—again, in our case, those on remand— entering provincial prisons.

Paralleling the previous figure, Figure 2.3 presents the proportion of those in provincial/territorial custody on an average night in Canada's 13 jurisdictions who have not yet been sentenced. The variation continues to be huge. While only 18 per cent of Prince Edward Island's prisoners were on remand on any given day

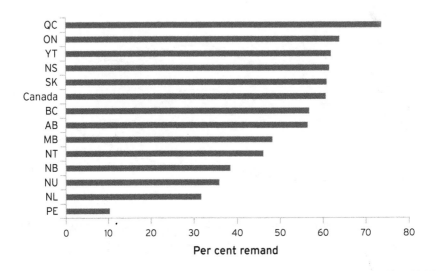

FIGURE 2.2 Per cent of admissions to provincial/territorial facilities not sentenced (remand)

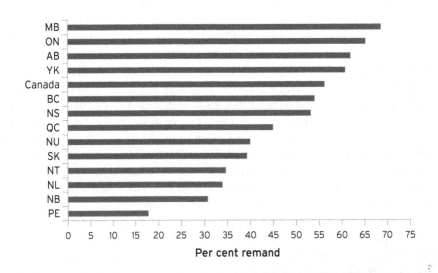

FIGURE 2.3 Per cent of provincial/territorial prison population that is not sentenced (remand)

in 2008, this figure rises to 69 per cent of Manitoba's inmates.[4] With bail laws in all jurisdictions being identical, it is clear that criminal justice practices (or culture) vary considerably. Nevertheless, in almost all Canadian jurisdictions, a significant proportion of those in prison are being punished without having been found guilty of an offence. Further, this inversion continues to increase over time, potentially further undermining any sense of restraint in the use of pre-trial detention.[5]

This reality reflects, in large part, legislative amendments introduced subsequent to the passing of the Bail Reform Act that have acted as additional impediments or hurdles to obtaining bail. Most obviously, Canada's law of bail has experienced a shift in the onus of proof with respect to release in a number of situations. Indeed, the absolute requirement that the prosecutor—rather than the accused—must prove the need for detention quickly suffered modifications subsequent to its enactment under the Bail Reform Act. By the mid-1970s, the onus was on accused persons to demonstrate why their release was justified in cases where the charge was laid while they were awaiting trial for another indictable offence, they were not residents of Canada, or they were charged with certain drug offences. By 2010, the list of circumstances in which the (legally innocent) accused would have to demonstrate why they should be released had expanded considerably to include circumstances where it was alleged that the offence involved 'organized crime', it was a terrorism offence, it involved the sale of firearms, or it involved the use of firearms, or other such matters.

In practice, this impediment to obtaining bail is even more formidable. By the end of the first decade of the twenty-first century, a naive observer in many courts (at least in Ontario) could easily conclude that accused persons held for a hearing to determine whether release was justified would have to demonstrate why they should be released in almost any circumstances. In a post-9/11 world, it would probably make little difference to the ultimate outcome of a bail hearing whether the accused or the Crown had to 'prove' their case if the allegation was terrorism or involved organized crime or firearms. While the introduction of these new reverse-onus provisions may be politically advantageous, the 'law in practice' would suggest that in all cases, no matter who, theoretically, had to prove what, it is almost certainly accused persons who would have to demonstrate to the satisfaction of the court why they should be released.

In addition to the new reverse-onus provisions, Canadians have also seen legislative expansion of the criteria for release that has made it more difficult to obtain bail. Specifically, the Criminal Code now (2011) states:

For the purposes of this section, the detention of an accused in custody is justified only on one or more of the following grounds:

(a)   where the detention is necessary to ensure his or her attendance in court in order to be dealt with according to law;

(b)   where the detention is necessary for the protection or safety of the public, including any victim of or witness to the offence, having regard to all the circumstances including any substantial likelihood that the accused will, if released from custody, commit a criminal offence or interfere with the administration of justice; and

(c)   if the detention is necessary to maintain confidence in the administration of justice, having regard to all the circumstances, including

(i)   the apparent strength of the prosecution's case,

(ii)   the gravity of the offence,

(iii) the circumstances surrounding the commission of the offence, including whether a firearm was used, and

(iv)   the fact that the accused is liable, on conviction, for a potentially lengthy term of imprisonment or, in the case of an offence that involves, or whose subject-matter is, a firearm, a minimum punishment of imprisonment for a term of three years or more.

(Section 515 [10])

It is easy to see how the 'secondary' ground has changed in the past 40 years. The original intent under the Bail Reform Act was that the two grounds would be considered separately. Presently, the judicial official can decide that it is a 'combination' of criteria or, perhaps, a little of each. More important is the test for future offending. In 1971, it was *substantial likelihood* that the accused would commit a criminal offence involving *serious harm* or an interference with the administration of justice. Forty years later, there still must be a 'substantial likelihood', but the offence in question can be *any* criminal offence. In addition, an explicit (separate) public interest ground has been added. This third ground—to maintain confidence in the administration of justice—is, obviously, quite an unusual reason for imprisoning a person without a finding of guilt, since it relates not to the accused but rather to what uninvolved members of the community *think* about the case. Court decisions (see Trotter, 2010) have suggested that it be invoked rarely and only in a narrow set of circumstances. Moreover, the test appears to be that of a reasonable person who understands the principles behind the law, the Charter, and the actual case.

However, Canada has not only witnessed legislative amendments that have rendered it more difficult to obtain bail; rather, we have also seen—in practice—an increasing use of more stringent release orders. Under the Bail Reform Act, the accused should be released on bail without conditions, a monetary component, or a surety unless the Crown can prove that a more onerous type of release is warranted. In fact, a 'ladder approach' is to be undertaken whereby the Crown must demonstrate why each form of release is inappropriate before he or she recommends a stricter level (Trotter, 2010). This hierarchy of forms of release is to ensure that accused persons are released in the least onerous manner possible.

Despite these guidelines, the use of sureties in bail cases appears to have become the norm rather than the exception in many Ontario courts. In an examination of eight separate Ontario courthouses, Myers (2009) found that the proportion of cases in which the justice of the peace required a surety in contested releases (i.e., cases with a full bail hearing) varied from 63 per cent to 100 per cent. Even with cases in which the Crown consented to the accused person's release, it was still shown—in seven of the eight courts—that sureties were required in at least 60 per cent of cases. In the remaining court, sureties were necessary 23 per cent of the time.

Further, it would seem that the use of sureties as the most common form of release order also extends to youth.[6] In a study of 199 youth bail cases across four Toronto bail courts, Myers and Dhillon (2011) found that 87 per cent of the youth released on bail were released with a surety.[7] Notably, the proportion of cases in which a surety was required varied from 94 per cent to 100 per cent in three of the courts but fell to 35 per cent in the remaining court. Similar findings were reported by Sprott and Doob (2010) when they reviewed a sample of 242 bail orders for accused who were released from a large youth court in Toronto. Specifically, 73 per cent of the sample required a surety for release.

Certainly from the perspective of the presumption of innocence, the frequent recourse to sureties is problematic. Indeed, a release order involving a recognizance with a surety is the second most onerous form of release (following a recognizance with a surety and a deposit). A surety must be found who can demonstrate to the court that he or she will be able to pay a certain amount of money if the accused fails to appear for court or violates a condition of release. The theory of the surety appears to be that accused people are more likely to abide by release conditions because otherwise their friend or relative will lose the specified amount of money. It is also assumed that the surety will have a direct influence on the accused person in ensuring compliance with all release conditions (in part because the surety stands to lose money if the accused violates any condition of release).

Equally disconcerting is the parallel with the past. Specifically, one is tempted to conclude that sureties have, in effect, been substituted for the bail bondsmen. Clearly, two important differences between these practices exist: money does not have to be deposited with the court in order to achieve release, and typically the surety is someone who has a relatively close relationship to the accused. Nonetheless, one is equally tempted to agree with Friedland (2007) when he suggests that while this change is an improvement, it is not much of one.

Moreover, the onerous nature of current release orders in bail extends well beyond the frequent use of sureties. Indeed, many of the forms of release—including 'surety release'—typically involve conditions being placed on the accused once in the community. Within the same rights protecting philosophy of the Bail Reform Act, Trotter (2010) argues that bail conditions should be approached with restraint and made the least burdensome as possible, given the coercive elements attached to them. Specifically, there are punishments for not abiding by them (e.g., arrest, detention, forfeiture of money, etc.) and the conditions themselves limit various freedoms (e.g., movement, association, communication, etc.).

The current reality appears to be in striking contrast to this argument. In Myer's study (2009) of eight bail courts in Ontario, the accused persons in nearly all consent releases and virtually all releases following a 'show cause' hearing had conditions attached to their release. More notably, over 50 per cent of accused had more than five conditions placed on their consent release order. With contested releases, this proportion only increased (often dramatically) for the majority of the courts under study.

While the principle of limited court intervention enshrined in the Youth Criminal Justice Act (YCJA) might suggest a reduced use of conditions on bail release orders of youth as compared to adults, the opposite seems to be true (Moyer & Basic, 2004; Moyer, 2005; Varma, 2002). Varma (2002) reports in her study of a Toronto bail court that all of the youth who were released on bail had conditions attached to their order. Similar findings were found by Moyer and Basic (2004) in their study of two urban courts in Ontario under the Young Offenders Act. In more recent research, Sprott and Doob (2010) report that 67.4 per cent of those released by the justice under the YCJA have 6 or more conditions placed on their release order. In fact, more than a quarter of those released (28.3%) had 8 or more conditions. While Sprott and Myers (2011) note an average of 6 conditions placed on youth released on bail, Myers and Dhillon (2011) found 9.3 conditions—on average—attached to youth release orders, with over 40 per cent of their sample having more than 10 conditions.

Potentially as disconcerting as the *number* of conditions placed on accused persons' release is the *scope* of conditions. The Criminal Code (s. 515[4]) enumerates a number of standard conditions that can be placed on accused persons released on bail. However, many conditions appear to fall under the catch-all provision that directs the accused to 'comply with such other reasonable conditions specified in the order as the justice considers desirable' (s. 515[4][f]). This broad discretion has seemingly resulted—at least as indicated in the few existing studies on bail conditions and given the limited information available for analysis—in a host of conditions that are routinely imposed but frequently appear to have little relation to the facts of the alleged offence and do not seem to be 'necessary to give effect to the criteria for release' (Trotter, 1999, p. 241). Rather, it has been suggested (Sprott & Doob, 2010; Myers & Dhillon, 2011; Myers, 2009) that conditions such as 'attend school each and every day, each and every class', 'be amenable to the rules and discipline of the home', or 'attend counselling and assessments as directed by the surety' may serve broader social welfare objectives, impose paternalistic treatment efforts (especially with female young offenders), or simply constitute tools of risk governance.

Faced with the options of being detained or being released with what, from the accused person's perspective, may look to be unreasonable or unnecessary conditions, the accused has a difficult choice: accept the conditions and be released or risk remaining in custody until the case is resolved. Few accused choose the latter alternative. However, while this decision may arguably be wise in the short term, it carries the potential for even more onerous effects in the long run. Specifically, the greater the number of conditions on a release order, the greater the likelihood that the accused will breach one of these conditions—a circumstance that can result in an additional criminal charge of failure to comply with a court order. When numerous bail conditions are coupled with a relatively lengthy period of time on bail awaiting the completion of the case,[8] the opportunity to acquire this administration of justice charge significantly increases (Sprott & Myers, 2011).

And, in fact, approximately 12 per cent of all cases of adults charged in Canada in 2009 involved the criminal offence of 'failure to comply with a court order' as the most significant charge in the incident—an offence widely accepted, in almost all cases, to involve a violation of a bail order. When one recalls that this criminal offence is, in effect, the result of criminalizing ordinary behaviour (e.g., going out at night becomes criminal when it violates a curfew), it is even more remarkable that roughly one in eight adults charged with a criminal offence was charged with violating bail conditions. We suspect that this administration of justice offence is highly affected by two local policies: the placing of unreasonable or unnecessary conditions on bail orders and the strict enforcement of these bail orders. Given these underlying 'cultural' factors, it is perhaps unsurprising to note the huge variability across Canadian jurisdictions in the proportion of all adult cases involving these (predominantly) bail violations. This variation is shown in Figure 2.4. Yukon appears to dominate the Canadian landscape with almost 25 per cent of all of its adults in 2009 facing—as their most serious charge— 'failure to comply with an order'. In Ontario, the proportion exceeds 10 per cent. Even in Prince Edward Island, approximately one out of every 25 adults charged with a criminal offence faced this charge.

And the numbers do not improve for youth. Indeed, bail violations also comprise a non-trivial proportion of the most serious charges that youth face in Canada. In 2009, 12.2 per cent of all youth charged with an offence were charged with a fail to comply with an order.[9] More importantly, 89 per cent of youths accused of violating a bail condition in 2009 were criminally charged rather than dealt with by a formal or informal diversionary measure. In contrast, only 43 per cent of youths recorded as being apprehended by the police for *any* offence were formally charged that year.

A vicious circle is seemingly being created whereby the criminal justice system produces, in effect, its own crime. Particularly in cases where an accused is, in fact, convicted of a charge of failure to comply with a bail order, another entry is added to this offender's criminal record, rendering it more difficult for the individual to obtain bail in the future. Indeed, the court tends to take administration of justice offences very seriously, likely interpreting them as signs of disrespect for, and of wilful disregard of, court orders (Sprott, 2006). Even in cases where an accused is again released on bail, the court is likely to impose even more onerous conditions,

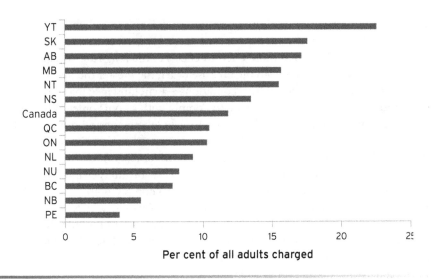

FIGURE 2.4 Per cent of all adults who were charged in 2009 who faced, as their most serious charge, a charge of 'Failure to comply with an order'

creating even greater opportunities for the accused to breach the new release order. This 'feedback model' becomes especially disconcerting when one recalls that many of the original bail conditions may have been unnecessary or unreasonable. Further, research with youth (Sprott & Myers, 2011) has shown that it is not uncommon for criminal charges related to the original bail hearing to be ultimately withdrawn.

Our return to the past is perhaps most visibly illustrated through our current (and increasing) lack of restraint in the use of pre-trial detention—not only in terms of actual numbers of accused held in custody while still presumed innocent, but also with regard to legislative amendments that have made it more difficult to obtain bail and current practices of frequent recourse to more (rather than less) onerous release orders. However, present parallels with our pre–Bail Reform Act era can also be located in our failure to defend other normative principles of a system of bail. Most notably, goals of equality are being strained. Illustratively, Parliament recently passed legislation on credit for pre-sentence custody that not only fails to fulfill its stated purposes but has a discriminatory effect on any accused held in remand who is ultimately found guilty and handed down a custodial sentence.

Since 1972, courts have been told that when handing down a sentence, they can take into account any time spent in (pre-sentence) custody (Manson, 2004/5). Traditionally, two rationales have been offered for this practice. On the one hand, conditions of remand are typically said to be more unpleasant than the facilities for sentenced prisoners. Provincial and territorial correctional ministries also tend not to offer rehabilitative programs to remand prisoners because of the short and unpredictable length of time that they spend in custody. On the other hand, various forms of conditional release from prison for those serving ordinary custodial sentences (e.g., remission, day parole, full parole, temporary absences, statutory release) do not apply to those in pre-sentence custody.

For these reasons, judges traditionally (at least until 2010) gave, typically, between 1.5 and 2 days credit against the sentence for each day spent in pre-sentence custody. This convention was altered in March 2009 when the government introduced a bill deceptively labelled the Truth in Sentencing Act. As stipulated in its press release, the primary purpose of the legislation was to 'strictly limit the amount of credit that may be granted for time served in custody prior to sentencing, bringing greater certainty and clarity to the sentencing process' (Department of Justice, Canada, 2009). Specifically, the bill would

- make it the general rule that the amount of credit for time served be capped at a 1-to-1 ratio, i.e., give only one day of credit for each day an individual has spent in custody prior to sentencing;
- permit a credit to be given at a ratio of up to 1.5 to 1 only where the circumstances justify it;
- require courts to explain the circumstances that justified a higher ratio; and
- limit the pre-sentencing credit ratio to a maximum ratio of 1 to 1 for individuals detained because of their criminal record or because they violated bail, with no enhanced credit being granted under any circumstances.

With support from all three opposition parties, the bill was made law.[10] In effect, it presumes that 1 day in pre-sentence custody is equivalent to 1 day in sentenced custody. A judge can move from a 1:1 credit up to 1.5 days credit off the sentence for each day in pre-sentence custody only when reasons are given and the accused person was not detained as a result of a criminal record. In sum, all accused should presumptively get only one day off their sentences for each day in pre-sentence custody, with this 1:1 ratio constituting the maximum for those originally detained because of a criminal record.

The impact of this bill, which came into effect in February 2010, is not immediately obvious. While it might appear, on the surface, to create equity across accused whereby those in remand would no longer be unfairly *advantaged* (with each day spent in pre-trial detention counting, in effect, 1.5 to 2 days toward their release, while those serving no time in pre-trial detention are unable to benefit from this 'extra' credit), this legislation actually *disadvantages* any accused in pre-trial custody. Specifically, it would appear that those drafting this legislation (conveniently) forgot that sentenced prisoners do not normally serve their full custodial sentences in Canada. Rather, they are generally released at (if not before) the two-thirds point of their sentence—a practice rooted in the routine remission of one-third of custodial sentences for provincial prisoners and statutory release at the two-thirds point of custodial sentences for federal prisoners. As such, each day of the prison sentence served by offenders post-conviction counts—in effect—1.5 days toward their release.

It is precisely to ensure that any time served pre-sentence (in remand) counts exactly the same as time served post-sentence that pre-trial detention time must be given the same credit as time spent in prison following sentence. Indeed, anything less than a 1.5:1 credit would result in unequal treatment between those offenders detained before trial and those with no pre-trial detention.[11] A simple example suffices to make the point. Accused A is sentenced to 90 days in prison. Having served no time in pre-sentence custody, this offender will serve no more than 60 days in a provincial institution, with the remainder of the sentence being remitted. Accused B should also be sentenced to 90 days in prison. However, this offender serves 30 days in pre-trial detention. Under previous legislation, these 30 days would be generally credited with a 1.5:1 ratio (representing 45 days). As such, this individual would still be handed down a 45-day prison sentence (90-day sentence—45 days credit). Of these 45 days, he or she would serve no more than 30 days (given remission). In total, Accused B would serve 60 days in custody (30 in remand and 30 post-conviction)—exactly the same as Accused A.

Under the current legislation, the 30 days of pre-trial detention served by Accused B would be presumptively credited with a 1:1 ratio (constituting 30 days). This offender would be given a 60-day prison sentence of which he or she would, in effect, serve 40 days (with remission). In total, Accused B (who should serve exactly the same sentence as Accused A) would serve 70 days in custody (30 in remand and 40 post-conviction) rather than the 60 days served by Accused A.[12] In other words, for the vast majority of Canadian prisoners, the current legislation unfairly disadvantages those offenders who have spent time in pre-trial detention. Specifically, those serving time in pre-sentence custody are now not only serving time in less favourable settings, but are getting *less* credit for their prison time than are those serving sentences after being found guilty.[13]

PART III: CHANGING PHILOSOPHIES

It would seem that Canada's bail system is, in many respects, moving away from the rights-protecting philosophy underlying the Bail Reform Act. We tend to agree with Trotter (2010) that Canadians continue—relatively speaking—to enjoy a 'liberal and enlightened' system of bail. Nonetheless, both legislative amendments and actual policy or practices over the last 40 years would seem to suggest that we are returning—in a number of important ways—to a past in which pre-trial detention could be characterized, at least to some degree, as excessive, unfair, and inequitable. The more difficult question becomes one of trying to make sense of this shift.

The answer, we would argue, appears to be rooted in two separate—albeit intertwined—changes in mentality. On the one hand, Canada has not been immune to wider pressures toward greater punitiveness in its responses to crime and criminals. In the name of public safety, the Canadian government—particularly since 2006—has introduced numerous legislative amendments whose goal has been largely to (appear to) be 'tough on crime'. As we have argued elsewhere in this text (Webster and Doob, chapter 4), Canada has increasingly adopted criminal justice policies that not only lack restraint in the use of imprisonment (if not blatantly encourage incarceration as the response par excellence to criminals) but have also arguably been crafted largely for political purposes rather than as informed policy. Indeed, it is not difficult to see the parallels within the smaller microcosm of bail of such measures as the recent expansion of mandatory minimum penalties or the abolition of either accelerated parole review or the faint hope clause with the increasing list of reverse-onus provisions or the reduction in the amount of credit given for pre-sentence custody at sentencing. Indeed, the politicization of crime would appear to have touched most stages of the criminal justice system.

On the other hand, it would seem that the principal players in the criminal court process have increasingly adopted a culture of risk aversion. Within the context of bail, this risk-averse mentality translates into vigorous attempts to avoid releasing accused who might subsequently commit crimes while on bail. Given that we have yet to perfect a means of distinguishing those who will, in fact, offend once released on bail, a risk-averse culture in the bail system has created, in practice, a generalized incentive to avoid—as long as possible—releasing anyone with more than a non-trivial likelihood of committing a crime.

This primordial concern with risk is illustrated with reference to the Ontario Crown Policy Manual. The section on bail hearings not only highlights, through the direct reference to three cases (*May/Iles*, *Hadley*, and *Yeo*),[14] the potential for tragedy when one makes the 'wrong' decision, but also calls attention to the consequences of a 'wrong' decision—for the Crown personally as well as institutionally—by reminding counsel of the inquests surrounding such tragedies in which 'issues surrounding bail hearings, including the conduct of Crown counsel and the exercise of Crown discretion, came under careful scrutiny' (Ministry of Attorney General, Ontario, 2005). This section is equally intriguing in what it fails to highlight. Specifically, while the three referred cases clearly involve the worst kinds of crimes, they represent only a miniscule proportion of crimes committed on bail. Indeed, it is notable that they happened 19, 14, and 10 years ago (at the time of writing). Further, one is never given a sense of the denominator that, at least in Ontario, constitutes a substantial number of people who are released on bail every day, the majority of whom go unnoticed because they do not commit any crime while awaiting trial.[15]

Not surprisingly, Crown attorneys who are concerned about their reputation as well as genuinely worried about public safety would choose to play it safe by opposing bail and, by extension, ensuring that no harm can come to either them or their organization by making the 'wrong' decision. In fact, any rational decision-maker in our current risk-averse society will favour detention precisely because the incentives to oppose release are greater than those to grant release. Table 2.1 outlines several costs and benefits of bail decisions for the decision-maker. Most importantly, when one considers a decision to 'release' (top row) by any decision-maker, all of the possible costs relative to reoffending by the accused person are of a public nature and can easily implicate the decision-maker. In contrast, the benefits of release are hidden and, perhaps more importantly, do not accrue to the decision-maker. As such, the decision-maker can only lose by releasing or recommending release of the accused person. The reverse scenario is no less true. When one considers a decision to detain (bottom row), the potential costs are completely hidden, while the benefits to the decision-maker are more salient. In brief, the choice is simple. The decision to release has potentially large costs and almost no benefits. The decision to detain has costs that are hidden and do not become attached to the decision-maker, while the benefits are direct and can be attributed to the decision-maker (Webster, Doob and Myers, 2009).

TABLE 2.1   The risks to the decision-maker of bail decisions

| Decision | Costs and Benefits of Bail Decisions | |
	Possible Costs	Possible Benefits
Release (for any decision-maker)	• Harm to the public if the accused reoffends (public) • Public criticism of decision-maker if the accused commits an offence on release (public)	• Supporting presumption of innocence (hidden) • Savings to offender (e.g., no loss of job) (hidden) • Savings to society (no correctional costs; no social assistance costs related to accused person's loss of employment) (hidden)
Detain or hold for bail hearing (if police officer), oppose bail (if prosecutor), or deny bail (if judicial officer)	• Offender may lose job (hidden) • Offender may not be able to support family (hidden) • Incarceration costs (hidden) • Distortion of sentencing (hidden)	• No public criticism • No offences can be attributed to decision-maker • If detained, no offences while on bail

Empirical evidence appears to support this risk-averse behaviour. Despite falling crime rates in Canada since the mid-1990s,[16] longitudinal data (albeit for only a few years) for Ontario (as Canada's most populous province) clearly show that the police—as the front-line decision-makers—are increasingly likely to avoid making the decision to release an accused person. Figure 2.5 illustrates this change. This figure suggests that although the number of criminal court cases in Ontario during this period was relatively stable (the top line), the number of them that started with a bail hearing was increasing (bottom line). The net result of these two facts is that an increasing proportion of cases start their court lives in bail court (the middle line). In other words, police officers (arresting officers and/or officers-in-charge, who can also

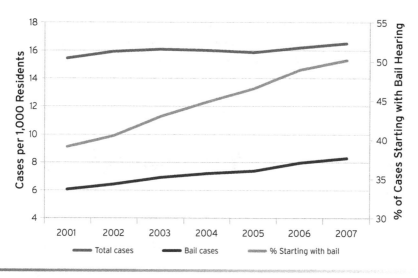

FIGURE 2.5   Ontario caseload: Total and cases with bail hearings

order that an accused person be released on bail) seem increasingly prone to sending the case to court for the Crown or a judicial officer (typically a justice of the peace without legal training in Ontario) to decide whether to release the accused. In fact, accused persons were more likely to be detained for a bail hearing than released by police on an appearance notice following the laying of charges in Ontario in 2007.

Bail hearings have also changed dramatically once cases reach criminal court. Most notably, these bail cases are being processed more than in the past. As shown in Figure 2.6, bail hearings take an increasing amount of time and a larger number of appearances to be completed in Ontario. While few comparative studies exist that permit an understanding of the actual operations of bail court, research conducted in the early 1970s of Ontario's largest bail court (Koza & Doob, 1975a) was replicated 30 years later. This comparison provides a window into potential explanations for the increase in the average number of days and appearances required to determine whether an accused should be released on bail or, alternatively, held until trial. Table 2.2 compares these two time periods, giving a snapshot of the outcome of the cases seen on an average day. Most cases were resolved in one way or another at the first appearance in 1974. In striking contrast, the majority of cases in 2006 were adjourned to another date to appear in the same court. In fact, the most common outcome of a court hearing in 2006 was that nothing happened—another form of our growing risk aversion.[17] Indeed, no one in court appeared to be particularly interested in resolving bail matters quickly. In fact, most requests for adjournments came from the accused persons or their defence counsel. However, it is equally notable that neither the Crown nor the justice of the peace challenged (much less questioned) the vast majority of them. One is tempted to conclude that a generalized expectation exists that adjournments are somehow inevitable or acceptable and that, by extension, the need to make a determination of bail can be simply avoided for another day.

TABLE 2.2   Change in bail court processing on an average day in 1974 and 2006

	Year	
Case Outcome	1974	2006
Adjourned	15%	63%
Contested release	5%	2%
Release (by consent)	44%	10%
Contested detention	7%	2%
Detention (by consent)	0%	4%
Move to another court for plea or for full show-cause hearing (or other outcome)	29%	19%
Total	100%	100%

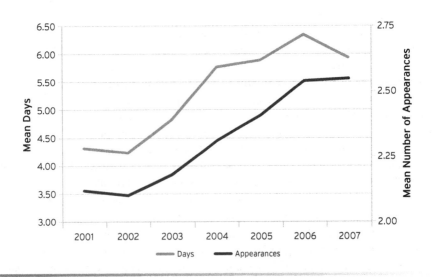

FIGURE 2.6   The mean length (time and appearances) of bail hearings (Ontario)

CONCLUSION

Our current bail regime is clearly different from that of our (pre–Bail Reform Act) past. Nonetheless, it would seem equally true that a number of similarities can be found, particularly in terms of concerns surrounding the protection or defence of fundamental principles of justice in pre-trial detention. Specifically, the rights-protecting parameters underlying the Bail Reform Act appear to have been diluted, to a certain degree, by the increasing lack of restraint in the use of pre-trial custody, an expanding list of obstacles to obtaining bail, more stringent types of release, and new forms of inequality. In fact, it is tempting to conclude that Canadians have in many respects returned to where our story began in the 1960s.

This return to the past suggests a shift in societal values. In particular, it would appear that Canadians are increasingly willing to risk sacrificing a number of the fundamental principles enshrined in the Bail Reform Act in the name of harsher punishment (or, at least, in appearing tough on crime) and risk avoidance. Within this context, the question becomes one of acceptable trade-offs. Indeed, the ramifications of such a change in mentality (and, by extension, in the structure and operations of our bail system) are numerous and far-reaching.

Most obviously, our large (and growing) remand population represents significant additional economic costs to the provincial governments. Illustratively, it cost approximately $60,000 per year to house a provincial prisoner in 2008/09 (Calverley, 2010). Within this context, it may be particularly relevant to remember that a substantial percentage of our tax dollars are being diverted into housing a population that has yet to have been found guilty of a criminal offence.

Institutionally, correctional institutions are also facing progressively greater challenges associated with the effective management of the remand population. Particularly given the unique characteristics of this population (i.e., unpredictability in terms of length of stay, the need for their separation from sentenced offenders, their frequent need to be transported to and from courthouses, and their lack of access to activities or programming), the day-to-day operations have quickly become an administrative nightmare, with serious repercussions for the safety of staff and inmates.

Further, the very nature of corrections is affected as the actual opportunities to provide correctional programming are decreasing. With longer stays in pre-trial detention, credit for time served at sentencing (even with a 1:1 ratio) significantly reduces an offender's actual custodial sentence. In fact, few sentenced offenders currently stay in correctional institutions long enough for treatment. In addition, the majority of provincial inmates—those on remand—do not even have access to programming, with the consequence that the time spent in pre-trial detention is, in fact, 'dead time' or, as corrections might refer to it, 'lost opportunities'.

Even within our criminal courts, risk-averse behaviour by the principal players in the bail process contributes to wider problems of court inefficiency and unnecessary delays in the delivery of justice. Moreover, the increasing number of days and appearances required to obtain a determination of bail would seem to suggest a distortion of the legislative intentions of bail. While the Canadian Criminal Code does not explicitly stipulate the number of court appearances during which the bail process is expected to be resolved, the fundamental principles of justice would certainly dictate that the process occur as quickly as possible.

On a more micro level, the bail process itself has devastating effects on the accused. When it is coupled with longer periods in remand and more onerous forms of release, the potential fallout for accused persons, their family, and society as a whole (which may be required to extend support) only exacerbates the situation. Further, unequal treatment between accused who served no pre-trial detention and those who did may negatively affect perceptions of justice and fairness.

And the list could go on. We often erroneously assess the bail system (and its ramifications) in isolation from other criminal justice agencies, if not from society in general. As such, we risk inaccurately weighing the costs and benefits of our current regime. A return to our pre-bail-reform past, rooted exclusively in short-term public safety concerns or desires to appear tough on crime, ignores the full range of implications that such a move would involve. Indeed, examining the past to learn from our mistakes is one thing. Returning to the past to relive those mistakes (albeit in different form) is another issue entirely.

CRITICAL THINKING QUESTIONS

1. Some police have suggested that if there is a reasonable and probable cause to charge someone with a criminal offence, then the person should be arrested and detained until trial. What issues does this suggestion raise?

2. Why do you think your province or territory has the rate of pre-trial custody that it does? Why might it be that your province or territory is different from Canada as a whole on this dimension and/or from other provinces and territories? How would you go about trying to find out why two provinces/territories differ in their use of pre-trial detention?

3. It has been argued that since the early 1970s, the use of sureties in the release of those accused of crimes has, in some parts of Canada, been a simple substitute for cash bail. If this is the case, should this move (from cash bail to sureties) be seen as an improvement in the administration of the release process?

4. Should decisions about bail for youths be made using the same principles and practices as bail for adults? What might be the arguments for and against having a separate regime for determining pre-trial release for youths?

5. If pre-trial detention is a punishment and conditions such as house arrest or curfews that are put on those released while awaiting trial are experienced as punishments, then should those who are found not guilty (or who have all charges dismissed by courts) be compensated for the punishments they

apparently did not deserve (unless, of course, the charges are dropped *because* the pre-trial punishment equals or exceeds that which the offender would receive if found guilty)?

NOTES

1   For convenience in this figure, we have—with apologies to our three Canadian territories—referred to provincial and territorial levels of incarceration simply as 'provincial imprisonment rate'.

2   We have chosen not to include a third category of provincial prisoners—often referred to in government statistical reports as 'other provincial prisoners'. This very small group largely constitutes those held in custody for various other reasons, most notably immigration issues (e.g., until they can be deported). While this group is not presented separately in Figure 2.1, it is included in the provincial total prisoner count. Further, any subsequent 'remand' data also exclude this third category of provincial prisoners.

3   There are, of course, two groups of unsentenced prisoners: those who are awaiting a bail hearing or a trial (or are being tried and are not yet convicted) and those who have been found guilty and are remanded in custody awaiting sentencing. The available data do not permit a separation of these categories of prisoners.

4   Notably, a comparison of the relative rankings of each of the jurisdictions in Figures 2.2 and 2.3 also shows considerable variability. For instance, while Quebec ranked highest across jurisdictions in terms of the proportion of its *admissions* who were in remand (roughly 75%), it ranked in the middle of all Canadian jurisdictions in terms of the proportion of its prison population (*counts*) who were in remand (45%). The difference in these values is explained by

this truism: the size of a prison population (counts) is a function not only of the number of individuals entering prison but also of how long they remain in custody. In Quebec, for example, while 75 per cent of those entering prison are on remand, this group remains in custody for a relatively short time, reducing the proportion of remand offenders in prison on any given day. Indeed, one needs to be particularly careful not to confuse *admission* data with prison *count* data, as they provide different descriptions of the remand population.

5   It is equally notable within this context that the median time spent in custody on remand has increased rather substantially from 1993 to 1995 (specifically, the average of the median number of days in remand for this three-year period) and from 2006 and 2008 (again, the average of the median number of days in remand for this three-year period) for all provinces for which data were available (NL, NS, NB, QC, ON, SK, BC, and YT). As such, Canada is not only sending a greater number of accused to remand but, once there, they are staying longer.

6   The pre-trial release decisions for youth were, at the time of writing (2011), governed largely by the same provisions as adults.

7   Equally notable, Myers and Dhillon (2011) found that in most of the observed bail cases, there was seemingly an automatic assumption that a surety was required in order for youth to secure a release order. With consent releases, the Crown proposed a surety release to the

court in most cases without any mention or consideration of other less onerous forms of release. In 'show cause' hearings, defence counsel would in most instances simply call the proposed surety to the stand following the reading in of the alleged facts of the case, again suggesting the generalized understanding that sureties are a necessary part of a bail plan.

8   And, in reality, the number of days required to resolve a case in criminal court is substantial. For youth cases, the median number of days from first to last appearance was 119 in 2008/09. In adult criminal court, the median number of days was 124 (Milligan, 2010; Thomas, 2010).

9   Again, it is safe to assume that most of the 'failure to comply with an order' charges were, in fact, violations of bail orders. In the youth criminal justice system, an additional offence—failure to comply with a disposition—exists that is typically the basis of charges of failure to comply with sentences (largely, failure to comply with a probation condition, which is categorized as a separate offence in the adult system).

10   Notably, the sponsor of the bill was also able to state that '[a]ll the provinces and territories have advocated strongly for Bill C-25 in the form in which it was presented to this chamber' (Senate of Canada Debates, 20 October 2009, p. 1520). Indeed, this Conservative senator quoted the attorney general for Ontario, Chris Bentley (a Liberal), who—like others with extensive experience with (and knowledge of) the criminal justice system—announced his unconditional support for the bill.

11   In fact, a recent Ontario Court of Justice decision (*R. v. Marvin Johnson*) drew the same conclusion. In a very clever and creative judgment, Justice Melvyn Green differentiated between the 'quantitative' issues (the conditional release issues) and the qualitative issues (conditions).

Conditions, he argued, are mitigating factors in deriving the appropriate sentences from which the 'quantitative' adjustments are made. Most cases—Judge Green decided—should receive the 1.5 days credit, which, he pointed out, was not meant to be 'exceptional'.

12   The calculations become more complicated when one looks at penitentiary sentences. Indeed, federal inmates sometimes serve as little as one-third of a prison sentence in custody, having been granted parole. For these cases, the appropriate credit for time served in pre-trial detention would necessarily have to be even greater than 1.5:1 in order to ensure equal treatment with those not having spent any time in remand.

13   While one might suggest that the various political parties simply did not understand the elementary arithmetic underlying the inequality of this bill, it is notable that the Bloc Québécois, which supported it, quoted a Supreme Court decision (*R. v. Wust*, 2000) that explicitly called attention to the fact that the 2:1 ratio reflects not only the harshness of the detention (absence of programs, etc.) but also the fact that none of the remission mechanisms contained in the Corrections and Conditional Release Act apply to that period of detention. Even more obvious, the New Democratic Party (NDP) also supported the bill, despite its justice critic having proposed two amendments in the House of Commons that would have changed the presumptive credit to 1.5:1, precisely to address the question of inequity inherent in the 1:1 proposal. Notably, both amendments failed by votes of 10 (against) to 1 (in favour) (Standing Committee on Justice and Human Rights, 1 June 2009, minutes). In a similar fashion, the Liberal committee chair of the Senate Committee on Justice and Legal Affairs recommended

the same amendments to the full Senate, citing as justification that the amount of pre-sentence credit that was contained in the original bill (1:1) did not reflect conditional release and remission provisions of the law. The amendment failed by a vote of 44 (against) to 30 (in favour). Remarkably, one of the senators who voted for the (Liberal) amendment—Senator Jerahmiel Grafstein—had served as executive assistant to John Turner, the Liberal minister of justice who introduced the 1971 Bail Reform Act (Friedland, 2007, p. 102). Equally notable, 19 Liberal senators were absent for the vote and only 1 Conservative senator did not vote. One suspects that the absences were purposeful: the Liberals did not want to be seen as being responsible for 'killing' 1-for-1 credit in the Senate.

14 In the first two cases, the murder of the spouse took place after domestic violence charges had been laid and the accused man had been released on bail. In the last case, an accused person had been released on bail and committed the essentially random murder in broad daylight of a young woman jogging in Burlington, Ontario.

15 A similar phenomenon occurs with conditional release from penitentiary. In 2008/09, there were 7,248 offenders who completed their time on full parole or statutory release (not including those serving indeterminate sentences). Completion can occur either because the offender successfully completes the release or is revoked (for a breach of conditions or a criminal offence). Full parole for ordinary offenders is quite rare. In fact, most (62%) of those who completed parole in 2008/09 received 'accelerated parole review' and thus were presumptively released largely because they had been convicted of non-violent,

non-drug offences and it was their first penitentiary sentence. Only 544 (7.5%) of the 7,248 were regular parole releases. Given that the parole system, like the pre-trial release system, has become increasingly risk averse, it is unsurprising that very few of those released on parole (regular or accelerated) commit offences. Nevertheless, we suspect that most Canadians would see those offenders in the community on parole as being quite dangerous. They might be surprised that in 2008/09, only 11 had their parole revoked for a violent offence, constituting 0.8 per cent of those who completed, in one way or another, their parole that year.

16 This conclusion holds whether one looks at the overall number of crimes reported to the police, the number of violent crimes reported to the police, or, more recently, Statistics Canada's 'crime index' measures (total or violence) that weight the severity of each reported crime according to an index of its relative seriousness (setting Canada's overall index at 100 for 2006).

17 Arguably, the increase in the number of appearances in bail court could simply reflect a lack of adequate court resources, which would create court backlog. The difficulty with this argument is twofold. On the one hand, a problem of backlog would largely increase only the number of days to complete the bail process but not the number of appearances—which is clearly not the case in Ontario. In fact, it would appear that it is precisely the rise in the number of appearances that is producing the increase in the number of days. On the other hand, it can be observed during periods in which the criminal court caseload has declined (reducing the strain on court resources) that the number of appearances to resolve the question of bail has nonetheless continued to increase.

REFERENCES

Calverley, D. (2010). Adult Correctional Services in Canada, 2008/2009. *Juristat*, *3*(3).

Canadian Committee on Corrections. (1969). *Toward unity: The report of the Canadian committee on corrections.* Ottawa: Queen's Printer.

Department of Justice, Canada. (2009, March 27). The Government of Canada introduces legislation restricting credit for time served. Press release (C-25), 27 March. Retrieved 4 November 2011 from http://www.justice.gc.ca/eng/news-nouv/nr-cp/2009/doc_32345.html.

Doob, A.N., & Cavoukian, A. (1977). The effect of the revoking of bail. *R. v. Demeter. Criminal Law Quarterly, 19*(2), 196–202.

Friedland, M.L. (1965). *Detention before trial: A study of criminal cases tried in the Toronto Magistrates' Courts.* Toronto: University of Toronto Press.

Friedland, Martin L. (2007). *My life in crime and other academic adventures.* Toronto: Osgoode Society.

Hagan, J., & Morden, C.P. (1981). *The police decision to detain: A study of legal labeling and police deviance.* In C.D. Shearing (Ed.), *Organizational Police Deviance: Its Structure and Control* (pp. 9–28). Toronto: Butterworths.

Hill, S.C., Tanovich, D.M., & Strezos, L.P. (Eds.). (2004). *McWilliams' Canadian criminal evidence* (4th ed.). Aurora, ON: Canada Law Book.

Kellough, G., & Wortley, S. (2002). Remand for bail: Bail decisions and plea bargaining as commensurate decisions. *British Journal of Criminology, 42*, 186–210.

Koza, P., & Doob, A.N. (1975a). Some empirical evidence on judicial interim release proceedings. *Criminal Law Quarterly, 17*, 258–72.

———— & ————. (1975b). The relationship of pre-trial custody to the outcome of a trial. *Criminal Law Quarterly, 17*, 391–400.

Manns, J.D. (2005). Liberty takings: A framework for compensating pretrial detainees. *Cardozo Law Review, 26*(5), 1947–2022.

Manson, A. (2004/5). Pre-sentence custody and the determination of a sentence (or how to make a mole hill out of a mountain). *Criminal Law Quarterly, 49*, 292–350.

Milligan, S. (2010). Youth Court Statistics 2008/2009. *Juristat, 30*(2). Statistics Canada Catalogue No. 85-002-X. Ottawa.

Ministry of the Attorney General, Ontario. (2005). *Crown policy manual.* Retrieved 7 September 2010 from http://www.attorneygeneral.jus.gov.on.ca/english/crim/cpm/2005/BailHearings.pdf.

Moyer, S. (2005). *A comparison of case processing under the Young Offenders Act and the First Six Months of the Youth Criminal Justice Act.* Report prepared for the Department of Justice Canada. Ottawa: Government of Canada.

————, & Basic, M. (2004). *Pre-trial detention under the Young Offenders Act: A study of urban courts.* Report prepared for the Department of Justice Canada, Research and Statistics Division. Ottawa: Government of Canada.

Myers, N. (2009). Shifting risk: Bail and the use of sureties. *Current Issues in Criminal Justice, 21*(1), 127–47.

————, & Dhillon, T.K. (2011). *The criminal offence of entering any Shoppers Drug Mart in Ontario: Criminalizing ordinary behaviour with youth bail conditions.* Unpublished manuscript. Toronto: Centre of Criminology.

National Council of Welfare. (2000). *Justice and the poor.* Ottawa: National Council of Welfare.

Ritchie, L. (2005). *A report on the bail process in the criminal justice system.* Unpublished honours thesis, University of Waterloo, London, ON.

Sprott, J.B. (2006). The use of custody for failing to comply with a disposition: Cases under the Young Offenders Act. *Canadian Journal of Criminology and Criminal Justice, 48*(4), 609–22.

Sprott, J., & Doob, A.N. (2010). Gendered treatment: Girls and treatment orders in bail court. *Canadian Journal of Criminology and Criminal Justice, 52*(4), 427–41.

Sprott, J.B. and Myers, N.M. (2011). Set up to fail: The unintended consequences of multiple bail conditions. *Canadian Journal of Criminology and Criminal Justice.* 53(4), 404–23

Thomas, J. (2010). Adult criminal court statistics, 2008/2009. *Juristat, 30*(2).

7Statistics Canada Catalogue No. 85-002-X. Ottawa.

Trotter, G.T. (2010). *The law of bail in Canada* (3rd ed.). Scarborough, ON: Carswell.

Varma, K.N. (2002). Exploring 'youth' in court: An analysis of decision-making in youth court bail hearings. *Canadian Journal of Criminology, 44*(2), 143–64.

Webster, C.M. (2007). *Remanding the problem: An examination of Ottawa Bail Court.* Report presented to the Ministry of Attorney General, Court Services Division, Ottawa.

———, Doob, A.N. and Myers, N.M. (2009). The parable of Ms. Baker: Understanding pre-trial detention in Canada. *Current Issues in Criminal Justice, 21*(1), 79–102.

CASES CITED

R. v. McDonald (1998), 127 C.C.C. (3d) 57.

R. v. Marvin Johnson (2011). Toronto Ontario Court of Justice. Released 23 February 2011.

R. v. Wust (2000), 1 S.C.R. 455, 2000 SCC 18.

STATUTES CITED

Canadian Charter of Rights and Freedoms (1982).

Criminal Code, R.S.C. 1985, c. C-46 (as amended).

3

A Trip from Thoughtful to Thoughtless: Murder Sentencing in Canada

Allan Manson

INTRODUCTION

Because of the gravity of the offence and the often visceral nature of responses to dramatic and well-publicized intentional killings, the sentencing response to murder provides an interesting example of how penal policy evolves. As in most nineteenth-century countries, Canada's first Criminal Code imposed the death penalty in all murder cases.[1] Hanging was the prescribed form of capital punishment, subject only to commutation by the federal cabinet. Public and political questioning of capital punishment began in the 1950s. As the debate heated up, the Canadian Parliament introduced new legislation in 1961 that divided murders into capital and non-capital categories.[2] While the last hanging in Canada took place on 11 December 1962 at the Don Jail in Toronto,[3] it was not until 1976 that the death penalty was finally abolished. In its place, Parliament established a scheme of first- and second-degree murder with mandatory life sentences for both. The distinction lay in the parole ineligibility period. For first-degree murder, it was 25 years. For second-degree murder, it was a period between 10 and 25 years set by the trial judge after receiving a recommendation from the jury, if it chose to make one. What was unique about the new scheme was a process for reconsidering parole ineligibility after 15 years, known not surprisingly as 'the 15-year review' or in the vernacular 'the faint hope clause'. This novel mechanism is the major subject of this chapter.

THE CANADIAN SENTENCING SYSTEM

For over a century, the Canadian sentencing system was based, except in cases of murder, on individualization, with no principles or purposes included in the Criminal Code. The available penalties were stipulated offence by offence in the

Criminal Code with prescribed maxima.[4] Eventually, in the latter half of the twentieth century, a handful of mandatory minimum penalties were introduced, most particularly with respect to repeat convictions for impaired driving. In 1995, the government of the day introduced legislation that provided four-year mandatory minimum sentences for 10 offences if committed with a firearm.[5] Since its election, the current government has embarked on a pointed campaign to increase the number of offences that carry mandatory minimum sentences. Although this legislative effort has extended to drug offences, organized crime offences, and even car theft for repeat offenders, the majority of offences in the Criminal Code still only have a prescribed maximum sentence.

The only major change to the Canadian sentencing scheme occurred in 1996. Parliament inserted into the Criminal Code a statement of purpose, a list of potential sentencing objectives, and a set of principles. No priority was articulated among the principles and objectives, although proportionality was described as a 'fundamental principle'. Consequently, some observers have described this legislative effort as establishing a 'cafeteria' approach. If the sentencing judge wants ribs, they are available; if the judge is a vegetarian, there is a vegetarian option. In other words—and subject to the occasional articulation of guidance from an appellate court for a particular type of offence—individualization and a potential amalgam of principles and objectives continue to provide the basic framework for sentencing.[6]

The Supreme Court of Canada has also become active on the sentencing front. While it has rejected most of the constitutionally based 'cruel and unusual' challenges to mandatory minimum penalties, it has recognized the 1996 principles as a new initiative to address over-incarceration and, in particular, the large and inordinate proportion of Aboriginal offenders in Canadian prisons and penitentiaries. This has led to encouragement of restorative objectives when appropriate. At other levels of the judiciary, we are witnessing an increased acceptance of proportionality as the engine for sentencing decisions.[7]

MURDER SENTENCING IN CANADA
The Abolition of Capital Punishment

Canadians began questioning capital punishment in the 1950s. Soon thereafter, in 1961, legislation was passed dividing murder into capital and non-capital categories. Essentially, capital murder was restricted to 'planned and deliberate' killings and the killing of a member of a prescribed set, which included police officers and jail guards. In slightly different forms, this approach continued until the political debate about capital punishment came to fruition in Parliament in 1975, when an abolition bill was presented by the governing Liberal Party. Although there had been no executions in Canada since 1962 because of commutations by the federal cabinet, at the time of the debate there were still a small number of people in jail with death warrants awaiting a decision on commutation.

The abolition debate was conducted vigorously in Parliament, in the media, and in public discourse. In Parliament, the issue was raised almost daily for many months. The 'retentionists' would use egregious examples of actual cases to argue for the continued need for a capital penalty. One such case, often cited as a justification for the death penalty, took place in 1972.[8] A man took a train to Toronto from Montreal, stole a car, and then robbed a bank. He was confronted outside the bank by two police officers. The man from Montreal was armed. He shot and killed one officer and seriously wounded the other. The story of the officer who was killed, Constable Maitland, was dramatically tragic. He left a young wife and three small children. One day during the debate in Parliament, a member named Andrew Brewin rose to read a letter he had received from Mrs. Maitland, the dead officer's widow and a constituent of Brewin's. She explained that neither she nor, when he was living, her husband supported capital punishment, and she urged the members of Parliament to vote for its abolition. While it is impossible to know what actually influenced the parliamentarians, Mrs. Maitland's letter may well have been a turning point. Capital punishment was formally abolished on 26 July 1976 with respect to any offences committed before or after that date. A decade later, a motion to revive the debate was defeated in Parliament.

The New Murder Sentencing Regime

While the parliamentary debates in 1975 and 1976 were heated, the substantive focus that consumed the attention of members of Parliament was the legitimacy of the death penalty, not the proposed substitutes of first- and second-degree-murder with mandatory life sentences and minimum parole ineligibility periods of 25 and 10 years respectively. However, the legislation also contained a proposal for the review of parole ineligibility. The review plan applied to all first-degree murder life sentences and any second-degree life sentences where the trial judge imposed a period of ineligibility greater than 15 years. Essentially, the plan would permit the offender to apply to a court to have the ineligibility period reconsidered in light of the circumstances of the offence and the offender's situation after 15 years of confinement.

The review procedure was not discussed in Parliament, but was scrutinized line by line by a parliamentary committee. The original proposal suggested that the review be conducted by a panel of three superior court judges. In committee, a member who had previously been a trial lawyer persuaded his colleagues to amend the scheme to employ a jury. Ordinarily, Canadian juries have no decision-making role in sentencing, but this suggestion struck a responsive chord, since it would put the responsibility for reducing the minimum period of confinement in the hands of representatives of the community in which the offence occurred.

The original legislation imposed no restrictions on the ability of an offender to apply for review other than having to have served 15 years toward the sentence. As well, the jury decision for or against reduction was based on a two-thirds majority. Given the visceral and idiosyncratic nature of responses to the question of punishment for murder, the ability to persuade eight jurors seemed to be a good threshold. During the first decade of experience, the relevant courts developed procedural rules and interpreted the statutory provisions in ways that ensured fair hearings without re-litigating the issue of guilt. As well, accommodation was made for the role of survivors to provide a victim-impact statement.

EXPERIENCE WITH THE 15-YEAR REVIEW

The first two 15-year reviews took place in 1987. Both cases, one in Quebec and one in Ontario, involved the killing of a police officer followed by capital prosecutions that led to the death penalty. These sentences were commuted by statute as a result of the abolition of capital punishment in 1976 and transformed into first-degree murder sentences. With life sentences for murder, the counting towards parole eligibility commences upon arrest, not sentencing. Hence, both prisoners were eligible to apply for a review in 1987. Interestingly, the Quebec case succeeded in a reduction, while the Ontario case failed.

Surprising to many observers, there have been relatively few applications for 15-year reviews. However, many applicants were successful. The data in Table 3.1, recorded as of 12 April 2009,[9] show the situation over a period of more than 20 years. It is true, as the relevant minister regularly reminds us, that almost 83 per cent of review applications are successful, but given the small proportion of eligible prisoners who apply (17.45%), this means that only 14.43 per cent of eligible prisoners received a reduction in parole eligibility from the 15-year review process.

Obviously, a process of self-selection has influenced prisoners' decisions on whether to apply for a review or not. One can only guess why this is, but there are some plausible suggestions. First, 15-year reviews are generally conducted in the place where the offence occurred and often generate a great deal of contemporary media attention. Some prisoners might prefer to let their case lay dormant, out of the public eye. Second, there can be concern that an unsuccessful application may

TABLE 3.1   Cases with more than 15 years' parole ineligibility: Those eligible to apply for review, those who applied, and those who received a reduction, 1987–2009

Number of offenders serving life sentences with more than 15 years' parole ineligibility	1,792
Number of prisoners eligible for s. 745 application	991
Number of eligible prisoners who have had reviews	173 (17.45% of eligible)
Number of prisoners who received some reduction	143 (14.43% of eligible)

prejudice a future parole application. A third reason is perhaps the recognition that, in order to succeed, one needs to show some good evidence of progress and positive change. Accordingly, prisoners may want to wait until they have received minimum-security status, or at least medium security, before seriously considering an application. Whatever the reasons, most cases that have gone forward have proven to be good cases.

Still, there have been some notorious applications that have affected the process by generating amendments. The inevitably doomed effort of Clifford Olson, one of Canada's most infamous serial killers, was met with a campaign to prohibit similar cases from occupying a public forum. Other victims continued to press for complete repeal. In 1997, the minister of justice amended the process by limiting access to reviews and diminishing the prospect of success. There were three major changes. First, anyone who was convicted after 9 January 1997 (the date of proclamation in force) of a multiple murder or a murder after having already been convicted of a murder would be disentitled entirely from applying.[10] Second, there would no longer be an absolute right to a hearing. Upon application, the chief justice of the province in which the offence occurred must consider the application and other written material to determine whether, on a balance of probabilities, the application has a reasonable prospect of success.[11] Only if the chief justice is satisfied that there is a reasonable prospect of success will a jury be empanelled to hear the application. The third change imposed a jury unanimity requirement.[12] After 1997, the prisoner needed to persuade all 12 jurors that he or she was entitled to a reduction in the period of parole ineligibility. While it was anticipated by some that this would have a significant impact on the number of successful applications, research has shown that the success rate has not changed substantially.[13]

It is important to remember that a jury has the power to reduce parole eligibility to a number of years less than 25. Accordingly, a successful application does not mean immediate eligibility. Moreover, once the reduced eligibility date is reached, this only opens the door for a parole application. From 1987 to 2009, of the 143 successful applicants, 130 have been released on parole. Of those released prior to 12 April 2009, 14 have been returned to custody, 11 have died, 3 have been deported, and 1 was on bail for a new charge.[14]

From the data presented above, a number of important observations can be made about the 15-year review process. First, eligible prisoners have been very self-selective in deciding whether to apply. One might conclude that, for the most part, only good cases go forward. Second, successful cases have occurred in every province. Since the decision maker is a 12-person jury made of ordinary Canadians, the degree of successful applications across the entire country, including in highly conservative provinces, suggests a high degree of social acceptability. Third, of the 130 prisoners who have obtained parole after a favourable section 745.6 ruling, 9 have been returned to custody for breaching a parole condition and one was charged with a new offence, robbery. Clearly, released prisoners have an infinitesimal impact on crime in Canada.

Because of new legislation discussed below, it is necessary to explain one other aspect of Canadian sentencing that has existed for many years. All murder sentences are life sentences. Many years ago, Canadian courts reached the logical conclusion that no sentence could be consecutive to a life sentence. This makes complete sense given that the life-imprisonment warrant only expires upon death. It would be fatuous to contemplate a warrant for an additional sentence taking effect consecutively—that is, only upon the death of the prisoner. This means that all additional sentences, even a new life sentence, must be served concurrently with the original life sentence. But how does this affect parole eligibility? First, section 745(b) of the Criminal Code provides that a person convicted of second-degree murder who has 'previously been convicted of culpable homicide that is murder, however described' shall be sentenced to life imprisonment with no parole eligibility for 25 years. So, a subsequent murder necessarily imposes a concurrent life sentence with a 25-year parole ineligibility period starting on the date of arrest for that murder. Second, section 120.2(2) of the Corrections and Conditional Release Act provides that a person serving a life sentence who receives an additional determinate sentence is only eligible for parole after serving the parole ineligibility period attached to the life sentence plus the period of ineligibility required by the new sentence. It is important to note that the aggregation of parole ineligibility periods applies only to fixed sentences and not to a new life sentence. The rationale behind this exclusion seems clear. The multiple murderer already has a 25-year ineligibility period. Moreover, the subsequent killing would have an obvious negative impact on the prospect of a successful parole decision in the future.

RECENT EFFORTS TO RESHAPE THE MURDER SENTENCING REGIME

Until 25 March 2011, the Conservative Party comprised the Canadian government and led a minority Parliament. Notwithstanding its minority status, the government of Stephen Harper managed to move its 'law and order' rhetoric, expressed frequently during its two electoral campaigns, into a legislative agenda. This agenda has been dominated by a number of new mandatory minimum sentences and other measures that will have the effect of limiting judicial sentencing discretion. However, it has included two bills intended to dramatically affect major aspects of murder sentencing. First, Bill S-6 repealed the 15-year review for any cases arising from a murder committed after its passage and will create new procedural hurdles for cases already in the system.[15] Second, the goal of Bill C-48 was apparently to permit a judge to make the 25-year parole ineligibility periods for first-degree murder consecutive in cases of 'multiple murders'. The 'backgrounder' prepared by the Library of Parliament explains that the bill's intention was to afford 'judges the opportunity to make the parole ineligibility periods for multiple murders consecutive rather than concurrent.'[16] Curiously, these two bills were given 'cute' subtitles in the fashion of some American legislatures. Respectively, they are called 'Serious Time for Serious Crime' and 'Protecting Canadians by Eliminating the Sentencing Discount for Multiple Murders'. Both bills made their way successfully through the legislative process with only limited opposition. In the latter part of March 2011, the government, fearing a possible defeat on non-confidence grounds (which would happen on 25 March 2011), hurried a number of bills to royal assent. Two of those were S-6 and C-48. Accordingly, while not yet proclaimed in force, at the time of writing they represent the law of Canada.

Explaining the legislative process in this situation is a bit complicated because the government prorogued Parliament in December 2009, leaving the original bills to die on the order paper. After Parliament resumed, it was necessary to reintroduce them, along with a large number of other bills, either in the Senate or the House of Commons. Bills S-6 and C-48 were reintroduced in 2010 verbatim from the predecessor bills. This means that the House of Commons and Senate have had two opportunities to consider each of these bills. When bills are presented in Parliament, speeches are made by their sponsors and some limited opportunity for questions is provided. Then, the legislative process refers proposed bills to specialized committees. In the House of Commons, this is the Committee on Justice and Human Rights; in the Senate, it is the Committee on Legal and Constitutional Affairs. From 2009 until 2011, in relation to Bills S-6 and C-48 and their identical predecessors, these two committees engaged in lengthy hearings and heard a large number of witnesses, some more than once. The minutes of these proceedings are rich with details that reveal much about the political and substantive rationale behind this legislative effort to change murder sentencing. In committee, the nature of the presentations, the kinds of questions asked by committee members, and the responses to them reveal a repetitive and shallow substantive discussion. While a few committee members attempted to probe witnesses in a serious manner, most simply assumed their partisan roles.

It is worth examining some of the speeches in Parliament and the testimony in committee. Since Bills S-6 and C-48 both deal with murder sentencing and, in particular, the parole ineligibility periods, they involve common themes and even occasionally the same witnesses in committee. Accordingly, it will be useful to review them together, breaking down the testimony into three categories: governmental witnesses, victims or victim advocates, and non-governmental witnesses.

Governmental Witnesses

The governmental witnesses include the minister of justice, his political delegates, and official representatives of Justice Canada and other federal agencies. When S-6 was introduced in the Senate, its sponsor was Senator Claude Carignan. He raised the issue of public confidence saying that 'for many Canadians, the availability of the faint hope clause is eroding their confidence in the integrity of the justice system.'[17] This comment suggests that there is something broken in the system that needs to be repaired. However, throughout the debates, the only problem identified by governmental witnesses was characterized as a 'truth in sentencing' issue. It was argued on a number of occasions that there is something dubious about a sentencing judge pronouncing a life sentence with no parole eligibility for 25 years and following this with an explanation of the possibility of a 15-year review. While this claim may have a hollow ring, the real impetus for the bill was explained by Minister Robert Nicholson when he appeared before the House Committee. He said:

> Many refer to the faint hope regime as the loophole for lifers that can undermine the protection of society, because the system affords leniency to murderers, whose crimes demand severe punishment. Even worse, and perhaps most importantly, victims have told me about the additional trauma inflicted on their families and loved ones. They live in constant dread that the killer who robbed them of their loved one may one day bring forward a faint hope application. This review process forces victims to relive the details of the horrible crimes they have suffered again and again.
>
> We want to spare these victims the anguish of parole eligibility hearings. We believe the justice system must not put those rights of individuals ahead of those of victims and law-abiding Canadians. The measures proposed in Bill S-6 are in direct response to these concerns.[18]

This focus on a perception of the victim's perspective was echoed by Bob Dechart, a member of the House Committee who had recently been appointed parliamentary secretary to the minister. After a few questions from committee members to witnesses about the potential impact of S-6 on rehabilitation, Mr. Dechart tried to end the discussion by saying:

> With respect, gentlemen, this bill is not about rehabilitation. I hear, a lot, that people can be rehabilitated, people should be rehabilitated, we need to give people incentives to be rehabilitated. That's not what this bill is about. This bill is about respecting victims and their families and truth in sentencing, so people will have faith in our criminal justice system, so they can go to bed at night and rest easy knowing that murderers are behind bars where they ought to be, and that the sentences the judges and juries impose upon convicted murderers are actually served by them.
>
> That's what this bill is about, and that's the problem this bill is designed to solve.[19]

There can be little doubt that Mr. Dechart's words reflect the true motivation behind the bill. However, they raise a serious question about how much this sentiment truly reflects the views of victims and to what extent those views should shape penal policy. Here, it is interesting to note how the minister responded to questions about how much homework he had done before introducing this legislation. When the predecessor to S-6 was presented in the House of Commons, the bill's sponsor, the parliamentary secretary to the minister of justice, gave an initial speech and was then asked some brief questions. One member of Parliament asked him about Canada's actual experience with the 15-year process. He answered: 'It is not a question of numbers. The victims, not the numbers, should be the basis for the bill.'[20]

This frank response was reflected in much of the governmental testimony, which did not offer any empirical or principled support for the bill beyond reconfigured versions of 'what Canadians want and what victims need.' How the minister knew what Canadians want is open to question. On the victim's perspective, however, there is some indication. During his appearance in committee on Bill S-6, the minister was pressed about the number of victims with whom he had consulted about the 15-year review process. In a number of his responses, he evaded the question, saying only that when he travels to major cities he makes a point 'of hearing from victims'. He also mentioned his contact with Sharon Rosenfeldt, a victims advocate and mother of a victim of notorious serial killer Clifford Olsen. Ms. Rosenfeldt gave testimony in committee, discussed below.

When officials from the Department of Justice, Corrections Canada, and the National Parole Board appeared before the committees, their testimony was restricted to explaining processes, explaining part of the proposed legislation, and providing data about the 15-year review process. Commissioner Don Head of Corrections Canada provided the most recent data on the 15-year review process, confirming what is outlined above: that only a small number of eligible prisoners apply, but that a high proportion of applications are successful. The chair of the National Parole Board, Harvey Cenaiko, shed some light on the histories of those people who had had there parole ineligibility reduced and were subsequently released by the board on day or full parole:

> These 136 offenders had a total of 649 supervision periods—526 on day parole and 123 on full parole. Of the 526 day parole supervision periods granted, two offenders had their parole revoked as the result of a new non-violent offence. The offences were for obstructing a peace officer over 15 years ago and for uttering a threat to cause death or harm in 2009–10. Of the 123 full parole supervision periods, nine offenders had their parole revoked as the result of a new non-violent offence. Two offenders had their parole revoked as the result of a new violent offence. The new violent offences were for robbery over 15 years ago and for assault with a weapon about eight years ago.[21]

An interesting exchange took place when Mr. Cenaiko was asked by a senator whether he was satisfied with the current scheme and whether the proposed changes were justified. He politely demurred, answering only that the board will apply the law and 'will continue to assess risk on lifers, whether they are eligible for parole at 15 years, at 20 years or 25 years.'

The only criticism of Bill S-6 came from the Office of the Correctional Investigator. In essence, the correctional investigator is the ombudsman for federal prisoners. The office dates back to the 1970s, but its framework and mandate are now established by Part III of the Corrections and Conditional Release Act, the same statute that governs the penitentiaries and the parole system. The Office of the Correctional Investigator has regular and current contact with penitentiaries through correspondence and through the on-site visits of its investigators. The current correctional investigator, Howard Sapers, began his remarks by describing the penitentiary environment as 'increasingly harsh, tense, crowded, volatile, and stressed', adding that these conditions are presenting serious challenges to the ability of the Correctional Service of Canada to 'provide safe and effective custody' as well as access to programs intended to respond to those factors that contribute to crime, such as 'substance abuse, family violence, histories of abuse, and trauma'. He reported that 'only 2% of an annual $2.5 billion expenditure is spent for this purpose'. Specifically with respect to Bill S-6, he said:

> Effectively increasing the incarceration rate by curtailing or eliminating parole eligibility needs to be carefully considered in the context of the capacity, intervention, and programming challenges already facing Canada's correctional authority.
>
> The faint hope clause is tied to the abolishment of capital punishment in 1976. It was intended to motivate offenders serving long-term sentences. It does not guarantee that the offender will be granted parole. The concept of faint hope expressly recognizes the capacity of an individual offender to change, to be rehabilitated, and to become responsible and law-abiding, even after committing a most serious offence.
>
> Bill S-6 will likely increase the period of time long-term offenders will wait before receiving correctional programming. Extended periods of idle time will most definitely impact on motivation levels and the ability of long-term offenders to participate in programs, especially as they age in custody and their health inevitably deteriorates.
>
> ... [I]t seems to me that we need to consider proposed criminal justice legislation in the context of striking an appropriate balance between measures designed to incapacitate and deter against the equally important principles of reintegration and rehabilitation.[22]

One would have thought that these comments from such an authoritative figure would have generated a more thoughtful debate. Instead, they seem to have been dismissed by the government's members on the House Committee. Mr. Sapers received a lecture from Mr. Dechart, who reminded everyone that the government is 'trying to design a system that respects the victims.'

When Bill C-48 was introduced in the House of Commons, it was presented by Daniel Petit, then the parliamentary secretary to the minister of justice. Mr. Petit explained that the bill was 'another example of the government's ongoing commitment to protect the families and loved ones of murder victims.' He added: 'Our government is following through on its commitment to make Canadian streets and communities safer by ensuring that offenders who are found guilty of serious crimes serve a sentence that reflects the severity of those crimes. The amendments to the Criminal Code in Bill C-48 are an important part of this commitment.'

In discussing the proposed new 'multiple murder' provisions, Mr. Petit stressed that the trial judge would retain discretion on whether to impose consecutive 25-year periods of ineligibility. However, his concluding remarks returned to the issue of confidence. He suggested that ordinary Canadians 'find it hard to understand that the justice system gives the most serious criminals—those who have committed multiple murders—access to parole despite the horrific circumstances of their murders and the number of lives they have taken.' He clarified this argument by referring to the current regime in which life sentences for murder are always concurrent, regardless of the number of victims. The implication, repeated only in the testimony of victims, was that victims wanted to see a specific part of a sentence attributable to their case. In other words, a global life sentence would be insufficient if no part of it could be identified and isolated as a response to a particular crime. This was a theme articulated a number of years ago in a private member's bill that dealt with sexual assault and the role of concurrent sentences. That bill did not pass, but the concept was resurrected in C-48.

The minister of justice returned to the Senate Committee to urge the passing of C-48. He repeated the bill's underlying rationale:

> However, the issue before us that Bill C-48 seeks to address is that, under Canadian law as it now stands, 25 years is the maximum period for which a convicted first- or second-degree murderer may be prevented from applying for parole, no matter how many lives that person may have taken.
>
> Many Canadians are perplexed by this. They cannot understand why the law cannot account, in a concrete way, for the fact that more than one innocent life has been lost. They justifiably criticize the current 25-year maximum parole ineligibility period as a symbolic devaluation of the lives of victims that appears to give multiple murderers a 'volume discount' for their crimes.
>
> This bill responds to those criticisms. It is based on the proposition that killing more than one person reflects a higher degree of moral blameworthiness and ought to allow the imposition of additional periods of parole ineligibility.[23]

Again, one notes how the minister framed his argument with the assertion that many Canadians are perplexed and critical of the current regime without offering any real support for this proposition. In the Senate, the minister was asked for an assurance that the language of the bill was sufficient to achieve its ostensible goal.

This was a legitimate question given the ambiguous nature of the triggering phrase in the bill:'who is convicted of murder and who has already been convicted of one or more other murders'. The minister, with support from a lawyer from the Department of Justice, explained that the amendment was 'designed to apply to multiple murders that occur in the same criminal incident and to multiple murders where murders are committed in different incidents'. According to the witnesses, this effect occurs even when the verdicts and convictions occur at the same trial, since the sentence for each count is imposed separately in sequence.

Victims and Victim Advocates

On each bill, a number of days in committee were devoted to hearing both from individuals who had experienced the loss of a loved one as a result of a murder and from representatives of agencies or associations with the mandate of speaking on behalf of victims. Most of the personal accounts were related to the notion often called 're-victimization' and how it is triggered by the prospect of the release of a convicted murderer and by the opportunities to participate in the release processes.

I do not intend to detail the testimony of the individual witnesses who provided accounts of tragic and gruesome events that surrounded particular killings. They spoke personally and eloquently of their grief and suffering. In one session, a father recounted the sexual assault and killing of his daughter and a grandmother spoke of the abduction, torture, and killing of her grandson. The common theme was the lasting and haunting nature of their thoughts about their loved ones. The father summarized his view succinctly:'I just want that man to serve his full 25 years. If they decide at that time that he is not worthy of parole, another 25 years, for me, is just fine. Life is life. He took a life, he should forfeit a life.'[24] Just reading these testimonies leaves one with an enormous sense of sympathy. The effect on the parliamentarians who heard it in person must have been more dramatic.

Much of the testimony was directed to Bill S-6 and the impact of the 15-year review process. From an advocacy perspective, a number of witnesses who work with and advocate for victims gave testimony. One witness was the director of advocacy and awareness from the Canadian Resource Centre for Victims of Crime, a 'national, non-profit advocacy group for victims and survivors of serious, violent crime'. She explained her support for Bill S-6 in these terms:

> The intense anguish felt by homicide survivors is aggravated by the provisions in our law that allow for offenders of first- or second-degree murder to seek, and in most cases be granted, a reprieve on their parole eligibility periods. Consider the following example: An offender is held in custody for three years awaiting trial for a murder. He is convicted, but has several appeals that drag through the courts for an additional seven years. By the time the court process is finally finished, the family is subject to the

prospect of a section 745 hearing just five [*sic*] years later. Even if the offender does not apply immediately, it hangs over the family's head, wondering if he will apply.

The judicial review process is tantamount to cruel and unusual punishment for homicide survivors, who lose their faith in a criminal justice system that removes from them the small measure of justice they thought they had won on behalf of their loved one. Section 745 of the Criminal Code is contradictory. Offenders convicted of first- or second-degree murder should serve the time the court intends them to before being eligible to apply for parole. The changes put forward in this legislation will lessen the suffering that these families feel by further restricting access to judicial reviews and eventually eliminating the process for all murders.[25]

She returned to the topic of confidence in the justice system and 'truth in sentencing' by saying that the 15-year review process 'takes those offenders deemed to be the worst offenders and grants them an opportunity to avoid the sentence imposed upon them.' In her view, the process harms victims if they attend the judicial reviews because, aside from reliving painful events, they must 'sit in court and listen to the offender describe his accomplishments and aspirations.'

Another witness was Sharon Rosenfeldt, the president of Victims of Violence. Ms. Rosenfeldt is the mother of one of the victims of Clifford Olson. She and her late husband have played influential roles in the victims' movement and have often contributed to law-reform initiatives. Her name was used on a number of occasions by other witnesses, including Minister Nicholson, to show the extent of their consultations. While her testimony was directed to support Bill C-48, she also spoke about the 15-year review process. Before ending her presentation to the House Committee, Ms. Rosenfeldt provided a compelling personal perspective on the experience of dealing with 15-year reviews:

> I can tell you one thing: it's tough. It's tough after 29 years, it's tough after 26 years, and I'm not so sure why we have to go through it. I have been around a long time; I understand laws and I understand people who work with offenders. Honestly, I'm not a vindictive person. I know all offenders aren't like Clifford Olson. I know that.
>
> Honest to God, it's tough. I'm still coming down from it. I'm turning 65. When can I put my son to rest? My husband is gone. The last time he had his eyes open, he had brain tumours. He was right out of his mind and rolling on the floor. He climbed out of his bed and he was screaming, 'Parole? Clifford Olson?' I don't think I can take it anymore.
>
> I'm so sorry; I know we're not supposed to be emotional. I know better than that; I truly do. I know better than that. I didn't mean for this to take place. It really is tough, though. There has to be a way. If this bill isn't passed, maybe . . .[26]

One can imagine the impact of Ms. Rosenfeldt's support given her combined roles as both the head of a national victims' organization and the parent of a murdered child.

Susan O'Sullivan, the recently appointed federal ombudsman for Victims of Crime gave testimony on both bills. With respect to S-6 she said:

> I have had the chance recently to talk to some victims and victim advocacy groups about the issue. Unfortunately, I have not conducted exhaustive consultations at this stage, as time did not permit. As such, the information I am presenting here represents those groups I did have a chance to talk to but cannot be taken to represent all victims as a whole.
>
> During my discussions it was made abundantly clear to me that there is strong support for Bill S-6 based on three main areas it addresses: accountability, transparency, and compassion.
>
> My third point is compassion, and it cuts to the heart of the matter for victims. The grief victims experience is devastating, and for those strong enough to try to move forward in life, having to rehash the crime and the trauma at a hearing can feel like reliving the worst time of their lives over and over again. Yes, victims can choose not to attend a hearing, but like anyone, victims often feel a strong compulsion to be there in person and to stand up for the very person who cannot—the victim.[27]

On Bill C-48, Ms. O'Sullivan said in support that it 'addresses two specific concerns that victims have raised again and again: the need for accountability for each life taken, and the anxiety and emotional toll victims face when an offender is granted a parole hearing.' On the first point, she explained that accountability is 'the desire' to see that the 'loss of their loved one's life is considered and valued and that the offender is held responsible for each life he has taken.' Like other witnesses on C-48, her testimony extended to the parole process, and she recounted her recent attendance as an observer at Clifford Olson's parole hearing:

> I can tell you, after talking with Sharon Rosenfeldt, that these hearings can be very difficult. Some victims choose not to participate in parole hearings, but for those who do, preparing victim impact statements and sitting in the same room with the offender who stole the life of a son or daughter can make wounds fresh again. And the impact of that hearing is not limited to just the two days the parole board meets and makes its decision. It comes years in advance when victims know that an offender's parole ineligibility period is coming to an end. It comes months in advance when the victims are advised that the offender will be having a hearing and they need to prepare. And it continues after the hearing as families try to continue to heal. These hearings involve time, cost, and often travel for victims. For those who may be unwell or who have medical issues, this can be especially challenging.[28]

Ms. O'Sullivan, with her long background in policing, was an impressive witness. However, her testimony went beyond matters of policy and invoked the personal experiences of Ms. Rosenfeldt to give context to her remarks.

Non-governmental Witnesses

Both the House and Senate Committees heard, on both bills, from an array of groups and organizations that were not affiliated with government and did not represent victims. These witnesses fell into three categories: professional groups that represent lawyers; groups that work with, and advocate on behalf of, female and male prisoners; and human rights organizations. These groups included the Canadian Bar Association, the Canadian Council of Criminal Defence Lawyers, the Ontario Criminal Lawyers' Association, Le Barreau du Québec, the John Howard Societies of Ontario and Canada, the Canadian Association of Elizabeth Fry Societies, and the Canadian Civil Liberties Association. All of these groups opposed both Bill S-6 and Bill C-48. While one would not want to belittle the preparation of their individual submissions, it is fair to say that they struck common chords, although they sometimes used different elements in their arguments. The consistent theme was that the current murder sentencing regime is not a problem and does not need to be changed. As well, they argued that concern and respect for the loss experienced by victims should not be the sole motivation for a major change in penal policy. To avoid repetition, I can capsulize their positions:

On Bill S-6:
a) The process contemplated when capital punishment was abolished is working well as demonstrated by how juries comprised of ordinary Canadians can distinguish between good cases and bad cases.
b) The 15-year review provides fairness to the life imprisonment regime, permitting the legal system to take an individual look at the person convicted of first-degree murder in light of the circumstances of that murder and the person's conduct over at least 15 years.
c) The 15-year review process encourages rehabilitation.
d) The evidence shows that released murderers do not present a risk to society.
e) The regime accommodates the views of victims at every stage.

On Bill C-48:
a) A life sentence is the longest sentence that can be imposed, and regardless of parole eligibility, it lasts for life.
b) The National Parole Board makes decisions on the basis of risk, and dangerous prisoners convicted of heinous crimes are unlikely candidates for release, in particular the often repeated examples of Clifford Olson, Paul Bernardo, and Russell Williams.
c) In the current system, persons convicted of murder are, on average, not released until they serve slightly more than 28 years in custody.

d) The notion that anyone feels aggrieved by concurrent sentencing to life imprisonment with no parole eligibility for 25 years is illusory.

Some of the submissions contained arguments and comments that are worthy of individual attention. Appearing on Bill S-6 on behalf of the Canadian Civil Liberties Association, Nathalie Des Rosiers discussed the needs of victims:

> However, it is probably not completely appropriate to equate compassion and respect for victims with a diminished commitment to the rehabilitation principle. Indeed, that is not what victims often say. In our research when we ask victims what they need, they say that they want respect and acknowledgement and access to services. The large gaps that are identified in victims' services are very important. It is interesting for a civil libertarian to say this, but if we are to continue to have a constitutional law system that is devoted to the presumption of innocence, we must invest in an adequate response to victims. They go hand in hand. You cannot have the public engage and respect the presumption of innocence, with all the cost that has for victims, without engaging fully with their needs.[29]

Joseph Di Luca, on behalf of the Criminal Lawyers' Association, testified in relation to C-48 as follows:

> It may come as no surprise to members of this committee that the Criminal Lawyers' Association does not support Bill C-48. In our view, this piece of legislation is looking for a problem, as opposed to being a piece of legislation aimed at fixing a problem. Put simply, I ask you what is the problem that this piece of legislation is aimed at correcting? Is there really a sentence discount for multiple murders, or is that an issue of optics, which, when properly understood, reveals no operative discount at play.[30]

Phil Downes, representing the Canadian Council of Criminal Defence Lawyers, commented on the way in which the current government gave provocative names to its justice legislation:

> Let me start by saying briefly a word about the title of this proposed legislation. It does not go in particular to any problems with the substance of it, which I will get to in a minute. The bill is called the 'Serious Time for the Most Serious Crime Act.' This trend on the part of governments of all stripes to engage in naming legislation with some catchy phrase when it is a serious piece of legislation is, in our respectful submission, somewhat insulting to the people of Canada. Proposed legislation like this is not a marketing exercise or some sort of grade-school mnemonic. It is our submission that we should try to avoid this kind of somewhat inflammatory

language in naming our pieces of legislation because it results in a suggestion, in my submission respectfully, that it is patronizing and does not treat
this kind of legislation with the seriousness that it deserves.[31]

An important dimension was added to the discussion by Kim Pate, executive
director of the Canadian Association of Elizabeth Fry Societies. She explained her
involvement with women prisoners who had sought judicial review and took care
to point out that some, not all, had been convicted of killing abusive partners. In
her testimony, she discussed the experiences of 'battered women' and how a
personal history of abuse can influence not only behaviour but also responses to
the judicial system.

Only a few individual witnesses appeared in committee on these bills, mostly
academics. However, the most significant individual witness was Rick Sauvé, a
man who had been convicted of first-degree murder in his youth and had successfully had his parole ineligibility reduced to 15 years in 1994. Given the time it
took for the judicial review process, and the subsequent procedures of the National
Parole Board, he was well into his seventeenth year before being released on full
parole. After the committees heard the human side of victimization, Mr. Sauvé's
testimony gave them an opportunity to see the human face of a remarkable man
who had received the benefit of the 15-year review. He now works for Lifeline, an
agency that provides help and support to lifers in the penitentiary system. He
explained how prisoners respond to the judicial review process: '[T]hey expose
themselves, and it's a trial of their character by the people of that community.'[32]
He provided his view on the nature of rehabilitation:

My belief is that people should be returned to their community, earn the
right to be returned to the community, when they've completed their
rehabilitation. They're no longer considered a risk to the community. If
somebody's considered a risk, then they shouldn't be returned to the
community.

I don't think there's any number . . . there's no magic number that you
can put on when somebody's rehabilitated. It's a process that starts inside,
and the person has to demonstrate that. It's not an easy process to get by
the National Parole Board, to earn your way from maximum security
down to minimum security, and then to find a community that's willing to
accept you. It's a long process.

During exchanges with the committee members, Mr. Sauvé provided examples
to support his views, many of which came from his Lifeline experience working
with prisoners convicted of murder. He observed:

If the risk is such that the person shouldn't be reintegrated into the community, they stay in prison. And there are many men and women who are

never going to get out. They're going to die in prison. I've worked with at least 16 people who have died from natural causes while serving their life sentences.

But the longer you keep people in, the harder it is to reintegrate them into the community. One of the things I studied when I was working on my thesis and I've witnessed in my work is that young offenders who come in and are sentenced to a life sentence and have a seven-year minimum are not getting out in seven years. Many of them are staying in 10, 15, or 20 years. And it's harder to reintegrate them into the community because their mental age and their experience in the community are the same when they go back out as they were when they came in. Their development is blunted.

I took a guy out on a pass just the other day. He is serving for second-degree murder. He was sentenced to 12 years. He's been in for 23 years. The problem was, he couldn't get into programs. They just weren't available, so he was in a lot longer than was necessary. He'd never seen a cell-phone before. He had never seen some of the new money that is out. So trying to help him reintegrate into the community is a challenge. The longer you keep people in, the harder it is to reintegrate them.

In answer to a question about the prospect of increased violence if the 15-year opportunity is removed, Mr. Sauvé agreed. He explained his position by imagining a person in a maximum security prison looking forward to a minimum of 25 years 'and probably a lot longer'. Sauvé asked, 'What does he have to look forward to?', and expressed his concern about the safety of 'the staff, the volunteers, the visitors, the nursing staff—all those people are the public who are working inside the system'. Rick Sauvé gave the committees a chance to see a product of the 15-year review process. But more importantly, he provided them with significant insights into how the penitentiary and parole processes work, from the perspective both of a prisoner and of someone who now works with prisoners. Notwithstanding his articulate and understated testimony, the majority of committee members supported both bills.

CONCLUSION

In reviewing the speeches in Parliament and the committee hearings on Bill S-6 and C-48 and their predecessors, one cannot mistake the government's goal in making significant changes to Canada's murder-sentencing regime. The government has combined a commitment to appearing 'tough on crime' with a concern to come out publicly and squarely on the victim's side. This is the constant message from all governmental witnesses who appeared before the House and Senate Committees on Bills S-6 and C-48, both of which passed both Houses and received royal assent on 23 March 2011. The only exception was Howard Sapers, the correctional investigator who found himself in his usual controversial position in opposition to governmental policy.

Significantly, the new approach was not predicated on any study or broad consultation. Equally significant was the government's blanket refusal to listen, or respond, to the criticisms of academics and practitioners who questioned the need for these changes. While the 'victim's voice' was consistently in support of these bills, it was not the product of any broadly based consultation and reflected the views of only a few individuals who have been involved with 15-year reviews. Advocates for victims will understandably give prominence to the role of victims. But when they appear before parliamentary committees, they need to be questioned on more than simply whether they support a piece of legislation. They need to be asked how the legislation promotes the real interests of victims. With respect to witnesses who have suffered as a result of crime, parliamentary committees need to ensure that their tragic experiences are not manipulated for partisan purposes. These witnesses deserve respect and sympathy for their personal loss and the challenges they have encountered within the legal process. They need to be supported. However, by its very nature, criminal justice is often a dirty business. Inevitably, it produces pain, grief, and heartache to which we cannot be indifferent. The central question is this: how much principle can be sacrificed in order for the criminal justice system to be seen as responding to the experience of a person who has suffered?

There remains some concern about whether C–48 is worded precisely enough to achieve its objective of ending concurrent sentences for multiple murders. One can foresee an argument that the legislation only applies to someone who has previously been convicted of murder and not to someone who is convicted at the same time for a number of murders. This is the problem that arises from using the phrase 'who has already been convicted of one or more other murders'. While we know the view of the minister and his officials on this interpretative question, courts will almost certainly be asked to examine this issue. Of course, even the minister's view, which depends on a sequence of conviction and sentencing, does not apply if an individual is convicted on a single count of an indictment that names multiple victims. This could happen in a bombing situation that results in multiple deaths.

Bills S–6 and C–48 reflect the government's general approach to justice legislation and sentencing in particular. The justice agenda of the Harper government has shown indifference to empirical data and the opinions of experts. More significantly, the government accepts the controversial notion of general deterrence and the dubious proposition that increased incarceration reduces crime. This might appear to be a curious strategy at a time when the reported rates for most crimes, including murder, are decreasing and when federal budget planning is promoting austerity in every sector except corrections. However, the various bills, when presented, were always accompanied by an emotional chord, an argument that the bills supported victims and enhanced societal safety. While both are laudable concerns, they cannot become labels that are attached superficially, speciously, and without scrutiny. They need to be promoted in ways that serve more than just the government's choice about how it wants to present itself. Still, the legislative strategy has been successful with little or no opposition in the last Parliament. The Liberal Party, the major opposition party at the time, supported the legislation, apparently concerned about appearing 'soft on crime'. Moreover, with the exception of a few Bloq Québécois and New Democrat members, the debates were timid and arid. And committees that have produced much valuable work in the past have become rubber stamps. It is a sad day for criminal justice policy in Canada.

CRITICAL THINKING QUESTIONS

1. Is there something special about the crime of murder that demands a different approach to the development of criminal policy?

2. In an ideal world, if there is a reform issue that needs to be addressed, what would the proper stages be for the development of a new criminal law policy? Which groups, governmental or otherwise, ought to participate in this process?

3. Given the importance of the victim's perspective, how should policy-makers seek out this perspective? Is there a value in the tragic story of an individual victim?

4. This chapter has argued that there is a growing trend of little to no informed debate on issues. What can be done to change this?

5. If the public were educated on the complexities of the bills that were being debated, do you think they would have wanted them to become law? Why or why not?

NOTES

1 See Criminal Code, 1892 (Can.) 55–6 Vict., c. 29, ss. 935–49

2 *An Act to Amend the Criminal Code (Capital Murder)*, S.C. 1960–1, c. 44, s. 1

3 This was the hangings of Turpin and Lucas. See R. Hoshowsky, *The Last to Die: Ronald, Turpon, Arthur Lucas and the End of Capital Punishment in Canada* (Toronto: Dundurn Press, 2007).

4 Occasionally, an anomalous mandatory minimum sentence was introduced, but this was rare. See s. 377 in the 1927 Criminal Code, R.S.C. 1927, c. 6, which provided a minimum penalty for

automobile theft until it was repealed with the introduction of the revised 1955 Code, S.C. 1953–4, c. 51.

5 Firearms Act, S.C. 1995, c. 39, ss. 141–50.

6 A more structured scheme of guidance was proposed by the Canadian Sentencing Commission in its 1987 report, but owing primarily to opposition from the judiciary and the bar, this was not adopted. See *Sentencing Reform: A Canadian Approach* (Ottawa: Supply and Services Canada, 1986). The commission's mandate expired with that report.

7   See *R. v. Arcand* (2010), 264CCC(3d) 134 (Alta. CA).

8   See *R. v. Vaillancourt*, [1974] O.J. No. 9 (Ont. CA).

9   See Canada, *Corrections and Conditional Release Statistical Overview 2009* (Ottawa, Public Safety Canada, 2009), 105. Although the 2010 data are available showing a new total of 178 review decisions and the same rates of success, the 2010 figures inexplicably use a smaller eligibility set that does not conform to data from earlier reports. Accordingly, I have relied on the 2009 data in which the eligibility set conforms to earlier data.

10 See Criminal Code, s. 745.6(2), enacted by S.C. 1996, c. 34, s. 2, proclaimed in force on 9 January 1997.

11 See ibid., s. 745.61.

12 See ibid., s. 745.63(3)

13 See J. Roberts, Determining parole eligibility dates for life prisoners: Lessons from jury hearings in Canada, (2002) *Punishment and Society*, *4*, 103.

14 *Supra*, note 9.

15 In Canada, sentencing is determined by the law extant at the time of the offence. Accordingly, it is unconstitutional to retroactively increase parole eligibility.

16 Robin MacKay, Legal and Legislative Affairs Division, Library of Parliament, *Legislative Summary of Bill C-48: An Act to amend the Criminal Code and to make consequential amendments to the National Defense Act (Protecting Canadians by Ending Sentence Discounts for Multiple Murders Act)*, Publication No. 40-3-C48E.

17 See *Hansard*, Debates of the Senate, 28 April 2010, p. 26, per Senator Carignan.

18 See *Evidence*, Standing Committee on Justice and Human Rights, 2 November 2010.

19 See ibid., 16 November 2010.

20 See *Hansard*, Debates of the House of Commons, 12 June 2009, per Daniel Petit.

21 *Proceedings of the Senate Committee on Legal and Constitutional Affairs*, 16 June 2010.

22 See *Evidence*, Standing Committee on Justice and Human Rights, 18 November 2010; *Hansard*, 15 November 2010.

23 Minister of Justice, *Proceedings of the Senate Committee on Legal and Constitutional Affairs*, 2 March 2011.

24 *Proceedings of the Senate Committee on Legal and Constitutional Affairs*, 17 June 2010.

25 Director of Advocacy and Awareness from the Canadian Resource Centre for Victims of Crime, *Proceedings of the Senate Committee on Legal and Constitutional Affairs*, June 17, 2010.

26 Sharon Rosenfeldt, *Evidence*, Standing Committee on Justice and Human Rights, 7 December 2010.

27 Susan O'Sullivan, *Evidence*, Standing Committee on Justice and Human Rights, 18 November 2010.

28 Ibid., 2 December 2010.

29 *Proceedings of the Senate Committee on legal and Constitutional Affairs*, 17 June 2010.

30 *Evidence*, Standing Committee on Justice and Human Rights, 30 November 2010.

31 *Proceedings of the Senate Committee on Legal and Constitutional Affairs*, 17 June 2010.

32 Rick Sauvé, *Evidence*, Standing Committee on Justice and Human Rights, 16 November 2010.

4

Maintaining Our Balance: Trends in Imprisonment Policies in Canada[1]

Cheryl Marie Webster and Anthony N. Doob

INTRODUCTION

This could have been a very short chapter. Indeed, there is no formal imprisonment policy per se in Canada to present or examine. While Canada has official policy statements about what should happen to prisoners (e.g., the Corrections and Conditional Release Act and the Prison and Reformatories Act), it does not have an explicit set of policies on who should be imprisoned. Nevertheless, Canada has had—implicitly and, in some cases, explicitly—a large number of policies and practices that, taken together, might constitute policy in this area. More importantly, we will argue that Canada has had, at least until very recently, a relatively consistent approach to imprisonment that can be described and discussed.

However, even with a body of 'unofficial' policies and practices on imprisonment to examine, this chapter might still have been very short. Specifically, this tangled set of largely unstated directives regarding those who should be imprisoned in Canada has resulted in an arguably uninteresting trend. As we will demonstrate, Canada has had a relatively stable imprisonment rate for over half a century. It could be argued that our 'lack of policy' on imprisonment has meant that Canada simply imprisons approximately 100 adults (plus or minus about 20) per 100,000 residents and has done so 'forever'. Given that one does not normally investigate the reasons for constants, there may be little more to say about Canadian imprisonment policies.

But there are other reasons to suggest that Canada's relative stability is itself interesting and worthy of examination. Canada's stability is somewhat anomalous in the international sphere, standing in stark contrast with the trends in imprisonment rates of its two obvious comparators: the United States and England & Wales. Canadian levels of incarceration also appear to constitute the exception to the view expressed by the director of the Centre for Crime and Justice Studies at King's College London, who stated that '[r]egardless of the variation in prison populations between capitalist countries, the general trend in [their] use of imprisonment . . . is an upward one. Most capitalist countries have witnessed significant growth in their prison populations' (Garside, 2010, p. 18). In fact, variability in trends is not hard to find. As Snacken (2010) notes, trends in European prison rates vary considerably, increasing in some countries, while remaining stable or decreasing in others.

In the end, it appears that there is, in fact, a story to be told about Canadian imprisonment policies. An examination of Canada's levels of incarceration may shed light on several of the factors contributing to a nation's penal landscape and, by extension, the relationship of the state to its citizens. Particularly given the research on explanations of variations in imprisonment rates in various nations (see, for example, Garland, 2001; Ruth and Reitz, 2003; Whitman, 2003; Tonry, 2004a, 2004b; Gottschalk, 2006; Newburn, 2007; Downes, 1998; Lappi-Seppälä, 2008) as well as the growing interest—in a number of countries—in the manner in which prison populations might be controlled or decreased (for instance, see Lappi-Seppälä, 2000; Gartner, Doob, & Zimring, 2011), a better understanding of the various ways in which Canada has maintained relative stability in incarceration is timely and relevant.

This chapter begins (Part I) with a description of trends in imprisonment rates in Canada. This pattern is subsequently contextualized within a broader framework through a cross-national comparison of levels of incarceration in the United States and England & Wales as Canada's closest comparators. Part II examines possible explanations for Canada's stability, focusing on historical, structural, and cultural factors that may have contributed to Canada's patterns in imprisonment rates. Part III concludes the chapter by considering the very recent rise in incarceration in Canada, which may be signalling a break with our tradition of stability.

PART I: TRENDS IN CANADIAN IMPRISONMENT RATES[2]

A glance at the last 100 years of imprisonment rates in Canada reveals a striking finding (Figure 4.1).[3] Canada has experienced relative stability in incarceration since the late nineteenth century. Even restricting our time frame to the past 50 years for which we have more detailed data, the conclusion is the same. While there has clearly been some fluctuation—from a low of 83 per 100,000 residents in 1974 to a high of 116 in 1994—there is no consistent trend. In fact, the level of incarceration has hovered around 100 per 100,000 residents for more than a half-century, with the 2009 rate being slightly higher at 110 per 100,000 residents in the general population.

Further, this stability in imprisonment generally holds (Figure 4.2) for both federal (housing those sentenced to two years or more) and provincial institutions (those sentenced to less than two years and those in pre-sentence custody). Indeed,

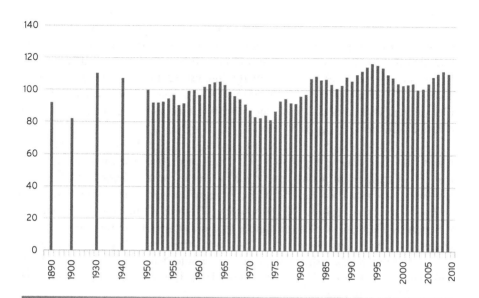

FIGURE 4.1   Total Canadian imprisonment rate per 100,000 residents

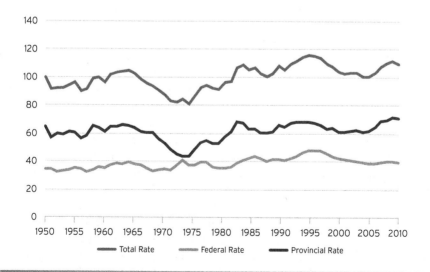

FIGURE 4.2   Total, federal, and provincial/territorial adult imprisonment rate per 100,000 residents

the overwhelming conclusion from these data is one of Canadian blandness: little change in over 50 years. This blandness becomes even more striking when contrasted with Canada's two closest comparators: the United States and England & Wales. These countries are particularly interesting for comparative purposes because of their multi-dimensional affinities to Canada. Indeed, the close similarities among these three nations are not only linguistic in nature but also historical, cultural, economic, and geographical.

Despite these affinities, Canadian imprisonment rates follow a strikingly different pattern over time. Figure 4.3 presents incarceration data for all three countries. By putting them in the same figure with the same scale, we wish to make two obvious points. First, American rates of imprisonment prior to the mid-1970s were—in terms of comparison with other Western countries—high, but not ridiculously high. Jail population figures (those in remand and those serving sentences of a year or less) were not available until 1980. Had these data been available, we estimate that the American rate would have been, prior to 1975, approximately 140 to 150 per 100,000 residents. Canada's rate was roughly 100 during the same period.

Second, the trend in Canadian rates of imprisonment diverges from that of both the United States and England & Wales. In the former case, the difference is dramatic. Between 1970 and 2002, the combined state and federal prison incarceration rates increased fivefold. With the jail populations, the 2008 US rate was 759 per 100,000 residents. Given that the United States is the most obvious comparator with Canada and the country that has the largest influence on us, the relative stability in Canadian imprisonment rates is striking. Even in comparison to England & Wales, the anomalous nature of Canada's levels of incarceration is obvious. Although the English imprisonment rate in 2009 was 'only' about 40 per cent higher than the Canadian rate, the trends in the two countries are quite different. Taken as a whole, the level of incarceration in England & Wales more than doubled between 1960 and 2003, reaching approximately 153 per 100,000 residents in 2009. Equally notable, this enormous variation in imprisonment rates across these countries cannot be explained by crime rates. Simplistically, incarceration might be seen as a crime-control mechanism. As crime increases, the state resorts to more imprisonment to reduce crime. Either through deterrence or incapacitation, it is assumed that crime and imprisonment are directly correlated.

This explanation, however, finds little empirical support. Illustratively, Figure 4.4 compares the homicide rates of Canada, the United States, and England & Wales on the same graph (but *not* the same scale). We use homicide because it is measured in comparable ways across countries. Notably, the trends in each country's overall crime rates (as well as overall violence rates) are similar to—albeit not identical with—the trends in to the homicide rates (though absolute rates are not comparable because of variation in definitions and data availability). In reading Figure 4.4, it is important to note that the scale for US homicide (on the right side of the figure) is different from that for Canada and England & Wales (which use

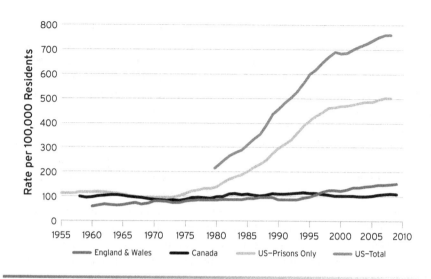

FIGURE 4.3   Total imprisonment (rate per 100,000 residents): Canada, England & Wales, United States

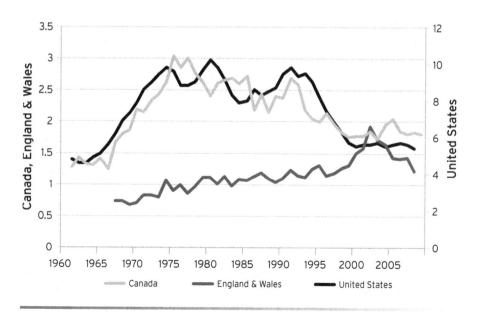

FIGURE 4.4   Homicide rates: Canada, England & Wales (left scale) and the United States (right scale) per 100,000 residents

the scale on the left). More fundamental for our current argument, these data show that imprisonment rates are not, to any substantial degree, related to levels of crime. While the shapes of the curves for the US and Canadian homicide rates are remarkably similar (though the US rate is about three times the Canadian rate), their patterns of imprisonment are strikingly different. Similarly, although the trends in incarceration of England & Wales and the United States are alike, their patterns of homicide differ. As scholars (Tonry, 2007, 2008; Lappi-Seppälä, 2008) have repeatedly argued, crime and imprisonment rates are not correlated. By extension, Canada's stability in its levels of incarceration cannot be simply explained by crime.

In fact, explanations for Canada's trend in imprisonment rates reside elsewhere. We have argued (Doob & Webster, 2006; Webster & Doob, 2007) that an understanding of those factors contributing to Canada's levels of incarceration is likely to come from an examination of the country itself. We propose that Canada's relative stability is largely the product of a unique and complex interaction of country-specific cultures, histories, and political institutions that combine in intricate ways (for a similar explanatory model, see Lappi-Seppälä, 2008).

PART II: EXPLAINING CANADIAN STABILITY IN IMPRISONMENT RATES

Our starting point is the recognition that Canada has not been immune to wider pressures to adopt more punitive imprisonment policies. A glance at several of the changes introduced in Canadian policy and legislation over the past 25 years suggests that many of those same forces contributing to higher incarceration rates in countries like the United States and England & Wales have also affected Canada. In fact, it would appear that Canada demonstrates many of the standard signs frequently associated with increases in a country's levels of imprisonment. For instance, we have seen the expansion of mandatory minimum penalties, increased maximum sentences, and more restrictive parole criteria.

When these changes—which have led to increased incarceration elsewhere—are juxtaposed with our continued stability in imprisonment rates, we are faced with an intriguing conundrum. It would appear that the secret to unravelling this mystery resides in Canada's ability to counter or balance these wider punitive pressures with more moderating forces. Specifically, the wider punitive forces have been given only limited expression within the Canadian context. A few examples suffice to illustrate the process.

A Balanced Response

One of the most widely discussed legislative changes associated with increases in the rates of incarceration is the introduction or expansion of mandatory minimum prison sentences. Canadian politicians have introduced this type of legislation under the guise of 'tough on crime' rhetoric. Although the empirical evidence supporting the belief that more punitive measures reduce crime is almost completely absent (Doob & Webster, 2003; Nagin, Cullen, & Jonson, 2009), slogans like 'Serious crime must mean serious time' (with mandatory minimum sentences as their vehicle) appeal to those who are unaware of the data demonstrating that they are false. The assumption is that 'tough' frontal attacks on any problem automatically solve it.

Mandatory minimum sanctions have always been a part of Canadian criminal law. However, their use has traditionally been limited, introduced only sporadically and usually imposing only relatively short sentences (with a few notable exceptions, such as homicide). Further, mandatory minimum sanctions have not generally been applied to high-volume offences, with the exception of impaired driving offences, which (currently) have mandatory minimum sanctions of a $1,000 fine (first offence) and short prison sentences (subsequent offences).

Canada's Parliament broke with this reserved approach in 1996 by legislating approximately a dozen mandatory minimum penalties of four years in prison for serious crimes with firearms. They were applied to serious violent offences (e.g., robbery, assaults, sexual assaults, manslaughter) in cases in which no mandatory minimums had previously existed. On the surface, this new legislation constituted a significant break with the past. Additionally, these changes contradicted policy statements that had been part of Canadian thinking for many years by imposing mandatory minimum sentences when there was no evidence that they were needed for any purpose other than that of a political nature. Indeed, the political need to look 'tough on crime' trumped the need for sensible policy.[4]

Mandatory minimum sentences had previously been seen as broadly inappropriate. Illustratively, the government issued a 'policy statement on sentencing' in 1984 (along with a sentencing bill that died on the order paper) that noted that '[m]andatory minimum sentences have been criticized on the basis of their rationale, their effectiveness, and their appropriateness' (Government of Canada, 1984, p. 60). Similarly, the Canadian Sentencing Commission reported in 1987 that '[t]he vast majority of the submissions received by the Commission argued for the abolition of mandatory minimum penalties' (p. 179) and recommended that for all offences other than murder and high treason, mandatory minimum penalties be abolished (p. 189). These views are completely consistent with current informed thinking (e.g., Tonry, 2009).

More important for our current purposes, one might have expected such a dramatic change from no mandatory minimum to a four-year mandatory minimum sanction to have had a measurable impact on imprisonment rates, especially since a number of different (violent) offences simultaneously received the new penalties. However, an examination of Figures 4.1 and 4.2 shows that it is very difficult to find any evidence that these mandatory minimum sentences had an effect on overall imprisonment rates. Indeed, it would seem that Canada was able to contain their impact, giving them only limited expression.

In fact, there is reason to believe that the four-year mandatory minimum sanctions had little effect on actual sentences. While these new penalties clearly increased the sentences that *some* offenders received, it is likely that the 'new' sanctions would not significantly differ from those that would have been handed down under the prior legislation for *most* offenders. Given the seriousness of the offence and the fact that those offenders falling under these new mandatory minimum sentences would frequently have criminal records—often serious—it is probable that they would already have been dealt with harshly by Canadian judges. Hence, this new legislation would have a considerably muted effect, contributing little to prison populations.

This same balance between tough-on-crime approaches and more reasonable punishment policies can be seen a decade later. The object of one of the first 'crime bills' following the election of the Conservative government in 2006 was to increase the 1996 mandatory minimum penalties for certain gun crimes. The government's press release spoke of 'enhancing the mandatory minimum penalty provisions of the Criminal Code' for crimes involving firearms, but did not explicitly mention that the then penalty was already 4 years. The new provision—as introduced—would raise the mandatory minimum for a first robbery using a handgun or restricted weapon (but not a shotgun or rifle, which had been included in the original 1996 legislation) from 4 to 5 years. For second and third offences, the mandatory minimums would have been 7 and 10 years, respectively.

Consistent with our hypothesis of countering more punitive forces, it is notable that by the time the bill was passed, the 10-year mandatory minimum sentence had disappeared. Further, the increase still only applied to some firearms. As in the past, the expected impact on imprisonment would be minimal, only affecting a subset of serious offences involving firearms.

The Mechanisms

This same story appears repeatedly (see Webster & Doob, 2007). Despite wider pressures toward more punitive provisions, Canada has largely managed to counter them with moderating forces. Consequently, the real question becomes one of understanding the mechanisms permitting this 'balanced response'—that is, what remains to be explained are the factors that have encouraged or enabled this tempered approach. We argue that the answer resides in a combination of country-specific historical, structural, and cultural factors that have shielded Canadians from rising imprisonment rates.

Historical Factors

One of the most powerful forces countering wider pressures toward harsher imprisonment policies and practices lies in Canadian history. A glance at Canada's criminal law and the numerous formal statements of criminal justice policy addressing the issue of criminal sanctions over the past 50 years leaves little doubt about Canadian tradition vis-à-vis imprisonment policies. The predominant *leitmotif* running through these documents is that of an official culture of restraint in the use of incarceration. Canada has consistently shown deep scepticism about imprisonment as an appropriate response to crime.

Canada's caution in the use of prison sentences was explicitly written into the Criminal Code in 1996. Section 718.2 states:'A court that imposes a sentence shall ...take into consideration the following principles:...An offender should not be deprived of liberty, if less restrictive sanctions may be appropriate in the circumstances, and ...all available sanctions other than imprisonment that are reasonable in the circumstances should be considered for all offenders, with particular attention to the circumstances of aboriginal offenders.' This clause supports the inference that 'high imprisonment' policies are not part of Canadian official policy. It becomes even more compelling when one recalls that this general statement about restraint was largely uncontroversial when the bill was being debated in Parliament—precisely during an era in which other nations were promoting the notion that 'prison works'.

However, while the need for restraint in the use of imprisonment for adult offenders was elevated—for the first time—to a legislated principle in these amendments to the Criminal Code, this statement constitutes only part of a long history of recognition by government and government-appointed commissions of the overuse of incarceration. It is not difficult to find statements urging restraint in the use of imprisonment. As early as 1969, the Canadian Committee on Corrections (the 'Ouimet Committee') released a comprehensive analysis of the manner in which Canada punishes offenders. Reflecting, we believe, the general consensus at the time, the report concluded that 'in all cases where there has been no finding of dangerousness, sentences of imprisonment should be imposed only where protection of society clearly requires such penalty. . . . The Committee wishes to emphasize the danger of overestimating the necessity for and the value of long terms of imprisonment except in special circumstances' (p. 190). It would seem that Canada did not have much confidence in the crime-controlling effects of imprisonment.

These same sentiments were echoed in various reports of the Law Reform Commission of Canada. In fact, its first report to Parliament in 1976–7 demonstrated general scepticism regarding the ability of the criminal justice system to reduce crime. It suggested that not only should Parliament show restraint in what it criminalizes but in the case that an act (e.g., theft) is criminalized, the less serious instances of criminal offences should be diverted outside of the normal criminal process. Even in sentencing, the commission recommended restraint:'[T]he cost of criminal law to the offender, the taxpayer and all of us must always be kept as low as possible. . . . The harsher the punishment, the slower we should be to use it. . . . The major punishment of last resort is prison. . . . As such it must be used sparingly. . . . Positive penalties like restitution and community service orders should be increasingly substituted for the negative and uncreative warehousing of prisoners' (Law Reform Commission of Canada, 1976, pp. 24–5).

In 1977, a House of Commons subcommittee chaired by a future minister of justice, Mark MacGuigan, went even further by concluding that '[s]ociety has spent millions of dollars over the years to create and maintain the proven failure of prisons. . . . Thus, before entering into a multi-million dollar construction program, less costly, and more productive alternatives should be introduced.' Further, it affirmed that '[i]f we continue to conceive of imprisonment as a sort of universal . . . [solution] to the problems of crime in our society, we will do nothing more than repeat old prescriptions for failure. . . . Imprisonment will be a useful social technique only to the extent that its purposes and limitations are clearly understood' (pp. 35–7).

In 1982, the government of Canada released a booklet entitled *Criminal Law in Canadian Society*, which was described, in the preface (above the signature of the Honourable Jean Chrétien, minister of justice), as 'setting out the policy of the Government of Canada with respect to the purpose and principles of the criminal law. . . . Never before has the Government articulated such a comprehensive and fundamental statement concerning its view of the philosophical underpinnings of criminal law policy.' This document reiterated the sentiments expressed earlier by the Law Reform Commission of Canada: 'The criminal law should be employed to deal only with that conduct for which other means of social control are inadequate or inappropriate, and in a manner which interferes with individual rights and freedoms only to the extent necessary for the attainment of its purposes' (Government of Canada, 1982, Principle (a), p. 59). With respect to sentencing, the policy was clear: 'In awarding sentences, preference should be given to the least restrictive alternative adequate and appropriate in the circumstances' (Principle [i], p. 64).

It is equally notable that although imprisonment policies ultimately reflect political decisions, it should not be assumed that the two main political parties in Canada have differed dramatically in their orientation to the criminal law. For instance, when the Progressive Conservative Party formed the government in 1984, it instituted a review of government programs, including the justice system. The justice system report, completed in 1985 and submitted to the government task force (the 'Nielsen Task Force'), noted that '[t]he use of incarceration in Canada has become a concern on a number of levels . . . . Incarceration costs approximately 10 to 15 times as much . . . as community-based [sanctions]. . . . At the same time as there are concerns about the costs . . . doubts about its value are also prevalent. . . . Correctional administrators consistently report that a large proportion of persons in their jails do not belong there. . . . There is also a paucity of alternative punishments which are less costly and less debilitating than prison' (Study Team Report, 1985, pp. 322–3).

A similar message of restraint emerged from the Canadian Sentencing Commission in 1987. Its report recommended that imprisonment only be imposed to protect the public from violence or in circumstances in which another sanction could not be devised that would reflect the gravity of the offence or the repetitive nature of the offender's conduct; or in which it would inadequately protect the public or the integrity of the administration of justice, or in which the offender would not comply with non-custodial sanctions (Canadian Sentencing Commission, 1987, p. 154). This commission also noted that its endorsement of a policy of restraint in the use of imprisonment was consistent 'with the recommendations of almost every group that has examined the criminal justice system from the Brown Commission in 1848 to the Nielsen Task Force in 1986' (p. 165). The Progressive Conservative government's 1990 policy document *Directions for Reform* noted: 'Imprisonment is generally viewed as of limited use in controlling crime' and 'Reducing this dependency on prisons is needed to achieve greater effectiveness, balance, and restraint in our system' (p. 10).

Perhaps the most surprising statement about imprisonment came from a Conservative-dominated committee of the House of Commons that was examining crime prevention: 'From the evidence presented . . . the members of the Committee are convinced that threats to the safety and security of Canadians will not be abated by hiring more police officers and building more prisons' (Standing Committee on Justice and the Solicitor General, 1993, p. 2). After presenting comparative imprisonment rates showing that the United States imprisonment rate was, then, about four times higher than that of Canada, the committee stated: 'If locking up those who violate the law contributed to safer societies then the United States should be the safest country in the world' (p. 2). In fact, the committee chairman—a Progressive Conservative and former RCMP officer—noted that [t]here was a lot of agreement that we can't just continue to build more jails. . . . If anyone had told me when I became an MP nine years ago that I'd be looking at the social causes of crime, I'd have told them that they were nuts. . . . I'd have said "Lock them up for life and throw away the key." Not anymore' (Vienneau, 1993).

And the list goes on. We have outlined only a few of the statements from official reports that would suggest that restraint in the use of imprisonment has been an integral part of criminal justice culture in Canada for decades. Table 4.1 presents some of these reports. The sheer number of these formal statements—extending across over 30 years of criminal justice policy—underlines the degree to which restraint in the use of imprisonment is part of Canada's criminal justice tradition. High imprisonment rates have historically been perceived as problems to be addressed. Indeed, imprisonment has been seen as a necessary but unproductive part of society to be minimized as much as possible. However, with no empirical evidence of a consistent decrease in Canadian incarceration, the value of this historical factor is not in its impact on the government's actions or in changing practices. Rather, this official culture of restraint would seem important in protecting Canada from some of the broader forces propelling other nations toward more punitive policies. Indeed, it has arguably provided the outer boundaries within which punishment is conceptualized and decided.

TABLE 4.1   A sample of reports proposing restraint in the use of imprisonment

Department of Justice, Canada: *Juvenile Delinquency in Canada. The Report of the Department of Justice Committee on Juvenile Justice* (1965)

Ministry of the Solicitor General, Canada: *Toward Unity: Criminal Justice and Corrections. Report of the Canadian Committee on Corrections* (the 'Ouimet Committee') (1969)

Law Reform Commission of Canada. *Our Criminal Law* (1976 and following)

House of Commons, Canada. *Sub-committee on the Penitentiary System in Canada* (the 'MacGuigan Report') (1977)

Government of Canada. *Criminal Law in Canadian Society* (1982)

Government of Canada. *Sentencing* (1984)

Government of Canada, Task Force on Program Review. *The Justice System* ('Neilson Task Force') (1985)

Canadian Sentencing Commission. *Sentencing Reform: A Canadian Approach* (1987)

Standing Committee on Justice and Solicitor General. *'Taking Responsibility' Report of the Standing Committee on Justice and Solicitor General on Its Review of Sentencing, Conditional Release and Related Aspects of Corrections* (the 'Daubney Report') (1988)

Government of Canada. *Directions for Reform: A Framework for Sentencing, Corrections and Conditional Release* (1990)

Standing Committee on Justice and the Solicitor General. House of Commons, Canada. *Crime Prevention in Canada: Toward a National Strategy.* (1993)

Federal-Provincial-Territorial Working Group. *Corrections Population Growth: Report for Federal/Provincial/Territorial Ministers Responsible for Justice* (1996, 1997, 1998, 2000)

Department of Justice, Canada. *A Strategy for the Renewal of Youth Justice* (1998)

Structural Factors

In recent decades, penal populism has been a reoccurring theme as scholars have noted the increasing degree to which criminal justice issues have become politicized and influenced by public opinion in many Western democracies (Pratt, Brown, Brown, Hallsworth, & Morrison, 2005). This politicization of crime policy has been identified as a powerful force in the trend toward more punitive approaches to criminal behaviour (e.g., Beckett, 1997; Roberts, Stalans, Indemaur, & Hough, 2003). Illustratively, both American and English judges and politicians—influenced by the perceived increasingly punitive public mood—have contributed to the escalation of their respective prison populations through an increased use of imprisonment (Tonry, 2001; Millie, Jacobson, & Hough, 2003).

Notably, Canada seems to have largely escaped this phenomenon. We would argue that the distinction between Canada and many other Western democratic countries is rooted largely in structural differences. Specifically, Canada's political and juridical systems are structured in such a manner that insulates or buffers government and judicial officials from the wider forces of popular punitiveness.

In the political realm, Canada's federal system creates a division of labour whereby the federal government is responsible for criminal law, while the provinces/territories are responsible for its administration. Thus Canadian provincial and territorial governments have no direct power to modify the criminal law despite playing the largest role in the administration of justice. This distinction creates and maintains a two-tiered political structure that isolates or at least distances the federal government—with its power to increase punitiveness within the criminal justice realm— not only from provincial/territorial demands but also from those of the general public.

Indeed, crises in crime are largely local issues. Therefore, it is the provincial/territorial governments that are particularly susceptible to populist punitive talk, but they have no legislative power over sentencing. Further, appeals court judges are appointed by the federal government. Thus, no structural mechanisms exist that would allow local citizens' groups to have a direct influence in the creation of laws that have a direct impact on imprisonment policies as has been the case in such US states as California (e.g., in its introduction of three-strikes legislation; Vitiello, 1997). In fact, Canadian politics have consistently shown a broadly based disinclination by (federal or provincial/territorial) governments to support referenda on any subject (Lipset, 1989). Hence, sentencing policies are left in the hands of the federal Parliament (which, until recently, considers government initiatives crafted by career civil servants) and judges (who are appointed for life, not elected).

In a similar distancing fashion, those criminal justice controversies receiving national attention have typically raised only questions of the administration of justice. In this way, the government of Canada can deflect concern back to the provinces, clearly reducing the pressure on the federal government to change the law. With maximum penalties for most offences being considerably higher than the maximum sentences ever awarded, the federal government can also legitimately imply that it has no responsibility for apparently lenient sanctions. Moreover, the Crown has always had the right in Canada to appeal lenient sentences.

As Lipset (1989) notes, political party discipline is strong in Canada compared to that in the United States. The vast majority of bills passed by Parliament originate with the government rather than with individual legislators, and thus Canadian bills tend to make the government responsible for financial and other effects on the provinces (e.g., social and opportunity costs of increased imprisonment). Further, this process ensures that other governmental departments have input (either prior to or at the cabinet table) with regard to the impacts of the proposed bill. The consideration and harmonization of these multiple interests and concerns may be important in ensuring more moderate legislation.

This same moderating process occurs when changes to the criminal law are considered. Specifically, the division of criminal justice labour between the federal and provincial/territorial governments ensures that changes to the criminal law will involve consultation between the two 'partners'. In fact, Roberts (1998) suggests that because of the shared federal-provincial responsibility, the federal government has been reluctant to legislate criminal justice policy without a consensus—at least among the largest provinces. Not surprisingly, the result (until recently) has been a time-consuming process, making it unlikely that quick-fix politically motivated legislation would be introduced in response to unusual circumstances that arise in isolated cases. Further, this consultation process has meant that the (more punitive) demands of more conservative provinces are frequently tempered or moderated by those of more liberal jurisdictions.

Beyond these structural effects of the shared responsibility for criminal law matters, many of the key players in criminal justice issues also have the advantage of being insulated, to some degree, from swings in public opinion. Canadian judges are the most obvious example. The judicial selection procedures in Canada provide that judges, at all levels, are appointed—rather than elected—without formal confirmation hearings (although formal private review procedures for assessing applicants for judicial appointments exist in many jurisdictions). Thus judges are less vulnerable to public sentiments that—certainly recently—have demanded punitive responses to crime. Similarly, while there is some evidence (Russell & Ziegel, 1991) that judges often have ties to the particular government that appointed them, the political background of the Canadian judiciary is not typically known or obvious to most observers. In this way, Canadian judicial decisions are less likely to reflect the party line of those in power or in opposition.

More broadly, the administrative organization of the federal government has also ensured that other players in criminal justice matters are distanced from popular punitive pressures. Specifically, it is non-elected civil servants and non-governmental experts—not politicians—who are most likely to be in charge of the actual form of criminal justice reforms in Canada. Indeed, the process of writing legislative bills in Canada is dominated by civil servant experts who almost always remain in their positions independent of changes in government. Borrowing, to some degree, from the British aristocratic culture and its recognition of and reliance on elite opinion, non-partisan, non-elected authorities have played a powerful role in creating moderate criminal justice policy in Canada. While the minister of justice and the federal cabinet ultimately determine any modifications of criminal law introduced into Parliament, it is this former group of specialists who have tended to define the need for changes and the exact nature of these changes.

Clearly, the Canadian federal system, the judicial selection procedures, and the administrative organization all play a role in shielding Canada from wider punitive forces. However, this focus neglects one of the crucial structural issues central to the determination or alteration of imprisonment rates. Specifically, the distribution of power also exerts a decisive influence on the degree to which custodial sentences are used. Notably, sentencing power in Canada has always remained firmly in the hands of judges. In fact, Friedland (2004, p. 472) argues that 'the judiciary has—perhaps with the federal government's tacit approval—become the dominant player in the development of the criminal justice system.' This responsibility for sentencing has prevailed even in the face of serious threat. In particular, the Canadian Sentencing Commission recommended in 1987 a very weak form of sentencing guidelines that would be created by a commission and confirmed by Parliament. Despite the fact that these presumptive guidelines would still have left enormous power to sentence with the sentencing judge, the proposal was rejected, in part because guidelines of any kind were seen as a radical departure from traditional policy.

This concentration of power in sentencing has been important in tempering pressures toward more punitive sanctions. Most obviously, Canadian judges have generally been left alone to make decisions about how to sentence. This independence stands in striking contrast to practice in a number of other Western democracies that have witnessed considerable volatility in the divisions of power among those governing sentencing. Illustratively, the 1990s in England were characterized by Ashworth (2001) as a 'battleground between the government and the senior judiciary' (p. 81) in which 'the judiciary and the legislature . . . vie[d] for supremacy in sentencing' (p. 84). As a result, the changes in sentencing laws in England & Wales during this period constituted nothing less than a 'torrent of legislation' as the government attempted to outflank the judiciary by implying that its sentencing was too lenient in some spheres, making mandatory sentences a necessity (p. 80).

While Canadian judges have not completely escaped legislative restrictions on their power, the degree to which Parliament has managed to curb their autonomy in sentencing matters has been considerably less. In fact, the judiciary has almost exclusively determined the degree to which imprisonment is to be used as a criminal sanction. The legislated maximum penalties are dramatically higher than sentences that are normally handed down, giving judges wide latitude. Further, sentencing is individualized, since judges can choose from a broad range of sentencing purposes whereby almost any sentence can be justified. Finally, many of the principal legislative modifications in sentencing matters, such as mandatory minimum sentences for serious violent offences carried out with a firearm, and the inclusion of principles and purposes of sentencing in the Criminal Code were likely seen as benign by the majority of judges.

Within this framework, Canadian judges have arguably acted as a stabilizing force in the use of imprisonment. Despite legislative freedom to increase the punitiveness of sentences, there was no notable change in the proportion of convicted cases sentenced to prison, nor in the overall mean prison sentence length handed down, over the 1994/95–2003/04 10-year period, according to available national (albeit incomplete) data (Thomas, 2004, p. 10). Indeed, Canadian judges appear to lack enthusiasm for more punitive responses to crime and criminals. This approach contrasts dramatically with those of the United States and England & Wales.

Illustratively, Ashworth suggests that the English judiciary—whether voluntarily or through increasingly punitive sentencing guidelines—'[s]teadily, and with relatively little legislative encouragement . . . increased their use of imprisonment to the extent that between early 1993 and early 1997 the prison population rose by 50 percent' (2001, p. 81).

Cultural Factors

Beyond the historical and structural factors that appear to have shielded Canada from wider punitive trends characteristic of other similar nations, Canadians also seem to possess certain cultural values that have limited the enthusiasm for increased imprisonment. These beliefs have permeated not only the political but also the popular culture. Specifically, Canadians appear to lack the moral taste for harshness—on an individual level—as well as faith—on the political level—in the effectiveness of more punitive sanctions in addressing crime.

Although the general public in Canada has not been immune to calls for harsher policies and practices (Doob, 2000; Roberts et al., 2003), research has shown that the majority of Canadians do not strongly support 'get tough' strategies as a solution to crime (Public Safety and Emergency Preparedness Canada, 2001). While a similar literature (Peter D. Hart Research Associates, 2002; Applegate, Cullen, & Fisher, 2000) exists on Americans' willingness to support less punitive responses to crime and criminals, comparative studies (see, for example, Adams, 2003; Lipset, 1989) contrasting Canadian and American core values suggest that Canadians are different from Americans in a number of fundamental ways. Of particular interest to our current purposes, it is noted that '[a]ttitudes toward violence are, in fact, among the features that most markedly differentiate Canadians from Americans' (Adams, 2003, p. 52). While Canada is characterized as less violent and more communitarian in its core values, the United States distinguishes itself as more individualistic and more accepting of violence.

As evidence of these cultural values, public opinion data are often invoked. However, given the continuing debate surrounding the inferences that one should draw from public opinion polls to capture popular culture (Doob, 2000), we have chosen to focus on several judicial decisions and government policies as reflections (as well as reaffirmations) of Canadian core values. While, at least until recently, legal and governmental institutions have generally led (rather than followed) public opinion in Canada, we would argue that—at a minimum—these forms of official culture delineate the outer margins of what popular culture is willing to accept.

Canada's more communitarian values are likely at the root of its resistance to many of the exclusionary practices adopted by other nations toward offenders. Drawing on Tonry's contention that one of the forces that allowed for the recent growth in imprisonment in England was the portrayal of the offender as no longer deserving of being considered (and, consequently, treated) as a full citizen (with all of the inherent rights), the 2002 Supreme Court of Canada decision to give prisoners serving penitentiary sentences the right to vote (*Sauvé v. Canada*) stands in stark contrast to the disenfranchisement policies of the United States and England (Uggen & Manza, 2002; Hurd, 2004). Similarly, Canada abolished capital punishment in 1977 and has made no serious attempts to create the American-equivalent sentence of life without parole.

As a similar expression of Canadian core values, Canada has officially rejected the use of imprisonment as a response to intolerance toward a particular—often racial—group. As Tonry (2004b) has suggested, nations experience regular cycles of sensibility during which they display different degrees of non-acceptance of others. Certainly in the United States, the 'war on drugs' arguably reflected a period of intolerance toward African-Americans who were labelled as 'bad people'— a view congenial to the fundamentalist right for whom distinctions between good and evil are rooted in the individual rather than in social forces that may have produced the original criminal behaviour. One can find a similar phenomenon in England, whose 'three-strikes' provision for certain drug offences introduced in 1997 was described by Ashworth (2000) as 'symbolic'—designed to create resentment of certain types of offender and at the same time to bolster the political fortunes of the Government' (p. 180).

While Canada has certainly not been immune to racist attitudes, with disadvantaged groups such as black and Aboriginal Canadians continuing to be overrepresented in Canada's prisons (Commission on Systemic Racism in the Ontario Criminal Justice System, 1995), its response—at least in terms of its expression through laws related to imprisonment—has clearly been different from the United States. Illustratively, the government of Canada attempted in 1996—through targeted legislation (section 718.2[e], as quoted above)—to *reduce* the incarceration level of its most disadvantaged and imprisoned group: Aboriginal Canadians. This legislative change was passed with no real opposition being raised in either Parliament or the media. Similarly, specialized courts dealing exclusively with Aboriginal people were established in some locations and have not received notable public criticism.

However, the cultural component of Canada's shield against wider pressures for harsher sanctions extends beyond popular culture. Indeed, Canadian *political* culture has also played a role in minimizing the impact of punitive forces that would otherwise lead to policies associated with increased imprisonment. Specifically, crime has not been—at least until very recently—a central focus of any of the principal political parties. Indeed, Canadian political parties have rarely used crime issues to construct political platforms, favouring instead a more balanced or moderate response to crime (Meyer & O'Malley, 2005). Illustratively, the federal ministry responsible for federal penitentiaries concluded in 2005 on its official website that

> [m]ost Canadians feel safe in their communities. Conveying these findings to the public is important to counter-balance media portrayals of crime as a pervasive problem. Compared to other issues, the majority of Canadians do not view crime as a priority issue for the government. This information

is helpful in ensuring that the government's response to the crime problem is kept in perspective. (Public Safety and Emergency Preparedness Canada, 2001)

In fact, a glance at the campaign platforms of the principal Canadian political parties in 1997—an election year deeply embedded in an era of increasing incarceration rates in many Western nations—provides an illustration of the lack of politicization of crime in Canada.[5] Illustratively, one of the principal foci of the New Democratic Party (NDP) was on 'the links between social conditions and crime'. Specifically, this party proposed to 'start by being tough on the causes of crime', as a society with growth in unemployment and insecurity as well as child poverty 'is sowing the seeds of crime in its own backyard' (New Democratic Party of Canada, 1997, p. 33). Perhaps not surprisingly, the Liberal Party also highlighted the need to address 'the underlying factors which lead to criminal behaviour' by reducing 'unemployment, poverty, inequality, family violence, illiteracy, lack of affordable housing, and poor education' (Liberal Party of Canada, 1997, p. 88).

More surprising was the similar focus of the Progressive Conservatives. After noting that they agreed with Canadians who 'have been saying for many years now that the justice system is too soft on criminals', this party recognized that 'an ounce of crime prevention is worth a pound of cure. Keeping young people in school, early intervention in the lives of young people in trouble, and education of young people in general about the consequences of crime, do more to prevent crime than any other kinds of action' (Progressive Conservative Party of Canada, 1997, p. 34). Even the Reform Party of Canada placed 'crime prevention' as its first point, noting their belief that 'the key to crime prevention is to strengthen families and communities, rather than rely exclusively on the judicial, parole and prison systems' (Reform Party of Canada, 1997, p. 15).

Yet, this emphasis on crime prevention should not suggest that there were no harsh proposals. Indeed, the Reform Party platform simultaneously called for such punitive measures as 'truth-in-sentencing'[6] for violent offenders; legislation whereby violent offenders who commit a second violent crime would be declared dangerous offenders; the repeal of the 'faint hope' clause; proposals to 'tighten up' on parole; changes to the definition of a 'youth'; and the publication of names of youths convicted of offences (Reform Party of Canada, 1997, pp. 15–16).

Nor was this political party alone in suggesting tough responses to crime and criminals. Both the Liberals and the Conservatives wanted changes to the Young Offenders Act that would strengthen its punitive bite. Notably, the Liberals highlighted the various ways (e.g., longer sentences for certain violent offences; new measures for certain serious violent offenders allowing for their transfer to adult court) in which it had ensured 'that the punishment better match[ed] the severity of the crime' (Liberal Party of Canada, 1997, p. 86). During the same election, the Progressive Conservatives proposed to 'lower the age of application of the Young Offenders Act from 12 to 10, give judges more power to impose mandatory treatment or therapy on troubled youths, make it easier to transfer serious violent crime cases involving young offenders to adult courts', and enact a Parental Responsibility Act to make the parents of young offenders financially responsible for their children's criminal acts (Progressive Conservative Party of Canada, 1997, p. 35). Even the NDP proposed to reform the Young Offenders Act 'so that age is only one of several factors considered in determining consequences' and to increase sentences and bail conditions for gang-related crimes (New Democratic Party of Canada, 1997, pp. 34–5).

However, these tougher responses were moderated—to varying degrees—by softer proposals. For example, the Liberal Party affirmed that 'minor, first-time offenders should be treated differently than serious, violent offenders', emphasizing that the party had already made 'changes to sentencing laws to encourage courts to distinguish between serious, violent crime requiring prison time and less serious, non-violent crime that can be handled more effectively in the community' (Liberal Party of Canada, 1997, p. 84). Further, it also proposed 'alternatives to incarceration for low-risk, non-violent offenders, such as sentencing reforms, community diversion programs, greater use of risk assessment techniques, and alternative sanctions' (Liberal Party of Canada, 1997, pp. 84–5).

This call for restraint in the use of incarceration was also apparent in the Progressive Conservative political platform, which proposed 'a tough but realistic approach [to making Canada's communities safe] that combines effective programs of crime prevention with a crackdown on criminals.' Its prevention initiatives included promises to 'support and expand any programs shown to help teach young people to be good citizens and to lower youth crime, give judges more flexibility in using alternative sentencing for first-time, non-violent offenses, and develop rehabilitation programs for young offenders that put the emphasis on basic education and social skills, personal responsibility and community service' (Progressive Conservative Party of Canada, 1997, p. 35).

This more balanced strategy vis-à-vis crime and criminals was also evident in the political platform of the New Democratic Party of Canada, which suggested that 'the solution to crime lies in both holding individuals responsible for their actions and social and economic policies that build safer, more responsive communities' (New Democratic Party of Canada, 1997, p. 34). While several of this party's proposals for preventing crime included increasing sentences or introducing tough measures for specific crimes (e.g., gang-related crimes, intimidation of witnesses by accused, corporate misconduct, and white-collar crime), the majority of them focused on preventive intervention programs (e.g., child care, support for parents, labour policies that encourage employers to respect family obligations, programs for street youth to help treat dependencies and develop skills for community participation, literacy programs, assistance for children with behavioural and learning disorders). Even the Reform Party of Canada acknowledged that 'Canadians generally agree that it is in society's best interest to try to rehabilitate criminals' (Reform Party of Canada, 1997, p. 16). While this party also affirmed that it felt that 'the pendulum has swung too far to one side', it proposed to 're-establish balance in our corrections system by reassessing prisons and parole with [our] safety in mind', which would include relying heavily on 'good old-fashioned work as rehabilitation therapy for criminals' (Reform Party of Canada, 1997, p. 16).

The restrained approach of Canada's political parties stands in stark contrast to the longer-term politicization of crime that has occurred in nations like the United States or England & Wales whereby politicians from the two main political parties in each country have positioned themselves as tough on crime, neither wanting to be associated with softer responses to crime (Beckett, 1997; Millie et al., 2003). As a result, a new bipartisan consensus has emerged in these nations that has significantly reduced any opposition—or even discussion of alternative measures—to incarceration as a response to crime. With no other message being heard, it is not surprising that the general public has willingly accepted rising imprisonment rates. Further, it is likely—as Newburn (2007) argues with regard to England—that the recent occupation by the Labour Party of the law-and-order territory traditionally monopolized by the Conservative faction has served to force the latter political party toward even more punitive policies.

Arguably, Canada's reluctance until 2006 to promote tough-on-crime policies resides, at least partially, in the scepticism that Canadian politicians have historically shown toward the effectiveness of criminal punishment in reducing crime. The policy statement from the government of Canada in 1982 sets the general tone of Canadian political culture as it relates to sentencing by affirming that '[i]t is now generally agreed that the [criminal justice] system cannot realistically be expected to eliminate or even significantly reduce crime' (p. 28). Similarly, the Canadian Sentencing Commission (1987) recommended that judges hand down proportionate sentences and that the 'standard' set of utilitarian sentencing purposes be given minimal application. Indeed, this commission was quite sceptical about the ability of a sentencing judge to protect society, suggesting that '[i]ntuitively, at least, one would rather resort to a security guard than to a sentencing judge to protect one's home' (p. 148).

This rejection of the notion that 'punishment stops crime' was reiterated in the political realm in 1996 by the then Canadian minister of justice, who affirmed that just as 'war is too important to be left to the generals . . . [c]rime prevention is too important to be left to the lawyers, or the justice ministers, or even the judges. . . . In the final analysis, crime prevention has as much to do with the [minister of] . . . Finance, [the minister of] . . . Industry, and [the minister of] . . . Human Resources Development, as it does with the [minister of] Justice' (Rock, 1996, pp. 191–2). While this message has not always been expressed so clearly, the lack of a general endorsement from politicians of the notion that judges are well placed to solve the 'crime problem' has ensured relative ambivalence on the part of Canadians vis-à-vis tough-on-crime measures.

This political culture differs dramatically from that of the United States or England & Wales. In both cases, these countries have endorsed the view that crime can best be addressed through high imprisonment policies. Illustratively, British Home Secretary Michael Howard acknowledged in 1993 that although his criminal justice policies would increase the use of custodial sentences, he did not 'flinch from that. We shall no longer judge the success of our system of justice by a fall in our prison population. . . . Let us be clear. Prison works' (cited in Newburn, 2007, p. 438). In the United States, the popularity of so-called three-strikes (and related sentencing) policies illustrates the same optimism in the ability of the state to reduce crime rates through harsher sanctions.

PART III: LOSING OUR BALANCE?

The trend in Canadian imprisonment rates over the past five decades is clearly one of stability. However, even stable patterns experience variability. Within this (statistical) perspective, the rise in Canadian imprisonment rates from approximately 103 to 110 per 100,000 residents from 2005 until 2009 would normally be ignored, especially since rates had reached 116 per 100,000 residents in 1994 without invoking serious concern about a new 'trend' or 'culture of imprisonment'. Yet, a broader perspective raises questions about the interpretation of this recent increase. Specifically, it may be a sign that Canada is witnessing a weakening of several of the factors that have traditionally shielded Canadians from high imprisonment. From this standpoint, we would argue that the past five years merit special consideration.

Drawing from Gottschalk (2006, 2009), we suggest that if this recent increase in Canadian levels of incarceration is, in fact, signalling the beginning of a new era in imprisonment policies, the root of this (potentially paradigmatic) shift would appear to reside—at least to some extent—in changes in politics. As this scholar reminds us, 'Criminal justice is fundamentally a political problem, not a crime and punishment problem' (2009, p. 467). As such, political needs may override the need for sensible or coherent policy.

Until 2004, the largely majority governments at the federal level gave a certain political stability to the country.[7] Since 2004, Canadians have been governed only by minority governments—first under a Liberal minority, from 2004 to 2005, and subsequently under a Conservative minority, from 2006 to 2011.[8] During neither of these minority governments did any obvious coalitions exist that could give Canadians any political stability. As such, the government no longer had easy political authority.

Further, this political instability coincided with a federal election in January of 2006 at a time when crime was particularly salient, in large part because of the highly publicized murder of a young white woman in the shopping area of downtown Toronto. Arguably as a simple strategy to attract votes, politicians in English Canada joined together in promulgating the view that crime was becoming a significant threat to public safety, politicizing crime to an extent not yet seen in the Canadian political context.

Indeed, tough-on-crime platforms were adopted by all three national parties. With the exclusion of the separatist Bloc Québécois, which continued to view crime as the consequence of broader societal forces, the policies on crime that were developed for the 2006 election by the other (national) political parties were largely distinguishable only in their details. All three parties recommended—some for the first time—the toughening of penalties through mandatory minimum sentences, the end or the significant curtailment of conditional sentences, and the introduction of new Criminal Code offences. Further, the NDP joined with the Conservatives in advocating reverse-onus provisions on bail for various offences and deterrence-based sentencing. To this already punitive list, the Conservative Party distinguished itself by proposing the repeal of the faint hope clause and changes to the credit at sentencing for time spent in pre-sentence custody—both of which were subsequently accomplished—as well as the creation of the presumption-of-dangerous-offender designation for certain offenders and the removal of the right to vote from prisoners.

While Canadian political parties continue to demonstrate general consensus surrounding the use of imprisonment, the significant change is that they are no longer promoting moderation or balance. Notably, none of the 2006 political platforms of the national parties contained any references to restraint in the use of incarceration—either through discussions of community sanctions for minor or first-time offenders or through alternative sanctions. Similarly, crime prevention was generally only raised within the context of youth. Even notions of rehabilitation and treatment were generally absent. Rather, the predominant approach involved punishment. Although the NDP mentioned 'root causes of crime' as the last 'pillar' in their approach to ending violence (following 'firm punishment and deterrence' and 'enhanced resources for enforcement'), the moderation of the past is noticeably absent.

At least until 2011, Canadians have lived in an era in which crime is squarely on the political agenda and harsher punishment is the response par excellence running through the vast majority of the crime and criminal justice bills. Even the national opposition parties for the most part either publicly supported the government's tough-on-crime policies—and, by extension, high imprisonment practices—or simply evaded taking sides by avoiding parliamentary votes. Clearly, the dominant message of the government (and, implicitly, the opposition) between 2006 and 2011 was that 'prison works' and hence incarceration was no longer a problem that should be minimized. Rather, imprisonment was heralded as the primary vehicle to resolving crime.

By extension, concerns with imprisonment costs were no longer seen as obstacles. Indeed, what was new in this period was the federal government's willingness to promote and finance additional penitentiary space and provincial governments' lack of clear opposition to policies that would increase their own prison costs. A simple example makes the point. When the mandatory minimum sentences were being discussed in the Department of Justice in the 1990s, we were told by a number of people involved in the development of the law that estimates were made of the cost of the proposals and that the actual proposals were crafted, to some extent, with these estimates in mind. While our informants differ as to whether they expected an impact on imprisonment, there was clearly concern about the costs.

In contrast, the mandatory minimum sentences first introduced in 2006 raised little discussion (or apparent concern) about costs. The government estimated that these provisions would likely increase the federal penitentiary population by about 300–400 prisoners. At that point, the government expected to spend about a quarter of a billion dollars over the subsequent several years for new penitentiaries (Clark, 2006). By 2010, the government appeared to be of the view that $9.5 billion would be needed in the next few years to build new *federal* penitentiaries to respond to its various initiatives (Zlomislic, 2010). Clearly, the view being propagated was that unprecedented financial investment is justified—if not natural—because harsher sanctions were being promoted by the government as an effective crime-reductive strategy.

But this has not been the only change taking place on Canada's political front. It would also appear that new legislative proposals for harsher policies and practices have largely been designed without the benefit of advice from those knowledgeable on criminal justice policy. Most obviously, much of the recent (more punitive) legislation seems to have been constructed with little attention to the criminological research demonstrating little—if any—favourable effect of such policies on crime (e.g., see Doob & Webster, 2003; Tonry, 2008; Nagin et al., 2009).

Further, many of these legislative proposals reflect the devalued role of civil servants as subject-matter experts and the corresponding ascension of public opinion in determining policy. For decades, the views of the public on matters of crime and criminal justice were understood as 'beliefs' rather than as carefully formed attitudes based on an informed assessment of the evidence (Doob & Roberts, 1983). As such, the government traditionally relied on public servants to provide knowledgeable policy advice. The very recent past would suggest that this approach may be changing, as the government is now responding to an uninformed public rather than attempting to lead or educate them.

Illustratively, proposals like the Truth in Sentencing Bill (which reduced the credit given for pre-sentence custody at sentencing) largely reflect political expediency catering to the public's (simplistic) understanding of the issues (as encouraged by the government) rather than concern with good (read: informed) policy. Indeed, the notion of attributing one day's credit (off one's prison sentence) for one day in pre-sentence detention sounds—at least at first glance—to be fairer and more equitable than the previous practice of granting 1.5 to 2 days—until, that is, one recalls that almost no one in Canada serves his or her full sentence as it was handed down. Remission of one-third of the full sentence (for provincial prisoners) and statutory release (of federal sentences) at the two-thirds point in the sentence are almost automatic. As such, offenders who are *not* paroled (and few federal or provincial prisoners are paroled) will almost certainly only serve two-thirds of their custodial sentence. Consequently, each day that they serve as a *sentenced* prisoner is credited as 1.5 days. Under the new legislation, by only giving one day credit toward the sentence for each day in pre-sentence custody, pre-sentence custody now counts *less* than time served in prison post-sentence. Hence, total days in custody for any prisoner who spends time in pre-sentence custody will, in effect, be longer than that of a prisoner who is handed down the identical sentence but who spends no time in pre-sentence custody.

Despite this glaring violation of equity and, by extension, a potential constitutional challenge, the bill was passed. Symptomatic of the underlying problem, it is notable that when we raised this same issue before the House of Commons Committee considering the bill, a Conservative member of the committee explained privately to one of us that although he knew that our 'figures were right', his constituents liked the bill and therefore he would be voting for it. Similarly, a Liberal committee member indicated that his party had decided to support this bill, which even he agreed made no sense. With politics trumping good policy, its passage was clearly penal populism at its best.

CONCLUSION

Predicting the future is always a dangerous endeavour. Indeed, as baseball philosopher Yogi Berra reminds us, 'It's tough to make predictions, especially about the future.' In the case of imprisonment policy, this warning may be even more true. Indeed, the very factors that we argue affect incarceration rates are themselves inherently unstable. Further, changes in some of these predictors are difficult to interpret, as their effects may ultimately be countered by other factors.

What is certain is that Canada has maintained relative stability for a significant period of time. This reality is even more impressive when one compares it to the trends in other similar nations, which have witnessed an overall increase in their levels of imprisonment. While Canada has clearly not been immune to wider pressures for harsher policies and practices, it has been able to balance these trends with more moderating forces. The simple maintenance of the status quo in imprisonment rates should—in our opinion—be viewed as a notable accomplishment.

However, it is equally true that several signs of change exist on the Canadian horizon, particularly within the political realm. Most obviously, there has been an increase in Canadian imprisonment rates in the first decade of this century. Further, this rise is likely to be the result of the weakening of several of the structural and cultural factors that have historically minimized the impact of forces that would otherwise have likely led to policies associated with increased imprisonment. Indeed, we have recently seen signs of the politicization of crime, the reduction in reliance on expert advice, and a growing promotion of prison as an effective solution to crime. Finally, several of these changes have also emerged as explanatory factors in countries that have experienced increased levels of incarceration (see, for instance, the case of New Zealand [Pratt & Clark, 2005; Pratt, 2008] or that of the Netherlands [Downes & van Swaaningen, 2007]).

While this apparent shift in Canadian politics would seem to constitute a real threat to Canada's long-standing tradition of restraint in the use of imprisonment, its long-term impact is still very uncertain. Canada has a long history of successfully countering or balancing wider pressures toward harsher sanctions, limiting their expression in the criminal justice arena. Although Canadians may momentarily have lost this balance, this does not necessarily mean that equilibrium cannot be regained—either by devising new strategies to re-balance these wider punitive forces or by reorganizing or strengthening those that currently exist. In addition, we know that harsher sanctions—even once legislated—are not invariably enforced (e.g., see Zimring, Hawkins, & Kamin, 2001). Indeed, judges and prosecutors have been shown to circumvent laws that they feel are in conflict with standard criminal law principles (Tonry, 2009; Harris & Jesilow, 2000). It would not be surprising to see such adaptations on the part of Canadian sentencing judges, particularly with legislation like the Truth in Sentencing Law as a means of reducing any (unfair) inequity between those who spend time in pre-sentence custody and those who do not.

Further, not all of the recent criminal justice legislation is likely to increase incarceration. For instance, Bill C-19 (39th Parl., 1st Sess.), which became law in 2006, created an offence in addition to 'dangerous operation of a motor vehicle' (maximum sentence: 5 years for ordinary offences, 10 years if bodily harm resulted, and 14 years if death resulted from the offence). The new law created the offence of 'dangerous operation of a motor vehicle while street racing', which imposes a maximum sentence of 5 years, or 14 years (if bodily harm resulted), or life in prison (if death was the result). The latter penalty is the same as 'criminal negligence causing death'. Since the actual offence is criminal negligence causing death while street racing, one wonders if this additional offence actually accomplishes anything. Clearly none of this family of offences will affect imprisonment rates.

More broadly, it has proven difficult to find any obvious patterns or internal coherence to the current government's political program (Malloy, 2010). As just one example, Bill C-25 (39th Parl., 2nd Sess.) would have changed the sentencing provisions for youth such that a youth sentence *could* have the objectives of denouncing unlawful conduct and individual and general deterrence—purposes excluded by the 2003 Youth Criminal Justice Act. Certainly at face value, this act of 'putting deterrence into the Youth Criminal Justice Act' would likely increase the severity of sentences by making them longer.

However, the actual effect of this bill on sentences is much less clear, since the sentence itself is still subject to the proportionality requirement. In addition, the multiple hurdles to imprisonment embedded in the Act were not changed. Further, sentences still were required, within proportionality, to be the most rehabilitative possible. The waters only became murkier when this bill was reintroduced as Bill C-4 (40th Parl., 3rd Sess.) after earlier dying on the order paper. At this point, it only contained denunciation and *individual* deterrence. Given that these purposes would be trumped by proportionality, it is hard to see how these new tough-sounding ('deterrence and denunciation') provisions would make much difference as long as judges were to follow the law. More importantly, we could not identify any coherent or principled approach to these legislative proposals.

Within this context, it would seem almost impossible to identify, with any confidence, the direction that criminal justice matters will take in the future. We continue to be hopeful—albeit less optimistic than in the past (Webster & Doob, 2007)—that Canada will not become the next nation to be swept up in a truly punitive tide. However, the recent challenges to our balanced approach to crime and criminals are multiple in nature and broad in scope. Given that these challenges may constitute a significant break with the long-standing traditions and practices that have defined and guided Canadian imprisonment policy for over 50 years, we would certainly suggest that there is reason for concern. Or, as Professor Yogi Berra noted, 'The future isn't what it used to be.'

CRITICAL THINKING QUESTIONS

1. Choose a recent election in your municipality, province/territory, or at the federal level. Were policies that could affect imprisonment a feature in the platforms of one or more of the parties? Do these policies look as if they could have affected imprisonment rates? Do the parties or candidates differ in any substantial way?

2. Should we expect crime rates and imprisonment rates to be related across time within a jurisdiction (such as a province or country) or across jurisdictions?

3. In Canada, how do the various levels of government (municipal, provincial, and federal) influence imprisonment rates?

4. What should be the role of public opinion in determining imprisonment rates?

5. Look at a recent newspaper or news Internet site for stories about crime or the criminal justice system. What is the explicit or implicit message that comes from these stories about Canada's or your community's rate of imprisonment?

NOTES

1 Parts of this chapter have been derived from Doob and Webster (2006) and Webster and Doob (2007).

2 We are using 'counts' (not admissions) as the numerator of our measure of 'rate of imprisonment'. This is the number of adults in prison on an average night serving sentences or awaiting trial/sentencing as well as a small number of 'others'—typically awaiting deportation.

This number is expressed as a rate per 100,000 people in the total population (not just adults) and constitutes the most common indicator of the use of imprisonment.

3 Data for the occasional years prior to 1950 were obtained from the policy statement *Criminal Law in Canadian Society*. Other data come from Statistics Canada. Because Statistics Canada has changed its definitions of certain categories (e.g., violence) from time to time, the end dates for some of these figures vary somewhat. In addition, estimates of imprisonment, crime, and every other criminal justice indicator used in this chapter vary to some degree, depending on exactly when the data were accessed.

4 Specifically, the government was legislating at this time its unpopular long-gun registry under which any Canadian who possessed a rifle or shotgun would be required to register it. The 'tough on offenders' legislation was a political attempt to balance the 'tough on gun owners' registry.

5 In the earlier election during this decade (1993), the political platforms of the four principal political parties were even 'softer' in their responses to crime and criminals. Crime was not included in the NDP campaign document and the Progressive Conservatives affirmed that

'the answer [to making our streets and communities safe] does not lie in simply building more prisons and getting more police. If that were true, then the United States would be the safest place on Earth' (Progressive Conservative Party of Canada, 1993, p. 26). Even the Reform Party—in its statement about crime— simply noted its support for 'a judicial system which places the punishment of crime and the protection of law-abiding citizens and their property ahead of all other objectives' and which the party promised to work toward through its proposals for 'amendments to criminal law which ensure greater certainty in sentencing, a more stringent parole mechanism, adequate punishment for young offenders, and the creation of inmate work program' (Reform Party of Canada, 1993, p. 6). The Liberals promised gun control, some 'tough' changes for serious crimes and young offenders, and some crime prevention.

6 Traditionally meaning that people would serve all or most of their stated prison sentence.

7 In fact, all but two periods between 1968 and 2004 (totalling roughly 3 of these 36 years) saw majority governments in Canada.

8 This chapter was completed in early 2011, just prior to another national election.

REFERENCES

Adams, M. (2003). *Fire and ice: The United States, Canada, and the myth of converging values*. Toronto: Penguin Canada.

Applegate, B., Cullen, F., & Fisher, B. (2000). Public opinion about punishment and corrections. In *Crime and justice: A review of research*. Chicago: University of Chicago Press.

Ashworth, A. (2000). *Sentencing and criminal justice* (3rd ed.). London: Butterworths.

———. (2001). The decline of English sentencing and other stories. In M. Tonry & R.S. Frase (Eds.), *Sentencing and sanctions in Western countries*. New York: Oxford University Press.

Beckett, K. (1997). *Making crime pay: Law and order in contemporary American politics*. New York: Oxford University Press.

Canadian Committee on Corrections. (1969). *Toward unity: The report of the*

Canadian Committee on Corrections. Ottawa: Queen's Printer.

Canadian Sentencing Commission. (1987). *Sentencing reform: A Canadian approach.* Ottawa: Supply and Services Canada.

Clark, C. (2006, May 4). Crackdown takes aim at guns, sentencing: Tories want mandatory minimums imposed and house arrest eliminated in certain cases. *Globe and Mail.*

Commission on Systemic Racism in the Ontario Criminal Justice System. (1995). *Report of the Commission on Systemic Racism in the Ontario Criminal Justice System.* Toronto: Queen's Printer for Ontario.

Corrections population growth: Report for federal/ provincial/territorial ministers responsible for justice. (1996). Ottawa: Ministry of the Solicitor General.

Department of Justice Canada. (2006, May 4). Minister of justice proposes tougher mandatory minimum prison sentences for gun crimes. press release. Retrieved 14 January 2011 from http:// www.justice.gc.ca/eng/news-nouv/ nr-cp/2006/doc_31800.html

Doob, A.N. (2000). Transforming the punishment environment: Understanding public views of what should be accomplished at sentencing. *Canadian Journal of Criminology, 42*(3), 323–40.

———, & Roberts, J.V. (October 1983). An analysis of the public's view of sentencing. A report to the Department of Justice, Canada.

———, & Webster, C.M. (2003). Sentence severity and crime: Accepting the null hypothesis. In M. Tonry (Ed.), *Crime and justice: A review of research* (Vol. 30). Chicago: University of Chicago Press.

———, & Webster, C.M. (2006). Countering punitiveness: Understanding stability in Canada's imprisonment rate. *Law and Society, 40*, 325–67.

Downes, D. (1998). The buckling of the shields: Dutch penal policy 1985–95. In R. Weiss & N. South (Eds.), *Comparing prison systems.* Amsterdam: Gordon and Breach.

———, & van Swaaningen, R. (2007). The road to dystopia? Changes in the penal climate of the Netherlands. In M. Tonry (Ed.), *Crime and justice: A review of research* (Vol. 35). Chicago: University of Chicago Press.

Friedland, M.L. (2004). Criminal justice in Canada revisited. *Criminal Law Quarterly, 48,* 419–73.

Garland, D. (2001). *The culture of control: Crime and social order in contemporary society.* Chicago: University of Chicago Press.

Garside, R. (2010). Why does Britain have such a high prison population? In J. Collins & S. Siddiqui (Eds.), *Transforming justice: New approaches to the criminal justice system* (pp. 75–8). London: Criminal Justice Alliance.

Gartner, R., Doob, A.N., & Zimring, F. (2011). The past as prologue? Decarceration in California then and now. *Criminology and Public Policy, 10*(2), 287–325.

Gottschalk, M. (2006). *The prison and the gallows: The politics of mass incarceration in America.* Cambridge, UK: Cambridge University Press.

———. (2009). Money and mass incarceration: The bad, the mad, and penal reform. *Criminology and Public Policy, 8*(1), 97–109.

Government of Canada. (1982). *The criminal law in Canadian society.* Ottawa: Government of Canada.

———. (1984). *Sentencing.* Ottawa: Government of Canada.

Hansard. (2005). Proceedings of the Standing Senate Committee on Legal and Constitutional Affairs (Issue 17). *Evidence,* June 22. Retrieved from http://www. parl.gc.ca/38/1/parlbus/commbus/

senate/ com-e/lega-e/17eva-e.htm?Lang
uage=E&Parl=38&Ses=1&comm_id=11

Harris, J.C., & Jesilow, P. (2000). It's not the
old ball game: Three strikes and the
courtroom workgroup. *Justice Quarterly,*
17, 185–203.

Hurd, D. (Right Honourable Lord Hurd of
Westwell) (2004, July). Are prison
reformers winning the arguments : The
2004 Prisoners' Education Trust Lecture.
Prison Service Journal, 154, 3–5.

Lappi-Seppälä, T. (2000). The fall of the
Finnish prison population. *Journal of*
Scandinavian Studies in Criminology and
Crime Prevention, 1, 27–40.

———. (2008). Trust, welfare, and political
culture: Explaining differences in
national penal policies. In M. Tonry
(Ed.), *Crime and justice: A review of*
research (Vol. 37). Chicago: University of
Chicago Press.

Law Reform Commission of Canada.
(1976). *Our criminal law*. Ottawa:
Ministry of Supply and Services.

Liberal Party of Canada. (1997). *Securing our*
future together. Ottawa: Liberal Party of
Canada.

Lipset, S.M. (1989). *Continental divide: The*
values and institutions of the United States
and Canada. Toronto: C.D. Howe
Institute, Canadian-American
Committee.

Malloy, J. (2010, September 7). Why does the
Harper government do what it does?
Beats us. *Globe and Mail*. Retrieved
17 January 2011 from http://www.
theglobeandmail.com/news/opinions/
why-does-the-harper-government-do-
what-it-does-beats-us/article1694280/

Meyer, J., & O'Malley, P. (2005). Missing the
punitive turn? Canadian criminal justice,
'balance', and penal modernism. In
J. Pratt, D. Brown, M. Brown, S. Hallsworth, & W. Morrison (Eds.), *The new*
punitiveness: Trends, theories, perspectives.
Cullompton, UK: Willan.

Millie, A., Jacobson, J., & Hough, M. (2003).
Understanding the Growth in the prison
population in England and Wales.
Criminal Justice, 3(4), 369–87.

Nagin, D.S., Cullen, F.T., & Jonson, C.L.
(2009). Imprisonment and reoffending.
In M. Tonry (Ed.), *Crime and justice: A*
review of research (Vol. 38). Chicago:
University of Chicago Press.

Newburn, T. (2007). 'Tough on crime': Penal
policy in England and Wales. In
M. Tonry (Ed.), *Crime and justice: A review*
of research (Vol. 36). Chicago: University
of Chicago Press.

New Democratic Party of Canada. (1997).
A framework for Canada's future: Alexa
McDonough and Canada's NDP platform.

Peter D. Hart Research Associates. (2002).
Changing public attitudes toward the
criminal justice system. Open Society
Institute. Retrieved from http://www.
soros.org/initiatives/usprograms/focus/
justice/articles_publications/publica-
tions/hartpoll_20020201

Pratt, J. (2008). When penal populism stops:
Legitimacy, scandal and the power to
punish in New Zealand. *Australian and*
New Zealand Journal of Criminology,
41(3), 364–83.

———, & Clark, M. (2005). Penal populism
in New Zealand. *Punishment and Society,*
7(3), 303–22.

———, Brown, D., Brown, M., Hallsworth,
S., & Morrison, W. (Eds.). (2005). *New*
punitiveness: Trends, theories, perspectives.
Portland, OR: Willan Publishing.

Progressive Conservative Party of Canada.
(1993). *Making government work for*
Canada: A taxpayer's agenda.

———. (1997). *Let the future begin: Jean*
Charest's plan for Canada's next century.

Public Safety and Emergency Preparedness
Canada. (2001). Public fear of crime and
perceptions of the criminal justice
system. Retrieved from http://www.

psepcsppcc.gc.ca/publications/
corrections/200111_e.asp

Reform Party of Canada. (1993). *Blue Sheet: Principles, policies & election platform*.

Roberts, J.V. (1998). The evolution of penal policy in Canada. *Social Policy and Administration, 32*(4), 420–37.

———, Stalans, L.J., Indemaur, D., & Hough, M. (2003). *Penal populism and public opinion: Lessons from five countries*. New York: Oxford University Press.

Rock, the Honourable A. (1996). Keynote address: Crime, punishment and public expectations. In J.M. Brisson & D. Greschner (Eds.), *Public perceptions of the administration of justice*. Montreal: Canadian Institute for the Administration of Justice.

Russell, P.H., & Ziegel, J.S. (1991). Federal judicial appointments: An appraisal of the first Mulroney government's appointments and the new Judicial Advisory Committees. *University of Toronto Law Journal, 41*(1), 4–37.

Ruth, H., & Reitz, K.R. (2003). *The challenge of crime: Rethinking our response*. Cambridge, MA: Harvard University Press.

Snacken, S. (2010). Resisting punitiveness in Europe? *Theoretical Criminology, 14,* 1362–806.

Standing Committee on Justice and the Solicitor General. (1993, February). *Crime prevention in Canada: Toward a national strategy*. Twelfth Report of the Standing Committee on Justice and the Solicitor General. Dr. Bob Horner, MP, Chairman. House of Commons, Canada.

Study Team Report. (1985). *The justice system: A study team report to the Task Force on Program Review (Nielsen Task Force)*. Ottawa: Supply and Services Canada.

Subcommittee on the Penitentiary System in Canada. (1977). *Report to Parliament*. Ottawa: Minister of Supply and Services.

Thomas, M. (2004). Adult criminal court statistics, 2003/04. *Juristat, 24*(12), 1–23.

Tonry, M. (2001). Unthought thoughts: The influence of changing sensibilities on penal policies. *Punishment and Society, 3,*167–81.

———. (2004a). *Punishment and politics: Evidence and emulation in the making of English crime control policy*. Devon, UK: Willan.

———. (2004b). *Thinking about crime: Sense and sensibility in American penal culture*. New York: Oxford University Press.

———. (2007). Crime does not cause punishment: The impact of sentencing policy on levels of crime. *South African Crime Quarterly, 20,* 13–20.

———. (2008). Learning from the limitations of deterrence research. In M. Tonry (Ed.), *Crime and justice: A review of research* (Vol. 37). Chicago: University of Chicago Press.

———. (2009). The mostly unintended effects of mandatory penalties: Two centuries of consistent findings. In M. Tonry (Ed.), *Crime and justice: A review of research* (Vol. 38). Chicago: University of Chicago Press.

Uggen, C., & Manza, J. (2002). Democratic contraction? Political consequences of felon disenfranchisement in the United States. *American Sociological Review, 67,* 777–803.

Vienneau, D. (1993, February 13). Canada must fight crime's social causes panel of MP's urges. *Toronto Star,* p. A1.

Vitiello, M. (1997). Three strikes: Can we return to rationality? *Journal of Criminal Law and Criminology, 87*(2), 395–481.

Webster, C.M., & Doob, A.N. (2007). Punitive trends and stable imprisonment rates in Canada. In M. Tonry (Ed.), *Crime and justice: A review of research* (Vol. 36). Chicago: University of Chicago Press.

Whitman, J.Q. (2003). *Harsh justice: Criminal punishment and the widening divide between America and Europe*. New York: Oxford University Press.

Zimring, F.E., Hawkins, G., & Kamin, S. (2001). *Punishment and democracy: Three strikes and you're out in California.* New York: Oxford University Press.

Zlomislic, D. (2010, August 7). Ottawa's prison plan won't work, critics say. *Toronto Star.*

CASES CITED

Sauvé v. Canada (Chief Electoral Officer), 3 S.C.R. 519 (2002).

STATUTES CITED

Criminal Code, R.S.C. 1985, ch. C-46 (as amended).

5

Youth Justice Policy Reform: The Youth Criminal Justice Act

Richard Barnhorst

Youth justice legislation governs how the criminal law deals with people who are not considered adults under the criminal law. In over a century of youth justice legislation in Canada, there have been three youth justice statutes. The most recent, the Youth Criminal Justice Act (YCJA), came into force in 2003. This chapter discusses the reform process that led to the YCJA. It begins with a brief overview of the evolution of youth justice legislation and then explains the policy objectives and major components that distinguish the YCJA from previous youth justice statutes. It examines the policy development process that preceded the introduction of the bill in Parliament as well as the parliamentary proceedings that culminated in the enactment of the YCJA. The chapter also discusses implementation activities and assesses the impact of the Act over its first several years. The conclusion is a consideration of factors that contributed to the passage of the YCJA and to the achievement of its objectives.

YOUTH JUSTICE PRIOR TO THE YOUTH CRIMINAL JUSTICE ACT

Prior to 1908, children and youths in Canada were treated basically the same as adults under the criminal law. There was no separate youth justice law or youth justice system. Children and youths received harsh punishments (e.g., whipping) for a wide range of offences, and they were sent to the same prisons as adult criminals.

In 1908, Canada passed its first youth justice statute, the Juvenile Delinquents Act (JDA). Although enacted under the federal government's criminal law power, it took a child welfare approach to offending by children and youths.[1] The Act made no distinction between 'neglected' children and 'delinquent' children. The focus was on treatment, not accountability. Decisions were to be based on the 'best interests of the child'. The broad definition of juvenile delinquent included not only offences that were offences for adults but also offences that were offences only for children (status offences), such as truancy and 'unmanageability'. The age range of 'juveniles' was 7 up to 16, 17, or 18, depending on the province. Separate juvenile courts were established, and court proceedings were to be informal and private. Custody sentences were indeterminate in length.

In the 1960s and 1970s, there were increasing concerns about individual rights and keeping less serious offenders out of the youth justice system. After 20 years of discussion and debate, these concerns were reflected in the Young Offenders Act (YOA), which came into force in 1984. In contrast to the JDA, the YOA attempted to blend and balance competing principles of criminal law and child welfare. It emphasized protection of society, recognized that young offenders were to be held accountable, permitted deterrence as a sentencing principle, and introduced legal rights for youth. On the other hand, the YOA retained much of a welfare approach by emphasizing the needs of youth, stating principles so broadly that a welfare approach could be justified, and permitting sentences that were disproportionate to the seriousness of the offence in order to address the welfare or treatment needs of youths.

The YOA also removed status offences, introduced determinate sentences, and created a uniform age range to be covered by the Act (from age 12 up until the eighteenth birthday). Diversion of cases from the youth court was permitted, and the court process itself was made more like an adult criminal court process.

THE YOUTH CRIMINAL JUSTICE ACT (2003): CRIMINAL LAW AND RESTRAINT APPROACH

The YOA was replaced by the Youth Criminal Justice Act (YCJA) in 2003. The YOA, for many years, had been widely criticized in the media, in public opinion surveys, and by politicians as too lenient on young offenders. As noted by the parliamentary committee that reviewed the YOA, 'Generally, the public believes that youth court judges are too lenient, that youth crime, particularly violent youth crime, is on the rise and longer sentences are necessary' (Standing Committee on Justice and Legal Affairs, 1997). The pressure for change was clearly in the direction of 'getting tough' with young offenders through longer sentences and greater use of custody. However, other critics, including some academics and the federal Department of Justice (DOJ), identified problems with the YOA that did not necessarily suggest that the legislation needed toughening. The DOJ highlighted the following (Department of Justice, 2002):

■ The YOA lacked a clear and coherent youth justice philosophy.
■ Pre-trial detention and custody sentences were being overused. Statistics indicated that Canada had one of the highest youth incarceration rates in the world.

- The courts were overused for minor cases that could be better dealt with outside the courts.
- Sentences were often unfair and disproportionate to the seriousness of the offence.
- Disproportionate sentences were often inappropriately based on the welfare or mental health needs of youths.
- The system did not make a clear distinction between its responses to serious violent offences and its responses to less serious offences.
- The process for transfer to the adult court resulted in unfairness, complexity, and delay.
- There was considerable variation among the provinces/territories in charges, court cases, pre-trial detention, and sentencing.

The YCJA addressed these problems by shifting the orientation of youth justice to a criminal law and restraint approach. This shift is reflected in the criminal law principles of the Act, the absence of welfare principles, the clear objectives of reducing the use of the courts and incarceration, and the structuring of decision-making toward achieving the objectives. The YCJA has maintained certain aspects of the YOA, such as the legal rights of youths, but it differs significantly from the YOA in the following areas.

Youth Justice Principles

The YCJA emphasizes accountability and proportionality. Youths are to be held accountable through meaningful consequences and measures that promote rehabilitation and reintegration. Accountability must be proportionate to the seriousness of the offence and consistent with the reduced maturity of youths. The Act also provides that holding youths accountable in a fair and proportionate manner can make a *contribution* to the protection of the public in the *long term*. The Act recognizes that there are many factors outside the youth justice system that can have an equal or greater effect on public protection than the activities of the youth justice system.

The YCJA, like the YOA, stresses the importance of rehabilitation. Unlike the YOA, the YCJA requires that rehabilitative measures be within a proportionate response to the offence. It prohibits the youth justice system from imposing an intervention that is disproportionate to the seriousness of the offence in order to address a youth's child welfare or mental health needs.

The YCJA reflects a policy of restraint in the use of the youth justice system, particularly in the use of the courts, pre-trial detention, and custody sentences. The preamble of the Act states that Canada should have a system that 'reserves its most serious interventions for the most serious crimes and reduces the over-reliance on incarceration for non-violent young persons.' This principle is based on a view that youth justice intervention may cause more harm than good and has often been an ineffective, costly overreaction to much of youth offending. In attempting to ensure that restraint is exercised, the YCJA structures the decision-making process to a much greater extent than did the YOA and the adult criminal law. The relatively strong and detailed provisions for key decisions, such as sentencing, indicate a recognition that decision-makers in the youth justice system needed more legislative direction if some of the problems under the YOA were to be avoided.

The YCJA also distinguishes the role of the youth justice system from the roles of other systems dealing with youth, such as child welfare and mental health. For example, it is clear that custody and pre-trial detention cannot be used as a substitute for welfare and mental health needs.

Use of the Court

Reducing the use of the court is a clear objective of the YCJA. In contrast to the YOA, the YCJA encourages the use of extrajudicial measures by specifying several non-court options for police and prosecutors, including no further action, informal warnings, cautions, and extrajudicial sanctions. The YCJA provides principles and guidelines that encourage police and prosecutors to reorient their general approach to responding to youth crime. Rather than assume that the normal response is to charge the youth, they must in all cases first assess whether an extrajudicial measure would be adequate to hold the youth accountable.

The Act further provides that extrajudicial measures may be used with repeat offenders. This principle is intended to counter the tendency under the YOA to restrict alternative measures to first-time offenders. The Act also strongly indicates to police and prosecutors that it should be exceptional for first-time, non-violent offenders to be taken through the court process.

Pre-trial Detention

The YCJA's objective of reducing incarceration includes reducing the use of pre-trial detention. The Act prohibits the use of detention as a substitute for child welfare, mental health, or other social measures. The underlying policy is that it is unfair to use the criminal justice system to incarcerate youths in order to address their non-criminal behaviour or needs, particularly when other youths who are accused of similar offences but do not have such needs would not be detained.

The Act also creates a presumption that detention is not necessary for public safety if the youth, if later found guilty, could not be sentenced to custody. The rationale is that it is generally unfair to incarcerate a presumed-innocent youth at the pre-trial stage if the youth cannot be incarcerated if found guilty of the offence.

Sentencing Principles

The YCJA sets out a new approach to youth sentencing that is much more specific and directive than either the YOA or the Criminal Code. The purpose of youth sentencing under the YCJA is to hold a youth accountable for the offence by imposing sanctions that are just, have meaningful consequences for the youth, and promote rehabilitation, thereby contributing to the long-term protection of the public.

Denunciation, deterrence, and incapacitation, which are sentencing objectives for adults under the Criminal Code, are not sentencing objectives under the YCJA. In excluding deterrence, the Act is aligned with research that shows that increasing the severity or length of sentences has no effect on the commission of further crime by the individual offender or other offenders (Doob and Cesaroni, 2003; Doob and Webster, 2003).

Proportionality is a fundamental sentencing principle of the YCJA: less serious cases should result in less severe sentences and more serious cases should result in more severe sentences. Proportionality was not a requirement under the YOA. Indeed, the Supreme Court of Canada concluded that it was appropriate under the YOA to impose a sentence that was disproportionately severe or intrusive if the youth had needs that required a greater degree of intervention than would be warranted by the seriousness of the offence (*R. v. J.J.M.*, [1993] 2 S.C.R. 421). This is prohibited under the YCJA.

Proportionality reflects the Act's restraint policy. However, proportionality alone may not reduce the use of custody. For example, a criminal justice system could have proportionate sentences where the most minor offences receive one day in custody and the most serious receive years in custody. The Act, therefore, restricts custody to serious and repeat offenders.

Adult Sentences

The YCJA eliminates the YOA process of transfer to adult court prior to a finding of guilt. The decision on whether to impose an adult sentence is made in youth court after a finding of guilt on a relatively serious charge. Instead of basing the decision to transfer on the 'best interests' of the youth and the protection of society, the YCJA allows an adult sentence only if, after taking into account that a youth is to be held to a lower level of accountability than an adult, the judge determines that a youth sentence would not be long enough to hold the youth accountable.

Amendments to the YOA in 1995 included a presumption that youths, 16 years of age or older, who were charged with certain very serious offences would be transferred to adult court. This meant that the onus was on the youths to persuade the youth court that they should remain in youth court. The YCJA initially expanded the range of offences that would trigger a presumption that an adult sentence should be imposed. It also lowered the age at which the presumption would apply from 16 to 14, although provinces could choose to retain age 16. The presumptive offence provisions were subsequently ruled unconstitutional by the Supreme Court of Canada (*R. v. D.B.*, [2008] S.C.J. No. 25). The Supreme Court decided that a principle of fundamental justice is that youths, in comparison to adults, are entitled to a presumption of diminished moral blameworthiness or culpability and that requiring youths to persuade the court that a youth sentence should be imposed violated this principle.

POLICY DEVELOPMENT PROCESS PRIOR TO INTRODUCTION OF YCJA

The substantial changes contained in the YCJA were the result of a seven-year reform process, beginning in 1995 and ending with the passage of the Act in February 2002.

The Federal-Provincial-Territorial Task Force on Youth Justice

The federal and provincial/territorial (FPT) ministers of justice established a task force of government officials to review the YOA and the youth justice system. The federal government and all provincial/territorial governments, except Quebec, were represented. Quebec refused to participate on the ground that it had already done its own review of the application of the YOA in Quebec. More than 80 per cent of the task force consisted of provincial/territorial officials.

The task force produced a 650-page report (Federal-Provincial-Territorial Task Force on Youth Justice, 1996). The task force did not question 'the fundamental framework and direction of the YOA'. It made few legislative recommendations to address many of the serious problems with the YOA (e.g., the use of court and custody, described earlier). Instead, the vast majority of recommendations were non-legislative in nature. For example, there were proposals related to risk/need assessment tools, FPT financial arrangements, guidelines, and 'best practices'. By emphasizing non-legislative recommendations, such as the development of diversion guidelines by provinces, rather than legislative amendments, the task force promoted flexibility and discretion for the provinces. This approach limits the extent to which federal legislation and judicial decisions can affect the operation and costs of the system, which are largely borne by provinces. However, non-legislative approaches can increase the likelihood of interprovincial variation in how youths are dealt with across the country.

Many of the legislative recommendations supported increased provincial control over the system. For example, the recommendations called for transferring from judges to provincial correctional officials the authority to decide whether a sentenced youth would be placed in secure or open custody. Several other legislative recommendations focused on toughening the legislation. For example, the task force recommended that more youths be transferred to the adult court; that it be clarified that the Criminal Code's dangerous offender and long-term offender designations apply to youths; and that the identity of 'dangerous' youths who receive youth sentences be published. A police and prosecutorial perspective was reflected in the recommendations to weaken the protections for youths who make statements to the police.

The task force made only two minor legislative recommendations relating to pre-trial detention and sentencing. It proposed that child welfare considerations alone should not constitute a ground for pre-trial detention and that consideration be given to a youth sentence that would be similar to the adult conditional sentence of imprisonment.[2] Regarding transfer to adult court, the task force recommended that the process be changed to a post-adjudicative process in youth court to determine whether an adult sentence should be imposed.

Parliamentary Committee Review

Another part of the review of the YOA and the youth justice system was a review conducted by the House of Commons Standing Committee on Justice and Legal Affairs. The committee invited the views of a broad range of people and organizations, including judges, prosecutors, defence lawyers, police, child welfare agencies, victims, parents, young offenders, and others. The committee's non-legislative recommendations included education campaigns for the general public and youth justice professionals, allocation of 5 per cent of the federal criminal justice budget to crime prevention, and the shifting of resources from custodial institutions to community-based services.

Although the mandate of the standing committee seemed to indicate that the committee would take a more comprehensive approach to legislative reform than was taken by the FPT task force, it did not do so. Its legislative recommendations were narrow in scope and did not question the basic philosophy and orientation of the YOA.

The standing committee and FPT task force reached similar conclusions in some areas, suggesting changes that would

- increase the use of alternatives to the court and custody sentences for less serious offences, although the standing committee and the task force primarily proposed non-legislative approaches, such as increased funding of alternatives;
- change the process of transfer to adult court to a post-adjudicative adult sentencing determination in youth court;
- weaken the legal protections of youths with regard to publishing their identities; and
- allow judicial discretion to admit a youth's statement to the police even though the police violated the youth's legal protections, if admitting the statement would not bring the administration of justice into disrepute.

The standing committee also proposed that the minimum age jurisdiction be lowered so that the youth court would be able to deal with children aged 10 and 11 alleged to have committed offences causing death or 'serious harm'. Prosecution in these cases would occur only if the attorney general consented and the youth court agreed.

The Federal Department of Justice

In May 1998, the federal minister of justice released the policy paper *Strategy for the Renewal of Youth Justice* (Department of Justice, 1998), which was the federal government's response to the standing committee's report. The paper indicated that the federal government agreed with most of the standing committee's recommendations. However, it went beyond the limited recommendations of the committee, announcing that the YOA would be replaced by a new youth justice statute in order to underscore the government's commitment to reform and to send a signal to Canadians that a new legal approach to youth justice was being taken. The paper set out a policy framework that identified problems under the YOA and described the policy directions that would later be contained in the provisions of the YCJA, discussed above.

The new legislation would recognize that there is a clear distinction between the small number of violent young offenders and the vast majority who are nonviolent. It would expand alternatives to court and increase the range of community-based sentences. This direction suggested a comprehensive approach that not only would respond to the pressure for toughening the legislation but would also address the evidence-based concerns about overuse of the courts and custody for less serious offenders. It signalled a two-pronged approach of being tough on violent and serious repeat offenders and softer on less serious offenders.

The policy paper was most specific in describing the tougher proposals regarding presumptive adult sentences, publication of the names of young offenders, and judicial discretion to admit youths' statements despite police noncompliance with legal safeguards. The specificity in these areas was consistent with the view that it was politically advantageous to show serious commitment to being tough on youth crime. The government rejected the parliamentary committee's recommendation to lower the minimum age of criminal responsibility to 10 in exceptional circumstances. The policy paper noted that the small number of under-12 'offenders' could be dealt with more effectively by parents and the community or, if necessary, the child welfare or mental health systems.

The federal Department of Justice also established a new Youth Justice Policy section to replace a small young offenders unit. The director general and four lawyers constituted a legal policy team and were the federal officials most directly involved in the legislative initiative. The team obtained research and statistical information on youth justice issues from academic criminologists. The Youth Justice Policy section also contained a program team that was responsible for funding and administrative matters related to a range of time-limited projects (e.g., pilot projects) to be run by community organizations and provincial governments.

Draft Legislation and Consultation

In the relatively short period of four months, beginning in the fall of 1998, the DOJ legal team developed draft legislation. During this period, there was considerable consultation between federal officials and senior officials from provincial/territorial governments through meetings of the FPT Coordinating Committee of Senior Officials (CCSO). The confidential discussions at these meetings included the review of draft legislation. No other individuals or organizations in the country had the opportunity to review the wording to be used in the bill that would be presented to Parliament. This exclusive consultation process gave the provinces/territories considerable opportunity to attempt to influence the content of the new legislation.

The special access of the provinces/territories to the federal justice policy process reflects the partnership in criminal justice between the federal government, which is constitutionally responsible for criminal law and procedure, and the provinces/territories, which are responsible for the administration of the criminal justice system. Provinces/territories can be affected by changes in the federal criminal law, and they thus seek to be involved in the changes, in part, to prevent what they consider to be potentially negative consequences. On the other hand, the achievement of federal policy objectives can be affected by provincial decisions related to how the law is applied, such as funding decisions and policies regarding charging, pre-trial detention, sentencing, and correctional programs.

If provincial/territorial officials at the CCSO meetings were opposed to the federal proposals, they could object at the meetings and could also raise their concerns with their deputy ministers, who, in turn, could raise the concerns with their ministers. The FPT ministers of justice have regular meetings at which issues and proposals related to criminal justice, including youth justice, are discussed. How the issues are resolved at these meetings can have a significant impact on the substance of legislative reform. Prior to the meetings at which YCJA issues were addressed, federal officials would brief their minister and advise on options, including possible compromises to accommodate provincial objections.

The federal government's broad policy direction left considerable scope regarding how it should be turned into specific legislative provisions. Numerous judgments on policy matters were made by the DOJ legal team in designing and drafting the legislation. For example, the government's objective of reducing custody sentences left open such important issues as the types of cases eligible for custody and how restrictive the provisions should be. Draft legislation developed by the legal team required approval by the deputy minister and minister before the YCJA bill was introduced in Parliament. Subject to these approvals, the legal team had an influential role regarding the substance of the legislation.

LEGISLATIVE BILLS AND PARLIAMENTARY PROCEEDINGS

In March 1999, Bill C-68, the first version of the YCJA, was introduced. The minister's press release on the bill emphasized tough-sounding provisions related to presumptive adult sentences and publication of the names of serious violent offenders (Department of Justice, 1999). The emphasis on toughness was consistent with the belief that it was better politically to be seen as tough on youth crime. Predictably, the news media also tended to focus on the harsher aspects of the bill, thus creating an impression with the public that the YCJA was a 'tough on crime' statute (see Doob & Sprott, 2004, for a discussion of the 'selling' of the Act versus what was actually contained in the Act). After prorogation of Parliament in June 1999, the bill was reintroduced as Bill C-3 in October 1999.

House Committee: Witnesses

The Standing Committee on Justice and Human Rights held meetings on Bill C-3 from November 1999 to October 2000. After a first meeting in which federal officials provided an overview of the bill, approximately 55 witnesses appeared over the next several months (Standing Committee on Justice and Human Rights, *Hansard*, 30 November 1999–29 March 2000). Witnesses were from a variety of sectors, including provincial governments, academics, lawyers, police organizations, victims' groups, and Quebec organizations.

Most witnesses (other than most witnesses from Quebec) supported the broad principles and general direction of the YCJA. However, their views were often conflicting on specific parts of the bill. The following highlights some of the views from the various sectors and demonstrates differences of opinion regarding key parts of the bill.

Extrajudicial Measures

Most witnesses, including the police, supported the objective of the bill to reduce the use of court and increase the use of extrajudicial measures. However, when witnesses commented on specific provisions, differences of opinion surfaced. For example, a provincial government was opposed to the presumption that extrajudicial measures should be used with non-violent first offenders and the requirement that police consider the use of extrajudicial measures before charging. This provincial government claimed that these provisions were intrusions by the federal government into provincial jurisdiction over the administration of justice. In contrast, academics and lawyers not only agreed with the provisions but also recommended that they be strengthened by authorizing a judge to send a case back to the prosecutor for further consideration of extrajudicial measures if the judge felt that it was a case that did not appear to require the use of the court to hold the youth accountable.

Pre-trial Detention

The YCJA provisions intended to reduce the use of pre-trial detention were generally not controversial, although there were concerns about the 'complexity' of the presumption against detention. The presumption was considered complex by some because it required consideration of the restrictions on custody sentences, which were in a separate part of the bill. A legal clinic lauded the provisions and supported the rationale that it is generally unfair to lock up presumed-innocent youths at the pre-trial stage if they could not be sentenced to custody if found guilty. However, a provincial government opposed the presumption against detention as well as the bill's prohibition on using pre-trial detention to address child welfare or mental health problems. It claimed that these provisions were unnecessary and could complicate bail hearings.

Youth Sentences

In general, the proposed sentencing principles, including the restrictions on custody, were supported, or at least not opposed, by most witnesses. However, provincial governments as well as police organizations objected to the exclusion of deterrence and denunciation from the sentencing principles, even though they failed to provide any research evidence in support of their position. Lawyers' organizations and legal academics supported the restrictions on custody, but some were concerned that the restrictions were not restrictive enough. Provincial governments were opposed to the new approach to custody sentences, which provided that two-thirds of the sentence would be served in custody and the last one-third—to promote reintegration of the youth—would be served in the community under supervision. The provinces claimed that this would automatically reduce the maximum custodial sentence available for serious violent offenders and could undermine public confidence in the youth justice system. Others, including some academics and non-governmental organizations (NGOs), supported the new custody and supervision order, although they recommended that the authority of correctional officials to hold a youth after the two-thirds point should be more limited.

Some legal academics and NGOs objected to the provisions that permitted provincial governments to opt out of implementing some of the new sentencing options. They argued that allowing this flexibility to provincial governments would increase the likelihood of disparity in sentencing throughout the country and would unfairly deny to youths in some provinces the same range of community-based sentences.

Adult Sentences

There was widespread support for a post-adjudicative adult sentencing process. However, there was major opposition to the presumptive adult sentence provisions, one of the few areas of the bill that reflected a 'get tough' approach. Academics, lawyers' organizations, and NGOs were strongly opposed. Some were opposed to any presumption, and others were particularly opposed to lowering the age at which the presumption would apply and adding the commission of a third serious violent offence to the list of presumptive offences. In contrast, a provincial government was concerned that the test for an adult sentence omitted the protection of society as the paramount consideration, as was provided in the YOA. A police organization objected to 14 as the age at which the presumption of an adult sentence should apply and proposed that it apply to 12- and 13-year-old youths as well.

Statements

The amendment to weaken the legal protections regarding youths' statements to police was consistent with recommendations of provincial attorneys general, the FPT task force, and the Standing Committee. Lawyers' organizations and some

NGOs were strongly opposed to the amendment. They argued that allowing judges to circumvent long-standing procedural safeguards was inconsistent with research findings that youths were vulnerable when dealing with police and required the safeguards when deciding whether to make a confession or waive their right to counsel. In contrast, a police organization argued that there should be no special legal protections for youths and the same common law rules that apply to statements made by adults to police should apply to youths.

Publication

The YCJA kept the privacy protections of the YOA except that it allowed the publication of the identity of a youth who received a youth sentence for a presumptive offence (an offence for which it would be presumed that the youth should receive an adult sentence). Academics, lawyers' organizations, and NGOs were strongly opposed to this provision, arguing that it would weaken a cornerstone of the youth justice system and a youth's prospects for rehabilitation.

Minimum Age of Criminal Responsibility

Retaining age 12 as the minimum age of criminal responsibility was supported by most witnesses, particularly lawyers' organizations and NGOs. However, a legal academic, police organizations, and a provincial government wanted children under 12 to be subject to the criminal law in certain situations if the offence was serious.

The Government's Response: Bill C-7

After the federal election in the fall of 2000, the majority Liberal government reintroduced the YCJA bill as Bill C-7 in February 2001. It was essentially the same as C-3. Although the federal government inserted more than 160 amendments, these were mainly minor changes. One of the more significant changes concerned the admissibility of statements by youths to police. In response to concerns raised by lawyers' organizations and others, C-7 removed the broad judicial discretion to admit statements in cases in which the police had violated the legal safeguards for youths. Instead, it provided that an exception to strict compliance with the safeguards would be permitted only if the non-compliance was a 'technical irregularity'.

The federal government's decision to propose only minor changes in response to the testimony of committee witnesses raises the question of why the government did not propose more substantial changes. This question is largely answered in Part G of this chapter (p. 127), which discusses several factors that contributed to the passage of the YCJA. However, two specific areas—the presumptive offence provisions and the loosening of the restrictions on publication of a youth's identity—highlight other factors that also affected the government's resistance to change in these areas. As discussed above, there was strong and widespread opposition to these parts of the bill. There was also no research evidence or sound policy reason to support the provisions. However, these were proposals on which the federal government had been very specific in its initial policy document, *Strategy for the Renewal of Youth Justice*. Based on its understanding of public opinion, the government used these proposals to emphasize its major message to the public and the media—it was taking serious violent youth crime seriously. These proposals were the two main get-tough proposals contained in the bill. If the government had abandoned these proposals, it would have undercut one of its main reasons for introducing the legislation—to respond to the public's lack of confidence in the youth justice system and the public perception that the system was too lenient on youths who commit serious offences. The argument that public perceptions of the youth justice system were based on inaccurate understanding of how the system operated was not persuasive. From a political perspective, it was the public perception, whether accurate or not, that mattered and the YCJA was intended to respond to that perception. The combination of these factors with others, such as the push from the right wing to make the provisions even harsher, made it highly unlikely that these get-tough proposals would be removed from the bill.

The government made one change to its initial presumptive offence provisions. It had initially proposed that the age at which the presumption of an adult sentence would apply would be lowered from 16, as under the YOA, to 14, but it modified this provision by proposing that provinces could choose to set the age at 15 or 16 rather than 14. Although this change raised serious concerns about unequal treatment of youths based on their province, the government made this change to respond to opposition from Quebec. As noted earlier, most witnesses from Quebec opposed the entire bill and wanted the YOA retained. The government had been attempting to counter many of Quebec's concerns by arguing that the YCJA contained flexible provisions that would allow Quebec to continue, in most respects, with the approach to youth justice that it had taken under the YOA. Enabling Quebec to use age 16 would allow that province to have the same age as under the YOA and make it easier for Liberals from Quebec to deal with Quebec critics of the YCJA.

Bill C-7 was referred to the Standing Committee, and five witnesses appeared: the federal minister of justice and representatives of four provincial governments. Manitoba and Saskatchewan expressed basically the same objections that they had indicated at their previous appearance before the committee on C-3. New Brunswick and Prince Edward Island, two provinces that had not appeared on C-3, were less critical of the bill than other provinces had been and focused their concerns, in part, on implementation issues and the need for increased federal cost sharing.

Amendments were proposed by opposition members of the committee, including more than 3,000 amendments by the Bloc Québécois, which delayed the committee process. The committee, which had a majority of Liberal members, rejected the opposition's proposed amendments, voted in favour of C-7, and returned the bill to the House of Commons for third reading in May 2001.

Third Reading—House of Commons

At third reading, the Liberal majority in the House was able to pass the bill over the objections of the opposition parties. Members of each party gave speeches summarizing their positions on the bill (House of Commons, *Hansard*, 29 May 2001).

The Liberal members of Parliament who gave speeches restated how the YCJA addressed the problems under the YOA and the evidence upon which the YCJA was based, such as the high rate of youth custody sentences. Liberal MPs from Quebec refuted criticisms that had been made by the Bloc Québécois, such as that the bill was not flexible enough to allow Quebec to provide rehabilitation programs. They expressed their disappointment with the Bloc's 'misinformation campaign', which was intended—they suggested—to influence public opinion in Quebec against the YCJA. They also stated that, despite the positive claims made by the Bloc about how the YOA operated in Quebec, the province dealt harshly with youths by committing minor offenders to custody and transferring a high number of youths to adult court.

A speech by the minister's parliamentary assistant criticized the Ontario government's recently released, 'get-tough' proposals, which included automatic adult sentences for 16- and 17-year-olds charged with serious offences, an expanded range of offences that would be presumed to require an adult sentence for 14- and 15-year-olds, increased length of youth sentences, and removal of the focus on alternatives to custody.

The parliamentary assistant commented that Ontario's proposed automatic adult sentences were

> part of Ontario's call for adult time for adult crime. This may be a catchy sound bite but it is a terribly flawed youth justice policy. . . . Ontario's proposal neglects to take into account that judges, after having heard all the elements of the case before them and after consideration of the facts, are best placed to determine whether a youth sentence would be adequate to hold the young person accountable or if an adult sentence is appropriate. Ontario apparently does not trust its own prosecutors to use their judgment, consider the circumstances of a particular offence, and apply for an adult sentence in appropriate cases.

He also criticized Ontario's recommendation to remove the focus on alternatives to custody, arguing that alternatives were needed to address the problem of large numbers of minor and non-violent offenders in custody. He noted: 'Ontario locks up more than 12,000 young persons a year. Ontario has one of the highest rates in the country of incarcerating first offenders found guilty of minor theft. Ontario has been criticized by its own provincial auditor for wasting taxpayer dollars by failing to use more alternatives to custody.'

The Canadian Alliance MPs called the bill 'hopelessly flawed' and 'doomed to failure'. They identified several specific recommendations that had been put forward by their party and rejected by the government. The recommendations, which were similar to Ontario's, called for making the law much tougher.

Bloc Québécois MPs repeated what they had been saying since 1999 and what most witnesses from Quebec said before the parliamentary committees. They claimed that 'everyone' in Quebec was opposed to the bill and that the YOA should be retained. They considered the bill to be 'repressive' and claimed that it would prevent rehabilitation because it would be too difficult to sentence youths to custody and to keep them in custody long enough to rehabilitate them. They particularly objected to the restrictions on custody sentences, the principle of proportionality, giving youths credit at sentencing for time spent in pre-trial detention, and releasing youths after two-thirds of the custody sentence to serve the remainder of the sentence under community supervision.

The Progressive Conservatives agreed with the bill's philosophy and emphasis on rehabilitation but argued that the bill was an attempt to 'please everyone'. As a result, the 'complex, convoluted' bill would achieve none of its objectives. They wanted the minimum age of criminal responsibility lowered to 10, increased disclosure of information on young offenders with schools, and the inclusion of deterrence and denunciation as sentencing principles.

The NDP primarily focused on the complexity of the bill, concerns about delay in the courts, and the need for adequate federal resources provided to provinces to implement the legislation.

Senate

The Senate Committee on Legal and Constitutional Affairs began hearings in September 2001. The committee heard from many of the same witnesses who had testified before the House Committee. The testimony was similar in most respects to what the House Committee had heard (Standing Senate Committee on Legal and Constitutional Affairs, 2001).

However, unlike the House Committee hearings, the Senate Committee heard from provincial politicians. The attorneys general of Manitoba and Saskatchewan made basically the same arguments that their officials had made to the House Committee. The Ontario attorney general was strongly opposed to the bill. He stated that his proposals would result in 'adult time for adult crime'. The proposals were contained in a draft 'bill' entitled 'No More Free Ride for Young Offenders Act'. The proposals, described above, reflected the most extreme get-tough approach to youth justice of all witnesses who appeared before either parliamentary committee.

The Senate Committee did not accept Ontario's recommendations but made several minor recommendations of its own. The only committee recommendation that was approved by the Senate as a whole was to replicate the wording of the sentencing provision in the Criminal Code that non-custodial alternatives should be considered for all offenders, with particular attention to the circumstances of Aboriginal offenders. The bill was referred back to the House for consideration of the proposed amendment. The Senate's decision to send the bill back to the House was unusual. A factor behind this decision may have been the growing concern among senators that the House, on a range of matters unrelated to youth justice, was not showing sufficient respect for the unelected Senate; by sending the YCJA back to the House, the senators could demonstrate the Senate's legislative role.

The Senate's proposed amendment was much weaker than other provisions in C-7 dealing with restrictions on custody for all youths. Thus, the proposed amendment was unnecessary but not problematic, and so the government agreed to its inclusion in the legislation. Bill C-7 received royal assent in February 2002.

IMPLEMENTATION OF THE YCJA

The coming into force of the YCJA was delayed until 1 April 2003 to allow time for provinces and others to prepare for the implementation of the Act. In contrast to the approach under the YOA, the Department of Justice initiated several activities to encourage implementation that was consistent with the objectives of the new legislation.

In 1999, when the first version of the YCJA was introduced in Parliament, the DOJ and provincial/territorial governments reached a cost-sharing agreement under which the federal government agreed to transfer nearly $1 billion to the provinces over a five-year period. Unlike the less structured funding agreement under the YOA, the funds were to be used by the provinces in ways that were consistent with federal policy objectives, such as the development of extrajudicial measures and community alternatives to custody sentences. Therefore, financial incentives to change the system were in place years before the YCJA was passed.

The DOJ also established the Youth Justice Renewal Fund to provide money to provinces, NGOs, and Aboriginal organizations to carry out activities consistent with the YCJA. Numerous pilot projects were funded to test innovative ideas regarding extrajudicial measures, alternatives to pre-trial detention, sentencing, and reintegration. The fund supported education programs and materials for youth justice professionals. It was also used for YCJA educational materials for youths and the general public and 'capacity-building' projects that were intended to help Aboriginal communities provide alternatives to detention and custody so that Aboriginal youths could be dealt with in their own communities.

The DOJ also initiated its own professional education program. It developed explanatory materials on the Act, including *YCJA Explained*, a comprehensive, online explanation of the Act for professionals. The DOJ also conducted one- to two-day professional education sessions in every province and territory.

IMPACT OF THE YCJA

Despite the claims by opponents of the legislation that it was 'doomed to failure' and would not achieve its objectives, according to statistics from the Canadian Centre for Justice Statistics, the YCJA has been successful in achieving most of its objectives, particularly the reduction in use of the court and custody sentences (see Bala, Carrington, & Roberts, 2009, for a detailed discussion on the impact of the YCJA on the use of court and custody). The Act achieved these objectives without an increase in police-recorded youth crime, which has declined under the YCJA (Dauvergne & Turner, 2010).

Charging and Police Diversion

In keeping with the Act's objectives, charging has decreased and police diversion of cases through extrajudicial measures has increased. There has been an almost complete reversal in the incidence of laying charges and police diversion. Under the YOA in 1999, 63 per cent of chargeable youths were charged and 37 per cent were diverted, while under the YCJA in 2009, 42 per cent of chargeable youths were charged and 58 per cent were diverted (Canadian Centre for Justice Statistics, 2010a). This change in police behaviour occurred without evidence of net widening (Bala et al., 2009).

Use of the Court

The major objective of reducing the use of the court has been achieved. Youth court cases declined by 23 per cent between 2002/03 and 2008/09 (Milligan, 2010). After a large initial drop, the number of youth court cases has remained relatively stable. Since 2002/03, there have been declines in court cases in all provinces and territories, with declines of more than 20 per cent in seven jurisdictions. Court cases have declined significantly in all major offence categories.

Custody Sentences

The major objective of reducing the use of custody sentences has also been achieved. The number of custody sentences dropped from 2002/03 to 2008/09 by an astounding 60 per cent. All provinces had significant decreases, ranging from 48 to 79 per cent (Canadian Centre for Justice Statistics, 2010b)

The percentage of guilty cases resulting in custody sentences also dropped, from 27 per cent in 2002/03 to 15 per cent in 2008/09 (Milligan, 2010). Instead of more than one in four guilty cases resulting in custody in the last year of the YOA, only one in about seven guilty cases did so in 2008/09. The percentage of guilty cases resulting in custody also dropped significantly in all provinces and territories.

Canada's overall youth incarceration rate, which includes both custody and detention, has declined by almost 50 per cent under the YCJA, from 13 youths per 10,000 in 2002/03 to 7 youths per 10,000 in 2008/09 (Reitano, 2004; Calverley, Cotter, & Halla, 2010). Since a significant decline in 2003/04, the youth incarceration rate has been stable.

Pre-trial Detention

Despite the YCJA provisions intended to decrease the use of pre-trial detention, there is evidence of an increase under the YCJA (Canadian Centre for Justice

Statistics, 2010c). In 2008/09, the average daily number of youths in remand was 16 per cent higher than in 2003/04. Comparisons of remand rates (the number of youths in remand per 10,000 youths in the population) also indicate some increase under the YCJA (Canadian Centre for Justice Statistics, 2010c). Based on statistics from the 10 provinces, the overall remand rate increased from 3.3 in 2003/04 to 3.8 in 2008/09. Seven of the 10 provinces had increases in their remand rate, with the largest increases in Manitoba and Saskatchewan. Manitoba's remand rate rose from 8.94 in 2003/04 to 16.95 in 2008/09. Saskatchewan's rate rose from 7.8 in 2003/04 to 10.23 in 2008/09.

Toughening the Law

There were three main areas in which the YCJA toughened the law: presumptive adult sentences, publication of a youth's identity after a youth sentence for a presumptive offence, and judicial discretion to admit a youth's statement despite a 'technical irregularity' by the police.

The toughening provisions have apparently had little, if any, impact. The toughest provisions, the presumptive adult sentence provisions, are no longer part of the law, having been ruled to be unconstitutional by the Supreme Court of Canada in 2008 (*R. v. D.B.*, [2008]). In addition, there have been no reported court cases allowing the publication of a youth's identity after a youth sentence for a presumptive offence or allowing the admission of a youth's statement on the basis of a 'technical irregularity'.[3] Courts have rejected prosecutors' arguments that police violations were technical, and they have required that the police rigorously comply with the legal safeguards regarding youths' statements (see, for example, *R. v. S.S.*, [2007]).

FACTORS THAT CONTRIBUTED TO THE PASSAGE OF THE YCJA

The YCJA reform process was long and contentious, but in the end, the YCJA became law and it has had remarkable success in achieving most of its policy objectives. It has also received international recognition as progressive legislation that is a model for reform in other countries. (see, for example, Solomon & Allen, 2009).

After initial pressure to make the law tougher, the YCJA brought in a new approach to youth justice that included some tougher measures. However, the main emphasis of the Act is not on making the youth justice system tougher but rather on reducing its use through less charging, less pre-trial detention, and fewer custody sentences; establishing coherent criminal law principles; and structuring the discretion of judges and other decision-makers. Without attempting to give a comprehensive explanation of why the Act passed, some influential factors can be identified.

Areas of Agreement

There was general agreement on a perceived need for change—a broad consensus that youth justice legislative reform was required. Public opinion polls indicated that the public lacked confidence in the YOA, and the minister acknowledged that it was the most unpopular of all federal statutes. The disapproval of the YOA created a situation in which it appeared that 'something must be done' even though it was not clear what exactly that something was. The unpopularity of the YOA spurred the minister not simply to amend the YOA but to replace it with a new statute with a new name, thereby suggesting that the government would introduce comprehensive reform that went beyond the relatively narrow legislative recommendations of the parliamentary committee.

There was also considerable agreement about some of the key problems that the YCJA was intended to address, such as the overuse of the court and custody for less serious offenders. It was widely accepted that having one of the highest youth incarceration rates in the world was something that needed to be changed. There was disagreement on how the problems should be addressed, but in general, the FPT task force, the Standing Committee, parliamentary witnesses, and political parties did not claim that changes were unnecessary in these areas.

Similarly, many of the basic principles in the legislative proposals were not seen as controversial, except by most Quebec witnesses and the Bloc Québécois. These principles included accountability, meaningful consequences, proportionality, rehabilitation, distinguishing between serious violent offences and less serious offences, and separating the role of youth justice from the roles of the child welfare and mental health systems. Agreement or at least an absence of opposition on these principles meant that the arguments were about how they should be applied, not about whether they were appropriate. Of course, there was major controversy over other principles, such as those related to the presumptive adult sentence provisions and the publication of the identity of youths found guilty of presumptive offences.

Majority Government

Majority government, combined with political commitment and party discipline, was a significant factor in ensuring passage of the legislation. The Liberals had a majority of members in both the House and the Senate as well as on the parliamentary committees that reviewed the bill. Thus, although there was considerable opposition from get-tough critics, including other political parties and some provincial governments, the Liberals' majority meant that they did not need to make compromises in order to get the YCJA passed. It is likely that a minority government would have compromised much more to accommodate the right wing, particularly since it often seems more politically popular to be seen as being tough on crime.

Two-Pronged Approach to Reform

The government took a two-pronged approach to youth justice reform. The new legislation would be tough on violent and serious repeat offenders through changes such as the new presumptive adult sentence provisions, but it would be soft on minor offenders through such changes as sentencing fewer minor offenders to custody. This approach allowed both the 'right' and 'left' in the youth justice field to find parts of the bill that they could support.

Size and Complexity of the Legislation

The size and complexity of the legislation was the focus of much criticism but may have helped in the passage of the YCJA. It was frequently pointed out that the YCJA was more than twice the length of the YOA, and it was often claimed that the YCJA was too complex and difficult to read. However, the youth justice process is, in fact, complex, and the many policy objectives and issues in a such a large statute made it difficult to characterize the whole Act in simple, media-friendly terms. Few people were totally supportive or totally opposed to it, in part, because of its size and the diversity of its issues, ranging from diverting minor offenders from court to deciding which youths should receive an adult sentence.

Parliamentary Witnesses

Although the final version of the YCJA was essentially the same as the original bill introduced three years earlier, witnesses before the parliamentary committees appear to have been important nevertheless. Witnesses who supported legal rights of youths and the need for restraint in the use of the system helped to counter the views of the get-tough critics. The 'rights and restraint' viewpoint and the Quebec perspective were important in demonstrating that there was not unanimity in the views of witnesses. The conflicting positions of opponents of the bill—seen as too soft by some and too harsh by others—tended to cancel each other out. They allowed the Liberals to claim that they were taking a balanced approach that was a reasonable middle ground in a highly contentious and complicated area of justice policy. After intense scrutiny and discussion for several years, it was clear that new youth justice legislation would not satisfy everyone.

Quebec

The most sweeping opposition to the YCJA came from the Bloc Québécois and numerous witnesses from Quebec. A major theme of their opposition was that the YCJA was too punitive. It was in the political interest of the Liberal government not to further antagonize Quebec by giving in to the opponents who wanted the YCJA to be made much harsher. The opposition from Quebec helped to counter the opposition from get-tough critics. Therefore, the efforts of Quebec opponents to defeat the YCJA played a significant role in ensuring that it became law and that it retained many provisions that were considered too lenient by right-wing critics.

Research and Statistics

Research and statistics played an important role in supporting many of the government's policy directions. Statistics supported the proposals for reducing the use of the court, increasing the use of extrajudicial measures, and reducing the over-reliance on incarceration. Research findings supported the emphasis on alternatives to custody and the exclusion of deterrence from the Act. Throughout the three years that the legislation was in Parliament, opponents of the YCJA did not produce credible statistics or research to counter the government's evidentiary basis for its proposals.

FACTORS THAT CONTRIBUTED TO THE ACHIEVEMENT OF THE YCJA'S POLICY OBJECTIVES

The factors discussed above help to explain why the YCJA was passed by Parliament, while the following factors help to explain why the YCJA, after coming into force, has achieved most of its policy objectives.

Clear Policy Objectives

Unlike the YOA, the YCJA is relatively clear in its policy objectives for the youth justice system and in addressing how the system needed to change. Although many factors can affect whether the objectives are achieved, it is presumably helpful to those working in the system to know what Parliament intended. Thus, while there is always room for interpretation and discretion in the application of the law, clarity in the policy directions has assisted decision-makers, including the Supreme Court of Canada. For example, in *R. v. C.D.; R v. C.D.K*, [2005], the Act's objective of reducing incarceration influenced the Supreme Court's decision to adopt a narrow interpretation of 'violent offence', which is one of the threshold criteria for a custody sentence.

Structuring Decisions

It appears that the YCJA's structuring of decisions through relatively strong and directive provisions helped to achieve legislative objectives. It is noteworthy that the most dramatic impacts have been achieved in the two areas in which the Act is most detailed in terms of decision-making rules—extrajudicial measures and custody sentences. In contrast, there is evidence to suggest that the objective of reducing pre-trial detention has not been achieved. Unlike extrajudicial measures and sentencing, the part of the Act dealing with pre-trial detention contains few new provisions and they are applied within the general and vague Criminal Code framework for adults. The limited impact of the pre-trial provisions suggests that reducing pre-trial detention may require provisions that are separate from the Criminal Code and more specific and directive in nature.

System-Wide Reform

The YCJA addresses all stages of the youth justice process. This system-wide scope allows a co-ordinated approach to reform. Changes at the front end of the system can have an impact on the achievement of back-end objectives. The extrajudicial measures provisions, in reducing the number of cases coming into the courts, may have helped to reduce the number of custody sentences. At a minimum, keeping youths out of the courts means that if they are later found guilty of an offence, they will have no criminal record or a shorter record. The YCJA sentencing provisions allow judges to take account of prior findings of guilt, and the research suggests that a youth's criminal record was a primary factor in judges' decisions to impose custody under the YOA (Carrington & Moyer, 1995).

A New Statute Rather Than Amendments

By passing a new statute instead of amending the YOA, the government made it clear to youth justice professionals that the legislative changes did not simply tinker with the existing rules but rather heralded a fundamentally new approach to youth justice decision-making. For example, the sentencing principles were entirely different and much more specific than those under the YOA. This meant that much of YOA case law was no longer relevant and that judges, prosecutors, and defence counsel would have to change their thinking and practices regarding what constituted an appropriate sentence. In concluding that deterrence was not a sentencing objective under the YCJA, the Supreme Court of Canada stated: 'The *YCJA* created such a different sentencing regime that the former provisions of the *YOA* and the precedents decided under it, including the decision of the Supreme Court of Canada in *M.(J.J.)*, are of limited value. The focus must be rather on the relevant provisions of the new statute' (*R. v. B.W.P; R. v. B.V.N.*, [2006]).

Professional Education

Professional education was probably important for the effective implementation of the Act. The DOJ and the provinces/territories put considerable effort and money into educating the people, particularly professionals, who would be involved in implementing the YCJA. Although it is difficult to measure the impact of professional education, it is likely that educating judges, police, prosecutors, defence counsel, and probation officers promoted an understanding of the YCJA and increased the chances of more consistent application of the law and achievement of its objectives.

Funding

Funding of programs is essential to the implementation of youth justice legislation. For example, the recognition in law of new sentencing options or extrajudicial measures is of little value if the funds are not available to implement them. Unlike the experience under the YOA, the main FPT funding agreement was structured to encourage funds to be used by the provinces and territories in ways that were consistent with the YCJA's policy objectives. The increase in federal funding, although not as much as many provinces wanted, helped to enable the system to change, including shifting it away from the high use of custody and courts.

Length of the Reform Process

The long process of reform meant that the YCJA was under discussion in the youth justice field for several years before it was passed by Parliament. By the time it came into force, professionals working in the system were familiar with the legislative proposals and probably had a good understanding of the new policy directions. In addition, the long process of getting the bill through Parliament did not prevent the new federal funding, discussed above, from being transferred to the provinces. The FPT funding agreement was in place a few years before the Act came into force, thus allowing time for the increased funding to take effect and for the focus to shift to community-based alternatives.

Provincial Implementation

The provinces/territories had a large role in determining whether the YCJA policy objectives were achieved. The funding decisions by the provinces/territories are especially important because the provinces/territories, not the federal government, pay most of the youth justice system costs. Their decisions on programs, training, policies, and funding can make a significant difference at each stage of the youth justice process. Although there continues to be provincial variation in aspects of the system, the overall changes in the youth justice system in Canada suggest that provinces/territories have implemented the YCJA in ways that generally support its key policy objectives.

CRITICAL THINKING QUESTIONS

1. Should the level of youth crime be a measure of the success or failure of the Youth Criminal Justice Act? Why or not?

2. The YCJA emphasizes accountability, proportionality, and rehabilitation. What are the meanings of these terms and how do they relate to one another under the YCJA?

3. The YCJA legislative process reflects four long-standing and competing perspectives on youth justice reform: (1) increased harshness/'get tough'; (2) legal rights and restraint; (3) treatment/welfare of youth; (4) provincial control. Explain each of these perspectives. Which sectors or groups tend to be associated with these perspectives?

4. A significant factor in the continuing high use of pre-trial detention under the YCJA is the large number of detained youths who are charged with breaches of probation conditions and bail conditions. These breaches typically involve behaviour that would not be considered criminal if the conditions were not part of a court order (e.g., curfew violations, not attending school). Should the law permit pre-trial detention of youths charged with these offences? Why? If they were not allowed to be detained, what should be the response if they continue to breach conditions?

5. Should youth justice legislation permit a court to impose an adult sentence on a youth? If not, why not? If so, under what circumstances should the law permit a court to conclude that a youth should not be treated as a youth and should be sentenced as an adult? See section 72 of the Youth Criminal Justice Act, which can be found at the Department of Justice Canada website: http://laws-lois.justice.gc.ca/eng/acts/Y-1.5/index.html. See also the decision of the Supreme Court of Canada in *R. v. D.B.*, [2008] S.C.J. No. 25, which can be found at the Supreme Court of Canada website: http://www. scc-csc.gc.ca/decisions/index-eng.asp.

NOTES

1   Child welfare, which deals with abused and neglected children, is the responsibility of the provinces.

2   A conditional sentence of imprisonment essentially means that the offender is sentenced to a term of imprisonment, but that term can be served in the community subject to conditions. If a condition is violated, the offender may be imprisoned.

3   This conclusion is based on a review of all cases reported in Quicklaw's monthly report, *Youth Criminal Justice Netletter*, from April 2003 to November 2011.

REFERENCES

Bala, N., Carrington, P., & Roberts, J. (2009). Evaluating the Youth Criminal Justice Act after five years: A qualified success. *Canadian Journal of Criminology and Criminal Justice, 51*(2), 131–67.

Calverley, D., Cotter, A., & Halla, E. (2010). Youth custody and community services in Canada, 2008/2009. *Juristat, 30*(1), 1–35.

Canadian Centre for Justice Statistics. (2010a). *Incident-based crime statistics, by detailed violations and police services, 1998–2009.* Accessed via Beyond 20/20 Web Data Server at http://ccjsccsj.statcan.gc.ca/

———. (2010b). *Youth court statistics, guilty cases by type of sentence, 1991/92 to 2008/09.* Accessed via Beyond 20/20 Web Data Server at http://ccjsccsj.statcan.gc.ca/

———. (2010c). *Youth correctional services, average counts of young persons in provincial and territorial correctional services.* Accessed via Beyond 20/20 Web Data Server at http://ccjsccsj.statcan.gc.ca/

Carrington, P., & Moyer, S. (1995). Factors affecting custodial dispositions under the *Young Offenders Act. Canadian Journal of Criminology, 37*(2).

Dauvergne, M., & Turner, J. (2010). Police reported crime statistics in Canada, 2000. *Juristat, 30*(2), 1–37.

Department of Justice, Canada. (1998). *A strategy for the renewal of youth justice.* Ottawa: Department of Justice, Canada.

———. (1999, March 11). Minister of justice introduces new Youth Justice Law. Press release. Ottawa: Department of Justice, Canada.

———. (2002). *The Youth Criminal Justice Act: Summary and background.* Ottawa: Department of Justice, Canada.

Doob, A., & Cesaroni, C. (2003). *Responding to youth crime in Canada.* Toronto: University of Toronto Press.

———, & Sprott, J. (2004). Youth justice in Canada. In M. Tonry & A. Doob (Eds.), *Crime and justice: A review of research*

(Vol. 31, pp. 185–242). Chicago: University of Chicago Press.

———, & Webster, C. (2003). Sentence severity and crime: Accepting the null hypothesis. In M. Tonry (Ed.), *Crime and justice: A review of research* (Vol. 30, pp. 143–95). Chicago: University of Chicago Press.

Federal-Provincial-Territorial Task Force on Youth Justice. 1996. *A review of the Young Offenders Act and the youth justice system in Canada*. Ottawa: Department of Justice, Canada.

House of Commons. (2001, May 29). *Hansard*. http://www.parl.gc.ca/

Milligan, S. (2010). Youth court statistics 2009/10. *Justistat, 30*(2), 1–37.

Reitano, J. (2004). Youth custody and community services in Canada, 2002/03. *Juristat, 24*(9), 1–27.

Solomon, E., & Allen, R. (2009). *Reducing child imprisonment in England and Wales—lessons from abroad*. Prison Reform Trust. http://www.juvenilejusticepanel.org/resource/ items/l/e/lessons%20from%20 abroad%20httpwwwprisoreformtrust orgukstandardaspid=1933.pdf

Standing Committee on Justice and Human Rights, House of Commons. (2000). *Hansard*, 30 November 1999–29 March 2000. http://www.parl.gc.ca/

Standing Committee on Justice and Legal Affairs. (1997). *Reviewing youth justice*. Thirteenth Report of the Standing Committee on Justice and Legal Affairs. Ottawa: House of Commons. http://www.parl.gc.ca/

Standing Senate Committee on Legal and Constitutional Affairs. (2001). *Hansard*, 27 September 27–8 November 2001. http://www.parl.gc.ca/

CASE LAW

R. v. B. W.P; R. v. B. V.N., [2006] S.C.J. No. 27.

R. v. C.D.; R. v. C.D.K., [2005] S.C.J. No. 79.

R. v. D.B., [2008] S.C.J. No. 25.

R. v. S.S., [2007] O.J. No. 2552 (C.A.).

6

Aboriginal Justice Policy in Canada

Scott Clark and Tammy Landau

A frequently quoted passage from the report of the Aboriginal Justice Inquiry of Manitoba (1991) unequivocally sums up the relationship between Aboriginal people and the justice system:

> The justice system has failed Manitoba's Aboriginal people on a massive scale. It has been insensitive and inaccessible, and has arrested and imprisoned Aboriginal people in grossly disproportionate numbers. Aboriginal people who are arrested are more likely than non-Aboriginal people to be denied bail, spend more time in pre-trial detention and spend less time with their lawyers, and, if convicted, are more likely to be incarcerated.
>
> It is not merely that the justice system has failed Aboriginal people; justice has also been denied to them. For more than a century the rights of Aboriginal people have been ignored and eroded. (p. 1)

The Royal Commission on Aboriginal Peoples (RCAP) concurred in the Manitoba inquiry's findings and recommendations and was clear in extending the failure of the justice system to include Aboriginal peoples in Canada generally, not just those living in Manitoba. According to James MacPherson, a lawyer working for RCAP, a powerful message expressed by federal, provincial, territorial, and Aboriginal governments in the course of RCAP's consultations was that '[t]he current Canadian justice system, especially the criminal justice system, has failed the Aboriginal people of Canada—Indian, Inuit and Métis, on-reserve and off-reserve, urban and rural, in all territorial and governmental jurisdictions' (Royal Commission on Aboriginal Peoples, 1996, p. 27).

Almost all policies directed at Aboriginal peoples in Canada, including those concerned with criminal justice, are designed and implemented by federal, provincial, and territorial governments and a variety of related bodies. In the case of criminal justice, the related bodies include the Royal Canadian Mounted Police (RCMP), the Supreme Court of Canada, and, occasionally, as we will see, lower courts. This has resulted in a complex mix of complementarities, which occasionally lead to positive change, and contradictions, which more often have resulted in confusion and failure to address problems. Our focus in this chapter will be on policy-making by the government of Canada, the Supreme Court of Canada, and the Ontario Court of Justice together with the Ministry of the Attorney General of Ontario (which will henceforth in this chapter be referred to as the Attorney General of Ontario).

The federal government is ultimately responsible for setting policy in the area of criminal justice and Aboriginal peoples by virtue of its unique authority: first, in terms of its responsibility for the Criminal Code; and, second, because it has the highest degree of constitutional responsibility for Aboriginal peoples across the country. This responsibility is set out in several pieces of federal legislation, most notably the Indian Act, and is clearly reflected in section 35 of the Canadian Charter of Rights and Freedoms. The Ontario Court of Justice and the Attorney General of Ontario, which provide our example of provincial policy engagement, are engaged in the administration of justice, including the application of the Criminal Code (as are courts and offices of attorneys general in the other provinces and territories). The Supreme Court of Canada has an impact on Aboriginal issues through its rulings that bear directly on Aboriginal people in the criminal justice system. These rulings must be taken into account by trial courts and by all levels of government in policy-making.

Before proceeding, we must provide a brief explanation of the legal categorization of Aboriginal peoples. The Indian Act first came into force in 1876 and has since been amended numerous times. The Act refers only to Aboriginal people who are registered with the federal Department of Indian and Northern Affairs as having 'status'—that is, as being a member of a band, which is the federal government's formal administrative designation for Indian government. The existence of bands is linked to the granting of reserve lands to certain groups of Aboriginal people by the Crown during the course of Canada's history. 'Non-status' Indians are not entitled to register as having status under the Indian Act and therefore are not entitled to band membership and normally do not live in reserve communities. Inuit and Métis are not covered by the Indian Act and, like non-status Indians, do not benefit from federal government developmental and support programs to the same extent that First Nations people do who are registered as status Indians under the Indian Act.[1] At the same time, the Crown, represented primarily by the federal government, has fiduciary obligations to all Aboriginal peoples,[2] whereby it is obliged to interact with Aboriginal peoples in a manner that affirms the unique historical relationship and respects contemporary Aboriginal rights.[3]

A further point worth noting is that Aboriginal people in Canada, whether status, non-status, Métis, or (to a lesser extent) Inuit increasingly live in urban settings. According to Statistics Canada (2009a), 54 per cent of Canada's Aboriginal population lived in an urban centre in 2006. The stereotype of Aboriginal people living in isolated northern communities no longer holds true, a fact that has major implications for policy development in most social arenas, including criminal justice.

This chapter is structured in the following way. First, we address the overrepresentation of Aboriginal people in the criminal justice system as an indicator of the extent of the problems facing Aboriginal people in Canadian society generally and in the justice system specifically. Second, we identify the concept of systemic discrimination as a means of examining and analyzing problems in the relationship between the criminal justice system and Aboriginal people. The explanatory tool of systemic discrimination provides us with certain themes that we will follow through the chapter. Next we examine three specific policy initiatives that have been implemented to address the problems: (a) amendments to the Criminal Code regarding the sentencing of Aboriginal offenders, together with the subsequent Supreme Court of Canada ruling in *R. v. Gladue*; (b) the establishment of the Gladue (Aboriginal Persons) Court in Toronto by the Ontario Court of Justice and the Attorney General of Ontario; and (c) the federal Aboriginal Justice Strategy, to date the most comprehensive attempt to design and implement policies and programs aimed at alleviating the stresses between the criminal justice system and Aboriginal people. As part of the examination of the three policy initiatives, we discuss their effectiveness and impacts. We conclude the chapter with suggestions for change.

OVERREPRESENTATION: THE EXTENT OF THE PROBLEM

The failure of the criminal justice system for Aboriginal people is manifested in many ways, perhaps most notably in the extreme overrepresentation of Aboriginal individuals as incarcerated offenders. In its 2008/09 annual report, the Office of the Correctional Investigator made the following comment:

> It is distressing to note that despite many well intentioned efforts and reforms to address the plight of Aboriginal people in the criminal justice system, the incarceration rate for Aboriginal people has increased from 815 per 100,000 in 2001/02 to 983 per 100,000 in 2005/06. Aboriginal rates of incarceration are now almost nine times the national average. One in five federally incarcerated offenders is a person of Aboriginal ancestry. Among women offenders, the overrepresentation is even more dramatic—an astounding 32% of women in federal penitentiaries are Aboriginal. (2009)

Statistics Canada (2009b) has provided data that expand on the overrepresentation issue. In 2007/08 Aboriginal adults accounted for 22 per cent of admissions to sentenced custody in federal, provincial, and territorial correctional institutions.[4]

Yet they represented only 3 per cent of the total Canadian population. The proportion of Aboriginal adults in provincial and territorial institutions continues to increase relative to non-Aboriginal adults. Between 1998/09 and 2007/08, the proportion increased from 13 to 18 per cent for males and from 17 to 24 per cent for females. Rates of incarceration of adult Aboriginal offenders vary by province and territory, as do the proportions of Aboriginal inmates compared to the relative proportions of Aboriginal people in the general population. In 2007/08, according to Statistics Canada, 'in Quebec the representation of Aboriginal adults in provincial and territorial sentenced custody is two times their representation in the province's general population. In Saskatchewan, the representation is seven times greater' (2009b, p. 9). The same report also notes that '[a]mong the provinces, the representation of Aboriginal adults in custody was higher in the west. For example, in Saskatchewan, Aboriginal adults represented 81% of the admissions to provincial sentenced custody while they represent 11% of the general population in this province' (p. 5).

Similarly, incarceration rates for Aboriginal youth are significantly higher than for non-Aboriginal youth. In 2005/06, Aboriginal youth represented 31 per cent of admissions to sentenced custody and 23 per cent of admissions to remand. However, they accounted for only 6 per cent of Canada's youth population (Statistics Canada, 2008). As Doob and Sprott (2007) have shown, comparative youth incarceration rates and sentence lengths vary by jurisdiction, at least in urban settings. The fact remains, however, that Aboriginal youth—like their adult counterparts—are overrepresented in the criminal justice system generally and in corrections in particular.[5]

One of the immediate effects of over-incarceration is the negative impact on incarcerated individuals. Landau (2006), for example, has described the dire conditions of the territorial jail in Iqaluit, Nunavut. Almost all the inmates are Inuit (reflecting Nunavut's 85 per cent Inuit population). Overcrowding is a serious problem, and there is essentially no programming, particularly for the two-thirds of the inmate population who are in custodial remand.[6] Offenders who come from distant communities accessible only by air are not visited by their families, and once released, offenders often have difficulty returning to their home communities. Other problems—such as gang recruitment in jails in the western provinces—are major concerns. However, it is unrealistic to expect otherwise until the incarceration rate of Aboriginal offenders declines significantly and Aboriginal people, especially younger people, are given educational and employment opportunities equal to those of the non-Aboriginal population.

Aboriginal people are overrepresented as offenders, as victims, and in correctional facilities. The overrepresentation figures are both startling and an effective indication that relations between Aboriginal people and the justice system are seriously flawed. In the words of the Supreme Court of Canada, '[t]he figures are stark and reflect what may fairly be termed a crisis in the Canadian criminal justice system.'

SYSTEMIC DISCRIMINATION: A FRAMEWORK FOR ANALYSIS

There are many specific examples of overrepresentation, and they occur throughout the justice system. The Supreme Court of Canada noted the following in its judgment in *R. v. Gladue*:

> Not surprisingly, the excessive imprisonment of aboriginal people is only the tip of the iceberg insofar as the estrangement of the aboriginal peoples from the Canadian criminal justice system is concerned. Aboriginal people are overrepresented in virtually all aspects of the system. As this Court recently noted in *R. v. Williams*, [1998] 1 S.C.R. 1128, at para. 58, there is widespread bias against aboriginal people within Canada, and '[t]here is evidence that this widespread racism has translated into systemic discrimination in the criminal justice system'.[7]

In this forthright statement the Supreme Court justices referred to an important concept: systemic discrimination. When considering explanations for Aboriginal overrepresentation, or for any specific problem regarding the justice system and Aboriginal people, it is useful to think about this concept. Dickson-Gilmore and La Prairie define discrimination (for our purposes, 'systemic discrimination') as tending 'to arise from the unconscious implementation of structures or policies which were not intended to be discriminatory but which, owing to the manner in which they interact with larger social structures, have a negative impact on members of certain groups' (2005, p. 55). The Aboriginal Justice Inquiry of Manitoba provides a similar definition: 'The term "systemic" discrimination is used where the application of a standard or criterion, or the use of a "standard practice," creates an adverse impact upon an identifiable group that is not consciously intended' (1991, p. 100). Negative comparisons and systemic discrimination can be seen in all phases of the criminal justice system, including policing, courts, and corrections. It is a problem that affects not only Aboriginal people, but also other racialized and minority groups, as demonstrated, for example, by the Commission on Systemic Racism in the Ontario Criminal Justice System (1995).

Why are Aboriginal people overrepresented as offenders and victims? And why does systemic discrimination exist in the criminal justice system? The Royal Commission on Aboriginal Peoples identified two viable explanations, each of which has a degree of currency in government thinking and academic literature: socio-economic marginality and colonialism.

The first, socio-economic marginality, refers to structural problems that lead to the social and economic marginality of Aboriginal people. Even a basic investigation leaves no doubt that Aboriginal individuals and entire communities are marginalized in Canada. The median income in 2006 for Canada's non-Aboriginal population was $33,394, while the median income for the total Aboriginal population was $22,366 and for First Nations people $19,114 (Statistics Canada, 2010).[8] As well, Aboriginal employment rates were significantly lower than the non-Aboriginal rate for the same period: 81.6 per cent for the non-Aboriginal population compared to 65.8 per cent for the total Aboriginal population and 60.4 per cent for First Nations people (Statistics Canada, 2010). Employment rates in remote and isolated Aboriginal communities are significantly lower than the overall Aboriginal employment rates, which include urban Aboriginal people, who are more likely to have jobs.

Compounding the problem of relatively low income and employment rates is a host of other unacceptable social and living conditions facing Aboriginal people, especially those living in remote and isolated areas. Many authors, agencies, and inquiries have documented seriously substandard levels of housing, education, and health care for Aboriginal communities. In 2006, the proportion of First Nations dwellings requiring major repairs was 45 per cent, compared to 7 per cent for the non-Aboriginal population. While 25 per cent of the non-Aboriginal population between 25 and 54 years of age had attained a university degree by 2006, the comparative numbers for the Aboriginal population were 7 per cent (First Nations), 9 per cent (Métis), and 4 per cent (Inuit).[9]

The high rates of tuberculosis currently seen in Aboriginal communities are significant indicators of the effects of socio-economic marginalization—a combination of poverty, poor housing, and poor health care. According to Health Canada, '[s]tudies have shown that First Nation people are more at risk than other Canadians of getting TB infection. Some of the root causes are related to poor socio-economic conditions where they live' (Health Canada, 2010). A further indicator of structural social and economic marginality is the high rate of suicide among Aboriginal people, especially youth. In a 2007 report published by the Aboriginal Healing Foundation, the authors write that while the suicide rate for the Canadian population has declined, the rates among Aboriginal people have increased. They state that the suicide rate among Inuit is '6 to 11 times higher than the general population' (Kirmayer, Brass, Holton, Paul, Simpson, & Tait, 2007, p. xv).

And finally, we see that social and economic marginalization, which includes the problems noted above, also contributes to the overrepresentation of Aboriginal people in the criminal justice system. In the words of RCAP,

> Cast as a structural problem of social and economic marginality, the argument is that Aboriginal people are disproportionately impoverished and belong to a social underclass, and that their over-representation in the criminal justice system is a particular example of the established correlation between social and economic deprivation and criminality. . . . There is no doubt in our minds that economic and social deprivation is a major underlying cause of disproportionately high rates of criminality among Aboriginal people. (1996, p. 42)

RCAP's other viable explanation for Aboriginal overrepresentation in the criminal justice system has to do with the colonial experience.[10] According to RCAP, 'The relationship of colonialism provides an overarching conceptual and historical link in understanding much of what has happened to Aboriginal peoples' (1996, p. 47). RCAP also noted that colonialism is a historical relationship characterized by 'particular and distinctive historical and political processes that have made Aboriginal people poor beyond poverty' (p. 46). A relatively early explanation of the links between colonialism and overrepresentation was contained in a 1988 report prepared by Michael Jackson for the Canadian Bar Association. In that report, Jackson spoke of a colonial relationship whereby cultural alienation, territorial dispossession, and social-economic marginalization became increasingly pronounced among Aboriginal peoples. According to Jackson, '[t]his process of dispossession and marginalization has carried with it enormous costs of which crime and alcoholism are but two items on a long list' (Jackson, 1988, p. 218). In other words, the impacts of colonialism have contributed in significant ways to the overrepresentation of Aboriginal people in the criminal justice system.

POLICY DEVELOPMENT: ATTEMPTS TO ADDRESS THE IMPACTS OF SYSTEMIC DISCRIMINATION

We will now turn to some of the policies that have been designed and implemented with a view to addressing problems arising from systemic discrimination. Again, we will look at three examples: first, changes in the Criminal Code regarding sentencing introduced by the government of Canada and subsequently elaborated upon by the Supreme Court of Canada; second, the establishment of the Gladue (Aboriginal Persons) Court in Toronto by the Ontario Court of Justice and the Attorney General of Ontario; and, third, the federal Aboriginal Justice Strategy. A common aim of all three initiatives has been to reduce the overrepresentation of Aboriginal people in the criminal justice system. As we examine the three cases, we will consider the impacts that systemic discrimination arising from socio-economic marginalization and colonialism has on existing conditions and on the effectiveness of the initiatives.

Sentencing Policy and Aboriginal People

In 1996, the government of Canada introduced the first comprehensive set of Criminal Code amendments regarding sentencing. As Rudin points out, before the amendments came into force 'sentencing was the exclusive purview of judges who balanced the principles of deterrence, denunciation, incapacitation, and rehabilitation in their own personal fashion, subject only to appellate review' (2007, pp. 40–1). The amendments, reflected in section 718 of the Criminal Code, introduced a degree of restriction on judges' decision-making by imposing legislated sentencing guidelines. The primary aim of the amendments was to reduce the frequency of carceral sentences imposed by Canadian courts.

The most significant element of the amendments, as far as Aboriginal people are concerned, was section 718.2(e): 'A court that imposes a sentence shall also take into consideration the following principles: . . . (e) all available sanctions other than imprisonment that are reasonable in the circumstances should be considered for all offenders, with particular attention to the circumstances of aboriginal offenders.' Perhaps especially with respect to Aboriginal people, the federal government wanted to tackle the problem of over-incarceration in its sentencing reforms.

Rudin points out that '[a]s with much legislation, the actual meaning of section 718.2(e) remained somewhat vague until the Supreme Court of Canada released its decision interpreting the section in 1999 in the case of *R. v. Gladue*' (2007, p. 42). The *Gladue* appeal arose from a sentencing decision handed down by a trial court judge in British Columbia in the case of Jamie Gladue, an Aboriginal woman convicted of murder. The sentence, which involved incarceration and probation, was appealed on the grounds that the trial judge had not adequately considered the circumstances and heritage of the offender as an Aboriginal person according to section 718.2(e). The judge's decision was based, in part, on the notion that because Ms. Gladue lived in an urban setting and not in a reserve community, she was estranged from her Aboriginal heritage and way of life. The judge therefore concluded that Ms. Gladue was not subject to section 718.2(e) whereby all reasonable and available sanctions other than imprisonment should be considered for all offenders, especially Aboriginal offenders. The British Columbia Court of Appeal upheld the ruling of the trial court judge, and the case then went to the Supreme Court of Canada.

In its response to the appeal, the Supreme Court left no doubt as to its position regarding Aboriginal overrepresentation and section 718.2(e):

> These findings [regarding Aboriginal overrepresentation] cry out for recognition of the magnitude and gravity of the problem, and for responses to alleviate it. The figures are stark and reflect what may fairly be termed a crisis in the Canadian criminal justice system. The drastic overrepresentation of aboriginal peoples within both the Canadian prison population and the criminal justice system reveals a sad and pressing social problem. It is reasonable to assume that Parliament, in singling out aboriginal offenders for distinct sentencing treatment in s. 718.2(*e*), intended to attempt to redress this social problem to some degree.[11]
>
> It arises also from bias against aboriginal people and from an unfortunate institutional approach that is more inclined to refuse bail and to impose more and longer prison terms for aboriginal offenders.

The Supreme Court's judgment was progressive. It added weight to the government's concerns about Aboriginal overrepresentation, and affirmed the underlying principle and general guidance in section 718.2(e). The court also recognized the roles played by poverty, marginalization, and systemic discrimination in the overrepresentation of Aboriginal people. Significantly, the court's judgment supported the idea—contrary to the British Columbia trial court judge—that Aboriginal people in urban areas, as well as in reserve communities and more remote and isolated areas, should be considered under section 718.2(e).

The Supreme Court recognized the importance of sentencing alternatives for both Aboriginal and non-Aboriginal offenders. In the Aboriginal context, alternatives are generally categorized under the umbrella 'restorative justice.' As noted in the quote above, the court referred to 'restoring a sense of balance to the offender, victim, and community, and in preventing future crime.' This is very much a restorative approach to dealing with crime. However, as Roach and Rudin point out, '[a]lthough the court recognized the congruence between restorative justice and aboriginal justice, it also realized that such programmes are relatively rare and stressed the need to consider all possible alternatives to imprisonment for aboriginal offenders even if those alternatives do not have a cultural component' (2000, p. 356).

The lack of adequate restorative justice programming is addressed in the mandate of the Department of Justice Canada (Justice Canada) through its Aboriginal Justice Strategy, our third example of policy development presented later in the chapter. Suffice it to say at this point, the availability of viable, community-based restorative justice programming does not meet the levels conceived by the Supreme Court. In the absence of such alternatives, Aboriginal offenders continue to be sent to jail at significantly higher rates than non-Aboriginal offenders. Roach and Rudin (2000) predicted one year after the *Gladue* judgment that while it was positive in many respects, it was not likely to reduce the rate of incarceration of Aboriginal offenders, a prediction that appears to have been accurate. As noted above in our discussion of overrepresentation, while Aboriginal people represent only 3 per cent of the total Canadian population, the proportion of Aboriginal adults in provincial and territorial institutions continued to increase substantially relative to non-Aboriginal adults between 1998/99 and 2007/08, the period immediately following the Supreme Court's judgment in *Gladue*. Why is this so?

While the Supreme Court in *Gladue* was progressive in some respects, it was less helpful in others. Rudin notes that the court stated that section 718.2(e) did not automatically mean an Aboriginal person would receive a lesser sentence, and it further said that when convicted for a serious violent offence, an Aboriginal person would likely receive the same sentence as a non-Aboriginal offender.[12] As Rudin points out, '[i]n the subsequent case of *R. v. Wells*—a conditional sentencing case—the court continued to send some mixed messages as to the impact of s. 718.2(e) in cases of violence' (2007, p. 43). According to Anand, '[i]f one of the functions of the Supreme Court is to clarify the law and provide effective guidance to lower courts, then *Gladue* is a failure' (2000, p. 414). Rudin continues with the following regarding vagueness in the *Gladue* judgment:

What the court did not do in *Gladue* was to indicate to a sentencing judge how she was to obtain the information she needed to sentence according to the new provisions found in the *Criminal Code*. It was not clear how a legal system that had contributed to the over-incarceration of Aboriginal people was suddenly to reconstitute itself to redress the same problem that it had a hand in creating. (2007, p. 43)

It is not unusual for Supreme Court rulings to be written in a relatively general manner, at which point governments and the lower courts are left to assign practical meaning and manage the realities on their own. In the case of the *Gladue* ruling, this is precisely what happened in Toronto on the initiative of the Ontario Court of Justice, as described later in our next example of policy development. Other jurisdictions have not been so effective in adapting to *Gladue*.

Other, perhaps more serious, concerns have been raised with respect to the *Gladue* judgment. In referring to a 2001 article by Stenning and Roberts, the editors of the *Saskatchewan Law Review* describe the authors' view of the *Gladue* judgment as 'bad criminal justice policy' (Board of Editors, 2002, p. 1). Stenning and Roberts (2001) make three main points. First, they maintain that Aboriginal overrepresentation does not derive from discriminatory sentencing practices, as assumed by Parliament when it passed section 718.2(e) as part of the sentencing provisions. Rather, they say, overrepresentation stems from a complex variety of factors, including higher offending rates because of socio-economic marginalization and discrimination in other areas of the criminal justice system such as policing, a point corroborated by Dickson-Gilmore and La Prairie (2005, p. 42). It is these problems that must take priority over sentencing, according to Stenning and Roberts. Second, they argue that the Supreme Court's *Gladue* judgment loses sight of the important ideal of parity in sentencing. They say that other groups, such as African-Canadians in Ontario, also suffer from socio-economic marginalization and systemic discrimination, but that *Gladue* aims to give Aboriginal offenders preferential consideration, a development that contradicts the parity ideal. While this assertion has been debated at length, one's view may depend on how section 718.2(e) is read: are other groups adequately recognized in the first part of the clause, or do the final nine words give unequal recognition to Aboriginal offenders? Third, Stenning and Roberts argue that the alternatives to which the court vaguely refers are essentially non-existent (a point also recognized by most other authors). Often judges are thus left in a quandary when trying to adhere to the intent of *Gladue*. These factors lead Stenning and Roberts to conclude that section 718.2(e) and the *Gladue* judgment combined to create 'empty promises' for Aboriginal people and that neither the legislation nor the judgment would result in a decrease in Aboriginal overrepresentation. The latter assessment is consistent with the view of Roach and Rudin (2000) and the ongoing incarceration rates noted above.

The article by Stenning and Roberts elicited considerable reaction, primarily in the *Saskatchewan Law Review*, where it was published (Brodeur, 2002; Cairns,

2002; Daubney, 2002; Rudin & Roach, 2002). These critiques were followed by a rejoinder by Roberts and Stenning (2002). We will not review the debate in detail, but will identify some particular points that continue to be problematic with respect to Aboriginal sentencing and over-incarceration.

There is a danger, identified by Roach and Rudin (2001), that section 718.2(e) and *Gladue* might result in net widening for Aboriginal offenders. Their concern is that judges might choose to apply conditional sentences as an alternative to imprisonment in instances where a less serious sanction might have been ordered prior to the arrival of section 718.2(e) and *Gladue*. As Roach and Rudin explain, '[c]onditional sentences, however, can result in net widening if they are ordered in cases where less intrusive sanctions would ordinarily have been ordered. . . . There are real grounds for concern that conditional sentences are resulting in net widening as judges apply them to offenders who would not normally have been subjected to actual imprisonment' (2000, p. 369).

The use of a conditional sentence is more serious than commonly understood. It is not a probationary sentence, but a prison sentence of under two years to be served in the community under certain conditions set by a judge.[13] The breaching of the conditions associated with such a sentence could automatically lead to the actual incarceration of the offender for the remainder of his or her term. If Roach and Rudin are right and judges are applying conditional sentences when they would normally have handed down a less serious sentence, such as a probation order, a fine, or a suspended sentence, then net widening is occurring in terms of more serious sentences. The upshot, according to Roach and Rudin, is that '[a]t the most basic level, it is clear that prison populations have not decreased to the same extent as conditional sentences have been ordered. With over 28,000 conditional sentences being ordered in their first two years of existence, prison populations have not been reduced to nearly the same extent' (2000, p. 369).

A related concern is that judges may impose a conditional sentence of greater duration than they might have if they had handed down a sentence of actual incarceration at the outset. This is especially concerning in light of the fact that Aboriginal offenders, especially in the western provinces, are disproportionately likely to breach their conditions. The result may be that when Aboriginal offenders are sent to prison for the remainder of their sentence after a breach, they may be incarcerated longer than if they had been sent to prison in the first place.

The problem of breaching conditions, whether linked to fine payment, probation orders, or conditional sentences, is a serious one for Aboriginal offenders, and it is largely tied to social and economic marginalization. Dickson-Gilmore and La Prairie (2005) argue that Aboriginal people are at higher risk of offending, reoffending, and breaching conditions because of their relative marginality in Canadian society. This marginality is characterized by the problems noted earlier in the chapter: poverty, unemployment, low educational attainment, poor housing, and poor mental and physical health. Dickson-Gilmore and La Prairie are careful to note that the severity of these conditions and the degree of Aboriginal marginality vary among different groups and in different parts of the country. In this connection, they discuss the emergence of a growing 'Aboriginal underclass', comprising mainly registered Indians living in reserve communities (2005, pp. 35–6). Relatively speaking, this group is the most disadvantaged among all Aboriginal groups in the country and therefore at greatest risk. Overall, however, Dickson-Gilmore and La Prairie confirm that social and economic marginality resulting from a history of living the colonial experience contributes to Aboriginal people's higher risk of offending, reoffending, and breaching conditions. In the case of conditional sentences, this means a disproportionate likelihood of being sent to jail.

Have the policies represented by the Criminal Code amendment in the form of section 718.2(e) and the subsequent Supreme Court judgment in *Gladue* had their intended effects? Certainly, the scale of the problem of Aboriginal over-incarceration was recognized and the relevant motivation was present. Government and judicial support for the concept of alternatives to incarceration—restorative justice—was strongly indicated. However, not much appears to have changed. Aboriginal offenders continue to be incarcerated at levels significantly higher than non-Aboriginal offenders. Judges have relatively little recourse to sentencing alternatives at the community level. Net widening through the use of conditional sentences and the breaching of conditions are still serious potential problems. And the question of parity in sentencing raised by Stenning and Roberts is an issue that remains unresolved and continues to be debated.

Perhaps the difficulty lies in the intersection of two realities: first, the enormous scope of the problem and, second, and the limitations of the justice system, whether through Criminal Code amendments or Supreme Court decisions, in coming to grips with the fundamental issues underlying Aboriginal overrepresentation. The Royal Commission on Aboriginal Peoples, among many others, has shown us that overrepresentation stems from the colonial experience and from social and economic marginality. The resulting conditions facing Aboriginal people as a whole create a higher risk of their being involved in the system as offenders or victims. These are the fundamental problems that must be addressed in a comprehensive and proactive way. Perhaps then the policy changes introduced by the minister of justice and the Supreme Court will have greater impact.

The Gladue (Aboriginal Persons) Court in Toronto

Toronto's Gladue Court is a policy success story. The court was born of a need to design ways to apply section 718.2(e), a problem that, almost two years after the *Gladue* judgment, was still problematic for judges. The Aboriginal population in the census metropolitan area of Toronto is young and growing, according to Statistics Canada: 'In 2006, 26,575 Aboriginal people lived there, a 31% increase from 2001' (Statistics Canada, 2009c, p. 5).[14] In view of the size of Toronto's Aboriginal population and recognizing that section 718.2(e) and the *Gladue* judgment were motivated by a serious problem and were aimed in the right direction, the Ontario Court of Justice and the Attorney General of Ontario established the country's first and, to date, only Gladue Court, or Aboriginal Persons Court, at Old City Hall in downtown Toronto. Since then, Gladue Courts have been established in two additional Toronto locations, as well as one in Sarnia, and Gladue caseworkers now prepare reports for courts in Toronto, Hamilton, Brantford, Kitchener-Waterloo, Milton, and Guelph.

The main aim of the court is to adhere to section 718.2(e) and thereby keep Aboriginal offenders out of jail if this were to be at all reasonable and possible. The primary challenges facing the judges are these: knowing when an accused person is, in fact, Aboriginal; knowing the background and circumstances of an offender as an Aboriginal person; and knowing what alternatives to incarceration might be possible and reasonable for the individual offender. When the court was established, judges needed help with these questions and Gladue caseworkers became an invaluable resource in providing that help. Pre-trial detention was a particularly serious issue requiring attention. Justice Knazan of the Ontario Court of Justice (2003) points to the recognition by those working in the criminal courts that once an individual has been imprisoned for a pre-trial period, the likelihood is higher that she or he will also receive a custodial sanction at sentencing. Judges may not be aware that they can be influenced by the fact of pre-trial detention (which assumes a greater risk of some form) and subsequently imposes a sentence involving further prison time. Higher rates of pre-trial detention for Aboriginal accused, particularly in view of a lack of appropriate community-based pre-trial alternatives, may then translate into an increased likelihood of custodial sentences. The Gladue Court, primarily through the work of the caseworkers, has attempted to address this problem.

Justice Knazan (2003) notes that the court stressed four key approaches to trying to adhere to section 718.2(e): identification of Aboriginal accused as Aboriginal; resources in the form of professionals expert in the area, including *Gladue* caseworkers who could provide the judge with essential background information on individuals and make the links to communities and community resources for purposes of providing alternatives; bail (and, by extension, the reduction of pre-trial detention); and courtroom atmosphere, by which the court made certain physical and process modifications to make Aboriginal offenders and victims feel less traumatized while in court. We will focus on bail as an important aspect of the Gladue Court's innovative approach. The question of bail is also useful for our purposes because it relates directly to issues we discussed earlier regarding section 718.2(e) and the *Gladue* decision.

In its examination of Manitoba courts, the Aboriginal Justice Inquiry of Manitoba identified the denial of bail and pre-trial detention as concurrent problems commonly facing Aboriginal accused (1991, pp. 221–4, 360–1).[15] The commissioners noted that, according to analyses of provincial court data, Aboriginal men and especially women were significantly more likely to spend time in pre-trial detention than non-Aboriginal accused. A major reason for the difference was the higher likelihood that an Aboriginal accused would be denied bail. This view was also held by the Supreme Court in *R. v. Gladue*.[16] However, to the extent that unequal denial of bail and pre-trial detention are realities, at least in some jurisdictions, the causes of the problems lie in underlying practices. When a judge or justice of the peace makes a decision regarding bail and pre-trial detention, she or he considers the following basic questions: "'Is this a dangerous person?" and "Is this a person who can be trusted?'" (Aboriginal Justice Inquiry of Manitoba, 1991, p. 100; see note 14). The Manitoba commissioners point out that while these questions are important, they are 'inherently subjective' (1991, p. 100). They are subjective in the sense that the information required by the decision-maker contains a bias that often works against the accused Aboriginal person. For example, information regarding education, employment, income, and permanent residency, which is typically sought from the accused, generally favours non-Aboriginal individuals, who are significantly more likely than Aboriginal accused to have completed a certain level of education, have a job, earn a steady income, and have a permanent residence in the area where the alleged offence was committed. Thus, bail is less likely to be granted to Aboriginal accused than to their non-Aboriginal counterparts. Consequently, according to the Manitoba commissioners, pre-trial detention is more common for Aboriginal accused.

The Gladue Court judges recognized the problems with bail and pre-trial detention identified by the Manitoba inquiry and the fact that nowhere does the Criminal Code specifically address the question of bail for Aboriginal offenders. However, as Justice Knazan says, '[a]ll the same, the Toronto Gladue Court addresses the particular circumstances of Aboriginal offenders at the bail hearing as an important part of considering "all available sanctions other than imprisonment that are reasonable in the circumstances" as s.718(2)(e) requires' (2003, p. 11). This is a significant policy decision by the court, one premised on the realization, noted by Knazan, that '[a]s any lawyer knows . . . the bail hearing becomes the most important proceeding because a detention order will effectively pre-determine the sentence as one of imprisonment. . . . Pre-trial detention is an obstacle to applying s.718(2)(e) and *R. v. Gladue* because imprisonment occurs before the judge can fulfill her role of considering the unique circumstances of Aboriginal offenders' (2003, pp. 11–12). The Gladue Court took its justification for its policy directly from the Supreme Court's judgment in *Gladue* when it said in paragraph 65 that Aboriginal over-incarceration is the result of a number of factors, including 'bias against Aboriginal people and from an unfortunate institutional approach that is more inclined to refuse bail and to impose more and longer prison terms for Aboriginal offenders.'[17] The Gladue Court's creative approach to bail decisions enables it to adhere more closely to the intent of section 718.2(e) and the *Gladue* judgment. Simply stated, the court gives consideration to granting bail when most other courts would not (Knazan, 2003, pp.13–14).

One of the Manitoba inquiry's 'inherently subjective' factors in decision-making regarding bail is the ability of the accused person to pay the cost of bail—to provide a surety. For Aboriginal people, who are less likely to be employed or to have an income and who are often alienated from family and community, making bail is a real problem. Pre-trial detention is almost inevitably the result in many courts. In Gladue Court, however, every effort is made to accommodate individuals who cannot provide a surety by assessing the individual's risk and by developing a pre-trial release plan. Bail is not guaranteed, but it is a real possibility for those who qualify by the standards set by the court. The court now has an Aboriginal Bail Program supervisor who is associated with the Toronto Bail Program and who interviews and screens accused without sureties for eligibility for release. The Toronto Bail Program agreed to adapt its guidelines so that Aboriginal persons without a surety, including those with histories of failing to appear in court, can be considered for supervision. And, as Justice Knazan points out in an update to his 2003 paper, '[t]here is enough community commitment that the Court can consider some innovative conditions of release, such as daily reports by cellphone, house arrest in shelters and twice weekly appearances in court' (2005, p. 5). Release plans are carefully monitored by court staff.

Pre-trial detention or remand is a serious problem across the country for both Aboriginal and non-Aboriginal accused. Up to 60 per cent of admissions to provincial or territorial jails are remands, while approximately 40 per cent are sentenced individuals. This places significant stress on the correctional system, as well as on the individuals in remand. As Rudin says, '[t]he importance of release on remand cannot be stressed. Numerous studies have shown that those held in custody on remand are more likely to plead guilty and be found guilty than those who are released pending trial' (2007, p. 53).

Typically, Aboriginal people are placed in custodial remand because they have a higher rate of failure to appear for court hearings. This is not surprising given their difficult backgrounds and marginal living conditions discussed elsewhere in this chapter. However, the opportunity to be granted bail and avoid pre-trial detention as offered by the Gladue Court and the Toronto Bail Program has been a positive development for many Aboriginal accused in Toronto. Knazan and Rudin, as well as a three-year evaluation by an independent consultant (Campbell Research Associates, 2008), confirm that the assessment, planning, and monitoring process instituted by the Gladue Court is effective. The court's bail program has the added benefit of removing some pressure from Toronto's overcrowded jails. Finally, and perhaps most significantly, the bail program contributes to the Gladue Court's achievement of its overall goal to adhere to section 718.2(e) by helping Aboriginal people stay out of jail.

The success of the Toronto Gladue (Aboriginal Persons) Court is interesting for several reasons. It adheres to the principles underlying section 718.2(e) and set out in the Supreme Court's *Gladue* decision. Implicit in this approach is the recognition that Aboriginal people have been subjected to a colonial experience that has left a highly disproportionate number of them in conditions of social and economic marginality. The Gladue Court is aware that these realities have made Aboriginal people more likely to be at risk of offending, reoffending, failing to appear in court, and being incarcerated. These are substantial problems, of course. But is it especially significant in this case that effective policy decisions were made, not at the level of the government of Canada or the Supreme Court, but at a relatively local level by a small number of players working as judges in the Ontario Court of Justice and other engaged professionals. They have implemented policy changes that are making a positive difference for Aboriginal people in Toronto.

The Aboriginal Justice Strategy

In 1991, the government of Canada implemented a five-year Aboriginal Justice Initiative (Department of Justice Canada, 2010b). The initiative's home was Justice Canada, although it was established as a cost-sharing program with provincial and territorial governments. Its main purpose was to support community-based justice projects such as diversion programs, community involvement in sentencing, and mediation and arbitration processes for civil disputes. In 1996, the government renewed and expanded the initiative and changed its name to the Aboriginal Justice Strategy (AJS). In 2002, the AJS was renewed for a further five years, and in 2007, it was renewed until 2012. The AJS is the primary and most comprehensive federal policy with respect to Aboriginal people and criminal justice.[18]

According to Justice Canada, '[t]he Aboriginal Justice Strategy (AJS) is a response to the well documented fact that Aboriginal Canadians are over-represented in the justice system both as victims and offenders' (Department of Justice Canada, 2010a). Justice Canada has identified the overall objectives of the AJS as follows:

- To help reduce crime and incarceration rates in Aboriginal communities with community-based justice programs;
- To increase the involvement of Aboriginal communities in the local administration of justice;
- To provide better and more timely information about community justice programs funded by AJS; and
- To reflect and include Aboriginal values within the justice system. (Department of Justice Canada, 2010a)[19]

In this part of the chapter, we will focus on whether the objectives of the AJS are relevant to the needs and aspirations of Aboriginal communities and whether the AJS is making a positive contribution to the problems facing Aboriginal people in the criminal justice system. Our immediate challenge, however, is that there has been little research either on the effectiveness of the AJS or on community-based justice alternatives in Canada. The following analysis is therefore somewhat theoretical, while recognizing the need for intensive primary information collection and evaluative research at the community level.

Justice Canada notes that during the 2008/09 fiscal year, the AJS funded 124 programs that served approximately 400 Aboriginal communities. Funded projects continue to vary somewhat in terms of specific purpose and structure; however, they all reside within the restorative justice rubric. In the North, for example, community justice committees are funded to carry out a variety of functions, including family group conferences, elder counselling, and spousal mediation. Sentencing circles and healing circles continue to be supported in other regions.

Is this approach effective? Justice Canada would have us believe it is. The final report of the summative evaluation of the AJS dedicates the paragraph below to conclusions on the question 'To what extent have community-based programs had an impact on crime rates in the communities where they are implemented?' Recall that this question refers to one of the four main objectives of the AJS. The conclusion reads as follows: 'Individuals who participate in the AJS programs are more likely to get rehabilitated than those who are sent into the mainstream justice system. The recidivism study conducted in support of this evaluation indicates that offenders who participate in AJS-funded programs are approximately half as likely to re-offend as are offenders who do not participate in these programs' (Department of Justice Canada, 2007, p. 47).[20]

Yet why are rates of Aboriginal overrepresentation still so high? As the following pages indicate, there are some who have been critical of the AJS itself. For example, referring to earlier evaluations of the AJS that paint a rather bleak picture of federal efforts to resolve justice issues, Dickson-Gilmore and La Prairie make the following point:

> What is clear in even these most recent evaluations is that we continue to implement essentially similar policies and approaches, all of which seem to maintain the same, remarkably unspectacular outcomes, and we continue to fail to address the underlying assumptions upon which those policies rest. As long as we continue to stand firm in our current direction, without looking closely at what we are standing upon, very little is likely to change in regard to Aboriginal people and justice, community or otherwise. (2005, p. 217)

The concern expressed by Dickson-Gilmore and La Prairie raises questions, beginning with the way one defines 'community'. They note that community has typically been defined as some variation on the theme of 'sociality, time and space', where people interact in a certain identifiable area over a certain time period. But, as Dickson-Gilmore and La Prairie explain, each of these concepts is in itself vague. Further, they point out that community is often defined to suit the needs of a researcher for purposes of information collection and analysis, or government for administrative reasons (2005, pp. 5–7). These are top-down approaches to defining community that often do not serve the interests of the community itself. Proulx attributes this hegemonic approach to defining community to 'historically and geographically specific colonial discourses and practices', including legislation such as the Indian Act (2003, p. 152). The alternative is a bottom-up definition 'which recognizes that communities are self-defined by people as a reflection of their local interactions and participation' (BC Resources

Community Project, 1998, p. 3; quoted in Dickson-Gilmore & La Prairie, 2005, p. 8). In other words, people are capable of defining themselves as a community according to the criteria that matter most to them. Further, the community—not a researcher or government officials—is best able to identify its needs, aspirations, and appropriate approaches to addressing problems. The community must, at the very least, be directly engaged with government in defining issues and creating innovative solutions, although the lack of meaningful engagement between federal government departments and Aboriginal communities has been documented many times (e.g., Dickson-Gilmore & La Prairie, 2005; Proulx, 2003; Warry, 1998; Ross, 1996).

This is a critical point for many reasons. Consider, for example, the relevance of culture in federal justice policy development. The problem of Aboriginal over-representation in the system is seen to exist, in large part, because the dominant justice system is socially and culturally out of step with the needs of Aboriginal people and the dynamics of Aboriginal communities. In response, governments (the federal government, in particular) and related organizations such as the RCMP claim to have initiated 'culturally relevant' or 'culturally appropriate' community-based alternatives as an effective way to address problems. The AJS, for example, is replete with references to Aboriginal culture and values. However, for such claims to be valid, it is essential for funding bodies such as Justice Canada to take very seriously the proposals developed by communities and community-based groups. In every case, discussion must take place and culturally relevant justice alternatives supported if reasonable. Regrettably, this has not always happened, and until recently, the literature (e.g., Dickson-Gilmore & La Prairie, 2005) and Aboriginal communities and groups expressed the concern that the government's top-down approach prevented the initiation of culturally relevant and effective community-based alternatives.

On a more positive note, it appears that Justice Canada, since the initiative began in 1991, has improved in its ability to enter into effective dialogue with provincial and territorial governments and with the Aboriginal communities and community groups proposing alternative justice programs. In past years, it was clear that not only was Justice Canada failing to enter into meaningful engagement with communities, but to varying degrees it was imposing its misunderstanding of culturally relevant programming on communities. Ironically, perhaps, the misunderstanding was based to some extent on the idea that 'culturally relevant' was synonymous with 'traditional' as understood by Justice Canada. It appears the department has learned more recently that the essential question is this: what approaches would best meet the needs of communities, whether traditional, non-traditional, completely new, or an amalgam? Cultures change, a fact that characterizes all cultures. Governments and Aboriginal communities alike would do well to accept this reality and understand that 'traditional' or ill-defined 'culturally appropriate' policies and programs will not necessarily meet the needs and aspirations of Aboriginal communities.

Is the AJS achieving its objectives? While a full answer to this question would require more space than we have in this chapter, it is fair to say that Justice Canada has improved its approach to consulting with communities and community groups and to supporting effective community-based programs. However, the rates of overrepresentation of Aboriginal people in the criminal justice system continue to be astoundingly high. Why is this so?

The first reason is fairly obvious. If we accept that the AJS is contributing positively to effective community-based alternatives and if we also accept that AJS-funded programs reduce recidivism rates, then why isn't the federal government substantially increasing the budget of the AJS to allow the number of funded programs to expand beyond the 124 funded in 2008/09? Indeed, it is uncertain at this point that the AJS will be renewed at all in 2012. Such policy decisions are made at the highest levels of the government of Canada, including the Privy Council Office and the Treasury Board.

Two other problems with regard to policy and practice negatively affect the development of community-based alternatives and the reduction of overrepresentation. First—and this is a serious critique of the mainstream justice system—the system often fails to support the attainment of community goals by not doing its part to make the intersections between Aboriginal communities and the dominant system work effectively. Second, the apparent unwillingness of the federal government to address fundamental factors underlying Aboriginal overrepresentation in the criminal justice system continues to be a major impediment to solving the problem.

With regard to the first point, we see instances of the dominant system not fulfilling its essential responsibilities in making the intersection of dominant approaches and AJS-funded community alternatives viable. For example, we have witnessed occasions where a long-standing and effective Community Justice Committee has been shut out of the business of rehabilitating young offenders simply because a newly arrived RCMP detachment commander did not agree with the concept of restorative justice and therefore would not divert pre-charge cases to the local committee (although restorative justice was claimed to be a fundamental aspect of RCMP policy). The irony in this example is that Community Justice Committees receive funding support from the AJS, which, like the RCMP, is a federal government institution. Similarly, we have witnessed a judge referring a man convicted of spousal assault to a Community Justice Committee for 'traditional counselling' as part of his probation order when, in fact, the committee was not at all prepared to deal with such offenders. The judge acknowledged never having spoken with the local committee about what they could and would take on. The mainstream justice system must fulfill its part of the bargain if innovative community-based approaches are to work. The mainstream system is, after all, still the dominant system. New approaches will only work if the dominant system allows them to proceed and works closely with communities (Clark, 2011). This will change only under exceptional circumstances in the development of self-government, circumstances that include a significant degree of Aboriginal autonomy in the administration of justice.

Even more serious is the social and economic marginality of Aboriginal people in Canada. Earlier in this chapter we addressed the unacceptably high rates of poverty and unemployment and the substandard levels of housing, education, and health care currently experienced in Aboriginal communities. Again, in the words of the Royal Commission on Aboriginal Peoples, '[t]here is no doubt in our minds that economic and social deprivation is a major underlying cause of disproportionately high rates of criminality among Aboriginal people' (1996, p. 42). Similarly, the Supreme Court of Canada recognized the extent of the problem in *Gladue*: 'It is clear that sentencing innovation by itself cannot remove the causes of aboriginal offending and the greater problem of aboriginal alienation from the criminal justice system. The unbalanced ratio of imprisonment for aboriginal offenders flows from a number of sources, including poverty, substance abuse, lack of education, and the lack of employment opportunities for aboriginal people.'[21]

Like the decision to sustain the AJS, policy decisions required to address issues of marginalization are largely the responsibility of the federal government. However, while the government continues to address those issues through various departments (e.g., Aboriginal Affairs and Northern Development Canada; Health Canada), its efforts never seem to be enough. Social and economic marginality remains a critical problem, and rates of overrepresentation continue to rise. We believe that the failure to effectively address this challenge through a comprehensive strategy is the single most important policy issue with regard to the overrepresentation of Aboriginal people in the criminal justice system. Adequate resources must accompany such a strategy, and open and in-depth consultations with Aboriginal communities and organizations are needed. The problems will not be resolved quickly, in part because they have developed over many years and in part because they are so serious. But the government of Canada, together with provincial and territorial governments and Aboriginal communities and organizations, must make reversing the marginalization of Aboriginal people a policy priority.

CONCLUSION

The design and implementation of Aboriginal criminal justice policy in Canada continues to face major challenges. Rates of overrepresentation of Aboriginal people in the system are still extremely high, and systemic discrimination is an ongoing reality. Yet we have seen improvements. The legislated amendments to the Criminal Code, in recognizing how unequal life chances contribute to offending and victimization among Aboriginal people, as well as in recognizing the value of sentencing alternatives, were significant advances in federal policy. Similarly, the expanded recognition of the same realities by the Supreme Court of Canada in *Gladue* was major step forward. The fact that the sentencing amendments and *Gladue* stimulated the creation of the successful Gladue Courts in Toronto is testament to their importance in the effort to reduce the overrepresentation and over-incarceration of Aboriginal people.

The overall achievement of Justice Canada's Aboriginal Justice Strategy is less certain. There is no doubt that many projects funded by the AJS have been successful. Officials managing the AJS have recognized in recent years that a genuinely active engagement of Aboriginal communities in policy and program design and implementation is essential if local justice alternatives are to be effective. However, if the AJS has indeed evolved into an effective supporter of viable community alternatives, then the higher-level policies of the federal government should include the strategy's continuation and an increase of its resources.

The role of the mainstream justice system is an additional area of concern. Given that the system will continue to be dominant, it is important to ensure the intersections between the mainstream structures, such as police and courts, and Aboriginal communities remain viable. The mainstream structures have important roles to play, and they must work to fulfill those roles. Similarly, communities must strive to make the arrangements work from their side.

Underlying any policy development with respect to Aboriginal peoples in Canada are fundamental issues of social and economic marginalization. Thanks to the conclusions drawn by many experts and expert bodies, such as the Royal Commission on Aboriginal Peoples, we know that poverty and unequal life chances contribute to the overrepresentation of Aboriginal people in the criminal justice system. Overcoming those historic and persistent challenges should be the first goal of governments and Aboriginal organizations and communities. Significant progress toward the achievement of that goal will finally set the conditions whereby justice policy will truly be able to make positive and long-lasting changes for Aboriginal people.

CRITICAL THINKING QUESTIONS

1. Discuss the various models that have been used to account for Aboriginal overrepresentation in the criminal justice system. Which model do you think accounts best for the unacceptably poor social and economic conditions of Aboriginal people in Canada? Give reasons to support your answer.

2. How is section 718.2(e) designed to address Aboriginal overrepresentation in the criminal justice system? Does it threaten the concept of parity in sentencing for all Canadians? Give reasons to support your answer.

3. There is increasing evidence of systemic discrimination against many racialized groups in the Canadian criminal justice system, resulting in their overrepresentation at various points in the process. Do you think it might be valuable to apply any of the approaches to Aboriginal overrepresentation in that context? Why or why not? Give specific reasons to support your argument.

4. Would it be desirable, or even possible, to establish one or more Aboriginal justice system completely separately from the mainstream justice system in Canada?

5. What government policies would you change or implement in order to address the overrepresentation of Aboriginal people in the criminal justice system in Canada?

NOTES

1 'Indian' is employed in this description of the Indian Act, as it is the legal term used in the legislation. However, status and non-status Indians are now generally referred to as First Nations people.

2 'Fiduciary' is a legal term referring to 'one who holds anything in trust' or 'who holds a position of trust or confidence with respect to someone else'. In this case, the Crown is in a fiduciary position—a position of trust—with respect to Aboriginal peoples. As such, the Crown is obliged to use its rights and powers for the benefit of Aboriginal peoples.

3 Two Supreme Court of Canada cases defining the fiduciary obligations of the Crown with respect to its responsibilities under the Charter of Rights and Freedoms are *Guerin v. R.*, [1884] and *R. v. Sparrow*, [1990].

4 The essential difference between federal and provincial/territorial carceral sentences is the length of the sentence. Federal sentences are for two years or more, while provincial/territorial sentences are for a maximum of two years less one day.

5 Statistical data should be viewed with caution. It is notoriously difficult to ensure the accuracy of census counts of Aboriginal people and even more difficult in terms of crime-related data. Statistics Canada (2005) has acknowledged the challenges. That said, Statistics Canada provides the best available data and the most useful for our purposes here.

6 The related issues of bail, pre-trial detention, and custodial remand are discussed in detail later in this chapter.

7 *R. v. Gladue*, [1999] 1 S.C.R. 688, para. 61.

8 According to Statistics Canada, '[m]edian total income includes earnings from all sources including employment income as well as government transfers. The median income is the middle value where half of the specified population earns more and half the population earns less' (Statistics Canada, 2010).

9 It is worth noting that the employment and educational attainment figures for the Aboriginal population may be inflated because of the difficulty in surveying Aboriginal people. It is possible that Statistics Canada achieved a disproportionately high response rate from Aboriginal individuals who had a job or a university degree compared to those who did not.

10 The colonial experience for Aboriginal peoples from the time of early French and British contact has been characterized by attempts by the colonial powers to control Aboriginal lands and natural resources. Many mechanisms of colonial control have been imposed, including violent relocation and restrictive legislation (most famously through the Indian Act). Some authors (e.g., Proulx, 2003) refer to colonialism and post-colonialism as part of the same process through history to the present.

11 *R. v. Gladue*, para. 64.

12 Ibid., para. 79.

13 Amendments to the Criminal Code introduced by the minister of justice in 2005 removed certain categories of offence from the possibility of being considered for a conditional sentence. Those offences include all serious personal injury offences as defined in the Criminal Code, such as all forms of sexual assault.

14 These figures will be substantially higher now and, in fact, were probably unrealistically low in 2006 owing to difficulties in identifying and counting Aboriginal people in the city.

15 Pre-trial detention is also known as custodial remand. A judge or a justice of the peace can deny a bail application and order pre-trial detention on the basis of any one of the three following criteria established in the Bail Reform Act of 1972, codified in section 515 of the Criminal Code, and modified more recently: (a) to ensure the attendance of the accused in court; (b) to ensure the protection or safety of the public and to protect against criminal offences before the trial; and (c) to maintain confidence in the administration of justice.

16 *R. v. Gladue*, para. 65.

17 Ibid.

18 Further renewal is uncertain at the time of writing.

19 The third of the four AJS objectives— 'To provide better and more timely information about community justice programs funded by AJS'—may or may not be successfully achieved; however, it is not included in our analysis.

20 The authors of the evaluation admit that the recidivism study had methodological limitations; however, for present purposes, we can accept the study's general findings.

21 *R. v. Gladue*, para. 65.

REFERENCES

Aboriginal Justice Inquiry of Manitoba. (1991). *Report*. Vol. 1: *The justice system and Aboriginal people*. Winnipeg: Queen's Printer.

Anand, S. (2000). The sentencing of Aboriginal offenders, continued confusion and persisting problems: A comment on the decision in *R. v. Gladue*. *Canadian Journal of Criminology*, 42(3), 412–20.

BC Resources Community Project. (1998). Geography Department, University of Northern British Columbia, Prince George, BC.

Board of Editors. (2002). Colloquy on 'Empty promises: Parliament, the Supreme Court, and the sentencing of Aboriginal offenders'. *Saskatchewan Law Review*, 65(1), 1–2.

Brodeur, J-P. (2002). On the sentencing of Aboriginal offenders: A reaction to Stenning and Roberts. *Saskatchewan Law Review*, 65(1), 45–52.

Cairns, A. (2002). Seeing and not seeing: Explaining mis-recognition in the criminal justice system. *Saskatchewan Law Review*, 65(1), 53–62.

Campbell Research Associates. (2008). Evaluation of the Aboriginal Legal Services of Toronto Gladue Caseworker Program. http://aboriginallegal.ca/docs/Year_3.pdf

Clark, S. (2011). The Nunavut Court of Justice: An example of challenges and alternatives for communities and for the administration of justice. *Canadian Journal of Criminology and Criminal Justice*, 53(3), 343–70.

Commission on Systemic Racism in the Ontario Criminal Justice System. (1995). *Final Report*. Ontario: Queen's Printer.

Daubney, D. (2002). Nine words: A response to 'Empty promises: Parliament, the Supreme Court, and the sentencing of Aboriginal offenders'. *Saskatchewan Law Review, 65*(1), 35–43.

Department of Justice Canada. (2007). *Aboriginal Justice Strategy summative evaluation: Final report*. Ottawa: Department of Justice Canada.

———. (2010a). Department of Justice Canada Aboriginal Justice Strategy: Funding guide. http://www.justice. gc.ca/eng/pi/ajs-sja/pub/guide.html

———. (2010b). The Aboriginal Justice Strategy. http://www.justice.gc.ca/eng/pi/ajs-sja/index.html

Dickson-Gilmore, J., & La Prairie, C. (2005). *Will the circle be unbroken? Aboriginal communities, restorative justice, and the challenges of conflict and change.* Toronto: University of Toronto.

Doob, A.N., & Sprott, J.B. (2007). The sentencing of Aboriginal and non-Aboriginal youth: Understanding local variation. *Canadian Journal of Criminology and Criminal Justice, 49*(1), 109–23.

Health Canada. (2010). First Nations, Inuit and Aboriginal health: Tuberculosis (TB). http://www.hc-sc.gc.ca/fniah-spnia/diseases-maladies/tuberculos/index-eng.php

Jackson, M. (1988). *Locking up Natives in Canada: A report of the Canadian Bar Association Committee on imprisonment and release.* Ottawa: Canadian Bar Association.

Kirmayer, L.J., Brass, G.M., Holton, T., Paul, K., Simpson, C., & Tait, C. (2007). *Suicide among Aboriginal people in Canada.* Ottawa: Aboriginal Healing Foundation.

Knazan, Judge B. (2003). *Sentencing Aboriginal offenders in a large city—the Toronto Gladue (Aboriginal Persons) Court.* Paper presented at the National Judicial Institute Aboriginal Law Seminar, Calgary.

Knazan, Judge B. (2005). *The Toronto Gladue (Aboriginal Persons) Court: An update.* Paper presented at the National Judicial Institute Aboriginal Law Seminar, St. John's.

Landau, T. (2006). Plus ça change? 'Correcting' Inuit Inmates in Nunavut, Canada. *Howard Journal of Criminal Justice, 45*(2), 191–207.

Office of the Correctional Investigator. (2009). *Annual report of the Office of the Correctional Investigator 2008–2009.* http://www.oci-bec.gc.ca/rpt/annrpt/annrpt20082009-eng.aspx#2.6

Proulx, C. (2003). *Reclaiming Aboriginal justice, identity, and community.* Saskatoon: Purich Publishing.

Roach, K., & Rudin, J. (2000). *Gladue:* The judicial and political reception of a promising decision. *Canadian Journal of Criminology, 42*(3), 355–88.

Roberts, J.V., & Stenning, P. (2002). The sentencing of Aboriginal offenders in Canada: A rejoinder. *Saskatchewan Law Review, 65*(1), 75–95.

Ross, R. (1996). *Returning to the teachings.* Toronto: Penguin.

Royal Commission on Aboriginal Peoples. (1996). *Bridging the cultural divide: A report on Aboriginal people and criminal justice in Canada.* Ottawa: Minister of Supply and Services Canada.

Rudin, J. (2007). *Aboriginal peoples and the criminal justice system.* Report prepared for the Ipperwash Inquiry (Ontario).

———, & Roach, K. (2002). Broken promises: A response to Stenning and Roberts' 'Empty promises'. *Saskatchewan Law Review, 65*(1), 3–34.

Statistics Canada. (2005). *Collecting data on Aboriginal people in the criminal justice system: Methods and challenges.* http://www.statcan.gc.ca/pub/85-564-x/85-564-x2005001-eng.pdf

———. (2008). Youth custody and community services in Canada, 2005/2006. *Juristat, 28*(8). http://www.statcan.gc.ca/pub/85-002-x/85-002-x2008008-eng.pdf

————— (2009a). 2006 Census: Aboriginal peoples in Canada in 2006: Inuit, Métis and First Nations, 2006 Census. http://www12.statcan.gc.ca/census-recensement/2006/as-sa/97-558/p3-eng.cfm

—————. (2009b). The incarceration of Aboriginal people in adult correctional services. *Juristat, 29*(3). http://www.statcan.gc.ca/pub/85-002-x/2009003/article/10903-eng.pdf

—————. (2009c). *2006 Aboriginal Population Profile for Toronto.* http://www.statcan.gc.ca/pub/89-638-x/2009001/article/10825-eng.pdf

—————. (2010). *Aboriginal statistics at a glance.* http://www.statcan.gc.ca/bsolc/olc-cel/olc-cel?lang=eng&catno=89-645-X

Stenning, P., & Roberts, J.V. (2001). Empty promises: Parliament, the Supreme Court, and the Sentencing of Aboriginal Offenders. *Saskatchewan Law Review, 64*(1), 137–68.

Warry, W. (1998). *Unfinished dreams: Community healing and the reality of Aboriginal self-government.* Toronto: University of Toronto Press.

LEGISLATION CITED

Bail Reform Act, S.C. 1970–71–72, c. 37.

Constitution Act, 1982, being Schedule B to the *Canada Act 1982* (UK), 1982, c. 11.

Criminal Code (R.S., 1985, c. C-46).

Indian Act (R.S., 1985, c. I-5).

CASES CITED

Guerin v. R., [1984] 2 S.C.R. 335.

R. v. Gladue, [1999] 1 S.C.R. 688.

R. v. Sparrow, [1990] 1 S.C.R. 1075.

R. v. Wells, [2000] 1 S.C.R. 207.

R. v. Williams, [1998] 1 S.C.R. 1128.

7

Domestic Violence and Problem-Solving Courts

E. Jane Ursel

In 1990 the first specialized domestic violence (DV) criminal court was introduced in Winnipeg, Manitoba, amidst quite a bit of controversy. Judges and defence lawyers decried such an imposition, while women's organizations and shelter workers applauded the innovation. In 1997 Ontario followed suit, and today there are seven jurisdictions—Newfoundland, New Brunswick, Ontario, Manitoba, Saskatchewan, Alberta, and the Yukon—with domestic violence courts in operation (Ursel, Tutty, & LeMaistre, 2008). These changes provide an interesting case study in policy initiatives that changed the administration of justice across Canada. How did such a controversial policy come to be seen as a natural evolution in the administration of the courts within a decade? This chapter will situate domestic violence courts within the larger trend toward problem-solving courts and examine why the policy of specialized DV courts has gained such momentum in the past few years. In addition, it will consider what problems these courts were designed to address and how successful the courts have been in dealing with the identified problems. Because each province has structured its specialized court quite differently, I will provide some comparative analysis; however, for a detailed description of court operations and outcomes, I will use the Winnipeg Family Violence Court (FVC) as a case study.

POLICY CHANGE: REDEFINING DOMESTIC VIOLENCE

Until the mid-1980s, wife abuse was perceived by most Canadians as a personal tragedy rather than a serious crime (MacLeod, 1980). The redefinition of wife abuse from personal tragedy to social problem has its origins in the feminist movement of the late 1960s and early 1970s. The feminist movement's rallying cry—'The personal is political'—opened all forms of women's subjugation to social and political analysis, revealing gender inequalities and leading to demands for reform. Violence against women emerged as a central concern in the early 1970s when grassroots women's organizations established emergency shelters for abused women, being the first to do so. Over time the concept of wife abuse broadened to include same-sex relationships, common-law relationships, and so on, and the term 'domestic violence' came to be more frequently used.

By the 1980s, Canadian society was beginning to acknowledge that domestic violence was a serious social issue and some specialized programs, such a shelters and transition houses, started to receive government funding. At the same time attorneys general across Canada began to issue policy directives to police, advising them that in cases of domestic abuse 'where there were reasonable and probable grounds that a crime had occurred, charges should be laid, regardless of the relationship between the victim and the accused' (Ursel, 1991, p. 268). These directives were designed to change the predominant police practice at the time, which was to *not* make an arrest or lay charges when called to a domestic assault incident. This charging policy was a direct response to criticism by women's groups and shelter workers whose clients told them time and again that they had called the police but 'nothing happened'.

The charging directive laid the groundwork for more comprehensive changes within the criminal justice system (CJS). Arrest data provided communities, for the first time, with concrete and calculable measures of the incidence of domestic violence. While shelter workers had for years identified the pervasiveness of wife abuse, their claims were often dismissed as anecdotal. Rising police arrest rates, however, provided a measure that could not be so easily dismissed. Not surprisingly, the arrest rates for domestic assaults began a steady rise in every jurisdiction in which charging directives were issued and implemented. In Winnipeg, for example, 629 individuals were arrested for a domestic assault in 1983, the year the directive was issued, while the number had increased to 1,200 in 1989 (Ursel, 1991). Importantly, increased numbers resulted in increased visibility in the courts. Court reporters began to notice these cases and became aware of how differently domestic violence cases were resolved compared to other criminal matters. As court reporters began to write about these cases, the public visibility of domestic violence increased, and this in turn had a major impact on public awareness and public attitudes. The following are some examples of the press coverage in Winnipeg: 'Days of Terror Net Suspended Term', *Winnipeg Sun*, 18 December 1987; 'Wife Abuser's Jail Sentence to be Appealed', *Winnipeg Free Press*, 8 February 1990; 'Woman Terrified of Husband—Out of Jail in 8 Weeks', *Winnipeg Sun*, 7 February 1990; 'Justice—More or Less—Two Cases Point Out Vast Gap in Sentencing', *Winnipeg Sun*, 16 February1990.

Within two weeks in February 1990, three articles in two Winnipeg newspapers decried the inadequacies of the courts in dealing with domestic violence matters. Newspaper articles reinforced the ongoing lobbying by women's organizations. Press coverage of DV cases provided the evidence used by opposition politicians during question period in the legislature. In short, a directive to lay charges made a previously 'invisible' crime visible and domestic violence became a political issue. On 15 September 1990, the Winnipeg Family Violence Court was opened. The sequence of events that directed attention to the courts in Manitoba was quite similar to that in Ontario.

> On March 8, 1996—International Women's Day—Arlene May, a 39-year old mother of five, was shot to death in her Collingwood, Ontario, home by her ex-boyfriend Randy Isles, who then killed himself. The next day, on March 9, 1996, the *Toronto Star* launched its award-winning, eight part series that examined society's response to spousal abuse. What the *Star* reporters concluded upon completing their investigation was that the criminal justice system was not responding to spousal abuse, at least not in any meaningful way, nor had it ever seemed to do so. (Dawson & Dinovitzer, 2008, p. 120)

In 1996, the Ontario government announced that Toronto would have the first two DV courts in the province, one at Old City Hall (K-Court) and the other in North York. One year later, additional DV courts were implemented in Brampton, Hamilton, London, North Bay, Oshawa, and Ottawa. In 2001, the Ontario government made a commitment to introduce DV court programs in all of its 55 court jurisdictions (Dawson & Dinovitzer, 2008).

THE LIMITS OF THE TRADITIONAL JUSTICE SYSTEM

The demand for court specialization was based on the assertion that the traditional paradigm of the CJS was ill-equipped to respond to domestic violence cases. Critiques of the CJS highlighted a number of assumptions and policies within the system that confounded attempts to adjudicate domestic violence matters. A primary concern was that the CJS 'is organized around discrete incidents and official investment in incidents is shaped by their legal seriousness and probabilities of conviction . . . but domestic violence typically involves multiple incidents, sometimes of escalating seriousness, with little physical evidence and few witnesses' (Worden, 2000, p. 233). Second, because of the adversarial nature of the criminal justice process, it is assumed that 'both sides' are committed to winning 'their case'—that is, that the victim has the same interest as the Crown attorney in public conviction, punishment, and rehabilitation. However, victims of domestic violence have diverse motivations for seeking CJS intervention (Ford & Regoli, 1993; Ursel, 1998b, 2002). Third, many victims face collateral legal issues such as divorce, custody, and child support proceedings. In short, DV cases typically involve a process rather than a discrete incident. They are complex and messy rather than being straightforward evidentiary matters.

Historically, measures of success within the CJS have been one-dimensional, focusing on outcome rather than process and mired in single-incident frameworks. This tended to lead to a non-interventionist attitude in DV cases. Police are not motivated to arrest because nothing happens when they do—the case is stayed. Prosecutors are discouraged from proceeding because the victim is ambivalent about testifying and they don't have much evidence beyond victim testimony. As a result of these attitudes, many cases never got to court and those that did were not resolved to anyone's satisfaction, as indicated by the press coverage, cited above, and in the literature (Ursel, 1998a; Worden, 2000; Dawson & Dinovitzer, 2008). However, given the complexity of DV cases, determining a better intervention model was a challenge.

At the time DV courts were being introduced in Canada, a number of US states were exploring models of specialization frequently referred to as problem-solving courts (Ptacek, 1999; Casey, 2004). As a result, the advocates for change began to diversify. Lobbying by women's organizations and press coverage still played important roles in pressing for reform within the CJS, but legal practitioners began to join the voices for change. While judges and Crown attorneys working in specialized courts don't lobby, they do speak to their colleagues. Judges and prosecutors from different provinces visited Winnipeg and Toronto to see the courts in action. Data collected from the Winnipeg Family Violence Court were being shared across Canada (Ursel, 2000). In the United States, specialization took the form of problem-solving courts and judges were often the innovators of change: '[Judges] are excited about this not because they are re-engineering the world, but because they feel they are exercising a meaningful role as a judge' (Chief Judge Judith Kay of the New York Court of Appeals, cited in Lane, 2003, p. 956).

The combination of different pressures on government— internally from judges and prosecutors and externally from lobby groups and the press—often reached a critical threshold when tragic DV incidents or homicides occurred. Between 1999 and 2010, specialized DV courts steadily grew in number across Canada, while problem-solving courts proliferated in the United States. The specialized courts were attempting to structure a better response to the challenges that DV cases presented. The problems articulated across North America were the same.

1. Despite the charging directives issued in the early 1980s, service providers and researchers continued to document police reluctance to charge in DV cases (Ferraro, 1989; Jaffe, Wolfe, Telford, & Austin, 1986).
2. When police did arrest, prosecutors were often reluctant to proceed because of the ambivalence of the victim and the fact that they were usually the only witness (Worden, 2000).
3. In the rare cases where an accused was arrested, prosecuted, and convicted, the sentences were inappropriately light given the nature of the crime. For example, the most frequent disposition in Winnipeg courts

prior to specialization was a conditional discharge (Ursel & Hagyard, 2008).

4. Finally, and most importantly, there was a serious 'lack of fit' between the complex reality a victim was contending with and the one-dimensional operation of a traditional criminal court. This 'disconnect' not only drove the demand for a different type of court but has continued to challenge the CJS to intervene in a just and effective manner that does not re-victimize the victim.

REDEFINING JUSTICE: DOMESTIC VIOLENCE AND PROBLEM-SOLVING COURTS

Practitioners in the social service and justice systems were facing a dilemma. There prevailed a strongly held belief that domestic violence must be treated as a crime in order to protect the victims, yet the outcomes of criminal justice interventions were woefully inadequate. Concurrently, across North America, advocates and practitioners were identifying similar problems in courts dealing with offenders who were addicted to drugs or were mentally ill. On the face of it there doesn't seem to be a lot in common among drug addicts, spouse abusers, and the mentally ill, but court personnel were seeing these cases recycle regularly through court; clearly, the traditional penalties and/or rehabilitation programs imposed at sentencing were perceived to be having no effect. The judiciary's frustration with the revolving door of justice experienced by these chronic reoffenders was evident:

> I think the innovation that we're seeing now is the result of judges processing cases like a vegetable factory. Instead of cans of peas, you've got cases. You just move 'em, move 'em, move 'em. One of my colleagues on the bench said: 'You know, I feel like I work for McJustice: we sure aren't good for you, but we are fast. (Chief Justice Kathleen Blatz, cited in Lane, 2003, p. 955)

Out of this frustration, the Miami–Dade County Drug Court opened in 1989. This innovative and specialized court linked drug-addicted offenders to judicially monitored treatment. The court's approach was to prioritize treatment, monitoring, and rehabilitation. Drug treatment courts changed the role of the judge from neutral arbitrator and trier of fact to a participant in an interdisciplinary treatment team. Courts such as this call upon judges to use their judicial authority to motivate individuals to accept needed services, and to monitor their compliance and progress (Winnick, 2003). The monitoring occurs through judicial review, a requirement that offenders appear before the sentencing judge on a regular basis to account for their behaviour while in treatment. Winnick (2003) identifies this practice as a problem-solving court, stating: 'These cases require the courts to not only resolve disputed issues of fact, but also to attempt to solve a variety of human problems that are responsible for bringing the case to court' (p. 1055). This concept, referred to as therapeutic jurisprudence, has provoked a debate about whether the use of judicial authority to coerce an offender to accept treatment is a violation of due process (Casey, 2004). Notwithstanding this debate, there have been no court challenges, to date. Perhaps the defendants' acceptance of this model of intervention is facilitated by the fact that the heavy hand of justice which pressures them into treatment is balanced with their ability to avoid incarceration, if they comply. Problem-solving courts typically impose treatment as an alternative to jail: 'The difference in cost between treatment court and traditional adjudication is almost entirely due to the costs of incarceration' (Casey, 2004, p. 1486).

This concept of justice expanded rapidly across North America. The combined effect of disaffected citizens, outraged press, and a frustrated judiciary created fertile ground for problem-solving courts. By 2008, there were more than 2,500 problem-solving courts in the United States, including drug courts, DV courts, and mental health courts (Wolf, 2009). Typically these courts have been implemented where existing social or legal institutions have failed to stop the cycle of recurrent offending behaviour. These courts reject the single-incident framework of traditional courts, focusing instead on the history of the individual or couple in an attempt to develop an intervention strategy to change the offending behaviour.

As the concept of problem-solving courts expanded to different jurisdictions and to the adjudication of different crimes, variations in operation were introduced. For example, drug courts and mental health courts tend to focus primarily on the offender, while DV courts have a dual frame of reference, the victim and the accused. Thus, in DV courts, it is typically the case that a substantial component of the multidisciplinary team focuses on victim needs and support. In addition, DV courts vary in their approach to offender monitoring: some courts have judicial review and others rely on very assertive monitoring from community corrections. Despite the variety in court operations, DV courts are clearly situated in the problem-solving court model—that is, they approach the issue with a wide lens, a multi-disciplinary team, and a focus on ending the revolving-door effect of chronic reoffending.

CANADIAN DV COURTS: COMMON PROBLEMS— DIFFERENT SOLUTIONS

Because the Canadian Criminal Code is federal and criminal charges are the same across the country, one might expect that the structure and administration of specialized DV courts would also be the same across Canada. However, the administration of provincial courts, which hear the majority of the DV cases, is the responsibility of the provinces. This makes it possible for each province, often each city, to design its DV court according to the characteristics of the community it serves. Some courts emphasize rigorous prosecution, with a very strong focus on enhanced evidence collection, while others are focused on diversion and early intervention. Thus, the implementation of DV courts are a product of pragmatic matters like volume and court caseloads, as well as policy-makers' and practition-ers' views of the most effective design for the outcome they want to achieve. Although there is marked variation in DV courts across Canada, there are some standard components that are typically associated with problem-solving and DV court:

1. *A system for identifying domestic cases in order to stream them into a different court process.* This occurs at the police level and is often associated with some form of specialized DV unit within the police service.
2. *Separate court rooms or, in smaller jurisdictions, separate days in which all mat-ters before the court are DV cases.*
3. *Specialized prosecutors with training and/or experience in prosecuting domestic matters.*
4. *A victim-services program with specialized DV counsellors.*
5. *A treatment program for abusers.* This is often a specialized unit in probation.

These five components ensure that the DV cases are separated from other offences and earmarked for a specialized court with specialized staff to respond to the offender and the victim.

While it is not possible to discuss all of the different models of court specializa-tion in this chapter, I will point to some of the most obvious distinctions in differ-ent jurisdictions before proceeding to a more detailed description of the Winnipeg Family Violence Court. For a detailed analysis of different court models in four jurisdictions in Canada, see Ursel et al. (2008). Differentiation occurs within a number of areas.

1. *Criteria for inclusion.* In some jurisdictions (e.g., Winnipeg and Calgary), the court will deal with all family violence matters, including child abuse and elder abuse, as well as, intimate partner abuse, while in other jurisdictions the specialized court will deal only with intimate partner violence cases (Toronto K-Court).
2. *Judicial review.* A number of courts in Canada have instituted a process of judicial review. This court-intensive form of monitoring, having offend-ers return to court regularly to report to the judge on their progress in treatment, is manageable in a location where the total caseload may be only a few hundred accused a year. However, in cities that have 2,000 or 3,000 cases a year, setting aside sufficient court time for judicial reviews is not feasible. The specialized court in the Yukon (Hornick, Boyes, Tutty, & White, 2008) and New Brunswick includes judicial reviews.
3. *Range of court processes included.* Some jurisdictions (e.g., Winnipeg) have special courts and specialized staff for bail hearings, sentencing courts for guilty pleas, and trial courts for contested cases. In short, Winnipeg

has specialization from the beginning to the end of the judicial process. Other courts only handle first appearances; this was the case in Calgary for the first four years of its operation. In 2001, Edmonton only had specialization at the trial court (Tutty, Ursel, & Douglas, 2008b).

4. *File ownership.* In this system, a Crown prosecutor assigned to a particular file will deal with that case and any subsequent appearances before the court involving that case (e.g., in cases of reoffending months or years later and/or in appeal cases). The intent is that the prosecutor becomes so familiar with the accused person's offending behaviour and the victim's circumstances that he or she can make a very strong case in court. It provides continuity for the victim over time, so that the prosecutor can develop a relationship of trust with the victim. Winnipeg has this system, and in some smaller jurisdictions with only one specialist prosecutor, there is de facto file ownership until the prosecutor leaves his or her position.

5. *Court emphasis.* Some specialized courts focus on early intervention, prioritizing support for victims and treatment for offenders over pursuing a conviction. Various courts across North America take this approach, such as the North York court in Ontario, modelled after Dade County court in Florida, and the HomeFront Program in Calgary. These courts, in comparison to courts in Toronto or Winnipeg, are more closely modelled after the original problem-solving courts, with much more focus on rehabilitation than on conviction. Other courts (e.g., the K-Court in Toronto), modelled after the San Diego court, are designed to pursue vigorous prosecution through increased co-operation between prosecutors and police. In these courts, judges play a more traditional role as neutral arbitrators. The focus is on enhanced evidence collection, with the use of audio and video statements, as well as photographs of the victim's injuries, medical reports, and transcripts of 911 tapes. The intent is to be able to proceed with a prosecution with or without victim co-operation (Dawson & Dinovitzer, 2001). Finally, there are courts that attempt to include all of the above components—that is, vigorous prosecution, especially for repeat offenders, and early intervention strategies, including diversion for first-time offenders. In these courts the judges play a traditional role as triers of facts; however, their decisions around sentencing are informed by greater knowledge of the dynamics of domestic violence and better information on the couples' histories. Winnipeg is a good example of this model.

FREQUENT OUTCOMES IN SPECIALIZED COURTS

Despite the considerable diversity in models of DV courts across Canada, some consistent results have been reported in jurisdictions that have released data about their courts. The first and most frequent observation that most courts report is the increase in the number of cases coming to court. This is a result of greater numbers of calls to police and increasing arrest rates. Calgary, Winnipeg, Saskatoon, Toronto, and Moncton have all noted this pattern. It appears that the introduction of a specialized court and all of the publicity that surrounds it have the effect of increasing public awareness of the danger of domestic violence. Further, the existence of a specialized court may give victims greater confidence that their situation will be treated seriously and respectfully (Tutty, George, Nixon, & Gill, 2008). The existence of the specialized court also had an impact on police arrest rates (Ursel & Hagyard, 2008). This reveals the interactive dynamic of the CJS. If you make a change in one part of the system, such as the courts, you will see changes in other components of the system, such as police and corrections. This may occur for two reasons. First, police may be more inclined to arrest if the existence of a specialized court gives them the confidence that an arrest will have consequences and not just end in a stay of proceedings. Second, in a number of jurisdictions that were introducing specialized courts, the police were part of the discussion in planning the court and arrest policies at the police level were reaffirmed.

A second outcome found in all of the jurisdictions with a DV court was the expansion of victim services to include people whose partner had been charged. This development evolved differently in each jurisdiction. In Calgary, for example, the provision had been an integral part of the plan for the court from the beginning (Hoffart & Clarke, 2004). In Winnipeg, the Women's Advocacy Program pre-existed the introduction of the specialized court, and the increasing volume of clients resulted in an expansion of the service and its eventual integration into the large, province-wide Victim Services Branch of the Manitoba Department of Justice.

A third outcome found in most jurisdictions with a DV court is the expansion of treatment programs for batterers. The strong rehabilitative thrust associated with specialized courts resulted in early referral to counselling in the North York and Calgary courts and in the sentencing of the offender to treatment in the Winnipeg court and the K-Court in Toronto. The jurisdictions had to respond to meet the growing demand for treatment programs. In some provinces, the primary responsibility for delivering treatment was assigned to specialized probation programs (e.g., in Winnipeg and Calgary), while in other jurisdictions it resulted in expanded funding for treatment programs delivered by non-governmental agencies.

The above three common outcomes of court specialization suggest a concerted attempt to respond to the limitations of the traditional justice paradigm identified above. The development of victim services and treatment programs for batterers are consistent with the multidisciplinary nature of problem-solving courts. However, it should be emphasized that court specialization can, at best, only improve the system; it cannot solve the problem of domestic violence. Domestic violence is an inherently complex problem and the criminal justice system has a limited intervention role. The paradox of the CJS is that it is at once very powerful (at times a matter of life or death) and profoundly limited. At certain points in time, a quick police response, a denied bail request, or a jail sentence may be critical in preventing a domestic homicide, but these cannot, in and of themselves, prevent the cycle of violence. While the specialized courts constitute an important piece of the puzzle in DV prevention and intervention, they continue to face many challenges. The question is whether they are more effective at addressing these challenges than are the traditional courts.

THE WINNIPEG FAMILY VIOLENCE COURT

This court provides a good case study of specialization because it now has 20 years of experience and continuous evaluation. The Winnipeg Family Violence Court monitoring project, the source of data used in this chapter, began with the opening of the court on 15 September 1990. It collects data on all cases that have been processed through the court, more than 30,000 cases to date. To consider the community context in which the court operates, it is helpful to know that Manitoba has a population of one million people and approximately 670,000 are Winnipeg residents. While some court components exist in towns outside of Winnipeg, the full service is Winnipeg based.

The components of specialization are listed roughly in the order that an individual encounters them in the justice system. At the entry level, police label all the domestic cases, and police officers on duty are the first responders and usually the arresting officers. There is limited specialization in the Winnipeg police service—a DV co-ordinator and eight officers who do follow-up investigations in two of the busier districts. The provincial victim services program employs 52 staff who provide information, support, protection planning, assistance in applying for protection orders, court accompaniment, and referrals. They are located throughout the province with a core of 16 staff in Winnipeg.

Court-related components are specialized Crown attorneys, judges, and designated courtrooms. Winnipeg's Domestic Violence Unit consists of 17 Crown attorneys who specialize in the prosecution of all Winnipeg family violence cases, which are organized on a 'file ownership' basis. Prosecutors in this unit also do circuit court; that is, they prosecute cases in communities that have a visiting rather than a resident court, judge, and prosecutor. As a result, smaller communities, where a significant number of cases before the court are domestic assaults, have the benefit of a specialized prosecutor. When the Winnipeg court first began, 14 judges sat in the court; the volume increased so dramatically, however, that since 1992 most of the provincial court judges have rotated in the DV courtrooms. The final component consists of the designated courtrooms: one courtroom for bail hearings, several to hear guilty pleas, two trial courts for DV matters, and one child-friendly courtroom for child abuse trials. In total, this amounts to a minimum of 60 hours of court time a week.

While corrections is not a component of the court, it was dramatically affected by the introduction of the Winnipeg Family Violence Court. Both probation and institutional correctional officers play important roles as primary sources for treatment programs for convicted offenders. In diversion situations involving accused who receive a stay of proceedings with an order for counselling, the treatment is provided by non-governmental agencies.

THE IMPACT OF SPECIALIZATION

The rapid spread of specialized courts has resulted in a lively debate about whether they make a difference and whether the outcomes justify the expansion of resources associated with the DV courts. The data from the Winnipeg Family Violence Court indicate some significant improvements as well as some continuing challenges. For the purposes of this chapter, I will report data on intimate partner violence cases, excluding other family offences, such as child abuse or elder abuse. The following quick summary traces the changes from the point at which a call first comes through to police to the final sentencing outcome.

At the entry point to the criminal justice system, the number of calls to police increased, as did the percentage of calls that resulted in charges being laid. Winnipeg police records indicate that calls for service labelled as 'domestic' rose from 9,685 in 1990 to 14,662 in 2000 to 16,867 in 2007. Domestic calls are now the most frequent call for service in Winnipeg, constituting over 36,000 hours of police processing time annually. Police records also indicate that the ratio of arrests to calls for service rose from 7 per cent in 1990 to a peak of 36 per cent in 1993/4 and has fluctuated between 25 and 30 per cent since then (Ursel & Hagyard, 2008). Figure 7.1 demonstrates that the increase in spousal assault arrest rates in Winnipeg coincides with the opening of the specialized court.

One controversy surrounding the rising arrest rates is the issue of dual arrests. These are cases in which police attendance at an incident of domestic violence results in the partners accusing one another and the police arresting both, clearly an unintended consequence of pro-arrest policies. Prior to the aggressive arrest policy issued in 1993 by the Winnipeg Police Service, the overwhelming majority of cases (94%) involved a single arrest, and only 6 per cent of cases coming to FVC court involved charges of both parties. The dual arrest rate rose to 9 per cent in 1998 and then began to decline when police introduced training programs to help officers identify primary aggressors. In 2005, the dual arrest rate was 4 per cent, indicating that 96 per cent of all spousal assault cases resulted in a single person being charged.

VICTIM AND ACCUSED CHARACTERISTICS

The Winnipeg data are similar to that in other jurisdictions in that approximately 80 per cent of the victims are women and 83 per cent of the accused are men. The average age of the victim is 32, and the average age of the accused is 33. However,

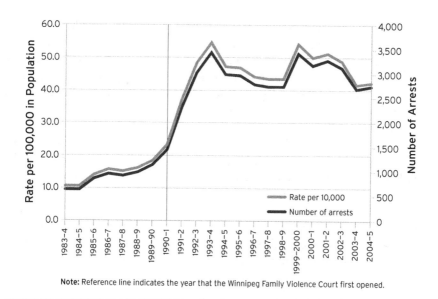

Note: Reference line indicates the year that the Winnipeg Family Violence Court first opened.

FIGURE 7.1   Rate (per 10,000) and number of arrests for spousal assaults in Winnipeg

the range in age was 16 to 83 for victims and 18 to 87 for the accused. Thus, while domestic violence is more prevalent in younger couples, it is not limited to the young. Information on the relationship of the victim and the accused indicates that the most frequent cases heard in FVC involved abuse in ongoing relationships: 36 per cent common law, 20 per cent boyfriend and girlfriend, and 16 per cent husband and wife. However, 24 per cent of all cases involved ex-partners.

Perhaps the most controversial data on characteristics of victims and offenders is the overrepresentation of individuals disadvantaged by low income and/or ethnicity. Individuals of Aboriginal origin, broadly defined, make up approximately 13 per cent of the population of Winnipeg but 39 per cent of the cases in FVC where ethnic origin was known. Aboriginal accused and victims were overrepresented by a factor of three. However, it is important to note that studies conducted by Statistics Canada, Amnesty International (2004), and Aboriginal women's groups consistently find that Aboriginal women are three times more likely to be abused by an intimate partner than non-Aboriginal women. Tragically, the presence of Aboriginal people in FVC may be an accurate representation of the incidence of violence in their lives.

The FVC data indicate that persons listed as unemployed (16%) or on welfare (33%) and persons with less than average education are also overrepresented in this court. Unfortunately, this overrepresentation is typical of most criminal courts. Critics of the justice system point to this overrepresentation of the disadvantaged as evidence of the negative consequences of criminalizing domestic violence

(Snider, 1990). However, it is important to note that 90 per cent of the calls to the police come from victims and/or their family. If the victims are as disadvantaged as their accused partner, this typically means that, unlike a middle-class victim, they may have no other source of help than the police. Winnipeg police data indicate that women of low income and/or Aboriginal origin are much more likely to call police than middle-class women. When police attend, if there is evidence that a crime occurred, they will arrest and charge the accused.

One way to assess whether arrest in these cases is appropriate, whether the accused really did pose a threat to the security of the victim, is to examine the accused's history of prior violence. Given that past behaviour is a good predictor of future behaviour, the finding that 76 per cent of the accused in FVC had a prior arrest for a crime against a person (typically an assault) suggests a serious potential for further violence. Most importantly, 48 per cent of those prior arrests had been for DV offenses. This suggests that the individual being arrested could reasonably be considered to pose a significant future risk to the victim.

THE COURT PROCESS AND OUTCOMES

In traditional court studies, the issue of conviction rates and sentencing is of primary concern. However, one of the distinguishing features of the specialized court is its commitment to providing an effective intervention in the cycle of violence, and this may not always be a conviction. In Manitoba, the guidelines for the Domestic Violence Prosecutions Unit encourage vigorous prosecutions, but not at the expense of re-victimizing the victim. In a sense, the Manitoba model lies between the more traditional model in the Toronto K-Court, which puts a high premium on convictions (Dawson & Dinovitzer, 2001), and the Calgary model, which prioritizes treatment over conviction for low-risk cases (Hoffart & Clarke, 2004). As a result, the Winnipeg FVC, with the victim's consent, offers a diversion program to first-time offenders judged to be low risk. However, prosecutors in the Domestic Violence Unit also have an impressive conviction rate for higher-risk accused.

The most frequent charge in DV cases is common assault. Between 1992 and 2005, common assault accounts for 61 per cent of all charges laid and 56 per cent of the cases in which it is the most serious charge. Breaches of court orders are the second most frequent charge, accounting for 43 per cent of all charges laid and 12 per cent of cases in which it is the most serious charge. In descending order of frequency of all charges laid, there are uttering threats and criminal harassment (20% of the 30,554 cases heard), assault with a weapon (12%), and aggravated assault and assault causing bodily harm (11%). In the same time period, there were 418 sexual assaults (or 1%) and 37 murders (or less than 1%).

Two important observations must be made about this pattern of charges. First, the frequency of breaches is one indication of offender patterns of reoffence. This is particularly true of chronic reoffenders. It is often the case that accused with a pattern of frequent reoffences will not be convicted on their assault charge because of victim reluctance to testify, but will be convicted on breaching conditions of no contact because police, who attended the incident, are able to testify to the breach (Ursel & Hagyard, 2008). Recidivism, as measured by repeat assaults on their partner, is common (Hornick et al., 2008), and despite the measures introduced with specialization, it continues to be a challenge to the courts and a major threat to victims. Second, the dominance of common assault as both the most frequent and the most serious charge in a case can be misleading. In traditional courts, the tendency is to put the most effort and the most resources into prosecuting the most serious charges. However, as Stark (2007) argues, domestic homicides often occur in cases where there has been only one previous arrest with a charge for a 'minor' assault. Thus, while some DV incidents follow a pattern of ever-increasing severity, there are also incidents, often among separating couples, in which the second attack is fatal. It is for this reason that victim-assistance workers must fully understand both the usefulness and the limits of risk-assessment tools and work with victims to develop an effective safety plan. Prosecutors, too, must have the full story of the couple's relationship. One must never assume that a common assault case is always a good candidate for diversion.

The conviction rate in FVC has increased from a low of 44 per cent in 1995/96 to a high of 56 per cent in 2004/05, which is similar to Toronto's K-Court conviction rate of 55.6 per cent (Dawson & Dinovitzer, 2008). Average conviction rates, however, can be misleading because they lump together single and repeat offenders, cases purposely diverted and cases vigorously prosecuted. The longitudinal data available in the Winnipeg FVC allow us to consider the conviction rate in light of the reoffence rates of the accused. Table 7.1 below identifies a direct relationship between conviction rates and reoffence history.

TABLE 7.1   Spousal conviction rate by single and repeat offenders (1992–2005)

Single/Repeat Accused	Number of Individuals	% of All Individuals	Conviction Rate (%)
1	15,082	58	37
2	5,456	21	48
3-4	3,533	14	54
5-6	1,110	4	57
7-10	607	2	62
11-23	219	<1	67
Total	26,007	100	46

At the same time that Crown attorneys pursued rigorous prosecution of repeat offenders, they also introduced a diversion program for low-risk, first-time offenders. This in part explains the low conviction rate among first-time offenders. In cases deemed eligible for diversion (approximately 10 per cent of all cases), the accused had the option of delaying their hearing until they could complete a treatment program. If prosecutors received a report from the counselling service that the referred clients did attend, participate, and complete their treatment, then the prosecutors would stay the proceedings. This process differs from the classic problem-solving court model operating in the Yukon, where the accused must plead guilty prior to entering treatment (Hornick et al., 2008), and also differs from the Calgary model, where a stay with peace bond occurs prior to treatment (Tutty, McNichol, & Christensen, 2008). Winnipeg does offer the incentive of having charges stayed, as is the case in Calgary, but it does retain the 'stick', the ability to proceed with prosecution if the accused does not complete treatment. In this regard, the Crown attorney 'persuades' the accused to co-operate and complete treatment, while in problem-solving courts this persuasion is exerted by the judge through the process of judicial review.

SENTENCING

Perhaps the most dramatic change resulting from specialization has been the radical shift in sentencing, a pattern that emerged within the first year of the establishment of the Winnipeg Family Violence Court. Prior to specialization, the most frequent disposition for individuals convicted of assaulting their partner was a conditional discharge (Ursel & Hagyard, 2008). This can be interpreted as 'Yes, the accused did the crime, but there is no treatment ordered, no punishment, and they are not left with a criminal record after the discharge period'—in short, from the perspective of the victim, no consequences. When specialization was introduced, the most frequent sentence became supervised probation with a treatment order, and the second most frequent sentence, incarceration. This change has had serious consequences for DV offenders.

An analysis of the cases from 1999 to 2005 shows that the overwhelming majority of convicted offenders (69%) received a sentence of one to two years of probation and court-mandated treatment. The second most frequent sentence was incarceration (25%); if we include intermittent sentences, the incarceration rate increased to 27.6 per cent of all convicted offenders. This is similar to the 31 per cent incarceration rate in the Toronto K-Court (Dawson & Dinovitzer, 2008). As for the less severe sentences, 12 per cent of all convicted offenders received a fine and 10 per cent received a conditional discharge. This represents a dramatic change from the period prior to specialization, when a conditional discharge was the most frequent sentence for convicted offenders. Most offenders now have multiple sentences, and a common combination is three to six months in jail and two years probation.

If we consider sentences for the most serious charges, we find that the highest rate of incarceration (38%) was for those convicted of sexual assault; the second highest rate (34%) was for persons who were convicted of major assaults (aggravated, assault causing bodily harm, etc.), and the third highest rate (32%) was for those convicted of breaches. While incarcerating individuals for breaches may seem extreme, since it is generally assumed that breaches are minor offences, our data indicates that persons sentenced with breaches had rather extensive criminal histories, specific to the family violence court.

Owing to the high rate of breach charges in 2005, the research team began collecting detailed information on conditions imposed on accused persons. At the time of arrest, conditions can be imposed either by police when the accused is released on their own recognizance or by a judge as a condition of their release (bail conditions). When a person has been convicted, they would have conditions imposed as part of their sentence (probation conditions). We now have breach information on 6,822 partner abuse cases over a three-year period.

When we compare offenders convicted for breaches alone (no other charge) to those offenders who were convicted of other charges, we find that the breach-alone offenders were almost twice as likely to have a prior record for domestic assault (47%) as those with no breach (27%) and more than twice as likely to have two or more prior convictions for domestic assault (23%) as those with no breach (10%). Similarly, those convicted of breach alone were more likely to have multiple prior convictions for general assault (39% versus 26%) and more than twice as likely to have prior convictions for assault with a weapon as offenders without breach charges. Finally, those convicted of breach alone were four times more likely to have a prior record for attempted murder, manslaughter, or murder than offenders without breach charges. Thus, the prior record of those convicted of breach alone indicates significant levels of violence in their past and their sentence may reflect the risk they pose to the victims.

RECIDIVISM AND OTHER CHALLENGES

One of the greatest concerns for victims, service providers, and practitioners in the justice system is whether the offender will commit a violent act again. For the victim, this is a measure of her risk; for the criminal justice system, it is a measure of its efficacy. Therefore, recidivism is a central issue in any assessment of differing court models of intervention. It was the chronic pattern of reoffending that motivated many policy-makers and practitioners to look to problem-solving or specialized courts as an alternative intervention model.

The FVC study identifies several measures of recidivism and factors that are correlated with recidivism, and Table 7.1 provides one example of the correlation between prior record and conviction rates. However, to get a clearer measure of reoffence patterns, we followed 2,443 individuals accused of a domestic assault in 2000 to see how many had reoffended three years later. We also looked at the nature of the reoffence. For example, were they charged with a breach alone, or were they charged with a new assault? Among these accused, 48 per cent were convicted, 41 per cent had their cases stayed, 8 per cent were diverted, and 3 per cent were either acquitted at trial or discharged.

TABLE 7.2   Recidivism rate by court outcome and type of new offence

Court Outcome	# Accused	New Offence	Breach Only	Total
Convicted	1,177	34%	17%	51%
Stayed	1,011	26%	6%	32%
Diverted	199	15%	2%	17%
Acquitted*	56	21%	13%	34%
Total	2,443	29%	11%	40%

*The 13 per cent acquitted who eventually were charged with a breach violated a protection order that their partner was granted.

Table 7.2 identifies a number of challenges for policy-makers and illustrates the complexity of DV cases. The first, most obvious result is that conviction is no guarantee of safety. The convicted offenders had the highest rate of recidivism, in both the reoffence (34%) and the breach-only (17%) categories, and Table 7.1 indicates that a person is most likely to be convicted if he or she has previously been before the FVC on a domestic matter. Because of the high recidivism rates, many women have witnessed their abuser convicted only to be abused by him again. At a minimum, these results should give all of us a better appreciation of victims' ambivalence about the justice system and their reluctance to testify. In addition, these results indicate that conviction alone is not enough and that treatment doesn't always work.

It would be wrong, however, to conclude from these results that convictions are useless. First, we don't want to return to past practices in which there were no consequences for assaulting one's partner, but we do need to explore practices that would be much more effective at providing safety for victims. Currently, when an accused is arrested, the victim has a period of safety (60% of accused spend one month or more in custody); with conviction, this period of safety is extended while the offender is in jail or while supervised on probation. Sometimes the period of safety allows the victim time to seek support and develop safety plans for herself and her children. However, as practitioners know, often the couple reconciles on or before the end of the period of incarceration or probation, and in these circumstances reoffences are likely to occur.

It is important to note that, among the convicted offenders, 17 per cent of their reoffences are for breaches alone. Convictions contribute to protection because the conditions of 'no contact, no communication' associated with most convictions allow police to intervene prior to an assault by arresting the offender on a breach. However, given that jail sentences are typically short—44 per cent are one year or less—and convicted offenders are most likely to reoffend, convictions provide only temporary protection.

One improvement on the temporary nature of the protection afforded victims involves directing chronic reoffenders to the Criminal Organization and High Risk Offender Unit (referred to as COHROU). COHROU is a probation program that provides very intense supervision (daily or twice daily contact) in combination with equally intense case supervision. There are three domestic violence COHROU units in Winnipeg, and each one can manage only 15 to 20 offenders. While COHROU is viewed as a very resource-rich program, its costs can be considered modest when measured against the costs of revolving-door court appearances, health and social welfare costs, and the incalculable suffering of families coping with chronic reoffenders. COHROU has had some significant successes with chronic repeat offenders, although no systematic evaluation of the program has been done to date. Yet COHROU is a promising possibility because it works with offenders, not just to control their access to the victim, but also to provide wraparound case intervention—housing, social assistance, life skills, and job training—to break old patterns of anti-social and violent behaviour. COHROU staff also have regular contact with the victims to keep them apprised of developments with the offenders, to check on the victims' sense of their own safety, and to refer them to necessary support services.

The more optimistic indicator from Table 7.2 is the finding that the lowest recidivism rates occurred among first-time offenders who were in the diversion program. This suggests that the specialized prosecutors are making good judgment calls on who are the low-risk offenders and that giving people options for treatment may reduce patterns of reoffence. These outcomes are consistent with the findings in Calgary and the Yukon, which also offer strong treatment options.

DO SPECIALIZED COURTS MAKE A DIFFERENCE?

Across Canada, six provinces and one territory have opted for specialized domestic violence courts and have increased the resources to support these courts. However, two questions remain, how do we measure whether these courts are able to provide a better quality of justice, and most importantly, do they contribute to keeping victims and their families safer than they were prior to specialization? In the four jurisdictions that have published evaluations—Winnipeg, Calgary, Toronto, and the Yukon—there is evidence that conviction rates have increased, that services for victims have expanded and treatment programs for offenders have increased. Further, there is evidence that specialized prosecutors are more likely to bring the full history of the couple to court rather than limiting their brief to a single inci-dent (Ursel et al., 2008).

Reports from specialized prosecutors indicate that they have a better under-standing of victims' circumstances and are less judgmental of victim ambivalence about testifying (Malaviya, 2008). Also, studies on treatment programs for abusers indicate that such programs can reduce recidivism, although the degree of reduc-tion varies from one study to another (Ursel & Gorkoff, 1996; Gondolf, 1999; Dobash, Dobash, Cavanagh, & Lewis, 2000). Many studies suggest that the earlier a treatment intervention occurs in the history of abusive behaviour, the greater the likelihood of sustained behavioural change.

Despite some of the significant improvements observed in most jurisdictions with specialized courts, there are still significant challenges. Specialization can result in competing pressures and expectations. On the one hand, there is the expectation that a specialized court will handle cases more rapidly, while on the other hand, there is the reality that specialization is associated with substantial increases in the number of cases coming to court. Moreover, as the system becomes better at tracking offenders, researchers are identifying a small percentage of chronic reoffenders (Gondolf, 2002; Ursel & Hagyard, 2008). While it is important to be able to identify these offenders, the system is struggling to design effective interventions for these perpetrators.

An ongoing challenge in our courts is how to make an adversarial legal system that requires proof 'beyond a reasonable doubt' less intimidating to victims. The expansion of victim services does provide an advocate for victims separate from the mandate of a prosecutor, and this has substantially reduced the phenomenon of re-victimizing the victim within the justice system. However, courts are still a frightening environment and convictions do not guarantee safety for victims and their families. Perhaps the best measure of the value of court specialization is not its ability, in a relatively short time, to solve all of the above problems, but the will-ingness of the practitioners in these courts to identify these challenges and explore ways to improve their responses to them.

Prior to specialization, the issue of domestic violence was largely hidden and the resources of the justice system that could be directed toward this crime were largely untapped. Canadian journalist Brian Vallee provides a stark reminder of why we need the resources of the justice system along with the social service sys-tem to keep victims safe. He contrasts the number of women who were victims of domestic homicide in Canada with the number of Canadian police officers and soldiers killed in the years 2000–06, a period in which Canada was heavily engaged in the war in Afghanistan. The death rate for domestic homicides was five times higher: 101 war and police casualties compared to 500 female domestic homicides (Vallee, 2008).

Domestic violence is all too often a matter of life or death. We need the power and authority of the justice system to intervene in these cases. It is instructive to learn from the Ontario Domestic Violence Death Review Committee (2007) that people murdered by their partners were less likely to have reported their abuse to the police than other victims of domestic violence. It is very important to make justice more accessible to the vulnerable and more effective in its interventions. In Manitoba, there is strong evidence that specialization has increased women's calls to police and there are some early indicators that this has improved women's safety. In the past, prior to specialization, Manitoba had one of the highest female domestic homicide rates in Canada. However, in the decade 1993–2003, after instituting court specialization and strong pro-arrest policies, Manitoba had the lowest female domestic homicide rate in western Canada and the third-lowest rate in the country. Creating specialized courts and specialized services increases the likelihood that victims will call for help. It is a first step toward engaging justice personnel at all levels in acknowledging the complexity of the issue and exploring new and more effective strategies for prevention and intervention.

CRITICAL THINKING QUESTIONS

1. In Canada, we have had two decades of policy changes within the criminal justice system to respond more effectively to domestic violence cases. Despite this, we do not see a dramatic decline in these offenses. What factors do you think may account for the persistence of these offences?

2. Why do DV offenders have such a high recidivism rate? How could the criminal justice system address this issue more effectively? Are there other institutions which may be more effective?

3. Despite the fact that the Canadian Criminal Code is federal and therefore the same across Canada, why do we see that the DV courts in different communities develop very different models of specialization. Do you think this is a good approach or does it become a barrier to a concerted national response?

4. If you were a prosecutor in a specialized domestic violence court how would you define success?

5. Many are concerned with sentence 'leniency' or the use of imprisonment. Given the complexities of domestic violence cases, should that be the main area of concern when thinking about responses to abusers? Why or why not?

REFERENCES

Amnesty International. (2004). Stolen sisters. http://www.amnesty.ca/resource_centre/reports/view.php/load=archview&article=1895&c=Resource+Centre+Reports

Casey, T. (2004). When good intentions are not enough: Problem solving courts and the impending crisis of legitimacy. *SMU Law Review, 57*, 1459–520.

Dawson, M., & Dinovitzer, R. (2001). Victim co-operation and the prosecution of domestic violence in a specialized court. *Justice Quarterly, 15*, 593–622.

——— & ———. (2008). Specialized justice: From prosecution to sentencing in a Toronto domestic violence court. In J. Ursel, L. Tutty, & J. LeMaistre (Eds.),

What's law got to do with it: The law, specialized courts and domestic violence in Canada (pp. 120–51). Toronto: Cormorant Press.

Dobash, R.E., Dobash, R.P., Cavanagh, K., & Lewis, R. (2000). *Changing violent men.* Newbury Park, CA: Sage.

Ferraro, K. (1989). Policing woman battering. *Social Problems, 36,* 61–74.

Ford, D.A., & Regoli, M.J. (1993). The criminal prosecution of wife assaulters. In N.Z. Hilton (Ed.), *Legal responses to wife assault* (pp. 127–64). Newbury Park, CA: Sage.

Gondolf, E.W. (1999). A comparison of four batterer intervention systems: Do court referral, program length, and services matter? *Journal of interpersonal violence, 14,* 41–61.

———. (2002). *Batterer intervention systems: Issues, outcomes, and recommendations.* Thousand Oaks, CA: Sage.

Hoffart, I., & Clarke, M. (2004). *HomeFront evaluation: Final report.* Calgary: Home-Front Evaluation Committee. http://www.homefrontcalgary.com/stistics/index.htm

Hornick, J.P., Boyes, M., Tutty, L., & White, L. (2008). The Yukon's domestic violence treatment option: An evaluation. In J. Ursel, L. Tutty, & J. LeMaistre (Eds.), *What's law got to do with it: The law, specialized courts and domestic violence in Canada* (pp. 172–96). Toronto: Cormorant Press.

Jaffe, P., Wolfe, D.A., Telford, A., & Austin, G. (1986). The impact of police charges in incidents of wife abuse. *Journal of Family Violence, 1*(1), 37–49.

Lane, E. (2003). Due process and problem-solving courts. *Fordham Law Journal, 30,* 955–1026.

MacLeod, L. (1980). *Wife battering in Canada: The vicious circle.* Ottawa: Canadian Advisory Council on the Status of Women.

Ontario Domestic Violence Death Review Committee. (2007). *Annual report to the Chief Coroner.* Toronto: Office of the Chief Coroner.

Malaviya, R. (2008). From shelter worker to Crown attorney: One woman's journey. In J. Ursel, L. Tutty, & J. LeMaistre (Eds.), *What's law got to do with it: The law, specialized courts and domestic violence in Canada* (pp. 46–68). Toronto: Cormorant Press.

Ptacek, J. (1999). *Battered women in the courtroom: The power of judicial responses.* Boston: Northeastern University Press.

Snider, L. (1991). The potential of the criminal justice system to promote feminist concerns. In E. Comack & S. Brickey (Eds.), *The social basis of law* (pp. 238–60). Halifax: Garamond Press.

Stark, E. (2007). *Coercive control: How men entrap women in personal life.* New York: Oxford University Press.

Tutty, L., Ursel, J., & Douglas, F. (2008). Specialized domestic violence courts: A Comparison of models. In J. Ursel, L. Tutty, & J. LeMaistre (Eds.), *What's law got to do with it: The law, specialized courts and domestic violence in Canada.* Toronto: Cormorant Press.

———, George, D., Nixon, K., & Gill, C. (2008). Women's views of programs to assist them with the justice system. In J. Ursel, L. Tutty, & J. LeMaistre (Eds.), *What's law got to do with it: The law, specialized courts and domestic violence in Canada* (pp. 21–45). Toronto: Cormorant Press.

———, McNichol, K., & Christensen, J. (2008). Calgary's HomeFront specialized domestic violence court. In J. Ursel, L. Tutty, & J. LeMaistre (Eds.), *What's law got to do with it: The law, specialized courts and domestic violence in Canada* (pp. 152–71). Toronto: Cormorant Press.

Ursel, J. (1991). Considering the impact of the battered women's movement on the state: The example of Manitoba. In E. Comack & S. Brickey (Eds.), *The social basis of law* (pp. 261–88). Halifax: Garamond Press.

———. (1998a). Eliminating violence against women: Social reform or co-optation in state institutions. In L. Samuelson & W. Antony (Eds.), *Social problems: Thinking critically.* (pp. 73–81). Halifax: Garamond Press.

———. (1998b). Mandatory charging policy: The Manitoba model. In K. Bonneycastle & C. Rigakos (Eds.), *Unsettling truths: Battered women, policy politics and contemporary research in Canada.* Vancouver: Vancouver Collective Press.

———. (2000). Winnipeg Family Violence Court report. In *Family violence in Canada: A statistical profile 2000.* Ottawa: Canadian Centre for Justice Statistics, Statistics Canada.

———. (2002). 'His sentence is my freedom': Processing domestic violence cases in the Winnipeg Family Violence Court. In L. Tutty & C. Goard (Eds.), *Reclaiming self: Issues and resources for women abused by intimate partners* (pp. 43–63). Halifax: Fernwood Press.

———, & Gorkoff, K. (1996). *The impact of Manitoba corrections partner abuse treatment program on recidivism.* Prepared for Manitoba Department of Justice, Winnipeg. RESOLVE Manitoba.

———, & Hagyard, C. (2008). The Winnipeg Family Violence Court. In J. Ursel, L. Tutty, & J. LeMaistre (Eds.), *What's law got to do with it: The law, specialized courts and domestic violence in Canada.* Toronto: Cormorant Press.

———, Tutty, L., & LeMaistre, J. (Eds.). (2008). *What's law got to do with it: The law, specialized courts and domestic violence in Canada.* Toronto: Cormorant Press.

Vallee, B. (2008). *War on women.* Toronto: Key Porter Books.

Winnick, B. (2003). Therapeutic jurisprudence and problem solving courts. *Fordham Law Journal, 30,* 1055–105.

Wolf, R. (2009). A new way of doing business: A conversation about statewide coordination of problem-solving courts. *Journal of Court Innovation,* Summer, 1–14.

Worden, A.P. (2000). The changing boundaries of the criminal justice system: Redefining the problem and the response in domestic violence. *Criminal Justice 2000, 2,* 215–66 Washington: US Department of Justice.

PART 1

SUGGESTED READINGS

Chapter 1

Cooley, D. (2005). *Reimagining policing in Canada*. Toronto: University of Toronto Press.

Beare, M., & Murray, T. (2007). *Who's calling the shots: Police and government relations*. Toronto: University of Toronto Press.

Brodeur, J.P. (2011). *The policing web*. New York: Oxford University Press.

Law Commission of Canada. (2006). *In search of security: The future of policing in Canada*. Ottawa: Ministry of Public Works.

Rigakos, G.T. (2002). *The new parapolice: Risk markets and commodified social control*. Toronto: University of Toronto Press.

Chapter 2

Current Issues in Criminal Justice, 21(1), July 2009. Special issue on bail in Australia, the United Kingdom, and Canada.

Friedland, M.L. (1965). *Detention before trial*. Toronto: University of Toronto Press.

Trotter, G.T. (2010). *The law of bail in Canada* (3rd ed.). Scarborough, ON: Carswell.

Chapter 3

Bottoms, A., & Roberts, J. (2010). *Hearing the victim: Adversarial justice, crime victims and the state*. Cullompton, UK: Willan.

Grant, I., Chunn, D., & Boyle, C. (1994). *The law of homicide*. Scarborough, ON: Carswell.

Tonry, M. (2011). *The Oxford handbook of crime and public policy*. Oxford, UK: Oxford University Press.

Chapter 4

Canadian Committee on Corrections. (1969). *Toward unity: The report of the Canadian Committee on Corrections*. Ottawa: Queen's Printer.

Crawford, A. (Ed.). (2011). *International and comparative criminal justice and urban governance: Convergence and divergence in global, national and local settings*. New York: Cambridge University Press

Gottschalk, M. (2006). *The prison and the gallows: The politics of mass incarceration in America*. New York: Cambridge University Press.

Tonry, M. (Ed.). (2008). Crime, punishment, and politics in comparative perspective. Vol. 36 of *Crime and Justice: A Review of Research*. Chicago: University of Chicago Press.

Chapter 5

Barnhorst, R. (2004). The Youth Criminal Justice Act: New directions and implementation issues. *Canadian Journal of Criminology and Criminal Justice*, 231–50.

Carrington, P., & Schulenberg, J. (2003). Police discretion with young offenders. http://www.justice.gc.ca/eng/pi/yj-jj/res-rech/discre/pdf/rep-rap.pdf

Department of Justice Canada. (2003). *YCJA explained. http://www.justice.gc.ca/eng/pi/yj-jj/ycja-lsjpa/ycja-lsjpa.html*

Doob, A., & Sprott, J. (2005). Sentencing under the Youth Criminal Justice Act: An historical perspective. In K. Campbell (Ed.), *Understanding youth justice in Canada* (pp. 221–41). Toronto: Pearson Prentice Hall.

Moyer, S. (2004). *A comparison of case processing under the Young Offenders Act and the First Six Months of the Youth Criminal Justice Act.* http://www.justice.gc.ca/eng/pi/yj-jj/res-rech/pdf/compar.pdf

Chapter 6

Borrows, J. (2002). *Recovering Canada: The resurgence of indigenous law.* Toronto: University of Toronto Press.

Dickson-Gilmore, J., & La Prairie, C. (2005). *Will the circle be unbroken? Aboriginal communities, restorative justice, and the challenges of conflict and change.* Toronto: University of Toronto.

Gosse, R., Youngblood Henderson, J., & Carter, R. (1994). *Continuing Poundmaker and Riel's quest: Presentations made at a conference on Aboriginal Peoples and justice.* Saskatoon: Purich Publishing.

Ryan, J. (1995). *Doing things the right way: Dene traditional justice in Lac La Martre, NWT.* Calgary: University of Calgary Press.

Chapter 7

Barasch, A.P., & Lutz, V.L. (2002). Innovations in the legal system's response to domestic violence: Thinking outside the box for the silent majority of battered women. In A.R. Robert (Ed.), *Handbook of domestic violence: Policies, programs and legal remedies* (pp. 173–201). New York: Oxford University Press.

Bell, M.E., & Goodman, L.A. (2001). Supporting battered women involved with the court system: An evaluation of a law school–based advocacy intervention. *Violence against Women, 7,* 1377–404.

Dobash, R.E., Dobash, R.P., Cavanagh, K., & Lewis, R. (2000). *Changing violent men.* Newbury Park, CA: Sage.

Ogrodnik, L. (2006). Spousal violence and repeat police contact. In L. Ogrodnik (Ed.), *Family violence in Canada: A statistical profile 2006* (pp. 11–19). Ottawa: Ministry of Industry.

SUGGESTED WEBSITES

Chapter 1

The Canadian Police College. http://www.cpc.gc.ca/en/home

The Police Executive Research Forum. http://www.policeforum.org

The Police Sector Council. http://www.policecouncil.ca/

Public Safety Canada. http://www.publicsafety.gc.ca/index-eng.aspx

Royal Canadian Mounted Police. http://www.rcmp-grc.gc.ca/

Chapter 2

Ontario Ministry of Community Safety and Correctional Services. http://www.mcscs.jus.gov.on.ca

Ontario, Ministry of the Attorney General. http://www.attorney-general.jus.gov.on.ca/english/crim/cpm/default.asp

Statistics Canada, Juristat. http://www.statcan.gc.ca/bsolc/olc-cel/olc-cel?catno=85-002-X&chropg=1&lang=eng

Chapter 3

Federal Ombudsman for Victims of Crime. http://www.victimsfirst.gc.ca/index.html

Justice Canada, Policy Centre for Victim Issues. http://www.justice.gc.ca/eng/pi/pcvi-cpcv/index.html

Public Safety Canada, National Office for Victims of Crime. http://www.publicsafety.gc.ca/prg/cor/nov/nov-bnv-eng.aspx

Chapter 4

Department of Justice Canada. http://www.justice.gc.ca/eng/index.html

François Lareau, LL.M., Lawyer/Avocat, Barreau du Québec. http://www.lareau-law.ca/droitpenal_.htm

Parliament of Canada. http://www.parl.gc.ca/LegisInfo/Home.aspx?Language=E&Mode=1&Parl=40&Ses=3

Public Safety Canada. http://www.publicsafety.gc.ca/index-eng.aspx

The Sentencing Project. http://www.sentencingproject.org/template/index.cfm

Chapter 5

Canadian Centre for Justice Statistics Profile Series. http://www.statcan.gc.ca/bsolc/olc-cel/olc-cel?catno=85f0033m&CHROPG=1&lang=eng

House of Commons Standing Committee on Justice and Human Rights. http://www.parl.gc.ca/CommitteeBusiness/CommitteeHome.aspx?Cmte=JUST&Language=E&Mode=1&Parl=40&Ses=3

Youth Justice, Department of Justice Canada. http://www.justice.gc.ca/eng/pi/yj-jj/index.html

Chapter 6

Justice Canada. http://www.justice.gc.ca/eng/index.html

Report of the Aboriginal Justice Inquiry of Manitoba. http://www.ajic.mb.ca/volume.html

Report of the Commission on First Nations and Métis Peoples and Justice Reform. http://www.justice.gov.sk.ca/justicereform/

Report of the Ipperwash Inquiry. http://www.attorneygeneral.jus.gov.on.ca/inquiries/ipperwash/index.html

Report of the Royal Commission on Aboriginal Peoples. http://www.ainc-inac.gc.ca/ap/rrc-eng.asp

Chapter 7

Canada's shelters for abused women. *Juristat: Canadian Centre for Justice Statistics, 27,* 1–20. http://publications.gc.ca/collections/collection_2007/statcan/85-002-X/85-002-XIE2007004.pdf

Family violence in Canada: A statistical profile. Ottawa: Canadian Centre for Justice Statistics, Statistics Canada. http://www.statcan.gc.ca/pub/85-224-x/4064472-eng.htm

Native Women's Association of Canada. http://www.nwac.ca/

PART 2
Related Policy Areas

OVERVIEW

While much focus is given to policy-making in traditional criminal justice policy areas (policing policy, sentencing policy, Aboriginal justice policy), less attention has been given to other areas of policy that merge with, and interact within, traditional criminal justice arenas. For example, as the following chapters reveal, various social, national, and international security policies relating to health, welfare, immigration, terrorism, organized crime, and technology have been politically framed and discussed through the lens of crime control. As Jonathan Simon has asserted (2007, p. 4), this framing of issues that traditionally fall outside of the criminal justice realm illustrates the shift toward 'governing through crime', which allows for the technologies, discourses, and metaphors of crime and criminal justice to be used to expand the range of issues that fall under the umbrella of criminal justice policy. However, as we will see in the following chapters, it is not a straightforward process whereby criminal justice policy expands into, and usurps, other policy areas. Rather, the relationship between criminal justice and social, or security, policies is uneven and complicated, and therefore tracing the evolution of policy responses sheds light on the importance of the social, political, and historical context.

In chapter 8, Fischer, Bibby, Argento, Kerr, and Wood trace the long history of drug law policy in Canada. The authors suggest that controlling drugs has always been a public policy issue. While the drugs that are the focus of intervention change, the discussion largely remains the same. Fischer et al. explain the tension inherent in Canadian drug law policy between the concepts of 'crime' and 'health', each of which provides very different assumptions that lead to different conse- quences in terms of policy, interventions, and professional responses. It is this tension that has characterized drug enforcement policy in Canada. And while there is clear recognition and evidence that health measures should be used in the treatment of drug users and offenders, drug policy has been dominated by the criminal law. Any treatment efforts and resources are funnelled through the crim- inal justice process rather than standing alone in health policy.

Kent Roach, in chapter 9, discusses the initial policy response to terrorism post-9/11 as reflective of the governing-through-crime paradigm. The passage of the massive new Anti-Terrorism Act (ATA, 2001), was symbolic—sending a signal that Canada would be tough on terrorism—and created many new terrorism crimes even though 9/11 was more an intelligence and law enforcement failure than a failure of the criminal law. Roach traces Canada's approach to policy- making since the passage of the ATA, including policy and legislation that broad- ened the range of human security threats and borrowed from other policy areas; for example, terrorism and threats to public health were included as risks to public safety and immigration law could be used as a mechanism for enforcing anti- terrorism law.

In chapter 20, Wendy Chan's analysis of welfare policy in Canada traces the increasingly punitive consequences for individuals who experience economic challenges and must rely on social assistance. Chan examines the dramatic shift in Canadian welfare policy toward tighter eligibility requirements, increased surveil- lance, and punitive sanctions for suspected fraud. This shift from social policy to criminal justice policy is linked to a recasting of welfare recipients as morally bankrupt and criminally blameworthy, and much of the driving force behind these reforms has been neo-liberal governance and the restructuring and retrenchment of the welfare state. Chan discusses the way in which welfare and punishment have come to work together in regulating social marginality and how the language of pathology and crime has been used to justify punitive measures. She also discusses the consequences of welfare reform in Canada and the particularly severe impact of such reform on women and racialized groups who rely on social assistance.

Through an analysis of a case study in chapter 11—the deportation of Tran Trong Nguyen to Vietnam in 2010—Anna Pratt examines the exercise of immi- gration penalty in Canada and its relationship with the crime-security nexus. She uses the Tran case to offer a glimpse into the diverse historical and contemporary intersections between the domains of criminal justice and immigration. In her examination of policy reform and legislation over the past four decades, Pratt maintains that a blurring of the boundaries between criminal justice and immigration occurred at the level of policy-making and that, as shown in the Tran case, national security came to be conflated with violent street-level criminality of youth gangs, who were seen to be the genesis of organized transnational crime syndicates. This conflation between national security and 'true' crime, along with extensive media coverage and public interest, enabled immigration enforcement to succeed where criminal justice enforcement had failed, namely the ultimate deportation of Tran Trong Nghi Nguyen.

In chapter 12, Margaret Beare discusses the expansion in focus on organized crime—a continual 'building on' of policy as opposed to 'going back'—which is influenced by significant international pressures on Canada to harmonize its policies with international law enforcement or run the risk of being viewed as soft on organized crime. Beare traces the evolution of organized crime policy in Canada, highlighting the interplay of local, national, and international forces, along with the politicization and expansion of the subject matter in recent years—for example, the inclusion of local gangs within the scope of the policy. According to Beare, policy initiatives do not reflect the complexity of the issue, cast an overly broad net, do not allow for a Canadian solution, and are politicized with the typical language of threat that is used to justify getting tougher against an enemy in our midst.

Lastly, Sara Smyth, in chapter 13, focuses on the policy challenges associated with cybercrime. Smyth asserts that cybercrime is now severe, pervasive, aggressive, and increasingly sophisticated and that this poses a significant threat to the Internet's viability as an essential element of our critical infrastructure. Smyth maintains that Canadian criminal justice policy has not been able to keep up with the rapid pace of technological growth and the evolving nature of criminal activity on the Internet. This suggests a need for other mechanisms of regulatory control, particularly those that involve third-party intermediaries who are in a better position—based on resources, information, or authority—than government actors to identify and prevent third-party misconduct.

REFERENCES

Anti-Terrorism Act (S.C. 2001, c. 41).

Simon, J. (2007). *Governing through crime: How the war on crime transformed American democracy and created a culture of fear.* New York: Oxford University Press..

8

Drug Law and Policy in Canada: Torn between Criminal Justice and Public Health

Benedikt Fischer, Meagan Bibby, Elena Argento, Thomas Kerr, and Evan Wood

INTRODUCTION

For decades, the 'drug problem' has had a strong presence in the media and popular discourse and has constituted a pre-eminent domestic public policy challenge in Canada (Fischer, 1999). While the specific facets of the drug problem have shifted and focused on different drugs over time—for example, cannabis in the 1960s or injection drugs in the 1990s—the basic tenets of the discussion have remained rather consistent (Giffen, Endicott, & Lambert, 1991; Fischer et al., 1998).

Typically debates have revolved around these questions: Should drug use be a crime, or is it a disease for which people should get treatment? Will law enforcement reduce rates of drug use or the availability of drugs on illegal markets? Should drug use be decriminalized or legalized in the interest of better policy? Where does 'harm reduction' fit in as an intervention framework (Fischer, Roberts, & Kirst, 2002; Cohen & Csete, 2006)? These key questions have been amplified by the emergence of HIV and overdose epidemics among illicit drug users starting in the late 1980s (Wood et al., 2003c; Kerr & O'Briain, 2002). Despite warnings of the impending epidemics and calls for action, policy-makers were slow to respond (Kerr & O'Briain, 2002; Strathdee et al., 1997b).

These questions also point to a fundamental tension between paradigms of crime and health that has existed in Canadian drug control throughout history. A century ago (1908–11), Canadian law-making rendered the supply and use of an ancient psychoactive drug—opium—a criminal offence and thereby laid the foundation for a criminalization approach to drug use that remains dominant today (Solomon & Green, 1988; Giffen et al., 1991). From the mid-century onward, however, mounting voices argued that drug addiction should mainly be thought about as a health problem that was dealt with by measures of prevention and treatment (Fischer et al., 2002; Giffen et al., 1991). These two frameworks rest in essentially different assumptions, leading to equally different approaches to policy, interventions and institutional mandates. Yet these tensions are not played out on an equal battlefield. The basic analytical thread of this chapter will be that drug policy in Canada is dominated by the hegemony of criminal control and enforcement over perspectives and measures of health (Solomon & Green, 1988; Fischer et al., 2002; Wood et al., 2003a). Criminal law and crime control are among the most powerful policy tools available, and consequently health interventions for substance use or addiction are subordinated to the existing crime-control framework. Outside of the area of sex work, this particular constellation is rather unique in Canada, and drug policy has been stuck in this conflict for half a century, hindering progress toward the implementation of more evidence-based policy (Young, 2004).

In this chapter, we will first give a brief history of drug law and policy and then provide an overview of illicit drug use and related key harms in Canada. Subsequently, we will focus on select forms of illicit drug use and describe key intervention and policy developments in recent years, set in the context of the above-described tensions between concepts of crime and health. Conclusions will reflect on options for more evidence-based drug policy in Canada.

A BRIEF HISTORY OF DRUG LAW AND POLICY

In 1908, in the context of severe socio-economic tensions between Chinese immigrants and the Anglo-Saxon population in British Columbia that culminated in violent anti-Chinese riots in Vancouver, the House of Commons passed the Opium Act, a criminal law that prohibited the manufacturing, importation, and sale of opium products in Canada (Giffen et al., 1991). With opium being mainly a Chinese socio-economic commodity, this step was aimed to curtail Chinese business activity (Solomon & Green, 1988; Giffen et al., 1991). Shortly thereafter—in 1911—the Opium Act was expanded to prohibit opium possession, thereby criminalizing the medical and cultural usages of this drug. Influenced by parallel drug prohibition efforts in the United States, the Canadian government added other psychoactive drugs—including heroin, cocaine, and cannabis—to the drug law's schedule by the late-1920s, drugs that were mainly seen as associated with non-white ethnic minorities (Giffen et al., 1991). However, drug enforcement initially focused almost exclusively on opium (Giffen et al., 1991). Over the coming years, a systematically expanding drug law enforcement apparatus emerged at the federal level under the Bureau of Narcotic Drugs, co-ordinating drug enforcement, prosecution, and input to law-making (Giffen et al., 1991; Fischer et al., 1998). In the mid-1920s, the Royal Canadian Mounted Police (RCMP) assumed the main responsibility over drug law enforcement in Canada, thereby seizing a new institutional *raison d'être* (Giffen et al., 1991).

TABLE 8.1   List of acronyms

BBV	blood-borne virus
CCC	Cannabis Compassion Club
CBT	cognitive-behavioural therapy
CDSA	Controlled Drugs and Substances Act
CSC	Correctional Service of Canada
DOJ	Department of Justice Canada
DTC	drug treatment court
HCV	hepatitis C virus
HAT	heroin-assisted treatment
IDU	injection drug user
MMS	mandatory minimum sentences
MMAP	Medical Marijuana Access Program
MMT	methadone maintenance treatment
NADS	National Anti-Drug Strategy
NEP	needle exchange program
NSP	needle and syringe program
NMPOU	non-medical prescription opioid use
POA	prescription opioid analgesic
PHSA	Provincial Health Services Authority
RCT	randomized controlled trial
RCMP	Royal Canadian Mounted Police
SCUK	safer crack-use kits
SCUS	supervised crack-use site
SIS	supervised injection site
VCH	Vancouver Coastal Health
VIDUS	Vancouver Injection Drug Users Study

By the 1940s, heroin use—with its largely white rather than ethnic user population—in the larger Canadian cities had replaced opium use as the main focus of drug enforcement (Giffen et al., 1991; Solomon & Green, 1988). Several expert committees had already called for treatment interventions rather than punishment for heroin addicts, even floating the idea of heroin maintenance programs akin to morphine maintenance programs that existed in the United States at that time

(Solomon & Green, 1988; Giffen et al., 1991; Fischer, 2000). While these ideas did not materialize, the drug law was expanded by key enforcement provisions extending far beyond those ordinarily available in the Criminal Code. For example, for 'possession for the purpose of trafficking' charges, the 'onus of proof' was reversed so that defendants had to prove their innocence rather than the Crown prove their guilt (Giffen et al., 1991). Certain offences entailed mandatory minimum punishments or even allowed corporal punishment (e.g., whipping) (Giffen et al., 1991). Enforcement personnel carried 'writs of assistance' providing blanket authorization for search or seizure in drug investigations, eliminating the need for case-specific warrants (Giffen et al., 1991). The modernized Narcotic Control Act in 1961 included a 'mandatory treatment clause' in the draft law. This provision would have allowed—at the discretion of the judge or prosecutor—incarceration for drug addicts to be substituted with commitment to mandatory (and possibly indefinite) treatment (Giffen et al., 1991; Fischer et al., 2002). However, this treatment clause never came into effect, hence eliminating the inclusion of treatment alternatives in the drug law (Giffen et al., 1991; Fischer et al., 2002).

In the 1960s, enforcement quickly shifted its focus toward cannabis use, which had been spreading rapidly, especially among young people (Green & Miller, 1975; Smart, 1983; Fischer, Ala-Leppilampi, Single, & Robins, 2003). Cannabis offences rose from a few dozen to several thousand in the late 1960s, most of which resulted in criminal sentences and records for offenders, causing considerable social controversy (Fischer, 1999). In response, the Liberal government established the Le Dain Commission of Inquiry into the Non-Medical Use of Drugs (the Le Dain Commission, 1969–73), which recommended that personal drug use not be subject to criminal punishment and that treatment be provided as the main intervention for drug addiction (Giffen et al., 1991; Fischer et al., 2003). The Commission's recommendations, however, had little effect on law or policy (Giffen et al., 1991; Fischer et al., 2003). Even though about 50 per cent of Canadians consistently expressed opposition to the criminal punishment of cannabis use, several attempts to decriminalize cannabis use failed in the following years (Giffen et al., 1991; Fischer et al., 2003). Instead, drug law enforcement increased cannabis arrests and charges, the vast majority of which were for simple drug possession (Dauvergne, 2009). In the late 1980s—parallel to the US 'War on Drugs'—'Canada's Drug Strategy' was launched, devoting the majority of its resources to drug enforcement rather than prevention or treatment (Fischer, 1994; Kerr & O'Briain, 2002). The subsequent renewal of the federal drug law—the Controlled Drugs and Substances Act (CDSA), enacted in 1996—maintained and cemented the criminalization of drugs and their use (Fischer et al., 2002). Rapidly rising numbers of overdose deaths as well as HIV and hepatitis C virus (HCV) infections among injection drug users (IDUs) emphasized the urgency for better prevention and treatment services, yet also pointed to the contributive role of enforcement in creating health risks for IDUs while entailing little change in enforcement practice (Strathdee et al., 1997b; Fischer, Popova, Rehm, & Ivsins, 2006). In fact, the numbers of drug offences enforced steadily increased from 56,817 in 1993 to 80,142 in 1999, mainly consisting of possession offences (61%) (Dauvergne, 2009). Subsequent iterations of the federal drug strategy continued to devote most resources to enforcement rather than prevention or treatment (DeBeck, Wood, Montaner, & Kerr, 2009; DeBeck, Wood, Montaner, & Kerr, 2006). Hence, the hegemony of criminal repression in Canadian drug law and policy—established and consistently expanded throughout the twentieth century—was effectively reinforced and carried into the new millennium.

EPIDEMIOLOGY OF DRUG USE AND HARMS

The category of 'illicit drugs' comprises a variety of drugs, one of which—cannabis— is commonly used in the general population. As elsewhere, the prevalence of cannabis use in Canada has fluctuated over time. While some seven per cent of adult Canadians reported past-year cannabis use in the early 1990s, two recent national surveys—the Canadian Addiction Survey (CAS) in 2003 and the Canadian Alcohol and Drug Use Monitoring Survey (CADUMS) in 2008—measured such use between 11 and 14 per cent, respectively (Adlaf, Begin, & Sawka, 2005; Health Canada, 2009a). However, the proportion of adolescents or young adults (including secondary or university student populations) reporting use has been much higher (30% or more) and now often exceeds tobacco use (Adlaf & Paglia-Boak, 2007; Adlaf et al., 2005). The proportion of cocaine use and other stimulants is low at one to two per cent as measured in large general population surveys, as use of these drugs is relatively uncommon in these samples (Health Canada, 2009a).

Other illicit drug use is largely concentrated in marginalized or high-risk populations. While a total heroin user population of 60,000 to 90,000 was estimated for Canada in 1997, this prevalence has likely shrunk and, in many settings, heroin use has been replaced with non-medical prescription opioid use (NMPOU) (Fischer, Rehm, Patra, & Firestone Cruz, 2006; Davis & Johnson, 2008; Fischer & Rehm, 1997). In street drug user populations, opioids are commonly co-injected with cocaine; for example, in the Vancouver Injection Drug Users Study (VIDUS)— a cohort study of some 1,600 IDUs in Vancouver regularly assessed since 1996—14 per cent reported injecting 'speedballs' (heroin and cocaine combined) daily in 2004 (Miller, Kerr, Strathdee, Li, & Wood, 2007). Since the 1990s, a resurgence of the use of other psycho-stimulants—for example, crack or methamphetamine— among street drug users has occurred, primarily due to easy and cheap availability, and crack has been cited as the most commonly used drug in many local street drug–use scenes (Haydon & Fischer, 2005; Leonard et al., 2008; Werb et al., 2010; Wood, Stoltz, Montaner, & Kerr, 2006).

Recent studies provide a general impression of key harms and costs related to illicit drug use in Canada. The economic cost burden for both licit and illicit drug use in Canada in 2002 was estimated to be $39.7 billion, or four per cent of the gross domestic product (GDP) (Rehm et al., 2006). As much as $8.2 billion—a relatively small share compared to alcohol and tobacco—was linked to illicit drug use. Notably, it is criminal justice costs that are proportionally highest for illicit drugs compared to the other substance categories. Specifically, while 20 per cent of the economic costs related to drug use was attributable to illegal drugs, illegal drugs account for 43 per cent of criminal justice expenditures (Rehm et al., 2006).

Mortality and morbidity constitute key harms related to illicit drug use; however, estimates on these indicators are crude, partly because data are not systematically collected across Canada. There are an estimated 1,000 to 2,000 accidental (e.g., overdose) deaths related to illicit drugs in Canada per year, although it is not clear which drugs are involved (Fischer, Rehm, & Blitz-Miller, 2000; Fischer et al., 2006a; Rehm et al., 2006). The province of British Columbia experienced a dramatic spike in drug-related overdose deaths in the mid-1990s, peaking at 417 annual deaths in 1998, primarily due to overdoses from combined heroin/cocaine injecting (Kerr et al., 2007; Buxton et al., 2009). Numbers of overdose deaths successively decreased in subsequent years due to the expansion of prevention and treatment interventions (Fischer et al., 2006a; Buxton et al., 2009). A recent study documented that the proportion of prescription opioid-related overdose deaths in Ontario doubled between 1997 and 2004 (Dhalla et al., 2009). In nine out of 10 cases, either alcohol or benzodiazepines—that is, other legal substances—were also involved in these deaths.

Key morbidity indicators for illicit drug use include blood-borne viruses (BBV) such as HIV/AIDS and HCV. Of the 2,623 recorded new HIV infections in Canada in 2008, 20 per cent were attributed to (injection) drug use; after decreasing trends, these rates have remained stable since 2003 (Public Health Agency of Canada, 2009). Among street drug users in Canada, HIV infection rates vary, from rates as low as less than three 3 per cent to 25 per cent or higher, depending on local risk patterns and networks (Health Canada, 2006; Fischer et al., 2005; Miller et al., 2006). Although less publicized, the drug-use-related burden of HCV is much higher. Among the estimated existing 250,000–300,000 HCV infections in Canada, about 50 per cent are estimated to be IDU-related, and 90 per cent or more of new infections are attributed to IDU transmission (Fischer et al., 2006c; Firestone Cruz et al., 2007). HCV rates among street drug–user populations are high, ranging from 40 to 90 per cent across Canada (Miller et al., 2002; Fischer et al., 2005; Wood et al., 2005a). Even though in some jurisdictions—for example, British Columbia—the rate of IDU-related HCV transmissions has decreased over the past decade owing to improved prevention measures (Buxton et al., 2009; Wood, Montaner, & Kerr, 2005), studies elsewhere have shown that drug users are HCV infected within one to two years of initiating drug-injecting behaviour, leaving a small window of opportunity for effective interventions (Maher, Li, Jalaludin, Chant, & Kaldor, 2007). In many settings throughout Canada, the above-described drug-use-related mortality and morbidity harms are disproportionately elevated within Aboriginal populations (Craib et al., 2003; Buxton et al., 2009).

INJECTION DRUG USE

In the past 25 years or so, IDU has been a major public health and policy concern in Canada and internationally, primarily due to the high morbidity and mortality burden (Strathdee et al., 1997a; Fischer et al., 2000). Several important factors are known to contribute to acute health risks among IDUs. First, the common co-injecting of heroin and cocaine ('speedballs') was associated with excessive 'binge-ing' patterns and other risk factors (e.g., sex work involvement), leading to infectious disease transmission, overdose, and other harms (Spittal et al., 2002; Craib et al., 2003; Leri et al., 2005). Recent data suggest that heroin/cocaine injecting has decreased, largely due to shifts in local drug cultures in which (non-injected) prescription opioid analgesics (POAs) and crack/cocaine have become increasingly prevalent (Fischer et al., 2005; Werb et al., 2010). Most street-involved IDUs in Canada are characterized by 'poly drug use' (Fischer et al., 2005; Leri et al., 2005; Werb et al., 2010). For example, in the 2006 I-Track study of IDUs across Canada, the most commonly injected drugs were cocaine (77.5%), morphine (45.9%), and hydromorphone (32.9%); the most commonly used non-injection drugs were cannabis (74.7%), crack (65.2%), and benzodiazepines (49.1%) (Health Canada, 2006). In the 2001 assessment of the pan-Canadian OPICAN illicit opioid user cohort, heroin (67.2%), cocaine (54.6%), and crack (54.6%), as well as POAs, were the most commonly used drugs, though drug-use patterns in both studies varied starkly across sites (Fischer et al., 2005). Among young IDUs in VIDUS, one-third reported injecting heroin and cocaine daily, with 10 per cent reporting crack smoking and 14 per cent injecting speedballs (Miller et al., 2007). Social and environmental determinants—for example, homelessness, injecting in public spaces, imprisonment, and law enforcement—are well-documented predictors of elevated morbidity and mortality risks among IDUs (Miller et al., 2004; Tyndall et al., 2006; Kerr, Small, & Wood, 2005). For example, use in public spaces often compels users to rush injecting and disregard rules of safer injecting out of fear of detection by police (DeBeck, Small, Wood, Li, & Kerr, 2009).

Following the outbreak of the HIV epidemic among IDUs in the 1980s, needle exchange programs (NEPs) were gradually established in Canadian cities in the 1990s (Hankins, 1998; Fischer et al., 2000). Owing to their initially controversial status—for example, NEPs were considered potentially illegal under the CDSA—the programs were expanded and operated hesitantly (e.g., 'one-for-one exchange') and hence prevented far less cases of HIV or other BBV transmissions than possible as had been demonstrated in other countries (e.g., Australia) with better implementation (Strathdee et al., 1997b; Hankins, 1998; Fischer et al., 2000). Seminal studies have demonstrated that NEPs effectively reduce IDU-related risk behaviours, specifically HIV transmission, among IDUs who utilize these services (Ritter, Ritter, Cameron, Ritter, & Cameron, 2006; Palmateer et al., 2010). In recent years, the reach and practices of NEPs have been improved and have facilitated better access to sterile syringes among IDUs (Kerr et al., 2010).

Following similar initiatives in Europe and Australia, a so-called supervised injection site (SIS) pilot project ('Insite') was established in Vancouver in 2003. The SIS pilot was based on a federal exemption from the CDSA, with the objective to assess the intervention's impact on mortality and morbidity among IDUs (Wood et al., 2004a; Small, 2007). In SIS facilities, IDUs can inject drugs in safe, clean, and supervised environments—with medical staff on standby in case of emergencies—in order to reduce risky injection practices or overdose risks (Broadhead, Kerr, Grund, & Altice, 2002; Small, 2007). Safe injection sites also provide drug and health information, as well as basic health care, social services, and treatment referrals (Broadhead et al., 2002; Wood et al., 2003b; Kimber, Dolan, van Beek, Hedrich, & Zurhold, 2003).

The Vancouver SIS has been most rigorously evaluated (Wood et al., 2006; Small, 2007; Wood, Kerr, Tyndall, & Montaner, 2008). For example, data has shown that the SIS has been linked to reduced public injecting and syringe discarding (Wood et al., 2004b; Petrar et al., 2007) and that its users are less likely to share needles and are more likely to engage in safer injection practices than control groups (Wood et al., 2005c; Stoltz et al., 2007; Kerr, Tyndall, Li, Montaner, & Wood, 2005). Furthermore, non-fatal overdose levels among SIS users remained stable, and referrals to addiction treatment increased (Wood, Tyndall, Zhang, Montaner, & Kerr, 2007). Despite its demonstrated positive results published in leading medical science journals, the current (Conservative) federal government has been determined to close Insite (Small, 2007; Dalton & Hall, 2010). The RCMP has repeatedly attempted to discredit research findings on the SIS, petitioning members of the Vancouver Police Department, addictions physicians, and the media to oppose the SIS exemption (Small, 2007). Its proponents have sought to protect the SIS legally, and to date, the higher courts in British Columbia have confirmed that the SIS is a health service within the operational jurisdiction of provincial health services and is constitutionally protected under the 'right to health' provision of the Canadian Charter of Rights and Freedoms (CBC News, 2010). While Insite remains open, its case has been heard by the Supreme Court of Canada and should be adjudicated later in 2011. As such, the struggle for/against the SIS has come to epitomize symbolically the tensions between the crime and health paradigms of drug-use control in Canada. Other Canadian cities are considering the establishment of SIS facilities, yet likely are awaiting the Supreme Court's decision before undertaking concrete steps.*

CRACK USE

While the 1980s saw North America confronted with a 'crack epidemic', a resurgence of crack use has occurred among Canadian street drug users in the past decade, as the drug is widely and cheaply available on local drug markets (Haydon

*Post-scriptum at time of text-editing: On 30 September 2011, the Supreme Court ruled that the Vancouver SIS was legitimate and protected under the Charter, and thus can remain open.

& Fischer, 2005; Werb et al., 2010). In the I–Track study, 32 per cent of IDUs reported crack use in the past six months, with rates over 50 per cent in Edmonton and Toronto (Health Canada, 2006). In the VIDUS cohort, crack-use prevalence increased from 7.4 to 42.6 per cent in the period 1996–2005 (Werb et al., 2010). While crack is typically smoked and not injected, the health and social risks of crack use are extensive (DeBeck et al., 2009; Werb et al., 2010). For example, crack users are at elevated risk for HIV and HCV transmission as well as premature mortality (Tortu, McMahon, Pouget, & Hamid, 2004; Fischer et al., 2006c; DeBeck et al., 2009). When comparing crack users and non-crack users in the OPICAN cohort, crack users were more likely to report HIV and HCV infection (Fischer et al., 2006c). Many of these problems are caused by risk behaviours other than crack use, reflecting the highly marginalized status of these populations. For example, many crack users are past or current drug injectors, involved in sex work, burdened by homelessness, use drugs mainly in public spaces, and feature extensive histories of imprisonment (Booth, Kwiatkowski, & Chitwood, 2000; Ross, Hwang, Zack, Bull, & Williams, 2002; Fischer et al., 2006c). Many crack users have intensive involvement in criminal activities—mostly property or drug acquisition crimes, yet also violent crimes, partly due to the stimulant psycho-pharmacological effects of crack as well as related to the volatile dynamics of crack markets (Goldstein & Kalant, 1990; Inciardi & Pottieger, 1994; Cross, Johnson, Rees Davis, & James Liberty, 2001; Fischer et al., 2006c).

A major challenge is that no effective and widely deliverable treatment options currently exist for crack (Van den Brink, 2005; Siqueland et al., 2004). Although cognitive-behavioural therapies (CBTs) are offered for crack use, they are rarely utilized, costly, and the majority of users entering such treatment quickly disengage from treatment or relapse (Carroll, Roundsville, & Gawain, 1991; Siqueland et al., 2004). Experimental studies with possible stimulant maintenance agents (e.g., disulfiram)—analogues to the concept of opioid maintenance treatment—for crack dependence have not been encouraging and do not promise ready clinical applications in the near future (Shearer & Gowing, 2004; Pani et al., 2010).

Given the recent prevalence and harms of crack use, there has been a great need for health-oriented interventions (Haydon & Fischer, 2005; O'Byrne & Holmes, 2008), specifically targeting the common sharing of crack-use paraphernalia and the possible transmission of BBVs (primarily HCV) among users (Haydon & Fischer, 2005; Fischer, Powis, Firestone Cruz, Rudzinski, & Rehm, 2008; Malchy, Bungay, & Johnson, 2008). To reduce these risks, local health service providers began disseminating so-called safer crack-use kits (SCUK) in select cities across Canada in the late 1990s (O'Byrne & Holmes, 2008). Modelled after the idea of NEPs, SCUKs provided crack users with a small kit that included safer 'crack pipe' materials (Pyrex stem, mouth piece, metal screen, etc.), together with safer drug-use information and safer sex resources (Haydon & Fischer, 2005; Malchy et al., 2008). Initially considered illegal, SCUK initiatives were not supported by public health authorities and were actively opposed by police (Haydon & Fischer, 2005;

O'Byrne & Holmes, 2008). While health authorities in Ottawa, Toronto, Winnipeg, and Victoria eventually shifted to supporting and implementing SCUK distribution, local, social, and political opposition saw SCUK initiatives suspended again in some sites (Landry, 2004; O'Byrne & Holmes, 2008; Malchy et al., 2008).

To date, only limited evaluation data on the impact of SCUK exist, partly because of the relative newness and limited implementation of these programs (Malchy et al., 2008; Fischer et al., 2008a). An Ottawa study found that the study sample of crack users had substantially reduced crack injection in the previous month (96 per cent to 78 per cent)—in favour of increased non-injection use—as a result of SCUK dissemination (Leonard, DeRubeis, & Birkett, 2006). While many crack users are already HIV or HCV infected and many engage in intensive crack binge-use patterns for which the availability of SCUK materials may be insufficient (Wood et al., 2005a; Shannon et al., 2008)—SCUK may function as an important way to connect with marginalized crack-user populations and thus provide them with basic education or refer them to health or treatment services (Haydon & Fischer, 2005; Malchy et al., 2008). More outcome evaluations on SCUK interventions are clearly needed. The concept of an experimental 'supervised crack-use site' (SCUS)—analogue to SIS for IDUs—has been discussed and proposed for various Canadian cities in recent years (DeBeck et al., 2009). While the necessary authorizations (including a CDSA exemption from the federal government) will undoubtedly be difficult to obtain, a recent proposal for an experimental SCUS study in Vancouver is in preparation.

HEROIN AND OTHER OPIOID USE

For decades, heroin was amply available on street drug markets and sold to users by street-level dealers at highly inflated prices, forcing most addicts into regular habits of acquisition—that is, property crime (Giffen et al., 1991; Courtwright, 1997; Fischer et al., 2006b). The proverbial 'heroin junkie' formed the core of the IDU population until the 1980s, when stimulants (e.g., cocaine and/or crack), as well as sedate medications (e.g., barbiturates and/or benzodiazepines) became increasingly available and patterns of 'poly-drug use' became increasingly common among heroin users (Fischer et al., 2005; Leri et al., 2005; Courtwright, 1997). Yet some significant changes have occurred in regard to opioid drug use in recent years. In the OPICAN study, the prevalence of heroin use had significantly declined in all but two study sites between 2001 and 2005, and instead the use of POAs had increased substantially in the study population (Fischer et al., 2005). POAs are pharmaceutical medications for pain care pharmacologically similar to heroin (Ballantyne, 2007). Increases in NMPOU were also observed in the United States, where such use had become prevalent not only among street drug–user populations but also among general—including student and adolescent—populations since the 1990s (Davis & Johnson, 2008; Boyd, McCabe, & Teter, 2006; Compton & Volkow, 2006). Extensive increases in levels of and harms associated with NMPOU have been documented in the United States. For example, past-year prevalence of NMPOU doubled from 6.5 million in 2000 to 12.5 million in 2007 among the general population (12 years+), with levels among secondary and post-secondary students substantially higher (Substance Abuse and Mental Health Services Administration, 2009a). POA-related emergency room admissions rose from 172,726 to 247,669 (43%) between 2004 and 2006 alone (Substance Abuse and Mental Health Administration, 2008a). POA-related substance-use treatment admissions rose from 16,674 in 1997 to 90,516 in 2007—more than fivefold—in just a decade (Substance Abuse and Mental Health Services Administration, 2009b). Finally, POA-related accidental poisoning deaths more than tripled, from 4,041 in 1999 to 13,755 in 2006, constituting a leading cause of death among healthy adults in the United States (Warner, Chen, & Makuc, 2009).

Canadian data are unfortunately much less systematic and comprehensive. The 2008 CADUMS reported the rate of NMPOU in the general population to be 0.5 per cent, though these data likely represent a substantial underestimation owing to methodological survey limitations; recent survey data have found a NMPOU rate of 6.5 per cent for the Ontario general population (Shield, Ialomiteanu, Fischer, & Rehm, 2011; Fischer, Nakamura, Iaolomiteanu, Boak, & Rehm, 2010). Secondary school surveys for Ontario and the Atlantic provinces have found rates of NMPOU as high as 19 per cent (Brands, Paglia-Boak, Sproule, Leslie, & Adlaf, 2010). The number of admissions for POA-use problems into addiction treatment programs in Ontario approximately doubled from 5,408 in 2004/05 to 10,131 in 2008/09 (Fischer, Nakamura, Rush, Rehm, & Urbanoski, 2010), and both opioid (e.g., methadone) maintenance and detoxification programs in Ontario have experienced substantive increases in POA-related admission (Brands, Blake, Sproule, Gourlay, & Busto, 2004; Sproule, Brands, Li, & Catz-Biro, 2009). Similarly, POA-related accidental poisoning deaths in Ontario doubled from 14 (1991) to 27 (2004) per million population and POAs may now be implicated in half of all drug-related accidental deaths in Canada (Dhalla et al., 2009; Fischer & Rehm, 2009).

While heroin and POAs are similar in their pharmacology, they present distinct challenges for interventions and policy. Heroin, from the production of its raw material (e.g., opium poppy in countries like Afghanistan or Myanmar) to its distribution to the end consumer on street markets, is a fully illegal product and subject to drug law enforcement (Fischer, Bibby, & Bouchard, 2010; Babor et al., 2010). While even large-scale seizures of heroin have been shown to have little effect on availability or pricing of heroin on Canadian street markets, heroin can fluctuate considerably in potency and purity, and so contributes to varying morbidity and mortality (Wood et al., 2003c; Fischer, Gittins, Kendall, & Rehm, 2009). Supply and distribution dynamics of POAs used non-medically are different, with 'diversion' from legitimate sources being a principal pathway (Inciardi et al., 2009; Fischer et al., 2010a). While a large extent of POAs used non-medically among the general population are sourced from family or friends (Substance Abuse and Mental Health Administration (SAMHSA), 2008b), POAs among street drug users are mainly obtained by so-called prescription shopping or 'double doctoring', obtained from drug runners or dealers, traded for other drugs, or—in exceptional instances—obtained by prescription fraud or robberies (Fischer et al., 2009; Joranson & Gilson, 2007; Inciardi, Surratt, Kurtz, & Cicero, 2007). The largest extent of these 'supply' activities for POAs clearly are difficult to enforce by traditional means of drug law enforcement (Fischer, Rehm, & Gittins, 2009). Specifically, North America consumes far more POAs than any other region in the world; overall consumption levels here have doubled in the past decade alone and population level data suggest that levels of NMPOU and harms are linked to the exceptionally high levels of POA availability (Compton & Volkow, 2006; Fischer, Gittins, & Rehm, 2008; International Narcotics Control Board, 2009). POA-rich environments have starkly curtailed local heroin markets in many Canadian cities in favour of POAs, particularly outside of major import cities like Vancouver or Montreal (Fischer, Patra, Firestone Cruz, Gittins, & Rehm, 2008; Fischer et al., 2009). However, possible interventions to reduce NMPOU problems by reducing overall POA supply come with considerable risks. POAs are important analgesic medications, and reductions in their supply or availability could severely undermine the quality of pain care (Hurwitz, 2005; Joranson & Gilson, 2005; Fischer & Rehm, 2008). The shift from heroin to POAs among active street drug users may have some potential upsides from a public health perspective, as POAs can be more predictable in potency and purity to users, which in turn may help avoid overdoses (Fischer et al., 2009). Most POAs can also be used orally, offering users the option of non-injection routes of administration, although many continue injecting (Fischer et al., 2009).

While heroin and POA misuse clearly represents challenges for individual and public health, treatment options also illustrate the tensions between crime and health interventions. Half a century ago, addiction physicians in Canada and the United States began experimenting with methadone—a synthetic and orally administered opioid drug—as a possible substitution treatment for heroin dependence (Halliday, 1963; Dole & Nyswander, 1965). Initially viewed as a potential crime reduction measure, 'methadone maintenance treatment' (MMT) quickly proved to be a rather simple yet effective treatment measure for heroin dependence (Fischer, 2000). Today, MMT is one of the most valued medical interventions, effective in reducing illicit heroin use, criminal behaviour, and BBV transmission risk among heroin-dependent individuals attracted into and retained in treatment (Ward, Hall, & Mattick, 1999; Faggiano, Vigna-Taglianti, & Lemma, 2003). In Canada, MMT quickly grew in use throughout the 1960s. By the early 1970s, there were 23 approved MMT programs with some 1,500 patients enrolled (Peachey & Franklin, 1985; Fischer, 2000). However, drug enforcement authorities increasingly opposed MMT, as it also represented a shift toward the 'medicalization' of the heroin-use problem and hence threatened to undermine the legitimacy and efforts of enforcement (Fischer, 2000). Using claims that methadone spread into illicit markets and simply 'maintained' dependence, law enforcement officials pressured regulators to tighten controls over MMT (Giffen et al., 1991; Fischer, 2000). In response, federal authorities imposed highly restrictive licensing, access, and practice regulations on MMT providers and patients in 1972 (Bishop, 1971; Fischer et al., 2002). Consequently, many physicians holding exemptions stopped providing MMT care, and the number of patients enrolled in MMT drastically declined by 65 per cent from 1972 to 1982, resulting in most undesirable outcomes from a public health perspective (Peachey & Franklin, 1985; Fischer, 2000). In the mid-1990s, federal authorities devolved authority over MMT-provider training and practice standards to provincial authorities, substantially liberalizing and simplifying these parameters (Brands, Brands, & Marsh, 2000). MMT providers can now obtain their (federal) exemption by a short training session, and clinical practice guidelines are mainly set and monitored by provincial Colleges of Physicians and Surgeons (Health Canada, 2009c). Shortly after the deregulation, MMT utilization increased dramatically in Canada. The number of MMT patients increased from 1,771 in 1996 to 22,098 in 2003, and the number of physicians holding an MMT exemption increased from 60 to 846 over the same period (Strike, Urbanoski, Fischer, Marsh, & Millson, 2005; Popova, Rehm, & Fischer, 2006). In 2009, more than 50,000 patients were enrolled in MMT in Canada and 1,318 physicians held a licence to provide MMT (Fischer & Rehm, 2011). Notably, a large proportion of the recent increases in MMT patients are due to POA rather than heroin misuse.

The Le Dain Commission's 'Treatment Report' (1972) had already recognized MMT's limitations, specifically in reaching and providing effective maintenance to long-term heroin addicts (Giffen et al., 1991; Fischer & Rehm, 1997). Even under optimal conditions, MMT at best reaches some 50 per cent of opioid users, with many rotating in and out of treatment (Fischer et al., 2002). In response to MMT limitations and given the increasing public health crisis concerning heroin injecting in the 1990s, several countries launched experimental trials of medical heroin prescription or 'heroin assisted treatment' (HAT) trials for MMT-resistant heroin addicts (Fischer et al., 2002; Fischer et al., 2007). The first such (observational) study was conducted in Switzerland (1995/98), followed by randomized controlled trials (RCTs) in the Netherlands, Germany, Spain, and England (Fischer et al., 2007). A similar study—entitled the 'NAOMI study'—was implemented, after years of preparation, in Canada from 2005 to 2008 (Gantry, Oviedo-Joekes, Laliberté, & Schechter, 2009). Originally planned as a multi-site trial in Vancouver, Montreal, and Toronto, the study was limited to the first two sites owing to a lack of eligible patients and also to resistance from parts of the addiction medicine community in Toronto (Gantry et al., 2009). At a cost of more than $10 million, the NAOMI study confirmed the general findings of other HAT trials—namely, superior treatment retention, decreased heroin use, less criminal activity, and superior physical and mental health improvements compared to controls (in MMT) (Fischer et al., 2007; Gantry et al., 2009; Oviedo-Joekes et al., 2009). While HAT is an expensive and logistically complex treatment (e.g., it requires special treatment clinics), the current federal government has not indicated a readiness to approve HAT as a regular treatment based on the positive study results (Fischer et al., 2007;

Gantry et al., 2009).Aside from major political barriers, HAT is an unrealistic treatment option for the growing population of individuals with POA—rather than heroin—dependence (Van den Brink & Haasen, 2006; Fischer & Rehm, 2006; Kerr, Montaner, & Wood, 2010).

CANNABIS

Cannabis use is highly prevalent in the Canadian population.While about one in nine Canadian adults are current users, one in three young adults use the drug (Adlaf et al., 2005; Health Canada, 2009a). When cannabis became drug law enforcement's main target in the 1960s, cannabis convictions rose from a mere 28 in 1964 to 19,929 in 1973, with the vast majority targeting cannabis possession— that is, use (Giffen et al., 1991; Fischer et al., 2003).While many charges resulted in fines or conditional discharges, they still imposed criminal convictions and records on defendants (Giffen et al., 1991; Fischer et al., 2003; Room, Fischer, Hall, Lenton, & Reuter, 2010). Reviews as far back as the Le Dain Commission (1972) recognized that criminalization of cannabis use was not likely to be effective on an individual level, nor did it constitute good public policy (Le Dain Commission, 1973; Giffen et al., 1991; Fischer et al., 2003). Public opinion polls have repeatedly shown that 50–60 per cent of Canadians think that cannabis use should not be criminally punished, although they do not necessarily oppose legal controls (Giffen et al., 1991; Fischer et al., 2003). Numerous political initiatives since the Le Dain Commission have set out to reform the legal status of cannabis use, yet so far without success (Giffen et al., 1991; Hyshka, 2009; Fischer et al., 2003). While the CDSA limited first-time offences of possession of small amounts of cannabis (less than 30 grams) to a summary conviction process only, with maximum penalties of six months imprisonment or a $1,000 fine (double for repeat offences), these offences still result in criminal convictions and records (Fischer et al., 2003).

More recently, both the House of Commons' Special Committee on the Non-Medical Use of Drugs and the Senate's Special Committee on Illegal Drugs (2002) presented reports that examined alternative law and policy options for cannabis-use control (Fischer et al., 2003). Consequently, successive Liberal governments tabled cannabis-control reform bills (C-38 in 2003 and C-17 in 2004) that proposed the exemption of small amounts (less than 15 grams) of cannabis from criminal punishment, proposing instead the imposition of a non-criminal 'ticket'-like penalty (Fischer et al., 2003; Collin, 2006). Interim drafts of the bill even extended the non-criminal fine for small amounts of cannabis supply production (e.g., several plants) for personal use. As such, these cannabis law reforms were similar to 'expiation notice' schemes implemented in several Australian states, where personal cannabis possession (and in some cases production) is punished by a non-criminal fine (Room et al., 2010). While generally considered successful, these schemes have resulted in concerns over potential net widening as well as use of enforcement discretion (Room et al., 2010).The above cannabis-control reform bills would have established factual decriminalization of personal cannabis possession in Canadian federal law, but neither of the bills received final readings, and they died when the Conservative government took office in 2006 (Collin, 2006; Hyshka, 2009). In the meantime, cannabis offences that were enforced increased from some 43,000 in 1987 to 62,500 in 2007, constituting the vast majority of drug offences enforced under the CDSA (Dauvergne, 2009). The largest proportion—70 to 75 per cent—targeted simple cannabis possession—that is, personal use (Fischer et al., 1998; Dauvergne, 2009). Notably, enforcement patterns for cannabis varied considerably across jurisdictions, with 80 per cent of the total of cannabis offences having been enforced in British Columbia, Ontario, and Quebec (Dauvergne, 2009).

On the health side, the number of individuals admitted to treatment for cannabis problems has increased in recent years. For example, in publicly funded addiction treatment programs in Ontario, 6,219 clients reported cannabis as their primary problem substance in 2000/01, representing 13 per cent of all clients; this figure increased to 33,780 in 2008/09 (Urbanoski, Strike, & Rush, 2005; Drug and Alcohol Treatment Information System, 2009). Notably, a sizable proportion of treatment admissions are diverted or 'coerced' referrals from criminal justice (e.g., as part of a sentence) or workplace (e.g., from drug-testing program) settings and are not necessarily users in need of treatment (Room et al., 2010; Drug and Alcohol Treatment Information System, 2009).

After several Canadian higher courts had heard legal challenges against blanket cannabis-use prohibition as enshrined in the CDSA and the barriers entailed for medicinal cannabis users, the federal government established the so-called Medical Marijuana Access Program (MMAP) in 2001. Through the MMAP, individuals with one of a list of pre-defined—and medically confirmed—severe illnesses (e.g., HIV/AIDS, cancer, glaucoma) could apply for an exemption from the CDSA in order to use cannabis for medicinal purposes (Health Canada, 2005). It took several years of jurisprudential interventions against standing federal law to move toward these health-oriented legal protections for medicinal cannabis use, underscoring the dominance of repressive drug control in federal policy (Hathaway & Rossiter, 2007; Lucas, 2008). Since its creation, the MMAP has been criticized for its overly complex procedures and restrictive eligibility criteria (Belle-Isle & Hathaway, 2007; Lucas, 2008). In 2009, only 4,029 individuals—out of an estimated 400,000 potential medical cannabis users (Canwest News Service, 2010)—were enrolled in the MMAP (Health Canada, 2009b). A larger number of medical cannabis users have been accessing cannabis supplies through so-called Cannabis Compassion Clubs (CCC), now in existence in many cities across Canada. CCCs are non-state charitable facilities providing individuals with confirmed medical needs with cannabis for therapeutic use (Hathaway & Rossiter, 2007; Lucas, 2008). The CCCs formally violate CDSA provisions, yet they exist on the basis of silent agreements between the providers and local law enforcement and rely on self-regulation (Belle-Isle & Hathaway, 2007; Hathaway & Rossiter, 2007). It is estimated that at least 10,000 Canadians regularly procure cannabis from CCCs (Hathaway &

Rossiter, 2007). In California, 200,000 patients now hold medical marijuana–use permits under California's Compassionate Use Act (Room et al., 2010). This development has been described as a form of 'side door' legalization of recreational cannabis use in the general population (Room et al., 2010).

Cannabis production is a vibrant industry in Canada. A Fraser Institute report assessed the annual value of 'grow op' sales in British Columbia alone to be roughly $3.64 billion (or 2.8 per cent of GDP) in 2000 (Easton, 2004). With more than 1.8 million cannabis plants seized in Canada in 2007, it is evident that this industry is widespread; the majority of cannabis production occurs in BC, Ontario, and Quebec, where 90 per cent of the cannabis was seized (National Intelligence Analysis, 2008). In the context of attempts toward easing penalties for personal cannabis use enshrined in federal law, law enforcement has increasingly focused on the 'supply side' of cannabis (Fischer et al., 2003). This emphasis resulted in a considerable increase in the number of cultivation incidents enforced since the late 1990s, more than doubling in some regions; in addition, several special initiatives were launched in select provinces, including 'snitch lines' for cannabis production, specialized tactical units ('green teams'), and the RCMP's appointment of a 'national co-ordinator for marijuana grow operations' (Malm & Tita, 2007). While there are unsubstantiated claims that green teams have been effective in decreasing grow ops within their target area, there is some evidence that these efforts displaced grow ops to neighbouring areas in many instances (Malm & Tita, 2007). Although law enforcement efforts have been enhanced to address the rising number of grow ops, in many cases police seize the drugs and equipment without laying charges (Chin, Dandurand, Plecas, & Segger, 2001; Bouchard, 2007).

DRUG USE IN CORRECTIONS

Due to intensive drug-use enforcement, a majority of illicit substance users, particularly IDUs, report a history of incarceration (Fischer et al., 2005; Jürgens, Ball, & Verster, 2009). For example, in the VIDUS cohort in Vancouver, 59 per cent reported a history of incarceration (Milloy et al., 2008). High rates of criminal justice involvement were also found in the OPICAN cohort, with 50 per cent of participants reporting arrest and 42 per cent reporting detention in the past year (Fischer et al., 2005). Although illicit drugs are strictly prohibited in correctional institutions, illicit drug consumption persists among inmates, many of whom have established drug-use habits (Kerr, Wood, Betteridge, & Lines, 2004). The Correctional Service of Canada (CSC) recently found that 39 per cent of male federal inmates and 33 per cent of females reported using illicit drugs in the past six months, with almost half of these injecting drugs, mainly opioids or cocaine (Zakaria, Thompson, Jarvis, & Borgatta, 2010).

Unfortunately, because of the lack of basic preventive interventions, many drug-related risks (e.g., HIV and HCV transmission) are common within correctional facilities (Small et al., 2005; Wood et al., 2005b). As sterile injecting equipment is not available, equipment sharing is common among IDU inmates, with up to 55 per cent of men and 41 per cent of women in federal prison reporting having used someone else's needle (Zakaria et al., 2010). Numerous international studies have demonstrated that incarceration is a powerful determinant of BBV transmission as well as—especially in the period immediately following release—overdose risk for IDUs (Seaman, Brettle, & Gore, 1998; Binswanger et al., 2007; Farrell & Marsden, 2008). Among CSC inmates who have ever tested, 4.6 per cent were HIV positive and 31 per cent were HCV positive, prevalence rates that are much higher than in the general population (Zakaria et al., 2010; Ubelacker, 2010). In Vancouver, it has been estimated that 21 per cent of HIV infections among IDUs were acquired in prison (Hagan, 2003). Despite the proven effectiveness of needle and syringe programs (NSPs) at reducing HIV and HCV risk (i.e., syringe sharing), the CSC has refused to implement such programs (Kerr et al., 2004; Jürgens et al., 2009). In the absence of NSPs, IDU inmates are provided with bleach for needle and syringe decontamination; this, however, is a suboptimal intervention and commonly ineffective procedure, and some inmates have trouble accessing this service (McCoy et al., 1994; Kerr et al., 2004; Zakaria et al., 2010). It has been observed that the absence of NSPs in prisons denies incarcerated IDUs the right to health under domestic and international law (Kerr et al., 2004; Martin et al., 2005). Conversely, CSC established MMT programming in 1998 (Sibbald, 2002). Initially only designed to continue MMT among patients who had been on treatment prior to incarceration, the program was expanded in 2002 to also initiate opioid-dependent inmates on MMT (Sibbald, 2002). Currently, some seven per cent of CSC inmates are enrolled in the MMT program, and the positive results reported are consistent with international evidence that MMT can be feasible and effective in correctional populations (Dolan, Hall, & Wodak, 1996; Larney, 2010).

CONDITIONAL SENTENCES AND COMPULSORY TREATMENT

Introduced in 1996, 'conditional sentencing' is a relatively new tool in Canadian criminal sentencing. It provides options for offenders—under strict and comprehensive conditions—to serve their sentence in the community or utilize individualized therapeutic measures in lieu of incarceration (Roberts & Cole, 1999; Roberts & Gabor, 2004; MacKay, 2007). Conditional sentences were expected to provide a cost-effective tool for rehabilitative justice, as well as for substance-use offenders, by way of integrating treatment orders for drugs and alcohol into sentencing (Roberts & Gabor, 2004; Marth, 2008; Wild, 1999). There were 42,941 conditional sentences imposed across Canada between 1996 and 1999, 11 per cent of which involved drug-related offences; this proportion increased to 20 per cent by 2006/07, underscoring the growing relevance in this area for and impact on substance-use treatment systems (Drug and Alcohol Treatment Information System, 2009; Roberts & La Prairie, 2000; Marth, 2008). However, these numbers may decrease if 'anti-crime' legislation proposed by the federal government to make certain drug offences ineligible for conditional sentencing is implemented (Department of Justice Canada, 2010).

The use of conditional sentencing has also been questioned owing to the lack of empirical evidence available on its effectiveness (Wild, Roberts, & Cooper, 2002). In a review of the issue, more than 50 per cent of the articles on compulsory treatment were non-empirical, evidence of program effectiveness was mixed, and, of the 18 studies measuring effectiveness, 83 per cent lacked a comparison group, calling into question the strength of their methodology (Wild et al., 2002). Conditional sentences have also been criticized for possible breaches of civil liberties, for the use of legal coercion in treatment, and for violations of patient confidentiality (i.e., information sharing between treatment and criminal justice agencies) (Wild et al., 2001; Klag, O'Callaghan, & Creed, 2005; Seddon, 2007). Furthermore, while relapse is recognized as a natural part of the treatment process, it is regarded as a violation of the offender's conditions from a criminal justice perspective and likely to result in punitive consequences—for example, the suspension of the conditional sentence and/or imprisonment (Conners, Maisto, & Donovan, 1996; Wild, 1999).

DRUG TREATMENT COURTS

Drug treatment courts (DTCs) were first implemented in the United States in the 1980s as a novel form of therapeutic justice and have since been adopted in Canada (Shichor & Sechrest, 2001; Hora, Schuma, & Rosenthal, 1999). According to the Department of Justice Canada, DTCs 'represent a concerted effort to break the cycle of drug use and criminal recidivism' by offering an alternative to incarceration (Department of Justice Canada, 2009a). The majority of DTCs utilize a multidisciplinary team approach, attempting to bridge criminal justice and health services and retain participants in the program (La Prairie, Gliksman, Erickson, Wall, & Newton-Taylor, 2002; Goldkamp, 2000; Bakht, 2005). Participants are typically non-violent offenders charged with drug crimes, with most programs requiring a guilty plea from the offender for acceptance (Fischer et al., 2003; Werb et al., 2007; Department of Justice Canada, 2009b). Once admitted, participants are obliged to attend treatment regularly, appear in court to discuss progress, and undergo random urinalysis testing (Chiodo, 2001; La Prairie et al., 2002). Rewards are offered to participants who demonstrate program compliance and successes (e.g., extended curfews, gift cards), and sanctions are given for breaching conditions (e.g., community service hours, short-term imprisonment); repeated breach of conditions may result in exclusion from the DTC and return to traditional court processing (Fischer et al., 2002; La Prairie et al., 2002; Department of Justice Canada, 2009b). The duration of offenders' involvement in DTC programs in Canada varies between eight and 18 months; participants must generally be drug-free for a period of time, comply with program conditions, and show evidence of life-skill improvements (i.e., employment, housing, education) in order to successfully 'graduate' (Department of Justice Canada, 2009b). DTCs exist in Toronto (established in 1998), Vancouver (2001), Edmonton (2005), Winnipeg (2006), Ottawa (2006), and Regina (2006), and more are in planning. Notably, the 'success' and program expansion of DTCs in Canada were announced by the government in 2001, before a federally funded evaluation of the Toronto DTC pilot project was completed and would have allowed for evidence-based decisions (Anderson, 2001; Fischer, 2003).

The rationale for the development of DTCs is primarily based on three main arguments, namely that DTCs (a) lower criminal recidivism rates, (b) reduce drug use, and (c) are a cost-effective alternative to incarceration (Shichor & Sechrest, 2001; La Prairie et al., 2002; Werb et al., 2007). Unfortunately, there is little evidence, especially in Canada, that DTCs achieve these benefits or that these exceed those achieved through voluntary treatment programs (Werb et al., 2007; Fischer, 2003). Recent evaluations reveal that graduation rates from DTCs are low, between six and 36 per cent, and programs retain less than half of DTC participants (Department of Justice Canada, 2009b). In an evaluation of the Vancouver DTC, within six months of leaving the program, 52 per cent of participants had new charges and 24 per cent had new convictions (Public Safety Canada, 2009). Furthermore, many evaluations have been characterized by methodological issues; for example, they have featured potential design biases toward findings in favour of DTC interventions (Anderson, 2001; Covington, 2001; Shichor & Sechrest, 2001; Fischer, 2003; Werb et al., 2007). Limited outcome data have made cost effectiveness analyses difficult, and although it has been claimed that the costs of DTCs are substantially lower than incarceration, there are questions about what costs are considered for these calculations (La Prairie et al., 2002; Department of Justice Canada, 2009b; Fischer, 2003). There have also been severe concerns that DTC operations undermine fundamental principles of justice as well as individual rights of the offender (Fischer, 2003; Werb et al., 2007; Stinchcomb, 2010).

OTHER RECENT DEVELOPMENTS

The above two case studies—conditional sentencing and drug treatment courts—are instructive, as they illustrate the dominance of criminal control tools in dealings with illicit drug users (Goldkamp, 2000; Fischer, 2003; Rush & Wild, 2003). If an offender does not comply with the extensive conditions imposed by either of the 'therapeutic justice' interventions, it is the criminal justice—and not the treatment—framework that prevails (La Prairie et al., 2002; Fischer, 2003). These new alliances between criminal justice and treatment are potentially problematic on several other levels, since they operate on paradigmatically different philosophies and objectives, many of which stand in tension with principles of good therapeutic care (Boldt, 1998; Goldkamp, 2000; Fischer, 2003). A further fortification of criminal justice principles was Bill C-15, a federal law that sought to establish mandatory minimum sentences (MMS) for select drug offences by, for example, increasing maximum penalties for cannabis production and rescheduling select substances from the CDSA's Schedule III to Schedule I (Dupuis & MacKay, 2010). Despite strong evidence that MMS have been unsuccessful, a renewed version of the bill was reintroduced in May 2010 and was awaiting second reading in the Senate at the time of writing (Gabor & Crutcher, 2002; Dupuis & MacKay, 2010).

These recent steps toward reinforcing the dominance of criminal justice in Canadian drug policy were politically bolstered by the new federal Conservative government's 'National Anti-Drug Strategy' (NADS), launched in 2007 (Department of Justice Canada, 2008). The NADS consists of only three elements, namely prevention, treatment, and enforcement (Department of Justice Canada, 2008). The concept of 'harm reduction', which is commonly used as an umbrella term for pragmatic public health measures like NEPs, SIS, MMT, and HAT and had been included in Liberal government iterations of Canada's Drug Strategy, had been purged. This change was out of step with various international developments, including the United Nation's 'Target Setting Guide', which emphasizes the importance of harm reduction measures in response to drug addiction (World Health Organization, 2005, 2009). The federal government also shifted the lead for the NADS from Health Canada, which had co-ordinated previous drug strategies, to Justice Canada, symbolizing the current dominance of criminal justice ideology.

DRUG LAW AND POLICY IN CANADA—*QUO VADIS*?

Current federal drug law and policy in Canada, with drug-user criminalization at its core, originally evolved as a tool of wider socio-ethnic control a century ago to become dominated by state-based ideologies and practices of crime control (Comack, 1986). Treatment or public health measures aimed at drug use mainly exist as measures subordinated to criminal justice and punishment-oriented interventions (Giffen et al., 1991; Fischer et al., 2002). Under the current abstinence-oriented federal government, efforts to shift drug policy toward more health- and evidence-based approaches have largely failed or have been generally hindered by ideological resistance or institutional inertia to maintain the status quo of criminalization (Fischer et al., 2003). It is worthwhile recalling that the RCMP survived elimination in the 1920s only because it assumed the role of federal drug law enforcement, and up to 9/11, it received a third of its institutional budget for drug enforcement (Giffen et al., 1991; Fischer, 1994). It is also noteworthy that select reforms (e.g., the MMAP or Insite) only occurred thanks to forceful interventions from the courts, not as a result of government-driven law- or policy-making (Mandel, 1994).

Much of the tangible burden of substance use (e.g., drug use in streets and other public places, overdoses, drug-related crime) occurs in Canadian cities and towns, and hence Canadian municipalities have taken an increasingly progressive approach to the drug problem (MacPherson, 2001; Small, 2007; O'Byrne &

Holmes, 2008). Many large Canadian cities—Vancouver is a leading example, partly due to the extreme nature of the drug problem in its Downtown Eastside—have developed their own drug strategies that, while recognizing a place for enforcement, emphasize measures of prevention, treatment, and public health (MacPherson, 2001; Toronto Drug Strategy Advisory Committee, 2005; DeBeck et al., 2008). In some cases, these policies have been supported by municipal policing strategies that view addiction as a health issue (Vancouver Police Department, 2006; DeBeck et al., 2008). Provincial jurisdictions usually shoulder the cost burden for drug-related health care, treatment, and criminal justice costs, and thus have also been supportive of facilitating more sensible public health policy options (MacPherson, 2001). To illustrate, the substantial expansion of MMT occurred under provincial stewardship once devolved from the federal level; NEPs are now integral components of many municipal public health departments across Canada; SCUK dissemination now occurs mainly under the auspices of select provincial or municipal public health authorities; and Insite was launched as a joint initiative by the City of Vancouver and the Vancouver Coastal Health Authority and has been actively defended by the BC government against federal intervention (Brands et al., 2000; Haydon & Fischer, 2005; O'Byrne & Holmes, 2008). In select municipalities, recreational cannabis use by adults is tolerated to some degree in public spaces, allowing for what may result in a gradual normalization of recreational cannabis use (Hathaway, 2004; Levine, 2003). While cannabis smoking stands in tension with current anti-smoking policy, cannabis policy reform would be given a major boost if provincial jurisdictions saw feasible ways to derive tax benefits from cannabis sale or production for personal use. Such reform could serve public health objectives—for example, by reducing black markets for cannabis, establishing quality control of cannabis products, promoting safer use—and the tax income generated could be substantial (Easton, 2004; Room et al., 2010).

CONCLUSION

This chapter reviewed key parameters of illicit drug–use epidemiology, law, and interventions in Canada as they have evolved over the last century, specifically within the particular constellation of conflicting paradigms of criminal justice and public health. Illicit drug use in Canada was originally viewed as a crime problem, and this framework has retained its dominance, despite increasing need and support for health interventions in recent decades. A crucial point to note is that many of the harms associated with illicit drug use described above (e.g., BBVs, overdose mortality, or even black markets) are not necessarily natural consequences of the use of illicit drugs, but in many instances a direct outcome of ineffective or harmful drug policy (e.g., repressive law enforcement aimed at drug use) (Babor et al., 2010; Kerr et al., 2005a). These policies of criminalization, however, are socially chosen and modifiable, yet their revision is an essential condition to the achievement of a more sensible—and less harmful—future policy approach to illicit drug use in Canada, one more aligned with principles of public health. One hundred years after the origins of criminal drug control in Canada, it is time for Canadian drug law and policy to arrive in the twenty-first century and embrace public and individual health as their guiding principles.

CRITICAL THINKING QUESTIONS

1. When thinking about the origins of drug control in Canada, to which extent was there real concern about a 'drug problem' or community health or safety? Why and how is it worthwhile to consider the origins of drug control from a perspective of social control?

2. Given the tension between crime- and health-oriented interventions in illicit drug use in Canada, why and how has criminal control prevailed over and dominated health-oriented approaches for so long?

3. When considering harms related to drug use, why is it important both to focus on and differentiate between the harms from use and the collateral harms from ineffective control or policy?

4. What are the key barriers to reform of drug policy toward more health- and evidence-based interventions in Canada, and what needs to happen to overcome these barriers effectively?

5. The authors contend that deriving taxes from the sale of cannabis would be beneficial, since these resources could be used for public health objectives— that is, by reducing black markets for cannabis, insuring the quality of cannabis products, promoting safer use, etc.—and could also generate significant income in the form of tax revenues. Do you agree with this rationale and policy approach?

REFERENCES

Adlaf, E.M., Begin, P., & Sawka, E. (2005). *Canadian Addiction Survey (CAS): A national survey of Canadians' use of alcohol and other drugs: Prevalence of use and related harms—a detailed report* Ottawa: Canadian Centre on Substance Abuse.

———, & Paglia-Boak, A. (2007). *Drug use among Ontario students 1977–2007: OSDUHS highlights.* CAMH Research Document Series (Rep. No. 21). Toronto: Centre for Addiction and Mental Health.

Anderson, J. (2001). What to do about 'much ado' about drug courts? *International Journal of Drug Policy, 12,* 469–75.

Babor, T., Caulkins, J.P., Griffith, E., Fischer, B., Foxcroft, D.R., Humphreys, K., et al. (2010). *Drug policy and the public good.* Oxford: Oxford University Press.

Bakht, N. (2005). Problem solving courts as agents of change. *Criminal Law Quarterly, 50,* 12–38.

Ballantyne, J. (2007). Regulation of opioid prescribing. *British Medical Journal, 334,* 811–12.

Belle-Isle, L., & Hathaway, A. (2007). Barriers to access to medical cannabis for Canadians living with HIV/AIDS. *AIDS Care, 19,* 500–6.

Binswanger, I., Stern, M., Deyo, R., Heagerty, P., Cheadle, A., Elmore, J., et al. (2007). A high risk of death for former inmates. *New England Journal of Medicine, 356,* 157–65.

Bishop, J.W. (1971). Methadone and the care of the narcotic addict: Report of a Special Joint Committee of CMA and the DNHW Food and Drug Directorate. *Canadian Medical Association Journal, 105,* 1193–201.

Boldt, R.C. (1998). Rehabilitative punishment and the drug treatment court movement. *Washington University Law Quarterly, 76,* 1205–306.

Booth, R.E., Kwiatkowski, C.F., & Chitwood, D.D. (2000). Sex related HIV risk behaviors: Differential risks among injection drug users, crack smokers, and injection drug users who smoke crack. *Drug and Alcohol Dependence, 58,* 219–26.

Bouchard, M. (2007). A capture-recapture model to estimate the size of criminal populations and the risks of detection in a marijuana cultivation industry. *Journal of Quantitative Criminology, 23,* 221–41.

Boyd, C.J., McCabe, S.E., & Teter, C.J. (2006). Medical and nonmedical use of prescription pain medication by youth in a Detroit area public school district. *Drug and Alcohol Dependence, 81,* 37–45.

Brands, B., Blake, J., Sproule, B., Gourlay, D., & Busto, U. (2004). Prescription opioid abuse in patients presenting for methadone maintenance treatment. *Drug and Alcohol Dependence, 73,* 199–207.

———, Paglia-Boak, A., Sproule, B.A., Leslie, K., & Adlaf, E.M. (2010). Nonmedical use of opioid analgesics among Ontario students. *Canadian Family Physician, 56,* 256.

Brands, J., Brands, B., & Marsh, D. (2000). The expansion of methadone prescribing in Ontario, 1996–1997. *Addiction Research, 8,* 485–96.

Broadhead, R.S., Kerr, T.H., Grund, J.-P., & Altice, F.L. (2002). Safer injection facilities in North America: Their place in public policy and health initiatives. *Journal of Drug Issues, 32,* 329–55.

Buxton, J., Skutezky, T., Tu, A., Waheed, B., Wallace, A., & Mak, S. (2009). The context of illicit drug overdose deaths in British Columbia, 2006. *Harm Reduction Journal, 6*:9.

Canwest News Service. (2010). New rules 'slap in the face': Medical marijuana advocates. http://www.canada.com/news/rules+slap+face+Medical+marijuana+advocates/1632440/story.html

Carroll, K., Roundsville, B., & Gawain, F. (1991). A comparative trial of psychotherapies for ambulatory cocaine abusers: Relapse prevention and interpersonal psychotherapy. *American Journal of Drug & Alcohol Abuse, 17,* 229–47.

CBC News. (2010). Ottawa to appeal injection site ruling. The Canadian Press. http://www.cbc.ca/canada/british-columbia/story/2010/02/09/bc-supreme-court-appeal-supervised-injection-site.html

Chin, V., Dandurand, Y., Plecas, D., & Segger, T. (2001). *The criminal justice response to marihuana growing operations in BC.* Abbotsford, BC: Department of Criminology and Criminal Justice, University College of the Fraser Valley.

Chiodo, A. (2001). Sentencing drug-addicted offenders and the Toronto drug court. *Criminal Law Quarterly, 45,* 53–100.

Cohen, J., & Csete, J. (2006). As strong as the weakest pillar: Harm reduction, law enforcement and human rights. *International Journal of Drug Policy, 17,* 101–3.

Collin, C. (2006). *Substance abuse issues and public policy in Canada: II, Parliamentary action (1987–2005)* (Rep. No. PRB 06-05E). Ottawa: Library of Parliament.

Comack, E. (1986). 'We will get some good out of this riot yet': The Canadian state, drug legislation, and class conflict. In S. Brickey & E. Comack (Eds.), *The Social Basis of Law.* Toronto: Garamond.

Compton, W.M., & Volkow, N.D. (2006). Major increases in opioid analgesic abuse in the United States: Concerns and strategies. *Drug and Alcohol Dependence, 81,* 103–7.

Conners, G., Maisto, S., & Donovan, D. (1996). Conceptualizations of relapse: A summary of psychological and psycho-biological models. *Addiction, 91,* S5–S13.

Courtwright, D.T. (1997). The prepared mind: Marie Nyswander, methadone maintenance, and the metabolic theory of addiction. *Addiction, 92,* 257–65.

Covington, J. (2001). Linking treatment to punishment: An evaluation of drug treatment in the criminal justice system. In C. Manski, J. Pepper, & C. Petrie (Eds.), *Informing America's policy on illegal drugs: What we don't know keeps hurting us* (pp. 349–81). Washington, DC: National Academy Press.

Craib, K.J.P., Spittal, P.M., Wood, E., Laliberté, N., Hogg, R.S., Li, K., et al. (2003). Risk factors for elevated HIV incidence among Aboriginal injection drug users in Vancouver. *Canadian Medical Association Journal, 168,* 19–24.

Cross, J., Johnson, B., Rees Davis, W., & James Liberty, H. (2001). Supporting the habit: Income generation activities of frequent crack users compared with frequent users of other hard drugs. *Drug and Alcohol Dependence, 64,* 191–201.

Dalton, A., & Hall, N. (2010, February 9). Ottawa seeks shutdown for BC safe-injection site. *Vancouver Sun.*

Dauvergne, M. (2009). Trends in police-reported drug offences in Canada. *Juristat, 29,* 1–25.

Davis, W., & Johnson, B. (2008). Presciption opioid use, misuse, and diversion among street drug users in New York City. *Drug and Alcohol Dependence, 92,* 267–76.

DeBeck, K., Kerr, T., Li, K., Fischer, B., Buxton, J., & Montaner, J. (2009). Smoking of crack cocaine as a risk factor for HIV infection among people who use injection drugs. *Canadian Medical Association Journal, 181,* 585–9.

————, Small, D., Wood, E., Li, K., & Kerr, T. (2009). Public injecting among a cohort of injecting drug users in Vancouver, Canada. *Journal of Epidemiology & Community Health, 63,* 81–6.

————, Wood, E., Montaner, J., & Kerr, T. (2006). Canada's 2003 renewed drug strategy—An evidence based review. *HIV/AIDS Policy and Law Review, 11,* 1–12.

————, Wood, E., Montaner, J., & Kerr, T. (2009). Canada's new federal 'National Anti-Drug Strategy': An informal audit of reported funding allocation. *International Journal of Drug Policy, 20,* 188–91.

————, Wood, E., Zhang, R., Tyndall, M., Montaner, J., & Kerr, T. (2008). Police and public health partnerships: Evidence from the evaluation of Vancouver's supervised injection facility. *Substance Abuse Treatment, Prevention and Policy, 3:*11.

Department of Justice Canada. (2008). *National Anti-Drug Strategy for Safer and Healthier Communities.* Department of Justice Canada. http://www. nationalantidrugstrategy.gc.ca/back-fich/doc2008_02_21_2.html

————. (2009a). *Drug treatment court funding program.* Department of Justice Canada. http://www.justice.gc.ca/eng/pi/pb-dgp/prog/dtc-ttt/index.html

————. (2009b). *Drug treatment court funding program summative evaluation: Final report.* Ottawa: Department of Justice Canada, Evaluation Division of Strategic Planning and Performance Management.

———. (2010). *Backgrounder: Conditional sentencing reform*. Department of Justice Canada. http://www.justice.gc.ca/eng/news-nouv/nr-cp/2010/doc_32497.html

Dhalla, I., Mamdani, M., Sivilotti, M., Kopp, A., Qureshi, O., & Juurlink, D. (2009). Opioid analgesic prescribing and mortality before and after the introduction of long-acting oxycodone in Ontario. *Canadian Medical Association Journal, 181*, 891–6.

Dolan, K., Hall, W., & Wodak, A. (1996). Methadone maintenance reduces injecting in prison. *British Medical Journal, 312*, 1162.

Dole, V., & Nyswander, M. (1965). A medical treatment for diacetylmorphine (heroin) addiction. *Journal of the American Medical Association, 193*, 646–50.

Drug and Alcohol Treatment Information System. (2009). *Substance abuse statistical tables: 2004–2009.* Toronto: Centre for Addiction and Mental Health (CAMH).

Dupuis, T., & MacKay, R. (2010). *Bill S-10: An act to amend the controlled drug and substances act and to make related and consequential amendments to other acts.* Ottawa: Library of Parliament, Canada.

Easton, S. (2004). *Marijuana growth in British Columbia* (Rep. No. 74). Vancouver: Fraser Institute.

Faggiano, F., Vigna-Taglianti, E., & Lemma, P. (2003). Methadone maintenance at different dosages for opioid dependence. *Cochrane Database of Systematic Reviews, 3*, 1–45.

Farrell, M., & Marsden, J. (2008). Acute risk of drug-related death among newly released prisoners in England and Wales. *Addiction, 103*, 251–5.

Firestone Cruz, M., Fischer, B., Patra, J., Kalousek, K., Newton-Taylor, B., Rehm, J., et al. (2007). Prevalence and associated factors of hepatitis C virus infection (HCV) in a multi-site Canadian population of illicit opioid and other drug users (OPICAN). *Canadian Journal of Public Health, 98*, 130–3.

Fischer, B. (1994). Maps and moves—The discrepancies between rhetoric and realities of Canadian drug policy. *International Journal of Drug Policy, 5*, 70–81.

———. (1999). Prohibition, public health and a window of opportunity: An analysis of Canadian drug policy, 1985–1997. *Policy Studies, 20*, 197–210.

———. (2000). Prescriptions, power and politics: The turbulent history of methadone maintenance in Canada. *Journal of Public Health Policy, 21*, 187–210.

———. (2003). 'Doing good with a vengeance': A critical assessment of the practices, effects and implications of 'drug treatment courts' in North America. *Criminal Justice, 3*, 227–48.

———, Ala-Leppilampi, K., Single, E., & Robins, A. (2003). Cannabis law reform in Canada: Is the 'saga of promise, hesitation and retreat' coming to an end? *Canadian Journal of Criminology and Criminal Justice, 45*, 265–97.

———, Bibby, M., & Bouchard, M. (2010a). Non-medical use and diversion of psychotropic prescription drugs in North America—A review of sourcing routes and control measures. *Addiction, 105*, 2062–70.

———, De Leo, J.A., Allard, C., Firestone Cruz, M., Patra, J., & Rehm, J. (2009). Exploring drug sourcing among regular prescription opioid users in Canada: Data from Toronto and Victoria. *Canadian Journal of Criminology and Criminal Justice, 51*, 55–72.

———, Gittins, J., Kendall, P., & Rehm, J. (2009). Thinking the unthinkable: Could the increasing misuse of prescription opioids among street drug users offer benefits for public health? *Public Health, 123*, 145–6.

————, Gittins, J., & Rehm, J. (2008a). Characterizing the 'awakening elephant': Prescription opioid misuse in North America: Epidemiology, harms, interventions. *Contemporary Drug Problems, 35,* 397–426.

————, Kalousek, K., Rehm, J., Powis, J., Krajden, M., & Reimer, J. (2006b). Hepatitis C, illicit drug use and public health: Does Canada really have a viable plan? *Canadian Journal of Public Health, 97,* 485–8.

————, Nakamura, N., Iaolomiteanu, A., Boak, A., & Rehm, J. (2010b). Assessing the prevalence of non-medical prescription opioid use in the general Canadian population: Methodological issues and questions. *Canadian Journal of Psychiatry—Revue Canadienne de Psychiatrie, 55,* 606–9.

————, Nakamura, N., Rush, B., Rehm, J., & Urbanoski, K. (2010c). Changes in and characteristics of admissions to substance use treatment related to problematic prescription opioid use in Ontario, 2004–2009. *Drug & Alcohol Dependence, 109,* 257–60.

————, Oviedo-Joekes, E., Blanken, P., Haasen, C., Rehm, J., Schechter, M., et al. (2007). Heroin-assisted treatment (HAT) a decade later: A brief update on science and politics. *Journal of Urban Health, 84,* 552–62.

————, Patra, J., Firestone Cruz, M., Gittins, J., & Rehm, J. (2008b). Comparing heroin users and prescription opioid users in a Canadian multi-site population of illicit opioid users. *Drug and Alcohol Review, 27,* 625–32.

————, Popova, L., Rehm, J., & Ivsins, A. (2006a). Drug use related overdose deaths in British Columbia and Ontario, 1992–2002. *Canadian Journal of Public Health, 97,* 384–7.

————, Powis, J., Firestone Cruz, M., Rudzinski, K., & Rehm, J. (2008c). Hepatitis C virus transmission among oral crack users: Viral detection on crack paraphernalia. *European Journal of Gastroenterology & Hepatology, 20,* 29–32.

————, & Rehm, J. (1997). The case for a heroin substitution treatment trial in Canada. *Canadian Journal of Public Health, 88,* 367–70.

————, & Rehm, J. (2006). Illicit opioid use and treatment for opioid dependence: Challenges for Canada and beyond. *Canadian Journal of Psychiatry, 51,* 621–3.

————, & Rehm, J. (2008). Nonmedical use of prescription opioids: Furthering a meaningful research agenda. *Journal of Pain, 9,* 490–3.

————, & Rehm, J. (2009). Deaths related to the use of prescription opioids. *Canadian Medical Association Journal, 181,* 881–2.

————, & Rehm, J. (2011). *Prescription Opioids Misuse, Harms and Control in Canada: A Research and Policy Issues Brief. Report to the Department of Justice of Canada.* Toronto: Centre for Addiction and Mental Health (CAMH).

————, Rehm, J., & Blitz-Miller, T. (2000). Injection drug use and preventive measures: A comparison of Canadian and Western European jurisdictions over time. *Canadian Medical Association Journal, 162,* 1709–13.

————, Rehm, J., Brissette, S., Brochu, S., Bruneau, J., el-Guebaly, N., et al. (2005). Illicit opioid use in Canada: Comparing social, health and drug use characteristics of untreated users in five cities (OPICAN study). *Journal of Urban Health, 82,* 250–66.

————, Rehm, J., & Gittins, J. (2009). *An overview of non-medical use of prescription drugs and criminal justice issues in Canada.* Ottawa: Department of Justice Canada.

————, Rehm, J., Patra, J., & Firestone Cruz, M. (2006b). Changes in illicit opioid use profiles across Canada. *Canadian Medical Association Journal, 175,* 1–3.

———, Rehm, J., Patra, J., Kalousek, K., Haydon, E., Tyndall, M., et al. (2006c). Crack across Canada: Comparing crack and non-crack users in a multi-city cohort of opioid and other street drug users. *Addiction, 101,* 1760–70.

———, Roberts, J., & Kirst, M. (2002). Compulsory drug treatment in Canada: Historical origins and recent developments. *European Addiction Research, 8,* 61–8.

———, Single, E., Room, R., Poulin, C., Sawka, E., Thompson, H., et al. (1998). Cannabis use in Canada: Policy options for control. *Options Politiques, 19,* 34–8.

Gabor, T., & Crutcher, N. (2002). *Mandatory minimum penalties: Their effects on crime, sentencing disparities and justice system expenditures.* Ottawa: Department of Justice Canada, Research and Statistics Division.

Gantry, C., Oviedo-Joekes, E., Laliberté, N., & Schechter, M. (2009). The trials and tribulations of implementing a heroin assisted treatment study in North America. *Harm Reduction Journal, 6*:2.

Giffen, J., Endicott, S., & Lambert, S. (1991). *Panic and indifference—The politics of Canada's drug laws.* Ottawa: Canadian Centre on Substance Abuse.

Goldkamp, J. (2000). The drug court response: Issues and implications for justice change. *Albany Law Review, 63,* 923–61.

Goldstein, J., & Kalant, H. (1990). Drug policy: Striking the right balance. *Science, 249,* 1513–21.

Green, M., & Miller, R. (1975). Cannabis use in Canada. In V. Rubin (Ed.), *Cannabis and culture* (pp. 497–520). The Hague: Mouton Publishers.

Hagan, H. (2003). The relevance of attributable risk measures to HIV prevention planning. *AIDS, 17,* 911–13.

Halliday, R. (1963). Management of the narcotic addict. *British Columbia Medical Journal, 5,* 412–14.

Hankins, C. (1998). Syringe exchange in Canada: Good but not enough to stem the HIV tide. *Substance Use & Misuse, 33,* 1129–45.

Hathaway, A. (2004). Cannabis users' informal rules for managing stigma and risk. *Deviant Behaviour, 25,* 559–77.

———, & Rossiter, K. (2007). Medical marijuana, community building, and Canada's compassionate societies. *Contemporary Justice Review, 10,* 283–96.

Haydon, E., & Fischer, B. (2005). Crack use as a public health problem in Canada— Call for an evaluation of 'safer crack use kits'. *Canadian Journal of Public Health, 96,* 185–8.

Health Canada. (2005). *Frequently asked questions—Medical use of marihuana.* http://www.hc-sc.gc.ca/dhp-mps/marihuana/about-apropos/faq-eng.php

———. (2006). *I-Track: Enhanced surveillance of risk behaviours among injecting drug users in Canada—Phase I Report* Ottawa: Surveillance and Risk Assessment Division, Centre for Infectious Disease Prevention, Health Canada.

———. (2009a). *Canadian Alcohol and Drug Use Monitoring Survey (CADUMS): Summary Results for 2008.* Ottawa: Health Canada. http:// http://www.hc-sc.gc.ca/hc-ps/drugs-drogues/stat/_2008/summary-sommaire-eng.php

———. (2009b). *Marihuana for medical purposes—Statistics (5 June 2009).* http://www.hc-sc.gc.ca/dhp-mps/marihuana/stat/_2009/june-juin-eng.php

———. (2009c). *Methadone Program.* http://www.hc-sc.gc.ca/hc-ps/substancontrol/exemptions/methadone-eng.php

Hora, P., Schuma, W., & Rosenthal, J. (1999). Therapeutic jurisprudence and the drug treatment court movement: Revolutionizing the criminal justice system's response to drug abuse and crime in America. *Notre Dame Law Review, 74,* 439–538.

Hurwitz, W. (2005). The challenge of prescription drug misuse: A review and commentary. *Pain Medicine, 6,* 152–61.

Hyshka, E. (2009). The saga continues: Canadian legislative attempts to reform cannabis law in the twenty-first century. *Canadian Journal of Criminology and Criminal Justice, 51,* 73–91.

Inciardi, J., & Pottieger, A. (1994). Crack cocaine use and street crime. *Journal of Drug Issues, 24,* 273–92.

———, Surratt, H., Cicero, T.J., Kurtz, S., Martin, S., & Parrino, M. (2009). The 'Black Box' of prescription drug diversion. *Journal of Addictive Diseases, 28,* 332–47.

———, Surratt, H.L., Kurtz, S., & Cicero, T.J. (2007). Mechanisms of prescription drug diversion among drug-involved club- and street-based populations. *Pain Medicine, 8,* 171–83.

International Narcotics Control Board. (2009). *Narcotic drugs: Estimated world requirements for 2009. Statistics for 2007* (Rep. No. E/INCB/2008/2). New York: United Nations.

Joranson, D.E., & Gilson, A. (2005). Drug crime is a source of abused pain medications in the United States. *Journal of Pain and Symptom Management, 30,* 209–301.

———, & ———. (2007). A much-needed window on opioid diversion. *Pain Medicine, 8,* 128–9.

Jürgens, R., Ball, A., & Verster, A. (2009). Interventions to reduce HIV transmission related to injecting drug use in prison. *The Lancet Infectious Diseases, 9,* 57–66.

Kerr, T., & O'Briain, W. (2002). Drug policy in Canada—The way forward. *Canadian HIV/AIDS Policy & Law Review, 7,* 27–32.

———, Fairbairn, N., Tyndall, M., Marsh, D., Li, K., Montaner, J., et al. (2006). Predictors of non-fatal overdose among a cohort of polysubstance-using injection drug users. *Drug & Alcohol Dependence, 87,* 39–45.

———, Montaner, J., & Wood, E. (2010). Science and politics of heroin prescription. *The Lancet, 375,* 1849–50.

———, Small, W., Buchner, C., Zhang, R., Li, K., Montaner, J., et al. (2010). Syringe sharing and HIV incidence among injection drug users and increased access to sterile syringes. *American Journal of Public Health, 100,* 1449–53.

———, Small, D., & Wood, E. (2005a). The public health and social impacts of drug market enforcement: A review of the evidence. *International Journal of Drug Policy, 16,* 210–20.

———, Tyndall, M., Li, K., Montaner, J.S.G., & Wood, E. (2005b). Safer injection facility use and syringe sharing in injection drug users. *The Lancet, 366,* 316–18.

———, Wood, E., Betteridge, G., & Lines, R. (2004). Harm reduction in prisons: A 'rights based analysis'. *Critical Public Health, 14,* 345–60.

Kimber, J., Dolan, K., van Beek, I., Hedrich, D., & Zurhold, H. (2003). Drug consumption facilities: An update since 2000. *Drug and Alcohol Review, 22,* 227–33.

Klag, S., O'Callaghan, F., & Creed, P. (2005). The use of legal coercion in the treatment of substance abusers: An overview and critical analysis of thirty years of research. *Substance Use & Misuse, 40,* 1777–95.

La Prairie, C., Gliksman, L., Erickson, P., Wall, R., & Newton-Taylor, B. (2002). Drug treatment courts—A viable option for Canada. Sentencing issues and preliminary findings from the Toronto drug court. *Substance Use & Misuse, 37,* 1529–66.

Landry, F. (2004, August 28). Crack kits condemned: Seen as fueling addiction. *Winnipeg Sun.*

Larney, S. (2010). Does opioid substitution treatment in prisons reduce injecting-related HIV risk behaviours? A systematic review. *Addiction, 105,* 216–23.

Le Dain Commission. (1973). *Final report of the Commission of Inquiry into the Non-Medical Use of Drugs*. Ottawa: Information Canada.

Leonard, L., DeRubeis, E., & Birkett, N. (2006). *City of Ottawa public health safer crack use initiative: Evaluation report*. Ottawa: University of Ottawa.

———, DeRubels, E., Pelude, L., Medd, E., Birkett, N., & Seto, J. (2008). 'I inject less as I have easier access to pipes': Injecting, and sharing of crack-smoking materials, decline as safer crack-smoking resources are distributed. *International Journal of Drug Policy, 19*, 255–64.

Leri, F., Stewart, J., Fischer, B., Jürgens, R., Marsh, D.C., Brissette, S., et al. (2005). Patterns of opioid and cocaine co-use: A descriptive study in a Canadian sample of untreated opioid-dependent individuals. *Experimental & Clinical Psychopharmacology, 13*, 303–10.

Levine, H. (2003). Global drug prohibition: Its uses and crises. *International Journal of Drug Policy, 14*, 145–53.

Lucas, P. (2008). Regulating compassion: An overview of Canada's federal medical cannabis policy and practice. *Harm Reduction Journal, 5*, 1–13.

McCoy, C.B., Rivers, J., McCoy, H.V., Shapshak, P., Weatherby, N., Chitwood, D.D., et al. (1994). Compliance to bleach disinfection protocols among injecting drug users in Miami. *Journal of Acquired Immune Deficiency Syndromes, 7*, 773–6.

MacKay, R. (2007). *Bill C-19: An act to amend the criminal code (conditional sentences of imprisonment)*. Ottawa: Library of Parliament Canada.

MacPherson, D. (2001). A framework for action: A four pillar approach to drug problems in Vancouver. City of Vancouver. http://vancouver.ca/fourpillars/pdf/framework.pdf

Maher, L., Li, J., Jalaludin, B., Chant, K., & Kaldor, J. (2007). High hepatitis C incidence in new injecting drug users: A policy failure? *Australia and New Zealand Medical Journal, 31*, 30–5.

Malchy, L., Bungay, V., & Johnson, J. (2008). Documenting practices and perceptions of 'safer crack use': A Canadian pilot study. *International Journal of Drug Policy, 19*, 339–41.

Malm, A., & Tita, G. (2007). A spatial analysis of green teams: A tactical response to marijuana production in British Columbia. *Policy Sciences, 39*, 361–77.

Mandel, M. (1994). *The Charter of Rights & the legalization of politics in Canada*. Toronto: Thompson Educational Publishing.

Marth, M. (2008). Adult criminal court statistics, 2006/7. *Juristat, 28*, 1–21.

Martin, R.E., Gold, F., Murphy, W., Remple, V., Berkowitz, J., & Money, D. (2005). Drug use and risk of bloodborne infections: A survey of female prisoners in British Columbia. *Canadian Journal of Public Health, 96*, 97–101.

Miller, C.L., Kerr, T., Strathdee, S., Li, K., & Wood, E. (2007). Factors associated with premature mortality among young injection drug users in Vancouver. *Harm Reduction Journal, 4*:1.

———, Strathdee, S., Spittal, P., Kerr, T., Li, K., Schechter, M., et al. (2006). Elevated rates of HIV infection among young Aboriginal injection drug users in a Canadian setting. *Harm Reduction Journal, 3*:9.

———, Tyndall, M., Spittal, P., Li, K., Palepu, A., & Schechter, M.T. (2002). Risk-taking behaviours among injecting drug users who obtain syringes from pharmacies, fixed sites, and mobile van needle exchanges. *Journal of Urban Health, 79*, 257–65.

———, Wood, E., Spittal, P.M., Li, K., Frankish, J.C., Braitstein, P., et al. (2004). The future face of coinfection: Prevalence and incidence of HIV and hepatitis

C virus co-infection among young injection drug users. *Journal of Acquired Immune Deficiency Syndromes, 36*, 743–9.

Milloy, M., Small, W., Tyndall, M., Lai, C., Montaner, J., & Kerr, T. (2008). Incarceration experiences in a cohort of active injection drug users. *Drug and Alcohol Review, 27*, 693–9.

National Intelligence Analysis, Criminal Intelligence, RCMP. (2008). *Drug situation in Canada 2007* (Rep. No. PS61-14/2007E-PDF). Ottawa: Royal Canadian Mounted Police.

O'Byrne, P., & Holmes, D. (2008). Evaluating crack pipe distribution in Canada: A systems change case study. *Addiction Research Theory, 16*, 181–92.

Oviedo-Joekes, E., Marsh, D., Guh, D., Brissette, S., Krausz, M., Anis, A., et al. (2009). Scientific and political challenges in North America's first randomized controlled trial of heroin-assisted treatment for severe heroin addiction: Rationale and design of the NAOMI study. *Clinical Trials, 6*, 261–71.

Palmateer, N., Kimber, J., Hickman, M., Hutchinson, S., Rhodes, T., & Goldberg, D. (2010). Evidence for the effectiveness of sterile injecting equipment provision in preventing hepatitis C and human immunodeficiency virus transmission among injecting drug users: A review of reviews. *Addiction, 105*, 844–59.

Pani, P.P., Trohu, E., Vacca, R., Amato, L., Vecchi, S., & Davoli, M. (2010). Disulfiram for the treatment of cocaine dependence. *Cochrane Database of Systematic Reviews, 1*, 1–50.

Peachey, J., & Franklin, T. (1985). Methadone treatment of opiate dependence in Canada. *British Journal of Addiction, 80*, 291–9.

Petrar, S., Kerr, T., Tyndall, M., Zhang, R., Montaner, J., & Wood, E. (2007). Injection drug users' perceptions regarding use of a medically supervised safer injection facility. *Addictive Behaviors, 32*, 1088–93.

Popova, S., Rehm, J., & Fischer, B. (2006). An overview of illegal opioid use and health services utilization in Canada. *Public Health, 120*, 320–8.

Public Health Agency of Canada. (2009). *HIV and AIDS in Canada: Surveillance report to December 31, 2008*. Ottawa: Surveillance and Risk Assessment Division, Centre for Communicable Disease and Infection Control.

Public Safety Canada. (2009). *Drug treatment court of Vancouver (DTCV): Evaluation summaries*. http://www.publicsafety.gc.ca/res/cp/res/_fl/2008-ES-18-eng.pdf

Rehm, J., Baliunas, D., Brochu, S., Fischer, B., Patra, J., Popova, S., et al. (2006). *The costs of substance abuse in Canada, 2002*. Ottawa: Canadian Centre on Substance Abuse.

Ritter, A., & Cameron, J. (2006). A review of the efficacy and effectiveness of harm reduction strategies for alcohol, tobacco and illicit drugs. *Drug and Alcohol Review, 25*, 611–24.

Roberts, J., & Cole, D. (1999). *Making sense of sentencing*. Toronto: University of Toronto Press.

———, & Gabor, T. (2004). Living in the shadow of prison: Lessons from the Canadian experience in decarceration. *British Journal of Criminology, 44*, 92–112.

Roberts, J.V., & La Prairie, C. (2000). *Conditional sentencing in Canada: An overview of research findings*. Ottawa: Department of Justice.

Room, R., Fischer, B., Hall, W., Lenton, S., & Reuter, P. (2010). *Cannabis policy: Moving beyond stalemate*. New York: Oxford University Press.

Ross, M.W., Hwang, L.Y., Zack, C., Bull, L., & Williams, M.L. (2002). Sexual risk behaviours and STIs in drug abuse treatment populations whose drug of choice is crack cocaine. *International Journal of STD and AIDS, 13*, 769–74.

Rush, B., & Wild, T. (2003). Substance abuse treatment and pressures from the criminal justice system: Data from a provincial client monitoring system. *Addiction, 98,* 1119–28.

Seaman, S., Brettle, R., & Gore, S. (1998). Mortality from overdose among injecting drug users recently released from prison: Database linkage study. *British Medical Journal, 316,* 426–8.

Seddon, T. (2007). Coerced drug treatment in the criminal justice system: Conceptual, ethical and criminological issues. *Criminology and Criminal Justice, 7,* 269–86.

Shannon, K., Rusch, M., Morgan, R., Oleson, M., Kerr, T., & Tyndall, M. (2008). HIV and HCV prevalence and gender-specific risk profiles of crack cocaine smokers and dual users of injection drugs. *Substance Use and Misuse, 43,* 521–34.

Shearer, J., & Gowing, L. (2004). Pharmacotherapies for problematic psychostimulant use: A review of current research. *Drug and Alcohol Review, 23,* 203–11.

Shichor, D., & Sechrest, D. (2001). Introduction: Special issue on drug courts. *Journal of Drug Issues, 31,* 1–6.

Shield, K.D., Ialomiteanu, A., Fischer, B., & Rehm, J. (2011). Assessing the prevalence of non-medical prescription opioid use in the Canadian general adult population: Evidence of large variation depending on survey questions used (unpublished).

Sibbald, B. (2002). Methadone maintenance expands inside federal prisons. *Canadian Medical Association Journal, 167,* 1154.

Siqueland, L., Crits-Christoph, P., Barber, J., Connoly Gibbens, M., Gallop, R., Griffin, M., et al. (2004). What aspects of treatment matter to the patient in the treatment of cocaine dependence? *Journal of Substance Abuse Treatment, 27,* 169–78.

Small, D. (2007). Fools rush in where angels fear to tread: Playing God with Vancouver's supervised injection facility in the political borderland. *International Journal of Drug Policy, 18,* 18–26.

Small, W., Kain, S., Laliberté, N., Schechter, M., O'Shaughnessy, M.V., & Spittall, P. (2005). Incarceration, addiction and harm reduction: Inmates experience injecting drugs in prison. *Substance Use and Misuse, 40,* 831–43.

Smart, R.G. (1983). *Forbidden highs: The nature, treatment, and prevention of illicit drug use.* Toronto: Addiction Research Foundation.

Solomon, R., & Green, M. (1988). The first century: The history of non-medical opiate use and control policies in Canada, 1870–1970. In J. Blackwell & P. Erickson (Eds.), *Illicit Drugs in Canada: A Risky Business* (pp. 88–116). Toronto: Nelson Canada.

Spittal, P., Craib, K., Wood, E., Laliberté, N., Li, K., Tyndall, M., et al. (2002). Risk factors for elevated HIV incidence rates among female injection drug users in Vancouver. *Canadian Medical Association Journal, 166,* 894–99.

Sproule, B., Brands, B., Li, S., & Catz-Biro, L. (2009). Changing patterns in opioid addiction. Characterizing users of oxycodne and other opioids. *Canadian Family Physician, 55,* 68–9.

Stinchcomb, J.B. (2010). Drug courts: Conceptual foundation, empirical findings, and policy implications. *Drugs: Education, Prevention, and Policy, 17,* 148–67.

Stoltz, J., Wood, E., Small, D., Li, K., Tyndall, M., Montaner, J., et al. (2007). Changes in injecting practices associated with the use of a medically supervised safer injection facility. *Journal of Public Health, 29,* 35–9.

Strathdee, S.A., Patrick, D.M., Archibald, C.P., Ofner, M., Cornelisse, P.G.A., Rekart, M., et al. (1997a). Social determinants predict needle-sharing behaviour among injection drug users in Vancouver, Canada. *Addiction, 92,* 1339–47.

———, Patrick, D.M., Currie, S.L., Cornelisse, P.G., Rekart, M.L., Montaner, J.S., et al. (1997b). Needle exchange is not enough: Lessons from the Vancouver injecting drug use study. *AIDS, 11,* F59–F65.

Strike, C., Urbanoski, K., Fischer, B., Marsh, D., & Millson, P. (2005). Policy changes and the methadone maintenance treatment system for opioid dependence in Ontario, 1996 to 2001. *Journal of Addictive Diseases, 24,* 39–51.

Substance Abuse and Mental Health Administration. (2008a). *Drug Abuse Warning Network, 2006: National estimates of drug-related emergency department visits* (DAWN Series D-30, DHHS Publication No. [SMA] 08-4339). Rockland, MD: Office of Applied Studies, Substance Abuse and Mental Health Administration.

———. (2008b). *Results from the 2007 National Survey on Drug Use and Health: National findings* (NSDUH Series H-34, DHHS Publication No. SMA 08-4343). Rockville, MD: Office of Applied Studies, Substance Abuse and Mental Health Services Administration.

———. (2009a). *Results from the 2008 National Survey on Drug Use and Health: National Findings* (NSDUH, Series H-36, HHS Publication No. SMA 09-4434). Rockville, MD: Office of Applied Studies, Substance Abuse and Mental Health Services Administration.

———. (2009b). *Treatment episode data set (TEDS) highlights—2007. National Admissions to Substance Abuse Treatment Services* (DASIS Series: S-45, DHHS Publication No. (SMA) 09-4360). Rockville, MD: Office of Applied Studies, Substance Abuse and Mental Health Services Administration.

Toronto Drug Strategy Advisory Committee. (2005). The Toronto drug strategy: A comprehensive approach to alcohol and other drugs. City of Toronto. http://www.toronto.ca/health/drugstrategy/pdf/tds_report.pdf

Tortu, S., McMahon, J., Pouget, E., & Hamid, R. (2004). Sharing of noninjection drug-use implements as a risk factor for hepatitis C. *Substance Use and Misuse, 39,* 211–24.

Tyndall, M., Wood, E., Zhang, R., Lai, C., Montaner, J., & Kerr, T. (2006). HIV seroprevalence among participants at a supervised injection facility in Vancouver, Canada: Implications for prevention, care and treatment. *Harm Reduction Journal, 3:*36.

Ubelacker, S. (2010). Needle exchange needed to curb rising HIV rate in Cdn prisons: Advocacy groups. http://proxy.lib.sfu.ca/login?url=http://proquest.umi.com/pqdweb?did=2015598871&sid=1&Fmt=3&clientId=3667&RQT=309&VName=PQD

Urbanoski, K., Strike, C., & Rush, B.R. (2005). Individuals seeking treatment for cannabis-related problems in Ontario: Demographic and clinical profile. *European Addiction Research, 11,* 115–23.

Vancouver Police Department. (2006). *Vancouver Police Department drug policy.* Vancouver.

Van den Brink, W. (2005). Epidemiology of cocaine and crack: Implications for drug policy and treatment planning. *Sucht, 51,* 196–8.

———, & Haasen, C. (2006). Evidence-based treatment of opioid dependent patients. *Canadian Journal of Psychiatry, 51,* 635–46.

Ward, J., Hall, W., & Mattick, R. (1999). Role of maintenance treatment in opioid dependence. *The Lancet, 353,* 221–6.

Warner, M., Chen, L.H., & Makuc, D.M. (2009). *NCHS data brief: Increase in fatal poisonings involving opioid analgesics in the United States, 1999–2006* (Rep. No. 22). Hyattsville, MD: US Department of Health and Human Services, Centers for Disease Control and Prevention, National Center for Health Statistics.

Werb, D., DeBeck, K., Kerr, T., Li, K., Montaner, J., & Wood, E. (2010). Modelling crack cocaine use trends over 10 years in a Canadian setting. *Drug and Alcohol Review, 29,* 271–7.

———, Elliott, R., Fischer, B., Wood, E., Montaner, J., & Kerr, T. (2007). Drug treatment courts in Canada: An evidence-based review. hiv/aids *Policy and Law Review, 12,* 12–17.

Wild, C., Roberts, A., & Cooper, E. (2002). Compulsory substance abuse treatment: An overview of recent findings and issues. *European Addiction Research, 8,* 84–93.

Wild, T.C. (1999). Compulsory substance abuse treatment and harm reduction: A critical analysis. *Substance Use & Misuse, 34,* 83–102.

———, Newton-Taylor, B., Ogborne, A.C., Mann, R., Erickson, P., & Macdonald, S. (2001). Attitudes toward compulsory substance abuse treatment: A comparison of the public, conselors, probationers, and judges' views. *Drugs: Education, Prevention & Policy, 8,* 33–45.

Wood, E., Kerr, T., Lloyd-Smith, E., Buchner, C., Marsh, D.C., Montaner, J.S.G., et al. (2004a). Methodology for evaluating Insite: Canada's first medically supervised safer injection facility for injection drug users. *Harm Reduction Journal, 1,* 9.

———, Kerr, T., Small, W., Jones, J., Schechter, M.T., & Tyndall, M.W. (2003a). The impact of a police presence on access to needle exchange programs. *Journal of Acquired Immune Deficiency Syndromes, 34,* 116–18.

———, Kerr, T., Small, W., Li, K., Marsh, D.C., Montaner, J.S.G., et al. (2004b). Changes in public order after the opening of a medically supervised safer injecting facility for illicit injection drug users. *Canadian Medical Association Journal, 171,* 731–4.

———, Kerr, T., Spittal, P.M., Li, K., Small, W., Tyndall, M.W., et al. (2003b). The potential public health and community impacts of safer injecting facilities: Evidence from a cohort of injection drug users. *Journal of Acquired Immune Deficiency Syndromes and Human Retrovirology, 32,* 2–8.

———, Kerr, T., Stoltz, J., Qui, Z., Zhang, R., & Montaner, J. (2005a). Prevalence and correlates of hepatitis C infection among users of North America's first medically supervised safer injection facility. *Public Health, 119,* 1111–15.

———, Kerr, T., Tyndall, M., & Montaner, J. (2008). The Canadian government's treatment of scientific process and evidence: Inside the evaluation of North America's first medically supervised safer injection facility. *International Journal of Drug Policy, 19,* 220–5.

———, Montaner, J., & Kerr, T. (2005b). HIV risks in incarcerated injection-drug users. *The Lancet, 366,* 1834–5.

———, Stoltz, J., Montaner, J., & Kerr, T. (2006). Evaluating methamphetamine use and risks of injection initiation among street youth: The ARYS study. *Harm Reduction Journal, 3*:18.

———, Tyndall, M., Zhang, R., Montaner, J., & Kerr, T. (2007). Rate of detoxification service use and its impact among a cohort of supervised injecting facility users. *Addiction, 102,* 916–19.

———, Tyndall, M., Spittal, P., Li, K., Anis, A.H., Hogg, R., et al. (2003c). Impact of supply-side policies for control of illicit drugs in the face of the AIDS and overdose epidemics: Investigation of a massive heroin seizure. *Canadian Medical Association Journal, 168,* 165–9.

————, Tyndall, M., Stoltz, J., Small, W., Lloyd-Smith, E., Zhang, C., et al. (2005c). Factors associated with syringe sharing among users of a medically supervised safer injecting facility. *American Journal of Medical Sciences, 1*, 50–4.

World Health Organization. (2005). *Status paper on prisons drugs and harm reduction* Copenhagen: WHO Regional Office for Europe.

————. (2009). *WHO, UNODC, UNAIDS Technical Guide: For countries to set targets for universal access to hiv prevention, treatment and care for injecting drug users.* Geneva: World Health Organization.

Young, A.N. (2004). *Justice defiled: Perverts, potheads, serial killers and lawyers.* Toronto: Key Porter Books.

Zakaria, D., Thompson, J., Jarvis, A., & Borgatta, F. (2010). *Summary of emerging findings from the 2007 National Inmate Infectious Disease and Risk-Behaviours Survey.* Ottawa: Corrections Service of Canada.

9

Terrorism and National Security Policy-Making in Canada

Kent Roach

INTRODUCTION

This chapter will examine national security policy-making in Canada since the terrorist attacks of 11 September 2001. This policy-making process has been complex and controversial. It has involved both Parliament and the courts, and these institutions have responded to a variety of domestic and international pressures. Canada's initial response to 9/11 was the enactment of a massive new anti-terrorism law, the Anti-Terrorism Act (henceforth the ATA).[1] This law fit into a pattern of 'governing through crime'[2] because it created many new terrorism crimes even though 9/11 was more of an intelligence and law enforcement failure than a failure of the criminal law.[3] Criminal law was used as a symbolic means to signal that Canada would be 'tough on terrorism'.

In subsequent years, however, the Canadian government took a more nuanced approach based on a broader human security agenda. This approach included the 2004 enactment of the Public Safety Act, which provided a legislative framework for increased aviation security efforts and increased information sharing within government, and enabled the executive to respond better to a broad range of emergencies. The Act also contemplated increased protection and surveillance of critical infrastructure such as pipelines, electricity lines, and airports, and increased control over dangerous materials such as explosives and toxins.[4] In the same year, the government released its first official national security policy that was designed to provide a response to 'all risks' including terrorism and threats to public health from natural disasters and pandemics.[5] Such an all-risk human security approach has elements of neo-liberal governance and crime prevention, and it employs both the private and public sectors in an attempt to manage risks.[6]

Another characteristic of Canada's national security policy-making is how it has intersected with Canadian immigration and multiculturalism policy. In 2002, Canada signed a safe third-country agreement with the United States that prohibited refugee applications to Canada once a person had reached the United States. This was a response to American concerns about Canadian immigration policy as well as to the 1999 arrest of Ahmed Ressam, a failed refugee applicant to Canada who attempted to enter the United States to commit acts of terrorism. Nevertheless, the safe third-country agreement was a blunt and over-inclusive anti-terrorism tool that decreased the number of refugees who came to Canada. Canada also relied on immigration law as anti-terrorism law by using security certificates to subject five non-citizens alleged to be associated with Al-Qaeda to indefinite detention. When used as anti-terrorism law, immigration law allowed forms of indeterminate detention and secret evidence that would not be accepted under regular criminal law. The regular criminal law was, however, subsequently used to successfully prosecute a number of Canadian citizens for being involved in terrorist activities both at home and abroad.

The use of immigration law as anti-terrorism law also raised other human rights issues; there was concern, for example, that detained non-citizens, if deported to countries such as Egypt and Syria, would face torture. Canada's commitment not to be complicit with torture was challenged in the post-9/11 era. Public inquiries were conducted to examine the actions of Canadian officials in relation to Maher Arar and other Canadian citizens held on suspicion of terrorism and tortured in Syria. Concerns were also raised about the treatment of detainees that the Canadian Forces handed over to Afghan security officials. One might have expected that the Canadian Charter of Rights and Freedoms would have provided unequivocal and absolute protection against torture, as does international law. Unfortunately, as a sign that due process may at times be for crime control and may attempt to legitimate repressive measures,[7] the Supreme Court of Canada in 2002 refused to rule out the possibility that deportation to face torture could be justified under the Charter in 'exceptional circumstances'[8] and the Federal Court of Appeal held that the Charter would not apply in Afghanistan even if detainees were transferred from Canadian to Afghan officials in a situation that carried a substantial risk of torture.[9]

The action of Canadian security officials in the Arar and other similar cases might not have come to light or been reviewed unless media and public pressures had caused the government to appoint extraordinary public inquiries into these matters, inquiries that have been conducted independently of government by sitting or retired judges. Nevertheless, the low visibility of much executive action is reinforced by the widespread use of secrecy in national security matters.[10] It is also affirmed by the Canadian government's failure to follow the recommendation of recent commissions of inquiry to create review bodies that could keep pace with the increased intensity and integration of the government's national security activities.[11]

National security policy-making in Canada has been influenced by a variety of international pressures. There were widespread but false rumours that some of the 9/11 plotters had entered the United States through Canada. One part of the Patriot Act—labelled 'defending the Northern Border'—reflected American concerns about security threats from Canada in a heavy-handed manner. In the immediate aftermath of 9/11, Canadian officials co-operated with American security officials in secret and problematic ways. In 2002, the Royal Canadian Mounted Police (RCMP) disclosed full terrorism investigative files to their American counterparts without vetting the information for its relevance, accuracy, and reliability or attaching the usual restrictions or caveats on the Americans' subsequent use of the Canadian information. Included in these files was inaccurate information that labelled Canadian citizens Maher Arar and his wife as Islamic extremists with links to Al-Qaeda. This information likely played a role in the decision to detain Arar when he was transiting through the United States and then to render him to Syria, where he was tortured and detained for almost a year.[12] The Canadian government subsequently apologized to Mr. Arar and paid him $10.5 million in compensation. The Bush government made no apologies, and Arar was allowed to remain on the American watchlist, even under President Obama. Arar's lawsuit against American authorities has been thwarted by claims of state secrecy. Arar has become something of a hero in Canada, while the American government apparently still considers him a security threat.

Canada acquiesced to the continued detention of Omar Khadr, a Canadian citizen, at Guantanamo Bay. Khadr eventually pled guilty to killing an American solider in Afghanistan when he was 15 years old. Although the Canadian government made some diplomatic attempts to persuade the Americans that it was not appropriate to detain the severely wounded teenager in Guantanamo, it has refused publicly to criticize American actions in detaining and trying him before a military commission. The Canadian government's actions have shown little concern over the facts that Khadr was only 15 years old at the time of the incident and that he has been treated harshly by the Americans. In 2005, however, a Canadian court enjoined CSIS officials from continuing to interrogate Khadr at Guantanamo. In 2008, the Supreme Court of Canada held that the results of previous interrogations should be disclosed to Khadr because Canadian officials had breached the Charter by participating in violations of international human rights committed against Khadr at Guantanamo.[13] In 2010, the Supreme Court held again that the Canadian interrogation of Khadr at Guantanamo had breached his Charter and international human rights but refused—because of concerns with interfering with the government's foreign policy-making responsibilities—to order that Canada ask the Americans to repatriate Khadr.[14] The government responded to the decision by issuing a diplomatic note requesting that the United States not use information obtained from Canadian officials in its prosecution of Khadr before a military commission. A subsequent case found that this diplomatic note—which the United States did not agree to respect—did not provide an effective remedy, but the government appealed and obtained a stay of this ruling and the appeal was found moot in light of Khadr's subsequent decision to plead guilty before an American military commission.[15]

Canada, as well as the United States, has been influenced by the demand of the United Nations (UN) Security Council that every country enact tough anti-terrorism laws, including laws prohibiting the financing of terrorism. One of the reasons the ATA was enacted so quickly after 9/11 was the perceived need to be able to report to the UN Security Council that Canada had complied with Resolution 1373. Laws against terrorism financing as promoted by the UN and other bodies require lists of terrorists to be distributed to financial institutions that then effectively enforce the laws. The executive designation of terrorist groups and individuals by the UN and domestic jurisdictions, including Canada, makes a person a terrorist outlaw without a trial or any discernable due process. A person or group listed as a terrorist receives no prior notice of the listing decision and a limited right of judicial review after the decision has been made. In Canada, at least one person, Liban Hussein, was wrongfully listed as a terrorist under both UN and Canadian lists, an error that was corrected by the government after more than six months and considerable harm to Hussein.[16] In addition, the United Nations listed Abousfian Abdelrazik, a Canadian citizen, as a terrorist on the basis of secret intelligence, and he had to secure a court order to be allowed to return to Canada from Sudan.[17] International bodies such as the Security Council of the United Nations are increasingly making policy in criminal justice matters, and they seem to be at least as attracted to emotive appeals to victims' rights over due process rights and questionable assumptions that tough laws will prevent crimes as domestic legislatures are.[18]

Canada has not responded to all international demands for tough new anti-terrorism policies. United Nations Security Council Resolution 1624, adopted on 14 September 2005,[19] called upon all states to take steps to prevent incitement to commit acts of terrorism. The criminalization of speech is a problematic anti-terrorism strategy both because it burdens freedom of expression and because criminal prosecutions of such speech may be counterproductive. The Canadian approach to criminalizing speech associated with terrorism has so far been relatively cautious, and Canada has enacted no new laws in response to Resolution 1624. Indeed, Canada has been relatively sensitive to concerns that political and religious speech not be associated with terrorism, and it amended the ATA when it was still before Parliament in November 2001 to provide that 'for greater certainty, the expression of a political, religious, or ideological thought, belief or opinion' will not constitute a terrorist activity unless the expression satisfies the other definition of terrorist activities.[20] Canada did, however, strengthen the ability of the state to seize and remove hate propaganda from the Internet[21] and it created a new offence of mischief to religious property,[22] both on the basis of concerns about the connection between hate speech and terrorism. Although a Commons committee in March 2007 called for the enactment of the new offence of glorifying terrorism for the purposes of emulation[23] and a similar offence was enacted in Britain in 2006, Canada has not yet enacted such an offence.

Although Canadian national security policy continues to evolve, enough has occurred since 9/11 to allow for an evaluation of the policy-making process. The frequent interchange among Parliament, civil society, and the courts underlines the complex and controversial nature of national security policy-making in Canada. This chapter will critically evaluate the respective roles of Parliament and the courts with regard to some of the most important features of Canadian anti-terrorism law. The first part will examine and assess the contributions of Parliament and the courts to the fundamental issue of how to define terrorism and terrorist activities. The second part will focus on legislative and judicial treatments of the controversial new anti-terrorism powers of investigative hearings and preventive arrests. The third part will examine legislative and judicial treatment of security certificates issued under immigration law. Each of these topics could require a chapter in its own right, but my focus will be on what post-9/11 developments tell us about the national security policy-making process.[24] In other words, how have the policy issues been defined, framed, and sold to the public, and what is their likely effectiveness in achieving multiple goals, including preventing terrorism, respecting rights and liberties, responding to American security concerns, and ensuring that Canada plays its role in the international struggle against terrorism. I will also relate these aspects of national security policy-making to other forms of criminal justice policy-making discussed in this book.

THE DEFINITION OF TERRORISM AND TERRORIST ACTIVITIES

The ATA Debate

Bill C-36, containing what was to become the ATA, was introduced in Parliament on 15 October 2001. It weighed in at over 170 pages of legislative text that for the most part had been quickly drafted in the large and tragic shadow of 9/11. Although it was not enacted with the same rapidity as the USA Patriot Act—a speed that had prevented many American legislators from reading the text of that law—the debates about the ATA were rushed. The federal government took the position that because UN Security Council Resolution 1373 required all nations to enact laws against terrorism and the financing of terrorism and to report to a new United Nations Counter-Terrorism Committee by the end of 2001, Canada's Bill C-36 would have to become law by the end of 2001. It was in fact proclaimed in force on 18 December 2001.[25]

Perhaps because the government felt secure with its majority position in Parliament and was committed to legislating in response to 9/11, there was a robust debate about the ATA in committees in the Commons and the Senate. Books were written about the bill, and the media produced extensive analyses of its potential effects on civil liberties.[26] Groups representing Aboriginal people, unions, charities, refugees, and lawyers, as well as watchdog review agencies such as the Privacy and Access to Information Commission and the Canadian Human Rights Commission, all voiced their concerns about the bill as originally drafted to Commons and the Senate committees. The committees made some important recommendations, some of which were adopted as amendments to the bill. The result has been described as 'the most balanced example of legislative activism to date'[27] and one that demonstrated the ability of Parliament to take rights considerations into account. The committees certainly made important contributions to the ATA, but party discipline and closure were imposed to end the parliamentary debate, leading some members of Parliament, such as former prime minister Joe Clark, to criticize the process as 'a travesty of democracy'.[28] As will be seen, the courts have found a few parts of the ATA to be wanting under the Charter.

The omnibus and complex nature of the ATA made it difficult for interested persons and parliamentarians to assess all parts of the Act. Much of the debate revolved around the definition of terrorist activities, the introduction of investigative hearings and preventive arrests, and the effects of the law on charities. The implications of the more technical parts of the Act relating to signals intelligence, terrorist financing, and government secrecy received less attention. The important role that immigration law and in particular security certificates would play as anti-terrorism law was also largely ignored,[29] as were issues related to the review of national security activities. Bill C-36 affirmed that Parliament could enact omnibus measures and restructure much of the legal framework with respect to terrorism investigations and trials. Nevertheless, Parliament could not always focus on issues that would emerge in the future. The first criminal charges under the ATA was not laid until 2004, and in the meantime, Canada relied on immigration law security certificates as its prime response to terrorism, even though these instruments were not included in the ATA or subject to substantial debate after 9/11. The issues of information sharing and review of the RCMP's national security activities raised by Canada's involvement in the Maher Arar case were also not on Parliament's agenda in the immediate aftermath of 9/11.

The ATA Debate about the Definition of Terrorist Activities

United Nations Security Council Resolution 1373, enacted immediately after 9/11, called on all states under the mandatory provisions of Chapter VII of the United Nations Charter to ensure that terrorism was treated as a serious crime, but the resolution did not attempt to define terrorism. That difficult and controversial task was left to each domestic government. Many countries opted for broad and arguably over-broad definitions of terrorism that in turn gave police, prosecutors, and judges, as well as those in the private sector who were called on to enforce laws against terrorist financing, more discretion in determining whether a person was a terrorist.

Much of the ATA debate focused on the definition of terrorist activities that was to be included for the first time in the Criminal Code. As first introduced, the

ATA would have defined terrorist activities to include serious disruptions of essential public or private services so long as such activities were politically or religiously motivated and designed to intimidate a segment of the public with regard to its security or to compel a government or any person to act. The only exemption from this sweeping prohibition was for 'lawful advocacy, protest, dissent or stoppage of work'. This broad definition of terrorism inspired the widespread concern among many civil society groups that the Act would brand many illegal protests and strikes as terrorism. This concern led to amendments—before the bill became law—that dropped the requirement that exempted protests must be lawful.[30] Parliament was able to amend the bill to reflect the widespread concern that the initial definition of terrorist activities was too broad and would apply to illegal protests and strikes.

Groups representing Muslim and Arab Canadians and others expressed the concern that the unusual requirement that the prosecution establish a political or religious motive for a terrorist activity might also result in a process in which a person's political or religious views were used against them in a terrorism prosecution. Again, Parliament was responsive to these concerns and provided that the expression of religious, political, or ideological thought or opinions would not normally be considered terrorist activities.[31] These amendments demonstrate the ability of legislative debate and legislative committees to improve a bill before it is enacted and to respond to concerns expressed by some that proposed legislation would violate rights. As such, the ATA debate can be seen as an exercise in 'governmentality',[32] as the government made some strategic concessions but was also able to ensure that a large new act to criminalize terrorism was enacted in the Criminal Code in part to comply with UN Security Council demands for such legislation.

The Supreme Court's Definition of Terrorism in Suresh

In 2002, the Supreme Court weighed in on the difficult issue of defining terrorism in *Suresh v. Canada*.[33] The court was confronted with an undefined reference to terrorism in the Immigration and Refugee Protection Act.[34] The court was aware of the difficulties of defining terrorism and commented that

> one searches in vain for an authoritative definition of 'terrorism'. The Immigration Act does not define the term. Further, there is no single definition that is accepted internationally. The absence of an authoritative definition means that, at least at the margins, 'the term is open to politicized manipulation, conjecture, and polemical interpretation' . . . Perhaps the most striking example of the politicized nature of the term is that Nelson Mandela's African National Congress was, during the apartheid era, routinely labeled a terrorist organization, not only by the South African government but by much of the international community.

After recognizing the difficulties of defining terrorism, the Supreme Court came up with its own definition of terrorism, which it then read into the undefined reference to terrorism in Canada's immigration law. It concluded:

> [F]ollowing the International Convention for the Suppression of the Financing of Terrorism, that 'terrorism' in s. 19 of the Act includes any 'act intended to cause death or serious bodily injury to a civilian, or to any other person not taking an active part in the hostilities in a situation of armed conflict, when the purpose of such act, by its nature or context, is to intimidate a population, or to compel a government or an international organization to do or to abstain from doing any act'. This definition catches the essence of what the world understands by 'terrorism'. Particular cases on the fringes of terrorist activity will inevitably provoke disagreement.[35]

This definition of terrorism is considerably narrower than the definition of terrorist activities in the ATA. The *Suresh* definition focuses on acts intended to cause death or serious bodily harm to non-combatants as opposed to the vaguer concept of endangering a person's life or causing a serious risk to health and safety or broader harms relating to property damage or disruption of essential services that are included in the ATA's definition of terrorism activities. The *Suresh* definition refers only to the concept of intimidating a population or compelling governments or international organizations to act. It does not resort to vaguer and neoliberal concepts—found in the ATA—of threatening security (including economic security) or compelling persons (including corporations) to act or to potentially discriminatory concepts that focus on the religious or political motives of alleged terrorists.

The restrained *Suresh* definition of terrorism, if adopted domestically, would minimize the chances that Aboriginal protesters, anti-globalization protesters, and the animal rights movement would be investigated as terrorist suspects. A restrained definition of terrorism that focuses on death and injury to humans can be defended on both the normative basis that it minimizes the risk of targeting dissent and on the practical basis that it guards against the misallocation of scarce investigative resources to dissenters. It could be argued, however, that the *Suresh* definition is under-inclusive in part because it does not include hostage taking, a tactic that has traditionally been used by terrorists. Nevertheless, the *Suresh* definition captures the essence of terrorism and would certainly apply to notorious acts of terrorism before and after 9/11. It suggests that courts can accomplish what some might argue is the legislative task of defining terrorism. A comparison of the Supreme Court's and Parliament's post-9/11 definitions of terrorism suggests that the former was inclined to err on the side of an under-inclusive definition of terrorism and the increased liberty that such a definition would provide. In contrast, Parliament was inclined to err on the side of an over-inclusive definition of terrorism and the increased state power that such a definition would provide.

The *Suresh* definition also departs from the ATA definition because it does not require proof of political or religious motive. Instead it distinguishes terrorism from ordinary crime by requiring that the intentional acts be committed to intimidate a population or compel a government or international organization to act. As will be seen, the political and religious motive requirement in the ATA was subsequently subject to a successful Charter challenge in the courts, and the Supreme Court of Canada's decision on its constitutionality is pending.

The Partial Invalidation of Parliament's Definition of Terrorist Activities in *Khawaja*

The first person charged under the ATA, Mohamed Momin Khawaja, successfully challenged the definition of terrorist activities under the Charter. The judge held that while the terrorism offences were not unconstitutionally vague or over-broad and had constitutionally sufficient fault requirements, the requirement of proof of religious and political motive was an unjustified violation of freedom of expression, religion, and association and an invitation to religious profiling of suspected terrorists. The judge struck down the political or religious motive requirement and severed it from the rest of the definition.[36] He noted that a number of other definitions of terrorist activities, including the Supreme Court's definition in *Suresh*, did not include political or religious motive as an essential element of terrorism.

Justice Rutherford's decision to strike down the political and religious motive requirement in *Khawaja* was controversial. Some commentators argued that it was nonsensical to define terrorism without regard to religious and political motive.[37] At the same time, the ruling responded to real concerns in society about targeting people as potential terrorists because of their religious beliefs.[38] The Ontario Court of Appeal subsequently reversed Justice Rutherford's decision; the appeal court concluded that terrorist activities were not protected forms of expression or religion under the Charter and that terrorists and not the law itself were responsible for stereotypes associating Islam with terrorism.[39] The Supreme Court of Canada has, however, recently decided to hear an appeal in this case, and a decision is pending at the time of this writing.

Although it would be wrong to conclude that Parliament was totally insensitive to concerns that its definition of terrorist activities could encourage discrimination against political and religious minorities, Justice Rutherford's decision in *Khawaja* suggests that the independent judiciary has a capacity to be even more sensitive to concerns about discriminatory profiling of unpopular minorities than the elected legislature. Such a finding is in accord with understandings of judicial review that stress the unique role of courts in protecting unpopular minorities.[40] At the same time, however, the Ontario Court of Appeal's decision to uphold the religious and political motive requirement and accept stereotypes associating radical Islam with terrorism as inevitable suggests that judicial concerns for the protections of minorities may not be uniform or consistent.

It is noteworthy that both Parliament and the courts in Canada were troubled by the religious and political motive requirement. This may indicate that Canada was more concerned about community relations with its growing Muslim populations than were countries such as the United Kingdom and Australia that accepted the political and religious motive requirement with little political or legal controversy. Interestingly, Singapore, which has a 15 per cent Muslim minority population, chose not to include religious or political motives in its definition of terrorism even as it, like Canada, largely accepted a broad British definition of terrorism that featured the religious and political motive requirement.[41] Although courts may be better than elected legislatures at protecting unpopular minorities and traditional rule of law values, they also have a limited range of remedies at their disposal. In *Khawaja*, Justice Rutherford simply struck out that part of the definition of terrorist activities that required the prosecution to prove that the acts were in whole or in part committed for a political, religious, or ideological purpose, objective, or cause. The perhaps unintended effect of this limited remedy was an expansion of the definition of terrorist activities so that it could potentially be applied to much ordinary crime. The Supreme Court in its pending decision will face the difficult choice of perhaps having to order a new trial for Khawaja should it find that Justice Rutherford was correct in holding that the religious and political motive requirement was an unjustified violation of freedom of speech and religion. Such results reveal the shortcomings of the courts and Charter litigation as an instrument of law reform. Courts are the captive of the issues that are argued before them. They cannot always see the big picture and they cannot rewrite laws from scratch.

Summary

The government has not revisited the definition of terrorist activities despite the judicial invalidation of the political and religious motive requirement in *Khawaja* and the Supreme Court's sanction of a more restrained definition of terrorism in *Suresh*. The government's decision not to revisit the definition of terrorist activities is in one sense not surprising. The definition of terrorism is inherently controversial, and the existing definition errs on the side of breadth.

The courts have been more responsive to definitional concerns than Parliament. The Supreme Court in *Suresh* refused to accept Parliament's failure to define terrorism in the Immigration and Refugee Protection Act and produced a restrained definition of terrorism that focused on intentional violence designed to intimidate populations or compel governments to act. Although legislatures may have incentives to err on the side of over-inclusion when defining terrorism, courts are not subject to these popular pressures and if anything may err on the side of under-inclusion. The trial judge in *Khawaja* was not persuaded by some legislative attempts to qualify the political and religious motive requirement and severed that requirement from Parliament's definition. This decision was responsive to minority concerns about the definition, but it also produced a definition of terrorist activities that was broader than even the definition intended by Parliament. The Ontario Court of Appeal, however, upheld the religious and political motive requirement, and an additional appeal decision is pending from the Supreme Court. Even if the Supreme Court has problems with the definition of terrorism, it will have limited remedies at its disposal. Defining terrorism is very difficult. An optimal definition may be more likely to emerge from an interplay or a dialogue between the legislature and the court. It would also have been helpful had the UN Security Council provided guidance to nations on how to define terrorism.[42]

INVESTIGATIVE HEARINGS AND PREVENTIVE ARRESTS
The ATA Debate

An important feature of the Anti-Terrorism Act was its expansion of police powers. One provision provided for preventive arrest when there were reasonable grounds to believe that a terrorist activity would be carried out and reasonable suspicion to believe that detention or the imposition of conditions was necessary to prevent the carrying out of the terrorist activity. The period of preventive arrest under the Canadian law was limited to a maximum of 72 hours and could see a judge release a person before this time.[43] The maximum 72-hour period was shorter than the 7 days then provided under British law, a period that was subsequently extended to 28 days.[44] At the same time, the effects of a Canadian preventive arrest could last much longer than 3 days. The suspect could be required by a judge to enter into a recognizance or peace bond for up to a year with breach of the bond being punishable by up to two years' imprisonment and a refusal to agree to a peace bond punishable by a year's imprisonment. Concerns were raised about preventive arrests. The government responded by amending Bill C-36 to require various officials to report on the number of times they used these powers.[45] These various reports did not reveal any use of preventive arrests.

A second new investigative power was the power to compel a person to answer questions relating to terrorist activities either in the past or the future.[46] The subject could not refuse to answer on the grounds of self-incrimination, but the compelled statements and evidence derived from them could not be used in subsequent criminal proceedings against the person compelled except for perjury charges. There was recognition that the subject of an investigative hearing had the right to retain and instruct counsel at any stage of the proceedings.[47]

Preventive arrests and investigative hearings were two of the most controversial provisions included in the ATA. They were criticized for departing from the traditional rules of the criminal law, and it was feared that once introduced into anti-terrorism law, they might spread to other areas of the law. In partial response to these criticisms, the ATA, after it was introduced, was amended to provide a renewable five-year sunset on these two provisions.[48] In addition, state officials were required under the law to provide annual reports on the use of both provisions.[49] These provisions demonstrated the ability of legislatures to provide some concessions to critics of the new powers while at the same time providing the police with the new powers. They were another example of the nuances and give-and-take of 'governmentality' or the 'art of government'.[50]

The Supreme Court's Decisions in the Air India Investigative Hearing Cases

The first and only attempt to use investigative hearings was made during the Air India trial. The application for the hearing was held in secret, without notice to the media or to the accused in the trial. The person compelled to testify challenged the constitutionality of the procedure. In *Application under s. 83.28*,[51] the Supreme Court upheld the constitutionality of the novel procedure in a 6:3 decision. Justices Iacobucci and Arbour JJ. held for the majority that the procedure did not violate section 7 of the Charter given that protections that compelled evidence or evidence derived from that evidence could not be used against the person except in cases of perjury prosecutions. At the same time, Justices Iacobucci and Arbour indicated that use and derivative use immunity should be provided not only in subsequent criminal proceedings as Parliament had intended, but also in subsequent extradition and immigration proceedings. This expansion recognized the international context of terrorism.[52] Additionally, they held that the hearings should be held subject to the traditional evidential rules and protections, including rules relating to relevance. It is not clear how well these rules designed to govern trials will apply to the potentially wide-ranging investigations conducted in investigative hearings.[53]

Two judges dissented on the basis that investigative hearings violated the institutional independence of the judiciary by requiring judges to preside over police investigations. These judges, along with a third judge, also dissented on the basis that the use of an investigative hearing in the middle of the Air India trial constituted an abuse of process because it was an attempt by the prosecution to gain an unfair advantage.

In the companion case of *Re Vancouver Sun*,[54] a majority of the court held that the presumption in favour of open courts applied to the conduct of investigative hearings. Two judges dissented on the basis that the open court presumption would make the hearing ineffective as an investigative tool and could harm the rights of third parties and intimidate witnesses. This dissent raised but did not resolve the connection between investigative hearings and the ability of Canadian officials to protect witnesses and recruit informers. In the end, the Supreme Court upheld investigative hearings but also subtly changed them to better comply with due process and free speech. The result was that investigative hearings featured more press freedoms and due process than comparable grand jury proceedings in the United States or new powers given to the Australian Security Intelligence Organization to obtain judicial warrants to compel people to answer questions that were relevant to terrorism investigations.[55] The Canadian approach was also less punitive than the British approach, which re-enacted a crime of refusing to provide information about terrorism that had originally been enacted to deal with terrorism in Northern Ireland and has been used to convict relatives of terrorists after 9/11.[56]

The February 2007 Parliamentary Debate over the Renewal of Preventive Arrests and Investigative Hearings

Parliament has traditionally not been an effective forum for the discussion of complex and sensitive security issues. In 1979, Professor Franks observed that the main reason for poor parliamentary debates about security matters was that 'Parliament and the public have not had an adequate information and knowledge base on which to base discussion.'[57] Unfortunately, little seems to have changed in Parliament more than a quarter of century later.[58] As will be seen, the partisan and largely uninformed debate over the expiry of preventive arrests and investigative hearings represented a new low.

On 9 February 2007 the government introduced a motion to extend investigative hearings and preventive arrests for a three-year period.[59] The government argued that the renewal was necessary for the prevention of terrorism and stressed that in 2004 the Supreme Court had held that investigative hearings were consistent with the Charter. The Conservatives, like the Liberals before them, relied on the argument that security legislation had been 'Charter-proofed'. Although such arguments reflected the important role of the Charter in policy formation, they focused on the minimum standards of the Charter and avoided the issue of whether the policy in question was wise or effective.

The minister of public safety spoke at length about the need for the provisions, stressing that investigative hearings had been upheld by the Supreme Court and asserting that preventive arrests entailed a minor invasion of rights that could save lives.[60] The Liberals, the New Democratic Party (NDP), and the Bloc Québécois all indicated that they would oppose the motion, with the NDP and the Bloc citing the mistreatment of Maher Arar, even though Mr. Arar was never subject to either a preventive arrest or an investigative hearing.[61] On 21 February 2007, Prime Minister Harper, in response to a question about judicial appointments, brought up a newspaper story that alleged that the RCMP was intending to use investigative hearings in its continuing Air India investigation and that a father-in-law of a Liberal MP had been named as a possible target of an investigative hearing.[62] The issue dominated Question Period and the media in the ensuing days. The Conservatives alleged that the Liberals' position would threaten the Air India investigation into 1985 terrorist bombings that killed 331 people, and the Liberals alleged that the prime minister had impugned the integrity of a member of Parliament. The leader of the Opposition demanded an apology from the prime minister for his remarks. The prime minister demanded that the Liberals apologize for not renewing the provisions.[63] Neither apology was made. Both parties raised questions of privilege against the other.[64] The debate was nasty and partisan. What quickly got lost in the debate was a discussion of the merits or dangers of investigative hearings and preventive arrests. On 27 February, the government's motion to renew the provisions for a three-year period was defeated by a vote of 159 to 124.[65] The focus on partisan issues, as well as lack of information about the new powers, meant that the powers expired without a sustained or informed debate about their merits or dangers. The debate demonstrated how expert opinions about security policy, like other parts of criminal justice policy,[66] are marginalized in the political arena, where crime is increasingly used as a symbolic issue and manipulated for partisan advantage.

Summary

Parliament responded to criticism of new police powers during the original Bill C-36 debate by requiring the government to report on the use of preventive arrests and investigative hearings and by placing a renewable five-year sunset on the provisions. The reports on the use of the provisions proved to be unhelpful because the government reported no actual use of the provisions and did not attempt to explain why they might be necessary in future terrorism investigations. The sometimes excessive secrecy that surrounds national security activities can hinder full and informed parliamentary debate about the provisions.

In February 2007, Parliament decided not to renew investigative hearings and preventive arrests, but its debate was characterized by partisan accusations as opposed to sober second thoughts or informed debate. It was reported in the media that the RCMP wanted to use investigative hearings in the Air India investigation, but investigative hearings were unlikely to fix the problems that plagued the investigation of the 1985 bombings. These problems included a lack of co-operation between the RCMP and the Canadian Security Intelligence Service (CSIS), poor handling of sources, and poor protection of witnesses. Investigative hearings were a coercive quick fix for deeper structural problems in terrorism investigations. Use of investigative hearings would also run the danger of making the person compelled to co-operate virtually immune from subsequent prosecution even if he or she was involved in terrorist activities.[67] Investigative hearings may be an example of a simplistic, symbolic, and inexpensive attempt to improve the difficult task of investigating and prosecuting terrorism cases.

Fortunately, it appears as if the handling of sources and witnesses in terrorism investigations involving both CSIS and the RCMP improved given the important role that two human sources have played in the prosecution of a Toronto terrorist plot. In the national security area especially, it is important to distinguish between visible and often symbolic acts of policy-making and much less visible reforms to security intelligence, policing, and prosecutions. In any event, since the 2007 repeal, the minority Conservative government attempted to reintroduce into the Criminal Code investigative hearings and preventive arrests, but so far without success. As a result of gaining a majority in the 2011 election, the Conservative government will likely now reintroduce both preventive arrests and investigative hearings, perhaps without either the reporting or sunset requirements that were originally provided. Such a move would represent a normalization of what in 2001 were seen as extraordinary powers. At the same time, it would represent a largely symbolic attempt by the government to communicate that it was tough on terrorism.

In contrast to Parliament's misinformed and partisan performance in 2007 when it refused to renew preventive arrests and investigative hearings, the Supreme Court made more reasoned decisions in holding that investigative hearings were justified under the Charter. The majority and minority decisions in the court's 2004 decision contended with the merits and dangers of investigative hearings, whereas the February 2007 debate in Parliament on renewal did not. The end result of both processes were perhaps counter-intuitive, with the Supreme Court upholding the use of investigative hearings and Parliament voting against the minority government and deciding not to renew investigative hearings. The Supreme Court decisions may provide evidence that due process challenges under the Charter can be used to legitimate crime-control measures. Nevertheless, the court did not simply approve of investigative hearings but subtly changed them so as to increase protections for those compelled to co-operate and for freedom of the press. At the same time, investigative hearings can now be reintroduced with the Charter seal of approval. The effects of the Charter on national security policy-making are varied and subtle.

IMMIGRATION LAW SECURITY CERTIFICATES
The Original Debate

Security certificates that were used to detain and deport non-citizens suspected of being a risk to national security were included in immigration law before 9/11. The Supreme Court upheld security certificates in 1992 under the Charter, stressing that while the person subject to a security certificate would not have access to information used to support the certificate that, if disclosed, would harm national security, he or she would nevertheless receive a summary of such information. The case involved a person thought to be involved in organized crime. The court indicated that while

> the first day of the hearing was conducted *in camera*, the respondent was provided with a summary of the evidence presented. In my view, these various documents gave the respondent sufficient information to know the substance of the allegations against him, and to be able to respond. It is not necessary, in order to comply with fundamental justice in this context, that the respondent also be given details of the criminal intelligence investigation techniques or police sources used to acquire that information.[68]

This 1992 case underlines how 'due process can be for crime control' in the sense that repressive measures—in this case the use of secret evidence—could be held as consistent with the due process protections of the Charter.[69] This case also underlines how authorities can use the shortcut of immigration law proceedings with respect to non-citizens suspected of involvement in crime. Immigration law has a lower standard of proof than criminal law and allows the use of secret evidence that is not allowed in criminal courts. In other areas, including with respect to gang crime and war criminals, the government has used immigration law as a less restrained alternative or supplement to the criminal law. Non-citizens do not have the vote, and courts have traditionally accepted departures from standards of adjudicative fairness in immigration proceedings that would not be tolerated in criminal trials.[70]

Security certificates were not included in the ATA, but they were included in a revised Immigration and Refugee Protection Act that was debated and passed after six days in the Commons before 9/11. After an eight-day debate in the Senate, the new law was passed at the end of October 2001. The new act, which came into force in 2002, changed the security certificate procedure by taking away a hearing that permanent residents were entitled to before the Security Intelligence Review Committee. The hearings before this body had reflected the fact that it was the review agency for CSIS that collects the intelligence that is used to support security certificates. The new act provided for judicial review in the Federal Court after a security certificate was issued. This raises issues about the respective ability of courts and expert agencies to review governmental conduct. The new act also provided for automatic detention and less frequent judicial reviews for non-citizens who did not have permanent resident status.

These immigration law amendments were partially encouraged by UN Security Council Resolution 1373, which called on all nations to ensure that refugee status was not abused by terrorists. Domestic states have an interest in keeping terrorists out, but the UN's endorsement of the use of immigration law as anti-terrorism law was puzzling given its international perspective.[71] There is a danger that immigration law will simply deflect terrorists from state to state and not prosecute and punish them. At the same time, immigration law often allows states to use secret evidence and very broad liability rules that would not be tolerated in criminal laws that could be applied to citizens. Canada was not alone in using immigration law as anti-terrorism law in the immediate aftermath of 9/11. The United Kingdom derogated from fair trial rights in order to detain indefinitely non-citizens suspected of being involved in terrorism who could not be deported without risk of torture,[72] and the United States used widespread detention and selective registration schemes for non-citizens immediately after 9/11.[73] Canada has, however, continued to use immigration law as anti-terrorism laws perhaps in part because secret intelligence obtained from other states can be used as secret evidence under immigration law but not under criminal law. The Canadian reliance on immigration law as anti-terrorism law also reflected the fact that until the Khawaja and Toronto terrorism prosecutions, Canada had enjoyed little success in obtaining convictions in terrorism prosecutions.[74]

The Use of Immigration Law as Anti-Terrorism Law

All security certificates are subject to judicial review, but the detainee cannot see the information given by the government to the court if the disclosure of the information would harm national security or any person.[75] This means that secret evidence is extensively used in security certificate proceedings.

Five security certificates were issued between 2001 and 2003 against men suspected of involvement in Al-Qaeda terrorism. Mohamad Mahjoub, an Egyptian, was detained starting on 26 June 2000. He is alleged to have worked both for bin Laden and with the Vanguards of Conquest, a group that wished to overthrow the Mubarek government. In 2007, he was released on strict conditions after a judge found that he would not be returned to Egypt within a reasonable amount of time and his controlled release would not threaten the security of Canada. His conditions of release include electronic monitoring, house arrest, no access to telephones or Internet, and only approved visits.[76] Mahmoud Jaballah, alleged to have terrorist ties with the Egyptian Al Jihad, was held on a security certificate since August 2001. In 2007, he was released on a very strict form of house arrest that limits all his contacts with the outside world.[77] Mohammed Harkat was detained on 10 December 2002, with allegations that he had ties to the Algerian Islamic Army Group. He was released in 2006 on strict bail conditions that amounted to house arrest. His security certificate was upheld by the courts in 2010 and it remains to be seen whether he will be deported to Algeria, where he alleges he will be tortured.

Two security certificate cases have so far collapsed. Adil Charkaoui from Morocco was detained from May 2003 on suspicions of involvement with Al-Qaeda, but in February of 2005, he was released on strict conditions on his fourth detention review. In 2006, some of these conditions were loosened,[78] and in 2009, the government abandoned his security certificate rather than disclose intelligence to him as required by the reviewing judge.[79] Hassan Almrei, from Syria, was detained from 19 October 2001. In 2005, he staged a hunger strike for more than 60 days in protest of his conditions of confinement in a remand centre designed for prisoners awaiting trial. At the end of 2009, a judge quashed the security certificate as unreasonable, holding that while the security certificate was reasonable in 2001, there was no evidence that Almeri had engaged in terrorism, was a member of a terrorist group, or was a threat to the security of Canada.[80] The prolonged legal proceedings over these security certificates demonstrate many of the difficulties that result from systems of indeterminate detention, the use of secret intelligence as evidence, and attempts to deport terrorist suspects to countries such as Syria and Egypt where they may be tortured.

Suresh and Deportation to Torture

Another terrorism-related security certificate involved Manickavasgam Suresh, who was arrested in 1995 under a security certificate that alleged he raised money for the Tamil Tigers. He was released on bail in 1998 on relatively lenient conditions involving weekly reporting to immigration officials and no contact with members of the Tamil Tigers.[81] His deportation to Sri Lanka was considered by the Supreme Court in early 2002 and is still pending. The court ruled that international law prohibited the use of torture and that section 7 of the Canadian Charter of Rights and Freedoms would generally prohibit deportation to face a substantial risk of torture. This decision demonstrates how the independent courts can consider human rights principles and apply them to protect unpopular persons who do not have much political support. That said, however, the Supreme Court also made the following oft-criticized statement:

> We do not exclude the possibility that in exceptional circumstances, deportation to face torture might be justified, either as a consequence of the balancing process mandated by s. 7 of the *Charter* or under s. 1. (A violation of s. 7 will be saved by s. 1 'only in cases arising out of exceptional conditions, such as natural disasters, the outbreak of war, epidemics and the like': Insofar as Canada is unable to deport a person where there are substantial grounds to believe he or she would be tortured on return, this is not because Article 3 of the CAT directly constrains the actions of the Canadian government, but because the fundamental justice balance under s. 7 of the *Charter* generally precludes deportation to torture when applied on a case-by-case basis. We may predict that it will rarely be struck in favour of expulsion where there is a serious risk of torture. However, as the matter is one of balance, precise prediction is elusive. The ambit of an exceptional discretion to deport to torture, if any, must await future cases.[82]

In addition to recognizing a possible exception that would allow deportees to face torture, the Supreme Court also indicated that it would interpret security threats quite broadly and would defer to executive determinations of whether there was a substantial risk of torture unless they were patently unreasonable. This decision demonstrates that in the immediate aftermath of 9/11, the Canadian courts were not immune from the trend to deference to the executive or from a willingness to entertain exceptions from fundamental principles such as the absolute right not to be tortured. Although courts may be the best-equipped institution to protect unpopular people and fundamental values in times of emergency, there are no guarantees that they will play this important role. Fortunately, however, no Canadian court has yet applied the *Suresh* exception to allow deportation to torture. In addition, the *Suresh* exception that would allow deportation to torture was rejected by the European Court of Human Rights in another post-9/11 case.[83]

Charkaoui and the Reform of Security Certificates

In a 2007 decision in *Charkaoui*,[84] the Supreme Court found that the rights of security certificate detainees to fair proceedings under the Charter were infringed because of the ability of the government to use secret evidence against the detainee that was subject to no adversarial challenge. The court indicated that while the protection of secrets was an important objective, there was a variety of less restrictive means that would provide for adversarial challenges to the secret evidence. The court suspended its declaration of invalidity for a year in order to allow Parliament to select a substitute for the full disclosure denied to the detainee. This is consistent with the idea that Charter litigation does not necessarily give the courts the final word on matters of policy and allows legislatures to craft a variety of responses to judicial decisions.[85] Parliament responded to the decision with new legislation that allowed security-cleared special advocates but not the detainees or their lawyers to examine and challenge the secret evidence used to support security certificates.[86] This was an important procedural change because it exposed secret intelligence to adversarial challenge and pushed more information into the open. At the same time, however, it fell short of invalidating the security certificate regime.

The Supreme Court's decision in *Charkaoui* did not by any means resolve all the outstanding issues with respect to security certificates. One limit on judicial policy-making is that courts are captives of the case before them. In *Charkaoui*, the court did not revisit or flesh out the *Suresh* exception for deportation to torture despite the fact that the government had attempted to rely on this exception to justify deportation of terrorist suspects to Egypt and Syria. In addition, the court avoided the issue of the length of indeterminate detention under security certificates, noting only that detainees could continue to seek review of the conditions of their detention and bring subsequent Charter challenges. Finally, the court rejected Adil Charkaoui's challenge that the security certificate regime violated equality rights because it accorded non-citizens accused of terrorism much fewer rights than citizens.

Summary

The courts have played a significant role in moderating the use of immigration law as anti-terrorism law under the controversial security certificate regime. The courts have prohibited deportation to countries such as Egypt[87] that traditionally tortured terrorist suspects and have required that security-cleared special advocates be able to see and challenge secret evidence that is used against security certificate detainees. The recent collapse of a number of security certificates suggests that the use of security certificates against terrorist suspects may have been misguided. Although the regime allowed the government to keep intelligence secret and indeterminately detain non-citizens believed to be associated with terrorism, the use of security certificates has been politically and legally controversial. Immigration law has less legitimacy than criminal law as a means to punish and detain terrorists. The elected government and Parliament may be reluctant to take responsibility for ending security certificates, but the independent courts are slowly taking such steps.

CONCLUSION

This chapter has demonstrated that some of the most critical issues in Canada's post-9/11 anti-terrorism law have been the subject of dialogue and interplay between the courts and legislatures. The courts in the security certificate cases have called attention to rights concerns that were not adequately addressed by Parliament. Thus, in *Suresh*, the Supreme Court ruled that deportation to a substantial risk of torture would generally violate the Charter, and in *Charkaoui*, it ruled that secret evidence should be subject to adversarial challenge. The executive has responded to *Suresh* by trying to make use of the court's exceptional circumstance qualification to allow deportation to torture. Parliament responded to *Charkaoui* by creating a new statutory regime for the use of special advocates who can challenge the secret evidence.

Both courts and legislatures have important roles to play in national security policy-making. Courts have an obligation to protect the rights of minorities and freedom of expression, while elected legislatures have a mandate to maximize protections for security and secrecy. The courts can scrutinize particular provisions or omissions in laws that may not command enough of the legislature's attention. At the same time, the legislature retains the ability to frame a court's ruling about a particular provision in the larger broader policy context and to expand the terms of the dialogue. The performances of both Canadian legislatures and courts since 9/11 have been mixed and inconsistent. The courts have improved the fairness of both investigative hearings and security certificates. Such judicial decisions demonstrate the ability of courts to address important issues that were either ignored by Parliament or handled in a manner that did not result in sufficient protections for the fair treatment of unpopular groups. At the same time, however, when reviewing anti-terrorism laws, the courts have a limited range of often blunt remedies, and they have less of a capacity to see the big picture. The Supreme Court's decisions with respect to both investigative hearings and security certificates have the potential to legitimize these procedures as 'Charter-proof' and dampen debate about the wisdom, fairness, and workability of such policies. Although the court has found that the lack of any adversarial challenge to secret evidence used in security certificates violated the Charter, it did not hold that long-term detention under security certificates was fundamentally unfair to or discriminatory against non-citizens. The courts can play a valuable role, but they will focus on individual cases and the specific issues that are presented to them. Legislatures have the potential to see the bigger policy picture, but they may also be inclined to neglect the rights of unpopular minorities.

Parliamentary treatment of security issues has also been mixed. Although the debate in late 2001 over the Anti-Terrorism Act was rushed and many important issues raised by the omnibus legislation were missed, it demonstrated that parliamentarians can contribute usefully to the review of complex and controversial anti-terrorism legislation. Important amendments were proposed by committees and made by the government after the ATA was first introduced in October 2001. These amendments included a tightening of the definition of terrorist activities and the imposition of renewable sunset and reporting requirements on investigative hearings and preventive arrests. The Canadian Parliament was more responsive to the Muslim minorities' concerns about the political and religious motive requirement than were legislatures in Australia or the United Kingdom. Parliament responded to the Supreme Court's decision in *Charkaoui* by creating a new institution of special advocates and declaring that unreliable intelligence—including that obtained through torture or degrading treatment—should not be used to support certificates. At the same time, Parliament only reformed security certificates when prompted by the courts. Parliament's refusal to rethink security certificates and the difficulties of deporting people to countries that engage in torture or subjecting them to indeterminate detention or house arrest will eventually require the courts to respond to pressing injustices in individual cases. Legislatures also have the resources to create and expand bodies that can review secret national security activities, though the Canadian government has rejected proposals by both the Arar and Air India commissions of inquiry to provide enhanced and permanent review mechanisms for the Canadian government's secret and increasingly integrated national security activities. Without such review, much national security activity by the executive may escape either judicial or legislative review.

The executive, with its access to secret information, remains the dominant actor in the national security realm, and there are concerns about the adequacy of either legislative or judicial supervision of the work of the executive, including supervision of police, immigration, security intelligence, and foreign affairs officials. The public inquiries that were held on the actions of Canadian officials in relation to Maher Arar and other Canadians tortured in Syria are examples of how the whole of government executive responses to terrorism can be reviewed, but public inquiries remain extraordinary instruments of accountability that are only appointed at the discretion of the government.

The executive also has a mandate to respond to international initiatives that may not always respect human rights sufficiently. The ATA was quickly enacted in part in response to UN Security Council Resolution 1373 and the perceived need to have a new law to report back to the Security Council's newly created Counter-Terrorism Committee. The Security Council, however, refused to provide guidance about the definition of terrorism or, in the first years, to integrate human rights concerns in its work.[88]

Secrecy poses a fundamental dilemma in national security policy-making. Policy-makers in Parliament and the judiciary risk making uninformed decisions if they do not have access to secret information, but if they do have such access, then they will not be able to use the secret information to justify their decisions. The government, including security intelligence agencies and the police, have the incentive to claim secrecy both to increase their own power and to hide their mistakes. Canada is particularly vulnerable to excessive use of secrecy because it relies on more powerful countries for much of its intelligence. Other democracies, such as the United States, the United Kingdom, and Australia, are more advanced than Canada in reviewing national security activities in part because they give some legislators access to secret information and allow review bodies to work together to review increasingly integrated national security activities. In Canada, such reviews have only been accomplished through public inquiries, but they are only appointed on an ad hoc basis and at the discretion of the government.

Canada's post-9/11 policy-making about terrorism demonstrates many of the themes observed in other criminal justice contexts. The initial response to 9/11, the enactment of the massive ATA, fits into patterns of 'governing through crime' and downplaying more difficult and fundamental responses involving the prevention of crime. The UN Security Council played an important role in encouraging Canada and other countries to criminalize terrorism after 9/11. Like domestic governments, the UN was attracted to the simplistic assumption that criminalization would help to prevent crime victimization, and it failed to respect human rights or observe due process in its own process. The post-9/11 policy-making process was not totally focused on security; both the governments and courts made some decisions that restrained security laws and activities with concerns about rights, and this process demonstrated both dialogue between courts and legislatures and the give-and-take of governmentality. The Canadian government's subsequent public security response to a wide range of risks, including terrorism, moved beyond the initial criminalization stage, but also demonstrated the hallmarks of neo-liberal governance in a 'risk society'. It should not be surprising that the terrorism context reflects many of the themes that affect criminal justice policy-making more generally. Courts and legislatures engaged in dialogue and shared policy-making in this area as they have done in other visible areas of criminal justice policy. Nevertheless, the day-to-day operations of the executive, including the police and intelligence agencies, are often invisible and thus not often subject to effective review.

CRITICAL THINKING QUESTIONS

1. Assess the roles that the Canadian Charter of Rights and Freedoms and rights considerations in general have played in the development of Canadian anti-terrorism law. Has the Charter restrained the state and/or has it also provided the state with legitimacy for new laws and practices? Has due process been for crime control? Has due process facilitated the give-and-take implicit in ideas of governmentality?

2. How does anti-terrorism law relate to the issue of governing through crime? What are the strengths and weaknesses of a crime-based response to terrorism?

3. Evaluate the use of immigration law as anti-terrorism law, and relate this to issues of multiculturalism and community relations?

4. Has the review of Canada's post-9/11 national security activities caught up to the increased intensity and integration of those activities? Should it?

5. Has Canada achieved an appropriate balance between safety and security in its post-9/11 responses to terrorism?

NOTES

1 Anti-Terrorism Act, S.C. 2001, ch. 43, s. 145.

2 Jonathan Simon, *Governing through Crime* (Oxford: Oxford University Press, 2007). For a similar though less pithy concept of 'the criminalization of politics', see Kent Roach, *Due Process and Victim Rights: The New Law and Politics of Criminal Justice* (Toronto: University of Toronto Press, 1999).

3 Kent Roach, 'The Dangers of a Charter-Proof and Crime-Based Response to Terrorism', in Ronald J. Daniels, Patrick Macklem, & Kent Roach, eds., *The Security of Freedom: Essays on Canada's Anti-Terrorism Bill* (Toronto: University of Toronto Press, 2001), 131.

4 S.C. 2004, ch. 15.

5 'This system is capable of responding to both intentional and unintentional threats. It is as relevant in securing Canadians against the next SARS-like outbreak as it is in addressing the risk of a terrorist attack.' Canada, *Securing an Open Society: Canada's National Security Policy*, April 2004, 10. For a defence of an all-risk national security policy, see Roach, *September 11: Consequences for Canada* (Montreal: McGill-Queen's University Press, 2003), ch. 7.

6 Ulrich Beck, *The Risk Society: Towards a New Modernity* (London: Sage, 1992).

7 Doreen McBarnet, *Conviction: Law, the State and the Construction of Criminal Justice* (Oxford: Oxford University Press, 1983); Richard Ericson, *The Constitution of Inequality* (Ottawa: Carlton University Press, 1983).

8 *Suresh v. Canada*, [2002] 1 S.C.R. 3 at para. 78

9 *Amnesty International v. Canada*, [2008] F.C.A. 441. Leave to appeal was denied by Supreme Court of Canada.

10 The Arar Commission concluded that the government had over-claimed secrecy. Commission of Inquiry into the Actions of Canadian Officials in Relation to Maher Arar, *Report of the Events Relating to Maher Arar* (2006).

11 The government ignored the recommendations of the Commission of Inquiry into the Actions of Canadian Officials in Relation to Maher Arar in *A New Review Mechanism for the RCMP's National Security Activities* (2006), and in 2010, it proposed legislation that would not even ensure that the commission that reviews complaints against the RCMP would have access to secret information as recommended by the Arar Commission. The bill would also not expand the jurisdiction of the Security Intelligence Review Committee or allow integrated review of security operations involving multiple agencies of the federal government as recommended by the Arar Commission. See Bill C-38, 40th Parliament, 3rd Session. The government also did not follow the recommendation contained in the report of the Commission of Inquiry into the Investigation of the Bombing of Air India Flight 182, *A Canadian Tragedy*, to increase the powers of the prime minister's national security advisor to review the efficacy and efficiency of the government's national security activities.

See *The Government of Canada's Response to the Commission of Inquiry into the Investigation of the Bombing of Air India Flight 182*, December 2010.

12 Ibid.

13 *Khadr v. Canada*, [2005] F.C. 1076; *Khadr v. Canada*, [2008] S.C.C. 25.

14 Ibid., [2010] S.C.C. 3.

15 Ibid., [2010] F.C. 715; *Canada v. Khadr*, [2011] F.C.A. 92.

16 E. Alexandra Dosman, 'For the Record: Designating "Listed Entities" for the Purposes of Terrorist Financing Offences at Canadian Law,' (2004) 62 *University of Toronto Faculty Law Review* 15. On international efforts to counter terrorism, see Craig Forcese, *National Security Law* (Toronto: Irwin Law, 2008), ch. 6.

17 *Abdelrazik v. Canada*, [2009] F.C. 580. He was delisted by the UN in 2011.

18 Roach, *Due Process and Victims' Rights: The New Law and Politics of Criminal Justice* (Toronto: University of Toronto Press, 1999).

19 S/Res/1624 (2005).

20 *Criminal Code of Canada*, s. 83.01(1.1).

21 Ibid., s. 320.1.

22 Ibid., s. 430(4.1).

23 Subcommittee on the Review of the Antiterrorism Act, *Rights, Limits, Security: A Comprehensive Review of the Anti-Terrorism Act and Related Issues*, March 2007.

24 These parts of the chapter draw on and update Roach, 'The Role and Capacities of Courts and Legislatures in Reviewing Canada's Anti-Terrorism Law' (2008) 24 *Windsor Review of Legal and Social Issues*, 5.

25 While United Nations Security Council Resolution 1373 called on states to enact laws against terrorism and the financing of terrorism, it reflected international disagreement in that it did not define terrorism. See Roach, 'Sources and Trends in Post 9/11 Anti-terrorism Law', in Goold and Lazurus, eds., *Human Rights and Security* (Oxford: Hart Publishing, 2007), for a critical examination of the resolution's influence on many post-9/11 anti-terrorism laws.

26 Daniels et al., eds., *The Security of Freedom*; David Daubney et al., eds., *Terrorism, Law and Democracy: How Is Canada Changing Following September 11?* (Montreal: Yvon Blais, 2002).

27 James Kelly, *Governing with the Charter* (Vancouver: University of British Columbia Press, 2005), 246.

28 Roach, *September 11*, 67.

29 For a notable exception, see Audrey Macklin, 'Borderline Security', in Daniels et al., eds., *The Security of Freedom*.

30 See Criminal Code, R.S.C. 1985. C-34 as amended, s. 83.01(b) (ii) (E).

31 See Criminal Code, s. 83.01 (1.1).

32 Graham Burchell et al., eds., *The Foucault Effect: Studies in Governmentality* (Chicago: University of Chicago Press, 1991).

33 [2002] 1 S.C.R. 3 at paras. 94–5.

34 S.C. 2001, c. 27.

35 *Suresh v. Canada*, [2002] 1 S.C.R. 3 at para. 98.

36 *R. v. Khawaja*, [2006] 214 C.C.C. (3d) 399 (Ont. Sup. Ct. J.).

37 Ben Saul, *Defining Terrorism in International Law* (Oxford: Oxford University Press, 2006); Michael Plaxton, 'Irruptions of Motive in the War on Terror' (2007) 11 *Canadian Criminal Law Review* 233.

38 Roach, 'Terrorism Offences and the Charter: A Comment on *R. v. Khawaja*' (2007) 11 *Canadian Criminal Law Review* 273; Julian Falconer and Sunil Mathai, 'The Anti-Terrorism Act and the Arar Findings: Democracy Protected or Democracy Eroded?' (2006) 21 *National Journal of Constitutional Law* 49.

39 *R. v. Khawaja*, [2010] ONCA 862 at para. 126–7.

40 See, for example, John Hart Ely, *Democracy and Distrust* (Harvard: Cambridge University Press, 1980).

41 See Roach, *The 9/11 Effect: Comparative Counter-Terrorism* (New York: Cambridge University Press, 2011), chs. 3 and 7.

42 Ibid., ch. 2.

43 Criminal Code, s. 83.3.

44 Prime Ministers Blair and Brown unsuccessfully tried to persuade Parliament to raise the limit to 90 and 42 days respectively. Prime Minister Cameron has subsequently indicated that the maximum period will be lowered to 14 days. See Roach, *The 9/11 Effect, supra* ch. 5.

45 Ibid., s. 83.31.

46 In our adversarial system, which respects the right to silence, the police cannot compel a person with relevant information to assist them in their investigation.

47 Criminal Code, s. 83.28.

48 Ibid., s. 83.32.

49 Ibid., s. 83.31.

50 Burchell et al., eds., *The Foucault Effect.*

51 [2004] 2 S.C.R. 248.

52 Iacobucci and Arbour JJ. concluded that '[i]n order to meet the s. 7 requirements, the procedural safeguards found in s. 83.28 must necessarily be extended to extradition and deportation proceedings. In *Branch, supra*, at para. 5, derivative use immunity was stated to apply both in subsequent proceedings where the witness is an accused subject to penal sanctions, and more generally to any proceeding which engages s. 7 of the *Charter*, such as extradition and deportation hearings. The protective effect of s. 83.28(10) would be significantly undercut if information gathered under s. 83.28 was used at the state's discretion in subsequent extradition or deportation proceedings. Therefore, where there is the potential for such use by the state, the hearing judge must make and, if

necessary, vary the terms of an order to properly provide use and derivative use immunity in extradition or deportation proceedings' (ibid., at para. 79).

53 For arguments that the various protections read in by the court might, if taken seriously, deprive investigative hearings of much of their utility as an investigative tool, see Hamish Stewart, 'Investigative Hearings into Terrorist Offences: Challenging the Rule of Law' (2005) 50 *Criminal Law Quarterly* C.L.Q. 376.

54 [2004] 2 S.C.R. 332.

55 Roach, 'The Consequences of Compelled Self-Incrimination in Terrorism Investigations: A Comparison of American Grand Juries and Canadian Investigative Hearings' (2008) 30 *Cardozo Law Review* 1089; Roach, 'A Comparison of Australian and Canadian Anti-Terrorism Legislation' (2007) 30 *University of New South Wales Law Journal* 53.

56 Clive Walker, 'Conscripting the Public in Terrorism Policing' [2010], *Criminal Law Review* 441.

57 C.E.S. Franks, *Parliament and Security Matters* (Ottawa: Supply and Services, 1979), 65.

58 Reg Whitaker, 'Made in Canada? The New Public Safety Paradigm', in G. Bruce Doern, ed., *How Ottawa Spends* (Montreal and Kingston: McGill-Queen's Press, 2005).

59 *Hansard*, 9 February 2007.

60 Ibid., February 2007, at 6650.

61 Ibid., at 6646.

62 Ibid., at 7125.

63 Ibid., at 7128.

64 Ibid., at 7133.

65 Ibid., at 7405–6.

66 David Garland, *The Culture of Control* (Chicago: University of Chicago Press, 2001).

67 Roach, 'The Consequences of Compelled Self-Incrimination in Terrorism Investigations' (2008) 30 *Cardozo Law Review* 1089.

68 *Chiarelli v. Canada*, [1992] 1 S.C.R. 711.

69 McBarnet, *Conviction*; Ericson, *The Constitution of Inequality*.

70 Macklin, 'Borderline Security', in Daniels et al., *The Security of Freedom*.

71 For criticisms of the Security Council's post-9/11 performance on terrorism-related issues, see Roach, *The 9/11 Effect*, ch.2.

72 The law was repealed after the House of Lords found this use of immigration law as anti-terrorism laws to be discriminatory and disproportionate to a terrorist threat that included citizens. *A v. Secretary of State*, [2004] U.K.H.L. 56.

73 David Cole, *Enemy Aliens* (New York: New Press, 2003).

74 Roach, *The Unique Challenges of Terrorism Prosecutions* (Ottawa: Government Services, 2010).

75 *Immigration Refuge Protection Act*, S.C. 2001, ch. 27, s. 78.

76 *Mahjoub v. Canada*, [2007] F.C. 171.

77 *Jaballah v. Canada*, [2007] F.C. 379.

78 *Charkaoui v. Canada*, [2006] F.C. 555.

79 Ibid., [2009] F.C. 1030.

80 *Almeri v. Canada*, [2009] F.C. 1263.

81 *Re Suresh*, March 1998, at http://decisions.fct-cf.gc.ca/en/1998/des-3-95/des-3-95.html

82 *Suresh v. Canada*, [2002] 1 S.C.R. 3 at para. 78 (citations omitted).

83 *Saadi v. Italy*, 37201/06 decision of Grand Chamber, 28 February 2008.

84 [2007] 1 S.C.R. 350.

85 Roach, *The Supreme Court on Trial: Judicial Activism or Democratic Dialogue* (Toronto: Irwin Law, 2001). Some argue that the notion of a dialogue between the courts and legislatures discounts the upper hand of the judiciary. See 'Symposium' (2007) 45 *Osgoode Hall Law Journal* 1ff.

86 See *Immigration and Refugee Protection Act Amendments*, S.C. 2008 ch. 3. The new legislation also prohibited the use of evidence in security certificate proceedings that was obtained by torture or cruel and degrading treatment. See the collection of essays on the case and legislation at (2008) 42 S.C.L.R. (2d) 251–440.

87 *Jaballah v. Canada*, [2006] F.C. 1230 at para. 83, refusing to hold that exceptional circumstances justified deportation to a substantial risk of torture in Egypt.

88 Roach, *The 9/11 Effect*, ch. 2.

10

The Criminalization of Poverty: Welfare Reform and the Policing of Welfare in Canada

Wendy Chan

A. INTRODUCTION

Numerous reports in recent years have documented the depth and persistence of poverty in Canada and the lack of improvement in the situation over the last several decades (Klein & Pulkingham, 2008; National Council of Welfare, 2010). Declining welfare-state provisions, combined with a globalized, neo-liberal marketplace, have led to the economic marginalization of many individuals and families in Canada. As the Canadian Centre for Policy Alternatives (CCPA) notes, the gap between the rich and the poor is greater than it was 20 years ago (Wallace, Klein, & Reitsma-Street, 2006, p. 3). The National Council of Welfare concurs, pointing out that over the past 30 years, there has been little sustained improvement in managing the depth of poverty in Canada (2010, p. 4). These problems are profoundly gendered and racialized. The experiences of women and people of colour are made more challenging owing, for example, to family responsibilities, to the lack of access to affordable child care, and to structural barriers in the labour market that result in higher rates of part-time and temporary work.

Combating the increased challenges of poverty has not, however, been accompanied by an increased empathy for poor people. In fact, public attitudes have gone the opposite direction, where poor people were blamed for their economic marginalization and demonized as the 'enemy within' (Sidel, 2000). The stereotypes of welfare recipients as lazy and undeserving are deeply entrenched in both public and policy discourses and have led to their ongoing stigmatization in Canada. Such stereotypes have also resulted in a form of victim-blaming where reliance on welfare is seen as a failure to make good choices, to be self-sufficient, and to take control of one's economic circumstances. As a result, the behaviour of welfare recipients is always regarded as suspicious, fuelling the widespread public perception that welfare recipients require vigilant surveillance and punitive management strategies to protect the public purse from being bilked. The most recent example of this can be found in British Columbia, where the current government plans to sue more than 300 welfare recipients to recover fraudulent claims and overpayments in order to preserve the integrity of the system (Shaw, 2010b). Manitoba and Ontario have also acknowledged that fraud and overpayment have cost the provinces millions of dollars, and their plans to tackle this problem include ever-greater surveillance of welfare claims (Welch, 2010).[1]

The policing of welfare recipients in Canada is not new. Individuals, particularly women, who rely on the state for support have always found themselves under constant scrutiny by both state officials and the public over their eligibility and entitlement for access to social assistance (Martin, 1992). The stereotyping and stigmatizing of welfare recipients as illegitimate and potentially criminal are common strategies employed by Western governments to justify reducing already meagre social programs and to punish poor people with punitive practices and sanctions for their deviance and marginality. The belief that greater administrative and fiscal efficiency will be achieved by 'tightening up the system' has led many provinces to hire more workers to scrutinize new welfare claims and to review current claims for continued eligibility.[2] Not surprisingly, critics contend that this is tantamount to a war against the poor, since these measures simply continue to penalize poor people, particularly when errors in payment are made by the state (MacLeod, 2010). Nonetheless, as governments have been faced with high levels of public debt, welfare policies in Canada have relied on these practices and views of welfare recipients to curtail significantly the number of people eligible to receive assistance and to justify dismantling social programs.

As in Canada, the retrenchment of the welfare system is taking place across most Western liberal democracies. The United States, Australia, and Britain are experiencing a significant withdrawal of government support for social programs, a greater emphasis on economic independence and self-reliance, and tougher sanctions for those who fail to comply. Many Western welfare regimes now have in place a wide range of both criminal and non-criminal (e.g., fines or repayment) penalties for individuals who violate the rules of welfare. In particular, Mosher and Hermer note that welfare fraud is now regarded as a major crime against the public, one deserving of widespread moral condemnation, intensive policing, and punishment (2005, p. 5). Yet a closer examination of welfare enforcement policies and practices reveals inconsistent and contradictory evidence regarding the extent to which welfare recipients are failing to abide by the rules of welfare. Rather, difficulties in navigating the complex rules and administrative errors play a significant role in what is constituted as fraud in the welfare system (Mosher & Hermer, 2005; Mirchandani & Chan, 2007). Despite these findings, welfare recipients have been cast as the villains in the way in which the problem of welfare fraud is framed and presented to the public.

In this chapter, I use the example of British Columbia to argue that welfare policies increasingly criminalize and penalize people for living in poverty.

I examine the most recent changes to welfare enforcement policies in British Columbia and interrogate the ideological underpinnings of these reforms to suggest that a key factor in BC, as elsewhere in Canada, has been the tendency to link concerns over welfare—and welfare fraud in particular—with the view of welfare recipients as morally bankrupt and criminally blameworthy. The intense policing of and preoccupation with welfare fraud have come at the expense of welfare recipients, leading not only to the increased surveillance of welfare recipients in Canada, but also to a vastly expanding category of the undeserving poor.

Section B of this chapter provides the contextual background for the reforms made to welfare policies in the last two decades. Neo-liberal forms of governance have been the driving force behind the degree and type of changes witnessed in the welfare system. Notions of responsibilization and self-sufficiency are key tenets of neo-liberalism, and they have come to reinforce ideas about who is deserving and who is undeserving of state support. When these ideas are combined with greater demands for fiscal management, the end result is the intense policing of who is entitled to social assistance.

Section C examines welfare policies in British Columbia, focusing particularly on the sanctions related to welfare fraud. I argue that the disentitlement of poor people to social assistance and the implementation of punitive policies are possible through a construction of welfare recipients as 'criminals' and undeserving.

Section D explores the gendered and racialized impact of punitive welfare policies. While all groups suffer from increased surveillance and policing by welfare authorities, women and racialized groups are more likely to experience harsher outcomes because of racist and sexist assumptions about their behaviour and the structural disadvantages experienced in the labour market and within society more generally. This chapter concludes with the view that rather than promote greater social equality through welfare reform, Canada—like other countries—has taken the opposite route and has exacerbated the social inequities already present by criminalizing and penalizing Canadians for being poor.

B. NEO-LIBERALISM AND CANADIAN WELFARE POLICIES

Scholars have often held that the rise of neo-liberalism in Canada started in the 1980s, when government debts and deficits began soaring out of control and efforts to reduce public spending led governments to seize upon the ideas of neo-liberalism to direct policy changes (Cohen, 1997; McBride & Shields, 1997; Peck & Tickell, 2002). The goal of the neo-liberal project was to lead people to believe, first, that the public sector could no longer be supported through taxes and thus ought to be abandoned in favour of the marketplace, and second, that this was a logical approach to the problem (Cohen, 1997, p. 99). This would only be possible through a multi-pronged approach, one that involved institutional and economic restructuring as well as the reinforcement of a particular set of cultural and ideological processes. Individualism and consumption would be positioned at the centre of the project where people's identities would be derived from their role as taxpayers or service users rather than as citizens or community members (Coulter, 2009, p. 26).

With neo-liberalism, greater emphasis is given to optimizing the conditions of the marketplace and capital accumulation. The following prescription aptly describes the neo-liberal approach:

> As many costs as possible should be shifted from the state and back on to the individuals, and markets, particularly labour markets, should be made as flexible as possible. . . . The presumption is always in favour of recreating the widest possible conditions for markets to flourish, which means removing as many restrictions on competition as possible, and empowering market agents by reducing the burdens of taxation. (Gamble, 2001, pp. 131–2)

Alan Sears points out that the creation and integration into the economy of a cheaper, more flexible, and more productive labour force are central to the neo-liberal project (1999, pp. 95–8). This has been made possible by reorganizing labour, with low-paying jobs displaced to developing countries. Wealthy nations will now be characterized by a dual labour market where a small core of well-paid, stable jobs would be buttressed by a larger periphery of precarious employment (Hartman, 2005, p. 60). Other key approaches in the translation of neo-liberal principles into public policies include: the privatization of services through contracting-out and outsourcing to the for-profit sector; the introduction of market principles into the public sector; user fees; public-private partnership arrangements for capital, operations, and/or the financing of institutions, programs, or infrastructure; the promotion and celebration of volunteerism, charity, or fundraising as a substitution for public investment; the deterioration of terms and conditions of employment; and a deterioration of standards more generally (Quadagno, 1998; Coulter, 2009). Under neo-liberalism, the private and public sectors are both subjected to the same evaluative criteria as for-profit institutions. In the process, the distinction between the public and private is blurred, the role of the state is eroded, and the needs of the public or the collective good are relegated to the margins in favour of profit and capital accumulation (MacGregor, 1999; Brodie, 2002).

The Neo-liberal Welfare State

The restructuring and retrenchment of the Canadian welfare state have been heavily influenced by a form of economic rationalism rooted in neo-liberal ideology. This approach takes the view that the solution to high levels of public debt can be managed through smaller government, carefully targeted social programs, and greater reliance on families and the private sector for services and support (Baker, 1997, p. 1). Successive Canadian governments have embraced these ideas in reforming the welfare state to manage the problems of rising program costs, increasing numbers of claimants, and structural changes in the labour market.

These ideas have also served as a rationale for shifting political agendas that gives the market greater primacy over the state. Program entitlement across most provinces is now less associated with such notions as 'guaranteed annual income' and more with the view that social support should be temporary, needs based, and designed to encourage independence and self-sufficiency (Baker, 1997, p. 2).

The presence of welfare-to-work policies in most provinces is a clear indication of the neo-liberal shift. While these policies are not new, the related programs expanded dramatically in the 1990s (Peck, 2001). Provinces now require mandatory participation in employment programs and active job-searching as a condition of entitlement. The focus on work ethics is a sharp reminder that welfare dependence is no longer acceptable. Dependency is framed as harmful, and employment and self-sufficiency are applauded. Daenzer points out that invoking policies that emphasize work ethics and personal responsibility allows government to manage expectations induced by the market by lessening state expectations and increasing individual guilt (2009, p. 242). The effect is not simply individuals having greater difficulty accessing benefits and being made to feel guilty for doing so; there is also a fundamental change that sees social citizenship being replaced with market citizenship. Previously, when all citizens were entitled to a base level of benefits, the market citizenship model defined entitlement as contingent upon one's attachment to the labour market (Brodie, 1997). While social citizenship grants benefits on the basis of a social right, market citizenship sees welfare benefits as a privilege. Baker and Tippin observe that employment under market citizenship is equated with independence and independence is equated with worthy citizenship (1999). The end result of this shift is that economic security becomes increasingly less secure for people who cannot demonstrate their attachment to the labour market. Furthermore, the requirement that poor people demonstrate that they deserve to be supported by the state means that if they cannot do so, they will be constructed as unworthy, morally suspect citizens (Breitkreuz, 2005).

Another major policy change influenced by neo-liberalism relates to the amount of support that the state is willing to provide. Benefit rates have decreased dramatically in the last decade, in many cases falling well below levels required for basic subsistence (Klein & Pulkingham, 2008). The Canadian Centre for Policy Alternatives points out that 'welfare is not, and has never been, "generous"' (2008, p. 8). Klein and Pulkingham tracked British Columbians on income assistance over a two-year period and found that the participants were unable to survive on current welfare benefits and that, therefore, their day-to-day life focused on struggling to meet basic needs such as food, shelter, health, and personal safety (2008, p. 10). The situation in the rest of Canada is similar insofar as benefit rates in other provinces have also been regarded as insufficient for basic survival (Caragata, 2003; Gordon, 2005). No longer would the goal of welfare be, as the architect of Canada's income security system stated, to provide a 'general sense of security' and offer 'a better life for the great mass of people and a potent antidote for the fears and worries and uncertainties of the times' (Marsh, 1943/1975, p. 7). Politicians and the media have carefully crafted the message that cuts should be made to welfare programs so that people will find welfare so unpleasant they will be driven to seek alternatives (Gordon, 2005, p. 60). Current benefit rates are symbolic of a government deeply contemptuous of poor people for failing to rise to the challenge of labour market changes. It matters not that the type of work available to the unemployed in today's labour market is badly paid, insecure, and alienating. Therefore, even as poverty rates in Canada continue to climb and the gap between rich and poor widens, the dominant discourse of poverty portrays welfare recipients as having bad habits and inadequate self-control (Reid & Tom, 2006, p. 403). According to neo-liberal ideology, poverty stems from bad decision-making rather than from structural changes to the labour market or inadequate government support (Brodie, 2008, p. 148). Other Western countries, such as Britain, the United States, and Australia, share a similar approach to welfare reform, and as in Canada, class inequality increased as welfare benefits were reduced (Schustereder, 2010). In these countries, the retreat of the welfare state was also a response to growing pressure for governments to control spending and to act as agents of social control through a rearticulation of the criteria governing entitlement to benefits (Bahle, 2003).

Despite all the evidence available highlighting the inadequacy of welfare benefits, the public campaign by politicians and the media continues to fuel the myth that welfare is too 'generous',[3] that it is promoting lazy and irresponsible behaviour, and that welfare recipients are getting something they do not deserve (Power, 2005). Understanding the negative campaign against welfare recipients involves recognizing, as many scholars have argued, that the purpose of welfare reforms is not concerned with alleviating poverty, but rather with reducing the dependency of individuals and families who rely on the state for support (Mosher, 2000; Sidel, 2000; Gordon, 2005; Wacquant, 2009). To the extent that reducing the number of people eligible to receive welfare benefits constitutes a savings for the government, efforts to shorten welfare rolls have been a key strategy of neo-liberal welfare policy reforms. Along with the requirement that recipients must demonstrate that they are actively seeking employment, the ideological assault on welfare recipients is an important aspect of program cuts and disentitlement. Arguably, one of the most publicized campaigns focuses on the denial of assistance for those who have engaged in welfare fraud. Many poverty activists and researchers have noted the vigour and enthusiasm with which the government has sought to manage the alleged problem of welfare fraud (Chunn & Gavigan, 2004; Mosher & Hermer, 2005; Mirchandani & Chan, 2007). For example, in Ontario, the presence of snitch lines and greater numbers of eligibility review officers (or welfare cops) are just two indicators of the government's belief that rampant fraud exists within the welfare system. However, there is no evidence, even from the government's own data, to suggest that the problem is out of control (Mosher, 2000). Yet the construction of welfare recipients as being criminal justifies and legitimizes the implementation of punitive sanctions and denial of support. It also effectively masks the realities behind life on welfare and the significant hardships experienced by poor people on a daily basis.

The use of an anti-welfare rhetoric that stereotypes and demonizes welfare recipients has given rise to unprecedented levels of surveillance in the lives of poor people. A key characteristic of current welfare policies is the presumption that welfare recipients are 'guilty until proven innocent', that their conduct needs to be closely supervised and remedied by restrictive and coercive measures, and that deterrence and stigma are necessary to modify the behaviour of welfare recipients (Wacquant, 2009, p. 79). Wacquant sums up the situation well: 'The law effectively assimilates welfare beneficiaries to *civic felons* for whom workfare will serve as an analogon of probation fit to ensure that they abide by the reaffirmed national norms of wage work and family morality, on pain of being effectively kept out of the citizenry' (2009, p. 80).

Various studies have described the constant surveillance experienced by welfare recipients and the impact it has on their lives. Collins's study of Canadian women on social assistance found that her research participants felt guilty for every little thing they did and that the loss of personal privacy due to the high levels of surveillance resulted in the loss of human dignity (2005, p. 23). Her participants noted that not only were they under surveillance to determine eligibility or to ensure they were conforming to the rules, but they were required to give up all kinds of personal information, all of which could then be scrutinized regardless of whether it pertained to welfare rules or not (Collins, 2005, p. 23). Other researchers found similar comments by welfare recipients, noting that their participants felt humiliated on a daily basis and experienced high levels of anxiety, paranoia, and stress from worrying about whether or not their actions would result in being denied support or being criminally punished (Seccombe, James, & Walters, 1998; Power, 2005; Gilliom, 2005; Gilman, 2008). Nonetheless, resistance to welfare surveillance remains widespread despite the fact that it increases the stress and fear of many welfare recipients. Attempts to supplement welfare benefits is a necessary survival strategy, particularly for many poor women seeking to care for their families (Gilman, 2008). As Gilliom notes, welfare recipients became 'artful managers of their financial lives—creating ways to come up with necessary (and forbidden) extra income without triggering the surveillance system' (2005, p. 73). He refers to this as the practice of 'everyday resistance' by poor people against the constant surveillance that accompanies the struggle to survive.

Henman and Marston (2008) observe that with the advent of increasing surveillance in our daily lives, inequalities persist insofar as the application and experience of surveillance is different for different people. In the context of the welfare state, people receiving welfare benefits experience different levels of surveillance than people receiving other forms of state benefits. Not surprisingly, welfare recipients experience far greater levels of intrusion into their lives than people receiving unemployment allowances for example (Henman & Marston, 2008, p. 192). Recent examples of increasing surveillance in Canada include the suggestions that welfare recipients be fingerprinted or subjected to mandatory addiction screening (Bobier, 1998; Berger, 2001). That these suggestions have not been discussed with respect to other groups receiving state benefits highlights the discriminatory and differential treatment of poor people.

These findings have led many researchers to argue that a culture of surveillance encompasses access to and receipt of welfare benefits. Hartman claims that increased levels of control over the lives of welfare recipients are a deliberate outcome of neo-liberal rationalities that seek to discipline poor people to become self-governing in the name of individual initiative and responsibility (2005, p. 69). The current system of surveillance differs from past practices insofar as a 'paternalist penal state' has overtaken a 'maternalist welfare state' (Wacquant, 2002, p. 382). Poor people are now constructed and treated as a 'troublesome population to be subdued and "corrected" through stern behavioral controls and paternalistic sanctions' (Wacquant, 2010, p. 79). As many scholars note, this approach highlights the convergence and inseparability of criminal law and welfare law to regulate social marginality (Beckett & Western, 2001; Chunn & Gavigan, 2004). Welfare and punishment are now part of a broad policy regime that manages labour and inequality, with welfare acting as the carrot and as punishment the stick (Haney, 2004). Ironically, while the neo-liberal attack on the welfare state led to a withdrawal of state support for poor people, it did not reduce the presence of the state nor the resources required to condemn and punish the poor (Chunn & Gavigan, 2004). It simply made more visible the coercive arm of the state as social programs were slowly dismantled.

The difference in the intensity and intrusion of surveillance can be attributed to the ongoing moral distinction—of 'deserving' and 'undeserving'—that characterizes the distribution of welfare resources. As noted earlier, welfare recipients are portrayed as individuals with moral or psychological deficiencies to the extent that the term 'welfare' generally connotes deeply held negative emotions or associations (Fraser & Gordon, 1994). A recent Canadian study found that while Canadians continue to support spending on social services for the poor, they favour reduced spending on welfare (Harell, Soroka, & Mahon, 2008). The researchers claim that the framing of welfare—in terms of need—typically evokes negative images and thus support is lessened when there is the belief that recipients can 'control' their situation (Harell et al., 2008). As a result, groups that are seen as the most deserving, children and the elderly, are given greater support than people on social assistance (Harell et al., 2008, p. 55). Little (1998) notes, however, how easily the 'deserving' can fall into the ranks of the 'undeserving'. For example, single mothers and racialized people have been attacked and vilified for failing to be independent, responsible, and self-sufficient (Fraser & Gordon, 1994; Seccombe et al., 1998; Quadagno, 2000; Sidel, 2000; Coulter, 2009). They are the 'undeserving poor', the 'welfare queens', the 'deviant' and the 'irresponsible' (Sidel, 2000). They are often discredited as illegitimate and according to politicians, the only recourse available is to take a 'tough-love' stance through the use of draconian measures to ensure that their continued dependency on the state will cease (Seccombe et al., 1998). As Sidel aptly points out, these designations leave no room for the considerable variation and complexity that characterize people's lives and the fact that many of us have relied, to varying degrees, on the state for support of one kind or another (2000, p. 75). In the neo-liberal context, these views have intensified as politicians become more pessimistic about solving the problems of poverty and focus instead on the dangerous and undeserving nature of the poor.

The consequences of increased surveillance are many. Along with the continued demonization of welfare recipients, the reinforcement of disadvantage and discrimination, and the dehumanizing impact of surveillance on welfare recipients, recent studies suggest that now, more than ever, the social exclusion of poor people is cemented through a punitive approach that permeates both penal and welfare institutions (Beckett & Western, 2001; Mosher, 2005; Mirchandani & Chan, 2007). Discussions of welfare and welfare reform are now characterized by the language of pathology and crime, and welfare dependency assumes a thoroughly negative connotation. British Columbia is no exception to these recent trends in welfare policy reforms. The management of welfare recipients has become increasingly more punitive as the provincial Liberal government promotes the view that if welfare recipients cannot be coaxed into seeking employment, then their poverty can only be resolved with more exclusionary and security-minded responses. As welfare fraud is given greater priority in the effort to create a more efficient welfare system, criminal penalties are now part of the various sanctions available to punish welfare recipients who fail to obey the rules.

C. POLICING WELFARE IN BRITISH COLUMBIA
Welfare Reform in BC

In 2002, under the leadership of the provincial Liberal government, welfare policies in British Columbia underwent unprecedented change owing largely to a massive deficit that needed to be tamed (Klein & Long, 2003). Inspired by welfare reform strategies in the United States, the changes proposed in British Columbia would borrow many of the most punitive ideas, with the imposition of time limits at the heart of these reforms. The government estimated it would save approximately $581 million in its operating budget as well as monies from closing 36 welfare offices and cutting 459 full-time positions within the ministry (Klein & Long, 2003, p. 4). The new legislation, the Employment and Assistance Act (BCEA) and the Employment and Assistance for Persons with Disabilities Act (BCEAPWD), took effect in April 2002.

According to the human resources minister at the time, the central goals of the restructuring program were to reduce caseloads and prevent abuse in the system by tightening up eligibility rules (Palmer, 2002). Welfare dependency was seen by the government as 'a waste of people's potential' and a problem that needed to be dealt with severely. Doing so would require a shift in culture, a 'fundamental change from a culture of entitlement to a culture of employment and self-sufficiency' (Palmer, 2002). The government's goals would be achieved through a number of policy reforms. First, rates and benefits would be reduced in many categories, resulting in, for example, a single employable person receiving only enough bene-fits to cover 45 per cent of his or her minimum living costs (CCPA, 2002, p. 20). Second, it was no longer possible for an individual to engage in paid employment while receiving welfare benefits. This practice had been seen as necessary by wel-fare recipients to meet their basic needs, given the inadequate support provided; moreover, it encouraged them to engage in the labour market (CCPA, 2002, 23). Now, any income earned would be deducted from the monthly total benefits received. Third, single parents with young children ages three or older would now be expected to return to work despite the fact that child-care subsidies had not increased. Fourth, welfare recipients would be required to complete employment plans, setting out job goals and training objectives, to demonstrate they were act-ively engaged in the labour market. They were also required to wait three weeks before receiving assistance—a measure that many critics argued was overly harsh (Reitsma-Street, 2002; Caledon Institute, 2002; Klein & Long, 2003). Fifth, post-secondary students were no longer eligible to receive assistance unless they had a disability. Sixth, eligibility rules would now only provide two years of support out of every five years. Once the two years were exhausted, no further support would be provided. Finally, welfare recipients were required to demonstrate that they had been financially independent for two years before being eligible for assistance.

For people with disabilities, the most significant changes were the replacement of old categories of disability classifications with new categories; new criteria were established for each category, making it more difficult for disabled people to dem-onstrate eligibility. The most controversial of these changes focused on the time limits imposed. The requirement that new claimants must wait three weeks and be actively searching for employment before making an official application, the chan-ges to eligibility whereby benefits were now available for only two out of five years unless an exemption applies, and the two-year independence rule requiring that an applicant must have worked 840 hours or earned at least $7,000 in the two years before making an application would most likely cause enormous hardship. The Canadian Centre for Policy Alternatives argued that this punitive strategy demonstrated the government's disregard for the welfare of their clients and was only concerned with reducing welfare caseloads at any expense (Klein & Long, 2003, p. 27). The CCPA wondered how realistic it was to expect someone without financial resources to engage in job searches or to expect that a person has to have a two-year history of employment before he or she could apply for support (p. 30). The CCPA also cited the many problems that have occurred in the United States, where imposing time limits on access to benefits had been in place for much longer, resulting in 'time-limited leavers [being] worse off in every measure than the non–time-limited leavers' (p. 28). It noted that these new rules 'represent a Canadian first—another fundamental repudiation of welfare as a right when in need' (p. 30). Indeed, public opposition to the two-year time limit was particularly intense. Activists pointed to leaked government documents showing that up to 19,000 individuals could potentially be facing time-limit sanctions and that ministry workers were doubtful that all recipients facing time limits would be able to find or maintain employment (Wallace & Richards, 2008). These concerns eventually made their way into the mainstream, culminating in a multi-pronged provincial campaign that resulted in the minister for human resources adding new exemptions that would prevent thousands of recipients from being cut off (Reitsma-Street & Wallace, 2004, p. 175).

The neo-liberal agenda of reducing welfare caseloads by disentitling individuals from access to state support, by aggressively pursuing and investigating cases of 'fraud', and by constructing recipients as 'never-deserving' has been largely successful insofar as welfare caseloads in British Columbia have been reduced since the reforms were implemented in 2002. Between 2001 and 2005, welfare caseloads dropped by 42 per cent, and the government saw this as an indicator that their approach was working (Wallace et al., 2006), arguing that more welfare recipients were now moving into jobs and becoming self-sufficient. However, a study conducted for the CCPA found that the reduced caseloads can be attributed to a system that was overly restrictive and too complicated for individuals to navigate alone, such that most people in need were not getting the assistance required (Wallace et al., 2006). Instead, they were either discouraged from applying, denied, or delayed assistance for not complying with the complex rules. The most recent attempt to restrict access to welfare benefits in BC was to deny or cut off welfare to individuals with outstanding warrants unless they qualify for an exemption or have the warrant resolved.[4] Critics argue that without a list of the type of indictable offences that could lead to a denial of benefits, many welfare recipients who had engaged in minor crimes would be unfairly punished by the policy.

As Reitsma-Street points out, these welfare reforms represent a stark departure from past practices in which British Columbia has been seen as one of the more progressive provinces in supporting low-income families (2002). While previous governments in BC have been engaging in welfare reform, the scope and depth of the proposals made by the Liberal government shocked many. The Caledon Institute for Social Policy (2002) sums up the government's social program agenda as one of 'restricted eligibility; income-testing; rate cuts, offloading to families and the community; user fees', among many other changes. The institute notes that while the Liberal government promised a 'New Era', BC voters most likely did not anticipate the reality that was emerging (Caledon Institute, 2002, p. 10). A report from the Social Planning and Research Council of British Columbia (SPARC) in 2008 confirms what many critics suspected—that welfare recipients were 'still left behind' by the inadequate support provided and that 'income assistance remains a legislated form of poverty in BC' (p. 12).

Sanctions and the Policing of Welfare Fraud

As part of the welfare reform package, changes were also made to the penalties imposed on people who fail to conform to the rules of receiving welfare benefits. Families face benefit reductions of $100 per month or face short-term disqualification if a recipient quits his or her job, is fired without cause, fails to pursue income or assets, or fails to engage in reasonable work searches. An entire family can be deemed ineligible for benefits if there is a failure to comply with the employment plan. The CCPA argues that these types of policies place welfare recipients in a no-win situation where welfare benefits don't meet basic living standards but if individuals make any attempt to supplement their income, they risk losing all their benefits (Klein & Long, 2003, p. 34).

The most punitive penalties in this set of reforms apply to the area of welfare fraud. The BC government defines fraud as 'receiving assistance as a result of providing information that a person knows is false or misleading'.[5] It identifies three categories of welfare fraud, with sanctions varying depending on the type of conviction. A Criminal Code conviction for fraud results in a lifetime ban, whereas a conviction under the Employment and Assistance Act (BCEA) or the Employment and Assistance for Persons with Disabilities Act (EAPWD) results in a one-year ban for first offence, a two-year ban for the second offence, and a lifetime ban for the third offence. Lastly, admitted fraud or fraud committed under a civil judgment carries the penalty of three months for the first offence, six months for the second offence, and one year for the third offence.[6] Convictions under the Criminal Code or the BCEA cannot be appealed, whereas a civil court judgment can be. Recipients may also be required to repay the assistance received if they are found to have been ineligible to have received the monies.

Part of the problem with this definition is the issue of intent insofar as it is assumed that recipients who are found guilty were aware that their actions were criminal. However, discerning the intentions of a welfare recipient can be tricky if the rules and regulations governing welfare are complex and continually changing. It is wholly unrealistic to expect welfare recipients to know the most recent rules for receiving assistance when caseworkers are not always up-to-date with current policies (Mirchandani & Chan, 2007). Furthermore, as Mosher and Hermer (2005) found in their study of welfare fraud in Ontario, failing to make a distinction between 'fraud' and 'error' reinforces the stereotypes of welfare recipients as 'criminals who prefer to exploit the system rather than work for a living' (p. 37).

Most scholars point out that fraud constitutes only 3 to 4 per cent of caseloads at best and that this has remained constant over the last several decades (Rachert, 1990; Carty, 1996; Mosher & Hermer, 2005). Nonetheless, various levels of government have always viewed welfare fraud as a serious threat to the welfare system, and the current BC government is no different. According to the Ministry of Human Resources, the sanctions for fraud are aimed at 'deterring and preventing fraud to ensure income assistance is provided to those most in need'.[7] More recently, the government's intent to sue welfare recipients for monies owed is justified on the grounds that the government needs to 'send a message to those who receive unwarranted money and refuse to pay it back' (Shaw, 2010a). The construction of welfare recipients as undeserving cheaters who need to be severely punished has widespread support. A recent editorial supporting the government's most recent initiative argues that 'Coleman is right to combat con artists, even if they are poor and it costs money, to preserve the integrity of the welfare system and to insure money is there for those legitimately in need' (Editorial, 2010). What has not been made known in this debate is why so many recipients were overpaid in the first place. The assumption made by the media and general public is that welfare recipients were engaging in fraudulent behaviour despite the fact that the minister notes that only some of these cases involved fraud (Shaw, 2010a). This most recent example once again reinforces the perception that welfare recipients cannot be trusted and their behaviour needs to be closely scrutinized.

The circumstances that give rise to a charge of welfare fraud typically involve the non-disclosure of income from other sources or the failure to disclose that a 'spouse' is also present in the household (Carty, 1996; Mosher & Hermer, 2005). Studies conducted in Ontario, where the pursuit of welfare fraud is at a fever pitch, document the problems welfare recipients have with accessing information and staying abreast of the very complex rules governing their access to benefits (Martin, 1992; Mosher & Hermer, 2005; Little & Marks, 2010). Researchers found that it was not unusual for a recipient to be unaware that disclosure was required until a charge of fraud had been made (Mosher & Hermer, 2005, p. 58). Similarly, welfare recipients' uncertainty about the definition of 'spouse' has resulted in many women losing their welfare benefits. As well, many women may not view the person living with them as a 'spouse' and therefore do not feel it is necessary to disclose this co-habitation to their caseworker. Yet even when there is no attempt to deceive the state, the tendency has been to label these situations as 'fraud' (Mosher & Hermer, 2005, p. 64).

Allegations of fraud often lead to intrusive investigations into all aspects of an individual's personal life. In British Columbia, there are more than 100 government workers investigating welfare fraud. They have been known to make unannounced home visits and, more recently, have turned to the use of social networking sites to investigate recipients (MacLeod, 2008). Welfare recipients report that breaches of privacy are commonplace despite government assurances that protection of privacy remains a priority (Mirchandani & Chan, 2007). They are often required to provide all manner of personal information in order to apply for and continue to receive benefits. This level of scrutiny leaves many welfare recipients reporting that even where they have not done anything wrong, they are made to feel as if they are latent criminals (Mirchandani & Chan, 2007, pp. 70–6). They point out how the whole process of accessing welfare benefits can be degrading and dehumanizing (Mirchandani & Chan, 2007, p. 76).

A marked difference between the reforms in 2002 and earlier periods is the significant increase in the daily surveillance of applicants and recipients as well as the implementation of a lifetime ban for those criminally convicted of fraud and for third-time offenders under the BCEA legislation. Critics contend that while the penalties for fraud have become significantly more harsh, the reasons many people are convicted of fraud haven't changed over the years (Carty, 1998;

Klein & Long, 2003; Mirchandani & Chan, 2007)—namely, the need to survive is a driving force behind the failure to declare extra income or personal assets (Mirchandani & Chan, 2007). Indeed, as the poverty rates in BC continue to climb because of increases in the cost of living, preventing welfare recipients from supplementing their assistance only adds to their misery and ensures they remain trapped in poverty. The high-profile death of Kimberly Rogers in Ontario, where the coroner's inquest found that the lifetime welfare ban she had been given was a contributing factor to her suicide, is a sharp reminder of the impact of punitive, zero-tolerance policies.[8] Rather than learn from the Rogers case, the BC government has taken the opposite approach by suing more than 300 welfare recipients for monies owed (Shaw, 2010a).

It has also been pointed out that while the new laws in British Columbia emphasize a punitive theme, they are not accompanied by a corresponding attempt to provide adequate support for those seeking employment. Furthermore, government claims that more money will be saved as a result of reducing the number of people who are ineligible for benefits will likely result in increased spending in order to pay for administrative costs associated with constant assessments of eligibility. Organizations like the National Council of Welfare question the extent to which a reduction in welfare caseloads is the result of more people finding gainful employment or the result of people having greater difficulty obtaining social assistance owing to more restrictive eligibility requirements. The effects of slashing welfare budgets have been well documented in Ontario as well as in the United States, where greater misery, increased poverty and homelessness, and possibly death are just a few of the dire consequences facing those most in need (Gustafson, 2009).

Chunn and Gavigan argue that the restructuring of welfare in Canada and the concomitant emphasis on surveillance and policing have shifted our understanding of 'welfare fraud to welfare as fraud' (2004, p. 220). They note that, now, poverty, crime, and welfare are inextricably linked and to be poor is to be culpable (Chunn & Gavigan, 2004, p. 220). Indeed, as other scholars have also highlighted, the criminalization of poverty is a trend that has taken hold across many jurisdictions such that, by the early twenty-first century, the 'war against poverty' has now been replaced by a 'war against the poor' (Larkin, 2007; Marston & Walsh, 2008; Wacquant, 2009). Where the state once provided support for those in need, now the poor are 'made into scapegoats of all the major ills of the country and . . . summoned to care for themselves lest they be hit by a volley of punitive and humiliating measures intended, if not to put them back onto the narrow path of precarious employment, then at least to minimize their social demands and thus their fiscal burden' (Wacquant, 2009, p. 74).

The policing of welfare fraud is a central pillar of this punitive strategy, and it is used by the state to reinforce the prevailing view that welfare recipients are almost always undeserving and potentially criminal. As Dianne Martin adds, 'The prosecution of welfare fraud is heavily imbued with the bias of the population at large against social assistance recipients, and is marked by stereotypical thinking, with the result that these offenders are punished much more severely than those who commit other frauds against the public purse' (1992, p. 93).

The criminalization of the poor has legitimated the reorganization of social services into instruments of surveillance and has allowed for the containment of the poor through incarceration (Wacquant, 2009, pp. 83–5). The policy reforms in British Columbia and elsewhere in Canada reflect what is happening in the United States, Britain, and Australia—that the criminal justice system and the welfare system are not only now working in tandem, but are becoming difficult to distinguish as the administrative procedures in the welfare system become entangled with the criminal justice system. The aggressive investigation and prosecution of welfare fraud in BC, the movement away from civil penalties only, and the overlapping goals and attitudes toward the poor in both systems suggest, as the CCPA observes, that this is truly a 'bad time to be poor' in BC (Klein & Long, 2003).

D. THE GENDERED AND RACIALIZED IMPACT OF WELFARE SURVEILLANCE

For welfare recipients, having to navigate the deeply entrenched negative image the public has of them is difficult enough, but for women and racialized individuals, the problem is compounded by further discriminatory treatment. Stereotypes such as 'welfare queen', 'bogus refugee', and 'lazy immigrant' continue to shape not just public attitudes but also policy discussions regarding access and entitlement to welfare (Seccombe et al., 1998; Sidel, 2000; Pratt & Valverde, 2002). This is exacerbated by media images that continuously portray the poor as failed individuals, dysfunctional, and pathological (Bullock, Wyche, & Williams, 2001). As noted earlier, these views have fuelled the demand for the dismantling or drastic reduction of government support for the welfare system in the belief that welfare produces a culture of dependency and that poor people need to be motivated to find work. The problem with these types of arguments is that welfare is not a gender-neutral or race-neutral program. A large portion of welfare recipients are women, often lone mothers, and their needs and real-life experiences are not contextualized in discussions regarding welfare reform (Polakow, 1999). As a result, they tend to experience the harshest impact when cuts are made or when services are curtailed. Nor is welfare race neutral when it comes to the treatment of welfare clients. Racial disparities and racial inequalities permeate the welfare system, and racialized individuals are often assumed to be receiving assistance illegitimately (Neubeck & Cazenave, 2002; Mirchandani & Chan, 2007).

The Attack on Welfare Mothers

Is it appropriate to prosecute and convict a woman who does not disclose income from employment when the earnings go to an abusive spouse and the non-disclosure is part of a pattern of compliance with his demands and avoidance of his anger? (Martin, 1992, p. 88)

The current system of welfare enforcement unfairly penalizes women and is, as Mosher argues, central to the management of women's disentitlement to welfare (2000, p. 31). She notes how the anti-fraud campaign in Ontario proved particularly troublesome for women. If a single woman or lone mother is collecting welfare benefits and is found to be living with a 'spouse', she may be charged and prosecuted for welfare fraud (Mosher, 2000, p. 44). Her entire life is turned upside down as investigators probe into all aspects of her life to determine if there is evidence of an intimate relationship (Martin, 1992). In some cases, women have been threatened with fraud charges if they don't admit to living with a spouse (*Falkiner et al. v. Director of Income Maintenance Branch*). This places women in an untenable situation where the outcome is likely the loss of benefits and she is left in a situation in which her alleged spouse may or may not provide some financial support (Mosher, 2000, p. 44). Furthermore, so important is the need to deter other women from engaging in similar acts that in cases where women have been convicted of welfare fraud, imprisonment remains an option for the courts during sentencing (Carruthers, 1995, p. 246).

Women in abusive relationships are made even more vulnerable by the punitive measures implemented in BC (Morrow, Hankivsky, & Varcoe, 2004). For example, the lifetime ban for welfare fraud can result in women being compelled to return to their abusive spouses if they have no other financial recourses. Similarly, with respect to abused mothers, the requirement to return to the labour market after her child turns three means that a woman may have to return to an abusive spouse if she is unable to find employment that meets basic survival needs. She also faces the possibility that her child may be apprehended by authorities if she does not protect the child from witnessing wife abuse (Mosher, 2000, p. 47). A report conducted in Ontario on abused women's experiences of the welfare system concludes: 'For many the experience of welfare is like another abusive relationship . . . Disturbingly, the decision to return to an abusive relationship is often the 'best' decision for a woman, in a social context of horrendously constrained options' (Mosher et al., 2004, p. v).

Clearly, single women, lone mothers, and even abused women on welfare do not evoke any sympathy. Rather, contemporary responses mirror historical reactions that perceived these women as 'incomplete' because they failed to fulfill the obligations of marriage, normalized motherhood, and a proper family life (Polakow, 1999, p. 242). They have not only ruined their own lives, but those of future generations as well (Fineman, 1991). Poverty continues to be viewed as a private, individual affair, and poor women's bad choices and misconduct, it is argued, should not be bolstered by a welfare system that would perpetuate these vices. Thus, women are regulated through welfare policies that promote the view that welfare is designed to be a temporary stopgap measure for a woman until she finds a male breadwinner or until she can obtain child support from the father of her children (Gordon, 1988). These stereotypes have fuelled the belief that the regulation, surveillance, and punishment of women are imperative not only to prevent fraud, but to ensure that women assume their proper role. As Dee Cook notes, 'this unequal and harsh treatment of lone mothers is justified as an indirect spur to "solve" their problems by marrying' (1989, p. 32).

Yet the harms women suffer as a result of restrictive eligibility requirements, punitive measures, intense surveillance, and inadequate benefits are many. In her study of lone mothers on social assistance in Ontario, Power found that her participants were very conscientious about learning the rules of welfare to ensure compliance (2005, p. 23). They were particularly concerned about how their behaviour would be perceived by others, as they were in constant fear of being reported to Children's Aid (Power, 2005). Other common themes expressed by women navigating the welfare system include frustration with the rules and with caseworkers' lack of flexibility and compassion (Lightman, Mitchell, & Herd, 2003). Many researchers point to the caseworkers' unrealistic demands for information as a major barrier to accessing welfare (Herd, Mitchell, & Lightman, 2005; Mirchandani & Chan, 2007; Kohler-Hausmann, 2007). The amount of information required, the process and frequency of providing information, and the often inappropriate requests for information created a climate of suspicion that left welfare recipients stressed out and constantly worried that they would be cut off (Mirchandani & Chan, 2007). All these barriers resulted in many women self-regulating their behaviour or engaging in a form of 'self-censorship' to avoid losing their welfare benefits (Little, 1998). The dehumanizing, degrading, and demoralizing process that accompanies women's attempts to apply for and receive welfare is a form of constant harassment by the state (Power, 2005; Herd, Mitchell, & Lightman, 2005). Not surprisingly, many women believe the welfare system is more concerned with controlling them than with helping them (Lightman et al., 2003). However, given their desperation, many are resigned to having to accept the ongoing surveillance of their lives and invasion of their privacy as the price for obtaining welfare benefits (Gilliom, 2001).

One of the key challenges women face as a result of these obstacles is having to muster the ability to care for their families, since being constantly scrutinized significantly affects their overall quality of life. The factors that contribute to women's poor quality of life—along with having to live their life under a 'giant microscope'—include physical and mental health problems, being unemployed, not eating well, fear that their kids will be apprehended, and poor quality of housing (Collins, 2005; Reid & Tom, 2006). When all these are combined with inadequate benefits to meet basic needs, women report resorting to hiding extra income as a necessary strategy for survival even though the consequences are severe (Edin & Lein, 1997; Swan et. al., 2008). As Mosher correctly points out, the cumulative harm of recent welfare reforms on women is staggering (2000, p. 48). Faced with a no-win situation, women are forced to adopt whatever means are necessary to survive, with the constant threat that they will be disentitled at any time. It is thus not an overstatement to suggest that welfare reforms have occurred at the expense of poor women and that any hope of achieving gender equality in the current climate seems doubtful (Mosher, 2000, p. 48).

Welfare Racism

The policing of welfare has had an equally devastating impact on racialized individuals. In the welfare discourse of who is deserving and who is undeserving of government support, people of colour have been portrayed as predominantly undeserving. Racist stereotypes continue to shape attitudes about welfare and have promoted the belief that poor people of colour live in poverty because they lack a work ethic (Quadagno, 1994; Gilens, 1996; Harell et al., 2008). Faulty assumptions about the culture and values of racialized communities have legitimated policies and practices that preserve rather than break down racial hierarchies. For example, one of the most enduring stereotypes about women of colour is that they are hyper-sexed and promiscuous, leading to the belief that they have children to obtain more welfare money (Abramovitz, 2006). As a result, many welfare jurisdictions have reduced welfare benefits for women with children or implemented earlier cut-off times, such as the three-year limit in BC. Little's (1998) research found that, historically, mother's allowance programs often excluded immigrant or Aboriginal women because they either did not qualify or could not provide the necessary documentation. Other racialized groups in Canada have not fared much better. Depending on their immigration status, many immigrants to Canada are not eligible for welfare benefits upon arrival because of restrictions in sponsorship arrangements. Refugees are consistently portrayed as undeserving recipients of Canada's 'generosity' (Razack, 2000; Pratt & Valverde, 2002). As well, Aboriginal people in Canada have been stigmatized for decades owing, in part, to their high rates of participation in the welfare system (Kendall, 2001).

The effect of racial stereotypes on welfare recipients has led to more punitive sanctions, increased levels of poverty, and greater economic, social, and political inequality. A recent report by the Standing Senate Committee on Social Affairs, Science and Technology found that public policies hinder rather than aid Canadians hoping to get out of poverty (2009, p. 30). Inadequate welfare support—or the 'welfare wall'—is a major barrier that acts as a 'subtle form of micro-colonialism of poor people by the state, disempowering them and deterring them from acting to improve their lives' (p. 30). Statistical data in Canada confirms that the poverty rates of racialized Canadians can be up to three times higher than those of white groups (Jackson, 2001; Lovell & Shahsiah, 2006). New immigrants to Canada are particularly vulnerable to poverty owing to the lack of recognition of their 'foreign' credentials and local work experience (Kazemipur & Halli, 2001). For racialized Canadians, the problems are exacerbated by a neo-liberal restructuring of the workplace that has left women, people of colour, immigrants, and Aboriginal people more vulnerable. They are more likely than other Canadians to experience high levels of unemployment, precarious employment, and exploitative working conditions in this 'new' economy (Gordon, 2005, p. 73). The 'racialization of poverty' in Canada is the result of institutional and structural racism combined with economic hardship and low socio-economic status (Galabuzi, 2001).

Racial disparities and discrimination in the welfare system have reinforced and multiplied the difficulties of racialized Canadians. In their study of welfare fraud, Mirchandani and Chan (2007) found that racialized welfare recipients experienced a host of problems in their attempts to access and receive welfare benefits. These problems ranged from language barriers and the lack of translators to differential treatment by caseworkers, excessive surveillance, and stigmatization in the eyes of the general public. People of colour were assumed to be guilty of engaging in welfare fraud, and many welfare recipients experienced mental health problems in their daily attempts to resist these labels. Mirchandani and Chan argue that racial politics are deeply embedded in the disenfranchisement of the poor and that welfare reform is not just an attack against poor people, but also an attack against people of colour (2007, p. 87). Other scholars concur that the welfare system promotes a racialized society insofar as the problem of racism in the welfare system is not simply a matter of a few bad apples, but is, instead, a socially structured and systemic phenomenon (Quadagno, 2000; Neubeck & Cazenave, 2002; Bonds, 2006). Neubeck and Cazenave (2002) use the term 'welfare racism' to refer to the many different forms and manifestations of racism associated with the policies and practices of the welfare system. They point to the way in which 'race' and 'welfare' have been routinely linked in attacks against the US welfare system by politicians through the use of coded terms like 'welfare chisellers' or 'welfare queens' (p. 37). The enforcement of mandatory welfare-to-work programs also rely on racist stereotypes, such as that people of colour are slothful and dependent and need to be prodded into employment through the threat of disentitlement (p. 38). Where people of colour fail to follow the rules of welfare, Schram et al. (2009) found that race influences decisions to sanction. Decisions tended to be based on racial status and stereotype-consistent traits, with the result that people of colour experienced higher levels of sanctioning and punishment by welfare administrators than white welfare recipients (Schram, Soss, Fording, & Houser, 2009, p. 413).

These empirical studies highlight the significant gap between the political rhetoric of welfare reform and the material realities of poor people of colour. The assumption that increased scrutiny, criminalization, and stigmatization are necessary to enforce the work ethic fails to recognize the problems of racism, the high levels of unemployment among people of colour, or the brutality of poverty in racialized communities. Not only does this pattern of discrediting racialized people limit their long-term prospects, but punitive welfare policies also contribute to the ongoing policing of racial hierarchies and the myth that people of colour on welfare are almost always undeserving and not needy. Until we begin to challenge this discourse of racialized welfare recipients as illegitimate, people of colour will continue to experience widespread social, political, and economic exclusion in Canada.

E. CONCLUSION

The concept that the welfare state provides a safety net for people experiencing economic challenges is increasingly difficult to sustain given the recent reforms discussed in this chapter. Rather, the provision of welfare in Canada has shifted dramatically over the past several decades, promoting the neo-liberal project at the expense of poor families. Tighter eligibility requirements, punitive sanctions, and increased surveillance are all critical elements of a welfare state more concerned with the bottom line and punishing poor people than with providing support for Canadians in need. In the process, not only are more Canadians disentitled from access to welfare benefits, but they are now routinely portrayed as unworthy of state support due to their deviance and fecklessness. As Kohler-Hausmann observes, 'the spectacle of surveillance and prosecutions rearticulated the stigma associated with welfare while exacerbating the hardships of poor families' (2007, p. 346). Thus, any hope of acknowledging the material difficulties of poor families is now completely expunged from public discussions of welfare reform (p. 346). Indeed, the evidence from British Columbia and elsewhere suggests that the emphasis on surveillance and enforcement has diverted public discussions from focusing on the conditions contributing to poverty to emphasizing protection of the public purse from undeserving and illegitimate claimants addicted to state dependency. Women and racialized people will continue to be marked as the 'enemy within' as their poverty and desperation continue to be narrowly cast as a product of their own pathology. Rodgers accurately describes the implications of these policy changes for Western welfare states:

> There is now little talk of social justice and equality as essential principles for the maintenance of social order . . . the pursuit of equality has been replaced by the maintenance of equity, and the idea of social justice has been collapsed into the meritocratic sounding notion of 'equal opportunities' which . . . tends to generate a sense of relative deprivation, social division and anomie rather than social harmony. (Rodgers 2008: 196)

Only by resisting these trends and addressing the problems of poverty can we hope to reverse the tide of criminalization in welfare policy development.

CRITICAL THINKING QUESTIONS

1. How has the media shaped our views about poor people and poverty in general?

2. If there are not enough jobs in the labour market, is the government justified in blaming poor people for their situation?

3. What might be a more just response to the problems of poverty?

4. Punishing poor people seems counterintuitive to creating a more inclusive society. Would you agree or disagree?

5. Do you think anti-poverty measures such as increasing the minimum wage or providing more low-cost housing would make a difference? What other anti-poverty measures would be useful?

NOTES

1 Welfare fraud in perspective, *Toronto Star*, 9 December 2009, A26.

2 Welfare reforms have varied significantly across provinces. All provinces have experienced a decline in social assistance benefits in the last two decades, with Ontario, Manitoba, Nova Scotia, and PEI slashing benefits to single employable individuals by almost 30 per cent or more during 1994–2003. See Kneebone and White (2009) for a more detailed discussion of these changes.

3 See Wallace, Klein, and Reitsma-Street's (2006) report, *Denied Assistance*, for the CCPA. They document the various anti-welfare comments made to justify greater difficulty in accessing welfare benefits in British Columbia.

4 BC to deny welfare to alleged criminals, CBC Online, 19 October 2009.

5 Ministry of Housing and Social Development (2009), Fraud and Sanctions Brochure.

6 See Part 7 (Eligibility), s. 5 (Fraud) of the *BC Employment and Assistance Manual* for further procedural details.

7 See Ministry of Human Resources website: http://www.mhr.gov.bc.ca/factsheets/2002/ fraud_sept.htm

8 We've learned little from Kim Rogers's death, *Globe and Mail*, 9 August 2002.

REFERENCES

Abramovitz, M. (2006). Welfare reform in the United States: Gender, race and class matter. *Critical Social Policy, 26*(2), 336–64.

Bahle, T. (2003). The changing institutionalization of social services in England and Wales, France and Germany: Is the welfare state on the retreat? *Journal of European Social Policy, 13*(1), 5–20.

Baker, M. (1997). *The restructuring of the Canadian welfare state: Ideology and policy*. Social Policy and Research Centre (SPURC), discussion paper 77.

———, & Tippin, D. (1999). *Poverty, social assistance, and the employability of mothers: Restructuring welfare states*. Toronto: University of Toronto Press.

Beckett, K., & Western, B. (2001), Governing social marginality. *Punishment and Society, 3*(1), 43–59.

Berger, P. (2001). Science misapplied: Mandatory addiction screening and treatment for welfare recipients in Ontario. *Canadian Medical Association Journal, 165*(4), 443–4.

Bobier, P. (1998, February 1–5). Privacy at risk: Finger-scanning for ideology and profit. *Government Computer*.

Bonds, M. (2006). The continuing significance of race: A case study of the impact of welfare reform. *Journal of African American Studies, 9*(4), 18–31.

Breitkreuz, R. (2005). Engendering citizenship? A critical feminist analysis of Canadian welfare-to-work policies and the employment experiences of lone mothers. *Journal of Sociology and Social Welfare, 32*(2), 147–65.

Brodie, J. (1997). Meso-discourses, state forms and the gendering of liberal-democratic citizenship. *Citizenship Studies, 1*, 223–42.

————. (2002). Citizenship and solidarity: Reflections on the Canadian way. *Citizenship Studies, 6*(4), 377–94.

————. (2008). We are all equal now: Contemporary gender politics in Canada. *Feminist Theory, 9*(2), 145–64.

Bullock, H., Wyche, K., & Williams, W. (2001). Media images of the poor. *Journal of Social Issues, 57*(2), 229–46.

Caledon Institute. (2002, July). *A new era in British Columbia: A profile of budget cuts across social programs.* Caledon Institute of Social Policy report.

Canadian Centre for Policy Alternatives (CCPA). (2002). *Reckless and Unnecessary.* Vancouver: Canadian Centre for Policy Alternatives.

————. (2006). *Growing gap, growing concerns: Canadian attitudes towards income inequality.* Toronto: Canadian Centre for Policy Alternatives.

Caragata, L. (2003). Neoconservative realities: The social and economic marginalization of Canadian women. *International Sociology, 18*(3), 559–80.

Carruthers, E. (1995). Prosecuting women for welfare fraud in Ontario: Implications for equality. *Journal of Law and Social Policy, 11*, 241–62.

Carty, K. (1996). *Politics, policy and government in British Columbia.* Vancouver: UBC Press.

Chunn, D., & Gavigan, S. (2004). Welfare law, welfare fraud, and the moral regulation of the 'never deserving' poor. *Social and Legal Studies, 13*(2), 219–43.

Cohen, M.G. (1997). What women should know about economic fundamentalism. *Atlantis, 22*, 97–107.

Collins, S. (2005). An understanding of poverty from those who are poor. *Action Research, 3*(1), 9–31.

Cook, D. (1989). *Rich law, poor law.* Milton Keynes, UK: Open University Press.

Coulter, K. (2009). Women, poverty policy and the production of neoliberal politics in Ontario, Canada. *Journal of Women, Politics and Policy, 30*, 23–45.

Daenzer, P. (2009). Canada: New ideology and social assistance in post-industrial society. In J. Powell & J. Hendricks (Eds.), *The Welfare State in Post-Industrial Society.* London: Springer.

Edin, K., & Lein, L. (1997). *Making ends meet: How single mothers survive welfare and low wage work.* New York: Russell Sage.

Editorial. (2010, May 27). Coleman is right to fight welfare fraud. *Province.*

Fineman, M. (1991). Images of mothers in poverty discourses. *Duke Law Journal*, 287.

Fraser, N., & Gordon, L. (1994). A genealogy of 'dependency': Tracing a keyword of the US welfare state. *Signs, 19*(2), 309–36.

Galabuzi, G. (2001). *Canada's creeping economic apartheid: The economic segregation and social marginalization of racialised groups.* Toronto: CSJ Foundation for Research and Education.

Gamble, A. (2001). Neo-liberalism. *Capital and Class, 75*, 127–34.

Gilens, M. (1996). Race and poverty in America: Public misperceptions and the American news media. *Public Opinion Quarterly, 60*, 515–41.

Gilliom, J. (2001). *Overseers of the poor: Surveillance, resistance and the limits of privacy.* Chicago: University of Chicago Press.

————. (2005). Resisting surveillance. *Social Text 83, 23*(2), 71–83.

Gilman, M. (2008). Welfare, privacy and feminism. *University of Baltimore Law Forum, 39*(1), 25–49.

Gordon, L. (1988). What does welfare regulate? *Social Research, 55*(4), 609–30.

Gordon, T. (2005). The political economy of law and order policies: Policing, class struggle and neoliberal restructuring. *Studies in Political Economy, 75*, 53–77.

Gustafson, K. (2009). The criminalization of poverty. *Journal of Criminal Law and Criminology, 99*(3), 643–716.

Haney, L. (2004). Introduction: Gender, welfare and states of punishment. *Social Politics, 11*(3), 333–62.

Harell, A., Soroka, S., & Mahon, A. (2008, September). Is welfare a dirty word? Canadian public opinion on social assistance policies. *Policy Options,* 53–6.

Hartman, Y. (2005). In bed with the enemy: Some ideas on the connections between neoliberalism and the welfare state. *Current Sociology, 53*(1), 57–73.

Henman, P., & Marston, G. (2008). The social division of welfare surveillance. *Journal of Social Policy, 37*(2), 187–205.

Herd, D., Mitchell, A., & Lightman, E. (2005). Rituals of degradation: Administration as policy in the Ontario Works Programme. *Social Policy and Administration, 39*(1), 65–79.

Jackson, A. (2001). Poverty and racism. *Perception, 24*(4), 6–7.

Kazemipur, A., & Halli, S. (2001). The changing colour of poverty in Canada. *Canadian Review of Sociology and Anthropology, 38*(2), 217–38.

Kendall, J. (2001). Circles of disadvantage: Aboriginal poverty and underdevelopment in Canada. *American Review of Canadian Studies, 31*(1), 43–59.

Klein, S., & Long, A. (2003). *A bad time to be poor: An analysis of British Columbia's New Welfare Policies.* Vancouver: Canadian Centre for Policy Alternatives and the Social Planning and Research Council of British Columbia.

Klein, S., & Pulkingham, J. (2008). *Living on welfare in BC: Experiences of longer-term 'expected to work' recipients.* Vancouver: Canadian Centre for Policy Alternatives and Raise the Rates.

Kneebone, R., & White, K. (2009). Fiscal retrenchment and social assistance in Canada. *Canadian Public Policy, 35*(1), 21–40.

Kohler-Hausmann, J. (2007). 'The crime of survival': Fraud prosecutions, community surveillance, and the original 'welfare queen'. *Journal of Social History, 41*(2), 299–354.

Larkin, P. (2007). The 'criminalization' of social security law: Towards a punitive welfare state? *Journal of Law and Society, 34*(3), 295–320.

Lightman, E., Mitchell, A., & Herd, D. (2003). *Suspicion and surveillance: Navigating welfare's bureaucratic maze.* Toronto: Social Assistance in the New Economy Project, Faculty of Social Work, University of Toronto.

Little, M. (1998). *No car, no radio, no liquor permit: The moral regulation of single mothers in Ontario, 1920–1997.* Toronto: Oxford University Press.

———, & Marks, L. (2010). Ontario and British Columbia welfare policy: Variants on a neoliberal theme. *Comparative Studies of South Asia, Africa and the Middle East, 30*(2), 192–203.

Lovell, A., & Shahsiah, S. (2006). *Mental wellbeing and substance use among youth of colour.* Toronto: Across Boundaries: An Ethnoracial Community Mental Health Centre.

McBride, S., & Shields, J. (1997). *Dismantling a nation: The transition to corporate rule in Canada.* Halifax: Fernwood Press.

MacGregor, S. (1999). Welfare, neo-liberalism and new paternalism: Three ways for social policy in late capitalist societies. *Capital and Class, 67,* 91–118.

MacLeod, A. (2008, January 22). Facebook used by officials to spy on welfare clients. *The Tyee.*

MacLeod, A. (2010, June 16). Lousy cases against 'overpaid' welfare recipients: Legal advocates. *The Tyee.*

Marsh, L. (1943/75). *Report on social security for Canada.* Toronto: University of Toronto Press.

Marston, G., & Walsh, T. (2008). A case of misrepresentation: Social security fraud and the criminal justice system in Australia. *Griffith Law Review, 17,* 285–300.

Martin, D. (1992). Passing the buck: Prosecution of welfare fraud; preservation of stereotypes. *Windsor Yearbook of Access to Justice, 12,* 52–97.

Mirchandani, K., & Chan, W. (2007). *Criminalizing race, criminalizing poverty.* Halifax: Fernwood Press.

Morrow, M., Hankivsky, O., & Varcoe, C. (2004). Women and violence: The effects of dismantling the welfare state. *Critical Social Policy, 24*(3), 358–84.

Mosher, J. (2000). Managing the disentitlement of women: Glorified markets, the idealized family, and the undeserving other. In S. Neysmith (Ed.), *Restructuring caring labour: Discourse, state practice, and everyday life.* Don Mills, ON: Oxford University Press.

———, Evans, P., Little, M., Morrow, E., Boulding, J., & VanderPlaats, N. (2004). *Walking on eggshells: Abused women's experiences of Ontario's welfare system.* Toronto: York University.

———, & Hermer, J. (2005). *Welfare fraud: The constitution of social assistance as a crime.* Ottawa: Paper prepared for the Law Commission of Canada.

National Council of Welfare. (2010). *Poverty profile 2007: Depth of poverty.* February.

Neubeck, K., & Cazenave, N. (2002). Welfare racism and its consequences. In F. Fox-Piven, J. Acker, M. Hallock, & S. Morgan (Eds.), *Work, welfare and politics.* Portland: University of Oregon Press.

Palmer, V. (2002, January 16). Massive welfare overhaul in the works. *Vancouver Sun.*

Peck, J. (2001). *Workfare states.* New York: Guildford Press.

Peck, J., & Tickell, A. (2002). Neoliberalizing space. *Antipode, 34,* 380–404.

Polakow, V. (1999). Savage distributions: Welfare myths and daily lives. In L. Kushnick & J. Jennings (Eds.), *A new introduction to poverty: The role of race, power and politics.* New York: New York University Press.

Power, E. (2005). The unfreedom of being other: Canadian lone mothers' experiences of poverty and 'life on the cheque'. *Sociology, 39*(4), 643–60.

Pratt, A., & Valverde, M. (2002). From deserving victims to 'masters of confusion': Redefining refugees in the 1990s. *Canadian Journal of Sociology, 27*(2), 135–61.

Quadagno, J. (1994). *The color of welfare: How racism undermined the war on poverty.* New York: Oxford University Press.

———. (1998, August 22). *Returning welfare states to markets: The transition from universalism to individualism.* San Francisco: Presidential address to 93rd annual meeting of ASA.

———. (2000). Another face of inequality: Racial and ethnic exclusion in the welfare state. *Social Politics, 7*(2), 229–37.

Rachert, J. (1990). *Welfare fraud and the state: British Columbia 1970–1977.* Unpublished master's thesis, Simon Fraser University, Burnaby.

Razack, S. (2000). 'Simple logic': Race, the identity documents rule and the story of a nation besieged and betrayed. *Journal of Law and Social Policy, 15,* 181–209.

Reid, C., & Tom, A. (2006). Poor women's discourses of legitimacy, poverty and health. *Gender and Society, 20*(3), 402–21.

Reitsma-Street, M. (2002, July 15). The new era of welfare. *Times Colonist.*

Reitsma-Street, M., & Wallace, B. (2004). Resisting two year limits on welfare in British Columbia. *Canadian Review of Social Policy, 53,* 170–7.

Rodgers, J. (2008). *Criminalising social policy.* Portland, OR: Willan Publishing.

Schram, S., Soss, J., Fording, R., & Houser, L. (2009). Deciding to discipline: Race, choice and punishment at the frontlines of welfare reform. *American Sociological Review, 74*, 398–422.

Schustereder, I. (2010). *Welfare state change in leading OECD countries: The influence of post-industrial and global economic developments.* Wiesbaden: Gabler.

Sears, A. (1999). The 'lean' state and capitalist restructuring: Towards a theoretical account. *Studies in Political Economy, 59*, 91–114.

Seccombe, K., James, D., & Walters, K. (1998). 'They think you ain't much of nothing': The social construction of the welfare mother. *Journal of Marriage and the Family, 60*, 849–65.

Shaw, R. (2010a, May 26). BC goes to court to recover welfare funds. *Times-Colonist.*

———. (2010b, May 27). Government accused of 'poor-bashing' for its plans to reclaim overpayments. *CanWest News Service.*

Sidel, R. (2000). The enemy within: The demonization of poor women. *Journal of Sociology and Social Welfare, 27*(1), 73–84.

Social Planning and Research Council (SPARC). (2008). *Still left behind: A comparison of living costs and income assistance in British Columbia.* Vancouver: Social Planning and Research Council.

Standing Senate Committee on Social Affairs, Science and Technology. (2009). *In from the margins: A call to action on poverty, housing and homelessness.* Report of the Subcommittee on Cities. Ottawa: Senate of Canada.

Swan, R., Shaw, L., Cullity, S., Roche, M., Halpern, J., Limbert, W., & Humphrey, J. (2008). The untold story of welfare fraud. *Journal of Sociology and Social Welfare, 35*(3), 133–51.

Wacquant, L. (2002). The curious eclipse of prison ethnography in the age of mass incarceration. *Ethnography, 3*(4), 371–97.

———. (2009). Punishing the poor: *The neoliberal government of social insecurity.* Durham: Duke University Press.

———. (2010). Crafting the neoliberal state: Workfare, prisonfare and social insecurity. *Sociological Forum, 25*(2), 197–220.

Wallace, B., Klein, S., & Reitsma-Street, M. (2006). *Denied assistance: Closing the front door on welfare in BC.* Vancouver: Canadian Centre for Policy Alternatives and Vancouver Island Public Interest Research Group.

———, & Richards, T. (2008, July 31). Why welfare time limits never flew. *The Tyee.*

Welch, M.A. (2010, June 7). Province finding more welfare fraud, overpayment. *Winnipeg Free Press*, B2.

LEGISLATION CITED

Employment and Assistance Act 2002.

Employment and Assistance for Persons with Disabilities Act 2002.

CASES CITED

Falkiner et al. v. Director of Income Maintenance Branch, Ministry of Community and Social Services and Attorney-General of Ontario, 1997, Appellants' Submissions on the Charter.

Immigration Penality and the Crime-Security Nexus: The Case of Tran Trong Nghi Nguyen

Anna Pratt

THE CASE OF TRAN TRONG NGHI NGUYEN

Tran Trong Nghi Nguyen came to Canada from Vietnam with his mother in 1993 when he was just 11 years old. He became a permanent resident and lived in Calgary with his mother and 9-year-old sister. He left school in grade 11 and found work as a skilled glass cutter. After his mother was disabled in a workplace injury, Tran became the sole income earner in the family and took on responsibility for the day-to-day demands of taking care of both his mother and his young sister.

In 2000, when Tran was 18 years old, he was convicted of two counts of trafficking in narcotics, and two years later, he was convicted of an assault involving a fight with a co-worker. Tran served a conditional sentence of two years less a day in the community for the drug offences and received a fine for the assault charge. In 2004, Tran was ordered deported on the basis of 'serious criminality', which, under section 36(1)(a) of the Immigration and Refugee Protection Act (IRPA, 2001, c. 27), applies in cases where the conviction for an offence is punishable by a maximum term of imprisonment of at least 10 years. It is not necessary that an individual actually receive a 10-year prison sentence, only that the offence with which he or she is charged—in this case trafficking in narcotics—*could* be punishable by a maximum term of 10 years or more. So, even though the provincial criminal court proceeded summarily against Tran, deemed that he did not represent a danger to the public, and sentenced him to two years less a day to be served in the community, under the administrative regime of IRPA, Tran was deemed a serious criminal and ordered deported.

Tran appealed his removal order to the Immigration Appeal Division (IAD) of the Immigration and Refugee Board (IRB) under section 67(1)(c) of the IRPA. This section grants to the IAD the power to grant exceptional relief from removal on humanitarian and compassionate grounds, including the best interests of the

TABLE 11.1   List of acronyms

CBSA	Canada Boarder Services Agency
CSIS	Canadian Security Intelligence Service
CIC	Citizenship and Immigration Canada
CISC	Criminal Intelligence Service Canada
IAD	Immigration Appeal Division (of the Immigration and Refugee Board)
FCC	Federal Court of Canada
IRB	Immigration and Refugee Board (of Canada)
IRPA	Immigration and Refugee Protection Act (2001)
SCC	Supreme Court of Canada

child if this applies.[1] Deemed a flight risk, Tran spent most of 2008 in detention. His first appeal was dismissed by the IAD on 10 January 2008. He applied to the Federal Court of Canada for judicial review of the IAD decision and received a stay of his deportation. On 4 September 2008, the Federal Court ordered that the appeal be returned to the IAD to be heard by a differently constituted panel. In its decision dated 7 April 2009, the IAD again dismissed Tran's appeal against his removal order (IAD File No. VA4-01093).

In this decision, the IAD was entirely preoccupied with Tran's alleged association with a Calgary gang called Fresh Killers (FK) and the implications of that association in light of the security concerns that heavily saturate the IRPA. The prioritization of security was held out as the justification for the rather wholesale dismissal of the quite considerable humanitarian and compassionate considerations raised by Tran's situation. Tran applied to the Federal Court for judicial review of this second IAD decision. In its decision dated 28 January 2010, the Federal Court upheld the judgement of the IAD. Tran Trong Nghi Nguyen reported to border service officers on 2 March 2010, and was deported to Vietnam.

Tran's case received very wide coverage and huge notoriety in the local Calgary press and even some in the national media over the six years that it wove its way through the courts. This coverage dovetailed with the equally extensive press coverage of multiple shootings of and by suspected members of the two main Asian-based street gangs on the streets of Calgary. Public fears and police frustration intensified as the Calgary Police Service seemed unable to put an end to the street violence and were frustrated in their attempts to prosecute suspected gang members in the criminal courts. This local panic merged with mounting national concerns surrounding the linked threats posed by dangerous foreign criminals and organized crime.[2] While most of those involved in street-level criminal activity in Calgary were citizens and therefore not removable, Tran's status as a permanent resident made him vulnerable to deportation even though he had lived in Canada with his family since he was a child. Immigration enforcement would ultimately succeed where criminal justice had failed. Tran's precarious citizenship status made him vulnerable to what is known as the 'double punishment' of migrants convicted of crimes: Tran had already been punished by the criminal justice system for his prior offences, but was then doubly punished for these crimes when he was expelled from Canada.

In the context of the larger political campaigns surrounding criminal immigrants and organized crime, Tran's case quickly became emblematic of the scandal of dangerous foreign criminals and gangster violence. As put by his lawyer, Sharma Harsanyi, Tran 'had somehow become the public face of organized crime in Canada' (Harsanyi, 2010). Popular outrage focused on his status as a foreigner who was taking advantage of an excessively permissive immigration system and a legal system overly preoccupied with due process and judicial review. Tran had been deemed a serious criminal and ordered deported because he had been convicted of an offence that carries a penalty of 10 years or more. However, because he had only been sentenced to two years less a day, he retained the legal right to appeal his removal (a right he would have been denied had he been sentenced to two years or more). This enraged many, like Calgary member of Parliament (MP) Art Hanger, who blasted federal laws for allowing Tran so many appeals: 'You cut those avenues off and force them out of the country. Let's change the law.' He added: 'They don't deserve due process like all ordinary citizens of the nation. They've already violated the trust that was given to them when they came here, or allowed to come here' (CBC News, 22 October 2008). Tran's case had come to represent for many all that is wrong with an immigration system that allows 'violent foreign criminals' to delay their removal by taking advantage of legal appeals and rights.

By the time he was deported in 2010, Tran, who had lived in Canada since he was a child, who had but three relatively minor and dated criminal convictions, and who had never been convicted under the Canadian Criminal Code of any offences specifically relating to gang membership, had become the poster boy for the gangster problem in Calgary and for the foreign criminal threat to Canadian national security and public safety. As observed by his lawyer, Sharma Harsanyi,

> The heightened fear of the public, stoked by the sensationalist media, resulted in Tran facing a frenzied outcry for his removal. As a former hearings officer and more recently an immigration lawyer, I have appeared in hundreds of immigration hearings and appeals. I know, from personal experience, that there are many permanent residents, inadmissible on criminal convictions far more serious than Tran's, that are allowed to stay in this country. It was clear however, that the deck was stacked against Tran because of this 'persona'. (Harsanyi, 2010)

Tran's removal was upheld as a victory for a government deeply committed to the protection of the safety and security of its citizens. Speaking to a throng of reporters on 3 March 2010, Vic Toews, Canadian minister of public safety, flanked by Jason Kenney, minister of citizenship and immigration, lauded the work of the Canada Border Services Agency (CBSA) in removing 27-year-old Tran Trong Nghi Nguyen to Vietnam. Minister Toews proclaimed:

> I would like to congratulate the CBSA officials who were instrumental in removing Tran Trong Nghia [sic] Nguyen (Jackie Tran) from our country. I am pleased this serious convicted criminal will no longer pose a threat to the safety of Canadians and our communities ... This deportation provides another example of the outstanding work by the CBSA to remove serious criminals from this country. I would like to commend the professionalism and dedication of the CBSA officers who carried out this removal. Protecting the safety and security of our citizens is the most serious responsibility of the Government of Canada. (Ministry of Public Safety, 5 March 2010)

IMMIGRATION PENALITY AND THE CRIME-SECURITY NEXUS IN CANADA

In both content and optics, this triumphant announcement, together with the deportation it celebrated, was a grand performance of the sovereign authority of the Canadian nation-state to coercively control its borders in the name of protecting the public and nation from the crime-security threats posed by dangerous outsiders. Tran got caught up in the assemblage that is immigration penality.[3] This penality controls borders; polices non-citizens; identifies those who are dangerous, diseased, deceitful, or destitute; and refuses them entry or casts them out. Detention and deportation are the two most extreme and bodily sanctions of this immigration penality. Immigration penality is made up of diverse and intersecting state and non-state authorities, technologies, forms of knowledge, and regimes of rule. It includes a vast array of different state authorities—from public health, to social welfare, to criminal justice, immigration, border services, and security intelligence. It also includes a variety of non-state authorities, including the private security companies that police detention centres, the private airlines contracted for deportations, the airline personnel enlisted in the policing of travellers, the banks and bank tellers engaged in the policing of transnational organized crime and money-laundering offences, the legal aid staff who determine who will receive assistance for refugee claims, deportation appeals, and detention review hearings. Administrative, criminal, and human rights regimes intersect in many ways in the policing and punishment activities of immigration penality.

Tran was deported less for what he did than for what he represented. Indeed, Tran's story is but one entry in the much larger tale of the crime-security nexus and the governance of immigration penality in Canada. By crime-security nexus, I am referring to two simultaneous processes: the first is the way that certain forms of criminality have been reconceptualized and acted upon as threats to national security, and the second, conversely, is the way that the conception of national security has been radically reconfigured and extended to include governmental concerns with public safety and therefore to encompass a host of 'true' crimes that have been linked through organized crime and terrorism to national security. The very category of crime has become conflated with that of security, a process that began well before 11 September 2001, but which has gained considerable momentum since then.

Of particular interest in this chapter is the way in which Tran's case sheds light on the diverse historical and contemporary intersections between the domains of criminal justice and immigration. This chapter is loosely organized around the intersections at the levels of discourse, law and policy, and material technologies. The discursive intersections revolve around the emergence and entrenchment of this crime-security nexus in the governance of immigration penality. The law and policy intersections embed criminal justice definitions and determinations relating to danger to the public and criminality in the exclusionary provisions of immigration law and policy. The technological intersections are manifest in the application of material carceral sanctions and penal technologies in both criminal justice and immigration domains.

THE FORGING OF THE CRIME-SECURITY NEXUS IN CANADA

The discursive blending of crime and security preoccupations and definitions in relation to Canadian immigration penality must be understood in historical context. While overlapping and not clear-cut, broad transitions have taken place in the dominant logics governing exclusionary immigration law and policy in Canada, from the explicitly racist and moralizing logic of national purity, which characterized early Canadian nation-building, to the logic of national security driven by political ideology during the Cold War, to the crime-security nexus of the present. Throughout, criminality has always been an effective category for the exclusion of 'undesirables' from Canada, always intermingling with other preoccupations. The logic of (racial and moral) national purity had long interacted with criminality concerns in the governance of exclusionary immigration law and policy. And indeed, the influence of the logic of security had for some time been dominant, with wartime insecurities leading to the frequent use of discretionary powers to exclude 'subversives', 'enemy aliens', communists, anarchists, and the like. It is also the case that ethnic origin and imputed ideological threat were intensely intertwined. Further, in the absence of an official exclusionary category of 'political subversive' or 'ideological enemy', criminality provisions were frequently used to effect the detention and deportation of such 'threats' (Roberts, 1988; Avery, 1995; Avery, 1979).[4]

The explicitly racist and otherwise discriminatory exclusionary categories of immigration policy were delegitimized over the 1960s and 1970s. At the same time, however, the grounds for immigration exclusion on the basis of criminality and security proliferated. Moreover, while concerns about national security during the Cold War period had revolved around the threats to the political state posed by subversion, treason, espionage, and sedition, as the Cold War waned in the 1980s and 1990s, the logic of security was itself reconfigured to encompass the threats posed to public safety by international terrorism, organized crime, and a host of less 'exotic' true crimes now associated with organized crime. By the beginning of the twenty-first century, this blending of crime and security pre-occupations was explicit and deliberate.[5] As expressed by the Department of National Defence, '[T]he concept of security has expanded from denoting the safety of the state and protection against military danger to conveying the notion of freedom from fear and focusing on the security of people against a whole range of risks ("human security")' (Department of National Defence, 23 December 2002). Significantly, in this mandate, national security is now defined in large part through a criminal justice lens.

THE CRIME-SECURITY NEXUS IN CANADIAN IMMIGRATION LAW AND POLICY

Tran's case provides a glimpse into the ways that the domains of criminal justice and immigration intersect at the level of law and policy through the embedding of criminal justice preoccupations, definitions, and processes in the exclusionary provisions of immigration legislation and related policy documents. As noted above, the blurring of the boundaries between criminal justice and immigration began well before the terrorist attacks of 11 September 2001.

A process began in the mid-1950s and took hold through the 1960s that elevated human rights discourses and delegitimized the explicitly racist and moralistic immigration categories that had been promoted and rationalized by national purity discourses. The broadly discretionary, moralized, and explicitly racist provisions of the 1952 Immigration Act offended increasingly influential legal 'rights based' sensibilities and were contrary to the collectively and socially oriented tangents of welfare liberalism that had gained momentum in Canada. The influence of these discourses peaked in the 1970s with the passage of the 1976 Immigration Act and the creation of an independent administrative and legalized system of on-shore refugee determination. These developments have been conventionally represented as the triumph of liberal, democratic, and progressive values and interests (Kelley & Trebilcock, 1998; Dirks, 1995; Dirks, 1977; Hawkins, 1972). However, what this reading misses is the extent to which the 1976 Act represented the legalization, formal entrenchment, and expansion of the logics of risk and security, supplemented by criminality concerns.

Not only did the 1976 Immigration Act multiply and specify the crime-security–related grounds for inadmissibility, but a series of tough, enforcement-oriented immigration reforms over the 1980s and 1990s aimed to further exclude, through inadmissibility provisions or deportation, criminal migrants deemed to pose a threat to national security and public safety and to refuse refugee claimants who were similarly assessed.

The early 1990s ushered in a new era in the governance of immigration penality. The federal Liberals introduced Bill C-86 in 1992, which broadly defined and acted upon, to an unparalleled degree, the emergent threat of the criminal immigrant, especially that posed by organized criminals, and legally entrenched and intensified the coercive powers of immigration officers to enforce the Act and police the borders (Bill C-86, 1992 c. 49). Whereas the undesirable other of the past had been excluded through the mobilization of explicitly moralistic and racist discourses of national purity or through the justification of national security understood in more narrow, ideological terms, by the mid-1990s, the undesirable migrant came to be excluded through the mobilization of the crime-security nexus. Increasingly prominent law and order discourses and fears about organized criminal threats to national security entailed effects extending well beyond the criminal courts.

The powerful influence of this crime-security nexus is evidenced most dramatically by the unprecedented move in the mid-1990s to expand the working mandate of the Canadian Security Intelligence Agency (CSIS) to encompass crime and criminals as threats to national security. With the demise of traditional Cold War enemies and fears and in accordance with the increasing dominance of law and order concerns, CBSA maintains that organized and transnational crime now pose a monumental threat to 'various aspects of Canadian national security, law and order, the integrity of government programs and institutions, and the economy' (CSIS, Transnational Criminal Activity, November 2008). CSIS explains this expansion by referencing the effects of globalization, which it argues has created a world 'virtually devoid of national borders', providing vast opportunities for 'members of highly sophisticated and organized criminal syndicates to pursue a complex web of lucrative legal and illegal activities worldwide' (ibid.). However, the range of criminality included in the new operational mandate of CSIS is expansive:

> While still involved at the lower level with drug trafficking, prostitution, loan-sharking, illegal gambling and extortion … [organized criminals] have expanded their activities to a quasi-corporate level where they are active in large-scale insurance fraud, the depletion of natural resources, environmental crime, migrant smuggling, bank fraud, gasoline tax fraud and corruption. In addition, their frequent use of money earned from their illegal ventures to fund legitimate ones allows them to launder money and earn even more profits. They apply many of their criminal tactics in these legal business operations, never hesitating to use violence or murder to get ahead. (Ibid.)

National security, previously understood in strict sovereign relation to the political state, now encompasses social and national concerns with 'public safety'. As CSIS itself notes, 'In response to the rise of terrorism worldwide and the demise of the Cold War, CSIS has made public safety its first priority' (The CSIS Mandate,

February 2005). As I will discuss further a little later on, this extraordinary expansion and reconfiguration of the logic of national security to include everything from the run-of-the-mill, largely disorganized, violent, street-level criminality of youth gangs to highly organized, transnational criminal syndicates are what enabled the representation and ultimate expulsion of Tran as a serious criminal threat to national security.

By the turn of the century, the crime-security nexus was firmly in place, both at the levels of discourse and as entrenched in law and policy in relation to immigration penality. When the IRPA was first contemplated in 2000, its exclusionary concerns had been animated by the linked threats posed to national security by crime and fraud in the shape of transnational and organized crime. After the tragic events of 11 September 2001, this focus on organized crime was supplemented by the reinvigorated threat of terrorism. In June 2002, a new IRPA came into effect.[6] Its enforcement was promoted as the 'first and most important' departmental activity relating to the protection of the health, safety, and security of Canadians through the identification and removal of dangerous people. In addition to those deemed 'serious criminals', the IRPA also provides for the deportation without appeal of non-citizens, including permanent residents, refugees, and refugee claimants, using the broad and vague classifications of 'organized crime', 'terrorism', and 'security of Canada'. Moreover, the expanded inadmissibility provisions render those found to be 'serious criminals', 'organized criminals', or 'terrorists' ineligible to make a refugee claim and vulnerable to removal.

FROM 'DANGER TO THE PUBLIC' TO 'SERIOUS CRIMINALITY'

These developments provided the context for Tran's deportation. For the purposes of immigration penality (although not for the criminal justice system), Tran was guilty of 'serious criminality', a category of inadmissibility introduced by the IRPA in 2001. This category replaced the controversial 'danger to the public' provision that had been introduced with Bill C-44 in June 1994, on the heels of the so-called Just Desserts murder in Toronto in April of the same year of Georgina Leimonis (Bill C-44, 1995, c. 15). Tran's case resonates in several important ways with the Just Desserts case. In both instances, popular fears intertwined at the local level with police enforcement priorities and frustrations and with sustained, sensational media attention, and in both, these more local dimensions intersected with national law-and-order policy preoccupations. Moreover, both cases fuelled hype about racialized crime and criminals, dangerous foreigners, and criminality-based deportations. However, the Just Desserts case and danger-to-the-public deportations were not linked in any serious way to concerns about transnational or organized criminality and threats to national security. In contrast, these concerns were absolutely pivotal in Tran's case. These differences are worth spelling out in some detail.

Georgina Leimonis, a 22-year-old white woman, was shot and killed in 1994 in Just Desserts, a small cafe in an affluent neighbourhood in downtown Toronto. Four black men, Lawrence Brown, Gary Francis, O'Neil Grant, and Mark Jones, were charged with her killing. The massive media coverage of this event tended to gloss over the fact that, like Tran, these men had come to Canada as children and that one of them, Mark Jones, had actually been born in Trinidad—not Jamaica.[7] In July of the same year, Police Constable Todd Baylis (also white) was shot and killed by black, Jamaican-born Clinton Gayle who was under warrant for deportation at the time of the killing.

These murders, coupled with already heightened tensions between the black community and the police, triggered a massive public panic around the issues of race, crime, and immigration, a panic that the government seized upon and responded to swiftly and on several different fronts. The danger-to-the-public provision (s. 70(5) of Bill C-44) sanctioned the deportation without appeal of any non-citizen deemed by the minister of citizenship and immigration to represent a danger to the public. This included permanent residents who had been accepted into Canada as refugees under the *United Nations Convention Relating to the Status of Refugees* regardless of how long they have resided in Canada (*Convention Relating to the Status of Refugees*, 1951). This danger-to-the-public provision was one of a number of enforcement-oriented measures included in the bill that were designed to facilitate and expedite deportations.[8]

Shortly after Bill C-44 was tabled, on 7 July 1994, Sergio Marchi, then minister of citizenship and immigration, announced the 'Criminals First' initiative, a reorientation of Canada's detention and deportation priorities. Soon after, he also announced the creation of the Joint Immigration-RCMP Task Force to assist, among other responsibilities, in tracking down and arresting non-citizens with criminal records who were wanted for removal. Also in 1994, Citizenship and Immigration Canada (CIC) announced the creation of an organized crime section. Bill C-44 was thus the first of a flurry of government initiatives following the Just Desserts murder that aimed to get tough on 'criminal immigrants'—hence its informal reference as the 'Just Desserts Bill'.

The danger-to-the-public provision was a powerful manifestation of the rising influence of the logic of criminality in the governance of immigration enforcement and of the relative dominance of crime-security discourses vis-à-vis those discourses concerned with human rights and refugees. Section 70(5) removed the right of a permanent resident to appeal a deportation order to the Immigration Appeal Division (IAD) in cases where the individual had been convicted of a crime for which the maximum available penalty is 10 years or more and who had been deemed by the minister or her delegate to represent a danger to the public (known as the 'ministerial danger opinion'). This provision had applied to anyone who lacked the protections afforded by full citizenship, including, as noted, permanent residents and those who had been granted refugee status in Canada but who had not yet become citizens. With the enactment of this bill, those deemed a danger to the public joined those judged to be a threat to the national security to be one of the two groups denied access to the usual deportation appeals process.

The danger-to-the-public provision was eliminated in 2002 when the discretionary 'ministerial danger opinion' was replaced by the 'certainty' of strict legal criteria for the determination of serious criminality under section 36(1) of the IRPA. The replacement of the danger-to-the-public provision with the serious criminality provision was justified largely by reference to the need to eliminate the sweeping discretion of the ministerial danger opinion. This justification pleased those on the right of the political spectrum who were critical of discretion because of its association with an overly 'soft' and generous humanitarian ethos typical of the administrative welfare state. It also pleased those on the left who were critical of discretion because of its potential to introduce arbitrary or discriminatory bases for decision-making. Either way, the use of criminal justice convictions and sentencing maximums to determine inadmissibility was held out as a necessary solution to the problem of discretion.[9] However, as has been learned in a variety of other contexts, from welfare provision to the policing of wife abuse, efforts to stamp out discretion will inevitably fail, as it will always pop up at other locations. In this case, the discretion of the minister of immigration to issue a danger-to-the-public opinion has been replaced by the discretion that permeates the criminal justice system. The discretion of police in enforcement, the discretion of the prosecution in charging, and the discretion of judges in sentencing have become even more central in the determination of immigration inadmissibility, removals, and access to judicial review of such determinations.

Under the IRPA, removal for the reason of serious criminality is determined if there has been a conviction in Canada for an offence punishable by a term of at least 10 years or for an offence for which a term of more than six months has been imposed (IRPA, s. 36[1][a]). The right of permanent residents, or 'foreign nationals', to appeal a finding of inadmissibility for the reason of serious criminality is denied if there has been a conviction in Canada for a crime that was punished in Canada by a term of imprisonment of at least two years (IRPA, s. 64[2]). A sentence of two years or more also makes refugee claimants ineligible to have their claim for refugee protection referred to the IRB for a hearing (IRPA, s.102[2][a]).[10] Tran was ordered deported because his drug offence convictions carried a maximum possible sentence of 10 years or more. Because Tran was only sentenced to 2 years less a day for these convictions, he retained the right to appeal his deportation to the IAD on issues of law and humanitarian and compassionate grounds.

Further enhancing the discretion embedded in these provisions is the fact that many offences in Canada are subject to a wide spectrum of possible punishments. For example, a conviction for the offence of breaking and entering may result in a sentence ranging from an absolute discharge to life imprisonment. In addition, the range of offences captured by the serious criminality provision is very wide and includes many non-violent crimes, such as obtaining credit by false pretence, forgery, cattle theft, and trafficking in small amounts of marijuana or other narcotics (Weinrib & Galati, 1996, p. 57). It is also the case that the wording of this provision allows a person to be deemed inadmissible even if he or she had actually received a much lighter sentence than 10 years or more, as was the case with Tran. Moreover, police routinely overcharge suspects in order to provide more leverage in plea bargains. The reliance on offence and sentencing criteria for the purpose of determining whether someone is a serious criminal therefore imports into the domain of immigration penality the discretionary judgments that permeate the criminal justice system. This is particularly problematic when one considers other factors such as differential police enforcement practices and prosecutorial priorities and disparities in sentencing.

Although the serious criminality provision was intended to diffuse discretion and held out hope for some that it would therefore also limit the possibility for racist or otherwise discriminatory decision-making, in fact, the reliance on criminal justice definitions, practices, and decisions in the exclusionary provisions of immigration law and policy raises serious concerns about discrimination. Studies have repeatedly confirmed the presence of systemic and individual forms of racism and other kinds of discrimination in the administration of justice.[11] Because the serious criminality provision—just like its predecessor, the danger-to-the-public provision—is triggered by the broadly discretionary policing, prosecutorial, and sentencing decision-making of the criminal justice system, it necessarily applies and enforces the individual and systemic racism that traverses that system. Indeed, this racism is one of the core continuities between the previous regime that specified danger to the public and the contemporary framework of serious criminality. For example, under the danger-to-the-public provision, male members of the Jamaican community and Caribbean blacks were particularly vulnerable to being deemed a danger to the public and as such deported without appeal. Part of this vulnerability stemmed from the fact that for a variety of reasons many members of the Jamaican community have not applied for and received Canadian citizenship (the $200 fee for adults and $100 fee for children are likely factors here). Other reasons were offered for the particular vulnerability of Jamaican-born men to this provision, such as the following: that it was Jamaican nationals who were widely associated with the Baylis and Leimonis killings that fuelled the racist backlash that precipitated this reform; that racism has historically inflected Canadian immigration law and policy; and that racism is an endemic feature of the administration of criminal justice.[12]

The danger-to-the-public language exacerbated fears about racialized crime and immigration penality. The fears at the time of the Just Desserts killing centred on the dangers thought to be inherent in individual young black men rather than in street gangs made up of individual black men. But even though Jamaican 'posses' have been an explicit focus of official intelligence on organized crime for some time, criminality-based exclusions effected through the danger to the public provision were not associated with the trope of organized crime and national security to the extent that gang-based criminality is today. In Tran's case, the links between racialized street gangs and organized crime were much more prominent than was the case surrounding the Just Desserts killing and its enforcement aftermath. It is indeed significant that, in the hype surrounding Tran, the racialized youth gang violence on the streets of Calgary that had heightened public fears and attracted the attention of the police and local politicians dovetailed with the more general preoccupation with transnational and organized crime that had served as a critical linchpin connecting criminality and security at the level of national criminal justice and immigration enforcement policy since the early 1990s.

In the case of Tran, the organized and transnational crime threat described by CSIS to justify its unprecedented entry into the criminal justice domain at the level of national policy proved to be elastic enough to encompass not only the 'monumental' threat posed to public safety and national security (the twin peaks of the crime-security nexus) by highly sophisticated, technologically savvy networks of transnational organized criminals, but also included the largely disorganized, low-level criminality of violent youth street gangs. According to the logic of the crime-security nexus, street gang criminality now not only poses a criminal justice threat to public safety, but also—and by extension—presents a substantial threat to national security. The idea that street gang criminal activity sits at the low end of a continuum that leads at its other end to transnational criminal enterprises is widely accepted. As explained in a special feature on street gangs produced by the Criminal Intelligence Service Canada (CISC):

> Organized crime exists in more than one form. A challenge for police is to communicate with the public and officials in a way that explains and makes clear the continuum represented from street gangs through to international criminal enterprises. Organized crime needs to be recognized in its infancy as well as in its maturity if we are to be successful in dismantling it. (CISC Annual Report, 2006)

This expansive understanding of organized crime and its association with transnational crime and national security enabled the IAD's easy redefinition of a rather low-level homegrown criminal threat like Tran into a serious criminal, a dangerous foreigner, and a national security threat. This allowed the IAD to reject Tran's appeal on humanitarian and compassionate grounds first by determining in an administrative context that Tran was guilty of gang membership (in the absence of criminal convictions) and then by connecting this form of organized criminality to national security. As we shall see in the next section, once security became an issue, it could easily trump any humanitarian and compassionate factors raised by Tran's personal circumstances and pave the way for his deportation.

CRIME-SECURITY VERSUS HUMANITARIANISM

Tran's case highlights at a micro-level the more general contest between inclusionary humanitarian and protectionist discourses and expansive, exclusionary crime-security discourses that permeates immigration and refugee policy. While explicitly racist and discriminatory exclusions can clearly not be justified in the face of Canada's official commitments to equality, non-discrimination, and international human rights law, efforts to secure the nation and protect the public through assessments of risk and dangerousness appear as relatively unproblematic and objective and therefore legitimate justifications for the coercive operations of immigration penality. In the contest between humanitarian impulses and the quest for security, security has tended to come out on top. The predominance of the crime-security nexus and the ever-widening roster of crimes and criminals that have been reconfigured as national security threats through these linkages with organized crime and terrorism explain the ease with which the Immigration Appeal Board tribunal was able to dismiss the host of compelling and sympathetic humanitarian and compassionate dimensions of Tran's personal circumstances, dimensions that *by definition* should have been the tribunal's primary preoccupation (IRPA s. 67[1][c]).[13] Instead, the IAD was entirely preoccupied with Tran's alleged association with the Calgary street gang FK and the implications of this association in light of the heightened preoccupation with security that underpinned the writing of the IRPA. Quoting from the 2005 Supreme Court of Canada (SCC) *Medovarski* case, the IAD explained:

> The objectives as expressed in the IRPA indicate an intent to prioritize security. This objective is given effect by preventing the entry of applicants with criminal records, by removing applicants with such records from Canada, and by emphasizing the obligation of permanent residents to behave lawfully while in Canada. . . . Viewed collectively, the objectives of the IRPA and its provisions concerning permanent residents, communicates a strong desire to treat criminals and security threats less leniently than under the former Act. (*Medovarski v. Canada [Minister of Citizenship and Immigration]*, [2005], para.10)

In this light, the IAD imported as an aggravating factor 'association with a criminal organization' from the section of the IRPA that deals with the sentencing of smuggling and trafficking offences and determined that Tran's association with the FK gang represented such a pressing threat to security that it heavily outweighed any humanitarian and compassionate factors raised by Tran's personal circumstances. Expert testimony that Tran was very unlikely to reoffend, the absence since 2002 of any convictions for any crimes endangering the public, his expressions of remorse, and his demonstrated efforts at rehabilitation were all dismissed by the tribunal by reference to his imputed association with FK and the elevation of security concerns under the IRPA.[14] In this light, the host of humanitarian and compassionate factors relating to Tran's case were judged not to be sufficiently disproportionate as to outweigh the security concerns; indeed, it is difficult to imagine how any humanitarian and compassionate circumstances could ever displace the heightened preoccupation with crime-security. The tribunal acknowledged that Tran was well established in Canada, steadily employed, the sole provider for his disabled mother and caregiver for younger sister. Tran also carried out all household activities requiring manual effort and acted as English translator for his mother in all her daily affairs, including dealings with the workers' compensation system and frequent medical visits. As noted in the decision, 'The loss of his financial, emotional, physical, and language support would be very significant. There was minimal evidence to suggest a support network for Laura Tran outside of the appellant. The dependence of this disabled mother on her son is a significant factor which weighs in favour of the appellant' (IAD File No. VA4-01093, 7 April 2009, para. 38)

The tribunal also accepted that Tran was a de facto parent to his nine-year-old sister. He communicated with her teachers, schools, doctors. He attended all her medical appointments, drove her to and from school, provided financial support for her, and took her to the movies, McDonald's, the zoo. As the tribunal put it, he was the young girl's 'lifeline to Canadian society' (ibid., para. 44). Rather than interpreting these connections in Tran's favour, however, the IAD held that Tran's sister (and his girlfriend) was 'secondarily' in danger from those who might target Tran. In this very unusual twist, it was not the danger posed by Tran himself that was of concern to the tribunal. Indeed the tribunal clearly states that it did not believe that Tran himself posed *any* danger to the public. Rather, because he might be targeted (victimized) by others, 'his mere presence in Canada creates a secondary danger' (ibid., para. 42). Citing the best interests of the child, the judgment tribunal concludes, '[A]lthough I acknowledge the significant and important role the appellant plays in his sister's life, he also brings danger to her which mitigates the positive effect of his efforts to care for her' (ibid., para. 42).

Ultimately, the IAD concludes that the strong humanitarian and compassionate factors that weighed in favour of Tran—namely the severe effect of his removal on his family members—'are not so disproportionate as to outweigh the negative security interests which weigh against allowing the appeal' (ibid., para. 47). In the shadow of the crime-security nexus and its constituent linkages with organized crime and enabled by the much watered-down version of due process that applies in administrative settings, the tribunal 'tried' Tran for his association with an organized crime group and was able to connect the dots between Tran, street gangs in Calgary, organized crime, and national security in a way that the criminal justice system had failed to do. The tribunal carefully set the case up as a matter of national security, used that construction to trump Tran's compelling humanitarian and compassionate grounds, and paved the way for the application of the extreme and bodily sanctions of detention and deportation against Tran.

IMMIGRATION DETENTION: ADMINISTRATIVE OR PUNITIVE CONFINEMENT?

Canadian immigration legislation sanctions the use of coercive powers against non-citizens who have been targeted for detention and deportation. The debates around the uses of discretionary power in the administration of law and policy have been particularly pointed whenever the decisions that are taken entail serious consequences for the life and liberty of citizens. The administration of immigration legislation, in particular of those provisions that deal with the detention and removal of non-citizens, has tended to attract much less attention, even though it entails the very coercive consequences that, in the administration of criminal law, have generated so much concern.

While the bulk of this chapter has shown that there are significant points of intersection between the domains of criminal justice and immigration, intersections that I seek to capture through the use of the terms 'crime-security nexus' and 'immigration penalty', we should also be clear that the domains of criminal justice and immigration are not the same thing. The legal distinction between punitive and preventive administrative detention moves immigration detention from the ambit of criminal law into that of civil law. As such, the administrative nature of immigration detention decision-making does not carry with it the same obligation to provide all the same legal protections required under criminal law. While those who are detained may experience their detention as punishment, they need not have been charged with a crime and nor are they accorded the degree of rights and protections that would be theirs if they were actually being punished. For example, in detention review hearings, legal rules of evidence do not apply, access to legal counsel is limited, and the onus of proof is reversed so that those in detention have to prove that they should be released.

Immigration officers, who are civil servants employed by Citizenship and Immigration Canada, and adjudicators, who are members of the Immigration Division of the IRB, an independent adjudicative tribunal, have broad statutory powers to detain non-citizens.[15] Parliament has established two main grounds that justify detention: a likelihood that the person poses a danger to the public or, if not detained, a likelihood that the person will not appear for examination, inquiry, or removal. Immigration officers are also empowered to arrest without warrant, even when removal is not imminent. In addition to flight risk and danger to the public, 'foreign nationals' may be detained at any point in the process if an immigration officer is not satisfied with the accuracy of their identity and if they are deemed to be 'uncooperative' in efforts to establish their identity. Also introduced under the IRPA is the power to detain if it is deemed necessary in order to complete an examination—what some have called 'detention based on convenience' (IRPA, ss. 54–60).

In certain respects, the enforcement powers of immigration officers not only resemble but also exceed those of police officers. Immigration officers, for example, may detain a prospective immigrant or refugee if they are of the opinion that the person in question is not likely to appear for future immigration-related proceedings. While those charged with criminal offences may, after a hearing is held, be detained before trial because they are deemed to represent a flight risk or a danger to the public, it is nonetheless the case that the detention powers of immigration officers exceed those of police officers:

> Immigration Officers have powers beyond the range of any policeman [*sic*] or soldier in this country. There is no policeman who can arrest somebody because he thinks the guy won't show up for a hearing next week. If the

person doesn't show up, you issue an arrest warrant, but you can't decide Joe Blow isn't going to come next week, then go to his or her house, arrest them in their pyjamas and take them to detention. (House of Commons Standing Committee Hearings, 18 March 1998, p. 25)

IMMIGRATION ENFORCEMENT SOLUTIONS TO CRIMINAL JUSTICE PROBLEMS

Tran was detained on immigration hold for much of 2008 pending removal because he had been deemed to be a flight risk after missing an appeal hearing in early January. In October 2008, soon after the Federal Court had ordered a new deportation appeal hearing, Tran was released from detention on two $10,000 bonds and release conditions bearing a strong resemblance to those imposed by the criminal justice system when releasing on bail: living with his mother; remaining at his residence between 8:00 p.m. and 7:00 a.m. unless otherwise authorized by a CBSA officer for employment or a specific occasion; not possessing any illegal weapons; and abstaining from illegal drugs. Tran was subsequently rearrested and ordered detained again on 25 October after a police officer testified that he saw Tran out in public after his 8:00 p.m. curfew. On 14 November, Tran was released when it was determined that the officer had misidentified Tran on the night of the alleged breach. In August of the following year, Tran was again rearrested for breaching the condition of living with his mother. He was again released, this time because it was determined that his mother's decision to move into a subsidized apartment with her young daughter could not be held against him.

In the months leading up to Tran's deportation, a picture emerges of the sustained efforts of the local Calgary Police Service to target Tran: first through the collection of evidence to support conviction for gang membership offences and then, when this failed, through its repeated efforts to support his immigration detention and deportation through close monitoring of his release conditions and making submissions on the dangers he posed at his detention review hearings. When the local police gang task force in Calgary failed in its efforts to charge and convict Tran through the criminal justice system, an officer who had been very active in targeting Tran then acted as the key expert witness in Tran's appeal of his removal order, the officer's testimony serving ultimately to clinch the case for Tran's deportation.

The resort to deportation as a solution to a criminal justice problem is not a new phenomenon. There are ample historical examples of the deportation of criminalized undesirables from Canada as a supplement—or even as an alternative—to criminal justice prosecution: from the deportation of 'vagrants' during the Depression, to the deportation of immoral young women, to the deportation of communists and others who were thought to pose ideological threats to the political state, to the deportation of Chinese drug offenders in the past, and, more recently, the deportation of Jamaican-born men deemed dangers to the public.[16] A more recent example is the resort to civil avenues of deportation for suspected war criminals after efforts to prosecute under the war criminality provisions of the Canadian Criminal Code failed. Between 1987 and 1992, the government began four criminal proceedings against suspected war criminals in Canada, none of which resulted in criminal convictions.[17] As a result, in 1995, the government announced a shift in focus, from criminal prosecution to the civil avenues of denaturalization and deportation.[18]

In the pursuit of administrative as opposed to criminal proceedings, whether against suspected war criminals or against street-level gang members like Tran, cumbersome procedural safeguards of criminal prosecution are sidestepped, making punitive action in the form of deportation more likely. Important differences clearly exist between the denaturalization of suspected war criminals and the deportation of 'serious criminals', and the question of how to deal with those suspected of war crimes and crimes against humanity raises a host of complicated legal, political, and administrative issues. However, despite these differences, both instances demonstrate the heightened influence of the crime-security nexus and the degree of interchangeability between administrative immigration proceedings and criminal proceedings, and between detention and deportation and criminal punishment.

CARCERAL TECHNOLOGIES AND PENAL CONDITIONS

Notwithstanding the historical legal distinction between administrative detention and deportation and criminal justice punishment, those who become caught up in immigration penalty for whatever reason, criminal or otherwise, are acted upon as criminals—a trend that has intensified since the early 1990s. That detainees are 'administratively' rather than 'punitively' confined is largely irrelevant to those who are held in detention. In addition to intersections at the level of discourse and law and policy outlined above, the domains of criminal justice and immigration intersect in surprising ways at the level of material technologies. This is surprising because, even though immigration penalty is governed by an administrative legal regime and not a criminal law regime, it nonetheless deploys distinctly bodily penal technologies, usually assumed to be the preserve of criminal law enforcement: carceral confinement, bodily restraints, and forcible expulsion. Moreover, it is the very distinction between criminal law enforcement and immigration administration that enables the very extensive and sweepingly discretionary application of these traditional criminal justice technologies by immigration enforcement authorities.

As noted earlier, confinement in the form of immigration detention is not technically criminal punishment: it is administrative detention. Notwithstanding the historical legal distinction between administrative detention and criminal justice punishment, those who are suspected of violating immigration law for whatever reason, criminal or otherwise, are acted upon as criminals. The architecture, conditions, and regimes of immigration confinement are distinctly carceral.[19]

The technologies used in the policing of immigration detention also resemble those conventionally associated with criminal justice punishment. While the degree to which nineteenth-century reforms to the criminal justice system actually 'humanized' prison practices should not be overstated, the emergence of new modes of power that aimed to transform (through reform and rehabilitation programs) rather than merely control and punish prisoners had no echo in the context of immigration penality. The only objectives of the penal practices that are used in immigration detention are bodily subjection, control, and, ultimately, expulsion. The argument can also be made that criminal justice technologies have come to resemble immigration technologies—that they are less transformative than they are exclusionary, less oriented toward integration and rehabilitation than toward segregation and management, less about discipline than about risk. These important issues notwithstanding, there is an unmistakeable commingling and sharing of exclusionary and coercive technologies of control among criminal justice and immigration enforcement authorities.

Of particular salience is the use of body restraints on detainees. The use of handcuffs and leg irons or shackles is standard during transport to and from detention facilities. These may be further supplemented with a 'transportation belt', which secures handcuffed wrists at the waist level, if the guards judge that there is a risk of violence. Although justified by reference to the need to ensure safety and prevent escape, detention, handcuffs, leg irons, and transportation belts cannot help but evoke images of criminal justice penality and forcible confinement, bodily subjection, and punishment. The corporeality and brute forcefulness of these instruments of restraint are also powerfully reminiscent of medieval penality, particularly when linked with expulsion.[20] This association of forced bodily restraint and expulsion with pre-modern and early modern sovereign modes of penality (stocks, exile, and banishment) is heightened by tales of abuses and extreme bodily interventions that occasionally come to light, such as the forcible drugging and sedation of 'uncooperative' deportees or the sealing of the mouths of particularly unruly and vociferous deportees with duct tape (*Globe and Mail*, 1999).

The use of body restraints in the direct and physical subjection and control of bodies by force is commonly associated with criminal justice enforcement. Their use in conjunction with the expulsion of bodies from the nation in the non-criminal administrative context of immigration penality enforcement both demonstrates and reproduces the associations between the domains of immigration and criminal justice, between immigration and crime, between immigrants and criminals, as well as the coercive edge of sovereign power that permeates immigration penality.

SOVEREIGN POWER, THE FORTIFICATION OF BORDERS, AND THE NATIONAL ORDER OF THINGS

Sovereign power is thus not merely an archaic residue of the past. Indeed, it is a distinctly sovereign regime that is paramount in the governance of the particular sites and practices of immigration penality. No efforts are needed to transform 'deficient' outsiders into desirable citizens.[21] Like Tran, those who are deemed unwanted are physically confined and forcefully expelled. In this zone of exclusion, it is rules—not norms—that are the central features of the regimes that govern this site, and it is the bodies—not the souls, habits, or risks—of non-citizens that are directly targeted.

The distinction between administrative immigration detention and deportation and criminal punishment, as well as the long-standing tradition of judicial restraint in this area of public law and policy, hinges in large part on the notion of the sovereignty of nation-states. The legacy of the ideological national conception of sovereignty and the political conception of the sovereign rights and duties that derive from this legacy are remarkably resilient. As expressed in *Chiarelli v. Canada* (1992), 'the most fundamental principle of immigration law is that non-citizens do not have an unqualified right to enter or remain in the country. At common law an alien has no right to enter or remain in the country' (*Chiarelli v. Canada*, [1992] 1 S.C.R. 711). As was captured by the triumphant performance of sovereign power described at the start of this paper with respect to the successful deportation of Tran, this construction of state sovereignty in powerful conjunction with the crime-security nexus continues to justify even the most coercive examples of immigration penality: detention and deportation.

Discourses of national sovereignty continue to be dominant despite (or indeed because of) the growing recognition that global and transnational developments have increasingly unsettled the sovereignty of nation-states and the territorial borders that both constitute and are constituted by them. A global 'intensification of interconnectedness' (Inda & Rosaldo, 2002) has unsettled conventional constructions of the nation-state 'as common territory and time' (Hyndman & Roberts, 1998) and as the primary locus of citizenship.[22]

The deportation of 27-year-old Tran Trong Nghi Nguyen to his country of origin must be understood in relation to this broader context. The last few decades have witnessed the proliferation of efforts by Western industrialized countries to secure their territorial borders against 'undesirable' outsiders through the intensification and expansion of diverse national and transnational technologies of interdiction, containment, and expulsion in the shadow of the crime-security nexus.[23] This flexing of sovereign muscle and reassertion of the authority of the nation-state to control its geopolitical borders against the migration of undesirable populations come at the same time that 'global networks and flows' of goods, capital, information, and cultural symbols have decentred the authority of the nation-state and unsettled its traditional geopolitical borders.[24] In the face of a declining nation-state, this fortification of national borders and the intensification of efforts to reallocate 'subjects to their proper sovereigns' continually reassert and reconstitute the 'national order of things' (Malkki, 1995), 'sustain[ing] the image of a world divided into "national" populations and territories, domiciled in terms of state membership' (Walters, 2002). The expulsion of Tran Trong Nghi Nguyen to

Vietnam, his country of birth, is thus at the same time both a single instance of the forceful and bodily reassertion of sovereign power and the national order of things through the detention and deportation of dangerous foreigners, as well as but one entry in the larger story of the crime-security nexus and its dominance in the governance of immigration penality.

CRITICAL THINKING QUESTIONS

1. What is the 'crime-security nexus'? Provide specific examples of the different ways that this nexus has shaped the development of Canadian law and policy in the domain of immigration enforcement.

2. We often hear that the Canadian government attempts to balance humanitarian objectives with concerns for public safety and security. In what ways are the tensions between these policy objectives demonstrated in the case of Tran Trong Nghi Nguyen, and how are they resolved?

3. What connections can be traced between Tran's case and the influence and effects of globalization?

4. What is meant by the term 'immigration penality'? In what specific ways do the domains of immigration enforcement, border control, and criminal justice intersect, and why should we be interested in these intersections?

5. Why should we be interested in the deportation of Tran Trong Nghi Nguyen?

NOTES

1 As will be discussed a little later in the chapter, in this case, the best interests of Tran's young, dependent sister were a central concern in the appeal decision.

2 For coverage of the local Calgary panic surrounding gang violence, see, for example, *Calgary Sun*, 27 February 2009; *Calgary Sun*, 15 January 2009; CBC News, 2 January 2008; *Calgary Herald*, 10 October 2007; *Maclean's*, 19 September 2008; *Calgary Sun*, 24 February 2010. For a detailed review of the preoccupations at the national level with threats posed by dangerous foreign criminals associated with organized crime over the last few decades, see Pratt (2005). See also Chan (2006).

3 See Pratt (2005).

4 For further study of the different ways in which concerns about national purity,

national security, and criminality have influenced the governance of Canadian immigration penality, see also Valverde (1991); Strange & Loo (1997); Oikawa (1995); Kinsmen (2003); Carstairs (1999).

5 For a detailed examination of these developments, see Pratt (2005).

6 In fact, this legislation had been introduced well before 11 September 2001. On 6 April 2000, Bill C-31 was tabled (*An Act respecting immigration to Canada and the granting of refugee protection to persons who are displaced, persecuted or in danger*, 2000) to replace the 1976 Immigration Act (1976–7, c. 52, s. 1). In February 2001, a slightly revised version of this bill was reintroduced (*An Act respecting immigration to Canada and the granting of refugee protection to persons who are displaced, persecuted or in danger*, 2001,

c. 27 [Bill C-11]). It received royal assent in November 2001, and in June 2002, the new Immigration and Refugee Protection Act (IRPA) came into effect (Immigration and Refugee Protection Act, 2001 S.C., c. 27).

7 As the trial was subsequently slowed by allegations of racism and illegalities, the case was referred to as the 'justice deserted' case ('Just Desserts case a mess, judge reveals', *Globe and Mail*, 11 November 1998). The charges against Mark Jones were dropped, Lawrence Brown was sentenced to life for first-degree murder, and Gary Francis was sentenced to 15 years for manslaughter. O'Neil Grant was eventually acquitted, but he was deported to Jamaica in 2001, where he was killed in November 2007.

8 Including the expansion of the circumstances under which deportation orders are issued and the extension of the powers of immigration officers to arrest and search and seize (*CIC Update*, Ottawa, No. 8, April 1997, pp. 1–2).

9 For a discussion of discretion in the context of immigration decision-making, see Pratt (2005).

10 IRPA, s. 102(2)(A). While no ministerial opinion is required, a delegate of the minister of public safety and emergency preparedness reviews each case to decide whether a removal order should be issued by the Immigration Division (IRPA, s. 44[2]).

11 See, for example, Commission on Systemic Racism in the Ontario Criminal Justice System (1995); Royal Commission on the Donald Marshall Jr. Inquiry (1989); Mosher (1998); Wortley (1996); Ontario Human Rights Commission (2003); *Toronto Star*, Race and Crime Special Series (2002).

12 See Schwartz (1999). For a detailed discussion of the former danger-to-the-public provision, see 'Discretion, Danger to the Public and National Security' and 'Criminals First' in Pratt (2005).

13 This section grants to the IAD the power to grant exceptional relief from removal on humanitarian and compassionate grounds, including the best interests of the child. When considering whether special relief is warranted, the IAD is guided by the so-called *Ribic* factors:

1. the seriousness of the offence leading to the removal order;

2. the possibility of rehabilitation;

3. the length of time spent, and the degree to which the individual facing removal is established, in Canada;

4. the family and community support available to the individual facing removal;

5. the family in Canada and the dislocation to the family that removal would cause; and the degree of hardship that would be caused to the individual facing removal to his country of nationality. (*Ribic v. Canada [Minister of Employment and Immigration]*, [1985], I.A.B.D. No. 4)

These factors were endorsed by the Supreme Court of Canada in *Chieu v. Canada [Minister of Citizenship and Immigration]*, [2002] S.C.C. 3 [2002], and more recently in *Canada [Minister of Citizenship and Immigration] v. Khosa*, [2009] S.C.C. 12, [2009] 1 S.C.R.).

14 Despite arguments raised by Tran's lawyer, the IAB would be forgiven by the Federal Court for having reached outside of its jurisdiction by importing association/membership in an organized crime group (despite the absence of any criminal conviction for such offences) as an aggravating factor.

15 Detailed departmental guidelines on detention under IRPA are found in Citizenship and Immigration Canada's *Immigration Enforcement Manual*.

16 See Roberts (1988); Carstairs (1999); Valverde (1991); Avery (1979); Kinsmen (2009).

17 The 1994 the Supreme Court ruling in
   R. v. Finta, [1994] set a high burden of
   proof for these cases.

18 This allows the government to take
   action against suspected war criminals in
   Canada without actually having to prove
   in a criminal court that the person in
   question is a 'war criminal'. Instead,
   under section 10 of the Citizenship Act,
   citizenship may be revoked if it can be
   proven that 'they had entered Canada
   and/or obtained citizenship through
   misrepresentation, fraud, or the
   concealment of material facts' (CIC,
   'Canada's Program on Crimes against
   Humanity and War Crimes', 2005–6).

19 See Pratt (2001).

20 For an interesting examination of the
   penal genesis of deportation, see Walters
   (2002).

21 See also Simon (1998); Welch (2003).

22 See, for example, Holsten & Appadurai
   (1996); Sassen (1996); Sassen (2002); Isin
   (2000).

23 There is an extensive literature that
   examines the proliferation of enforcement measures, the fortification of
   territorial borders, and processes of
   'securitization' in the European and
   North American contexts. See Andreas
   (1998/99); Jamieson et al. (1998);
   Nagengast (1998); Flynn (2000);
   Fitzgerald (1995); Andreas (1999);
   Andreas & Snyder (2000); Simon
   (1998); Heyman (1999).

24 See Aas (2007).

REFERENCES

Aas, K.F. (2007). Analyzing a world in
   motion: Global flows meet criminology
   of the other. *Theoretical Criminology,
   11*(2), 282–303.

Andreas, P. (1998/99). The escalation of US
   Immigration control in the post-NAFTA
   era. *Political Science Quarterly, 113*(4),
   591–615.

———. (1999). Borderless economy,
   barricaded border. *NACLA Report on the
   Americas, 33*(3), 14–21.

———, & Snyder, T. (2000). *The wall around
   the West: State borders and immigration
   controls in North America and Europe.*
   Boulder, CO: Rowman & Littlefield.

Avery, D. (1979). *Dangerous foreigners.* Toronto:
   McClelland & Stewart.

———. (1995). *Reluctant host: Canada's
   response to immigrant workers, 1896–1994.*
   Toronto: McClelland & Stewart.

Calgary Herald. (2007, October 10). Justice
   system blamed for gang violence:
   Calgary's new police chief says lenient

sentences are crippling efforts to curb
   growing gang violence in the city.

Calgary Sun. (2009, January 15). Calgary
   gang ties proving deadly.

———. (2009, February 27). Calgary's gang
   war about revenge: Never-ending cycle
   of violence makes organized crime life 'a
   pretty asinine way to live'.

———. (2010, February 24). Young children
   joining gangs.

Carstairs, C. (1999). Deporting 'Ah Sin' to
   save the white race: Moral panic,
   racialization and the extension of
   Canadian drug laws in the 1920s.
   *Canadian Bulletin of Medical History/
   Bulletin canadien d'histoire de la medicine,
   16*(1), 65–88.

CBC News. (2008, January 2). Police brace
   for gang violence after downtown
   slaying. *CBC News.*

———. (2010). Gang member freed amid
   deportation fight. *CBC News.* http://
   www.cbc.ca/canada/calgary/

story/2008/10/22/tran-deportation-freed-bond.html

Chan, W. (2006). Crime, deportation and the regulation of immigrants in Canada. *Crime, Law and Social Change, 44*(2), 153–80.

Commission on Systemic Racism in the Ontario Criminal Justice System. (1995). *Report of the Commission on Systemic Racism in the Ontario Criminal Justice System.* Queen's Printer for Ontario.

Dirks, G. (1977). *Canada's refugee policy: Indifference or opportunism?* Montreal: McGill-Queen's University Press.

Dirks, G. (1995). *Controversy and complexity: Canadian immigration policy during the 1980s.* Montreal: McGill-Queen's University Press.

Fitzgerald, P. (1995). Repelling borders. *New Statesman and Society, 8,* 16–17.

Flynn, S.E. (2000). Beyond border control. *Foreign Affairs, 79*(6), 57–68.

Globe and Mail. (1998, November 11). Just Desserts case a mess, judge reveals.

Globe and Mail. (1999, January 20). Con Air is an airline with a difference.

Harsanvi, S. (2010). Myth of Jackie Tran. *Immigration Blog.* Retrieved 13 September from http://immlawyer.blogs.com/my_weblog/jackie-tran/

Hawkins, F. (1972). *Canada and immigration: Public policy and public concern.* Montreal: McGill-Queen's University Press.

Heyman, J. (1999). Why interdiction? Immigration control at the United States–Mexico border. *Regional Studies, 33*(7), 619–30.

Holsten, J., & Appadurai, A. (1996). Cities and citizenship. *Public Culture, 8*(2), 187–204.

Hyndman, J., & Walton-Roberts, M. (1998, December). *Transnational migration and nation: Burmese refugees in Vancouver.* Unpublished paper, 4.

Inda, J.X., & Renato, R. (2002). A world in motion. In J.X. Inda & R. Rosaldo (Eds.), *The anthropology of globalization: A reader* (pp. 1–12). Malden, MA: Blackwell.

Isin, E. (Ed.). (2000). *Democracy, citizenship and the global city.* London: Routledge.

Jamieson, R., et al. (1998). Economic liberalization and cross-border crime: The North American free trade area and Canada's border with the U.S.A. Part 1. *International Journal of the Sociology of Law, 26*(2), 245–72.

Kelley, N., & Trebilcock, M. (1998). *The making of the mosaic: A history of Canadian immigration policy.* Toronto: University of Toronto Press.

Kinsmen, G. (2003). National security as moral regulation: Making the normal and the deviant in the security campaigns against gay men and lesbians. In D. Brock (Ed.), *Making normal: Social regulation in Canada* (pp. 121–44). Toronto: Nelson.

Kinsmen, G. (2009). *The Canadian war on queers: National security as sexual regulation.* Vancouver: University of British Columbia Press.

Maclean's. (2008, September 19). Calls made for more resources on gang violence in Calgary.

Malkki, L. (1995). Refugees and exile: From 'refugee studies' to the national order of things. *Annual Review of Anthropology, 24,* 495–523.

Mosher, J.C. (1998). *Discrimination and denial: Systemic racism in Ontario's legal and criminal justice systems, 1892–1961.* Toronto: University of Toronto Press.

Nagengast, C. (1998). Militarizing the border patrol. *NACLA Report on the Americas, 32*(3), 37–43.

Oikawa, M. (1995). Cartographies of violence: Women, memory, and the subject(s) of the internment. In S. Razack (Ed.), *Race, space and the law: Unmapping a white settler society* (pp. 73–98). Toronto: Between the Lines.

Ontario Human Rights Commission. (2003). *Paying the price: The human cost of racial profiling inquiry report.* http://www.ohrc.on.ca/english/consultations/racial-profiling-report.shtml

Pratt, A. (2001). Sovereign power, carceral conditions and penal practices: Detention and deportation in Canada. *Studies in Law, Politics and Society, 23,* 45–78.

———. (2005). *Securing borders: Detention and deportation in Canada.* Vancouver: University of British Columbia Press.

Roberts, B. (1998). *Whence they came: Deportation from Canada 1900–1935.* Ottawa: University of Ottawa Press.

Royal Commission on the Donald Marshall Jr. Inquiry. (1989). *Discrimination against blacks in Nova Scotia: The investigation of the criminal justice system.* Halifax: Author.

Sassen, S. (1996). *Losing control: Sovereignty in an age of globalization.* New York: Columbia University Press.

———. (2002). *Global networks, linked cities.* London: Routledge.

Schwartz, B. (1999). Factum: The preventive function of section 15 of the Charter and the danger certificate system. *Manitoba Law Journal, 27,* 115–39.

Simon, J. (1998). Refugees in a carceral age: The rebirth of immigration prisons in the US. *Public Culture, 1998,* 577–606.

Strange, C., & Loo, T. (1997). *Making good: Law and moral regulation in Canada 1867–1939.* Toronto: University of Toronto Press.

Toronto Star. (2002, October 19–27). Race and crime special series.

Valverde, M. (1991). *The age of light, soap and water: Moral reform in English Canada 1885–1925.* Toronto: McClelland & Stewart.

Walters, W. (2002). Deportation, expulsion and the international police of aliens. *Citizenship Studies, 6*(3), 265–92.

Weinreb, A., & Galati, R. (1996). *The criminal lawyer's guide to immigration and citizenship law.* Aurora, ON: Canada Law Book.

Welch, M. (2003). *Detained: Immigration laws and the expanding I.N.S. jail complex.* Philadelphia: Temple University Press.

Wortley, S. (1996). Justice for all? Race and perceptions of bias in the Ontario criminal justice system—A Toronto survey. *Canadian Journal of Criminology,* October, 439–67.

LEGISLATION CITED

An Act to amend the Immigration Act, 1976, and to amend other Acts in consequence thereof (The Refugee Reform Bill), 1988, c. 35 (Bill C-55).

An Act to amend the Immigration Act, 1976, and to amend other Acts in consequence thereof (The Refugee Deterrents and Detention Bill), 1988, c. 31 (Bill C-84).

An Act to amend the Immigration Act, 1976, and to amend other Acts in consequence thereof, 1992, c. 49 (Bill C-86).

An Act to amend the Immigration Act and the Citizenship Act and to make a consequential amendment to the Customs Act, 1995, c. 15 (Bill C-44).

An Act respecting immigration to Canada and the granting of refugee protection to persons who are displaced, persecuted or in danger, 2001, c. 27 (Bill C-11).

Canadian Criminal Code, R.S.C. 1985, c. C-46.

Convention relating to the status of refugees, 28 July 1951, 189 U.N.T.S. 150, arts. 32–3, Can. T.S. 1969/6, entered into force 22 April 1954, accession by Canada 2 September 1969.

Immigration Act, 1952, R.S.C, c. 325.

Immigration Act, 1976–77, R.S.C., S.C., c. 52, s. 1.

Immigration and Refugee Protection Act, 2001 S.C., c. 27 (IRPA).

CASES CITED

Chiarelli v. Canada (Minister of Employment and Immigration) [1992] 1 S.C.R. 711.

R. v. Finta, [1994] 1 S.C.R. 701; [1994], 165 N.R. 1.

Medovarski v. Canada (Minister of Citizenship and Immigration) (T.D.), 2003 FCT 634, [2003] 4 F.C. 227.

Esteban v. Canada (Minister of Citizenship and Immigration), [2005] 2 S.C.R. 539, 2005 SCC 51.

Chieu v. Canada (Minister of Citizenship and Immigration), 2002 SCC 3, [2002].

Canada (Minister of Citizenship and Immigration) v. Khosa, 2009 SCC 12, [2009] 1 S.C.R.

GOVERNMENT DOCUMENTS

Canadian Security and Intelligence Service. (2005). *The CSIS mandate*. Backgrounder No. 1. Revised February 2005. http://www.csis-scrs.gc.ca/nwsrm/bckgrndrs/bckgrndr01-eng.asp

Canadian Security and Intelligence Service. (2008). *Transnational criminal activity*. http://www.csis.gc.ca/prrts/trnsntnl/index-eng.asp

Citizenship and Immigration Canada. (1997). *Update*. Ottawa. No. 8, 1–2.

Citizenship and Immigration Canada. Enforcement manual. *Detention*. http://www.cic.gc.ca/english/resources/manuals/enf/enf20-eng.pdf

Citizenship and Immigration Canada. (2002). *Ninth annual report. Canada's Crime against Humanity and War Crimes Program*. http://www.cbsa-asfc.gc.ca/security-securite/wc-cg/wc-cg2006-eng.html#fnr_1

Criminal Intelligence Service Canada. (2006). Annual report. http://www.cisc.gc.ca/media/media_2006/documents/highlights_2006_e.pdf

Department of National Defence. (2002). *Transnational crime: The next big threat?* Retrieved 23 December 2002 from http://www.forces.gc.ca/admpol/eng/doc/strat_2001/sa01_26_e.html

House of Commons Standing Committee Hearings. (1998). Transcript, 18 March, p. 25.

Ministry of Public Safety Canada. (2010). news release, 5 March.

12

Policy and Politics: The Evolution of Organized Crime Policies in Canada

Margaret E. Beare

INTRODUCTION

This chapter will examine some of the factors that go into the creation of policies, legislation, and policing practices pertaining to organized crime. Unlike some other areas of criminal conduct, 'organized crime' as a concept is burdened not only by its vagueness and breadth, but also by a mystique fed through popular culture and shaped by the rhetoric of those who have either a political or a policing agenda to promote. In short, organized crime can be exploited not only by the criminals who pursue the various forms of illegal activities, but also by policymakers, law enforcement agencies, and all others who can benefit from the rhetoric of, and responses to, organized crime. An understanding of policies related to organized crime requires an understanding of 'who gains and who loses' from the varying approaches.

This chapter begins with an examination of the changing factors that affect government policy-making specifically related to this nebulous topic of organized crime. Given the political attractiveness of the crime-fighting mantra, there is seldom a 'going back', rather a continual 'building on'. Hence one set of powers serves as the foundation for the next layer. Measures that initially appear to be extreme become normalized. It is this layering that the chapter addresses. While this tendency has long been true, the difference now is that the layers are no longer necessarily a response to conditions within any one jurisdiction, but are borrowed and are justified from afar. Policy-making increasingly reflects international pressures toward the harmonization of the laws, practices, and procedures relating to all aspects of the control of organized crime.

The very transnational nature of organized crime means that policies may be influenced as much by the international community as by domestic conditions. While one objective might be the global harmonization of policies, in practice harmonization is more akin to 'contagion' theory. Highly emotional security fears encourage jurisdictions to sign on to responses that appear to have no specific origin. Hence, what is accepted as desirable or necessary within the international community becomes the required strategy at home. This acceptance may reflect a fondness for enhanced powers and greater resources, a shared interpretation of the threat, or merely a sense of the appropriateness of being in step with policies in play elsewhere. This 'appropriateness of being in step' is made most urgent when sanctions are applied against countries that fail to respond to international agreements. Sanctions may include various 'blacklisting' measures that can influence the amount of aid or other forms of assistance received by a nation, or they may include the more general erosion of a country's positive recognition within the international community.

After examining the policy-making process, the chapter will discuss the initial entry of 'enterprise crime' into the Canadian Criminal Code. It will then describe policy developments in Canada, examining a diverse array of contemporary legislation, including enhanced policing powers and reverse-onus provisions that seek to fight organized crime by emphasizing 'criminal associations' and anti-money-laundering approaches.

THE POLITICS OF POLICY-MAKING

Both empirical evidence and ideological factors can determine the policies that governments ultimately pursue. For example, in both the policy debates and the legislation relating to young offenders, it is clear that politics plays a role, normally manifesting itself in the form of contrasting positions regarding 'what works'. Hence, when the House of Commons Standing Committee on Justice and Legal Affairs undertook a review of the Young Offenders Act (YOA), political tensions along party lines became clear and led to predictable debates: the Liberal majority emphasized crime prevention and rehabilitation; the Bloc Québécois opposed any changes and took the view that understanding youth justice was unique; and the Reform Party called for numerous 'get tougher' changes.[1] This level of political debate tends to be missing from discussions regarding organized-crime policy.

Drug traffickers and groups who are referred to as 'narco-terrorists' are portrayed as the poster criminals for organized crime, and therefore no sympathetic or rehabilitative orientation to policy is tolerated and certainly not advanced by any party. Being 'tough' on these specific criminals and organizations is seen to add to the security of citizens. No political party is strong enough, or perhaps courageous enough, to appear to be 'weak on organized crime'. The more relevant acknowledgement of the merits of demand reduction rather than tougher supply reduction strategies fails to hold political interest and hence also fails to offer viable alternative policies and approaches.

While there are numerous influences on government policy-making, the following diagram attempts to capture five of the main circles of influence at the

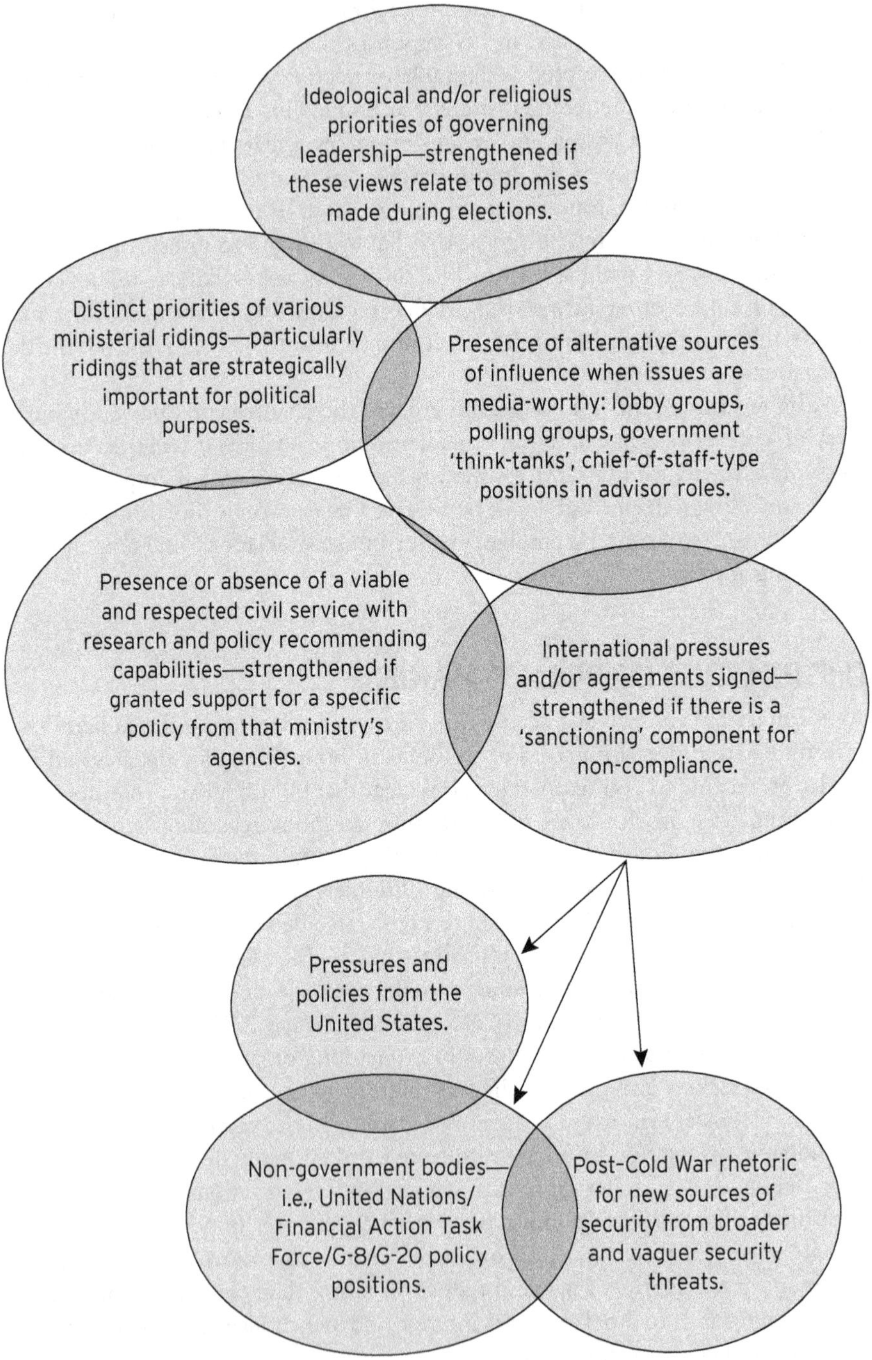

FIGURE 12.1 Spheres of influence on policy-making

domestic level, with links into the international sphere. A complicating factor is the significant overlap between and among these influences. Personal preferences of a leader may be fed back to him or her from a number of sources, including political parties, governments, supportive lobbyists, polls, or think tanks. A typical support-generating method of operation utilized by governments is to package an idea for the media and then use the media support to garner a 'demand for action' from the public. This demand is then used by government officials to justify the specific policy—a preference that they initiated in the first place. Any real or con- trived crisis can be exploited for this purpose. Government officials refer to 'win- dows of opportunity' when some catalytic event can be used to focus public attention on some needed change. These 'crises' allow the political party to present a politically advantageous response that can then be relayed back to the public via the media—often with the explanation that the public demanded the specific action. Various agendas can be advanced by exploiting the fear associated with and generated by specific forms of criminal conduct, including, of course, terrorism. Seizing an 'opportunity' is perhaps wise. 'Opportunism' is merely cynical.

The pressures are different when the focus shifts to international issues. Canada obviously wants to be, and be seen to be, a full participant in the international community. A network of agreements, conventions, 'recommendations', and treat- ies serves to narrow domestic decision-making. Daniel Alati (2010) examined the rapid international harmonization of perspectives, policies, and legislation per- taining to transnational organized crime. He traced how transnational organized crime moved from a position where it was seldom discussed in the legal discourse to its current position where we now have globally defined criminal offences and globally scripted responses to these international 'threats'. As indicated in Figure 12.1, all of the domestic pressures and influences combine with three key inter- national influences: the role of US officials in influencing global policy pertaining to transnational organized crime; the role of developed nations in influencing global policy pertaining to transnational organized crime (i.e., via G-7/G-8, mechanisms such as the Financial Action Task Force [FATF],[2] the United Nations [UN], and the European Union [EU]); and, finally, the shifting security priorities between the post–Cold War years and the post-9/11 years, which have recast transnational organized crime into a global security threat.

As with domestic influences, these international influences overlap. We find that the significant US players held key roles in the international non-state organ- izations. For example, Ronald Noble and Stan Morris, who both headed at vary- ing times the US Financial Crimes Enforcement Network (FinCEN), went on to hold leadership positions in FATF, Egmont (a network of Financial Intelligence Units), and Interpol.[3] Likewise, as Michael Woodiwiss argues,[4] the US-led 'war on drugs' was amenable to a shift to the 'war on organized crime', then to the inter- national 'war on money laundering', and finally to a focus on global terrorist financing—shifts that served both to justify the failure of the anti-drug efforts and to explain why there had been no significant impact on the amount, price, or purity of drugs within the United States. The rhetoric that positioned drugs as part of a much larger international criminal network served to 'explain' these limited results. The war on drugs was seen to fail in part because these criminals were 'really' part of a global organized crime conspiracy that had to be fought on different fronts with different strategies—policing strategies and military strategies that were backed up by powerful sanctions via a network of harmonized international agreements, conventions, and recommendations. Decades of spent resources and lives lost owing to enforcement-related corruption or criminal violence were the main results of the commitment to drug eradication.

In the post–Cold War environment, 'new security issues', 'non-traditional security threats', 'transnational crime threats', and 'regional security issues' were phrases used to capture and express an expanding array of insecurities. There was a tendency for cynics and critics to view the use of security rhetoric, including the sweeping of former serious crimes into the national security net, as an attempt on the part of national security agencies (CIA, CSIS, MI5, etc.) to secure their organizational futures. While there may have been some truth to these suspicions, the aftermath of 9/11 ensured that the organizations that could claim a national security mandate would survive well into the future.

In addition, critics have described the redefining of ordinary crimes as 'threats to national security'[5] as an example of the Americanization of Canadian law enforcement', requiring enhanced legislation and wider policing powers. It is a trend most visible in traditional organized crimes such as drug trafficking and money laundering (Beare & Schneider, 2007). Rather than being mere Criminal Code violations, these sorts of threats are now seen to require what Jean Paul Brodeur called 'high policing' (Brodeur, 1992).[6] The 'high-policing' model employs specific strategies such as reliance on greater surveillance, undercover operations, and enhanced police powers. It is typically political in the sense that the issues are seen to be relevant to governments and this political relevance legitimizes the intrusiveness of the strategies that are employed. The use of these strategies, and the rhetoric that accompanies them, brings a much wider population of offences and offenders to the interest of the police and, by extension, to both elected and unelected policy-makers.

RESEARCH-DRIVEN POLICY

The public service is one of the traditional sources of policy advice to ministers. The recent *Canada @ 150 Research Report*, which examines the future of the public service, begins with the recognition of a consensus that the role of the public servant is, among other things, to serve as researcher and supporter of science and technology and act as a trusted policy advisor, confident policy leader, and innovator (Canada, 2010). The politics of government ends at the level of the deputy minister. The 'servants' at or below that level are either to carry out in-house research or to commission the expertise of others to provide the best advice possible to their political masters. This vision of how research ought to serve policy-makers has been affected by changes within government during the last 20 years that have reduced and, in some cases, eliminated the in-house research capacities of most government departments. This separation of policy from research might work if there were sufficient funds and political will to invest in academic research units outside of government. However, the demise of the government in-house research capacity related to criminal justice issues coincided with federal funding cuts to criminology centres across the country.

With the downsizing of the government in the early 1990s, the majority of research units were disbanded and became strictly 'policy' units. Policy advisors now move in and out of departments with no expectation that they will be able to acquire substantive expertise. If they happen to arrive with knowledge relevant to their specific department, career opportunities will mean that they will soon move along to a higher position elsewhere. The policy advisors within government therefore shuffle around as they climb the government ladder. Ministers are no different in the sense that they arrive with little or no substantive knowledge of the issues for which they will be held accountable. Much like their policy advisors, ministers, on average, tend to move on to different responsibilities every two years. From 1984 to 2010 (26 years), there have been 16 ministers responsible for policing and correctional matters within the former Department of the Solicitor General and current Ministry of Public Safety Canada (formed in 2003). Between 2006 and 2010, 3 ministers have served in that portfolio under Prime Minister Harper. It is within this environment that we must examine policy-making on organized crime, a highly politicized policy area with direct international links and an increasing tendency to be framed with the rhetoric of 'national security threats'.

Few crimes are as soaked in politics as are those forms of criminality that are defined as 'organized crimes'. Policy-making in this area exposes the constant tension between thoughtful evidence-based policies and the much more popular 'get tough' responses that are voiced by virtually all political parties, both domestically and internationally. Critics maintain that matters of great importance to the operations of our jails, social order, civil rights, and enforcement have become fodder for political gain and on occasion simply reflect the religious or ideological whims of political leaders. In the words of Mr. Justice David Cole of the Ontario Court of Justice, '[Y]ou would think that you would want good policy development in the area of criminal justice—particularly in sentencing—but everything is done on the fly, and always with a view to quick political gain. All the academics know this. All the commentators know this' (quoted in Makin, 2009).

DEFINITIONAL ISSUES
Shifting from Traditional Crime Families and Gangs to Harm and Networks

What makes a crime 'organized crime'? In M. Beare's (1996) *Criminal Conspiracies*, organized crime is defined as 'a process' rather than as a type of crime or a type of criminal; it is the way in which crimes are committed rather than any specific type of crime. While the process conceptualization may still be valid, an important question remains: 'Process for what?' When one is describing the activities of organized crime, one might look at Mafia-type operations, since they are the criminal operations that have received the most attention. While the Mafia model is only one specific form of organized crime, for decades this structure was assumed to apply to any organized crime operation. Due to its more rigid, membership-oriented structure, it has a visibility that some other more fluid, looser, criminal networks do not have. The result: if the criminal operation did not look like a Mafia operation, then the criminal activity tended to be excluded from this organized crime definition.

A sophisticated operation of any sort will involve some degree of organization, will likely have some replaceable membership, and will have the capability to gain some advantage through the use of corruption or violence. However, from a policy perspective, it is important to ask whether all such crimes are worthy of special legislation, enhanced policing powers, longer sentences, and the expenditure of significant financial resources. The rhetoric suggests that there is something particularly threatening to society as a whole about those forms of criminality described as organized or transnational organized crime, with the notion of threat implying harm to society. If 'harm to society' provides a benchmark for the inclusion of an offence under the organized crime umbrella, an immediate problem is apparent: namely, financial crimes—crimes often committed by the financially powerful—are seldom referred to as organized crime, and yet in terms of harm, there is little doubt that financial crimes have wreaked havoc on economies around the world and have created untold personal disasters, including lost homes, lost jobs, lost pensions, and lost lives to suicide.

The continuing debate as to what to place under the definition of organized crime, plus the gradual recognition that criminal operations can involve both legitimate businesses as well as illegitimate operations, has led to a questioning of the merits of restricting the organized crime terminology to the more traditional rigidly structured and membership-based operations like the Mafia, outlaw bikers, or Triad-type groups. There is a growing recognition that some crimes may be *more* serious and *more* harmful, though they may not be 'organized' in any traditional manner that would fit a description of organized crime.

What the term 'organized crime' captures is important because it determines what conduct will be subjected to the greatest scrutiny and enforcement. We accept that organized crime will be targeted with specific criminal legislation and enhanced policing powers. Therefore, conduct that causes the greatest risk to society should wear the organized-crime label. However, internationally there is an increasing acknowledgement that criminal laws or strict policing forms of enforcement may in fact not be effective as a response against some of the most serious acts that impact countries around the globe. Corruption, environmental spillage and degradation, financial market manipulation, and various state crimes require not only a broad international response, but also a response that is quite different from strategies that target more traditional organized crimes. An example of this change can be discerned from the EU Council's decision to revise the mandate of Europol to include serious criminality as determined by the harm that it causes— harm that is not necessarily related to what is typically understood to be organized crime but that requires cross-border investigations and a multi-jurisdictional response (Dorn, 2009).

Shifting the organized crime focus to 'harm' encourages a focus on looser networks of criminals that involve a fluid blend of members who move easily from legitimate businesses to criminal enterprises (Australia, 1999; UN, 2011). This more recent view of the concept of 'organized crime' may meet with resistance. Biker wars and other visibly violent groups are attractive targets and far easier for the public, politicians, and perhaps even the police to understand than are the assorted criminal deal-making enterprises and massive financial frauds. Catchy headlines are a big part of the attraction to bikers and the Mafia. The Toronto newspapers (*Globe and Mail*, 2000, pp. A1, A3; *National Post*, 2000, p. A1; *Toronto Star*, 2000, p. A2) carried long articles and headlines about the sentencing of the 'Rothchilds of the Mafia' (the Cuntrera-Caruana 'kingpins') to long prison terms. The police were described as having arrested the 'Gretzky of Organized Crime'. Reference was made to the 'significant blow to so-called untouchables'. These grandiose claims are less easy to make when individual victims find themselves defrauded by financiers who have, through complicated schemes, moved the proceeds of their illegal activities offshore. The money is long gone and the tedious court case—if there is one—all too often drags on for years.[7] Shifting the focus of the media will not be easy. However, the public will eventually need to appreciate how fleeting the successes of high-profile drug and gang cases are, and what limited impact such arrests have on the overall criminal operations, let alone on the drug markets that sustain the operations.

THE EVOLUTION OF CANADIAN ORGANIZED CRIME LEGISLATION

The Canadian *Enterprise Crime Study Report* (Canada, 1983) was perhaps ahead of its time in adopting the term 'enterprise crime' instead of 'organized crime' in response to problems associated with the latter term. The report begins with the following quote from a previous report from British Columbia entitled *The Business of Crime*, according to which enterprise crime is considered to include

all types of criminal activity that are part of an ongoing arrangement between persons for the purpose of profit. It also includes the use of an existing organization to perpetrate or disguise criminal activities. *Use of the term 'organized crime' is avoided out of a desire not to restrict the reader's focus to a narrow view of the type of crime syndicate portrayed in the media.* That type of syndicate is included in the notion of enterprise crime, but so is a group of corrupt businessmen who use illegal methods to further their legitimate interests, as well as a corrupt labour union, and a group of individuals who organized themselves to import narcotics. (Canada, 1983; emphasis added)[8]

This report describes the similarities between enterprise crime and legitimate business in terms of how they are organized, and argues that this fact is of particular importance from a legislative, law enforcement, and prosecutorial perspective. The inclusion of white-collar crime is interesting in part because of the more recent tendency to exclude these types of crimes from organized crime discussions in Canada. The recent massive financial fraud cases indicate that we still take a blinkered view of what constitutes organized crime. In some of these examples the corporate criminals operated in a manner that met virtually all of the diverse requirements that would qualify them as organized criminals.

The interplay between Canadian and US organized crime rhetoric (rhetoric also now found in Australia and the UK) is a recurring theme in the Canadian reports. Following from the US focus on organized crime in the 1960s was a series of federal–provincial Canadian conferences held in 1965 and 1966. On 8 August 1967, the report of the January 1966 Federal–Provincial Conference on Organized Crime was released. The conclusions reached were quite dramatic. Organized crime was said to be entwined in nearly all fields of business and commerce. Moreover, it was alleged that 'those engaged in organized crime in Canada maintain a close working relationship and personal ties with many of the US crime syndicate . . . "the mafia"' (Beare, 1996, p. 143). The 1967 US Task Force on Organized Crime served to alert Canadians as well as Americans to the threats posed by criminal investment into legitimate businesses. The 'pollution' of legitimate business was a major justification for the passing of the 1970 US Racketeer Influenced and Corrupt Organizations Statute (RICO), drafted in part by Robert Blakey. RICO became the international model for responding to organized crime/racketeering. While it was assumed that Blakey was applying his 'new' RICO to the Mafia crime families within the United States, he emphasized that he intended the legislation to apply to a broader array of criminals. As he stated in 1982, 'There is nothing in RICO that says that if you act like a racketeer you will not be treated like a racketeer, whatever the colour of your shirt or your collar . . . people who run groups by extortion or violence or fraud ought to be called racketeers. And what they engage in is racketeering.'[9]

In 1982, Canadian government officials invited Blakey and officials from the UK to Ottawa to help devise a legislative framework to address organized crime in Canada. Blakey's perspective, presented in the earlier quote, was in keeping with the broader view of Canadian government officials as expressed in the *Enterprise Crime* document. Traditional street-level police strategies had come to be regarded as too limited in power and scope. The individual targets of these traditional policing strategies were non-essential to the existence of the criminal operations.

Arresting one or even many members of a criminal organization would not necessarily stop the organization from operating.

'Targeting upward' became the mantra. But even if this could have been an effective strategy, upper-echelon arrests within criminal syndicates were rare, and even when such convictions did occur, the criminals continued to run their criminal operations from within the walls of their prisons. This served to indicate that criminal individuals, criminal organizations, and criminal proceeds would all need to be the focus of law enforcement. One strategy alone would not be adequate. National and international working groups, conventions, and conferences expanded on earlier policy recommendations that flowed from a series of royal commissions, inquiries, and organized crime task forces. Targeting upward to capture upper-echelon criminals, shifting the focus from the individual criminals to the proceeds of crime, and recognizing that organized crime is an international enforcement problem that can be tackled only from a base of international collaboration and intelligence sharing, all eventually became embraced by law enforcement, resulting in a focus on criminal proceeds through the following strategies:

- Targeting up—away from a preoccupation with street-level busts
- King-pin focus—building cases against the leaders
- Focus on the money—'proceeds of crime' specialized enforcement units
- Anti-money laundering policies that extended beyond the police

Increasingly, countries became aware that not only did they share the same enforcement concerns, but in some cases they shared the same criminals and a portion of the same criminal proceeds. The crimes that were of the greatest concern were international in scope, and as such, the prevailing argument was that international approaches, involving collaboration in intelligence sharing and operational investigations, were required.

More practical, and possibly more lucrative during periods of fiscal restraint, was the view that these criminals were involved in numerous profitable crimes, the proceeds of which could be seized by governments. Locking up low-level operators would do little to disable the criminal operations, and while it was still occasionally essential to target key criminal figures, seldom was law enforcement able to get high enough to remove the top level. What did seem possible was to focus law enforcement's attention on the money, goods, and property acquired from organized crime. It was argued that upper-echelon criminals isolate themselves from the daily 'dirty' operations of illegal activity, becoming more directly involved when the illicit proceeds return cleansed and thus ready to be enjoyed or reinvested, perhaps in some legitimate venture.

As Canadian legislation evolved, at each point a catalytic event was seen to generate the next shift in enforcement strategy. In 1984, that catalyst was the *Pinto* case,[10] which involved a US drug trafficker who was convicted of laundering an estimated $40 million in US funds. He maintained a bank account in the name of a relative in Montreal, and because the money had already been deposited, the bank successfully argued that it was an 'intangible asset' and therefore could not be forfeited under existing Criminal Code provisions. The *Pinto* case served as the final straw for law enforcement and ushered in new legislation on the proceeds of crime. The challenge for policy-makers was how to package reforms for public and political consumption. The response to the challenge was twofold:

- First, provincial and territorial government support would need to be secured. This could be achieved by including a wide array of enterprise crimes (in addition to the designated drug offences typically prosecuted by the federal government) so that the provincial and territorial governments would benefit from the ability to seize assets.
- Second, the proceeds of crime legislation was included as one of the 51 separate initiatives that made up the National Drug Strategy. Therefore, the ability to seize assets was sold to the public not as some vague, draconian enforcement strategy to be used against crimes in general, but rather as a vital tool in the 'war against drug traffickers'.

'Targeting upward' had come to mean targeting the criminal proceeds rather than (or in addition to) the criminals. A series of 'original' pieces of Canadian legislation addressed this now preferred policy:

- Mutual Legal Assistance in Criminal Matters Act (1988), which allowed treaties to be signed with foreign jurisdictions to assist cross-jurisdictional law enforcement;
- Proceeds of Crime Legislation (1989), which allowed for the seizure and forfeiture of criminal proceeds and created the new offence of 'laundering';
- Act to Facilitate Combating the Laundering of Proceeds of Crime (1991), Regulations (1993)—a vaguely named piece of legislation that was actually a record-keeping requirement relating to the mandatory retaining of bank records for fixed periods of time; and
- Seized Property Management Act (Bill C-123) (1993), which set up a system to safeguard or dispose of seized items, either for the period between seizure and forfeiture or following a forfeiture order.

The increasing focus on international money laundering and criminal proceeds that developed fairly quickly during the 1980s and into the 1990s was made possible by the earlier policy shift—each change in thinking leading to new policies, new policing practices, and, in some cases, new legislation. This focus on the criminal proceeds meant that it was now necessary to trace illicit proceeds through the complex laundering schemes devised by criminals. Domestically, this led to the funding of Integrated Proceeds of Crime (IPOC) units within the RCMP. These specialized units included municipal and provincial police officers as well as forensic accountants, designated Crown prosecutors, and clerical support required for the complex anti-laundering cases.

DEVELOPMENTS DURING THE LATE 1990s AND BEYOND . . .

The next group of legislative initiatives continued to target 'dirty' or 'dangerous' proceeds derived from both legitimate and illegitimate sources, either as an attempt to combat criminal activity or for fear that funds could contribute to forms of terrorism. In addition, the legislation followed an international trend and began to target 'criminal associations'. In Canada, this meant a focus on outlaw biker-gang memberships or street-gang affiliations. Pressures either directly from the United States or through non-governmental bodies such as the Financial Action Task Force (FATF) appear to have had the greatest influence on Canadian policies during this period.

Law enforcement, and the legislation that authorized the enforcement practices, had by this point entered a precarious, or at least controversial, area. Front-line bank tellers and other such employees were now required to take on policing-type anti-money laundering detection duties and were tasked with predicting the future use to which legitimate funds might possibly be put in the detection of terrorist financing. In addition, legislation enabled the police to target those who 'facilitated' criminal activity even while not benefiting from that crime or even necessarily being aware that they were assisting criminals. These significant pieces of legislation greatly expanded the range of law enforcement.

First, Bill C-22 (the Proceeds of Crime Money Laundering Act) was enacted in 2000 and amended one year later to include terrorist financing (PCMLTFA).[11] If there was one specific piece of legislation that reflected the power of the international community (in the guise of the FATF) to exert direct influence on Canadian policy-making, Bill C-22 was it. Claiming that Canada was one of the last of the G-8 countries to have mandatory 'currency transaction reporting' for large and/or suspicious financial transactions, Canada basically *had* to enact this legislation.[12] This legislation made mandatory the reporting of suspicious transactions, created a cross-border reporting requirement, and also created FINTRAC (Financial Transactions Reports Analysis Centre of Canada).

Six years later, PCMLTFA was amended a second time with Bill C-25 (*An Act to amend the Proceeds of Crime [Money Laundering] and Terrorist Financing Act and the Income Tax Act and to make a consequential amendment to another Act*). This 2006 amendment to the PCMLTFA broadened the record-keeping and reporting measures applicable to financial institutions and intermediaries.[13] Under this legislation, money services, businesses, and foreign-exchange dealers had to register, and it allowed FINTRAC to disclose additional information to law enforcement and intelligence agencies. In addition to other enhancements, the legislation broadened the ability of Canadian agencies to share information with their foreign counterparts.

Second, while the above series of legislation and amendments targeted proceeds of crime and terrorist financing, another series of bills targeted criminal groups. In 1997, a significantly new direction in legislation took the form of Bill C-95, known as the anti-gang legislation. This 1997 legislation introduced into Canadian law the notion of 'participation in a criminal organization' as a triggering mechanism for additional powers for the justice system and enhanced sanctions for the convicted.

Bill C-95 was followed by Bill C-24 in 2002 (*An Act to amend the Criminal Code [Organized Crime and Law Enforcement]*). Bill C-24 served as a confirmation of the government's commitment to the 'membership' perspective. The enhanced legislation (C-24) was in part a response to concerns from law enforcement that the requirements under C-95 (what was called the 5-5-5 rule)[14] were too restrictive and hence too difficult to satisfy.

Canada did not choose to focus on criminal organizations in a vacuum; rather this approach was part of the United Nations Convention against Transnational Organized Crime, negotiated via a prolonged process in which Canada played a significant role. International pressures on Canada combined with three domestic events. First, during a federal election, Quebec demanded that the federal government intervene in Quebec's 'bloody biker war' between the Rock Machine and the Hells Angels. Second, this political demand peaked following the accidental death in 1995 of Daniel Desrochers, an 11-year-old boy who was caught in a biker bombing. The third event, which added to the pressure for what the media was calling 'anti-biker legislation', was the attempted murder of Montreal journalist Michel Auger, who was well-known for his reporting on the biker wars. Throughout this period, the police in Quebec, with the support of the Canadian Association of Chiefs of Police, lobbied for stronger powers to better enable the police to go after the outlaw bike clubs.

The new legislation (C-24) brought Canada more in line with the UN Convention against Transnational Organized Crime. Canada ratified the Convention in May 2002, and the Canadian legislation was proclaimed in January of that same year. Article 5 of the UN Convention against Transnational Organized Crime outlines what countries have agreed to bring into force in terms of the 'criminalization of participation in an organized criminal group' (United Nations, 2000, p. 3). Under the UN Convention, countries have agreed to criminalize the conduct of 'organized criminal groups'. The Convention used terminology that described the acts of participating in, facilitating, counselling, and/or actually committing a crime involving an organized criminal group. The Canadian legislation follows the dictates of the UN approach; it

- reduces the required number of members in the criminal organization from five to three;

- largely removes the requirement that the criminal organization have an ongoing pattern of criminality;

- increases the number of crimes that fall under the proceeds of crime legislation from what began as a 'selective' list of 24 offences to what are approximately 40 types of 'enterprise' crimes—to include most indictable offences;

- includes a 'justification scheme' (an authorizing mechanism) for law enforcers who commit certain acts that would otherwise be considered illegal during investigations; and

- broadens the forfeiture powers to include the profits of criminal organizations as well as the property that was used in a crime.

Three new offences, now found under section 467.11, 12, and 13 of the Criminal Code, were created:

- *participating* in activities of criminal organizations;

- *commission* of an offence for a criminal organization; and

- *instructing* the commission of an offence for a criminal organization.

In order for a person to be found guilty of the *participating* offence, it is not necessary for the prosecution to prove that the criminal organization actually committed the indictable offence, that the participation actually enhanced the ability of the criminal organization to commit the act, or that the accused was aware of the specific act that he or she might have been facilitating. Similarly, in cases involving the charge of 'commission of an offence for a criminal organization', it is not necessary for the prosecutor to prove that the accused knew the identity of any of the persons who constituted the criminal organization. And in the third new offence, 'instructing the commission of an offence for a criminal organization', it is not necessary for the prosecution to prove that an offence was actually committed, that the accused instructed a particular person to commit an offence, or that the accused knew the identity of all of the persons who constituted the criminal organization.

In response to the criticism that section 467.11(2) of the Criminal Code was overly broad, the Crown argued that the provisions were consistent with the provisions adopted by the UN Convention against Transnational Organized Crime. However, a comparison between the Canadian legislation and the UN Convention reveals some significant differences. The UN Convention requires that the prosecution prove that the accused took an active part in the activities of the organized group with the knowledge that his or her participation would contribute to the achievement of the criminal objective. Article 5(1)(a)(ii) of the UN Convention uses the words 'takes an active part' in the criminal activities or other activities of the organized criminal group.[15]

In contrast, the judge in *R. v. Beauchamp* (p. 30, para. 94) stated that Parliament was entitled to use general language, 'to rely on the courts to interpret its legislation harmoniously in accordance with the scheme of the *Criminal Code*, and also to avoid an unjust, inequitable or an absurd result.' The policy objective was to capture individuals who participated in or contributed to any activity of a criminal organization, no matter how that group might be structured or how diverse the range of 'participation' might be. A series of cases that attempted to challenge the constitutionality of this broad and arguably vague legislation revealed a willingness on the part of the courts to affirm Parliament's ability to leave room for interpretation on the part of judges. The prevailing view was that it was Parliament's intention that the definitions be broad so as to adapt to the ever-changing, fluid nature of organized crime.

BOX 12.1

R. v. Lindsay (2005 CanLII 24240 [ONSC] and Appeal 2009 ONCA 532) remains the important test case for the breadth and vagueness of this legislation. It was the first case of its kind in Ontario to utilize the amended sections of the Criminal Code that came into force as a result of the passage of Bill C-24. This case involved two men—Steven Patrick Lindsay and Raymond Lawrence Bonner, who were allegedly Hells Angels members. They were accused of attempting to extort $75,000 from a businessman in Barrie, Ontario. The accused were jointly charged with committing extortion for the benefit of, or at the direction of, or in association with a criminal organization, contrary to section 467.12 of the Criminal Code. While the two men never mentioned that they were members of the Hells Angels—and, in fact, never mentioned the Angels—the biker patch was visible on the back of their jackets when they walked away from the house in Barrie. The judge determined that the wearing of the jackets could be construed as evidence that the offence was committed 'in association' with a criminal organization.

In Toronto, 'Project Impact' involved the alleged 'Malvern Crew' and the rival 'GallowayBoyz'. Sixty-four individuals were arrested, and more than 40 accused were charged with 'participation in a criminal organization' by the Metropolitan Toronto Police and the Project Impact Task Force. The claim was made that the Malvern Crew was a criminal organization involved in drug trafficking, firearms, robbery, and attempted murder. The arguments that supported the classification of these gangs as criminal organizations was built on a 'tick-mark' method whereby separate characteristics were alleged to exist and were claimed to indicate a structured criminal operation involving

- turf/territory;
- nicknames;
- associates and wannabe members;

- rank order with a leadership structure (senior members 'instructing' youth members);
- hierarchy with networks of 'lesser' members; and
- emphasis on image and potential to intimidate (see Burnstein & Orlova, 2008).

This shift in policy, which now brings numerous 'participants' into the court charged with criminal organization offences, has had significant consequences for the justice system. The arrests of members of the Malvern Crew and similar 'anti-gang round-ups' illustrate the potential size of some of these mega-cases. While the courts defend this breadth, along with the lack of specificity as to when a person is either in or out of a criminal organization,[16] the resources required to transcribe wiretap conversations and to provide defendants with some form of defence are proving to be prohibitive. These costs, rather than Charter or constitutional considerations, may serve to place limits on the use of the legislation. Meanwhile, even as some critics continued to question the direction of the legislation, the government decided that it required strengthening.

The get-tough policy direction continued. In November 2005, Bill C-53,[17] commonly referred to as the Reverse Onus Forfeiture Act, was passed. The notion of a 'pattern' (or as found in the US RICO Statute, a 'pattern of racketeering activity') had been removed between the two versions of the Canadian criminal organizations bills (C-95 and C-24). It reappeared with Bill C-53. The legislation states that if there has been a 'pattern of criminal activity' (i.e., one criminal organization offence or two serious offences, indictable and punishable with more than five years) *and* income or assets *and* involvement in criminal organization or drug offences, then the property shall be forfeited if the state is satisfied on a balance of probabilities that legitimate income cannot account for the offender's property.

Critics raised a number of constitutional concerns, including broader issues regarding the growth of these reverse-onus powers. Traditionally, the Canadian justice system had guarded the principle that the state had to prove guilt or, put another way, that those who were charged did not have to prove their innocence. In addition, the justice system typically resists the notion of double punishments for the same offence. Given the breadth of these forfeitures and the fear that property unconnected to the current offence may be scooped up, critics claimed that the sanctions constituted cruel and unusual punishment. They argued that there was a mere pretence that the forfeiture of assets was not a punishment in addition to other punishments arising for the same offence.

By the mid-2000s, the policies regarding organized crime control had changed significantly from the 'original' 1989 proceeds of crime legislation, which had listed 24 offenses plus designated drug offenses as falling under the new legislative approach to combatting organized crime. The 1983 Canadian *Enterprise Crime* document had taken the view that criminal conduct by any number of criminal groups was to be considered 'organized crime' (although the report favoured the term 'enterprise crime'). White-collar crimes, financial frauds, political corruption, and illegal manipulation by labour unions were all to be considered, as were drug trafficking and other more traditional organized crimes. Twenty years later, the policing and legislative focus had become much more 'criminal membership' focused. While traditional organized criminals remained a concern, gangs came under greater scrutiny. Certain highly recognizable criminal groups, such as bikers and street gangs, became prime targets, with the public support for this enforcement heightened following a number of high-profile gang shootings. Hence 'gangs'—especially street gangs—became the target of choice.

The threat that required extraordinary powers now took the form of street criminals who used guns. Several separate legislative initiatives made the link between organized crime and street gangs and served to justify the various 'enhanced' penalties. In May 2006, Bill C-10, *An Act to amend the Criminal Code (minimum penalties for offences involving firearms)*, received first reading in the House of Commons. The primary objectives of Bill C-10 were to introduce mandatory minimum terms of imprisonment for individuals who committed serious or repeat firearm offences, and to create the new offences of break and enter to steal a firearm and robbery to steal a firearm. In November 2006, Bill C-35, *An Act to amend the Criminal Code (reverse onus in bail hearings for firearm-related offences)*, was tabled and as the name indicates, it proposed a reverse onus in bail hearings for certain offences involving firearms. Both of these bills came into force in January 2011.[18] The policies behind these new initiatives have been criticized by practitioners within the courts and the prison system, but arguments about the counterproductivity of these measures seemingly have had no impact on the federal government. The expertise of the officials working within the justice system and the empirical evidence that refutes arguments of deterrence have been ignored (Gabor & Crutcher, 2002; Gendreau & Goggin, 1999). While it is still too early to know the outcome, in February 2012 an Ontario Superior Court judge struck down a mandatory minimum sentence for a first offence of possessing a loaded firearm, ruling that the circumstances of the case did not warrant a three-year penitentiary sentence. The Judge argued that to impose such a sentence for what she called a 'foolish act' would constitute 'cruel and unusual punishment,' and would breach the charter.

With all of these legislative powers, it was still deemed essential to widen even further the swath of offences to which the powers could be applied. In August 2010, the federal government announced new regulations that designated several 'signature activities' of criminal groups as being 'serious offences'. Before these changes, the criminal acts perpetrated by criminal organizations had to meet the definition of 'serious offence' under subsection 467.1(1) of the Criminal Code. The government's concern was that some criminal activities of so-called criminal organizations failed to meet this criterion because the offences were not 'indictable offences punishable by sentences of five years or more'. In those cases, the police and prosecutors could not use the many special procedures available in organized crime investigations and prosecutions in areas such as peace bonds, bail, wiretaps, proceeds of crime, and parole eligibility.[19]

According to Justice Minister Rob Nicholson, these 'loop-holes' had to be closed. The answer was fairly simple: designate a number of additional offences as being 'signature activities' of organized criminals and thus give police more power to employ wiretaps and other investigative measures, while also lengthening jail terms for acts linked to organized crime. The signature activities (now designated 'serious offences') add a further 11 specific offences, including

- keeping a common gaming or betting house;
- betting, pool-selling, and bookmaking;
- committing offences in relation to lotteries and games of chance;
- cheating while playing a game or in holding the stakes for a game or in betting;
- keeping a common bawdy house; and
- various offences in the Controlled Drugs and Substances Act relating to the trafficking, importing, exporting, or production of certain drugs.

Noting the cuts in programs that focus on crime prevention and treatment, critics such as Liberal MP Mark Holland argued that the various crime bills were diversions to take the public's attention away from more controversial incidents: 'All the things that we know work, we know save money, save lives . . . they ignore. . . . This government, any time it gets into trouble . . . starts dumping on the table a rash of crime bills and more often than not, they're not thought through. This is about changing the channel'.[20]

DOLLARS, RESULTS, AND CHARTER PROTECTIONS

The policies that drive legislation and the enforcement strategies pertaining to organized crime are important because of the costs involved, as well as the additional impacts that some of the responses are having on the justice system and on the rights of the accused. Fighting organized crime is not cheap, and the costs extend beyond mere dollars. To lend a scientific appearance to the government's strategies, Public Safety Canada designed a Results-Based Management and Accountability Framework (RMAF)[21] to evaluate 'success' against a number of desired outcomes, including

- enhanced ability to investigate/prosecute organized crime offences/groups;
- increased knowledge and understanding of organized crime issues/tools;
- improved detection/targeting of organized crime offences/groups;
- enhanced partnerships (desired outcome not illustrated on the logic model);
- effective investigations (national/international);

- improved case preparation;
- effective prosecutions;
- disruption, dismantlement, deterrence, and incapacitation of criminal organizations; and
- enhanced public safety and security from organized crime.

While one might assume that a greater ability to detect and prosecute crime groups and to prepare better cases with more effective investigations is advantageous, what is not measured in the results-based framework is the *actual impact* in terms of a reduction in the amount of organized crime activity. One somewhat simpler measurement might tell a clearer story: Are illicit drugs harder to buy? Are they more expensive? Is the quality less pure? The answer to all of these questions is *no*. Law enforcement efforts may be accomplishing many things, but reducing the amount of drug trafficking or causing a significant reduction in money laundering might not be among those successes.

Rights and Charter protections must compete with these enforcement strategies. The philosophy of 'rounding up the group' and putting them out of business, together with seizing and forfeiting their assets, has had the result that organized crime investigations now tend to turn into mega-trials. What characterizes these cases is the expense, the length of the processes, the often dubious results, and the impact such cases have on the criminal justice system.

Protections such as the disclosure of all relevant information to the defence—as required following the *Stinchcombe* decision[22]—become a massive undertaking. According to the Department of Justice, '[D]isclosure ranged between thousands and tens of thousands of pages, although five prosecutors said that they had files with hundreds of thousands of pages.'[23] Yvan Poulin, a prosecutor with the Public Prosecution Service of Canada (PPSC), testified before the Standing Committee on Justice and Human Rights:

> Whenever we are dealing with organized crime, it automatically means there will be a mega-case. . . . It is thus that the gathering of sufficient evidence generally, and more often than not, requires very lengthy investigations involving the use of a whole gamut of tools that go all the way from simple shadowing to electronic surveillance, including work by undercover agents. The use of these investigation methods, given their nature and the duration of the investigations themselves, will necessarily generate a tremendous volume of evidence that must be collated, classified and disclosed. . . . The challenge therefore is to respect the principles set out in the *Stinchcombe* decision in a context in which the volume of evidence is, in every case, absolutely gigantic.[24]

Again, the issues that relate to mega-trials extend beyond the costs. The court process cannot handle the large number of suspects who are arrested at one time.

Given such constraints, the common scenario is for large numbers of charges to be laid, many charges to be dropped, some suspects to plead guilty, and a very few to be moved through the formal justice system. During this process, the criminal justice system is critically disrupted.

EVIDENCE OF SUCCESS VERSUS PROPAGANDA

Organized crime will never be eliminated. All comments to the contrary are either politically motivated or naive. The most that governments and law enforcement can do is decrease the demand for illicit goods and services, increase the risk of detection with some hope of deterring some people some of the time, and invest in crime-prevention programs. While one might argue that very sophisticated organized criminals cannot be persuaded to take up legitimate work, the same is not necessarily true of the various street-gang members who now fall under the more sweeping criminal organizations umbrella.

Criminal justice researchers generally agree that get-tough policies have little to do with either reducing crime or keeping society secure. It is notable that the backgrounder[25] to the Canadian government's legislation on stiffer penalties does a fairly thorough job of outlining why the legislation is inappropriate. It states that the existing research generally does not support the use of mandatory minimum sentences for the purpose of deterrence or for the purpose of reducing sentencing disparities (Gabor & Crutcher, 2002; Cohen, 2006). Research has found little difference in general recidivism rates regardless of the length of incarceration or whether the offender was given a prison or community sanction. In fact, some evidence indicates that prison produced slight increases in recidivism (Gendreau & Goggin, 2001; Roach, 2006), and therefore incarcerating offenders for longer periods results in increased prison costs that are not necessarily offset by any reduction in crime rates and recidivism.

However, research findings are currently having little to no impact on federal government policy-making—neither in relation to organized crime nor in relation to any other criminal justice issue. In response to receiving a briefing note from Correctional Service of Canada (CSC) officials pertaining to the likely negative impact on the prison system of some proposed new legislation, Prime Minister Harper stated that the hardest thing he has had to deal with is to 'get the bureaucrats on board'.[26] This frustration apparently stemmed from receiving research-based information from those people closest to the actual issues that conflicted with the get-tough political policies that he wished to introduce. Harper felt justified in publicly expressing his frustration with the 'kind of advice he has been receiving from the public service' and with the 'practical difficulties of working with bureaucrats' and 'getting them to move in the direction you want them to move'.[27]

Harper's direction was clear. On Monday, 10 January 2011, Conservative MPs travelled to their various ridings to announce more than $150 million in new spending for expansions to eight prisons, a plan that will add 634 beds. Laurie

Hawn, parliamentary secretary to Defence Minister Peter MacKay, said that the announcements were part of the government's tough-on-crime stance: 'We believe in spending money in a focused way to keep Canadians safe and keep our communities safe, and that's what this is all about.'[28] The total of this focused spending is estimated to be in excess of $601 million, to create 2,552 additional beds at institutions.[29] Criminologists responded with their research-based findings that refute the merits of turning to the prison system for all of the answers to crime. Quoting Irvin Waller, a crime-prevention expert at the University of Ottawa: 'It's going to cost you seven times as much to reduce crime through adding prison capacity as it would to invest in programs that teach effective parenting, programs that help kids get back into school.' Even the opposition parties demonstrated a degree of opposition to these measures—but their 'weak' opposition seemed largely restricted to the costs while acknowledging that the costs seemed particularly inappropriate 'when crime rates continue to drop and we are in bad economic times'.[30]

Advice from researchers across the country and from within government departments may become even easier to ignore in the future with the announcement that the census long form, which provides researchers with essential data related to many issues, including crime, is being eliminated. The head of Statistics Canada, Munir Sheikh, quit in protest over the Conservative government's decision to replace the long-form census questionnaire with a voluntary 'household' survey, warning that Ottawa's proposal for a voluntary survey won't work: 'Sheikh's resignation means the ballooning drama at the usually staid and low-profile agency is now a full-fledged political crisis for the Conservatives, who have been accused of turning their backs on evidence-based research.'[31]

During the fall of 2011, with a majority government, the Conservatives did not need to worry about the critics. With little allowance for debate, they introduced Bill C-10. This tough-on-crime omnibus bill, originally titled the Safe Streets and Communities Act, consisted of nine separate bills that previously had failed to pass.[32] In response to a Statistics Canada report (1 December 2011) that indicated that police-reported crime, including violent crime, was down significantly, Justice Minister Rob Nicholson stated that those numbers were not relevant to his government's legislation: 'We don't govern on the basis of statistics' (*Globe and Mail*, 2 December 2011). The Canadian Civil Liberties Association referred to the omnibus bill as 'Unwise, Unjust, Unconstitutional' (CCLA, 2011). Irwin Cotler summed it up as follows:

> If there is one common feature of these bills, it's the ignoring, marginalizing and mischaracterizing of the evidence. The Government holds out the crime bill as a purported means of crime reduction, yet studies show that the resulting prison overcrowding and use of mandatory-minimum sentences will ultimately result in more crime.[33]

The issue of evidence to support policy is not a Canadian problem alone, especially when policy decisions increasingly relate to justifying policy directives and agreements signed elsewhere. International pressures on Canada may be based on quite unattainable objectives, or even worse, ulterior objectives. The 2010 WikiLeaks included confidential government cables sent by Secretary of State Hillary Clinton and senior State Department officials that indicated that US-driven policy measures designed to control money laundering and terrorist financing are having a less positive impact than hoped—and less impact than their persistent rhetoric claims. The leaked cables catalogue a list of laundering methods that are not being curbed by the measures put in place under the various anti-laundering legislation and policies described in this chapter. Likewise, some countries have begun to resist some of the policies, accusing American officials of being heavy-handed and biased against Arab charities or individuals where evidence of wrongdoing is questionable or non-existent.[34] Two possible dangers require careful monitoring: first, a false belief in the unproven effectiveness of the various enforcement 'wars' (on crime in general, on organized crime, on money laundering, and on terrorist financing); and second, the possibility that some policies are driven by political agendas that have little to do with crime control. The costs involved must be matched with a clear appreciation of what is gained.

A contradiction appears in the advocated policies of the United Nations—a contradiction that is now replicated by the organized-crime policies of Western governments. In 2002, the UN carried out an international survey that created a typology of organized crime groups. This research emphasized the diversity in organized crime operations, including diversity of structure and operation.[35] Rather than rigid organized crime families and hierarchical structures, organized crime in some jurisdictions, and for some criminal markets, was found to consist of loose networks with the fluid involvement of participants. And yet international organizations such as the UN via the Convention against Transnational Organized Crime and the FATF process were instrumental in pushing forward harmonization policies that required the passing of legislation to criminalize specific crimes, including participating in organized criminal groups.[36]

Policies, legislation, and enforcement efforts intertwine—one driving the other two but not necessarily in any well-considered order. The result is a self-fulfilling prophesy in the sense that if legislation is created that works best with street gangs who announce their membership affiliations, or with outlaw biker gangs who wear their 'patches', or with remnants of Mafia families, then those groups become the target of law enforcement and the arrests become the proof that they do, in fact, account for the organized crime problems that the country experiences.

When people began to appreciate the reality of loose criminal networks, the blurring of legitimate and illegitimate operations, and the range of 'harms' not captured by traditional conceptions of organized crime, the international community moved instead to criminalize 'criminal associations' and proceed along what critics might argue to be the well-worn path that depicted organized criminals as distinguishable 'bad guys' in a capitalist sea of 'good guys'. Therefore, while the international community has become more harmonized, it remains unclear whether that harmonization is moving in the correct direction. Missed are the fluid networks of the more sophisticated criminal operations that may involve participants who are uncomfortably close to elites within politics, professional groups, police, and the financial establishment.

There will be no one legislative or enforcement answer to organized crimes, and many so-called organized criminals may be indistinguishable from more ordinary criminals. Traditional police work, together with a focus on demand reduction, may still be the best solution. However, policies pertaining to this topic will continue to be politicized. Politics, both domestic and international, will continue to play a significant role in the framing of the organized crime threats, and political parties will likely continue to speak with one voice on the need to get ever tougher on these criminals.

CRITICAL THINKING QUESTIONS

1. What potential biases upon the policy-making process are inherent in each 'sphere of influence on policy-making' (Figure 12.1) if a priority is given to any one of these influences?

2. Pressures exerted by the international community (as expressed via the UN, FATF, International Monetary Fund [IMF], World Bank, etc.) are encouraging a harmonization of policies and practices pertaining to the enforcement of transnational crimes. Discuss the gains and risks of this trend.

3. Organized crime appears to be an excellent topic for get-tough legislation—why? Discuss the potential impact of this legislation and policing strategies on the wider criminal justice system.

4. Discuss the interplay between politics and organized crime policy in Canada.

5. What are the advantages and disadvantages of using an organized crime policy framework to address street crime in Canada?

NOTES

1 See Bala (2005) as well as a discussion raised by Rochelle Direnfeld in an unpublished LLM paper looking at youth justice reform in Canada, submitted to Osgoode Professional Development, Summer 2010. However, debate only goes so far, and the party in power has a dominant say. Most recently, we see a Conservative influence in the naming of some of the recent bills. For example, Bill C-4, 'Sebastien's Law' (stemming from the killing of Sebastien Lacasse), was titled *Protecting the public from violent young offenders.* The offender in this case had already been sentenced as an adult and before final passage of this 'tougher' legislation.

2 The Financial Action Task Force (FATF) is a body created in 1989 by the Group of 7 (G-7) to address money laundering.

Each year an annual report is produced. The 40 recommendations made by the FATF serve as guidelines for the appropriate response to money laundering. This consensus-oriented body has turned to 'name and shame' techniques to encourage countries to adhere to its recommendations.

3　Beare (2003, pp. xiv–xv).

4　M. Woodiwiss, Transnational organized crime: The strange career of an American concept, in Beare (2003, pp. 3–34). See also Woodiwiss (2001); Naylor (1999, 2004, 2006).

5　See, for example, M. Beare, Introduction; M. Woodiwiss, Transnational organized crime; V. Mitsilegas, From national to global, from empirical to legal: The ambivalent concept of transnational organized crime; and R.T. Naylor, Follow-the-money methods in crime control policy—all in Beare (2003).

6　Brodeur (1992) originally appeared in 1983: J.P. Brodeur, High policing and law policing, *Social Problems*, *30*, 507–20.

7　The famous 1997 Canadian Bre-X case (which proved to be a fraudulently 'salted' gold mine in Borneo) might serve as an example. The case became notorious because of the astronomical rise in the price of Bre-X gold shares following the rumours of a massive gold reserve. Many powerful players and many countries were involved, but then the geologist, Michael de Guzman, exited his helicopter (250 metres in the air at the time), an evident suicide. Ten years later, in 2007, Bre-X's chief geologist, John Felderhof, went on trial in Canada but was acquitted of securities fraud. While he had apparently sold his stockholdings for $84 million in the months before the scandal hit, thousands of investors were not so fortunate.

8　Quote is taken from British Columbia, Ministry of the Attorney General, *The business of crime: An evaluation of the American Racketeer Influenced and Corrupt Organizations Statute (RICO) from a Canadian Perspective* (Victoria, BC, 1980), 2.

9　Taken from a transcript of proceedings that included a presentation made by Blakey at a solicitor general–hosted symposium on enterprise crime in Ottawa, 24–5 June 1982. Quoted in Beare (1996, p. 150).

10　*Royal Bank of Canada v. Bourque et al.*, [1984] 38 C.R. (3rd) 363.

11　First known as *An Act to facilitate combating the laundering of proceeds of crime*, it was amended post-9/11 and retitled the Proceeds of Crime (Money Laundering) and Terrorist Financing Act in 2001.

12　36th Parliament, 2nd Session, *Edited Hansard*, No. 79, 5 April 2000 [1525–725], and No. 80, 6 April 2000 [1110–250].

13　http://www.publicsafety.gc.ca/prg/le/oc/_fl/ogcrime06_e.pdf

14　Five members involved in crimes over a period of five years and committing indictable offences serious enough to be punishable by five years in prison if convicted.

15　See *R. v. Beauchamp*, [2009] ONSC, pp. 20–1, paras. 60–4, [2009 CanLII 37720 (ONSC)].

16　Legislation has withstood challenges in *R. v. Carrier*, *R. v. Beauchamp*; and *R. v. Lindsay*—but not uniformly; see the case from British Columbia, *R. v. Terezakis*, [2007] BCCA 384.

17　*An Act to amend the Criminal Code (Proceeds of Crime) and the Controlled Drugs and Substances Act and to make consequential amendments to another Act.*

18　See http://www2.parl.gc.ca/sites/lop/legisinfo/index.asp?Language=E&Chamber=N&StartList=A&EndList=Z&Session=14&Type=0&Scope=I&query=4881&List=stat

19 Government of Canada enacts new regulations to help fight organized crime, 4 August 2010, http://www.justice.gc.ca/eng/news-nouv/nr-cp/2010/doc_32531.html. According to the *Canada Gazette*, the official publication of the government, these regulations had been made on 13 July by order-in-council. Terry Stratton website: http://terrystratton.ca/EN/6372/116527

20 Organized crime law changes unveiled, last updated 4 August 2010, 11:41 p.m., at http://www.cbc.ca/canada/nova-scotia/story/2010/08/04/tories-organized-crime-nicholson.html#ixzz17Le5DXzO

21 See Public Safety Canada (2007/08), Summative evaluation of the measures to combat organized crime initiative: Final summary report, http://www.public-safety.gc.ca/abt/dpr/eval/mcoc-mlcco-eng.aspx

22 *Stinchcombe*, [1991] 3 S.C.R. 326 is the landmark Supreme Court of Canada decision on the disclosure of evidence in a trial.

23 Measures to combat organized crime: *Mid-term evaluation technical report*, p. 25, http://www.justice.gc.ca/eng/pi/eval/rep-rap/04/mcoc-mlco/tech/tech.pdf

24 40th Parliament, 3rd Session, Standing Committee on Justice and Human Rights, Evidence, Contents, 15 April 2010, at 1110, http://www2.parl.gc.ca/HousePublications/Publication.aspx?DocId=4423055&Language=E&Mode=1&Parl=40&Ses=3#T1110

25 Bill C-10: *An Act to amend the Criminal Code (minimum penalties for offences involving firearms) and to make consequential amendment to another Act*. Prepared by Wade Riordan Raaflaub Law and Government Division, 22 February 2007, revised 6 June 2007. http://www2.parl.gc.ca/Sites/LOP/LegislativeSummaries/Bills_ls.asp?lang=E&ls=c10&source=library_prb&Parl=39&Ses=1

26 CSC is one of the few divisions within the federal government that has been able to retain a strong research in-house capability and therefore is able to provide empirically based policy advice to ministers.

27 *Toronto Star* (2007).

28 CTV.ca News Staff, 10 January 2011, 9:42:57 p.m., Government pledges millions for prison expansions. At http://www.ctv.ca/CTVNews/TopStories/20110110/prison-upgrades-110110/

29 Gloria Galloway. Government faces hard sell for thousands of new jail cells, *Globe and Mail*. 10 January 2011, 9:08 p.m. At http://www.theglobeandmail.com/news/politics/government-faces-hard-sell-for-thousands-of-new-jail-cells/article1864948/

30 Ibid.

31 Bruce Campion-Smith and Richard J. Brennan. StatsCan chief quits over census furor. *Toronto Star*, 22 July 2010, http://www.thestar.com/news/canada/census/article/838401--census-furor-grows-engulfing-statistics-canada

32 See CBC News, 21 September 2011, 9 key elements of the crime bill. The full title of Bill C-10 is *An Act to enact the Justice for Victims of Terrorism Act and to amend the State Immunity Act, the Criminal Code, the Controlled Drugs and Substances Act, the Corrections and Conditional Release Act, the Youth Criminal Justice Act, the Immigration and Refugee Protection Act and other Acts.*

33 Irwin Cotler, member of Parliament for Mount Royal and the Liberal critic for justice and human rights: *Montreal Gazette*, 4 November, 2011; quoted in Canadian Centre for Policy Alternatives, 7 November 2011, Bill C-10 fact sheet.

34 Eric Lichtblau and Eric Schmitt. Cash flow to terrorists evades U.S. efforts. *New York Times*, 5 December 2010. http://www.nytimes.com/2010/12/06/world/

middleeast/06wikileaks-financing.
html?_r=1&ref=world

35 UNCICP (2002).

36 Article 5, p. 3. Other aspects of the UN
Convention included a focus on money
laundering, corruption, and obstruction
of justice. In addition, banks were to
keep accurate records and have them

available for law enforcement, and a
greater emphasis was put on international
co-operation, including with regard to
extradition, mutual legal assistance, and
information exchanges. http://www.
uncjin.org/Documents/Conventions/
dcatoc/final_documents_2/convention_
eng.pdf

REFERENCES

Alati, D. (2010). *Responding to global problems
locally: Understanding and evaluating the
process behind Canada's domestic response to
terrorism.* Unpublished LLM thesis,
Osgoode Hall Law School.

Australia, Queensland Crime Commission
and Queensland Police Service. (1999).
*Project Krystal: A strategic assessment of
organised crime in Queensland.* http://
www.cmc.qld.gov.au/data/portal/
00000005/content/
1865100114136453 9740.pdf

Bala. N. (2005). The development of
Canada's youth justice law. In K. Camp-
bell (Ed.), *Understanding youth justice in
Canada.* Toronto: Pearson/Prentice Hall.

Beare, M.E. (1996). *Criminal conspiracies.*
Toronto: Nelson Canada.

Beare, M., & Naylor, T. (1999). *Major issues
relating to organized crime: Within the
context of economic relationships.* Law
Commission of Canada, pp. 10–12.

Beare M.E. (Ed.). (2003). *Critical reflections on
transnational organized crime, money
laundering, and corruption.* Toronto:
University of Toronto Press.

Beare, M., & Schneider, S. (2007). *Money
laundering in Canada: Chasing dirty and
dangerous dollars.* Toronto: University of
Toronto Press.

British Columbia. (1980). *The business of crime:
An evaluation of the American Racketeer
Influenced and Corrupt Organizations
Statute (RICO) from a Canadian perspective.*

Victoria: Ministry of the Attorney
General.

Brodeur, J.P. (1992). High policing and low
policing. *Social Problems, 30,* 507–20.
Revised 1982 ASC paper: High Policing
and Law Policing. In K.McCormick
& L.Visano, *Understanding policing*
(pp. 277–99). Toronto: Canadian
Scholars' Press, 1992.

Burstein, P., & Alexandra, O. (2008).
Criminal organization legislation:
Politics and practice. In M.E. Beare
(Ed.), *Honouring social justice: Honouring
Dianne Martin* (pp. 251–70). Toronto:
University of Toronto Press.

Campion-Smith, B. & Brennan R.J. (2010,
July 22). Stats Can chief quits over
census furor. *Toronto Star.* http://www.
thestar.com/news/canada/census/
article/838401—census-furor-
grows-engulfing-statistics-canada

Canada, Department of Justice. (1983,
June-13). *Enterprise Crime Study report.*
Prepared by the Federal-Provincial
Ministers Responsible for Criminal
Justice Working Group. Ottawa.

Canada, Government of Canada. (2010).
Policy Research Initiative. Canada @150
research report. Part III: Canada's Public
Service in 2017 (full report found at
http://www.policyresearch.gc.ca/page.
asp?pagenm=01-toc; Part III at http://
www.policyresearch.gc.ca/page.
asp?pagenm=21-part3).

Canada, Statistics Canada. (2011, December 1).
Study: Perceptions of personal safety and

crime. http://www.statcan.gc.ca/daily-quotidien/111201/dq111201a-eng.htm

Canadian Association of Journalists. (2010). An open letter to Canadian journalists; website first released 11 June 2010. Retrieved 30 August 2010 from http://www.caj.ca/?p=692

Canadian Centre for Policy Alternatives (CCPA). (2011, November 7). Bill C-10 fact sheet. Manitoba office. http://www.policyalternatives.ca/sites/default/files/uploads/publications/Manitoba%20Office/2011/11/bill%20C-10%20nov%202011.pdf

Canadian Press. (2010, May 25). CIDA abortion advice ignored. http://www.theglobeandmail.com/news/politics/ottawa-ignored-cidas-advice-on-abortion-documents-reveal/article1579467/

CCLA (Canadian Civil Liberties Association). (2011). Omnibus crime Bill C-10. http://ccla.org/omnibus-crime-bill-c-10/

Cohen, G.J. (2006, January 9). Mandatory minimums not the solution. *Law Times* [Aurora, ON].

Dorn, N. (2009). The end of organized crime in the European Union. *Crime Law and Social Change, 51*, 283–95.

Gabor, T., & Crutcher, N. (2002, January). *Mandatory minimum penalties: Their effects on crime, sentencing disparities, and justice system expenditures.* Prepared for Research and Statistics Division, Department of Justice Canada. Ottawa.

Galloway, G. (2011, January 10). Government faces hard sell for thousands of new jail cells. *Globe and Mail.* At http://www.theglobeandmail.com/news/politics/government-faces-hard-sell-for-thousands-of-new-jail-cells/article1864948/

Gendreau, P., & Goggin, C. (1999). *The effects of prison sentences on recidivism.* Prepared for Solicitor General Canada. Ottawa, 1999.

Globe and Mail. (2000, February 26). Canadian mob kingpins jailed, A1;

Lengthy prison terms knock down untouchables, A3.

———. (2011, December 2). Though few fear crime, Conservatives move ahead with bill, A6.

Lichtblau, E. & Schmitt E. (2010, December 5). Cash flow to terrorists evades U.S. efforts. *New York Times.* http://www.nytimes.com/2010/12/06/world/middleeast/06wikileaks-financing.html?_r=1&ref=world

Makin, K. (2009, November 27). Canadian crime and American punishment. *Globe and Mail.*

Mitsilegas, V. (2000). *Money laundering counter-measures in the European Union: A new paradigm of security governance versus fundamental legal principles.* Ph.D. thesis, University of Edinburgh.

National Post. (2000, February 26). World's no. 1 mob chief undone by a phone card, A1.

Naylor, R.T. (1999). *Patriots and profiteers: On economic warfare, embargo busting and state-sponsored crime.* Toronto: McClelland & Stewart.

———. (2004). *The wages of crime: Black markets, illegal finance, and the underworld economy.* Ithaca: NY: Cornell University Press.

———. (2006). *Satanic purses: Money, myth, and misinformation.* Montreal: McGill-Queen's University Press.

Peters, B.G., & Pierre, J. (Eds.). (2004). *Politicization of the civil service in comparative perspective: The quest for control.* London: Routledge. http://site.ebrary.com.ezproxy.library.yorku.ca/lib/oculyork/docDetail.action?docID=10272602

Roach, K.W. (2006, February). Responding to gun violence. *Criminal Law Quarterly, 51*(2), 129–32.

Savoie, D. (2004). The search for a responsive bureaucracy in Canada. In Peters & Pierre (2004, p. 142). http://site.ebrary.

com.ezproxy.library.yorku.ca/lib/
oculyork/docDetail.action?docID=
10272602

Toronto Star. (2000, February 26). Drug lord
pleads guilty, A2.

———. (2007, January 11). Jailers fear PM's
justice overhaul, by T. Maccharles, A1, 22.

United Nations Centre for International
Crime Prevention (UNCICP). (2002).
*Assessing transnational organized crime:
Results of a pilot survey of 40 selected
transnational organized criminal groups in
16 countries.* Crime Reduction and
Analysis Branch Centre for International
Crime Prevention, United Nations

Office at Vienna, draft, August 2002;
published also in *Trends in Organized
Crime,* Winter 2000, *6*(2).

United Nations. (2000). *Convention against
transnational organized crime.* UN Office
for Drug Control and Crime Prevention.

———. (2011). *UNODC and organized crime.*
United Nations Office on Drugs
and Crime. http://www.unodc.org/
unodc/en/organized-crime/index.html

Woodiwiss, M. (2001). *Organized crime and
American power.* Toronto: University of
Toronto Press.

13

Internet Law and Policy from a Canadian Perspective

Sara M. Smyth

INTRODUCTION

Every new technology is both a burden and a blessing, and this is especially true with respect to the Internet.[1] This global communications infrastructure has been in a state of constant flux for the past several decades due to freewheeling human innovation. While this has provided us with new institutions, fresh ideas, and a keen awareness of creativity and intellectual freedom, something quite alarming has also taken place. Cybercrime is now severe, pervasive, aggressive, and increasingly sophisticated, and this poses a significant threat to the Internet's viability as an essential element of our critical infrastructure. This might come as a surprise to many given that the Internet flourished for decades with scarcely any regulation whatsoever.[2] The fact that it was such a successful engine of innovation and economic growth meant that regulation could largely be ignored in debates about Internet policy in Canada. However, the days of the Net as unregulated—or even as 'unregulable'[3]—must come to an end.

This presents a dynamic policy challenge because the Internet is a system of continuous transformation and complexity.[4] It contains hundreds of millions of computers, each connected to an intricate physical network that accepts input from an infinite number of users throughout the world simultaneously. As well, the computers can have many different software programs running on them that interact with other programs on other computers across the network.[5] Given the Internet's emergent and transnational properties, combined with the inherent vulnerabilities in its infrastructure, it is not surprising that attack patterns have evolved over time, with malicious activities being driven further underground, as well as to safe-haven jurisdictions.[6] Not only is the number of threats on the rise, the complexity and efficiency of attacks have increased precipitously over time.[7] Why this is the case, and what we can do about it, is the subject of this chapter.

It is clear that Canadian criminal justice policy has not kept pace with the rapid developments in computer technology witnessed during the past few decades. This can be attributed to the complexity of the issues raised and the difficulty of balancing public safety, as well as individual privacy, against the broader need for cybersecurity. Internet regulation is indeed feasible in Canada, but it must be multi-faceted and cannot emanate from a single source.[8] There are numerous points of control, involving both public and private actors. Predicting which intermediaries will succeed and what approach the law should adopt with respect to intermediary regulation is one of the most significant issues facing policy-makers in Canada today.[9]

A BRIEF OVERVIEW OF THE INTERNET

The Internet poses an exceptional challenge to policy-makers owing to its unique structure and design. It was born in the late 1960s, in the hushed corridors of university computer science departments and government research labs, as an American military tool that was part of a larger experiment to connect computers across the United States.[10] The founding engineers created a network built of many nodes, each connected to other nodes, so that even after a nuclear attack, it would be possible to use routes through the network without any degradation in the quality of the transmission.[11] They also realized that the network would be enormously efficient if messages could be broken down into small blocks.[12] The message blocks could be sent independently over the network and then reassembled at their destination.[13]

The Internet also has an 'end-to-end' design.[14] This means that all of the intelligence is placed at the ends of the network, on the software applications running on the user's machine.[15] No single entity can turn the system off or remove participants, and the number of 'nodes' or contributors can grow exponentially without degrading the function of the network itself.[16] There is also a common standard, or protocol, that enables computers to send and receive information over the network.[17] Transmission Control Protocols/Internet Protocols (TCP/IP) enable computers all over the world, each with unique Internet Protocol (IP) addresses, to send and receive information by establishing a connection over which packets of information can be transmitted according to a common 'language' and set of rules. This allows new technologies to be introduced into the network by end-users as long as they adhere to the basic protocols of communication.[18]

Naturally, the Internet would not have thrived and flourished had there not been an opportunity for ordinary users to connect with it. Thus, it is important that as the price of hardware, or computer processors and their related components, dropped in the late 1980s, the personal computer (PC) found its way into people's homes.[19] It is also critical that the personal computer of the 1980s—the mother of today's powerful PC—was designed to run software written by authors other than the manufacturer of the PC and one could easily upgrade it with new software without having to discard the hardware.[20] The PC was developed to be highly adaptable in that it was designed to run highly sophisticated commercial software, as well as homespun code, that can be created by amateurs, or individuals acting on their own, who only need to convince other users to run their programs. This introduces great diversity and inventiveness into the network, and it means that end-users can benefit from new innovations without having to understand how they work.

During the 1980s, software developers realized that performance growth in computer hardware would drive down costs to the point where computers would be affordable to ordinary consumers.[21] So they began designing software for the general public that was sold through a variety of distribution channels separately from hardware.[22] This led to the development of independent software firms, and as prices plunged, competition and innovation increased.[23] Public access to Internet-enabled software applications was also furthered by the creation of a multimedia branch of the Internet known as the World Wide Web.[24] As well, network service providers continued to emerge on the scene throughout the 1990s, providing links between the private computers connected to the Internet.[25]

This brief history illustrates that it was almost by chance that the Internet flourished so quickly and transformed our lives in ways that a more vigilant public might otherwise have wished. We cannot fault ourselves for failing to foresee that this miracle and wonder would give rise to so many problems in such a short time. The perpetual transformation and innovation of this medium give rise to significant security risks because the inherent design of the network influences the freedoms and controls that it enables.[26] In other words, the Internet has emergent and generative properties that both enable and evade regulatory control.[27]

THE CURRENT THREAT LANDSCAPE

The Internet is a dangerous place. Cybercrimes include theft, fraud, misdirection of communications, identity theft, theft of intellectual property, corporate espionage, system sabotage, data destruction, money laundering, child pornography, child luring, and terrorism, among others. Those with technical skills have joined forces with financially motivated criminals who want to steal personal information and financial assets.[28] Attacks can be perpetrated through the exploitation of vulnerabilities in the underlying software, and these intrusions can be attributed not only to hackers, but also to software manufacturers and users.[29] Moreover, cybercriminals are leveraging innovation at a rate that many target organizations and security vendors simply cannot match. A recent study conducted by TELUS and the Rotman School of Management at the University of Toronto indicates that Canadian organizations are experiencing high levels of breaches that are associated with outsiders, such as phishing, misuse of public Web applications, or viruses and malware.[30]

A robust, rapidly expanding online underground economy has also opened up new opportunities for criminals around stealing, packaging, and reselling information.[31] Participants include organized criminals, hackers for hire, disgruntled employees, as well as terrorists and their supporters.[32] Internet Relay Chat (IRC) servers and Web-based forums feature discussion groups that criminals use to buy and sell fraudulent goods and services. Items sold include credit-card data, bank account details, email accounts, full identities, and other information that can easily be exploited for financial gain.[33] Services include cashiers who transfer funds from stolen accounts into true currency, either through money transfers or online currency exchange, which is commonly known as 'cash out'.[34]

Malware authors and other criminals for hire also provide their skills, abilities, products, and services to others through the online underground economy. These include data acquisition and storage, access to systems, identity theft, and misdirection of communications. For example, a number of malicious tools are being sold online that provide access to identities, credentials, hacked hosts, and other exploits. Individuals can be hired to find vulnerabilities in a specific target, which could include, for example, a particular software application, operating system, or piece of hardware. If the vulnerability is found in a wide-reaching system, it can be used to deliver spam, spyware, or adware, which can be used for both malicious purposes and monetary gain.

The focus of online threats continues to be aimed at compromising end-users for financial gain, and attackers have honed their online fraud techniques.[35] The co-ordination of specialized groups for the production and dissemination of customized malicious code and phishing kits has led to a dramatic increase in malicious code threats.[36] Phishing kits, which are generic toolkits widely offered for sale on the underground economy, automatically create websites that mimic those of trusted financial institutions in order to steal financial information and other personal details from unsuspecting users.[37] This means that inexperienced intruders—normally referred to as 'script-kiddies' in the hacking nomenclature because they are not capable of writing their own programs (or 'scripts')—are able to exploit software security vulnerabilities with little effort and technical sophistication.[38] Experienced hackers have come to rely on these novices for the broad distribution of their malware.[39]

Threats are becoming more targeted, and one of the recent trends is away from the curious hackers who use their skills for bragging rights toward more sophisticated intruders who are primarily motivated by financial gain.[40] Computers are also more powerful than ever before, yet those who use them are not the computer-savvy scientists and academics of the recent past.[41] Social networking and constant online communication, as well as online banking, investing, and retail purchasing—in addition to the proliferation of communication devices, networks, and users—have created new opportunities for cybercriminals and more risks for ordinary users.[42] With increasing numbers of unsophisticated users conducting transactions online, attacks are proliferating at an alarming rate. In 2003, for example, SQL Slammer became the fastest computer worm in history, infecting more than 90 per cent of vulnerable systems in as little as 10 minutes.[43] Users can be blamed for opening infected email attachments and downloading malicious files onto their computers.[44] Yet adversaries are also reinvesting portions of their profits in developing new capabilities for circumventing modern security technologies, and in fact, even leading antivirus software vendors are finding it difficult to keep up with the amount of new malware.[45] This means that antivirus solutions are providing little defence and are rapidly being rendered obsolete.[46]

Attackers also regularly deploy botnets, or networks of infected computers, that can be used to send spam, launch network attacks, or disseminate malware.[47] The problem with botnets is their ability to harness the collective power of a large number of compromised computers to launch co-ordinated assaults, including distributing spam and phishing attacks, disseminating spyware and malicious code, and propagating denial of service attacks against an organization's website, all of which can have significant financial consequences.[48] As well, there has been a dramatic rise in the volume of spam being distributed across the Internet.[49] In one year alone, Symantec observed a 192 per cent increase in spam detected across the Internet, from 119.6 billion messages in 2007 to 349.6 billion in 2008.[50] Not only do spam emails diminish the personal and professional productivity of Canadians, they also raise significant security concerns.[51] They may contain spyware that tracks user activity or attempts to gain information. They can also contain viruses, worms, and other kinds of malicious code.

The lesson is that the future success of the Internet is at risk for the very same reasons that it triumphed almost overnight. The substantial increase in the rise of malicious code threats, combined with the inherent vulnerabilities in the Web, demonstrates the need for more proactive and co-operative security measures. Internet threats are now a global phenomenon, and if left unchecked, harmful activity allowed to fester in one region can easily spread worldwide, making it all the more difficult to locate the individual or group behind the attack. These concerns should remain at the forefront of our minds as we attempt to craft a policy approach that will meet the challenges posed by the increasingly sophisticated and aggressive Internet threat landscape.

EFFECTIVE SECURITY STRATEGIES AND COUNTERMEASURES

Given that the Internet is made up of both a physical structure, comprised of material property in the real world, and virtual content, consisting of information and ideas, attempts to control and monitor online behaviour can be directed at either the physical infrastructure of the Internet or the data circulating through its networks.[52] As a critical starting point, Parliament could criminalize conduct through substantive laws, such as those prohibiting hacking and identity theft, and back them up with tough penalties and rigorous enforcement. While this might seem trivial, it is absolutely essential given that there are a number of gaps in the current legal framework and existing provisions cannot address the sophisticated methods and means of attack now favoured by cybercriminals.

Canadian legislators have been far less insistent than their counterparts in other jurisdictions, such as the United States, in proposing specific legal remedies to address problems arising from the high rates of Internet penetration.[53] For instance, it wasn't until late 2009 that Parliament created a new legal framework to deal with the growing problem of identity theft.[54] Prior to this, the Criminal Code did not contain an identity theft offence at all. Furthermore, the Code contains provisions dealing with unauthorized access to computer systems, as well as mischief to data, and a general fraud provision that predates computer technology and the Internet.[55] However, these measures, which are primarily reactive rather than proactive, are not, either separately or together, capable of dealing with the most serious threats, nor are they sufficient to achieve the overall goal of deterring cybercrime offenders in Canada.[56]

It is puzzling that the Harper Conservatives, who are deeply committed to law-and-order policy, have done little to address the problem of cybercrime since they took office in 2006. The Harper agenda was revealed to Canadians with the publication of the 'Stand Up for Canada' election platform.[57] The confronting crime mandate did not focus on international security or terrorism, as one might expect, but instead dealt with law-and-order issues, such as protecting Canadians from those who commit serious and violent crimes.[58] Since that time, the Harper Conservatives introduced the aforementioned identity theft legislation, as well as anti-spam legislation. However, Bill C-27, also known as the Electronic Commerce Protection Act, did not become law before the second session of Parliament ended on 30 December 2009.[59] And it was only on December 15, 2010 that the Government of Canada passed the Fighting Internet and Wireless Spam bill, Bill C-28; up to that point, the prospect of Canada becoming a safe-haven jurisdiction for spammers was becoming an ever-increasing reality.

There are a variety of reasons why Parliament has been unwilling, or unable, to take a stand against cybercrime. Individuals and organizations may be leaving themselves vulnerable to cybercrime through a false sense of security, or a lack of awareness and even complacency, because intrusions are often undetected and underreported. Private companies, for their part, are often more concerned with negative publicity, which might result in harmful consumer or market reaction.[60] In the effort to protect their assets and their reputations, they are withholding valuable information about intrusions that could be instrumental in helping to combat cybercrime.[61] The result is that it is very difficult to determine how, and how often, victimizations are occurring, as estimates about the size and frequency of attacks tend to be based on anecdote and guesswork.[62] This makes it difficult for policy-makers to articulate why new laws are urgently needed.

Further, as I discuss in detail below, many civil liberties advocates have claimed either that the cybercrime threat is overblown or that the existing legal framework is capable of dealing with it, particularly given the privacy encroachments they fear. This criticism, which I believe is unfounded, has succeeded in generating a great deal of trepidation and controversy whenever Internet regulations have been proposed by Parliament. Another drawback is that the area is rife with technical terminology that can be intimidating to policy-makers, the media, and ordinary consumers, further contributing to the general sense of uncertainty, and lack of urgency, about cybercrime. Not only does this increase our vulnerability to attackers, it also means that, in spite of the fact that the cyber-security risks have increased proportionate to our dependency on computer technologies, Canadian policy-makers have either misunderstood or significantly underestimated the breadth and depth of the problem.

It is also clear that while conventional legal measures that focus on the underlying conduct could provide a strong foundation for combating cybercrime, they are unlikely to be effective, by themselves, at mitigating cybercrime because, as a global network, the Internet allows for the instant exchange of information between users throughout the world.[63] And given that the Internet is simply a neutral device for routing packets of data, which means that it doesn't discriminate between packets or route certain kinds of data differently than others, it imposes no restrictions upon end-users and, when it comes to censorship, it simply routes around it.[64] The Net's design structure means that when regulators try to impose content restrictions or criminal law prohibitions online, they are forever chasing a moving target.[65] Still more daunting, perhaps, is the fact that criminals can conceal their identities and relocate to jurisdictions where Internet service providers (ISPs) have trouble monitoring and filtering the increasing amount of traffic across their networks.[66]

Recall that the Internet is built on the TCP/IP suite of protocols for freely exchanging fragmented packets of any kind of communication, without impediment or delay. To exchange packets of data, all the system needs to know is the IP addresses of the machines to and from which the information is sent.[67] User identification is left for the participants to sort out.[68] Since the network wasn't designed with authentication in mind, it's easy for users to hide who they are.[69] This makes it time-consuming and expensive to enforce conventional legal measures on the Net. It is also one of the central reasons why the child pornography industry has continued to thrive and flourish online, despite the fact that Parliament has taken further steps to control it, including the enactment of what is arguably the broadest and most punitive criminal law regime in the Western world.[70] It makes little sense, in other words, for Parliament to focus most of its energies on punishing child pornographers while many potential—and current—cybercrimes are either undetected or unaddressed. This has generated significant exposure to risk for Canadian individuals and businesses, including exposure to financial losses, data breach liabilities, loss of clients and public confidence, and even, in the most extreme cases, actual physical harm.

Third parties have a critical role to play in helping to overcome the challenges that have proven so frustrating to policy-makers. Imposing liability upon intermediaries in order to identify and prevent third-party misconduct, instead of simply punishing wrongdoers, can be highly effective, particularly where a government's ability to regulate a specific problem is limited, while an intermediary's capacity to regulate, whether resulting from resources, information, or authority, is enhanced.[71] This is why the development of an effective regulatory framework must begin with identifying intermediaries, such as ISPs, which are best suited to regulate the conduct of third parties, notwithstanding the network's openness and protocol-based structure.

However, when there is a transfer of traditional forms of regulatory authority from the state to non-state actors, it can challenge fundamental democratic values, such as freedom of expression and association, as well as privacy, in ways that are traditionally reserved for public institutions.[72] This is particularly important when it comes to Internet regulation because the Internet is dynamic, enabling those who are regulated to participate in the ongoing development of the medium itself, through the production and distribution of content and code, as well in the creation and sharing of culture, both individually and collectively.[73] Without careful deliberation, attempts to mitigate risk can have the opposite effect of introducing new harms into the network, or of stifling innovation and communication, through excessive control over the transmission, substance, and accessibility of information.[74]

Software Security

One of the most obvious tactics in our cyber-security arsenal is to target the software vendors who develop the applications that make the Internet functional for end-users. On the surface, this holds significant appeal because flaws in software, which are usually caused by programming errors, are the primary way that attackers gain access to networks and are a determining factor in the amount of damage that is done.[75] Broadly speaking, software is the principal source of *all* computer security problems and the amount of software has increased commensurate to our reliance upon computers.[76] When millions of computer users all depend on the same software, vulnerabilities in the underlying code can spell disaster for multiple machines, and the problem is further compounded when computers are networked.[77]

By some estimates, there are up to 20 flaws per 1,000 lines of software code.[78] To put this in perspective, the Windows XP operating system has about 40 million lines of code and Windows Vista has more than 50 million lines of code.[79] As you might expect, hackers and other criminals exploit these vulnerabilities to spread malware, deface websites, modify and delete sensitive information, or take control of entire systems.[80] For their part, software manufacturers rush to market with poorly designed products riddled with vulnerabilities, yet they shoulder almost none of the harm that results from cybercrime intrusions and exploits.[81]

There is little or no market incentive for software publishers to produce reliable code because, from a purely economic perspective, *post hoc* security requires an expensive outlay of time and resources for little financial return, particularly given that, in today's marketplace, it is critical that software be deployed as quickly as possible in order to gain market share.[82] And, while code could be improved, most users wouldn't buy better-quality software, nor would they be willing to pay more for it, if vulnerable software, with more features, is available sooner for a lower price.[83] Frequently, software designers focus on getting an application to work, and the holes that interfere with functionality are their most important concern. As a result, security flaws aren't addressed until the end of the process, and the minimal effort expended on them is directly proportional to the urgency of the product release.[84]

This is not to suggest that software manufacturers ignore flaws altogether.[85] In fact, they invest considerable resources into the necessary evil of fixing bugs; however, latent defects carry perverse benefits because software producers use them opportunistically to create new strategic business opportunities. Software publishers have a powerful interest in maximizing their profits by monopolizing markets for upgrades and forcing consumers to purchase new versions of their products.[86] Defects provide a clever way of supplying new revenue within markets that are already saturated.[87]

Since software defects are always dealt with after distribution and standardization, there will inevitably be a 'window of vulnerability', given the time that it takes to develop a software update, or 'patch', during which attackers can exploit the security problems.[88] This problem is compounded by the fact that while the software industry has gotten better about releasing patches in a timely manner, there are still many examples of long delays.[89] Information about the vulnerability can quickly spread online, and worse yet, a hacker can create an automated exploit and make it available to a large pool of script-kiddies for them to use.[90] Yet, as long as the rush to market means that software companies continue to promote poorly tested software to consumers and we, the general public, continue to purchase their imperfect code, security will remain an add-on feature or, more or less, an afterthought. Consumers have not dealt with these problems with their feet because, quite simply, how does one suddenly abandon a product that has become the industry standard? Moreover, lack of knowledge and complacency have made it difficult to obtain the critical mass of consumers needed to hold software vendors accountable by refusing to purchase their products.[91]

Automatic patch services provide a helpful solution aimed at lowering the costs of maintaining a secure system for both businesses and consumers.[92] Many software manufacturers now offer automatic patch services that identify, download, and install relevant patches with minimal intervention from the user.[93] Yet many companies have been hesitant to implement automated patch-management tools because this requires giving outsiders a high degree of system access and there is also the concern that patches will introduce new problems and destabilize the networks.[94]

At the same time, businesses are running into expensive problems if they don't have an automated way to manage and deploy fixes.[95] Since major companies can have thousands of desktop computers, as well as hundreds of servers, they can be expected to devote thousands of man-hours to manual fixes.[96] As well, owing to the frequency with which patches are released—on average every 5.5 days—keeping current with the vulnerabilities and their related patches presents a daunting task.[97] Consequently, routine maintenance operations are frequently given precedence over patch management.[98]

Aside from these technical matters, legal rules have also been developed that insulate software manufacturers from liability. Consider, for example, the fact that these vendors use click-wrap agreements, which buyers must agree to on a take-it-or-leave-it basis, to negate the chance that they will be sued for defects in their products.[99] Software producers also rely on intellectual property laws to protect their source code.[100] While this gives them an incentive to invest in developing software without worrying that others will freely copy and distribute their code, the fact that production occurs in secret means that consumers have few facts when questions about quality and security emerge.[101] Without access to the source code, it is nearly impossible to assess the quality of the programming or to determine whether a particular vulnerability is present.[102] In this sense, effective security testing can only be done by the manufacturers, as they are the only ones with manual access and knowledge about the product.[103]

Software security problems come in many different shapes and sizes and so do the variety of possible solutions.[104] Thus, scholars have approached the problem from many different perspectives. For example, Kevin Pinkney and Douglas Barnes have suggested that policy-makers could focus exclusively on assigning liability to software developers and consumers under tort law.[105] Intuitively, this makes sense when we consider that hackers thrive on the careless programming practices of software manufacturers and the sloppy system administration and security measures undertaken by consumers. One suggestion put forward by Pinkney is to hold software manufacturers strictly liable for all harm caused by design flaws, allowing a security-related software failure.

Yet holding software manufacturers liable for defects in their products would place a chill on software development and innovation, as well as reduce incentives for other parties, such as consumers and ISPs, to take precautions. It would also delay output and increase the price of software for consumers, as manufacturers would likely pass on their increased production costs as well as accident costs.[106] In the United States, where many of the world's leading software manufacturers are headquartered, several doctrines under the Uniform Commercial Code (UCC) have served to protect sellers from liability, allowing them to shift the risks of software failure from themselves to the user, making it difficult to hold them liable under tort law.[107] Furthermore, if the government were to try to mandate performance standards for software, this would not likely succeed given that the technology advances so rapidly that the government could not keep up.[108]

Also keep in mind that the information technology community has been tirelessly working to develop new fixes, as well as internal policies and procedures for constructing software that was more secure.[109] For example, following a negative ruling from the US Federal Trade Commission, which could have led to fines totalling $2.2 trillion for a security flaw discovered in May 2003, Microsoft undertook a $100-million security initiative, called Trustworthy and Secure Computing, which led to major changes in security and development throughout the company.[110] Still, Microsoft maintains that even if a software product is designed and engineered to be secure, the number of vulnerabilities in large and complex products (with the features that will appeal to a broad set of users) simply cannot be reduced to zero.[111] Thus, while strict liability might reduce the number of vulnerabilities, it would not likely eliminate them, making it an unattractive option, especially considering the other potential negative outcomes discussed above. Another argument raised by software manufacturers about the buggy software they release into the marketplace is that these vulnerabilities do not determine whether or not a system is at risk. They maintain that if the skills of the intruder are sufficiently advanced, they will always be able to carry out an attack because they are so good at exploiting vulnerabilities in the software or in human nature.[112] These ideas are further explored in the next section.

Human Security

Networked systems are difficult to secure, and since complexity is the adversary of security, the systems of the future are likely to be inherently less secure.[113] No matter what kind of system is being dealt with, though, the weakest link is always the human being sitting in front of the computer.[114] Most people want security, but they don't really understand what it means and they don't want to have to interact with it. Indeed, many users find security intrusive and try to get around it whenever they can.[115] While a small number of users regularly update their anti-virus definitions, the simple tasks of properly configuring software (to use built-in security features) and applying patches are frequently neglected by even the most sophisticated users.[116] Many software consumers adopt a laissez-faire approach to cyber-security because of the lack of reliable information. Intrusions are largely undetected and unreported, which makes it easy for consumers to underestimate the risk and convince themselves that it won't happen to them.[117]

The fact that users are so trusting and compliant is also what makes them so susceptible to social engineering techniques. This is the hacker's idiom for the art of the con, or the ability to trick someone into doing something they wouldn't ordinarily do, such as revealing passwords and other sensitive information.[118] This is an esteemed technique to target users through phishing scams, which I discussed earlier. Alternatively, a criminal can pose as a trusted company insider, such as a network administrator, and get passwords and other valuable data directly from employees.[119] The beauty of social engineering is that it is an attack on the user, rather than on the system itself; even by requiring a user to visit a web page and execute the code, you quickly circumvent every security measure. Given that people are so easily taken in, it is always easier to target careless users than to bypass security or exploit technical vulnerabilities alone.[120]

It might make sense to give users a stake in fine-tuning the Internet, thus ensuring that they have an incentive, as well as a means, to participate in its maintenance and security. For instance, by expanding the number of people who view the code, such as in the case of open-source software, we can leverage the power of a diverse group of people to improve online security.[121] Only a small fraction of users can read source code, though, so the number of participants available for natural surveillance in cyberspace is negligible.[122] In fact, most users have no idea what the computer is doing when they tell it to do something. They are content to rely on blind faith.[123] And, consistent with the traditional client/server structural design of the Internet, most users would rather seek the advice of an expert, through a helpline, than deal with problems on their own.[124]

Nonetheless, there are precautions that ordinary users can take to protect themselves from the risk of intrusion, such as employing rigorous password administration, using correct system configuration, and installing security patches provided by manufacturers. This is why some commentators have suggested holding software consumers liable for negligence.[125] But how do we identify what is a 'reasonable' standard of care for the average consumer? And can we hold all consumers to the same standard? For example, if an attacker uses a botnet to perpetrate an attack, or loops and weaves his attack through numerous computers in multiple jurisdictions, should all of these victims be held liable to the same standard?[126] The inherent difficulties raised here are compounded by the lack of reliable information about intrusions, which leads consumers to misjudge risks. Moreover, the software industry maintains that sophisticated hackers can breach *any* standard of care—making the question of reasonable care even more difficult to ascertain.

Also keep in mind that, given the nature of the software industry, consumers cannot examine complex source code for vulnerabilities, and thus they are at the mercy of software producers, not only when they purchase a product, but throughout its entire lifespan.[127] Hacking is becoming increasingly sophisticated, and hackers continually search for previously unknown or undiscovered (i.e., unpatched) vulnerabilities to exploit. The delay in the time that it takes for a vulnerability to be discovered and a patch to be issued by the manufacturer means that hackers can readily identify and exploit design flaws before a company can release a patch to correct it. There are also many cases where consumers are unaware that a problem and a solution to correct it even exist.[128] Moreover, antivirus and anti-spyware software only provides protection against known vulnerabilities, which means that mandating the use of security software is not only likely to be difficult to enforce, but potentially ineffective.[129] Holding users liable for misjudging the risk of intrusion and the under-consumption of security would also release software manufacturers from liability and give them few incentives to prevent vulnerabilities in the first place.[130]

Recall, as well, that computer users don't only use software programs written by commercial software producers, although using programs written by unknown authors is an extremely risky thing to do.[131] Nevertheless, the inherent nature of computer-based technologies is to enable virtually anyone to produce code that other people can run on their machines.[132] Since not all software is produced by reliable programmers, and given that there is no obvious way for ordinary users to distinguish between benevolent and malevolent code, the Internet's ethos of mutual trust and reliance has become a significant problem. The obvious trade-off would be to try and do away with all of the user-generated content that proliferates on the Net. If this were even possible, it would stifle the ingenuity that we have come to value so much from this system.

Network Security

Given the flaws in software markets and the risks posed by ordinary users, it is unlikely that cybercrime can be dealt with by market forces alone. As the weakest link in the chain of communication, users are likely to mess things up, and relying on software vendors feels a little like trusting the fox to guard the henhouse. In a perfect world, we might be able to compel the fox to co-operate, but we'll never fully trust him. If targeting wrongdoers directly is ineffective owing to the anonymity of the Internet and the ease with which criminals can relocate to a jurisdiction outside the regulatory influence of Canada, policy-makers must decide between allowing the harm to continue and looking for other regulatory solutions.[133]

Internet service providers are valuable targets for regulation because they maintain primary control over the cables, wires, routers, and switches that transmit information in cyberspace. They also connect end-users with the Internet at large and they host content that is placed on their servers by others.[134] Their means of control include selecting content, channelling information to users, censorship (i.e., filtering and blocking), network access, user interaction (i.e., email, homepages, links), and so on.[135] In the complex Internet environment, the scope of this responsibility is enormous in the sense that ISPs can both enable and restrict public participation and discourse, which, in a democratic society such as ours, includes freedom of expression, association, and privacy in ways traditionally reserved for public institutions.[136]

Internet content filtering is now a pervasive global phenomenon, and it is viewed by many regulators as a panacea, or a simple way to deal with security challenges wrought by cyberspace, particularly in authoritarian regimes.[137] For example, China, as well as some other tightly controlled regimes, including Saudi Arabia and Singapore, has adopted a nation-wide filtering regime.[138] With blocking occurring at multiple points in the network and extending to a large variety of topics, China operates the most technologically advanced and extensive system of Internet censorship in the world.[139] Yet, Internet filtering, or blocking, and ISP regulation more generally are practices that have also spread throughout many industrialized democratic nations. For example, France ordered the Internet search engine Yahoo! to block French users from accessing a section of its site that auctioned Nazi memorabilia,[140] and the European Union recently implemented a sweeping data-retention directive, requiring ISPs to keep records of the data passing through their networks for a period of six months to a year.[141]

The growing international consensus around the importance of Internet filtering is most apparent with respect to online child pornography. In the most sinister ways imaginable, children are sexually abused and the images documenting their exploitation are now widely circulating on the Internet—a practice that is almost universally condemned.[142] The most popular tool that states are using to combat this insidious threat is a nationally based filtering scheme, primarily carried out by ISPs and local police agencies.[143] Countries that have implemented filtering technologies to deal with child pornography include Norway, Germany, Sweden, Denmark, Switzerland, Italy, the Netherlands, Finland, and even Canada.[144] Another way to deal with the problem of child pornography is to locate the source of the provider, or host, and issue a takedown notice. Australia has implemented a comprehensive 'notice-and-takedown' regime whereby the government directs ISPs to remove prohibited content from their servers.[145]

In the United States, the 'war on terror' initiative witnessed a massive expansion of electronic surveillance techniques, as the Bush administration sought to leverage its power to monitor otherwise inaccessible communications.[146] For example, the administration apparently authorized warrantless wiretaps on US-based Internet exchange points of certain ISPs, including AT&T and Verizon, in order to indiscriminately intercept communications passing through those networks.[147] These pernicious examples illustrate that it would be technically feasible for us to create closed Internet networks and to artfully monitor what Canadians are saying and doing online. Yet, we clearly do not want to implement such blunt measures because the benefits that could be achieved in terms of crime reduction would not outweigh the costs to our privacy, liberty, and freedom of expression. The diversity of the Internet would almost certainly be inhibited, as individuals might stop using it to exchange information on topics that could be considered controversial or unpopular for fear that they would suffer civil or criminal liability or be blocked from reaching their target audience.[148] Furthermore, private intermediary enforcement encouraged by government, through mandatory ISP filtering, provides no judicial safeguards or oversight to ensure accountability. Indeed, this unreviewable instrument of censorship would occur at the lowest level of visibility and provide no way for Canadians to know what information is forbidden to them, much less why.[149]

Since the Internet is so critical to our participation in democratic culture and public discourse, we need to be particularly mindful of the ISPs' pivotal role in defining our online experience, as we rely on them to gain access to the Internet, as well as to sift through and interact with a wealth of information online. The lack of openness that comes with the use of filtering software at the national level to restrict access to information on public networks (which is currently the practice in many countries around the world) has obvious public policy implications.[150] We don't want our ISPs to inhibit cultural participation, or political expression, or any other important online manifestation of a healthy functioning democracy.

The other thing to keep in mind is that while digital security tends to rely exclusively on preventive measures (i.e., firewalls, encryption, strong identification/authentication, antivirus, filtering/blocking, and so on), this strategy can only succeed if the countermeasures used are watertight; otherwise, someone will find a way to get around these preventive techniques.[151] Yet no technology is perfect, and thus, in addition to prevention, first-rate security must rely on detection and response mechanisms to identify wrongdoers and do something about them.[152]

Compelling—when necessary—ISPs to co-operate with police and disclose information is one of the few tools we have to detect and identify offenders and obtain valuable evidence in cyberspace. Parliament could require ISPs to scan computers, as well as individual email attachments, for infections; block email attachments with file extensions known to be associated with malware; and monitor their networks for the presence of botnet computers and then quarantine infected machines.[153] While some ISPs are already taking these steps, most have little incentive to take action on their own because they don't want to risk alienating their customers.[154] The focus instead has been on government-facilitated self-regulation by industry participants.[155]

Thus, Parliament would need to pass legislation to compel ISPs to comply with these measures because they are not legally enforceable under Canadian law. However, from a practical perspective, it would be time-consuming and expensive for an ISP to try to control the conduct of those who introduce malware into the network by identifying the transmissions that cause the problems and filtering out harmful code. The same is true with respect to quarantine or the idea that infected computers spreading malware are a risk to the community and need to be isolated. ISPs could administer the quarantine and also clean users' computers so that they could rejoin the Internet.[156] While quarantines have been used for centuries to contain infectious diseases like leprosy, to implement them on the Internet, we have to get around the problem of how they would work in the face of malware designed to evade them and how to ensure that people don't have their computers unjustifiably quarantined.[157] Furthermore, there's the issue of who gets to decide which computers should be quarantined. This problem doesn't arise on a private corporate or university network because the owners of the network get to make the decision.[158] But the Internet doesn't have a central decision-making authority, and even if ISPs were to administer the quarantines, someone would have to decide which computers should be isolated, for how long, and on what terms.

If Parliament were to enact laws forcing ISPs to police the Net, such as by barricading certain areas from view when they act as content hosts, removing content that is objectionable, or restricting access to certain entities with whom their customers wish to communicate, this would violate freedom of expression, a freedom that promotes not only popular speech but also unpopular and offensive viewpoints.[159] While there have been cases in which Canadian ISPs have filtered content hosted outside of Canada, the Telecommunications Act prohibits Canadian carriers from controlling the content or influencing 'the meaning or purpose of telecommunications carried by it' for the general public.[160] Yet this is not to suggest that ISPs shouldn't be encouraged, or even required, to assist law enforcement officials with enforcing Internet-specific regulations to the extent that it is both lawful and reasonable. However, given that the Internet is a transnational medium, there is a clear need for international co-operation. In fact, there has been increasing international consensus around the importance of a global initiative to combat cybercrime, particularly given that critical evidence, in the form of computer data, can be stored within any almost jurisdiction in the world.[161] This means that law enforcement agencies within the various countries must be required to preserve and facilitate access to the data quickly before it is deleted or otherwise destroyed.

Fortunately, Canadian policy-makers have not turned a blind eye to the need to ensure that a system of international co-operation for the sharing of computer data exists. As early as 2001, Canada signed the Council of Europe's Cybercrime Convention, which requires each signatory state to make it an offence to commit certain crimes using computer systems[162] and to grant new powers of search and seizure to its law enforcement officials, including the power to require an ISP to preserve a citizen's Internet activity records and to monitor user activity in real time.[163] It also requires law enforcement officials in each signatory state to assist those in other participating states by co-operating with 'mutual assistance requests' from police 'to the widest extent possible'.[164]

In keeping with these commitments, the Liberal government tabled the *Lawful Access Consultation Document,*[165] in 2002, which set out Parliament's argument in favour of enacting 'lawful access' regulations that would compel ISPs to install new interception and surveillance capabilities as they upgrade their networks and provide law enforcement officials with increased legal powers to access data.[166] Representatives of Justice Canada, Industry Canada, and the solicitor general of Canada held public consultations, and after receiving more than 300 submissions, Justice Canada released a summary of the results of the consultations.[167] Subsequently, in 2005, the Liberal government tabled Bill C-74, or the Modernization of Investigative Techniques Act (MITA).[168] The bill was a method of furnishing Canada with legislation similar to that of other countries and implementing the measures contained in the Cybercrime Convention.[169] The MITA passed first reading in November 2005, but died on the order paper when Parliament dissolved at the end of that month.[170]

The Harper Conservatives recently revived the MITA in the form of Bill C-46, or the Investigative Powers for the 21st Century Act, and Bill C-47, also known as the Technical Assistance for Law Enforcement in the 21st Century Act, which were introduced in the House of Commons together on 18 June 2009 by the minister of public safety. Both bills passed second reading in the House of Commons, but died on the order paper when the second session of the fortieth Parliament dissolved on 30 December 2009. The purpose of Bill C-46 was to modernize certain offences in the Criminal Code and the Competition Act to take into account new advances in communications technologies and to provide law enforcement agencies with new investigative tools better suited to confront computer crimes.[171] Among other things, the bill would make it possible for law enforcement agencies to make a demand or obtain a court order for the preservation of electronic evidence; would create new judicial production orders for obtaining data; would create warrants for obtaining transmission data in real time and for the remote activation of tracking devices in certain kinds of technologies; and would enable new production orders to be used by Canadian police who receive assistance requests from other countries. Bill C-47 addressed the same issues as the MITA, including technical interception capabilities and requests for subscriber information. Together, Bills C-46 and C-47 would have enabled Canada to finally ratify the Cybercrime Convention.[172]

These legislative proposals raise a number of critical issues, including the fact that Canada is one of the last of the G-8 nations to modernize its laws in this area.[173] Furthermore, Canadian police are operating under outdated laws, while Internet crime is on the rise.[174] Yet, when Parliament unveiled its lawful access policy, it was met with fervent opposition, with concerns expressed regarding both the costs to industry of implementing such a regime and the impacts upon the civil liberties of Canadians. Generally, those who oppose these measures claim that lawful access regulations are an overreaction to the cybercrime problem and that either the issues complained of are not widespread or our existing legal measures are sufficient to deal with them, particularly given the privacy and civil liberties encroachments they fear.[175]

Although the Charter does not apply to private entities, such as ISPs, the proposed lawful access measures would place ISPs in the role of agents of the state, either by compelling them to search for, collect, analyze, and share data with law enforcement agents, or by assisting police with the same activities. This raises the question of whether the recovery of electronic data by or from ISPs triggers the constitutional protections set out in section 8 of the Charter. That section provides the following: 'Everyone has the right to be secure against unreasonable search and seizure.' This issue has been dealt with in only one Canadian case to date.

In *R. v. Wier*,[176] an ISP, while repairing Wier's electronic mailbox, discovered attachments to an email message that appeared to contain child pornography. The ISP opened the attachments and found that they did contain child pornography. It informed the police of its findings and, upon request, forwarded a copy of the message to the police. The ISP also provided the police with Wier's billing address. Wier argued that the ISP was acting as an agent of the state and that the opening of the message and the forwarding of the message to the police were both warrantless searches. The Alberta Court of Appeal held that the ISP was acting as an agent of the state when it forwarded a copy of the message to the police at the request of the police officer.[177] The court classified the forwarding of the email as a 'warrantless search', which is presumed unreasonable and in violation of section 8.[178] This case establishes that if a private intermediary is collecting data for law enforcement purposes or carrying out some other type of surveillance function, the provisions guarding against unreasonable search and seizure may be engaged and the need for a valid search warrant may arise.

Since digital interceptions constitute a search or seizure, the statutory provisions authorizing them must also conform to the minimum constitutional requirements of section 8 of the Charter. In *R. v. Oakes,* the Supreme Court of Canada set out the analytical framework for determining whether the violation of a Charter right can be justified under section 1.[179] Generally, a constitutional guarantee can be limited if two conditions are met. First, the objective, which the legislative measures are intended to serve, must be sufficiently important to warrant overriding a constitutionally protected right or freedom.[180] It must relate to 'pressing and substantial' concerns in a free and democratic society before it can be recognized as sufficiently important.[181] Second, the means chosen to attain the objective must be reasonable and demonstrably justifiable in a free and democratic society. This involves a 'proportionality test' in which the courts must balance the interests of society against those of individuals and groups.[182]

It would be difficult to conclude that the proposed lawful access measures are not both pressing and substantial. Empirical data confirm that cybercrime has proliferated in the last decade or so, making it hard for anyone to argue that the threat to Canadians is exaggerated. As well, law enforcement officials in Canada currently have powers under Part 6 of the Criminal Code to intercept private communications; however, these procedural tools are insufficient to deal with crime on the Internet today. Since the legal provisions relating to lawful interception were drafted in the early 1970s, Canadians have witnessed dramatic changes in information technologies, including the mainstreaming of the Internet. The Code must be updated to reflect these developments.[183] For these reasons, Bills C-46 and C-47 would certainly meet the pressing and substantial aspect of the section 1 analysis.

It is also likely that the proposed measures would satisfy the other elements of the proportionality test, including the minimal impairment requirement and the requisite of proportionality between the Charter-infringing effects of the measures and the objective being sought. In attempting to justify the proposed legislation on these grounds, it is significant that these kinds of intermediary-enabled investigative techniques already exist in Canadian law.[184] For example, when a police officer enters a bank with a warrant to seize records, he or she does not actually seize the bank's computer system and search for the data him- or herself. Rather, bank officials are called upon to produce the information to police. The reason for this is twofold: first, it is more convenient for the bank, since its business operations are not interrupted; and second, it is more costly and efficient for the police.[185] The same considerations apply to ISPs, albeit to an even greater extent, given the inherent volatility of the data flowing through transnational computer networks.

The fact is that not all ISPs are in the habit of collecting and storing data that passes through their networks. This means that information that could be valuable to the investigation of a suspect for a computer-related offence can easily be destroyed or modified before it can be obtained and used for law enforcement purposes. There needs to be a way to compel the immediate safeguarding of volatile evidence that is specific to a particular Internet transaction or subscriber, particularly when there are reasonable grounds to believe that the data will assist in the investigation of a crime. Provided that interception is only used in limited cases, with respect to particular information about specific individuals who are suspected of illegal conduct, the risk of capturing other types of sensitive information, such as private communications, personal records or personal identification numbers (PINs), will be minimized. The proposed lawful access provisions will resolve a number of significant problems with respect to extraterritorial searches and timing issues because persons who are in possession or control of digital evidence will immediately be compelled to preserve and produce it, regardless of whether it resides on networks based in Canada or abroad. Thus, they are rationally connected to the goal of reducing the problem of crime on transnational computer networks, particularly those which originate in Canada.

Moreover, Bill C-47 would require ISPs to possess apparatus enabling law enforcement agents to intercept communications *after they obtain judicial authorization*. In other words, judicial authorization will be required for all interceptions according to the standards already set out in the Code, in addition to the requirements for security and confidentiality specified in Bill C-47.[186] And, consistent with our current privacy and constitutional protections, before issuing the order, the judge or justice must be satisfied that there are reasonable grounds to believe that an offence has been committed, that the data will afford evidence of the offence, and that the recipient of the order has possession or control of the data. These judicial safeguards are already required by the Code's search warrant provisions.

It is also important to consider that the requirement, contained in Bill C-46, for an ISP to preserve data and produce it for law enforcement officials would only arise after the issuance of a production order by a judge, in the same manner as is already provided for under section 487.012 of the Code.[187] Thus, proposed legislation would not give rise to a lower threshold of privacy protection; nor would it raise the spectre of 'continuous surreptitious surveillance' as some commentators have suggested.[188] Rather, it has privacy-protecting measures included within it, in addition to other safeguards to ensure oversight and accountability that satisfy the Charter's minimal impairment and proportionality requirements.[189]

Also bear in mind that most commercial websites do little, if anything, to protect users' privacy (in fact, many make money on advertising models that invade privacy); rather, the use of cookies, which track users from site to site and in some cases uncover their identity, as well as adware and spyware, by both legitimate and illegitimate entities, freely abounds.[190] Many of these features are automated and used to make money. Others target users in order to steal confidential information. Trojans, viruses, and worms also enable an attacker to control the victim's computer and steal confidential information, which is sold through the underground economy and/or used to commit serious crimes. These tools are commonly used to create backdoors into the computer, which open up a means for the remote control of the computer and the installation of other forms of malware, including keystroke-logging software.[191] These threats pose a greater harm to privacy than the means intended to combat them, especially given that the measures put forward by Parliament will be implemented in accordance with existing privacy and constitutional guarantees.

Bill C-47 also establishes special rules that enable designated law enforcement officials to obtain basic information about a subscriber from an ISP without a warrant or court order.[192] The Supreme Court of Canada has stated that as information collected by the state nears a certain type of 'core' personal and biographical information about an individual, the privacy interest becomes more important and the need for judicial authorization increases.[193] However, the issue of whether an individual has a reasonable expectation of privacy in customer name and address information held by an ISP has already been resolved by the courts. As long as the ISP enters into a service agreement with the user about disclosing the information for law enforcement purposes, name and address information will not be considered 'core personal information' that must be protected from disclosure without a warrant.[194] In other words, an individual does not have a reasonable expectation of privacy in his name and address when this information is disclosed without a warrant, in accordance with the terms of the subscriber agreement.

It appears that the question of compensation for costs incurred by telecommunication service providers, more than anything else, has been thwarting the implementation of lawful access legislation in Canada. Clearly, the purpose behind any third-party regulatory strategy should be that it will provide substantial social benefits, in this case, harm reduction, while not significantly impairing the ability of those same intermediaries to provide services to their customers. If Bill C-47 had become law, ISPs would have been required to face the costs associated with the implementation of new transmission apparatus or software into their networks, as well as with storing and deciphering data and providing it to law enforcement upon request. The financial cost associated with these requirements is an important issue, as network upgrades could cost millions of dollars.[195]

However, these expenditures must be weighed against the direct costs to Canadian organizations from network security breaches. These include costs related to notifying customers of compromises to their personal information; financial losses stemming directly from the security breach, including the resources expended to bring the network back online, which can translate into lost work product, increased labour costs, and a loss of profits;[196] and the expenses associated with implementing a solution to ensure that such incidents do not occur again in the future.[197] To put these figures into perspective, the annual loss to Canadian organizations per major incident or breach is C$423,469 per year and the average number of major incidents that these entities experience is a little over two per year.[198] For their part, ISPs must deal with the fact that attacks can cripple their networks and impair their ability to provide service to their customers. To manage these harms, ISPs must pay for more bandwidth and expensive network upgrades, which increases the cost of Internet service for consumers.

To return to the costs associated with the implementation of lawful access measures, ISPs would have likely passed the network upgrade expenses on to their subscribers, through service fees, resulting in an increased cost to consumers for Internet use in Canada. While the required costs may have been tolerable for large ISPs, smaller ISPs might have been put out of business and new providers might have been deterred from entering the marketplace altogether.

Parliament attempted to address these concerns by exempting, for a period of three years, telecommunication service providers with fewer than 100,000 subscribers from the requirements set out in Bill C-47.[199] The risk associated with this approach was that smaller ISPs, or those otherwise exempt from the requirements, would become havens for cybercriminals who knew that the networks couldn't be intercepted by law enforcement officials. Parliament also provided that in cases where the minister issued an order to a telecommunication service provider to comply with requirements to maintain intercept capability, the minister would have been required to provide reasonable compensation to the carrier for the costs of compliance.[200]

Given that most other major industrialized nations have already enacted these measures domestically, as the Cybercrime Convention requires them to do, the question is not whether or not Canada will implement interception capability requirements but how quickly and on what terms. The implementation costs of reasonable interception capability and the impact of the proposed requirements on the competitiveness of the Canadian telecommunications industry remain important issues which will undoubtedly have an impact on how lawful access legislation is structured and put into practice. The measures implemented in other jurisdictions can serve as useful models for determining the best approach to take in Canada on these issues.[201]

CONCLUSION

The Internet is now an essential component of our critical infrastructure. The viability of this important medium is threatened because as the number of users has rapidly increased during the past few decades, so too has the prevalence of online criminal activity. The high rate of Internet usage in Canada, coupled with robust privacy and constitutional protections, has meant that citizens are able, to a far greater degree than in many other nations, to publish and distribute opposing points of view. Canadian Internet users have also had the opportunity to engage in a variety of offensive and harmful online activities, such as accessing child pornography, which challenge our long-standing commitment to freedom of expression.[202]

Criminal justice policy has been unable to deal with the complexity of the issues raised in this area, such as the need to balance safety and security against privacy and civil liberties, as well as with the transnational nature of the criminality. Public policy has failed to keep up with the rapid pace of technological growth and the evolving nature of criminal activity on the Internet. This suggests a need for other mechanisms of regulatory control, particularly those that involve third-party intermediaries who are in a better position, based on resources, information, or authority, to identify and prevent third-party misconduct than government actors. At the same time, however, we must ensure that any new policy measures do not have the undesirable effect of stifling innovation or inhibiting the cultural flourishing and democratic participation that the Internet so freely enables.

Because of the Internet's unique architecture, ISPs have an essential role to play in helping to target online offenders. This would provide a valuable opportunity for industry participants to commit to practices that they would otherwise not be likely to adopt by themselves for fear of being undercut in the marketplace. However, lawful access is a complex and delicate issue because it involves issues of financial cost, competitiveness, privacy, technical capability, and the need to facilitate co-operation between law enforcement agents within Canada and abroad. The challenge is to implement measures that respond to technological transformation and globalization while ensuring that our privacy and constitutional guarantees are protected.

CRITICAL THINKING QUESTIONS

1. What are some of the challenges associated with estimating the true social and financial impact of cybercrime on the Canadian economy?

2. The Internet was designed to be open, with distributed control and mutual trust among users. Has this led to the emergence of new security threats? If so, how and why?

3. Consider the growth and complexity of the computing environment, and ask yourself what the future of cybercrime is.

4. What might Parliament do to better respond to developments in computer-related crime?

5. Is the Canadian legal framework capable of dealing with the cyber-security threats discussed in this chapter? Why or why not?

NOTES

1. Neil Postman, *Technopoly: The surrender of culture to technology* (New York: Vintage Books, 1993), 5.

2. Jonathan Zittrain, *The future of the Internet and how to stop it* (New Haven: Yale University Press, 2008), 9.

3. John Perry Barlow, 'A declaration of cyberspace independence', http://homes.eff.org/~barlow/Declaration-Final.html.

4. Bruce Schneier, *Secrets and lies: Digital security in a networked world* (New York: Wiley Computer Publishing, 2000), 6.

5. Ibid.

6. *Symantec global Internet security threat report—Trends for 2008*, 14, April 2009, 11.

7. Jonathan Walther, 'Meeting the challenge of automated patch management', SANS Institute, 19 July 2004, 7, http://www.sans.org/reading_room/whitepapers/

sysadmin/meeting-challenges-automated-patch-management_1468

8. Ronald J. Deibert and Rafal Rohozinski, 'Risking security: Policies and paradoxes of cyberspace security', *International Political Sociology*, 4 (2010), 15, 16.

9. Thomas F. Cotter, 'Some observations on the law and economics of inter-mediaries'. *Michigan State Law Review*, (2006), 67, 68.

10. Katie Hafner and Matthew Lyon, *Where wizards stay up late—The origins of the Internet* (New York: Simon and Schuster, 1996).

11. Ibid.

12. Ibid.,60.

13. Ibid.

14. Lawrence Lessig, *The future of ideas: The fate of the commons in a connected world* (New York: Vintage Books, 2001), 34–5.

15. Ibid.

16. Siva Viyanathan, *The anarchist in the library* (New York: Basic Books, 2004), 17.

17. Frances Cairncross, *The death of distance* (Boston: Harvard Business School Press, 1997), 11.

18. Deibert and Rohozinski, *supra*, note 8, 16.

19. Zittrain, *supra*, note 2, 11–18.

20. Ibid., 14–15.

21. Ibid., 19.

22. Bradford L. Smith and Susan O. Mann, 'Innovation and intellectual property protection in the software industry: An emerging role for patents?', *University of Chicago Law Review*, 7, (2004), 241, 245.

23. Ibid.

24. Hafner and Lyon, *supra*, note 10, 258; Zittrain, *supra*, note 2, 19.

25. Zittrain, *supra*, note 2, 29.

26. Lessig, *supra*, note 14, 35.

27. Deibert and Rohozinski, *supra*, note 8, 16; Zittrain, *supra*, note 2.

28. Robert W. Hahn and Anne Laney-Ferrar, 'The law and economics of software security', *Harvard Journal of Law and Public Policy, 30,* (2006), 282, 298.

29. Kevin R. Pinkney, 'Putting blame where blame is due: Software manufacturers and customer liability for security-related software failure', *Albany Law Journal of Science and Technology, 13,* (2002), 43, 46.

30. The *2008 Rotman-TELUS joint study on Canadian IT security practices* surveyed 300 Canadian IT security specialists from a wide range of public and private organizations. http://www.rotman.utoronto.ca/securitystudy/

31. *Symantec, supra*, note 5, 8.

32. Deloitte Development LLC, 'Cyber crime: A clear and present danger—Combating the fastest growing cyber security threat', (2010), 15, http://www.deloitte.com/assets/Dcom-UnitedStates/Local%20Assets/Documents/AERS/us_aers_Deloitte%20Cyber%20Crime%20POV%20Jan252010.pdf

33. Symantec Enterprise Security, 'Symantec report on underground economy: July '07– June '08', November 2008, 4, http://eval.symantec.com/mktginfo/enterprise/white_papers/b-whitepaper_underground_economy_report_11-2008-14525717.en-us.pdf

34. Ibid.

35. *Symantec, supra*, note 6, 12.

36. Ibid.,10. One growing form of social engineering is the 'phishing scam', which helps feed confidential data to criminals who then use it for fraud and theft. For example, an attacker poses as a legitimate business, such as a bank, by using an email that looks authentic. The email can redirect the victim to a fake website that is carefully designed to resemble the real company's site. Once there, the victim is tricked into entering personal and financial data. Hahn and Layne-Ferrar, *supra*, note 28, 290.

37. Ibid.

38. Reid Skibell, 'The phenomenon of insecure software in a security-focused world', (2003), *University of Florida Journal of Technology Law and Policy, 8*(2), 107, 111.

39. Hahn and Layne-Ferrar, *supra*, note 28, 296.

40. *Symantec, supra*, note 6.

41. Zitrain, *supra*, note 2, 45.

42. Deloitte, *supra*, note 32, 6.

43. R.F. Dacey, 'Effective patch management is critical to mitigating software vulnerabilities', US General Accounting Office, 10 September 2003, GAO-03-1138T, 4, http://www.gao.gov/new. items/d031138t.pdf. See also Walther, *supra*, note 7, 7. Note that the estimated cost of lost productivity to companies affected, within the first five days of the spread of this worm, was more than US$1 billion.

44. Jennifer A. Chandler, 'Liability for botnet attacks', *Canadian Journal for Law and Technology 13*.

45. Deloitte, *supra*, note 32, 4.

46. Ibid., 5.

47. *Symantec, supra*, note 6, 24. Note that bots are programs that are covertly installed on a user's machine to allow an attacker to remotely control it through a communication channel. These programs are available for purchase on the underground economy for as little as US$0.04 per computer.

48. Ibid., 24.

49. John Soma, Patrick Singer, and Jeffrey Hurd, 'Spam still pays: The failure of the CAN-SPAM act of 2003 and proposed legal solutions', *Harvard Journal on Legislation, 45*, (2008), 165. See also Government of Canada, 'Stopping spam: creating a stronger, safer Internet', Report of the Taskforce on Spam, May 2005, http://www.ic.gc.ca/eic/site/ ecic-ceac.nsf/vwapj/stopping_spam_ May2005.pdf/$file/stopping_spam_ May2005.pdf

50. *Symantec, supra*, note 6, 16.

51. Perry Cheung, 'The need for Canadian spam legislation', (2007) *Asper Review of International Business and Trade Law, 7*, 227, 228–9.

52. Deibert and Rohozinski, *supra*, note 8, 16.

53. Both Canada and the United States have high Internet penetration rates; in each country, almost three-quarters of the population have access to the Internet. See Ronald Deibert et al. (Eds.), *Access controlled: The shaping of power, rights and rule in cyberspace* (Cambridge, MA: MIT Press), 370.

54. Statues of Canada 2009, c. 28, Bill S-4, *An act to amend the Criminal Code (identity theft and related misconduct)*, received royal assent 22 October 2009.

55. Criminal Code of Canada, R.S.,1985, c. C-46. See ss. 342.1, 342.2, and 380.

56. Note also that the Personal Information Protection and Electronic Documents Act, R.S.C. 2000, c. 5 (PIPEDA) could address some of the problems discussed herein. Similarly, the Competition Act contains provisions dealing with deceptive and misleading representations that have been used to target misleading advertisements in the traditional media.

57. G. Bruce Doern, 'The Harper Conservative agenda: True blue or Liberal-lite?', in Bruce Doern (ed.), *How Ottawa Spends 2006–2007: In from the cold, the Tory rise and the Liberal demise* (Montreal: McGill-Queen's University Press, 2006), 8.

58. Department of Justice Canada, 'Canadian communities now safer as Tackling Violent Crime Act receives royal assent', http://www.justice.gc.ca/

59. This bill addresses spam and related threats from unsolicited email, including

identity theft, phishing, counterfeit websites, viruses, botnets, and spyware. It also grants an additional right of civil action to businesses and individuals targeted by those who perpetrate these harmful and malicious activities.

60. The TELUS-Rotman study found that brand damage or reputation impact was the primary concern of survey respondents in terms of the perceived impacts or costs of security breaches. As many as 81 per cent of the Canadian organizations surveyed indicated that this was their primary concern in the wake of a breach, followed by lost time due to disruption (66 per cent), litigation (66 per cent), and lost customers (67 per cent). TELUS-Rotman, *supra*, note 30.

61. In order to deal with this problem, Parliament could introduce a mandatory reporting law. This approach has been successfully implemented in California. The California Security Breach Information Act (S.B. 1386), 202 Cal. Stat. 915, mandates businesses to publicly disclose security breaches if the confidential information of a California resident could be compromised. See also *Symantec*, *supra*, note 5, 20.

62. Dacey, *supra*, note 43, 4. As many as 80 per cent of computer security incidents go unreported, in most cases because the organization was either unable to recognize that its systems had been penetrated (because there was no clear indication of this) or because it was reluctant to report the attack.

63. Note that the United States has one of the most long-standing and robust computer crime statutes in the world. Robert Morris was the first person convicted under this statute, the Computer Fraud and Abuse Act (18 USC 1030), for writing the world's first computer worm, in 1991. However, enforcement has proven difficult; in fact, the US Department of Justice has declined to prosecute in as many as 78 per cent of referred cases because of lack of evidence, and this is understandable given the anonymous and inter-jurisdictional nature of cyberspace. Hahn and Layne-Farrar, *supra*, note 28, 289 and 333.

64. This point originates from Internet pioneer John Gilmore, who famously quipped, 'The Net interprets censorship as damage and routes around it.' See Philip Elmer-DeWitt and David S. Jackson, 'First nation in cyberspace', *Time, 142*(2) (6 December 1993). Also see Lessig, *supra*, note 14, 37.

65. Deibert and Rohozinski, *supra*, note 8, 16.

66. *Symantec*, *supra*, note 6, 8. For example, technological tools, such as anonymizers and anonymous remailers, enable criminals to conceal their identities when browsing the Web or communicating with other users.

67. Lessig, *supra*, note 14, 32–3.

68. Zittrain, *supra*, note 2, 32. For instance, a website can demand that a user create an ID and password in order to access content.

69. Lessig, *supra*, note 14, 33.

70. Sara M. Smyth, 'A "Reasoned apprehension" of overbreadth: An alternative approach to the problems presented by S. 163.1 of the Criminal Code', (2009) *UBC Law Review 41*(1), 69.

71. Emily B. Laidlaw, 'A framework for identifying Internet information gatekeepers', *International Review of Law, Computers & Technology 24*(3), (2010), 263, 264.

72. Ibid.

73. Ibid., 266 and 269.

74. Deibert and Rohozinski, *supra*, note 8, 17.

75. Schneier, *supra*, note 4, 205; Skibell, *supra*, note 38, 108. See also Bruce Schneier,

'Foreword' in John Vega and Gary McGraw, *Building secure software: How to avoid security problems the right way* (Reading, MA: Addison-Wesley Professional, 2002), xix. Also see Dacey, *supra*, note 33.

76. Pinkney, *supra*, note 29, 67.

77. Ibid., 45.

78. Dacey, *supra*, note 43, 2.

79. Jason Hiner, 'The top five reasons why Windows Vista failed', ZDNet, 6 October 2008, http://www.zdnet.com

80. Michael Ena, 'Securing online transactions: Crime prevention is the key', (2008). *Fordham Urban Law Journal*, 35, 147, 153. For example, within a month following Google's release of a new Windows XP flaw, criminals exploited a bug through more than 10,000 online attacks launched from malicious web pages in the United States, Russia, Portugal, Germany, and Brazil. The flaw was discovered on 10 June 2010 by a Google researcher who went public about it five days later after failing to convince Microsoft to issue a patch to fix the problem within 60 days. See also Robert McMillan, 'Microsoft: 10,000 PCs hit with new XP attack', 30 June 2010, *CSO Online*, http://www.csoonline.com

81. Pinkney, *supra*, note 29, 46.

82. Skibell, *supra*, note 29, 108; Gary McGraw, 'A taxonomy of coding errors', in *Crimeware—Understanding new attacks and defenses* (Boston: Addison-Welsley, 2008), 40.

83. Scott Berinato, 'Software vulnerability disclosure: The chilling effect', *CSO: Security and Risk*, 1 January 2007, 3, http://www.csoonline.com

84. Pinkney, *supra*, note 29, 113.

85. Douglas A. Barnes, 'Deworming the Internet', *Texas Law Review, 83* (2004), 279, 294. Note that, in 2002, Microsoft halted all feature development of Windows products for two months

(costing an estimated US$200 million) in lost productivity in order to address security concerns. This led the company to implement a new training and development process that tried to address security at all stages of software development. As well, in 2003, the Federal Trade Commission (FTC) demanded that Microsoft improve the security in its passport information service or face fines of up to US$11,000 per violation. This led the company to undertake a US$100 million security initiative that was supposed to lead to changes throughout the company. See Skibell, *supra*, note 29, 107–8; and Hahn and Laney-Ferrar, *supra*, note 28, 312–13.

86. Note that patches, or software updates, are often free to download; however, in many cases, users are forced to upgrade by purchasing the newer version at a discounted price (requiring reinstallation of the software program).

87. Barnes, *supra*, note 85, 295.

88. Hahn and Laney-Ferrar, *supra*, note 28, 318.

89. Pinkney, *supra*, note 29, 116.

90. Ibid., 114.

91. Barnes, *supra*, note 85, 298.

92. Hahn and Laney-Ferrar, *supra*, note 28, 325.

93. Ibid.

94. Skibell, *supra*, note 38, 116. There seems to be a general reluctance to outsource IT security on the part of organizations. For example, the TELUS-Rotman study found that 40 per cent of the Canadian respondents indicated that their organizations did not allow outsourcing of security; however, organizations that outsourced were found to be less likely to experience breaches that could be prevented through network security technologies. TELUS-Rotman, *supra*, note 30.

95. Bob Violino, 'Patch management: Simplifying IT managers' lives while improving security', CIO, 1 August 2003, http://www.cio.com/article/29609/Patch_Management_Simplifying_IT_Managers_Lives_While_Improving_Security. Note that estimates have put the cost of manually managing patch deployment to be $14,400 per year.

96. Ibid.

97. Ibid. According to Intel, 'researching each of the 4,200 vulnerabilities published by CERT last year for 10 minutes would have required 17.5 weeks, or 700 hours of a researcher's time.' Note also that after the SQL Slammer attack, RBC Centura Banks issued a directive to bring their production servers up to date on required patches. Managers estimated that it would take more than 12, 000 man-hours to complete this task, including deploying and testing patches on more than 220 servers.

98. Walther, *supra*, note 7. Holding software manufacturers liable for defects in their products would place a chill on software development and innovation.

99. Skibell, *supra*, note 38, 122–4.

100. Such as trade secret, copyright, and patent law.

101. Barnes, *supra*, note 85, 292.

102. Pinkney, *supra*, note 29, 130.

103. Ibid., 131.

104. Hahn and Laney-Ferrar, *supra*, note 28, 286.

105. Pinkney, *supra*, note 29, 47.

106. Ibid., 70.

107. Ibid., 68 and 125. Examples include warranty disclaimers and limitations of remedy.

108. Hahn and Laney-Ferrar, *supra*, note 28, 337.

109. Ibid., 284.

110. Skibell, *supra*, note 38, 107–8.

111. Scott Charney, 'Establishing end to end trust', Microsoft Corporation, 2008; paper can be found at http://www.microsoft.com/mscorp/twc/endoendtrust/vision/default.aspx

112. Skibell, *supra*, note 38, 110.

113. Schneier, *supra*, note 4, 360–1.

114. Ibid., 266.

115. Ibid., 260–1. Most users are vastly ignorant of the harms that threaten them, until they are victimized themselves; and even then, many users simply attribute the problem to something else or ignore it altogether. For example, Schneier notes that if there are too many security alerts or warning signals, many computer users learn to ignore them or, even worse, disable them.

116. Barnes, *supra*, note 85, 298. See also Skibell, *supra*, note 38, 116. This includes both individuals and corporate entities.

117. Pinkney, *supra*, note 29, 67.

118. Kevin Mitnick and William L. Simon, *The art of deception: Controlling the human element of security* (Indianapolis: John Wiley and Sons, 2002).

119. Hann and Laney-Farrer, *supra*, note 28, 294. For instance, in a recent example of data theft, a Nigerian national living in California posed as the head of a business and tricked employees at ChoicePoint—a consumer data collection agency—to give him access to its files. The perpetrator used the information to create fake credit card accounts. The issuing banks lost approximately US$2 million (and ChoicePoint incurred US$2 million in costs notifying customers of the security breach.

120. Schneier, *supra*, note 4, 268.

121. Neal Kumar Katyal, 'Digital architecture as crime control', Yale Law Journal 112 (2003), 2261, 2265.

122. Ibid.

123. Schneier, *supra*, note 4, 264.

124. Zittrain, *supra*, note 2, 161. Note, however, that Canada already has effective cyber-reporting hotlines, including Cybertip.ca and Phonebusters. Parliament should encourage Canadians to use them.

125. Generally, this would require establishing the following: a duty to use reasonable care, a breach of that duty, a reasonably close causal relationship between the breach of duty and the injury, and actual loss/damage. Pinkney, *supra*, note 29, 75.

126. Ibid., 76.

127. Hahn and Laney Ferrar, *supra*, note 28, 314.

128. Ibid., 318.

129. Barnes, *supra*, note 85, 2451.

130. Pinkney, *supra*, note 29, 78.

131. Schneier, *supra*, note 4, 164.

132. Zittrain, *supra*, note 2, 59.

133. Ronald J. Mann and Seth R. Belzley, 'The promise of Internet intermediary liability', (2005) 47 *Wm. & Mary Law Review* 239, 256.

134. Jonathan Zittrain, 'Internet points of control', *Boston College Law Review* 4 (2002), 653, 664.

135. Laidlaw, *supra*, note 71, 267.

136. Ibid.

137. Deibert and Rohozinski, *supra*, note 8, 24.

138. Lawrence Lessig, 'The zones of cyberspace', *Stanford Law Review* 48, (1996), 1403. Zittrain, *supra*, note 134, 673.

139. Jonathan Zittrain and John Palfrey, 'Introduction', in Ronald Deibert et al. (Eds.), *Access denied: The practice and policy of global internet filtering* (MIT Press: Cambridge, MA, 2008), 3.

140. *Yahoo! Inc. v. La Lingue Contre le Racisme et l'Antisemitisme*, 379 F. 3d 1120, 1121–2 (9th Cir. 2004).

141. Directive of the European Parliament and of the council on the retention of data, Brussels, 3 February 2006, 2005/0182 (COD), http://www.ispai.ie/drfinal.pdf. Note also that the United Kingdom has compelled its ISPs to retain data for up to two years under the Regulation of Investigatory Powers Act, 2000.

142. Peng Hwa Ang, 'International regulation of Internet content', in William J. Drake and Ernest J. Wilson (Eds.), *Governing global electronic networks: International perspectives on policy and power* (Cambridge, MA: MIT Press, 2008), 319.

143. Ibid.

144. Deibert and Rohozinski, *supra*, note 8, 26. In November 2006, Canada's largest ISPs, including Bell, Rogers, Shaw, and TELUS, joined with Cybertip.ca to launch a new initiative to block Internet child pornography. Cybertip.ca receives complaints regarding websites hosting child pornographic images. Analysts assess the information, and the potentially illegal websites are forwarded to the appropriate law enforcement agency. Foreign-hosted Internet addresses (URLs) associated with child pornography are compiled on a list and provided to participating ISPs. The ISPs then automatically block access to addresses on the list. Note that this initiative is voluntary and not a legal requirement.

145. Classification (Publications, Films and Computer Games) Act of 1995, No. 63, 1995 (Australia).

146. Seth F. Kreimer, 'Censorship by proxy: The first amendment, Internet intermediaries, and the problem of the weakest link', *University of Pennsylvania Law Review 55*, (2006), 11, 24; Arthur J.

Cockfield, 'The state of privacy and privacy-encroaching technologies after September 11: A two year report card on the Canadian government', *University of Ottawa Law and Technology Journal 1*, (2003), 325. See also Electronic Privacy Information Center, 'Lawsuit seeks immediate release of FBI carnivore documents', 2 August 2000, http//epic.org/privacy/carnivore/8_02_release.html

147. Deibert et al., *supra*, note 53, 380.

148. Deibert and Rohozinski, *supra*, note 8, 28, point out that some non-democratic countries have followed the lead of the United States and claimed that the war on terror justifies their surveillance and opposition to minority viewpoints. In many countries, including Egypt, a combination of electronic surveillance and prosecution techniques is used to stifle minorities, such as the gay and lesbian community.

149. Kreimer, *supra*, note 146, 28.

150. Diebert and Rohzinski, *supra*, note 8, 25.

151. Schneier, *supra*, note 4, 9; Jonathan Zittrain and John Palfrey, 'Internet filtering: The politics and mechanisms of control', in *Access denied, supra*, note at 45–9. As Zittrain and Palfrey point out, no state has managed to implement a perfect system of technical filtering. There are two central problems inherent with nation-wide filtering of the Internet: either the system is overly broad in that sites which are not meant to be filtered are filtered, or it is not broad enough, which means that not all sites intended to be filtered are filtered. In addition, users can find a way to circumvent the filtering technology; thus, no country can completely succeed in filtering Internet content.

152. Schneier, *supra*, note 4, 9.

153. Chandler, *supra*, note, 44; Zittrain, *supra*, note 2, 166.

154. Zittrain, *supra*, note 2, 166. For example, ISPs generally don't want to take these steps because users might claim that they are not getting the service they paid for and, furthermore, because quarantined users need to be taught how to clean their machines, which is complicated.

155. Deibert et al., *supra*, note 53, 370.

156. Bruce Schneier, 'The plan to quarantine infected computers', *Forbes*, 11 November 2010.

157. Ibid.

158. Ibid.

159. *R. v. Sharpe*, [2001] 1 S.C.R. 45 at para. 21.

160. Statues of Canada 1993, c. 38. Section 36 provides: 'Except where the Commission approves otherwise, a Canadian carrier shall not control the content or influence the meaning or purpose of telecommunications carried by it for the public.' Note that Project Cleanfeed, the voluntary initiative targeted at foreign URLs hosting child pornography, has not sought or obtained approval from the CRTC. See Deibert et al., *supra*, note, 375.

161. Deibert and Rohozinski, *supra*, note 8, 20.

162. Including Internet fraud, child pornography, and offences relating to computer viruses. An additional protocol addresses hate propaganda. Note that Canada recently enacted legislation dealing with Internet fraud; however, there is no legislation specifically targeting computer viruses.

163. Article 16 requires signatories to adopt legislation to permit the preservation of computer data, including traffic data, for up to 90 days if it is relevant to an investigation. Article 18 requires signatories to draft regulations that

permit law enforcement officials to request computer data, as well as individual ISP service subscriber information. Article 20 requires that signatory states draft legislation to compel ISPs to permit law enforcement officials to monitor and collect the traffic data of their subscribers in 'real-time'. Article 21 requires signatories to draft legislation requiring ISPs to intercept and store data or to assist law enforcement officials in doing so.

164. Sara M. Smyth, 'Mind the gap: A new model for Internet child pornography regulation', *University of Ottawa Law and Technology Journal* 4(1), (2007), 59.

165. Canada, 'Lawful access consultation document' (Ottawa: Department of Justice and Industry Canada and Solicitor General Canada, 25 August 2002).

166. Lawful access is an investigative technique use by law enforcement agents and national security agencies that involves intercepting communications and seizing information where authorized by law. Michael Geist, 'Liberals try to resuscitate big brother plan for the Internet', http://www.michaelgeist.ca/

167. Nevis Consulting Group (General Editor), 'Summary of submissions to the lawful access consultation,' Department of Justice Canada, 28 April 2003, http://canada.justice.gc.ca/eng/cons/la-al/sum-res/index.html

168. 38th Parliament, 1st Session, 4 October 2004 – 29 November 2005.

169. Dominique Valiquet, 'Telecommunications and lawful access: The legislative situation in Canada', Library of Parliament, 21 February 2006, 3.

170. Ibid., 8.

171. Dominique Valiquet, 'Bill C-46: investigative powers for the 21st century act', Library of Parliament, 24 September 2009.

172. Ibid.

173. Clayton J. Pecknold, 'Police have to operate in the rotary phone era while cellphones, BlackBerrys and the Internet are a reality', *Times Colonist*, 25 September 2007.

174. Since 1995, the Canadian Association of Chiefs of Police has been asking for legislation requiring all telecommunication service providers to have the technical means to enable police to conduct lawful interceptions of their networks. Dominique Valiquet, 'Bill C-47: Technical assistance for law enforcement in the 21st century act', Library of Parliament, 28 July 2009, 2.

175. For example, following the 2002 *Consultation Paper on Lawful Access*, the Office of the Privacy Commissioner of Canada maintained that Parliament failed to demonstrate the existence of a serious problem that needed to be addressed. Similar sentiments were echoed by the British Columbia Privacy Commission as well as the Electronic Frontier Foundation. Note also that similar concerns were addressed by industry and members of the public in the 'Summary of submissions to the lawful access consultation document', *supra*, note 127.

176. 2001 A.J. No. 869 (Alta. C.A.) (Q.L.).

177. Ibid., para.11.

178. *Hunter v. Southam*, [1984] 2 S.C.R. 145; *R. v. Collins*, [1987] 1 S.C.R. 265, 278.

179. *R. v. Oakes*, [1986] 1 S.C.R. 103. Note that this is commonly referred to as the '*Oakes* test.'

180. *R. v. Big M Drug Mart Ltd.*, [1985] 1 S.C.R. 295, 352.

181. *Oakes, supra*, note 179, para. 69. There are three important aspects of the proportionality test. First, the measures enacted (giving rise to the Charter violation) must be carefully designed to

achieve the objective in question. In other words, they must be rationally connected to the objective. Second, the means chosen should impair the right or freedom 'as little as possible'. The legislation, in other words, must limit the right no more than reasonably necessary to achieve its objective. Third, there must be proportionality between the effects of the measures, which are responsible for limiting the Charter right or freedom, and the objective being sought.

182. Ibid., para.70.

183. Paul Weinberg, 'Wiretaps could raise the cost of web access', *Globe and Mail*, 28 July 2005, http://intperspectives. wordpress.com. In 2002, the Canadian Association of Chiefs of Police (CACP) released a response to Parliament's *Lawful Access Consultation Document* in which it maintains that, under the current regime, ISPs are not required to have interception capabilities, so that when a new technology or communication service is introduced, law enforcement agents must develop innovative methods to gain access to the networks. Canadian police are frustrated because they have no standard means by which to intercept a suspect's communications; this is why they are asking for legislation to compel ISPs to have the technical means to enable law enforcement officials to intercept communications built into their networks from the outset.

184. Laura Huey and Richard S. Rosenberg, 'Watching the web: Thoughts on expanding police surveillance opportunities under the cyber-crime convention', *Canadian Journal of Criminology and Criminal Justice 46*, (2004), 597, 598. Also see the comments made by Paul Harold Macklin, then parliamentary secretary to the minister of justice, in the *House of Commons Debates*, 138, 2nd Session, 37th Parliament, 29 September 2003, 7933–44.

185. Ibid.

186. Part 6 of the Criminal Code sets out the requirements that must be met to apply successfully for an authorization to intercept private communications. Before an authorization is issued, the judge hearing the application must be satisfied that it would be in the best interests of the administration of justice to authorize the electronic surveillance. Except in the case of certain specific offences, such as a terrorism offence, the judge must also be satisfied that other investigative procedures have been tried and have failed, that other investigative procedures are unlikely to succeed, or that there is an urgency such that other investigative procedures are impractical.

187. Issuance of the order is based on the existence of reasonable grounds to believe that an offence has been committed, in the case of a general production order, or on the existence of reasonable grounds to suspect that an offence has or will be committed, in the case-specific production orders. Note also that an organization, such as an ISP, can collect personal information without the knowledge and consent of an individual under section 7(1)(e)(ii) of PIPEDA if the collection is made for the purpose of making a disclosure that is required by law. An organization can disclose personal information without the knowledge and consent of an individual under section 7(3)(c. 1) of PIPEDA if the disclosure is made to a government institution and (iii) the disclosure will be made 'for the purpose of administering any law of Canada or a province.'

188. Daphne Gilbert, Ian R. Kerr, and Jena McGill, 'The medium and the message: Personal privacy and the forced marriage of police and telecommunications providers', *Criminal Law Quarterly 51*, (2005), 469, 500.

189. For example, pursuant to Bill C-47, all interceptions must be kept confidential and ISPs are required to guarantee the security of the contents of intercepted communications, data, and the identity of the individuals and organizations involved (clause 6[2]); requests for information must be made in writing and records must be kept for each request (clause 18); the commissioner of the RCMP, the director of CSIS, the commissioner of competition, or a chief of police will be required to verify, on a regular basis, that the requests comply with Bill C-47 and its regulations (clauses 20[1], 20[2], 20[3], 20[7], and 20[8]), and the privacy commissioner of Canada and/or the provincial privacy commissioners will have the power to conduct audits to determine whether the provisions relating to requests for information are being complied with (clauses 20[4] to 20[6]).

190. Schneier, *supra*, note 4, 170–5.

191. Aaron Emigh and Zulfikar Ramazan, 'Overview of crimeware', in Markus Jakobsson and Zulfikar Ramzan (Eds.), *Crimeware: Understanding new attacks and defenses* (Boston: Addison-Wesley, 2008), 29.

192. Note that the bill also sets out a number of 'extrajudicial protection measures', including records requirements and audits to determine whether the provisions in Bill C-47 and its regulations are complied with.

193. *R. v. Plant*, [1993] 3 S.C.R. 281.

194. For example, in *R. v. Ward*, [2008] ONCJ 335, the court found that given the contractual agreement entered into between the ISP and the user, as well as the information being sought, the customer's name and address did not fall within the protected 'biographical core of personal information' discussed by the Supreme Court of Canada in *Plant*. A similar decision was reached in *R. v. Vasic*, [2009] O.J. No. 685; and *R. v. Wilson*, [2009] O.J. No. 1067.

195. Weinberg, *supra*, note 183.

196. In 2008, the average cost per incident of data breach in the United States was US$6.7 million, an increase of 5 per cent from the previous year. Symantec, *supra*, note 5, 19.

197. Rotman-TELUS, *supra*, note 30, 5.

198. Ibid., 23.

199. Clause 68. This directly mirrors what was proposed in Bill C-74.

200. Bill C-74, s. 15.

201. For example, Parliament could commit to paying the costs by setting aside a substantial sum of money for that purpose, as was done in the United States. Parliament could also make reimbursement for all discretionary costs, as is the case in the United Kingdom. Requiring ISPs to pay the full implementation costs is another option, although this might jeopardize Canada's ability to maintain a competitive and fair communications industry.

202. Deibert et al., *supra*, note 45, 370.

PART 2

SUGGESTED READINGS

Chapter 8

Babor, T., Caulkins, J.P., Griffith, E., Fischer, B., Foxcroft, & D.R., Humphreys, K., et al. (2010). *Drug policy and the public good*. Oxford, UK: Oxford University Press.

DeBeck, K., Wood, E., Montaner, J., & Kerr, T. (2006). Canada's 2003 renewed drug strategy—An evidence based review. *HIV/AIDS Policy and Law Review, 11*, 1–12.

Fischer, B. (1999). Prohibition, public health and a window of opportunity: An analysis of Canadian drug policy, 1985–1997. *Policy Studies, 20*, 197–210.

Giffen, J., Endicott, S., & Lambert, S. (1991). Panic and indifference—The politics of Canada's drug laws. Ottawa: Canadian Centre on Substance Abuse.

Global Commission on Drug Policy. *War on Drugs—Report of the Global Commission on Drug Policy* (June 2011). http://www.globalcommissionondrugs.org/Report

Chapter 9

Bell, C. (2011). *The freedom of security: Governing Canada in the age of counter-terrorism*. Vancouver: University of British Columbia Press.

Daniels, R., Macklem, P., & Roach, K. (2001). *The security of freedom: Essays on Canada's Anti-Terrorism Bill*. Toronto: University of Toronto Press.

Forcese, C. (2008). *National Security Law*. Toronto: Irwin Law.

Kassam, K.-A.S. (2010). *Understanding terror: Perspectives for Canadians*. Calgary: University of Calgary Press.

Roach, K. (2011). *The 9/11 effect: Comparative counterterrorism*. New York: Cambridge University Press.

Chapter 10

Cohen, M.G., & Pulkingham, J. (Eds). (2009). *Public policy for women: The state, income security and labour market issues*. Toronto: University of Toronto Press.

Crowe, C., & Baker, N. (2007) *Dying for a home: Homeless activists speak out*. Toronto: Between the Lines.

Swanson, J. (2001). *Poor bashing: The politics of exclusion*. Toronto: Between the Lines.

Young, M. (Ed.). (2007). *Poverty: Rights, social citizenship, and legal activism*. Vancouver: University of British Columbia Press.

Chapter 11

Aas, K.F. (2007). Analyzing a world in motion: Global flows meet criminology of the other. *Theoretical Criminology, 11*(2), 282–303.

Chan, W. (2006). Crime, deportation and the regulation of immigrants in Canada. *Crime, Law and Social Change, 44*(2), 153–80.

Pratt, A. (2005). *Securing borders: Detention and deportation in Canada*. Vancouver: University of British Columbia Press.

Pratt, A. (2001). Sovereign power, carceral conditions and penal practices: Detention and deportation in Canada. *Studies in Law, Politics and Society, 23*, 45–78.

Roberts, B. (1998). *Whence they came: Deportation from Canada 1900–1935*. Ottawa: University of Ottawa Press.

Walters, W. (2002). Deportation, expulsion and the international police of aliens. *Citizenship Studies, 6*(3), 265–92.

Welch, M. (2003). Detained: Immigration laws and the expanding INS jail complex. Philadelphia: Temple University Press.

Chapter 12

Barton, A., & Johns, N. (Forthcoming). *The policy making process in the criminal justice system*. Oxford, UK: Routledge.

Brillo, B.B.C. (2010, August). Power politics in policymaking: The Anti-Money Laundering Act of the Philippines. *Research and Practise in Social Sciences, 6*(2), 43–61.

Hall, M. (2010). *Victims & policy making: A comparative perspective*. Collompton, UK: Willan Press.

Oliver, W.M., & Marion, N.E. (Eds). (2008). *The making of criminal justice policy in the United States: Essays on the role of the president, the Congress, and the public*. Lewiston, NY: Edwin Mellen Press.

Chapter 13

Brenner, S.W. (2006). Cybercrime Jurisdiction. *Crime, Law, Social Change, 46*, 189.

Goldsmith, J., & Wu, T. (2006). *Who controls the Internet?* Oxford, UK: Oxford University Press.

Lessig, L. (1999). *Code and other laws of cyberspace*. New York: Basic Books.

Smyth, S.M. (2010). *Cybercrime in Canadian criminal law*. Toronto: Carswell.

Wall, D.S. (2010). Micro-frauds: Virtual robberies, stings and scams in the information age. In T. Holt & B. Schell (Eds). *Corporate hacking and technology driven crime: Social dynamics and implications*. Hershey, PA: IGI Global.

SUGGESTED WEBSITES

Chapter 8

Canadian Centre on Substance Abuse. http://www.ccsa.ca/

Canadian Harm Reduction Network. http://www.canadianharmreduction.com/

Centre for Addiction and Mental Health. http://www.camh.net/

Chapter 9

Craig Forcese's national security law blog. http://craigforcese.squarespace.com/national-security-law-blog/

Department of Public Safety national security site. http://www.publicsafety.gc.ca/prg/ns/index-eng.aspx

Security Intelligence Review Committee website. http://www.sirc-csars.gc.ca/index-eng.html

Stop secret trials website. http://www.
homesnotbombs.ca/secrettrials.htm

Chapter 10

Canada without Poverty. http://www.
cwp-csp.ca/Blog/

Canadian Centre for Policy Alternatives.
http://www.policyalternatives.ca/

National Council for Welfare. http://
www.ncw.gc.ca/h.4m.2@-eng.jsp?
lang=eng

Ontario Coalition against Poverty. http://
www.ocap.ca/

PovNet. http://www.povnet.org/

Chapter 11

Amnesty International (AI). http://www.
amnesty.ca/

Canada Border Services Agency (CBSA).
http://www.cbsa-asfc.gc.ca/
menu-eng.html

Canadian Council for Refugees (CCR).
http://ccrweb.ca/

Citizenship and Immigration Canada
(CIC). http://www.cic.gc.ca/english/
index.asp

Global Detention Project. http://www.
globaldetentionproject.org/de/
home.html

No One is Illegal (Toronto). http://
toronto.nooneisillegal.org/

Chapter 12

Department of Justice, Canada. Publications. http://www.justice.gc.ca/
eng/dept-min/pub/index.asp_

House of Commons Committees,
Canada. http://www.parl.gc.ca/
CommitteeBusiness/ReportsRe-
sponses.aspx?Language=E&Mode=
1&Parl=40&Ses=3#expand

Law Enforcement. http://www.public-
safety.gc.ca/prg/le/index-eng.aspx

Public Safety Canada, Organized Crime.
http://www.publicsafety.gc.ca/prg/
le/oc/index-eng.aspx

Chapter 13

Bruce Schneier. http://www.schneier.
com

CATA Alliance. http://www.cata.ca/
Communities/caip/

Cybertip, Canadian Centre for Child
Protection. http://www.cybertip.ca/

Michael Geist. http://www.michaelgeist.
ca/

Public Safety Canada, Cyber Security.
http://www.publicsafety.gc.ca/prg/
ns/cbr/index-eng.aspx

INDEX

Note: Page numbers in **bold** refer to figures.

Aboriginal Bail Program, 149
Aboriginal Justice Initiative, 150; *see also*
    Aboriginal Justice Strategy
Aboriginal Justice Inquiry of Manitoba, 135, 139,
    147
Aboriginal Justice Strategy, 143, 150–4, 155;
    community-based alternatives in, 152–3,
    153–4; criticism of, 151; funded projects,
    150–1, 153, 155; objectives of, 150, 157n19
Aboriginal peoples, 3–4; ability to pay cost of
    bail, 148–9; breaching conditions, 145–6;
    colonial experience of, 141, 146, 156n10;
    conditional sentencing and, 145–6; defining
    'community,' 151–2; domestic violence cases
    in Winnipeg, 171; effects of over-
    incarceration, 138; employment and
    educational attainment, 156n9; harms from
    drug use, 193; income, 139–40; net widening
    for, 145, 146; overrepresentation in criminal
    justice system, 3–4, 95, 137–8, 140–1, 142,
    143, 144, 152, 153, 154; pre-trial detention
    and, 147, 148, 149; rates of incarceration,
    137–8; restorative justice, 143, 151, 153;
    sentencing policy and, 141–6; social and
    living conditions, 140; socio-economic
    marginality, 139–40, 145–6, 154; suicide rate
    and, 140; systemic discrimination and,
    139–41, 154; in Toronto, 146; tuberculosis
    and, 140; in urban settings, 136–7; welfare
    and, 265
Aboriginal women: domestic violence and, 171;
    mother's allowance programs, 265
Aboriginal youths: incarceration rates, 138;
    overrepresentation in criminal justice system,
    138; Youth Criminal Justice Act and, 125
accepted parole review, 55n15
accountability: police and, 24–6; in Youth
    Criminal Justice Act, 112, 113
Act to amend the Criminal Code (minimum
    penalties for offences involving firearms),
    314, 318
Act to amend the Criminal Code [Organized
    Crime and Law Enforcement]), 310, 313
Act to amend the Proceeds of Crime [Money
    Laundering] and Terrorist Financing Act),
    309–10
adware, 329, 344
Act to Facilitate Combating the Laundering of
    Proceeds of Crime, 308
African-Canadians, 144
Air India Flight 182, 11, 242; investigative
    hearings, 25, 233–4, 235
Alati, Daniel, 301
Alberta: domestic violence court in, 160
Alberta Court of Appeal, 342
Alberta Law Enforcement Review Board, 25
Almrei, Hassan, 238

alternative new force technologies and strategies,
    19
Amnesty International, 171
Anand, S., 143
anti-biker legislation, 310
anti-gang legislation, 310; Bill C-95, 310, 313
anti-spyware software, 337
Anti-Terrorism Act (ATA), 186, 222, 243; Bill
    C-36, 226–7; debate over, 226–7, 241–2;
    preventive arrests and investigative hearings
    in, 232–3, 234–5; definition of terrorism,
    227–8, 229, 230; expression of thought, 228;
    protests under, 228, 229; religious and
    political motive requirement for terrorism
    in, 231; Resolution 1373 and, 225; *see also*
    terrorism
anti-terrorism law: immigration law as, 223, 227,
    237, 238, 240, 247n72; *see also* Anti-
    Terrorism Act (ATA)
antivirus software, 337, 330
Application under s. 83.28, 233
Arar, Maher, 21, 25, 223, 224, 234, 242; case, 227
Arar Commission, 11
Arbour JJ., 233
arrest, preventive, 232–3; debate over renewal of,
    234–5
Ashworth, A., 93, 94, 95
attentive public, xxii–xxiii, xix
Attorney General of Ontario, 146
Auger, Michael, 310
Australia: jurisdiction over criminal law in,
    xvii–xviii; national security policy in, 243;
    'notice-and-takedown' regime in, 339; police
    research in, 7; welfare state in, 249
Australian Security Intelligence Organization, 233

bail: Aboriginal peoples and, 148–9; before
    reform movement, 32–6; cash, 33; conditions,
    41–2, 42–4; conditions for youth, 42; in
    Criminal Code, 2; at Gladue Court, 147–9;
    impediment to obtaining, 39–40;
    politicization of crime and, 47; risk-averse
    mentality and, 47–9; sureties in cases, 41;
    'tough on crime' philosophy and, 47, 51;
    violations, 43–4
bail bondsmen, 33, 41
bail hearings: adjournments, 49–50; amount of
    time and number of appearances, 49–50,
    51–2; change in processing on average day,
    50; consequences of 'wrong' decisions, 47–9;
    increase in number of, 55n17; mean length
    in time and appearances, **50**; Ontario total
    and cases with, **49**; police and, 48–9;
    reverse-onus provisions, 100; risks to
    decision-maker, 48
Bail Reform Act, 2, 31–2, 35–6, 46, 157n15;
    forms of release, 36, 40–1; grounds for

detention, 35; impediment to obtaining bail, 39–40; modifications, 36; presumption of innocence, 35; reverse-onus provisions, 39; rights-protecting parameters, 31, 32, 34, 36, 46, 51
Baker, M. and D. Tippin, 252
Baylis, Todd, 281, 283
Beare, M., 303
Bentley, Chris, 54n10
Berra, Yogi, 102, 104
biker gangs, 305, 310, 314, 319
bills: *C-3*, 119, 120–1; *C-4*, 104; *C-7*, 121–2, 123–4, 124–5; *C-10*, 314, 318; *C-15*, 206–7; *C-19*, 103; *C-22*, 309; *C-24*, 310, 313; *C-25*, 54n10, 103–4, 309–10; *C-27*, 331; *C-28*, 331; *C-36*, 226–7, 232; *C-44*, 280, 281; *C-46*, 341–2, 343, 344; *C-47*, 341, 342, 343, 344, 345, 346, 357n189; *C-48*, 63–4, 67–9, 70, 71, 72–3, 75, 76–7; *C-53*, 313; *C-68*, 118–19; *C-74*, 341; *C-86*, 279; *C-95*, 310, 313; *S-6*, 63–4, 64–7, 69–70, 71, 72, 75, 76–7
black Canadians, 95
Bloc Québécois, xv, 100, 122, 128, 299; credit for pre-trial detention, 54n13; debate over renewal of preventive arrests and investigative hearings, 234; Youth Criminal Justice Act and, 123, 124, 129
blood-borne viruses (BBV), 193, 194, 196, 204; *see also* hepatitis C virus; HIV/AIDS
Bonner, Raymond Lawrence, 312
botnets, 330, 337
Brewin, Andrew, 60
Bre-X case, 321n7
Britain: welfare state in, 249; *see also* England & Wales; United Kingdom
British Columbia: campaign against welfare fraud, 249, 258–62; drug-related overdose deaths, 193; 'grow-op' industry, 203; welfare policies, 249–50; welfare policy reforms, 256–8
British Columbia Court of Appeal, 142
Brodeur, J.-P., 5, 302
Brown, Lawrence, 281, 293n7
Brown Commission, 89
bureaucrats, xxi
Bureau of Narcotic Drugs, 189
Business of Crime, The, 305–6

Caledon Institute for Social Policy, 258
Calgary: domestic violence court, 172, 174
Calgary Police Service, 274, 288
California: Compassionate Use Act, 203
California Security Breach Information Act, 350n61
Canada @ 150 Research Report, 302
Canada Border Services Agency (CBSA), 21, 276, 279
Canada's Drug Strategy, 191, 207
Canadian Addiction Survey (CAS), 192

Canadian Alcohol and Drug Use Monitoring Survey (CADUMS), 192, 198
Canadian Alliance Party: Youth Criminal Justice Act and, 123–4
Canadian Association of Chiefs of Police (CACP), 26, 356n183
Canadian Association of Elizabeth Fry Societies, 74
Canadian Bar Association, 141
Canadian Bill of Rights, 30
Canadian Centre for Justice Statistics, 125
Canadian Centre for Policy Alternatives (CCPA), 248, 252, 257, 258, 259
Canadian Charter of Rights and Freedoms, xviii, 223; Aboriginal peoples in, 136; exception for deportation to torture, 239; investigative hearings in, 236; presumption of innocence, 30; 'right to health' provision, 195, 204; security certificates and, 236; security policy and, 234; pre-trial detention in, 30
Canadian Civil Liberties Association, 318
Canadian Committee on Corrections (Ouimet Committee), 34, 87
Canadian Human Rights Commission, 227
Canadian Resource Centre for Victims of Crime, 69
Canadian Security Intelligence Service (CSIS), 14, 235, 237, 279, 284; mandate of, 279–80
Canadian Sentencing Commission, 85, 88–9, 93, 98
cannabis, 191, 192; alternative law and policy options, 201; decriminalization of, 191; for medical purposes, 202–3; production industry, 203; reform bills, 201–2; treatment for, 202; use, 201–3, 208
Cannabis Compassion Club (CCC), 202–3
capital punishment, 58, 59–60, 95
Carignan, Claude, 64
Cenaiko, Harvey, 66
census, mandatory long-form replaced by voluntary survey, 318
Charkaoui (case), 239–40, 241, 242
Charkaoui, Adil, 238, 240
Chiarelli v. Canada, 291
child pornography, online, 332, 338–9, 342, 353n144
China: Internet content filtering (blocking), 338
ChoicePoint, 352n119
Chrétien, Jean, 88
Chunn, D. and S. Gavigan, 261
Citizenship and Immigration Canada (CIC): organized crime section, 281
civil servants, xxi; as subject-matter experts, 101, 102, 302–3
Clark, Joe, 227
click-wrap agreements, 335
Clinton, Bill, xv
Clinton, Hillary, 319
cocaine, 192, 194

cognitive-behavioural therapies (CBTs): crack use and, 196
Cold War, 277, 278
Cole, David, Justice, 303
Colleges of Physicians and Surgeons, 200
Collins, S., 254
Commission of Inquiry into the Actions of Canadian Officials in Relation to Maher Arar, 11, 244n11
Commission of Inquiry into the Investigation of the Bombing of Air India Flight 182, 11, 244n11
Commission on Systemic Racism in Ontario Criminal Justice System, 139
Committee on Justice and Human Rights, 64
Committee on Legal and Constitutional Affairs, 64
Communication Security Establishment (CSE), 14
communities: defining, 151–2; as problem in policing, 18–19; suspect ethnic or minority, 19
Community Justice Committee, 153
Computer Fraud and Abuse Act, 350n63
conditional sentences/sentencing, 145–6, 204, 206; breach of, 145–6, 175; drug law and, 204–5
conducted energy weapons. See tasers
Conservative Party. See Progressive Conservative Party
Constitution Act, 1867, xvii, xviii
Controlled Drugs and Substances Act (CDSA), 191, 201, 207
Cook, Dee, 264
cookies, 344
core personal information, 345
correctional institutions: drug use in, 203–4; jurisdiction over, xvii; remand population in, 51
Correctional Service of Canada (CSC), 203, 317
Corrections and Conditional Release Act, 63, 67, 79
Cotler, Irwin, 34, 318
Council of Europe: Cybercrime Convention, 341, 342, 346
courts: national security policy-making and, 241; policy-making role of, xviii–xix; Youth Criminal Justice Act and, 113
crack, 192, 194, 195–7; blood-borne viruses and, 196; health-oriented interventions, 196; HIV and HCV transmission, 196, 197; lack of treatment options, 196; mortality and morbidity and, 196
crime: globalization and, 9–10; as local issue, 91; perceptions of, xxii–xxiii, 101; politicization of, xiv–xvi, 99–100, 102; symbolic dimension of, xiii–xiv
crime prevention: political parties on, 96, 97, 100
crime-security nexus, 276–7, 284, 287, 289, 291; forging of, 277–8; versus humanitarianism, 284–6

criminal cases: number of days required to resolve, 54n8
Criminal Code of Canada, 6, 7; Aboriginal peoples in, 154; bail in, 2, 39–40, 42; conditional sentences in, 157n13; criminal organization offences, 311–13; definition of terrorist activities, 227–8; domestic courts and, 165; drug law enforcement, 191; federal responsibility for, 7, 10; identity theft in, 331; imprisonment in, 87; mandatory minimum sentences in, 93; multiple murder provisions, 68; murder sentencing in, 58; sentencing in, 59, 141–2; 'serious offences' of, 314–15; section 718.2(e) of, 144, 146, 147, 148; section 745, 63, 70; war criminality provisions, 289
Criminal Conspiracies (Beare), 303
Criminal Intelligence Service Canada (CISC), 284
criminal justice policy, xii, xv–xvi, xvii–xxiii; civil servant experts and, 92; concepts in, x–xii; distinctive features of, xii–xiv; ideology, xiv–xv ; journals, xiv; origins and sources, xvii–xix; policy community, xix–xx; recent interest in, xiv–xvii; study of, x–xvii
criminal justice system, xii; fragmentation of, xii–xiii; symbolic dimension of, xiii–xiv
Criminal Law in Canadian Society, 88, 90, 105n3
Criminal Organization and High Risk Offender Unit (COHROU), 177
criminal organizations, 309, 310–13; mega-cases, 313, 316–17; offences in Criminal Code, 311–13; 'serious offences' of, 314–15; 'signature activities' of, 314, 315; UN typology of, 319
'Criminals First' initiative, 281
Cross-Cultural Roundtable on Security, 19
cybercrime, 187, 326; challenges of enforcing policies, 330–3; federal government and, 331–2; human security and, 336–8; international co-operation and, 340–1; negative publicity from, 331; network security and, 338–41; new opportunities and risks, 329–30; precautions taken by users, 337; public policy and, 346; social engineering and, 336; software security and, 333–6; third parties and, 332–3; types of, 328; underground economy of, 328–9; users ignorant of harms, 352n115
cyber-reporting hotlines, 353n124
Cybertip.ca, 353n124, 353n144

Daenzer, P., 252
'danger to the public' provision, 280, 281–2, 283, 287
debt, government, 22
Dechart, Bob, 65, 67
Democrats, xv
Department of Indian and Northern Affairs, 136
Department of Justice Canada, xix, 131, 152, 316;

Aboriginal Justice Strategy, 143, 150–4, 155; review of youth justice system, 116–17; on Young Offenders Act, 111–12; Youth Justice Policy section, 117; Youth Justice Renewal Fund, 125

Department of National Defence, 278

Department of the Solicitor General, 303

Desrochers, Daniel, 310

Des Rosiers, Nathalie, 73

Dickson-Gilmore, J. and C. La Prairie, 139, 144, 145–6, 151

digital interceptions, 342–3, 343–4, 356n186; ISPs and, 356n183, 357n189; privacy and, 344–5

diplomacy, xx

Directions for Reform, 89, **90**

division of powers, federal-provincial/territorial, 91, 92, 118

domestic homicides, 173; battered women killing abusive partners, 74; death rate, 178; in Manitoba, 179

domestic violence, 161; arrest rates, 161; breaches and, 175, 177; challenges of cases, 162–3, 163–4; charge of common assault, 172–3; charging directive, 161; complexity of cases, 162, 163; diversion programs for offenders, 172, 174; dual arrests in, 170; limits of traditional justice system, 162–4; overrepresentation of disadvantaged peoples, 171–2; period of safety after arrest, 176; police arrest rates, 168; public visibility of, 161–2, 168; recidivism, 173, 175–7; spousal conviction rates in Winnipeg, **173**; treatment for offenders, 178; victim and accused characteristics, 170–2; in Winnipeg, 169, 170–2, **173**

domestic violence (DV) courts, 4, 160, 165; court emphasis, 167; criteria for inclusion, 166; differentiation across jurisdictions, 166–7; expansion of treatment programs for batterers, 168; expansion of victim services, 168, 178; file ownership, 167; impact on domestic violence, 168–9, 177–8; judicial review, 166; range of court processes included, 166–7; standard components of, 166; *see also* Winnipeg Family Violence Court

Doob, A.N. and J.B. Sprott, 138

Downes, Phil, 73–4

drug law and policy, 186; brief history of, 189–92; conditional sentencing, 204–5; enforcement, 191–2; harm reduction, 207; mandatory treatment clause, 191; possession for the purpose of trafficking charges, 191; treatment interventions in, 190, 191, 205

drugs, illicit, 192; Aboriginal peoples and, 193; in corrections, 203–4; harms and costs of, 192–3, 208; mortality and morbidity and, 193; overdose deaths, 193; treatment or public health measures, 207

drug treatment courts (DTCs), 164, 165, 205–6

Egmont, 301

elected officials, xx, xxii

Electronic Commerce Protection Act, 331

11 September 2001 terrorist attacks, xxiii, 11, 280; policing since, 2

emergency shelters, 161

Employment and Assistance Act (BCEA), 256, 259, 260

Employment and Assistance for Persons with Disabilities Act (BCEAPWD), 256, 259

England & Wales: addressing crime through imprisonment, 98–9; changes in sentencing laws, 93; homicide rates, 82–4; imprisonment rates, 82–4; imprisonment trends, 79–80; judiciary in, 93–4; political response to crime, 98; 'three-strikes' provision, 95

enterprise crime, 305–6, 314; *see also* organized crime

Enterprise Crime Study Report, 305–6, 313–14

Ericson, Richard, 17

European Union (EU): Internet filtering, 338

Europol, 305

Executive Research Forum, 7

failure to comply with a court order, 43–4, **44**, 54n9

'faint hope' clause, 58; repeal of, 96, 100; *see also* 15-year review

Fairchild, E.S., xxii

Federal Court of Appeal, 223

federal government (Parliament): administrative organization of, 92; jurisdiction over criminal law, xvii, 1, 6; minority versus majority governments, 99; responsibility for Aboriginal peoples, 136

federalism, xx

Federal-Provincial Conference on Organized Crime, 306

Federal-Provincial-Territorial Task Force on Youth Justice, 115–16

Federal Trade Commission (FTC), 351n85

Federation of Canadian Municipalities (FCM), 26

Felderhof, John, 321n7

15-year review, 58, 61–3; Bill S-6, 63–4; impact on victims, 69–70

Fighting Internet and Wireless Spam, 331

Financial Action Task Force (FATF), 301, 309, 319, 320–321n2

financial fraud, 306

FINTRAC (Financial Transactions Reports Analysis Centre of Canada), 309

First Nations people, 156n1; income, 140; *see also* Aboriginal peoples

'foreign nationals', 282, 287

FPT Coordinating Committee of Senior Officials (CCSO), 117, 118

France: Internet filtering, 338

Francis, Gary, 281, 293n7

Franks, C.E.S., 234

Frantino, Julian, 13
fraud: online, 329; welfare, 250, 253, 258–62, 263, 264, 266
Fresh Killers (FK), 274, 285
Friedland, Martin, 32–4, 41, 93; publicity for, 33–4

'GallowayBoyz', 312
gangs: national security and, 284; racialized, 283; biker, 305, 310, 314, 319; street, 309, 314
Gayle, Clinton, 281
Gilliom, J., 254
Gladue, Jamie, 142
Gladue (Aboriginal Persons) Court, 146–50, 154; Aboriginal Bail Program, 149; bail and, 147; locations of, 147; success of, 149–50
globalization, 9–10, 11, 279
global policy transfer, 7–8
Globe and Mail, 33–4
Gottschalk, M., 99
governance: police and, 24–6
'governing through crime', xxiii, 185, 186, 222, 243
governmental witnesses: bills S-6 and C-48, 64–9
Grafstein, Jerahmiel, 55n13
Grant, O'Neil, 281, 293n7
Green Party, xv
'green teams', 203
'grow-ops', 203
gun crimes: mandatory minimum penalties and, 86
Guzman, Michael De, 321n7
G-20 summit, 12–13, 13–14, 19, 24, 25

hackers, 328, 329, 330, 333, 335, 336, 337
Haggerty, Kevin, 17
Hanger, Art, 275
hanging, 58; see also capital punishment
Harkat, Mohammed, 238
harm reduction, 207
Harper, Stephen, 63, 76, 234, 303, 317, 331
Harsanyi, Sharma, 275
Hartman, Y., 255
Hawn, Laurie, 317–18
Head, Don, 66
Henman, P. and G. Marston, 254
hepatitis C virus infections: drug use and, 191, 193, 196
heroin, 190, 194, 197–201
heroin assisted treatment (HAT) trials, 200–1, 207
'high-policing' model, 302
HIV/AIDS: drug use and, 191, 193, 194, 196, 204
Hogg, Peter, xvii–xviii
Holland, Mark, 315
HomeFront Program, Calgary, 167
Home Office Police Research Unit, 7
homicide: rates in Canada, 82–4; in Canada, England & Wales, and US, 83; domestic, 74, 173, 178, 179

House of Commons Special Committee on the Non-Medical Use of Drugs, 201
House of Commons Standing Committee on Justice and Legal Affairs, 116, 299
Howard, Michael, 99
human security, cybercrime and, 336–8
Hussein, Liban, 225

Iacobucci, Justice, 233
identity theft, 330, 331
ideology: criminal justice and, xiv–xv
immigrants: welfare benefits and, 265
Immigration Act (1952), 278–9
Immigration and Refugee Board (IRB), 273
Immigration and Refugee Protection Act (IRPA), 228, 231, 280, 285; 'danger to the public' in, 280, 281–2, 283, 287; power to detain, 287; security certificates and, 237; 'serious criminality' in, 273, 280, 282
Immigration Appeal Division (IAD), 281, 284, 285; Ribic factors, 293n13; Tran's case and, 285, 286
immigration detention, 287, 289–90, 291; use of body restraints, 290
immigration law and policy: as anti-terrorism law, 223, 227, 237, 238, 240, 247n72; crime-security nexus in, 278–80; criminal exclusionary category in, 278; discretionary power in administration of, 286–8; racism in, 278; security certificates, 236–40
immigration penality, 186–7, 276, 277, 279, 287, 289, 291
impaired driving offences: mandatory minimum sanctions for, 85
imprisonment: addressing crime through, 82, 102; costs, 100–1; in Criminal Code, 87; culture of restraint, 86–90; impact on crime rates, 98; racism and, 95; remission of sentences, 45, 101; reports proposing restraint in, 90; stability in Canada's use of, 3; statutory release, 45–6, 101
imprisonment policies: balanced response to pressures to adopt more punitive, 84–6; cultural factors countering pressures to adopt more punitive, 94–9; enforcement of, 103; historical factors in countering pressures to adopt more punitive, 86–90; outcomes of, 317; pressures to adopt punitive; public attitudes towards, 94; structural factors in countering pressures to adopt more punitive, 90–4; unofficial, 79
imprisonment rates, 37, 79, 80–4, 81; comparing Canada, England & Wales, and US, 82–4, 83, 89; counts versus admissions, 104–5n2; crime rates and, 82, 84; increase in Canadian, 99, 102; stability in Canada's, 80–2, 84–99; trends in, 79–80, 80–4
incarceration. See imprisonment
income: Aboriginal peoples and, 139–40; earned while receiving welfare, 257; median, 156n8

Indian Act, 136, 151
injection drug use, 194–5; acute health risks from, 194; blood-borne viruses and, 191, 193; in correctional institutions, 204
innocence, presumption of, 30, 35; pre-trial detention and, 31
Insite, 195, 208
Institute for Strategic International Studies, 26
Integrated Border Enforcement Teams (IBETS), 20–1
Integrated Market Enforcement Teams (IMETS), 21
Integrated National Security Enforcement Teams (INSETS), 21
integrated national security policing, 20, 21
Integrated Proceeds of Crime (IPOC), 309
intelligence-led policing (ILP), 17–18
interest groups, xxi, xxii
inter- and intra-governmental relations, xx
Internet: brief overview of, 327–8; in Canada, 346; challenge of regulating, 326; 'end-to-end' design, 327; penetration rates, 349n53; proposed regulations, 331–2; surveillance, 339; threat landscape of, 328–30; see also cybercrime
Internet content filtering (blocking), 338–9, 354n151
Internet Protocols (IP) addresses, 327
Internet quarantines, 340
Internet Relay Chat (IRC), 329
Internet service providers (ISPs), 332, 333, 342; disclosure of information, 340, 345; digital interceptions and, 344, 356n183, 357n189; exempt from Bill C-47, 346; law enforcement and, 343–4; role in Internet regulation, 338, 339, 341, 347
interoperability, 15
Inuit, 136
investigative hearings, 235; Air India Flight 182 and, 233–4; in Anti-Terrorism Act, 232–3; debate over renewal of, 234–5
Investigative Powers for the 21st Century Act, 341–2, 343, 344
Ipsos Reid, 24
Iqaluit, Nunavut, territorial jail in, 138
I-Track study, 194, 196

Jaballah, Mahmoud, 238
Jackson, Michael, 141
Jamaican-born men, 283, 289
Joint Immigration-RCMP Task Force, 281
Jones, Mark, 281, 293n7
judges, xx; appeals court, 91; in problem-solving courts, 163; selection process for, 92; sentencing power of, 93–4
Just Desserts murder, 280–1, 283, 293n7
juvenile courts, 111; see also youth justice
Juvenile Delinquents Act (JDA), 110–11

K-Court (Toronto), 162, 166, 167, 168, 172, 173, 174
Kenney, Jason, 276
Khadr, Omar, 224–5
Khawaja, Mohamed Momin, 230
Khawaja case, 231, 237; definition of terrorist activities in, 230–1
Klein, S. and J. Pulkingham, 252
Knazan, B., Justice, 147, 148, 149
Kohler-Hausmann, J., 267

labour force: neo-liberalism and, 251
Landau, T., 138
Lawful Access Consultation Document, 341, 356n183
lawful access measures, 342, 343, 344, 355n166; costs of, 345–6
Law Reform Commission of Canada, 87, 88
Le Dain Commission of Inquiry into the Non-Medical Use of Drugs (Le Dain Commission), 191, 201–3; 'Treatment Report', 200
left, ideological, xv
legislation: moderating process of, 91–2; national security policy-making and, 241
legislative bills. See bills
Leimonis, Georgina, 280, 281, 283
Liberal Party, xv, 34, 122, 234; cannabis-control reform, 201–2; on crime, 96; debate over renewal of preventive arrests and investigative hearings, 234; Lawful Access Consultation Document, 341; moderate response to crime, 97; on youth crime, 96, 299; Youth Criminal Justice Act and, 123, 128
Lifeline, 74
Lindsat, Steven Patrick, 312
litigation: as interest-group activity, xviii–xvix
Little, M., 255, 265
local legal culture, xviii
long-gun registry, 105n4
Luca, Joseph Di, 73

M. (J.J.), 131
MacGuignan, Mark, 88
MacKay, Peter, 318
Maclean's, 34
MacPherson, James, 135
Mahjoub, Mohamad, 238
Maitland, Constable, 60
Maitland, Mrs., 60
malicious code, 329, 330
'Malvern Crew', 312–13
malware, 328, 329, 330, 333, 340, 344
mandatory minimum sentences, 59, 84–6, 93, 100; costs of, 100–1; drug offences and, 207; effect on actual sentences, 85–6; for gun crimes, 86
Manitoba: Aboriginal peoples in, 135; domestic homicides in, 179; Domestic Violence Prosecutions Unit, 172; remand population

in, 37; welfare fraud and overpayment in, 249; youth remand rates in, 127
Manitoba Department of Justice, Victim Services Branch, 168
Manson, A., 30
Marchi, Sergio, 281
Marion, N.E., xxii
Martin, Dianne, 261–2
May, Arlene, 162
Mears, D.P., xvi
media, xxii; domestic violence and, 161–2; organized crime and, 305
Medical Marijuana Access Program (MMAP), 202
Medovarski case, 285
methadone, 199
methadone maintenance treatment (MMT), 199–200, 207, 208; limitations of, 200; physicians holding exemptions, 200; in prisons, 204
Métis, 136; *see also* Aboriginal peoples
Metropolitan Toronto Police, 312
Miami-Dade County Drug Court, 164, 167
Microsoft, 335–6, 351n85
Military Intelligence, 14
Miller, Walter, xiv–xv
Ministry of Public Safety Canada, 303
Ministry of the Attorney General of Ontario, 136
Mirchandani, K. and W. Chan, 266
Modernization of Investigative Techniques (MITA), 341, 342
morphine maintenance programs, 190
Morris, Robert, 350n63
Morris, Stan, 301
Mosher, J., 264
Mosher, J. and J. Hermer, 249, 259
Moyer, S. and M. Basic, 42
municipal governments: drug problems and, 207–8; policing and, 6
murder: capital, 59; domestic homicides, 74, 173, 178, 179
murder sentencing, 2–3, 59–61; in Criminal Code, 58; efforts to reshape, 63–75; life sentences for, 63, 68; new regime in, 60–1; parole ineligibility, 58, 60–1, **61**, 63; parole ineligibility for multiple convictions, 63; victim's voices and, 76
Mutual Legal Assistance in Criminal Matters Act, 308
Myers, N., 41, 42
Myers, N. and T.K. Dhillon, 41, 42

Nagel, S. et al., xiii
NAOMI study, 200
Narcotic Control Act, 191
National Anti-Drug Strategy (NADS), 207
National Council on Welfare, 248, 261
National Drug Strategy, 308
National Institute of Justice, 7
National Parole Board, 72, 74

needle and syringe programs (NSPs), in prisons, 204
needle exchange programs (NEPs), 194, 207, 208
neo-liberalism, 2, 250; description of, 251; labour force and, 251; public policies and, 251; rise of in Canada, 250–1; welfare policies and, 250–6
net widening, for Aboriginal offenders, 145, 146
network security: costs of, 345–6, 357n201; cybercrime and, 338–41
Neubeck, K. and N. Cazenave, 266
New Brunswick: domestic violence court in, 160; remand population in, 37
Newburn, T., 98
Newburn, T. and T. Jones, xiii
New Democratic Party (NDP), xv; credit for pre-trial time served, 54n13; on crime, 96, 97; debate over renewal of preventive arrests and investigative hearings, 234; on youth crime, 97; Youth Criminal Justice Act and, 124
Newfoundland and Labrador: domestic violence court in, 160; remand population in, 37
Nicholson, Rob, 65, 315, 318
Nielsen Task Force, 88, 89, **90**
Noble, Ronald, 301
non-governmental witnesses: bills S-6 and C-48, 72–5
non-medical prescription opioid use (NMPOU), 192, 197–8, 199
non-Status Indians, 136, 156n1; *see also* Aboriginal peoples
Northwest Territories: remand population in, 37
Nunavut: remand population in, 37

offender monitoring, 164, 165
Office of the Correctional Investigator, 67, 137
Olson, Clifford, 62, 70, 71
online attacks, proliferation of, 329–30, 344; *see also* cybercrime
Ontario: domestic violence courts in, 160, 162; non-medical prescription opioid use in, 198; welfare fraud in, 249, 259, 253, 260, 263; youth crime response in, 123
Ontario Court of Appeal, 31, 230, 232
Ontario Court of Justice, 136, 146, 147; *R. v. Marvin Johnson*, 54n11
Ontario Crown Policy Manual: bail hearings in, 47
Ontario Domestic Violence Death Review Committee, 178–9
OPICAN study, 194, 197
opioid use, 197–201
opium, 188
Opium Act, 189
organized crime, 187, 280, 281, 298, 313–14; defining, 303, 303–5; globalization and, 9; Mafia model, 304, 306; national security and, 280, 284; as process, 304

organized crime policy, 303; costs of, 315–17; evolution of legislation, 305–9; focus on 'harm', 305; impact of, 316; influences on, 301; international harmonization of, 301, 320, 299; national security and, 302; policy-making, 298–9, 299–302; racialized dimension, 283–4; rhetoric in Canada and US, 306; strategies of, 307; 'targeting upwards', 307, 308

O'Sullivan, Susan, 71–2

Ouimet Committee. *See* Canadian Committee on Corrections (Ouimet Committee)

overrepresentation, in justice system: of Aboriginal peoples, 3–4, 137–8, 142, 144, 152, 154; effects of, 138

Parental Responsibility Act, 97

parole ineligibility, 58, **61**, 63, 68; review of, 60–1

Pate, Kim, 74

Patriot Act (US), 224, 226

penitentiaries: federal jurisdiction over, xvii; *see also* correctional institutions

people with disabilities: welfare policy reforms in British Columbia and, 257

personal computers, 327–8

Personal Information Protection and Electronic Documents Act (PIPEDA), 349n56, 356n187

Petit, Daniel, 67–8

phishing, 330, 336, 348n36; kits, 329

Phonebusters, 353n124

physicians: methadone maintenance treatment exemptions, 200

Pinkey, Kevin and Douglas Barnes, 335

Pinto case, 307–8

police: bail hearings and, 48–9; broader mandate of, 15–16; capacity and sustainability, 22–4; defined, 6; domestic assault incidents and, 161, 168; expenditures and projections, **23**; federal-municipal relationship, 8, 10; integration, 20–2 and; governance and accountability, 24–6; 'in decline' prior to 9/11, 5; interoperability of, 15; per capita, 8; political independence of, 8; powers under Bail Reform Act, 35; public, 6, 8; surveillance of, 24; trust in, 24

Police Foundation, 7

policing: in Canada, 5–9; costs of, 22; defined, 5–6; generalizations and hypotheses about Canadian, 8; government responsibility for policy, 6–7; growth in Canadian, 15; G-20 meetings and, 12–13, 13–14; integrated national security, 20, 21; intelligence-led, 17–18; international linkages in 'local' crime, 9–10; lack of Canadian national strategy, 10, 26, 27; policy, 6–8; post-9/11, 2, 9–13; reinvesting in, 14–15; research, 7; risk and, 17; security, 11–12, 20; security-based community, 18–19; spending on, 8, 14–15

Policing the Risk Society (Ericson and Haggerty), 17

policy: community, xix–xx; concept of, x–xi; policing, 6–8; public service advisors, 302–3; rational and evidence-based, xvi–xvii; research-driven, 302–3; uses of term, x–xi

policy-makers, xxi

policy making: evidence-based research and, 317–19; models of, xi; process of, xi–xii; xxiii; spheres of influence on, 299–301, **300**

policy networks, xix, xxi–xxiii

political parties, xv–xvi, 105n5; credit for pre-trial time served, 54–5n13; crime policies and, 95–8, 100; crime prevention and, 100

politicization: of crime and crime policy, 12–13, 90, 99–100, 102

poly-drug use, 194, 197

Poulin, Yvan, 316

poverty, 248; criminalization of, 261, 262; 'deserving' and 'undeserving' poor, 255–6, 265; gendered and racialized nature of, 248, 265; public attitudes towards, 248–9; victim-blaming, 248

Power, E., 264

prescription opioid analgesics (POAs), 194, 197, 199; supply and distribution dynamics of, 198–9

pre-trial detention, 2, 30–1, 157n15; Aboriginal peoples and, 147, 148, 149; in Bill C-3, 119; conditional release and, 45; credit for, 44–6, 51, 100; disadvantages to offenders having served, 45–6; impact on accused, 31, 52; justification for, 34; median time spent in, 53n5; presumption against, 2; presumption of innocence, 31; Truth in Sentencing Bill and, 101–2; Youth Criminal Justice Act and, 113, 126–7, 130

Prince Edward Island: remand population in, 37

Prison and Reformatories Act, 79

prisoners: right to vote, 94–5

prisons: growth in populations, 80; provincial jurisdiction over, xvii; sentenced versus remand population in, 36, **38**; *see also* correctional institutions

privacy: digital interception and, 344–5

Privacy and Access to Information Commission, 227

private police, 16–17

problem-solving courts, 163, 164–5, 174; popularity of, 165; *see also* domestic violence courts

Proceeds of Crime Legislation, 308

Proceeds of Crime Money Laundering Act, 309

Proceeds of Crime Money Laundering and Terrorist Financing Act, 309

Progressive Conservative Party, xv, 88, 96–7, 124, 202, 234, 235–6

'Project Impact' (Toronto), 312–13

proportionality, 59, 112, 114; test, 343, 355–6n181

Pross, A.P., xix

protestors, 13, 228

provincial/territorial governments: approach to drug problems, 208; domestic courts and, 165; policing and, 6; responsible for administration of law, xvii, 1–2, 7; youth justice and, 115
psycho-stimulants, 192
public criminology, xiv
public inquiries and commissions, 25
public policy, xi; *see also* policy
Public Prosecution Service of Canada (PPSC), 316
Public Safety Act, 222
Public Safety Canada, xix; Results-Based Management and Accountability Framework (RMAF), 315–16
public servants, xxi, 302–3

Quebec: Aboriginal peoples in provincial and territorial custody, 138; remand population in, 37, 53n4; Youth Criminal Justice Act and, xx, 122, 123, 124, 129; youth justice in, 115, 128

racialized people: welfare and, 255, 265–6
racism: in Canada, 95; 'serious criminality' and, 283, 266; welfare and, 265–6
racketeering, 306; *see also* enterprise crime; organized crime
RCMP. *See* Royal Canadian Mounted Police (RCMP)
reason, xvi
recidivism, 151, 153; Winnipeg Family Violence Court and, 173, 175–7, **176**, 178
Reform Party of Canada: on crime, 105n5; on crime prevention, 96; moderate response to crime, 97–8; youth crime and, 299
refugees, 223, 227, 280, 281; welfare benefits and, 265
rehabilitation: in Youth Criminal Justice Act, 112
Reitsma-Street, M., 258
remand population, 37–9, 51; admission versus count data, 37, **38**; in prisons, 36; *see also* pre-trial detention
Republicans, xv
research: policing and, 6–8; policy and, 302–3, 317
Ressam, Ahmed, 223
restorative justice, 143, 151, 153
Re Vancouver Sun, 233
Reverse Onus Forfeiture Act, 313
Rigakos, G.S., 16
right, ideological, xv
rights and freedoms, xviii; *see also* Canadian Charter of rights and Freedoms
risk: policing and, 17
Roach, K. and J. Rudin, 143, 144, 145
Roberts, J.V., 92
Rogers, Kimberly, 261
Rosenberg, Justice, 31

Rosenfeldt, Sharon, 66, 70–1
Royal Canadian Mounted Police (RCMP), 6, 8–9, 10, 21, 235; 2005 Strategic Plan, 20; Aboriginal peoples and, 136; 'culturally relevant' or 'culturally appropriate' community-based alternatives, 152–3; disclosure of terrorism investigative files, 224; drug law enforcement and, 189, 207; fiscal sustainability of, 23–4; funding for, 14; G-20 meetings and, 13; integrated policing and, 10, 20; investigations into management and leadership, 25; mandate, 10; organized crime and, 9; security policing and, 11–12; supervised injection sites and, 195; terrorism and, 10
Royal Commission on Aboriginal Peoples (RCAP), 135, 139, 140–1, 146, 154, 155
Rudin, J., 141, 143–4, 149
Rutherford, Justice, 230, 231
Ruth, Henry and Kevin Reitz, xvi
R. v. Beauchamp, 311–12
R. v. C.D.; R. v. C.D.K., 130
R. v. Gladue, 139, 142–4, 146, 148, 154; criticisms of judgment, 144–5
R. v. Lindsay, 312
R. v. Marvin Johnson, 54n11
R. v. McDonald, 31
R. v. Oakes, 343
R. v. Ward, 357n194
R. v. Wells, 143
R. v. Wier, 342

safer crack-use kits (SCUK), 196–7, 208
Safe Streets and Communities Act, 318
safe third-country agreement, 223
Sapers, Howard, 67, 75–6
Saskatchewan: Aboriginal people in provincial and territorial custody, 138; domestic violence court in, 160; youth remand rates in, 127
Saskatchewan Law Review, 144
Saudi Arabia: Internet filtering, 338
Sauvé, Rick, 74–5
Sauvé v. Canada, 94–5
Schram, S. et al., 266
Scottish Institute for Policing Research, 7
script-kiddies, 329, 334
Sears, Alan, 251
security-based community policing, 18–19
security certificates, 236–40, 241, 242; original debate, 236–7
security intelligence, 18
security policing, 11–12, 20
security policy, national, 18, 222, 223; courts and legislature and, 241; dilemma of secrecy in, 242–3; funding for, 14; gangs and, 284; integration of security and policing, 20; international pressures on, 224; organized crime and, 280, 284; process of, 226; RCMP and, 11–12; rhetoric, 302

Seized Property Management Act (Bill C-123), 308
Senate Committee on Legal and Constitutional Affairs, 124–5
Senate Special Committee on Illegal Drugs, 201
sentences: completion of, 55n15; concurrent life, 68; conditional, 100, 145–6, 175, 204, 206; federal versus provincial/territorial, 156n4; mandatory minimum, 59, 84–6, 93, 100–1, 207; remission, 45, 101; statutory release, 45–6, 101; time served calculations, 54n12
sentencing, 58–9; Aboriginal peoples and, 141–6; Bill C-3, 120; Bill C-48, 63–4, 67–9, 70, 71, 72–3, 75, 76–7; Bill S-6, 63–4, 64–7, 69–70, 71, 72, 75, 76–7; confidence in justice system and, 40, 64, 70; in Criminal Code, 59; federal jurisdiction over, 91; mandatory maximum penalties, 93; mandatory minimum penalties, 59; murder, 2–3, 58, 59–61, 63–75, 76; parity in, 144, 146; proportionality and, 59; 'truth in sentencing', 65, 70, 96; Winnipeg Family Violence Court and, 174–5; youth crime and, 126; in Youth Criminal Justice Act, 113–14, 131
'serious criminality' provision, 273, 280, 282, 289; offence and sentencing criteria, 282–3; racism in, 283; range of offences captured by, 282
Serious Incident Response Team (Nova Scotia), 25
Shearing, C.D. and P.C. Stenning, 5, 16
Sheikh, Munir, 318
Sidel, R., 255
Simeon, Richard, xx
Simon, Jonathan, xxiii, 185
Singapore: definition of terrorism in, 231; Internet filtering, 338
Snacken, S., 80
social engineering, 336, 348n36
Social Planning and Research Council of British Columbia (SPARC), 258
software: anti-spyware, 337; antivirus, 337, 330; flaws in, 333–4; holding users liable, 337; Internet filtering software, 339; open-source, 336–7; patches (updates), 334, 337, 351n86; privacy and, 344–5; public access to Internet-enabled, 328; security, 333–6; security features for users, 336; source code, 336–7; 'window of vulnerability', 334, 337
software manufacturers: liability and, 335–6; rushing to market, 333–4
Solomon, Peter, xi
sovereign power, 290–1
spam, 329, 330, 331
Special Investigations Unit (Ontario), 25
specialized courts: challenges with, 178; frequent outcomes in, 167–9; see also domestic violence courts; problem-solving courts
speech, criminalization of, 225

speedballs, 192, 194
Sprott, J. and A.N. Doob, 41, 42
Sprott, J.B. and N.M. Myers, 42
spyware, 330, 344
SQL Slammer, 329
Standing Committee on Justice and Human Rights, 119, 316
Standing Senate Committee on Social Affairs, Science and Technology, 265
Stark, E., 173
Statistics Canada, 105n3, 137–8, 171, 318
status Indians, 136, 156n1; see also Aboriginal peoples
Stenning, P. and J.V. Roberts, 144–5, 146
Stinchcombe decision, 316
Stolz, B.A., xxi
Stone, Deborah, xi
Strategy for the Renewal of Youth Justice, 116–17, 122
street racing: sentencing laws, 103
structured interaction perspective, xi
sub-government, xix, xx–xxi
substance-use offenders: compulsory treatment, 205; conditional sentencing, 204–5, 206; see also drug law and policy
suicide rate: Aboriginal peoples and, 140
summons to court, 32, 34
supervised crack-use site (SCUS), 197
supervised injection site (SIS), 195
Supreme Court of Canada, 138, 345; Aboriginal peoples and, 136; adult sentencing for youth, 114; definition of terrorism, 229, 231; Insite and, 195; investigative hearings in, 236; Khadr case and, 224–5; on overrepresentation, 139; prisoners' right to vote and, 94–5; security certificates and, 236–7; sentencing and, 59; torture of detainees and, 223; Youth Criminal Justice Act and, 131; youth sentencing and, 114. Cases: Application under s. 83.28, 233; Charkaoui (case), 239–40, 241, 242; Khawaja case, 230, 231; M. (J.J.), 131; Medovarski case, 285; R. v. C.D.; R. v. C.D.K., 130; R. v. Gladue, 139, 142–4, 146, 148, 154; R. v. Oakes, 343; Suresh v. Canada, 228–30, 231, 238–9, 240, 241
Suresh, Manickavasgam, 238–9
Suresh v. Canada, 228–30, 231, 238–9, 240, 241
sureties, 33, 41; youth and, 53–4n7
Symantec, 330
systemic discrimination, 139–41, 154

tasers, 19; public inquiries into incidents, 24, 25
Technical Assistance for Law Enforcement in the 21st Century Act, 341, 342, 343, 344, 345, 346, 357n189
Telecommunications Act, 340
TELUS-Rotman study, 328, 350n60, 351n94
terrorism: definition, 227–8; definition in Khawaja, 230–1; definition in Suresh, 228–30; financing legislation, 309; globalization and, 11; policing

global-local, 10–12; policy response to, 186, 222; preventing incitement to commit, 225–6; religious and political motive requirement, 230, 231–2, 232; risk of, 17

terrorist attacks, xxiii, 2, 5; *see also* 11 September, 2001

terrorist designation, 225

therapeutic jurisprudence, 165, 205, 206

Toews, Vic, 276

Tonry, M., 94, 95

Toronto: Aboriginal peoples in provincial and territorial custody, 146; terrorist plot in, 235, 237

torture, exception for deportation to, 239, 240, 242

'tough on crime' philosophy, 3, 12, 47, 75, 98, 317, 318; bail hearings and, 51; Canadian political parties and, 100; mandatory minimum sentences and, 84–5, 86; youth crime and, 117, 118, 123, 122, 124

Transmission Control Protocols/Internet Protocols (TCP/IP), 327, 332

Tran Trong Nghi Nguyen, 186, 273–6, 283; appeal of removal order, 273–4, 282, 285–6; coverage of case, 274; crime-security nexus in case of, 276–7; criminal background of, 273, 275, 285; deportation of, 273, 274, 280, 282, 291–2; detention of, 288; humanitarian factors versus security concerns, 285–6; Immigration Appeal Board tribunal, 285; targeted by police, 288

Trotter, G.T., 36, 41, 46

Trudeau, Pierre, 34

Truth in Sentencing: Act, 45, 103; Bill, 101–2

'truth-in-sentencing' measures, 65, 70, 96

tuberculosis: Aboriginal peoples and, 140

Turner, John, 34

Uniform Commercial Code (UCC), 335

United Kingdom: immigration law as anti-terrorism law, 237; national security policy in, 243; police research in, 7

United Nations (UN): Convention against Transnational Organized Crime, 310–11, 319; organized-crime policies, 319; Target Setting Guide, 207

United Nations Convention Relating to the Status of Refugees, 281

United Nations (UN) Security Council, 225, 243; Counter-Terrorism Committee, 226, 242; Resolution 1373, 225, 226, 227, 237, 242, 245n25; Resolution 1624, 225–6

United States: addressing crime through imprisonment, 98–9; crime policy in, xv; homicide rates, 82–4; immigration law as anti-terrorism law, 237; imprisonment rates, 82–4, 89; imprisonment trends, 79–80; jurisdiction over criminal law in, xvii–xviii; national security policy in, 243; online surveillance, 339; organized crime rhetoric

in, 306; Patriot Act, 224, 226; police research in, 77; political response to crime, xxiii, 98; problem-solving courts in, 163; software manufacturers' liability in, 335; 'war on drugs' in, 95, 191, 301–2; 'war on terror', xxiii, 339; welfare state in, 249

Ursel, J. et al., 166

US Federal Trade Commission, 335

US Financial Crimes Enforcement Network (FinCEN), 301

US Police Executive Research Forum, 7

US Racketeer Influenced and Corrupt Organizations Statute (RICO), 306, 313

US Task Force on Organized Crime, 306

Vallee, Brian, 178

values, core Canadian, 94–5

Vancouver: drug problem in, 208; supervised injection site in, 195

Varma, K.N., 42

victims and victims' advocates: bills S-6 and C-48, 69–72; murder sentencing and, 76

video cameras and phones: police surveillance and, 24

VIDUS study, 196, 203

violence against women, 160–1; *see also* domestic violence

Wacquant, L., 254

Waller, Irvin, 318

warrants, 34

Web-based forums, 329

welfare: attempts to supplement benefits, 254, 258–9; complexity of rules and regulations, 259, 264; decreasing benefit rates, 252–3; dependence, 252, 256; income earned and, 257; mothers and, 262–4; punishment and, 255; racism and, 265–6; women and, 263, 267

welfare fraud, 250, 253; in British Columbia, 249, 258–62; Criminal Code conviction for, 259; versus error, 259; failure to disclose 'spouse' is present, 260, 263; non-disclosure of income, 260, 264; in Ontario, 249, 253, 259, 260, 263; penalties for, 260–1; people of colour and, 266; sanctions and policing of, 258–62

welfare policies, 186; criminal law and, 255; enforcement, 249; gendered and racialized impact of, 250; reform in British Columbia, 256–8; reforms to, 256, 268n2; time-limit sanctions and, 257–8

welfare recipients: employment plans, 257; gendered and racialized impact of surveillance on, 262–6; policing of, 249, 250; racist stereotypes of, 265, 266; stereotypes of, 248, 249, 253–4, 259, 260, 261–2, 262; stereotypes of women, 263–4, 267; surveillance of, 254–5, 256, 260, 264, 267

welfare state: neo-liberal, 251–6; in Western nations, 249

welfare-to-work policies, 252, 266
white-collar crime, 306, 314
wife abuse, 160–1; welfare system and, 263; *see
    also* domestic violence
WikiLeaks, 319
'windows of opportunity', 301
Windows: Vista, 333; XP, 333, 351n80
Winnick, B., 164
Winnipeg: arrests for spousal assaults, **171**;
    COHROU units in, 177; domestic violence
    arrest rates, 161; domestic violence court in,
    160; Domestic Violence Unit, 169; Women's
    Advocacy Program, 168
Winnipeg Family Violence Court, 162, 163, 167,
    169–70; conviction rates in, 173–4; court
    process and outcomes, 172–4; impacts of
    specialization, 170; recidivism and other
    challenges, 175–7; sentencing in, 174–5;
    victim and accused characteristics, 170–2
Winnipeg Police Service, 170
women: violence against, 160–1; welfare system
    and, 262–4
Women's Advocacy Program (Winnipeg), 168
Woodiwiss, Michael, 301
World Wide Web (WWW), 328; *see also* Internet

YCJA Explained, 125
young offenders: Aboriginal, 125, 138; bail cases
    and, 41; bail violations and, 43; incarceration
    rates, 111, 126; judicial discretion to admit
    statement despite non-compliance by police,
    116, 117, 120–1, 127; legal protection
    regarding publishing of identities, 116, 121,
    127; remand rates, 127; transfer to adult
    court, 112, 114
Young Offenders Act (YOA), 3, 96, 97, 111, 131,
    299; alternative measures in, 113; charging
    and police diversion in, 126; criticisms of,
    111–12, 128; custody sentencing in, 126;
    parliamentary committee review of, 116; in
    Quebec, 115; rehabilitation in, 112; *see also*
    Youth Criminal Justice Act (YCJA)
youth crime: alternatives to court, 116;
    Department of Justice Canada review of,

116–17; 'get-tough' approach, 117, 124;
    non-custodial alternatives, 124; political
    parties on, 96–7; pre-trial detention and, 115;
    prior to Youth Criminal Justice Act, 110–11;
    provincial control over, 115; public
    perceptions of, 122; sentencing and, 115;
    transfer to adult court, 116
Youth Criminal Justice Act (YCJA), 3, 103, 110,
    111–14; accountability in, 112, 113; adult
    sentences in, 114, 120, 127, 129; alternative
    measures in, 113; areas of agreement, 128; bail
    conditions, 42; clear policy objectives, 130;
    draft legislation and consultation, 117–18;
    extrajudicial measures in, 119, 130–1; factors
    that contributed to achievement of objectives,
    130–2; factors that contributed to passage of,
    127–30; funding of, 125, 131, 132; impact of,
    125–7; implementation of, 125; legislative
    bills and parliamentary proceedings, 118–25;
    length of reform process, 132; minimum age
    of criminal responsibility, 121; as new statute
    rather than amendments, 131; offence
    provisions, 121–2; parliamentary witnesses,
    129; policy of restraint, 112–13; pre-trial
    detention in, 113, 119, 130; principles of,
    112–13; professional education and, 131;
    proportionality in, 112, 114; provincial
    implementation and achievement of policy
    objectives, 132; Quebec and, xx;
    rehabilitation in, 112; research and statistics
    and, 129–30; royal assent, 125; Senate
    hearings of Bill C-7, 124–5; sentencing
    principles of, 113–14, 131; size and
    complexity of legislation, 129; structuring
    decisions and achievement of objectives, 130;
    system-wide reform and, 130–1; third reading
    of Bill C-7, 123–4; two-pronged approach to
    reform, 128–9; use of courts in, 113
Youth Justice Renewal Fund, 125
Yukon: domestic violence court in, 160;
    problem-solving court in, 174

zero tolerance, xiii